The Life of
Ralph Waldo Emerson

BY

RALPH L. RUSK

NEW YORK

CHARLES SCRIBNER'S SONS

1949

RALPH WALDO EMERSON
AT THE AGE OF ABOUT FIFTY-ONE

To

MARGARET ANN, W. T.
MARIAN and ELLEN

PREFACE

EVER since I became acquainted with the numerous and rich manuscript sources that had been closely guarded for many years but were at last accessible, it has seemed to me that it ought to be possible to write, not merely a book about Emerson, but one fit to be called his life. The very plenitude of authentic records promised to make realizable, this time, the biographer's dream of re-creating an entire man, much as a novelist or dramatist of insight and imagination creates a character from a less restricted range of experience. The man that so good a critic as Matthew Arnold called the writer of the most important English prose of the nineteenth century, that man would turn out to be, not very surprisingly, no pale, emotionless specter. What he needed to be allowed to do was to reveal his private life and private thought, and now he could be allowed to do that.

In this book I therefore try to let him and his contemporaries speak for themselves and act as they did in real life, without much regard to our preconceived notions of them. Since Emerson was a child and acted as a child during a significant period of his growth, he relives here those years, though plainly he was not then a poet or an essayist. As he was much more affected by his early love affair than has been supposed, he betrays here his emotion and his sentiment, though they may seem out of character in a future philosopher—even a philosopher of so unorthodox a kind as he was to become. As his ideas grew slowly from slight beginnings, I let him show how they grew.

I am not wholly unaware of my lapses from the role of disinterested observer. A biographer does not shut his eyes to what he himself has experienced, but always reports another man's life in the light of his own. He cannot keep his own feelings completely masked as he witnesses the comic or tragic predicaments of his hero. He cannot quite conceal his admiration for some particular characteristic or his dislike for another. For my part, I am conscious of putting a high value on Emerson as an individualist struggling, though never with entire success, to keep his little area of personal freedom safe from encroachment. Yet, it seems to me, when I recall my conviction that his mind is no such simple thing as to be finally classified and filed away, but is conspicuously valuable for its flexibility and variety and even its contradictions, I slip quickly back into my unpartisan role.

Doubtless I have absorbed more from scholarly commentaries than my notes show, and yet I try to state my indebtedness whenever I am aware of it—except my frequent indebtedness to James Elliot Cabot and Edward Waldo Emerson. As executors and as editors they prepared the way. They were among the earliest biographers, and, though they wrote over sixty years ago, have hitherto been the only ones to draw to any extent upon original manuscripts. Their scope was limited, and it has now been possible to add greatly to the sources they preserved and put into some semblance of order but used only sparingly; yet their work was of greater worth to me than I am able to make clear in a few words.

I am conscious of many other obligations that deserve fuller acknowledgment than I can make. To the members of the Ralph Waldo Emerson Memorial Association, and particularly to Emerson's grandsons W. Cameron Forbes, Edward Waldo Forbes, and Raymond Emerson, I am thankful for the freedom I have had of a great collection and for help of many kinds. Over a long period of years, and often at the cost of much time and trouble, Mr. Edward Forbes has courteously responded to my almost continual requests for records difficult to find or perhaps nonexistent. I owe him a very special debt. Doctor Haven Emerson allowed me the use of the important family papers which he owns. Mr. Lewis S. Gannett, Mr. H. W. L. Dana, Mr. A. Le Baron Russell, and many others made it possible for me to quote from unpublished writings.

Grateful acknowledgment is due to the Harvard College Library, and especially to its Houghton Library, where most of the Memorial Association's manuscripts, together with other essential papers, are preserved. During the many months I spent in the Houghton Library I profited much by the expert aid of Mr. William A. Jackson and Miss Carolyn Jakeman. I have also had the friendly and effective co-operation of the Columbia University Libraries, the New York Public Library, the Union Theological Seminary Library, the Massachusetts Historical Society, the Concord Free Public Library, the Concord Antiquarian Society, the Emerson House in Concord, the Harvard Historical Society (of Harvard, Massachusetts), the Andover-Harvard Theological Library, the Abernethy Library of Middlebury College, and other libraries—more than can be named here.

I owe particular thanks to Miss Sarah R. Bartlett, Mrs. Howard W. Kent, Miss Anna M. Scorgie, Miss Jannette E. Newhall, Mrs. H. M. Foster, Miss Viola C. White, Miss Helen Stearns, Mrs. Marshall B. Fanning, Mr. William S. Parker, Mr. Bliss Perry, Miss Marjorie Nicolson, Miss Eleanor Tilton, Miss Mary E. Burtis, Mr. Frederick T. McGill, Mrs. William Elder, M. Louis Cazamian, and Miss Nora Scott.

The Columbia University Press, as well as the Memorial Association, granted me permission to draw freely upon *The Letters of Ralph Waldo Emerson*. The Houghton Mifflin Company made the *Journals of Ralph*

Waldo Emerson fully available to me. Mr. Odell Shepard gave me leave to quote from *The Journals of Bronson Alcott.*

The progress of the book was greatly helped by the John Simon Guggenheim Memorial Foundation's award of a fellowship in biography and by generous financial aid from the American Philosophical Society. Margaret Ann and W. T. White, my daughter and son-in-law, read my manuscript, greatly to its benefit. Mr. John L. Cooley, besides bringing me his Emersoniana, lent a practiced hand to the work of correcting both galleys and page proofs of my chapters; and Mrs. Walter R. Bowie read the page proofs of them. Mr. John Hall Wheelock of Charles Scribner's Sons was a wise and sympathetic adviser. My wife, Clara Gibbs Rusk, gave indispensable and much-valued aid from the time when the first preliminary note was made till the day when the last proof sheet was corrected.

Mr. Edward Forbes has supplied the picture of his grandfather which is reproduced in the frontispiece. The original was presumably a daguerreotype by Southworth & Hawes of Boston, but its early history is not now clear. That daguerreotype, or an enlargement of it, was very probably, I think, the same "large photograph, taken fifteen years ago," mentioned in Ellen Emerson's draft of a letter to Gisela von Arnim Grimm apparently begun in March of 1868. According to Ellen, the "large photograph" had been "contemptuously discarded" by the family in spite of the photographer's warning that "This may not be the Father, but it is the orator, the man as he stands before the world, and this will be the one picture valued by posterity, when all the others are forgotten." And it was only, she said, "within three months" that it had been rediscovered "in Southworth & Hawes's shop" and "dragged . . . from obscurity" and "admired and eagerly sought for." The same picture I have used, and, as I conjecture, the same Ellen described, was published by Alexander Ireland in the longer of his two biographies of 1882. In his prefatory note Ireland could give only an indefinite account of it. It was "reduced from a large one" sent to him "in 1867," but "taken probably a few years before." Yet, for some unexplained reason, he printed "Æt. 55" under his reproduction, thus affirming that the original was not earlier than 1857. When, however, the picture was republished in the first volume of the Centenary Edition it was dated 1854; and as that year was doubtless assigned by Emerson's son, the editor, it seems most probable. The evidence in favor of 1853, including some recently discovered, does not much weaken that probability, though it is a reminder of the very real uncertainty that still exists.

R. L. R.

New York
February 1949

CONTENTS

THE LIFE OF
RALPH WALDO EMERSON

1.

PROLOGUE:
WILLIAM AND RUTH EMERSON

For shame! O Emerson! Arise to industry! To glory!
—William Emerson's diary, October 13, 1795

WHEN William Emerson came home from the governor's house on Election Day he found a new son. Ralph Waldo had been born at a quarter past three that afternoon. There is good reason to believe that William Emerson felt the elation a father would naturally experience on such an occasion and the great relief a husband would naturally feel when his wife had passed safely through the ordeal of childbirth. But his diary, though it had some highly emotional passages, seldom seemed to him a fit place for the outpouring of sentiment. He made a laconic note of the favorable condition of Ruth, his wife. Whatever his parental feelings were, he concealed them perfectly as he jotted down the entry briefly recording the events of that busy day. He betrayed no more surprise than if he had known in advance the exact moment of the birth of his fourth child. And it seems probable that even with such foreknowledge he could not easily have canceled any of his engagements, for he was now a rather important man in Boston, the capital of Massachusetts.

In the same diary where he recorded the events of Election Day, May 25, 1803, he had already written the story of most of his mature years. He sometimes reviewed his career, partly to admonish himself against repeating old errors, but surely not without a mild feeling of satisfaction because of his successes. If his achievements seemed modest, they were mainly due to his own exertions. He had hardly known his father and had not found it easy to rise from the condition of a rather impecunious, if well instructed, country boy. Diary and family correspondence together vividly evoked not less than thirteen years of his past, carrying him back to the time when he was a young college graduate pleased with the prospect of eking out a slender salary from the Roxbury grammar school by keeping an evening school in winter and a girls' school in summer.

I

His pleasure in teaching dwindled rapidly. The inescapable double responsibility of discipline and instruction weighed heavily upon him, and his spirits were, as he said, "depressed with perpetual fatigue." He experienced no undue delay in getting his license to preach or in receiving his call to the little church at the village of Harvard, only a few miles across the hills from his native Concord. But even in the ministry his peace of mind proved to be short-lived. Indeed it may have had no life at all, for in his letter of acceptance, in March of 1792, his thoughts already seemed to dwell unhappily on the meager salary he was to receive. When he told his future flock that "it is God who assigneth us our station in life," he perhaps half consciously implied that for his own part he would not have chosen so small a place as Harvard. At his ordination past generations of New England preachers whose name he bore, and other reverend ancestors of different names, were so many firm cords binding him to the church. Living members of the family were present to encourage him, and his stepfather, Ezra Ripley, preached the ordination sermon. But whatever reason William Emerson had for singleness of heart, he was soon deeply discontented, for he found his parish torn by religious dissension and too poor to relieve him of his poverty.

He could not remember being free of debt since his twelfth year, but poverty now proved harder to endure than when he had been less conspicuous, and he formed a new resolve to acquire the virtue of frugality. He reminded himself in his journal: "Paid for a gold ring and buttons. Things, which I could very ill afford! Be careful in future." His proposal that his salary be pegged to commodity prices had some practical results and showed him no mean theoretical economist, but he involved himself more deeply by purchasing a farm. His increasing financial difficulties made him fear that a separation from his church would be necessary. Though such an act, in the face of the old New England custom of permanent pastorates, would, he felt, "be like suffering my hair and my eyes to be plucked out," it would be better than starvation.

It was pleasant enough to figure in the upper social set of the parish; and being a friend of the comparatively opulent Squire Kimball and of Henry Bromfield, the Roger de Coverley of the place, made up partly for one's own lack of the good things of life. Yet the young pastor could not be content with favors from great friends. He was weary of bachelorhood, "the life of a monk," as it seemed to him, but was without money to marry on.

He tired of parish dissension. Though the conservatives in his church yielded far enough to accept a new and less trinitarian hymnal, they finally rose in rebellion against instrumental accompaniment for religious songs. Both the liberal hymns and their instrumental accompaniment were innovations the music-loving pastor was responsible for. The visible symbol of his approval of these things was the bass viol he lent to the musicians. But whatever he did, he might offend somebody; and unfriendly critics, eager to stir up the too placid pool of village life, were sleepless in their vigilance.

It was true that he could turn to a variety of literary interests for consolation. He had, it seems, founded the first social library in the town, and he acted as its custodian. Besides, he had collected a little library of his own. He was enthusiastic about the fine things he discovered in Zimmermann on solitude, and he read Priestley's letters to a philosophical unbeliever. But, since he felt no wholehearted devotion to his Harvard church, his life seemed to lack a steady purpose.

Between readings he gave out books from the social library or played on his viol. He was uneasy because he saw that he read without method, and he caught himself spending too much time playing checkers and singing in the parlor. He resolved to be prudent but was soon at his checkers and singing again. On his twenty-sixth birthday he was compelled to reflect how much of his life had been carelessly spent. "Count the hours," he admonished himself, "which I have consumed in sleep, dress, amusements, and in mere saunterings, and what have I left? O let shame and compunction fill my soul . . . May God almighty take me into his holy keeping!" But, immediately descending again into the actual world where holy and profane things were inextricably jumbled, he added: "Planted my watermelons & musk melons. Wrote two prayers. Attended and prayed in town-meeting. Came home and read Tho. Reid's intellectual powers, which is now my *author* on hand. Meditate. Review my last year's journal."

No doubt new resolves were not wholly in vain, but he pleasantly discovered that "It is almost certain, that I can do as much in a day by spending one third of it in company, as by confining myself entirely." He not only sermonized and planted melons but arranged to have a new pair of breeches made and played games. He sermonized again, read "the april magazine," visited and drank wine, returned and played checkers. He was off to Boston for a round of visits, music, and other pleasures, with special attention to a family named Haskins. On the quarter day he could do little but look over accounts and pay debts. "May God help me," he ejaculated, "to be more pious and prudent."

His resolutions to study suffered many rude interferences. He blamed himself for spending a good part of the day foolishly, "trooping and training in town, and what not." "Would to God," he prayed, "my mind could so . . . embrace a subject, as to be diverted by nothing trifling or incidental!

Am lowspirited, poor wifeless, houseless, landless, and I am afraid almost friendless." Pained cries continued to punctuate the more complacent pages of his journals: "Began to sermonize. Failed. Retreated like a coward . . . For shame! O Emerson! Arise to industry! To glory! . . . Shake off sloth. Banish lustful thought and foolish, childish imaginations. . . . When shall I produce works, that in the opinion of my enemies, as well as friends, shall be deemed the joint effort of genius & habit?"

He finished Reid on the intellectual powers and was no doubt pleased with his perseverance to the end of such a weighty and edifying treatise. He wrote prayers and committed them to memory, and he contemplated. He got through Beattie on truth, read some political pieces, began "Wesley's testament," and finished "a Sicilian romance," presumably Mrs. Radcliffe's novel and certainly not the only one of hers that he became acquainted with. He resigned his office as librarian, apparently after getting into an argument at the library meeting and then once more regretting his lack of prudence. The library left his house the same day that he gave up his viol, and he felt vacant and listless. But the next day he sermonized, kept retired, and felt virtuous and happy. Once when he had tried in vain to write sermons, he sat in the hall of the tavern for an hour, watching the boys and girls dance. The last days of his twenty-seventh year found him reading *The Mysteries of Udolpho,* a story in which beauty and goodness tardily triumphed over villany, while Pyrenees or Apennines created an atmosphere of wild romantic loveliness or loneliness, and supernatural horrors got explained away. People in the village thought that his courtly manners sometimes bordered on pomposity, that he was too proud, that he asked grace too poetically when there was little on the table; but when he looked at himself he saw a very human, uncertain, distressed person.

Though Boston meant over thirty miles of not very easy roads, he managed to cover them now and then, keeping in touch with Doctor Belknap, a preacher, compiler of hymns, writer of fiction, biographer, and historian. Such a connection was a badge of culture, but William Emerson, in making the long journey, also had in mind other attractions than those of the versatile Doctor. By the summer of 1795 he was a not infrequent visitor at the house of the Haskins family in Rainsford's Lane. A cautious and deliberate lover, he did not wholly trust his own instincts. He was making his advances with the approval, if not on the advice, of his erratic but sometimes clever and even brilliant sister Mary. She let him know that she had considered the eligibility of the young women of her acquaintance and had made up her mind. It was she who urged him to think seriously of Ruth, tenth of the sixteen children of John Haskins, the well-to-do distiller.

The Haskins family was an interesting bit of humanity to examine. John Haskins had been of a bold, adventurous nature from his youth, when he had run away from home to follow the sea. Plying his cooper's trade as a member of the crew of a privateer, he had been taken captive by the Spaniards and afterwards by the French. Success as a business man in later years inevitably added to his willfulness and personal force, and he must have inspired admiration and pride as he strode up the aisle of Trinity Church on a Sunday, wearing his long red cloak and carrying his cocked hat in his hand. Ruth's mother, Hannah, also displayed a will of her own. She used stubbornly to refuse to follow her husband to Episcopalian Trinity, and, instead, would carry off a contingent of the Haskins children to Congregational Park Street Church. In Ruth herself, the Haskins will was subdued, perhaps not only by Haskins discipline but by her own gentler nature, yet it showed in her remarkable power of endurance and in her unwavering loyalty to principles and to friends. Now, in 1795, it was probably a decisive circumstance that she possessed a loyal friend of her own in Mary Moody Emerson.

"Be it as it may," Mary Moody informed her brother, "of the amiable Ruth I *must* write. . . . I have already told you that she is virtues self. And I repeat it, that in her look and manners is combined every thing which gives an idea of the whole assemblage of mild and amiable virtues. Added to this a natural good understanding and a uniform sense of propriety which characterises her every action and enables her to make a proper estimate of every occurance. Yet true it is, my dear Ruth, thou dost not possess *those energies,—those keen vibrations of soul* which seizes pleasure—which immortalizes moments and which give to life all the zest of enjoyment! But why should I regret this incapasity? If thou wert thus formed, thou wouldst be a very different being from what thou now art. . . . A thousand unborn sensations would impede the gentle accents of benevolence, which now dwell on those lips that seem open but in the cause of virtue!"

This was an honest, unadorned character analysis, calculated, not to stir the imagination of a young man, but to impress his judgment, and in William Emerson judgment ruled the imagination. There was no fateful result for a year or so. But on a June day in 1796, William rode out with Ruth "&," as he put it with his customary restraint, "talked with her on the subject of matrimony." Before the week was over he had bought a horse, and his trips to Boston multiplied until, on the 25th of October, in the long, many-windowed Rainsford's Lane house, he was married to the woman he somewhat meagerly described as "the pious and amiable Ruth Haskins." Their short wedding journey covered all the significant geography of William Emerson's life. They went from Boston to Concord, where they dined, and then on to the upland village of Harvard, where they found their neighbors and friends waiting to receive them.

The little village clung to the flanks of a ridge in a region of much natural beauty. Not far away was the long crest of Prospect Hill. From it one got a memorable view of Wachusett to the west and of Monadnock and other mountains to the northward. But it is not clear whether the pastor and his bride cared for these things. Winter was coming on, and they bought a cow and settled down on the farm. Toward the end of November the unrepentant bridegroom recorded: "Beautiful day. . . . we are poor and cold, and have little meal, and little wood, and little meat; but, thanks to a kind Providence, courage enough!" Soon he agreed to take a school in order to add $25 a month to the family income.

Early in the following year, thinking it proper to make a formal report on his matrimonial venture to his father-in-law, he assured him that "my expectations in regard to conjugal life, which never were notoriously modern, are happily answered." The bride wrote with perfect decorum to her sister Elizabeth, "Surely it cannot be reprehensible to love so good a sister; but it would be if I were to repine at our separation, while I am under the most endearing obligations to a friend nearer, than parents, or brethren; one, who is altogether worthy of my affections. Thus blessed, feign would I hush every rising murmur about distance from that little spot I once delighted in, as my home; and complain only of those imperfections in myself, that render me undeserving such a companion. I daily regret that, so little of that benign and heavenly disposition recommended in the gospel is discernible in my conduct."

Ruth's piety was habitual. A serious, religious tone appeared in many of her resolutions, letters, prayers, and journal entries and was by no means inspired simply by her sense of duty as the wife of a minister. An early prayer of hers commemorating a festival day in her religious life read like a liturgy. Once she copied a precept of self-reliant tone, "In things of moment, on thyself depend"; but in her recorded thoughts she was usually concerned with religious introspection. Generally she acted much and wrote little.

Late in the winter of 1798, the first child, Phebe Ripley, was born. "Joy and gratitude," William recorded, "swell our bosoms." Acts of kindness from the neighbors made life easier at the farmhouse-parsonage. But the mere business of getting a living for a growing family continued to absorb the energies of the pastor, though he was quite as deeply religious as his wife. "This world," he confessed, "which ought to have a very small share of my thoughts engrosses many of them." He feared that he was in danger of carrying his devotion to the family's temporal welfare "to an excess which my religion and profession will by no means justify."

He regarded his small salary and his strained personal relations with his parish as warnings that it was time for a change; and he seems to have decided that if help did not come soon from some other quarter he would set out for Washington, the paper city already agreed upon as the future federal capital, and make a new start in the world. He had a fine dream of founding there a more liberal church than the one he was tied to. But a timely opportunity for a less precarious change determined his future. The Ancient and Honourable Artillery Company of Boston asked him to preach their Election Day sermon in 1799; and his discourse, published as *Piety and Arms,* was doubtless decisive in getting him the invitation to the pastorate of the First Church in that town.

The First Church persuasively argued that Boston's need was greater than little Harvard's because of the "Alarming attacks that are made on our holy religion, by the Learned, the Witty & the Wicked, especially in populous & Sea Port Towns," and was obviously ready to offer him a better salary. It was a foregone conclusion that he would accept. Frankly reminding his village parishioners of their failure to ease his financial burden and of their chronic dissension, he begged them to let him go in charity and peace. Suddenly appreciative of his value and aware of the special expense that might be involved in settling his successor, they sent in a demand for $1300 as compensation for the loss of their pastor, but, when the Boston church offered $1000 as an ultimatum, accepted that sum. On Sunday, September 22, 1799, in spite of alarming signs of ill health, William Emerson preached both sermons at the Old Brick, the home of his new congregation.

He was undoubtedly pleased with the First Church's promise of a salary of $14 a week, a dwelling house, and an annual supply of twenty cords of wood; but, being prudent after seven years of unhappy experience, he qualified his gratitude with the observation that he was ignorant of the expenses of town life and could only express his confidence that his employers would deal justly with him. They were expected to see that he got a reputable maintenance if he performed his duties faithfully. And, as it turned out, both church and pastor kept their parts of this understanding.

The house occupied by the Emersons stood in Summer Street, near what is now the corner of Chauncy. In contrast to the noise and bustle in the vicinity of the Old Brick, half a mile away, here was almost bucolic peacefulness. The tinkling of cowbells could still be heard in a neighboring pasture, and the old parsonage, a gambrel-roofed wooden building, painted yellow and standing far back from the gate, had nearly an acre of land to itself, with orchard and garden and a row of elms and Lombardy poplars.

Other orchards and gardens, belonging to the estates of prosperous neighbors, made the region slightly reminiscent of the country villages William Emerson had known. The common, only a short distance away, was itself still a public cow pasture.

William Emerson had good reason to be hopeful. But Ruth, on the eve of her second confinement, seemed to have a premonition of ill fortune in Boston. She dreaded the prospect of "the useless ceremony, parade, and pomp, that almost necessarily are attached to a town life." She declared that she did not feel qualified to move in this new sphere, and in spite of the difficult winters at Harvard she kept her great preference for retirement and rural scenes. But she was a dutiful wife, and she remembered that in following her husband she was returning to her girlhood home "to dwell," as she said in her somewhat Biblical manner, "among my kindred and friends."

Though John Clarke, named after the late minister of the First Church, came safely into the world a few weeks after his parents had settled down in Summer Street, a major disaster was not far in the future. Within a year illness swept the transplanted household, and it is certain that William Emerson was dramatizing no imaginary grief when he made the brief entries in his diary on the final day of the ordeal: "Phebe is worse. Dies. Oh! my God, support me under this heavy loss!" Ruth Haskins Emerson wrote more calmly but with no less feeling: "Sept 28, 1800. Sabbath day, Died Phebe Ripley Emerson, the eldest child and only daughter of William and Ruth Emerson Her disorder was the disentery and canker. She was a lovely and charming flower . . . O gracious God, let us ever be more solicitous, that the ends thou didst design may be fully answered! Since thou has deprived us of one of the purest streams of our earthly happiness, do thou draw us to thee the fountain of inexhaustible felicity!" A third child, William, destined to outlive all his brothers and sisters but one, was born on the last day of July, 1801—"His perfect birth, and the good state of his mother fill our hearts with gratitude to God," wrote his father.

The minister of the First Church seemed to regard all of the cultured part of Boston as belonging to his parish. His calendar presented a jumble of engagements. He gave much time to the founding and encouragement of clubs, societies, and institutions intended to aid science, literature, and the arts. The school committee required his attention. The singing society met at his house. Across the Charles, in Cambridge, he attended the exhibition at Harvard as a member of the visiting committee; and he was soon due at a meeting of the overseers. He did not neglect the Humane Society or the Agricultural Society. He attended the club at Popkin's. He was driving himself hard and had little privacy for either thought or relaxation.

Even his outings were apt to have an air of official gravity. He sailed in the revenue cutter, a government vessel, when he got away for a few days to visit Cape Cod and to pitch quoits and to fish at an island on the return voyage. At another time he went "down on the water with the Select Men." He became a member of the Massachusetts Historical Society. He met with Kirkland and Popkin, fellow ministers of Boston churches, to arrange for the founding of the Physiological Society, or wrote his 304th sermon, or took his turn at lecturing before the Boston Philosophical Society, or had to prepare a Fourth of July oration, and, on the day of his oration, dine with the governor and attend an association meeting at Popkin's. He found he had to write something for the *Palladium,* a local newspaper. He studied chemistry. In January of 1803 he received a new honor, being appointed chaplain to the senate of the commonwealth; and before the year was out he was to receive a like honor from the council.

Though he was much in the public eye, he had the good sense not to overestimate his own value. "Good God!" he wrote in his journal, "What a slow being I am! I scarcely vegetate. I am sometimes noticed; but I am as stupid as an ass." Once after a meeting of the Philosophical Society, he recorded that that organization was flourishing and remarked, with some degree of self-satisfaction, "I thank a good Providence that this child of my brain is fostered, and promises to grow to mature age." But he was not boastful. Such prominence as he had already won was, after all, mainly to be credited, as he doubtless knew, to the pulpit he occupied.

His reputation as a preacher at the First Church in his early years there was enough to warrant the publication, by the summer of 1803, of half a dozen or more sermons; but these were by no means works of genius. They were not even very remarkable for any precocious Unitarianism or rationalism. With many other Congregational ministers of his time, he was drifting only half-consciously into the current of Unitarian thought, and in America this still lacked definite direction. Though he may well have been in a questioning mood—the least that could have been expected of a budding Unitarian—when he prayed for help "to frame just conceptions of Jesus Christ, and of the design and extent of his mission to mankind," he was orthodox enough to praise God for "the clear and glorious light of divine revelation" and for "sending from the realms of happiness thy blessed son, who was the brightness of thy glory and the express image of thy person, into this our sinful world." Yet he stressed very little the notion of eternal punishment; and, though it might seem to him that an "awful dispensation of providence" could cover his own purposes with darkness, no belief in the predestination of the soul seems to have troubled him. At times he held firmly to the doctrine of human depravity as well as to that of Christ's mediation. But he was more an Arminian denying an arbitrary and tyrannically administered scheme of salvation than a Calvinist holding to a belief in the absolute government of God. Wearying somewhat of the unqualified dogma of a threefold God, he was almost a Unitarian. If he hated to let go of the old hereditary doctrines, he also liked to be a cultured man and a catholic-minded gentleman.

Though he was not brilliant in his sermons, he could at least appeal to good sense. "His eloquence," according to one contemporary, "was of that bold and manly kind, that, when used in argumentative discourses, generally produces conviction without appealing to the passions; and in those of a didactick nature, enforces moral and religious truth, by its suavity and mildness." Obviously he thought one of the chief duties of the minister was to make religion a foundation for a just and temperate life, the life of reason and of religion combined.

Even though for him the happy pulpit warrior was one who did not confound the morality of the pagan Stoics with the religion of Christ, he was confident that truth would be safe without being locked up in the prison of a creed. What had seemed to some of his predecessors in the pulpit of the First Church the abomination of abominations of all Christendom he could tolerate. He could remark without acrimony that "The roman catholick church is going forward with spirit in Boston." It would not be unreasonable to imagine him as an unperturbed onlooker when the Church of the Holy Cross was dedicated in Boston and Bishop Carroll and the priests, mutely testifying to the fact that Catholicism was still foreign to New England, moved in procession from the residence of the Spanish consul.

His orthodoxy had not gone unquestioned at the time of his ordination. He read the radical Priestley and he seems to have owned a copy of *The Age of Reason,* deist Tom Paine's book that stripped religion of revelation. Perhaps he had summed up well his whole career as a preacher before he had commenced it. The functions of an enlightened divine, he had said, struck him with amazing beauty, and he was charmed with the idea of reforming mankind.

But if William Emerson was a liberal in religion he was a conservative in politics. Though in his clerical sphere he tried to keep clear of open political controversy and more than once declared his dislike of politics, those who heard his sermons and addresses could easily guess where his party allegiance lay. The chief danger he saw to the social structure was radical reform. He held to the opinion that society was a cake in which the richest and most refined ingredients enjoyed a natural right to be on the top layer. As he said in his sermon on the death of Governor Bowdoin's widow, he believed that "Talents, honours, and wealth hold a sort of natural sway over the opinions of mankind." He commended the founders of the Boston Female Asylum for their charity but at the same time felt it necessary to reassure his hearers, for these comprised, as a local newspaper reported, "most of the female merit and elegance of the town." If, he admitted, those in charge of the asylum entertained "the romantick notion of instituting an order of females in the community with new privileges, or of even conferring gentility on these children who are destined to service," they might with reason be accused of "disturbing the wholesome arrangements of society. But we," he declared, "are infected with no rage for modern innovation."

When he praised the early settlers in a Fourth of July oration, he remembered their unconquerable love of liberty, but he defined that liberty in much the same terms as those once used by the First Church's hero John Winthrop on a famous occasion. He correctly understood the doctrine taught by the Puritan leaders of Massachusetts Bay Colony. Concerning the liberty of the common people they had no illusions. They did not seek or wish "the freedom of an irrational, but that of a rational being." Their doctrine of equality was a very sober one. It was not an equality of wisdom that they believed in. And they did not teach "a parity of power, but of obligation."

He saw clearly that the liberty for which Americans had later been willing to fight against the mother country was the liberty to control their own wealth, and he held that it was not the Americans but the British who had resisted law and order. And while he drew an example for the world to admire from the American Revolution, he pointed a steady finger of warning toward the French one. "See there, ye vaunting innovators," he exclaimed, "your wild and dreadful desolations!" Even in the year 1802 he could see that the French, "after murdering the mildest of despots," had got a republic that was mere military despotism and slavery. And he reminded his fellow countrymen that "along with the political innovation, which was ravaging Europe, there came abroad an infidel philosophy, equally subversive of freedom, as of morals." If America should drink deeper of this foreign draught, she would be ruined.

In the parlor, in the pulpit, or on the public platform William Emerson made a more than respectable figure. The nearly contemporary engraving of him published in *The Polyanthos* showed his face long and narrow with deep lines that seemed to express courtesy, dignity, urbanity. The full head of hair, only slightly wavy, and combed straight back from the forehead, added to his air of elegance. The engraving, however, according to the editor of the little magazine that printed it, was only "sufficient to awaken a recollection of Mr. Emerson's features" and could not be called a likeness. It was certainly "not so alive as he"; and it was too somber to conjure up the image of "a very ready talker, with his friends" or a man who, though he was formal in manner and speech, had "a passionate love for the strains of eloquence."

On several of his friends and acquaintance he made a vivid impression. According to a fellow preacher practiced in observing and judging the characteristics of public speakers, William Emerson was "much more than ordinarily attractive" and had a "melodious voice," a clear enunciation, and an agreeable pulpit manner. James Russell Lowell's father saw in him "a handsome man, rather tall, with a fair complexion, his cheeks slightly tinted, his motions easy, graceful and gentlemanlike, his manners bland and pleasant." A Miss Eliza Quincy described him as a naturally good-looking man who dressed with great care and carried a gold-headed cane. "I think," she said, "he was proud of his well-shaped leg. He wore knee-breeches and black silk stockings, and when he sat down he placed one ankle on the other knee, for that showed his leg to the best advantage." Whether or not it was correctly reported that the tavern keeper knew him by his boots, the minister was undoubtedly an elegant, formal man.

In the spring of 1803, when his third son was born, William Emerson must have resembled very little the somewhat lifeless wood engraving in *The Polyanthos*. Probably well-informed Bostonians would have agreed that this liberal minister of the town's oldest church and chaplain of the Federalist senate was in his proper place when he sat at the governor's table on Election Day, a chief anniversary of the commonwealth. May 25 was only one of his many busy days. He kept a steady hand as he recorded the birth of Ralph Waldo. In the rest of his entry he betrayed only the slightest impatience. He included there the fact that two days earlier he had received a Mr. Puffer as his guest, "and," he grumbled with disciplined decorum, "here he has tarried." A complimentary remark on the Election Day sermon just preached by Puffer masked the host's desire for his guest to be gone. The diarist rounded out the story of the 25th by mentioning a club. He presumably found time to attend the club that evening. On the following day he was present to hear the "convention" sermon, part of the ceremonies of Election Week, and had the governor and others home to dinner with him, where they may have viewed his new son. On the 27th he was at a meeting of the Massachusetts Charitable Fire Society. He also dined on that day with Lady Temple, perhaps to bring her religious consolation, for he had only recently preached her mother's funeral sermon.

At times, no doubt, his hurrying from one appointment to another gave him a pleasant sense of importance and helped him to forget a fundamental conflict in character which he shared with a large part of humanity. But he was by no means a stupid person, and there it still was, plainly to be seen by his own eyes, the conflict between his love of mere gentility, of social pleasure, and of ease and his resurgent ambition to rise to industry and fame. Whatever qualities might be necessary for the successful pursuit of fame, it became clear to him that the achievement of even industry made demands that were discouragingly exacting. He was used to being frank with himself. Had his parishioners been fortunate enough to look into William Emerson's diary they might have read in it a sermon on human nature more eloquent than any the pastor ever preached from his pulpit.

Unfortunately he did not record in his diary his secret thoughts at the climactic moment of the week when he climbed into his pulpit and sat waiting to begin his sermon. The congregation may have misjudged him but doubtless thought him a calm, collected, confident, satisfied man. His wife, unwilling to trust anybody else to iron his lawn bands, had seen that all was in order before he left home. And now he was "very handsome" with the lawn at his throat and his black silk gown held correctly in place by the broad plaited band of black silk around the waist.

Ruth Emerson, calm and deliberate, served as the balance wheel in the daily routine performance of the Emerson domestic machinery and made little stir in public. Having unobtrusively put the final touches to the impressive dignity that would clothe her husband in his pulpit, she was willing to share with other members of his congregation the status of admirer and disciple. Perhaps her most conspicuous public appearances were before the altar of the First Church, where she is said to have carried her babies, each in turn, for baptism by her husband.

It seems unlikely that she was strong enough to play this part in the ceremony of May 29, 1803, when the four-days-old Ralph Waldo was duly entered in his father's bold hand in the baptismal record of the parish. But probably it was she who had chosen the boy's first name in honor of her brother Ralph Haskins, then "far absent in the Pacific Ocean" as supercargo on the ship of a Boston merchant. The second name came from the Emersons. It had repeatedly appeared among them since the seventeenth century, when Edward, grandson of the Thomas Emerson who had founded the American branch of the family, had married Rebecca, daughter of Cornelius Waldo. As William had recently noted in some genealogical jottings, it had recurred well into the eighteenth century, when his paternal grandparents, Joseph and Mary, had given it to two sons in succession, not content to allow it to go unused after the death of the first.

2.

BOSTON, 1803

This mart of commerce; this rich mine of wealth;
This field of plenty; residence of health . . .
Shall all things else but *genius* flourish here?
—Winthrop Sargent, *Boston. A Poem,* 1803

THE year 1803 was a good year for an American to be born in. On the day of Ralph Waldo's birth, Reuben Puffer, the guest of the Emersons, uttered some truths that turned out to be not wholly unrelated to that event. For nations, as well as for individuals, he said in his election sermon, there were times when heaven was propitious. Now the United States came forward to enjoy their day. The future hung upon the fate of America, and she was a spectacle watched by the whole world. Had the preacher of the election sermon been only slightly more prescient and had he not been addressing an audience predominantly Federalist, he might have pointed for proof to the territorial expansion then actually in progress. Thomas Jefferson, the man in the White House who seemed to cast a long, sinister shadow over State Street and Cornhill in Boston, was already negotiating with France for more suitable boundaries. News traveled slowly and any treaty had to be ratified by the Senate, but some weeks had now passed since the President's emissaries, though instructed only to buy French land about the mouth of the Mississippi, had suddenly agreed to purchase the whole of Louisiana, sprawling across the Western prairies and plains from the Mississippi to the Rockies. The Federalists, unable to discover any good in Jefferson, were soon filled with alarm and warned that

> Extended empire like expanded gold,
> Exchanges solid strength for feeble splendor.

But such fears were unfounded in the opinion of most Americans; and the republic really was, as Puffer said, coming forward now to enjoy its day.

Boston herself was just stepping forward to enjoy a new day of greatness among American cities. Since the century and more of her rule as the queen of English colonial towns, she had been eclipsed and surpassed both commercially and intellectually. But her future was again bright. Though she had fewer than thirty thousand people on her three hills and along the borders of her small peninsula, still literally almost an island, her wharves and warehouses already gave her the air of a metropolis. The Boston commercial world of 1803 was fast becoming an economic powerhouse that could, if properly harnessed, make the wheels of culture turn with exciting momentum. That commercial world was a solid fact not only in the experience of the aged business-minded distiller John Haskins but in the life of his son-in-law, the minister, for without the sustenance provided by it the thin spiritual flame of the First Church might have flickered and smoked.

If William Emerson could have found time during the overcrowded hours of May 25 to make the rounds of the waterfront and the chief business streets, he would unquestionably have been impressed by the rich stores of goods for sale. He might have got the key to the whole intricate pattern of commerce by stopping at Central Wharf, where his brother-in-law John Haskins Junior not only transacted auction, brokerage, and commission business but sold West Indian rum, claret, Burgundy and muscat wines, and a variety of French goods. Somewhere along the waterfront the brig *Eliza* was just in from Alicante with a cargo of brandy; the schooner *Sally* had arrived after a passage of twenty-nine days from Guadeloupe with various stores, including molasses that was no doubt intended to be made into rum; the ship *Mary* was in with salt from Lisbon; and there was newly arrived coastwise shipping. Shops and warehouses were crowded with a bewildering variety of desirable things: silk ribbons, men's silk hats, Italian artificial flowers, Roman violin strings, marble chimney pieces with hearths to match, thousands of excellent Havana segars, fine flour, first and second quality ship bread, haddock, pollock, herring, mackerel, hundreds of quintals of codfish and barrels of alewives and hogsheads of molasses, boxes of white and brown Havana sugar, Canton sugar, Calcutta sugar, Welsh's fresh chocolate, numerous chests of fragrant hyson and hyson skin and bohea and Souchong tea, tons of the best green coffee, bottled cider, pipes of country gin and Rotterdam gin, St. Vincent's rum, cherry rum, New England rum, St. Kitt's and Grenada rum, London porter, cognac, sherry, Madeira, Lisbon and Vidonia and Malaga wines, Bordeaux claret, table beer and strong beer by the barrel, kegs of tobacco, boxes of Turkey figs, prunes, muscatel raisins, fresh oranges, lemons, apricots, Baltimore flour, Richmond flour, pork, casks of rice, nuts, seeds, tons of whale oil, Georgia upland cotton and cotton from the Carolinas, hemp, bales of Madras handkerchiefs, plushes, umbrellas, fans, gloves, hose, ear jewels, ear hoops and knots, English and Genevan watches, finger rings, knee buckles, swords and hangers, gold and silver and tinsel epaulettes, satins, laces, broadcloths, calicoes, ginghams, cassimeres, chintzes, Marseille quiltings, sprigged and tamboured muslin, long lawns, Irish linens, sheeting, diapers, shawls, black and colored hats for men, razors, straw hats and bonnets as high as $15 each, fancy rosettes, veils, cloaks, mantles, silk gloves, superfine fancy colored kid gloves and shoes of the same material, sewing silks of all kinds, nankeens, dimities, elegant morocco and cabinet work shaving and dressing cases, satteen wood tea caddies with cut glass sugar basins, elegant family medicine chests, paints and water colors in scores of varieties.

But it would doubtless have been perfectly obvious to the calmly appraising mind of William Emerson that not only the fertilizer of mercantile wealth but a good deal of patient cultivation would be necessary to make the sandy soil of Massachusetts bear a rank harvest of marketable ideas, and that the Bostonians would have years of laborious waiting before their local renaissance could reach its height. Their town seemed to cry aloud for reform, even to its very streets and houses. Civic pride, shamed by what seemed a monstrous collection of shapeless structures, where the few symmetrical buildings were like rough-hewn diamonds in a mean setting, demanded domes, turrets, and spires to "parley with the setting sun." Winthrop Sargent, the current satirist and self-appointed spokesman for civic pride, was satisfied with the evidences of commercial prosperity. But he lamented in his poem *Boston* the depraved public taste that was offended by Shakespeare and patronized triumphant German dullness on a stupid stage. Literature was in disgrace, with ballads, foolish odes, and acrostics the order of the day. One reason why genius alone failed to flourish here, Sargent argued, was that poverty restrained it even in the midst of wealth. Writers needed encouragement if they were to survive. Sargent, a sort of New England Johnson, lashed with his scorn the social excesses and follies of the times and advised, with perhaps little more conviction than the author of *London* had done, that it would be better to fly from such scenes to rural joys, far surpassing the pleasures of the town. But his sincerity was unmistakable when he announced his ardent hope that in some more glorious day these envious spots would all be wiped away, leaving the name of Boston "unrivall'd on the chart of fame."

William Emerson, in spite of his unflattering estimate of himself as "Destitute of one particle of genius," was really significant as one of the leaders in the scheme for a future city notable for letters, arts, and sciences. The desire for cultural amelioration was a part of his religion. He had been used to praying, not only for a divine blessing upon the commerce, fishery, and manufactures which he now saw flourishing about him, but for a prospering of the "means of literature." He was just now witnessing, doubtless with little realization of the importance of the event, the arrival of a new worker who would prove to be far more effective than he in advancing the good cause. A week after the birth of his son Ralph Waldo he attended at the Park Street Church the ordination of William Ellery Channing, later famed both as the national Unitarian leader and as the harbinger of a new literary era in New England. There were a number of intellectual or political notables who also seemed to strengthen the town's claims to a place in the cultural sun. John Quincy Adams, future President, was a member of the First Church. Old John Adams, ex-President, emanated distinction when he came in from his suburban residence to receive honors on public occasions. Samuel Adams, a memorable figure of the Revolutionary era, had a few more months to live before being carried to the Granary Burying Ground with such pomp as the clergy, local officialdom, and the representatives of foreign countries could supply. Jeremy Belknap was dead by this time, but the older Robert Treat Paine, later a friend and adviser to William Emerson, much as Belknap had been, was still a justice of the state's supreme court.

Not farther away than Cambridge was a little group of professional scholars, and miscellaneous untitled ones were also leavening the dough of the whole community. Bostonians, if they wished to study Spanish or French, might find their way to William Emerson's own street, where Francis Sales held evening classes at home and stood ready to furnish translations, even from Italian or Portuguese, upon request. On the fringes of Boston, Susanna Haswell Rowson, an English-born teacher and ex-actress, removed her young ladies' academy from Medford to Newton and kept up the stream of fiction that had already made her one of the most widely read authors in America.

In the fine arts the renaissance, if European art was to have one in Massachusetts, still seemed to be in the distant future. Though Copley, one of the clever portrait painters of his time, was a native of Boston, he had now been an Englishman for a quarter of a century or more. Neither Gilbert Stuart, a Rhode Islander, nor Washington Allston, a South Carolinian, had yet arrived with brush and pigments to be a citizen of the town. Well-to-do families owned a few portraits, but, so far as the less fortunate were concerned, art hardly existed outside such hopeful institutions as the Columbian Museum. The Columbian still had to be taken into account, for though it had recently burned to the ground, it was rising again phoenix-like from its ashes, as the owner had promised, and would flourish at a new home in Milk Street. There it would soon display, for a moderate admission fee, a new selection of "elegant paintings," together with wax figures of historical personages, a perfect model of a mammoth's skeleton, and a surprising variety of both natural and artificial curiosities.

Its rooms would resound with "excellent Music on the organized and grand Piano-Fortes." Before the year was ended, the Columbian, emulated by the rival Washington Museum at the foot of the Mall, would combine literature and art in an exhibition of figures of Shakespearean characters. The Boston stage meanwhile offered entertainments ranging from tragedy to farce. In Federal Street *Hamlet* was played for the "first time these four years."

The pastor of the First Church could have given any of his culture-hungry fellow townsmen full information about the local scientific and learned societies. Once he had boldly joined John Quincy Adams, Josiah Quincy, John Lowell, Benjamin Bussey, and John Kirkland, later president of the college, in pledging contributions toward the purchase of apparatus and a library needed by the Society for the Study of Natural Philosophy. In spite of his too slender financial means, he was still a devoted organizer and promoter. Of all the Boston societies founded during his lifetime the Massachusetts Historical Society appealed most to this lover of method. It had realized Belknap's dream of a repository where historic objects and historical manuscripts could be preserved in order and in safety for the use of the learned and the curious. But it was only one of the rather numerous scholarly or scientific institutions watched over by William Emerson and his friends.

Boston's literary event of the year 1803 was the launching of *The Monthly Anthology*, with schoolmaster Phineas Adams at the helm. After six months, William Emerson was to take Adams's place, enlisting new recruits and giving the feeble but ambitious little *Anthology* a more significant direction. The society he would soon help form for the support of the magazine would be in some respects conservative, being made up of gentlemen conscious of their class. Yet nothing else in Boston would point more steadily toward the town's literary future than this society and the *Anthology*. The latter was the forerunner of *The North American Review*, and the society eventually instigated the founding of the Boston Athenæum.

Ralph Waldo, now still in his first year, would live to look back upon this era with some justifiable disdain, pricking and deflating its pretension with an epithet, "that early ignorant & transitional *Month-of-March*, in our New England culture." In their soberest moments the minister of the First Church and his fellow pioneers would doubtless have acknowledged the accuracy of every term of this verdict. They knew it was only early spring, but they were preparing for a summer which they themselves could hardly hope to enjoy.

3.

LOOKING OUT FROM HIS CORNER

❊

Thus, little by little, I became conscious where I was; and
to have a wish to express my wishes to those who could
content them . . . And, lo! my infancy died long since,
and I live.

> —St. Augustine, *The Confessions,* translated by
> E. B. Pusey, Book I

DURING his early infancy Ralph Emerson was not much distinguished from his brothers in extant family papers, and incidents in which he was concerned seemed mostly trivial to his elders, though they could not actually have been so in the life of any child. As early as his second year he was probably ordered to Concord, along with his brothers, to "inhale a large portion of rural and balsam air." When he was two years old his father sent him from Haverhill a promise to "bring home cake for little boys who behave well at the dinner table." In his third year he showed some imagination when he joined his brother William in pretending to carry the family news to their father, then in Maine, and to drink his health. He was overjoyed at the traveler's return but doubtless listened with more wonder than comprehension to tales of the voyage to Portland in a vessel described as hardly bigger than a punch bowl. By December of 1805 he was regarded as "rather a dull scholar"; and it is possible that he was already at school by that time. In the following March he was going to his teacher, a Mrs. Whitwell, "again." He got through a serious illness blamed on worms, and before his third birthday he was once more back in the dame school and naturally still unable to read well.

Presumably he had by this time discarded the yellow flannel that the pastor's children are said to have worn "when quite young," and had got into his dark blue nankeen jacket and trousers. He sometimes said his prayers to Mary Winslow, his father's ward, and repeated for her entertainment such profane pieces as "You'd scarce expect one of my age," "Franklin one night stopped at a public inn," and a part of the dialogue between Brutus and Cassius. But there is no proof that he was an infant prodigy, and some of the accomplishments Mary Winslow remembered may have belonged to a period several years later. The three-year-old scholar was certainly admonished because of his slow progress at school. Once, when it was a question of whether he or his brother William needed help more, Ralph was selected as the one to be drilled in his studies.

Yet he may have been acquiring quite as much informal as formal acquaintance with subjects worth knowing. Even at his age he may have caught some enthusiasm for the mysteries of science from his father, an amateur scientist and member of a scientific club. Once his father, after spending hours in preparation, viewed the total eclipse of the sun from neighbor Bussey's garden in company with "a congregation of astronomers." The boy could hardly have been ignorant of such doings as these, and he may have got an exaggerated notion of the dignity of men of letters when the genteel members of the Anthology Society came frequently to dine and to select articles for publication in the next number of their magazine. In Boston he had, fortunately, opportunities to see specimens of humanity ranging from refined to savage. Sometimes he may have found his best teachers on the streets. This would surely have been possible when, for several days, the town was host to ten Indian warriors, true and original Americans, as they themselves declared.

Boston's love of pageantry stimulated civic and national pride in juvenile minds. On the Fourth of July discharges of artillery and the ringing of bells saluted sunrise and sunset, and there were processions and noisy celebrations. At night crowds assembled on the common to witness the display of fireworks. The Emerson boys, with family history strengthening their patriotism, could hardly have escaped the general enthusiasm. Grandfather Emerson's death during the Revolution would have been a familiar story to them; and they must have heard their mother tell how, when she was seven years old, General Washington had taken her on his knee. But the Election Day that came on the last Wednesday in May was their favorite holiday. Weeks before the event, as the boys lay in bed at night, they counted in anticipation their Election Day pleasures. The chief adventure was the spending, on the common, of the ninepence allotted to each of them. The first time Ralph was old enough to have his money, so goes the family tradition, he injudiciously parted with all of it for a sheet of gingerbread but was immediately so filled with remorse that the compassionate keeper of the stall allowed him to return half of the purchase and gave him back half of the price.

Before he was four years old he had seen the beginning of one family disaster and the end of another. The birth of his fourth brother, Robert Bulkeley, seemed at first a propitious event. But Bulkeley was destined to live past middle age without developing mentally beyond the ability to pen a few childish, ink-blotted lines. John Clarke, the oldest brother, had found no New England climate that would heal his lungs. At home he continued to fail "notwithstanding the best advice that Boston affords, and the best attention we can give him." On the day of his death his father was overwhelmed with grief as he assured the questioning boy that he had been a good child and would go to heaven, and Ruth Emerson seems to have been crushed by the catastrophe. Ralph must at least have been sobered by a sense of insecurity, though he was so young that he could remember nothing in after years but sitting with the family in the parlor at the funeral.

Doubtless he was not oblivious of the changing moods of his father. William Emerson frequently felt disgust for worldly ambition but was apt soon to fall a victim to it again. He reproved his sister Mary Moody for false humility, a mask too flimsy to hide the pride which demanded that her relatives "have a *name* in the world." For himself, he told her, he began to see life in a different way and prized most highly the honors of the honest, quiet man. Yet by January of the following year he had felt a new upsurge of ambition and was experimenting with a private time table too exacting for a man of his uncertain health:

6 to 7 Dress
7 to 8 Read the scriptures Original
8 to 9 Read Practical authors
9 to 11 Sermonize. Write 4 pages.
11 to 12 Greek authors. Write a letter.
12 to 1. Latin authors. Write pro bono publico
1 to 2. Write for periodical publications.
2 to 3. Newspapers. Sermonize.
3 to 4 Read new publications & polemicks.
4 to 5 Read Philosophy. Mathematicks
5 to 6. Bookmaking
6 to 7. Read History. Sermonize.
7 to 9. Visit.
9 to 10. Write prayers.
10. to 11. Journalize. Devotions. Read.

His whole family must have been oppressed with anxiety when, that spring, he suffered "a profuse hemorrhage from the lungs, from the effects of which he never completely recovered." His doctors suggested Concord as a refuge from the east wind. He knew Concord weather better than they did and may not have followed their suggestion, but the very name of his native town must have been music in his ears in the tense days of strife between France and England when his own country stood precariously on the brink of war. He sometimes wished he had been born and bred among Quakers and was vexed beyond measure that the whole world should be kept in a constant tumult merely for the sport of a dozen or so madmen, as he said. As for local politics, the fate of the Federalism which was no doubt close to his heart seemed to be prophesied that summer in the magnificent spectacle of the funeral of Fisher Ames, its great leader.

At some earlier and happier period of his life the minister and his family might have gloried in the inauguration of a new church to take the place of the one now engulfed in the swirling commerce of the town. But he preached the last sermon in the Old Brick only in spite of what had appeared to him to be the restraining hand of God. An unforeseen "dispensation of providence . . . suspending the exercise of my ministry, seemed," he admitted, "to cover this purpose, and all my other purposes, with a veil of darkness." And, to add to his gloomy mood, there was the fact, quite plain to him, that he was leading a divided congregation to the new place of worship. Many resented the trading of the Old Brick for a new church barren of traditions. Even the parcel of dwelling houses built for the church as part of the bargain was not enough to salve their pride. The ill feeling remained tense, and one rude wit, not loath to remind the world of the bargaining that had been necessary in order to get William Emerson from the Harvard church, quipped:

> Alas! Old Brick, you're left in the lurch,
> You *bought the Pastor* and *sold the Church.*

William Emerson had the satisfaction of finishing and publishing *A Selection of Psalms and Hymns,* with its preface dated in August of 1808. His old theories of church music were now broadcast. Presumably there was a new interest in hymnology in his own household, where it became, sooner or later, a regular duty of the boys to learn hymns by heart. But the moods of the pastor were inconstant, and he was soon discontented with himself again. "The time was," he wrote that autumn, "when I hoped to be a light in the church; but now, gracious God, the very light that is in me seems to be darkness." A week later he had recovered his spirits somewhat and resolved once more, "God willing, strictly to adhere to method in pursuing my studies."

There were some reasons for a happier view of his fortunes. He was given $700 for the purchase of furniture, and on a fine day in November he moved into a new parsonage, the best of the four large dwelling houses that the purchasers of the Old Brick had built for the church. He had hardly settled his family there before his sixth son, Charles Chauncy, arrived safely. But the management of his household must by this time have demanded more and more of his strength, and as a new year approached, the minister sensibly resolved upon a less exacting but still orderly scheme for his own life:

New Plan

Before Breakfast. Prayers. Shave & dress. Biblical criticism.
Before Dinner Sermonize. Write a prayer. Walk.
Before Tea Newspaper. New publications. History. Billets, Letters, Business.
Before Supper Write pro bono publico.
Before bedtime Read.

In 1809, the year for which William Emerson devised his simplified diurnal schedule, his son Ralph was six years old. It may have been about this time that Ralph was taken for the sake of his health from Boston for a brief stay in Concord. There he tried dock tea and bathing as cures for some eruptive disease, perhaps what he afterwards remembered under the vague label of salt rheum. Even in Boston, he could not escape the supposedly curative baths. He rebelled till dislike of them, strengthened by fear of deep water, became a phobia. William Emerson's insistence on carrying out the doctor's advice stirred up long-lived resentment in the boy. Some forty years later Ralph could not forget the severity of a father "who twice or thrice put me in mortal terror by forcing me into the salt water off some wharf or bathing house, and . . . the fright with which, after some of this salt experience, I heard his voice one day, (as Adam that of the Lord God in the garden,) summoning us to a new bath, and I vainly endeavouring to hide myself."

Two other symbols of authority, Mrs. Whitwell and the Miss Nancy Dickson who succeeded her and who seems to have taught in the same dame school, left little more than their names in his memory. In old age William Furness could recall going with him to the ABC school kept in Summer Street opposite the wooden Trinity Church. Ralph himself was far more impressed by William Furness, with his red and white handkerchief adorned with illustrations of the Mother Goose tale of "The House that Jack Built," than by the rest of the school.

The third of Ralph's regular teachers, Lawson Lyon, made an unforgettable impression on some of his charges. Lyon was "a severe teacher, high-tempered, and flogged the boys unmercifully." He would make a big apple, the gift of some diplomatic pupil, illustrate the use of the terrestrial globe; and, after the apple had served this educational purpose, he would proceed to eat it with great satisfaction. He was a practical-minded man and was probably at his best in training boys for the counting room. But he seems to have meant little more to Ralph than Mrs. Whitwell or Nancy Dickson did.

Outside school the life of the very small boy must have been less gray than tradition paints it. In his declining years William Furness, recollecting how his friend once played with him and Sam Bradford on the floor, of the Furness home, declared that it was the only occasion, so far as he knew, when Ralph ever played as a normal child would have done. Probably Furness's memory was at fault, but even when the boy had no companions he must have had frequent opportunities to escape the boredom of unimaginative trivialities. There were ways of doing that without toys, and it is hard to believe that the only toy in the minister's household was the pictured box, originally filled with little story books, that may have inspired a passage in "Domestic Life." At any rate, the few incidents remembered by Ralph or by others from his early days did not add up to a realistic childhood for any boy.

Ralph showed some imagination when he offered to aid the woodsawer at work in the Emerson yard by doing the grunting for him. The yard was for a long time his chief playground, and "his mother used to warn him not to play in the streets for fear of meeting 'rude boys.' " He would "stand at the gate in a state of pleasing excitement half fear half hope that the 'rude boys' would come near enough for him to see them!" As "a little chubby boy" he trundled a hoop in Chauncy Place. He had never had a sled "and would not have dared to use one, for fear of the 'Round-Pointers,'—rough boys from Windmill Point and the South End, who 'were always coming;' taking Summer Street on their way to the Common, where they had pitched battles with the West-Enders." But some of these incidents reported so candidly by him were the reminiscences of an old man whose memory was failing, and, at best, they certainly did not tell the whole story.

It is true, however, that his Aunt Mary Moody Emerson loomed larger in Ralph's early life than did either his schoolteachers or his playmates. She was an extremely valuable, if only occasional, instructor, for she cared about ideas. Though she generally managed to disagree with her brother William, she was always welcome in his house. In October of 1809, he wrote her: "If it is a compliment to say that I love you, and that your residence in my family until death or matrimony separates us is necessary to my happiness, I confess I have been complimentary, and shall be so continually. . . . Again gladden with your voice & healing attentions our charming boys, who have lame legs, wounded hands, and other calamities, and whose minds and hearts afford a fine field for the display of talents such as their aunt possesses."

As she would one day jest to La Fayette, she had been "in arms" at the Concord Fight. She was in her thirties before Ralph, eventually to be her biographer, was old enough to recognize her peculiar virtues. In her early years she was a recluse with access to only a few books, one of which was a copy of *Paradise Lost* so mutilated that she could not then know the title or that Milton was the author. Once she was out of seclusion she learned rapidly, and she became a dangerous adversary in an argument. She even tried authorship, though her few articles in *The Monthly Anthology* were undistinguished and were possibly printed because of her brother's influence and after he had revised them. It was an exaggeration to claim that all her language was happy; but it was little more than the sober truth to call the diction of her letters and journals "inimitable, unattainable by talent, as if caught from some dream." If, as she said, the love of virtue was her particular gift from God, she was also gifted with a genius for doing the unexpected and unconventional thing, sometimes with supreme abruptness and awkwardness. She really delighted in success, in youth, in beauty, in genius, in manners; but her praise was often accompanied with the sting of reproof. "She surprised, attracted, chided and denounced her companion by turns, and pretty rapid turns." She prodded ambition into action. "Scorn trifles," she admonished, "lift your aims: do what you are afraid to do . . ."

She escaped wealth and was glad, for she believed it would have spoiled her. After due consideration she refused an offer of marriage from "a man of talents, education and good social position, whom she respected." She liked solitude and long found a kind of mystical delight in nature. Nature had taught her to say, "Alive with God is enough,—'t is rapture." But she was a bundle of contradictions. Whatever her mysticism amounted to, she continued to be both a fiery Calvinist and a liberal daughter of the Enlightenment. For many years she longed for death and was prepared for it, even to her shroud. But in spite of her secession from the world, she managed to keep open the one outlet to it through which she was able to exert the whole force of her character. Few had patience with her bad taste, her clownish defiance of proprieties, her cryptic style of speech and writing, and her cruel self-torment. But Ralph and one or two of her other nephews were among the exceptions to the rule and were richly repaid for their trouble.

William Emerson, though busy with his literary and scientific societies and prematurely broken in health, took his parental responsibilities seriously. When he was away from home in April of 1810 he wanted to hear that Ralph "regards his words, does not eat his dinner too fast, and is gradually resigning his impetuosity to younger boys." He admonished the three girls who seem to have been his wife's helpers and the children's nurses, and filled up his letter with remarks intended for the edification of the boys. "I offer this tribute," he told his wife, "on the altar of domestick affection and aid, which we together build, and the fire of which we suffer never to be extinct; and if you think . . . any portion of it . . . will assist you in fulfilling in my absence your domestick cares, you may cause it to be read or read it when the family may be assembled at the morning sacrifice."

For him the parental and priestly offices as well as vocabularies were closely related. At the First Church, Ralph stood in a class with Sam Bradford and other boys to repeat the catechism to the minister on the afternoons of communion Sundays. The catechizer bore a striking resemblance to the son who was helping to recite the answers. But William Emerson was not narrow in his insistence on religious and moral training. He lived up to the spirit of his own father's exhortation to him to "learn to read your Book and love your School." He had once warned his oldest son that "It will grieve me excessively to have you a blockhead; but it will excessively delight me to have you a bright scholar." He would soon round out more than ten years of service on the school committee in Boston. Recently he had concluded that the family tradition was not intellectual enough and had advised his mother not to overstress in her grandchildren the culture of the heart at the expense of the culture of the head.

By this time Ralph was old enough to get much of his education from casual contacts with persons. On convention morning of Election Week he might observe the behavior of the visiting ministers who came to the parsonage for breakfast, sometimes as many as a dozen of them. Some customs and manners of his later life grew from roots deep in his childhood, and memories of trivial happenings and of momentary delight in sense impressions remained as links to his past. Over fifty years later he would be served duck turnover on Thanksgiving Day "because he used to have one when he was a little boy." Christmas was generally little noticed in a community that still kept some of its Puritan characteristics, but Ruth Emerson had Episcopalian relatives. On Christmas Day the family circle was formed at the Haskins house in Rainsford's Lane. On New Year's Day Ralph doubtless accompanied his parents to the home of his Uncle Thomas Haskins, and on Twelfth-night they all went to Uncle Kast's house in Hanover Street. On Monday afternoons Grandfather and Grandmother Haskins were ready to serve tea to the assembled family. In winter they had a silver tankard of sangaree inside the fender, and at the proper time it went round for each person to drink from. Haskins's unmarried daughters, Aunts Nancy, Fanny, and Betsey, were in the background here, as they were in the background of Ralph's whole youth. Nancy and Fanny did little more than make tatting and bobbin, but Betsey could rise to the occasion when sister Emerson needed help in her household.

In the Emerson family an ordinary day began with a simple breakfast. There were family prayers in the morning, and everyone read his own verse of Scripture, the children taking part as soon as they could read. After breakfast Ruth Emerson retired to her own room for reading and meditation and was not to be interrupted. Thursday, Saturday, and Sunday were marked by special rituals. On Thursday, following the "lecture" in Chauncy Place, where clergymen from neighboring towns took turns preaching, William Emerson was apt to bring home some fellow ministers to dine. His dining room, decorated with portraits of Charles Chauncy and John Clarke, the earlier ministers of First Church for whom he had named two of his own sons, was a fitting place for such a gathering. Saturday had its salt-fish dinner, with vegetables, melted butter, and pork scraps; but in the evening the Sabbath began. No visits were received or made. The work basket was put aside, the parlor fireplace put in order, and the boys' clothes got ready for use on the following day. On Sunday Ruth Emerson, a good disciplinarian, was no doubt in complete control of her children as they set out for church. Even on so important an occasion she was ruled by good sense and was apt to forgo such vanity as a silk dress and wear one of plain cotton cloth. On Sunday evening, at the end of a full twenty-four hours of religious observance or quiet, the family was ready once more for simple social pleasures. If, as often, the deacons of the church and other friends came in, Ruth Emerson had a waiter prepared in the sideboard with decanters of wine and spirits.

For some years, presumably, this had been the typical social routine of the family of which Ralph was a part. But Ralph and his mother and brothers must have heard much, and with pride, of the life of his father outside the home. Even outside his church and his societies, William Emerson was a public figure, though not a great one. In his modest role of man of letters he had made himself known, at least to his fellow townsmen, as an editor, journalist, and historian. He had helped to found *The Christian Monitor,* but he was credited with no contributions to that journal except four discourses "with the prayers annexed to each." Escaping from the shadow of the pulpit, he wrote some "original compositions" and made "judicious selections" for *The Polyanthos,* another local publication. After a year and a half as editor of *The Monthly Anthology,* he had made way for a succession of editors and editorial committees. As a contributor he was counted on mainly for selections from British authors, brief notices of sermons, brief "Thursday lectures" of his own on religious or moral topics, and brief moral essays. Once he seems to have thrown off his habitual restraint and engaged in a sharp skirmish with some authors he accused of plagiarism. The *Anthology,* by mere coincidence, was to come to an end within a few weeks of his death, but not until long after he had resigned his seat "as an actual member" of the society, partly because, in the precarious state of his health, he had found it hard to keep up the pace of conviviality set by some of his more robust friends.

Except for the *Anthology* his editorial labor had been chiefly on his book of psalms and hymns. His historical writing was mainly comprised in his incomplete, posthumously published book on the First Church, a partial fruition of his desire to study "the great & learned men of this country," including his own predecessors in the Boston pulpit. The book, simple and orderly, showed a good deal of knowledge of New England history. The dramatic episode of Anne Hutchinson and the bitter battle between Chauncy and the enthusiasts who had Jonathan Edwards as their strong but not entirely loyal champion warmed the blood of the historian and made his style alive, but he often sank into a dull formality. A more serious fault was his strong bias on the side of the correct, intellectually well-groomed and predictable conservatives. He was a partisan of the elder John Winthrop and of Charles Chauncy, both shining knights wearing the favors of the First Church. He betrayed little comprehension of such complex minds as those of Roger Williams and Jonathan Edwards.

But his preaching, his attendance on learned societies, and his literary labors—persuasive examples for Ralph, however lacking they were in any extraordinary distinction—were fast drawing to a close. In February, 1811, he was too ill to give a wholehearted welcome to the "healthy, fat, black-eyed" daughter who was born before he could finish a letter begging Mary Moody to come by the earliest stagecoach. He now looked gloomily into the future of the family. "To my wife and children indeed," he reflected, "my continuance upon earth is a matter of moment, as, in the event of my decease, God only knows how they would subsist. And then the education of the latter!" A couple of weeks earlier he had recorded the last of more than two hundred marriages performed for his parishioners. On April 7 he added the infant Mary Caroline Emerson's name to his long list of baptisms. Meantime he had preached his last sermon.

He tried a voyage to Portland but in vain. He assumed as much gaiety as he could and jested about the conflicting advice of the doctors. They would eventually agree that the hemorrhage of the lungs he had suffered several years earlier probably had nothing to do with his final collapse.

Their post-mortem examination would show that "the lower orifice of the stomach was almost entirely closed by a schirrhous tumour, or hard swelling, which on the inside was ulcerated." But meanwhile the patient apologized for his mirth at the confusion of the learned men. "Threads of this levity," he confessed, "have been interwoven with the entire web of my life."

Next day it seemed as if he heard a voice from heaven ordering him to hand in his final accounts, but he was unshaken. "Whilst it is necessarily the knell of terrour and sadness to my terrestrial hopes," he explained as bravely as if he were still speaking from his pulpit, "it brings no dismay to my celestial expectations." When he died, on May 12, 1811, his sister Mary Moody Emerson, remembering his "state of long invalidity" and his "defective" theology, could not grieve for him.

The First Church voted to furnish mourning to the widow and family and directed that the male members of the society should wear black crape around the arm for six weeks "and that the females assume appropriate badges of mourning for the same time." The church and several other organizations arranged jointly to show proper honor to the dead. As the funeral procession moved from the First Church toward King's Chapel burying ground, the Ancient and Honourable Artillery Company marched before the hearse, while William and Ralph, the oldest surviving sons, walked behind it as mourners. Various delegations marched in line, and at the rear between fifty and sixty coaches lumbered along. Ralph, then eight years old, was more struck by the pomp and circumstance of the occasion than by grief; and as he marched up School Street and saw the procession sweep round the corner into Tremont Street, it seemed to him a grand sight.

4.

A BOY'S TROUBLED WORLD

How strange that all
The terrors, pains, and early miseries,
Regrets, vexations, lassitudes interfused
Within my mind, should e'er have borne a part,
And that a needful part, in making up
The calm existence that is mine . . .
—Wordsworth, *The Prelude,* Book I

THE First Church granted Ruth Emerson a temporary stipend of $25 a week, the full amount of her late husband's salary, and soon decided on a long-term plan that would give her $500 annually for a period of seven years. She was also to have, on certain conditions, the use of the parish house for one year, and this period was destined to be lengthened. She made the best disposition of her family she could manage. She sent Bulkeley to the relatives in Maine. She accepted Grandfather Ripley's offer to keep Edward that summer in Concord, where Ralph would also be by August, improving in general health but "afflicted by the humour." At the end of July she composed a prayer commemorating her husband's death, such a prayer as she had made long before at the death of her first child.

It was arranged that William Emerson's library should be sold at auction in August. Among the more than two hundred works to be offered to the public were some bearing the names of Ovid, Cicero, Livy, Longinus, Shakespeare, Swift, Pope, Ossian, Shenstone, and Goldsmith. There were also *The Spectator* and *The Rambler* and almost all the other famous series of eighteenth-century essays in English, besides Enfield's history of philosophy and certain writings of Descartes, Locke, and Paley. There were few American books, but one of them was Jonathan Edwards on the will. Fortunately a number of volumes not advertised, as well as some that were, remained in the possession of the family or were returned later. Though the proceeds from the auction may not have justified the sacrifice of the larger part of the library, the need for funds was great. And the historical sketch of the First Church, got into printable shape and copyrighted by the widow before the end of December, could hardly have earned enough to make a serious difference to her.

Mary Moody Emerson had yielded to her sister-in-law's plea for help, but had to be persuaded again to stay on and to resist the urgent invitations of other relatives who were competing for her services. Early in 1812 Ruth Emerson assured a relative in Maine that "could you but look into this house of distress, you would be convinced of the importance of her continuance here. Providence seems to have bestowed on her talents exactly suited to the exigences of this bereaved family. In short I do not think her place could be supplied to these *fatherless children* by any one on earth. I pray God to preserve her valuable life & enable me justly to appreciate so great a blessing. She possesses some traits of character that bear so strong a resemblance to my dear deceased husband as render her peculiarly dear to me, & I hope she will not ever leave me except for a visit or a *good Husband,* while she lives." Aunt Mary was thus growing more important in the eyes of the family. No ordinary housekeeper or governess, she even wrote the prayers which first Ralph's brother William and then Ralph himself "read aloud morning and evening," prayers that contained "prophetic and apocalyptic ejaculations" and "treasuries of piety" fit to inspire sermons.

On his ninth birthday Ralph was of the statutory age to enter the Boston Public Latin School; and then, or, almost certainly, a little earlier, he joined the group of boys described by a contemporary as "the most intractable and turbulent fellows, sixty or seventy in number, that ever met together to have Latin and Greek hammered into them." The school was, in 1812, at an unfortunate stage of its long history. It was, for one thing, unsettled and badly housed. The old brick building in School Street, close to the Emerson home, was being torn down to make way for a bigger one. The architect had designed a formidable three-story structure, partly of granite and, on the whole, better fitted to serve as a blockhouse on a frontier infested with Indians than as a place where boys might hope to study without sacrificing their eyesight. Ralph seems actually to have arrived before the old building was torn down and to have followed the school in its migration to an old wooden block on the Mill Dam, thence to a loft on Pemberton Hill, and finally back to School Street when the new building was ready. Even in the new quarters the boys had to be content with desks and seats of long, thick plank, too hard for jackknives.

The management was equally primitive. The headmaster, famed among schoolboys of the time, was William Biglow, nicknamed Sawney. His dramatic method of teaching could not have been altogether ineffective, for it made abstractions as concrete as the somewhat different pedagogical system of Charles Dickens's Dotheboys Hall would do. Biglow would flourish his cane as he demanded of a backward pupil what an active verb expressed. " 'I'll tell you what it expresses,' he resumes, bringing the stick down upon the boy's haunches with decided emphasis, 'it expresses an action and necessarily supposes an agent, (flourishing the cane, which descends again as before) and an object acted upon, As *castigo te*, I chastise thee; do you understand now, hey?' " Biglow's liking for liquor was no more controllable than his temper and already threatened to prove his undoing.

Ralph Emerson found the day under Biglow broken conveniently into two quite separate sessions, and the intermission was sometimes more pleasant for him than the authorities intended it to be. With other members of the lower classes he was sent off to spend a couple of hours in a special school for private instruction in writing and cyphering; but, as the South Writing School, kept by Master Rufus Webb, was on West Street, or close to it, temptingly near Boston's public playground and parade field, he "deliberately and continuously played truant, and enjoyed the stolen hours on the Common." Apparently he had the courage to do these things with the full knowledge that "bread-and-water confinement" would follow. On the more sober days when he arrived at his writing desk, however, he applied himself earnestly enough to make good progress. William Furness, his seat-mate in Webb's large, sparsely occupied room, never forgot how Ralph labored over his copybook, his tongue, half out of his mouth, working up and down in cadence with the strokes of his pen.

Playing truant on the common was only one of many extracurricular activities, ranging from mildly interesting to alluring, which were known to the small schoolboy. Getting away to the wharves, only a short distance from Summer Street, he could pick up shells out of the sand that vessels had brought as ballast. There were plenty of attractive stones. There was also gypsum; and its luminescence was a great marvel, never fully understood, but easily demonstrated by rubbing two pieces together in a dark closet. The boy would magnetize his penknife till it would hold a needle. He doubtless felt that he was voyaging through strange seas of thought when he meditated upon the fact, proved by actual experience, that blue and gamboge combined would make green in the pictures of mountains that he improvised. He got pleasure from "drawing vases by scrawling with ink heavy random lines, and then doubling the paper, so as to make another side symmetrical." He halloed at the pond, getting wonderful replies.

Certainly by this time he was practicing the art of poetry, and it could not have been beyond his powers "at the age of nine years" to compose "The Sabbath," now extant in a copy made by another hand many years later. "The Sabbath" advised, in general, observance of the Lord's day with attendance at church, with prayer, and with reading of holy books, and added some specific recommendations for certain contingencies and, undoubtedly, actual predicaments. If war prevailed, peace was to be prayed for; if famine, plenty. If a man sinned, he was to repent and make good resolves. The chief inspiration of both form and matter was perhaps the family hymnal. The impeccable orthodoxy of all seven stanzas was adequately illustrated in one of them:

> Remember your Redeemer's love,
> And meditate on things above,
> Forsake while you are here below,
> The path which leads to realms of woe.

But such piety did not always engross the thoughts of the youthful poet even on Sunday. At church he had a good opportunity to drift from poetic to philosophical moods until he was startled by the terrific snort some old parishioner made in a pocket handkerchief. Sitting in his pew he would amuse himself by "saying over common words as 'black,' 'white,' 'board,' etc., twenty or thirty times, until the words lost all meaning and fixedness, and," as he afterwards put it, "I began to doubt which was the right name for the thing, when I saw that neither had any natural relation, but were all arbitrary. It was a child's first lesson in Idealism."

There were the ventures into the water in Charles Street after school hours and the striking spectacle of the rope walks, primitive factories which, in those days, stretched their great length along many outlying Boston streets or along the water front. There was the ever present danger of raids by the tough North-Enders, South-Enders, and Round-Pointers. Once, when Ralph was ten or eleven years old and Edward was eight or nine, the two brothers were coming back into town over Charlestown bridge when they met a little ruffian who asked their names and where they lived. Finding that they did not belong to his quarter, he attacked Ralph and gave him a bloody nose; and soon both the Summer Street boys were in tears. Ralph later regretted that he had not got more of so invaluable a part of a boy's education.

He heard the old Boston street cries. John Wilson, the town crier, rang his bell at each street corner as he described a lost child or advertised an auction such as had done away with most of the Emerson family library. Wilson shouted "so loud that you could not hear what he said if you stood near." Ralph eventually learned his lesson that whatever the inhibiting influences of religious and moral training in the home, "a cultivated person has several social languages to use as occasion requires," and from boys in the street he doubtless picked up English that could be used "like a sharp stick among the rabble."

In common with other boys he loved the display of power, speed, and color in a large town. He was proud that he knew the fire engines as outsiders could not do—the Extinguisher, the Despatch, and the Cataract. There were the armories to pour out gay soldiery. There was the impressive procession of boys in uniform when the Washington Benevolent Association took to the streets. The procession might be nearly a mile long and would be escorted by elite companies of light infantry. Once there were fourteen grand divisions of marchers, each headed by a marshal with the national standard. The onlookers saw a forest of banners inscribed in honor of Washington, Independence, Peace, Commerce, Agriculture, Mechanic Arts, Fisheries, the Union, the Navy, and National Glory. The division of the Rising Generation alone contained upwards of four hundred youths, all dressed in beautiful uniforms, their hats and coats decorated with garlands of flowers. In war time, even more than in peace, the soldiery and the sea-fencibles were in evidence in the port.

In the autumn of 1812 war with Britain was about to begin seriously at last after dragging along for months. The catastrophic blockade would be delayed by the enemy until after the re-election of Madison, to be sure; but the election once over, "then, my countrymen," warned a Federalist paper, "prepare for war in earnest, taxes, annihilation of prosperity, and the whole phial of wrath, invited by a foolish, incompetent, and Frenchified set of rulers." But already there were some naval victories to temper the anger of the opposition, and Boston was an important naval base. The frigates *President, United States,* and *Congress* and the brig *Argus* left the harbor while the *Constitution, Chesapeake,* and *Hornet* were still being fitted out. The *Constitution,* designed by Joshua Humphreys with an eye to decisive superiority over British and French frigates nominally of the same class, had won her victory over the *Guerrière* within some two months after the declaration of war. The victorious ship already had a poet to celebrate her, and, though family tradition preserved only an uninspired line of his ballad on that subject, Ralph, as self-appointed laureate, now began to compose similar warlike pieces and recite them for his friends.

Aunt Mary hinted that he should commemorate the tragic day when Bostonians crowded the high ground and housetops near the harbor as Captain Broke's *Shannon* tauntingly showed her British colors and luckless Lawrence's *Chesapeake* followed her out to sea. But presumably Ralph did not find his muse propitious. As an extant copy of his verses on the Battle of Lake Erie was dated as late as 1814, he may have got part of his inspiration for them from what the Columbian Museum called its grand naval panorama of the fight. It is probable that others of his verses, now apparently lost, did not differ greatly in quality from these from "Perry's Victory":

When late Columbia's patriot brave
Sail'd forth on Eries tranquil wave
No hero yet had found a grave—
Within her watery cemetery.
But soon that wave was stained with gore
And soon on every concave shore
Reechoed with the dreadful roar
Of thundering artillery.

Though he preferred naval subjects, he was stirred by the Russian victories over Napoleon's retreating army, victories quite as important to America as the war against the British. Doubtless he envied his mother and his brother William when they went to King's Chapel, with the tickets given to the family, to hear homage sung to the Muscovites by a great chorus. Everybody knew of the doings at the Exchange Coffee House, where toasts were drunk to the Emperor Alexander, "The deliverer of Europe," and to General Kutuzoff, Prince of Smolensk. One of the inevitable transparencies showed Moscow wrapped in flames from which a Russian eagle was ascending with a scroll in his beak bearing the words *"Moscow is not Russia."* Within a year or two Ralph appropriately honored the Russians in one of the poetic panoramas in which he liked to show how history was molded by divine providence.

By June of 1813 Ruth Emerson was sending out another plea for aid from Mary Moody Emerson. Her affairs seemed to be coming to a crisis. She expected to have to give up the parish house before the end of the summer, "& then," she said, "the last visible connexion will be dissolved between this family & the society once so dear to my departed husband." By this time the church had chosen the Reverend Mr. Abbot, a bachelor, as the new pastor, and she was asked to accommodate him in her home. Again she urged Aunt Mary to hasten to her help. "What could I do?" she pleaded with her stubborn sister-in-law. "I could not refuse the wish of the society; but you know enough of my peculiarities to have some idea of the greatness of this trial. The belief that it might in some respects be beneficial to the children led me to consent—" Thus, just as she was counting on "retireing to some obscure retreat" she was, she regretted, "constrained to remain in the midst of this trying scene."

Other boarders meanwhile were coming and going, and it was not until some days after his ordination that John Abbot brought his things to the parsonage, whereupon Ruth Emerson appealed once more to Aunt Mary, astonished at the latter's calm persistence in keeping to her retreat at Waterford. "Why my dear sister," she tried to reason with Aunt Mary, "it was on the presumption of your aid I ventured to ingage to take a boarder that will occasion us so much care & time—Nor do I think it would be consistent with your or my views of propriety & respectability that I should take a person of this discription without a female friend or companion in the house besides I cannot find time in your absence to do even the necessary sewing of the family with my other cares & have now 4 or 5 shirts for the children which they need, waiting to be made when you return—" That autumn, with, as she supposed, less than three months of grace before she would have to leave the parish house, she was still trying in vain to persuade Aunt Mary, but at last her entreaties seem to have won a promise of help. In December she was hopefully listening till midnight to the stages as they rolled past, and before the end of January she had the pleasure of seeing the recalcitrant aunt arrive. It is reasonable to conjecture that Aunt Mary at once became the chief mentor of Ralph, supervising his home studies and inspiring him to efforts that the Latin School would never have got from him.

At any rate she was already a guide of whom he was fully conscious. She had long been his correspondent, perhaps since he was six or seven years old. By the spring of 1813 he had conquered enough of his awkwardness with the pen to write her in what is possibly the earliest letter of his to be preserved, a few scraps of news and something of his daily routine at the end of his tenth year:

"Boston April 16th 1813

"Dear Aunt

"I lately heard of our cousin Caspers death you do'nt know how affected cousin Rebecca was. I am much obliged to you for your kind letter. I mean now to give you an account of what I do commonly in one day if that is what you meant by giving an account of one single day in my life   Friday 9th I choose for the day of telling what I did. In the Morning I rose as I do commonly about 5 minutes before 6   I then help W$^{\underline{m}}$ in making the fire after which I set the table for Prayers. I then call mamma about quater after 6. We spell as we did before you went away   I confess I often feel an angry passion start in one corner of my heart when one of my Brothers get above me which I think sometimes they do by unfair means after which we eat our breakfast then I have from about quater after 7 till 8 to play or read   I think I am rather inclined to the former. I then go to school where I hope I can say I study more than I did a

little while ago. I am in another book called Virgil & our class are even
with another which came to the Latin School one year before us. After
attending this school I go to Mr Webbs private school where I write &
cipher I go to this place at 11 and stay till one oclock. After this, when
I come home I eat my dinner & at 2 oclock I resume my studies at the
Latin School where I do the same except in studying grammar after I
come home I do mamma her little errands if she has any then I bring in
my wood to supply the break-fast room. I then have some time to play
& eat my supper after that we say our hymns or chapters & then take our
turns in reading Rollin as we did before you went. We retire to bed at
different times I go at a little after 8 & retire to my private devotions &
then close my eyes in sleep & there ends the toils of the day. May 11 Samuel
Bradford went yesterday to Hingham to go to Mr. Colman's School. Your
little pensioner Eliza Twist if you remember her is now established in a
Charity School and doing pretty well. Cousin John sends his love to you
& is well. I have sent a letter to you in a Packet bound to Portland which
I suppose you have not received as you made no mention of it in your
letter to mamma. Give my love to Aunt Haskins & Aunt Ripley with Robert
& Charles & all my cousins & I hope you will send me an answer to this
the first opportunity & beleive me I remain your most dutiful Nephew

"R. Waldo Emerson

"M M Emerson"

But he had become a more sophisticated letter writer, and by the following year he had added to his circle of correspondents a brilliant Miss
Sarah Alden Bradford, a friend of Aunt Mary's who became a little later
the wife of his half uncle Samuel Ripley. For her benefit he discussed in
serious verses the virtues of Rollin's ancient history, an admirable introduction to hero-worship. Rollin's story of Athens delighted him, though
he regretted that the Frenchman had omitted the Trojan War,

> The burning city, and Æneas' flight
> With great Anchises on that fatal night.

Sarah Bradford was a skillful teacher, cleverly inciting him to scholarly
exercises that were to be personal favors to her. "Only think," she wrote
him, "of how much importance I shall feel in the literary world." Still
following hints she had given him, he turned to Vergil, praising

> Nisus and Euryalus too
> Those youthful heroes and those friends so true,

and he went on to furnish her with his own rhyming translation of a passage from the fifth eclogue.

He continued to compose letters in verse. He wrote elegies on departed relatives and friends and nonsense verses of pure doggerel. He was already the author of several pages of octosyllabic couplets laboriously labeled *The History of Fortus A Poem in One Volume Eigth Edition with Emendations By R W Emerson 1813. Embellished with Elegant Engravings by W. H. Furness.* The somewhat crude drawings made for him by his fellow bencher at Webb's school were well suited to the unpolished metrical romance. Fortus, singlehanded, slaughtered all but six score of the six score and twenty thousand warriors who opposed him in his most notable encounter, killed two dragons, and got possession of a magically guarded ring and, consequently, of an anonymous damsel, the only begetter of his valor, who by this time felt sufficiently sure of his constancy.

By 1814 the Latin School had reached a crisis. The school committee had first investigated, then warned, the tippling Biglow. It was decided that it would be wise to hire an instructor who would "unite to the learning of a scholar the manners of a gentleman," even if he required a higher salary. Biglow's eventual dismissal was the result of a gradual rise of sentiment against him followed by a slow response from the authorities. But the uproarious scenes of the sudden rebellion remembered by Ralph Emerson in later years could not have been entirely imaginary. The day after the storm the usher shortened his morning prayer to ten words, "Father forgive them for they know not what they do." Biglow was out. The school committee were soon arriving to introduce Benjamin Apthorpe Gould as the new master, and Gould ruled securely from that moment.

About this time a new blow fell upon the Emerson family in the death of three-year-old Mary Caroline, the only sister Ralph had known. Within a couple of years after her death he remembered her in lines addressed to a playmate who had suffered a similar loss:

Ne'er since my own loved sister met her doom,
Has such a pang assailed my bleeding heart
As when your sister felt the fatal dart.

But the time was to come when he could recall little more of Mary Caroline than that he "used to drag her to school in her wagon" and that she was fair and had beautiful eyelashes.

The war, impatiently endured by Bostonians from the first, was causing them new hardships. The press set up warning signposts along "The Road to Ruin" and boldly called for an end to this foolishness at the earliest possible moment. Plain citizens were alarmed by the high cost of living.

Few of them were so confident of getting an answer to the puzzle as was the youthful Lydia Jackson, a girl destined to be important in Ralph Emerson's later life; but even Lydia, set apart and protected from the turmoil of the time as she was, betrayed some anxiety when she wrote home to Plymouth from the academy she was attending at Dorchester:

"Tell me dear Father the reason of the excessive high price of provisions, when the earth has produced so bountifully? Every thing is extravagantly dear, yet every thing abounds, you are my Oracle dear parent, so you must expect me to question you on every, to me, inexplicable subject."

Even the *"LAUS DEO!"* that greeted Napoleon's abdication could not make people forget the financial, and perhaps military, disaster staring them in the face. Boston looked for a time as if it might become as lifeless as the miniature model of the town, showing wharves, stores, etc., which Joseph Duchesne exhibited in Summer Street and promised to illuminate brilliantly on the evening of July 4. At Washington, in August, the British blew up the Capitol and the President's house and destroyed the navy yard, and they were thought likely to be in Boston soon if drastic action was not taken.

But drastic action was taken. Boston quickly assumed the appearance of a garrison. Amid cheers of the citizenry the West Cambridge Light Infantry, the Concord Artillery, the Framingham Artillery, the Marlborough Light Infantry, the Worcester Artillery, the Milford Artillery, and the Hingham Riflemen began to arrive, together with contingents of light infantry from Westborough, Waltham, Haverhill, Quincy, and neighboring towns. Massachusetts and the other New England states were at last in the war, though their people were mostly prepared to fight as New Englanders, and not for the national government, and were eager to bring hostilities to an end at the earliest possible moment. Anyhow, as "A Peace Advocate" declared in the press, all the objects of the war had now been attained, for these were simply to renew and rekindle the spirit of hostility against Great Britain which was fast expiring in the East, to break down the Federalist party altogether, and to complete the ruin of the commercial states. The Hartford Convention, drawing New England into a regional federation and straining the cords that bound her to the Union, was soon to begin its sessions.

Ralph Emerson was old enough to share in the general excitement. The rejoicing over the American victory on Lake Champlain was allayed by the report that Baltimore was menaced by the British. In Boston Harbor the ferries to Noddle's Island, later known as East Boston, were kept busy carrying volunteers, mostly unfit no doubt, to work on the hastily planned defenses. One day the dry-goods dealers abandoned yardsticks and scissors

for picks and shovels; another day the merchants of Long Wharf patri-
otically toiled on earthworks or at least had good intentions. Members of
the board of health, printers and binders and booksellers, the bricklayers
and stonelayers, and the housewrights were ready to take their turns on
various fortifications about the town. In later years the "one military recollection" from Ralph's own experience as a participant would, according
to his mood, fit, pleasantly exciting, into the pattern of unforgettable memories of things past, or would seem only mock-heroic or mildly comic.
Probably, at the time, there was nothing very heroic about the trip to
Noddle's Island with the boys from the Latin School. Ralph "went with
the rest in the ferryboat, and spent a summer day," but he would not
remember that he did any kind of work. What impressed him most was
the trouble he and the other boys took to get water in their tin pails in
order to relieve their intolerable thirst.

So long as the Emerson family had the parish house on Summer Street
and the pension of $125 a quarter they could keep from destitution. For
a long time they were little disturbed in their possession of the place, and
it is difficult to understand why they left it as soon as they apparently
did. Pastor John Abbot, though he married without much delay, seems
never to have lived in the parsonage except as a boarder. He preached
only a few sermons at the First Church before he voyaged to Portugal for
health; and he did not return till near the middle of the next year and
then only to go into seclusion at Brighton. In the following October he
died, and his successor was not ordained till months afterwards. But there
is reason to believe that the Emersons gave up all claim to the parish house
sometime before the end of 1814 and lived for a while in Bennet Street.
It is possible that for a brief time they were with the Haskinses in Rainsford's Lane. Meantime the most disturbing fact was that every day the
rising prices and the prospect of a British attack from the sea made any
residence in Boston less desirable. The family began to turn their eyes
toward the country. On September 20, 1814, Aunt Mary wrote the relatives in Maine an account of the troubles and uncertainties that the Emersons faced in the capital.

"You will like to hear by a pen from this place, on which for some
time so dark a cloud has rested. The publick mind . . . became in the
most anxious and alarmed state, you know. Many of the inhabitants
hastened to hide themselves & property in the Country. For the two last
sabbaths the petitions of the Clergy denote 'fearfull uncertainty' . . . But
you know the unhappy division in opinion renders it difficult for an individual to judge of the preponderance of immediate danger. People of
good judgement, at the head of socity, think an invasion of this Town

propable. At any rate, we know that a most afflictive and humiliating war is depopolating and wasting the property lives of the Inhabitants! But so dark and misterious is the condition of man, ever since the apostacy, that one war raging, and one Country distroyed, is but an epitome of the whole earth. . . . As to our unprotected selves we are very calm as to immediate difficulty—But had we any thing to lose we s⁰ feel very different probably. We did not think of moving till last week many friends tho't it best And when we consider the price of wood & provisions which will be the consequence of the troops quarted already here it seems the best thing to go into the Country. But where? Father R has invited us there in case of being obliged to fly. And Ruthy has concluded, and has indeed sent to propose taking some part of their house & living by ourselves as it is impossible for her to board out with the children. . . . Either of Rev Brothers w⁰ take one of the boys were it in their power, and were they situated so that she could on the whole think it best. And as business is wholly checked there is not a single place to which either Ed. or Ralph can go. We are contemplating Andover as a good place for Boarders and Mrs T. Haskins has written to her friends today. You would think from this we are *cast down* but we are not. A low and humble state is generally without much change. We have some hope that this house may be given up, in that case Ruthy will not be in danger of immediate difficulty from debts. This letter will increase your comfort in having Bullkley. *Blessed be God who put it into your heart.* I have been desirous to try some new plan of life; but Ruthy will not consent to our seperation at this time. . . . I s⁰ like to describe the garrison like appearance of this Town, the incessant echo of martial musick, no day nor night excepted, but I have not time on this paper, nor inclination. . . ."

In spite of the uncertainties of war time, William, the oldest of the Emerson boys and the first ready for college, went to Cambridge that September, and within the week the family had a detailed account of what adventures a newly arrived freshman might experience there. Ralph doubtless pondered his own future in the light of his brother's report. Their mother, in her reply, showed the Spartan sternness that could temper her maternal affection. She wasted no tears over the dangers her son encountered among the young barbarians who had matriculated a year or two ahead of him. "You I trust will ever rise superior to these little things," she admonished William, "for though small indeed consume much time that might be appropriated to better purpose & far nobler pursuits. What most excites my solicitude is your *moral improvement* & *progress* in *virtue* . . . It is impossible for you to know any thing of the anxiety I feel for you . . . I fear I think almost too much about you; for should you not

be *all* you *ought* & *all I wish* I should be *very unhappy*—Let your whole
life reflect honour on the *name* you bear—You have it now in your power
to lay the foundation of future eminence in every thing praiseworthy &
excellent—I am happy I can say I feel a confidence in you that you will
be disposed to avail yourself of your advantages by making the best use
you can of them—"

Though William took such admonitions seriously and translated them
into action, Ralph continued to follow his bent toward a less strenuous
discipline that did not encroach too much on his favorite amusements.
Of these, verse-making served him most effectively as a protection against
overexertion at study. Yet his compositions were generally sober in tone
and were frequently pious. The death of his eighty-six-year-old grandfather Haskins in October, shortly before the Emersons left Boston for the
country, inspired the eleven-year-old boy to a characteristic effort. The
elegy he wrote was perfectly regular in both meter and theology. He betrayed no sense of incongruity as he transformed the man who had sailed
the seas on a privateer and had more than once been taken captive by
foreign ships into a merely conventional angel, singing and soaring, his
head "covered with a crown of gold" and his hands holding a harp.
Nothing was recognizable of the vigorous and proud old John Haskins
who would have been more at home in a red cloak and cocked hat.

5.

CONCORD GHOSTS AND OTHERS

In the long sunny afternoon
The plain was full of ghosts . . .
—"Dirge," Concord, 1838

JOHN HASKINS was buried in the family tomb under old Trinity Church on the last day of October. A little more than a week later Ruth Emerson wrote from Concord to her sister Fanny of her unhappiness on quitting "the town & the dear Mansion . . . immediately after the decease of our hon^d Father." But events continued to testify to the timeliness of her move to the country. If one of her late husband's seventeenth-century predecessors in the pulpit of the First Church could have come back to Boston in the last days of that autumn, he would doubtless have been convinced that the blockaded town had incurred divine displeasure. He might have pointed, with impressive logic, to the terrible warning of the recent earthquake. The shock, it was said, had been "preceded by a noise like that of a coach driven over the pavement" and was felt as far away as Concord. Concord, a town the British had never 'been able to occupy for more than a few hours, seemed, however, a comparatively safe retreat; and here Ralph's paternal grandmother and Ezra Ripley, his stern but generous stepgrandfather, welcomed the Emersons into the parsonage later known as the Old Manse.

The quiet village, more than any other place their ancestral home, had long had a peculiar attraction for Emersons. To Ralph's father, a native, it had seemed, in most respects, as good as a health resort, but much more than that. "The streams of Concord" were proudly paired with "the hills of Charlestown" in American tradition as he had expounded it. Once he had confessed, in a fit of nostalgia, that the little river town became dearer to him every day of his life: "Frequently in imagination I am bathing my limbs in its waters. The fine foliage of its trees, its pleasant hills and their beauteous prospects, and its extensive and verdant meads, often pass in review before my minds eye. Nowhere, sooner than in that lovely village would I pass the remnant of a life no longer useful . . ." His faith in its virtues had never afterwards been severely tried. His widow and Ralph, hitherto only occasional visitors in the town, were now beginning their first residence there.

On Sundays Ralph must have listened with some awe to Grandfather Ripley as the dignified man presided over his congregation in "the old, cold, unpainted, uncarpeted, square-pewed meeting-house, with its four iron-gray deacons in their little box under the pulpit." The country minister belonged to the rear guard of the Puritans, still believed in special providences, and had strong confidence in his prayers for rain. Though nominally a Unitarian in his later years, he was by no means a radical; and he could never be charged with sowing seeds of thought that could by any chance sprout into transcendental heresies.

He had written many sermons by this time, but probably not one of them was distinguished. A pen seemed fatal to the vigor of his expression. But when he spoke without script he was direct and forceful. "He had a foresight, when he opened his mouth, of all that he would say, and he marched straight to the conclusion." His prayers were far more interesting than his sermons, and as the boy listened for some affecting touch of nature, he must have contrasted him with the more formal and cool William Emerson of Boston. It was true that, because of "their remoteness from artificial society & their inevitable daily comparing man with beast, their inevitable acquaintance with the outward nature of man & with his strict dependence on sun, rain, wind, & frost; wood, worm, cow, & bird," these "old semi savages" in country parishes got "an education to the Homeric simplicity which all the libraries of the Reviews & the commentators in Boston do not countervail."

Ripley was stubbornly individual, but he loved people, had no studies and no occupations which company could interrupt, and was always ready to talk. Concord history was one of his specialties. He had an astonishing knowledge of the town's past, family by family, and he took very seriously his duty as patriarch. Riding about Concord with the old man, Ralph got vivid impressions of his own ancestors. One tale that stuck in his mind related how Grandfather William Emerson had defended his church against nine of its members that had stirred up a quarrel and "how every one of the nine had come to bad fortune or to a bad end." Ripley himself had been Grandfather Emerson's successor in his pastorate, had married his widow and acquired his land.

Grandfather Emerson became the Concord minister on the first day of the year 1766. By that time he had graduated from college, had finished the customary probationary period of schoolteaching, and was ready to settle down. Not long after he entered the house of the late pastor Bliss as a lodger he was wooing widow Bliss's daughter Phebe, and before the end of the year he married her. Even if his salary was only £100 a year he and Phebe could make a pleasant home on their small farm bordering on the Concord River. Their numerous tables and beds, their two pictures on canvas and three under glass, their books, their twenty-one cream-colored plates, their four large silver spoons, and their pair of silver tea tongs were, with their less pretentious possessions, enough for comfort. When the pastor set out for his church on a Sunday he may have made a more than decent appearance in his beaver hat, white wig, and black coat. The silver buckles at his knees and on his shoes would have given an added touch of distinction.

If his church was troubled with dissension and if some of its members, disliking his doctrine and regarding his discipline as high-handed and harsh, haled him before more than one council of sister churches, he knew how to suffer a severe rebuke and still come off victorious. His doctrine was apparently little more than the orthodox congregationalism of his time. With the lay members of his church, he signed a brief declaration of faith in "ye Covenant of Grace" and in "ye Word of GOD as the only Rule of our Faith & Practice"; but both pastor and flock tied themselves more firmly to old Puritan theology by adding the opinion that "ye shorter Cachesim of ye Assembly of divines" was an "excellent Compendium" of the word of God. It is said that, with all his firmness, he showed much kindness to the parishioners. When he first came, says a Concord tradition, the children, remembering the harshness of his predecessor, were afraid; but Grandfather Emerson's judicious praise was to them "like the sun coming from behind a cloud."

Grandfather Emerson was quite as much concerned with the stormy politics of the time as with his religious duties. He witnessed the funeral of the four victims of the "Boston Massacre," and he watched the temper of the capital with intense interest when some citizens became discouraged and began "to blame ye Destroyers of ye Tea & to lay ye Severity of ye present Measures, & ye Sufferings consequent upon it at their Door!" In the following autumn he was chaplain to the provincial congress, the rebellious provisional government of Massachusetts, then meeting at Concord. Early in 1775 he was busy recruiting minutemen; and at the general review in March he boldly exhorted the soldiers against submission to authority.

The redcoats soon arrived. A local tradition had it that at the first alarm of the British approach to Concord Grandfather Emerson appeared "with the others, his firelock in his hand" and that he raised the spirits of one frightened colonial by laying his hand on his shoulder and saying, "Don't be afraid, Harry; God is on *our* side." According to one historian, he was rash enough to advise fighting in the center of the village, saying, "Let us stand our ground . . . if we die, let us die here!" But it is probable that his main business during the subsequent encounter between minutemen and the king's men at the North Bridge was to stay close by his house in order to guard his family and to feed the frightened women and children who took refuge in his yard.

A month after Bunker Hill he wrote to his wife from the camp at Charlestown "that as y: Sword is drawn we Americans will never sheath it till all our Grievances are fully redress'd to our utmost Wishes!" On the anniversary of the Concord Fight he was ready with a prophecy of America's future greatness. A few months later, at the close of divine service, he asked and received leave of his church to go as chaplain to the army of the north, then at Ticonderoga. According to a family tradition, as he was setting out on his fatal journey he turned his horse at the bend of the road to look back once more at his home "as few men look—for he was taking a leave."

At Ticonderoga the enemy was 130 miles away, and there was no prospect of battle, but death could come in other ways. Toward the middle of September, while the American army lay rotting in a camp unprotected by the most elementary precautions against disease, the chaplain himself began to suffer from "a Sort of a mongrell Feaver & Ague." Without waiting for his pay, he started southward in a race with death. He got no farther than Rutland, where strange but friendly hands cared for him during his "long illness with the billious fever, attended with a tedious Diarrhea," and decently interred his body.

From his grandmother Phebe Bliss Ripley as well as from Ezra Ripley, Ralph must have heard the story of Great-grandfather Daniel Bliss, a predecessor of Grandfather Emerson in the same village church. Bliss had been pastor some twenty-five years when he died in 1764. Ripley doubtless knew the story well from the church records and from the extant family papers.

Bliss stood trial on fifteen articles of complaint brought against him by a few militant parishioners. His doctrine, discipline, and conduct were all attacked at once. The council which tried him was especially concerned over the charge that he had been wandering about from town to town, to the disturbance of other ministers and their parishes. He was, in the end, advised to acknowledge his faults publicly, to study the Scriptures and orthodox divines diligently, to take time to prepare his public appearances, and to avoid delivering any unsound and perplexing doctrines; but his accusers were reprimanded quite as sharply. He promptly made his submission, and when the quarrel broke out again a few years later, he had his church firmly at his back, and the crisis was soon past.

Great-grandfather Bliss was simply caught in the revivalist excitement stirred up by Whitefield. He was swept from his moorings, as other enthusiasts were, and fished for souls in strange waters. Ralph's father once unceremoniously dismissed three of his own ancestors, including Daniel Bliss, as followers of Whitefield "who were incapable of raising the tempest," as the English itinerant had done, but "were able, by means of dust and rubbish, to continue the troubled state of the atmosphere." Many besides Ezra Ripley must have known that when Whitefield preached to a great throng at Concord he was pleased because his hearers were "melted down," and took a special liking to Pastor Bliss, staying over night at his house "that we might rejoice together." Bliss "broke into tears" that night, but it was no unusual thing for strong minds to yield to the eloquence of Whitefield.

During all but about forty-three of Concord's one hundred and seventy-nine years of existence, the preachers in the town's pulpit had been Ralph's ancestors with the one exception of Ezra Ripley, but Ripley was the boy's stepgrandfather and almost an Emerson.

The pastorate of Edward Bulkeley, Ralph's ancestor in the sixth generation before his own, reached back some thirty-seven years from 1696, the date of his death. According to tradition Edward Bulkeley "once saved Concord from an attack of the Indian" because the red man feared the minister's prayers.

Peter Bulkeley, Edward's father, was remarkable for the ill temper he sometimes yielded to when he was tormented by bodily pains and for his severe dress, his extremely close-cropped hair, his too refined conscience, and his constant catechizing. But he was respected for solid virtues. His name must have become familiar to Ralph, for Peter Bulkeley was esteemed by all well-informed persons as one of the founders of the town. Driven out of England by Archbishop Laud's persecution of the nonconformists, he voyaged to the New World; and before the end of 1635 he and his flock, coming to a friendly understanding with the Indians of the Musketaquid country, dug rude shelters out of the hillside and gave the name of Concord to their new home.

Peter Bulkeley commanded some respect, not only in his own town and among the savages, but among the Puritan theologians who long kept the Bay Colony in a turmoil of controversy. He once served as co-moderator, with the great Thomas Hooker, of an important synod. He struggled with the treacherous subtleties of Puritan theology and succeeded so well in explaining them to his parishioners that he was persuaded to publish a series of sermons in a volume called *The Gospel-covenant; or the Covenant of Grace Opened.* He showed that though grace was free, a prerequisite to its operation was man's faith, and that good works, though not pre-requisite, were an inevitable result; but he also quietly assumed that the first act in the drama of salvation was God's arbitrary choice of those who should enjoy its benefits. The book would be for Bulkeley's Concord repre-sentative in the seventh generation after him not merely a symbol of a false and poisonous creed but a reminder of family and of Concord history.

It was not quite in vain that Bulkeley, like Hunt, Willard, Hosmer, Meriam, and Flint, once possessed the land, though there was reason for the earth's laughter when

> Each of these landlords walked amidst his farm,
> Saying, ' 'T is mine, my children's and my name's.'

No living person in Concord bore the surname Bulkeley and none of the first minister's land was in the possession of the Emerson family.

Concord was nevertheless the key to Emerson family history; and as late as 1814 nearly all of the American geography of Ralph's family could have been included in a circle a hundred miles in diameter with either Concord or Boston as the center. A radius of about thirty-five miles would have reached all but one or two outlying villages that mattered.

Ralph's great-grandfather Joseph Emerson, father of the Revolutionary William Emerson, was born in the town of Chelmsford, some ten miles to the north of Concord, but was known in later life as the minister of Malden. He graduated at Harvard, kept school at York in the District of Maine, settled at Malden in 1721, and, in the same year, married Mary Moody. She was the daughter of Father Moody, minister of York, a hearty, eloquent, magnetic man who would forbid an offended parishioner to leave the meetinghouse, crying out, "Come back you graceless sinner, Come back!" or, when members of his flock turned into the alehouse on a Saturday night, would follow them in, collar them, drag them out, and send them home. Both Joseph Emerson and Samuel Moody were, with Daniel Bliss, among the enthusiasts who labored in the fields that White-field had plowed.

Joseph and Mary lived largely for their children. Births dotted their calendar from 1722 to 1745 with remarkable regularity till the Christian names traditional in the family were nearly exhausted. "Conclude for ye future," Joseph wrote in his diary for 1738, "to write some of my Sermons at length, hoping they may be of some Service to my children & Relations when I am gone." Both parents had their hearts set on keeping up the family connection with the ministry. In 1763 the father sent William one of the choicest books in his library, with the admonition: "Dear Child!

your Mother & I are not a little concern'd for you—It was with a special view to the *Ministry,* that we have been at so great an Expense for your Education: If therefore your Genius & Disposition leads to it, & you should be qualify'd for it, both as to Gifts & Graces, it would be an inexpressible Addition to our Comfort & Joy." Joseph himself "read the Iliad, & said, he should be sorry to think that the men & cities he read of never existed"; and, according to a family story, he endangered William's health by insisting that the boy keep out of the hayfield and stay at his studies. Ralph would one day search the diaries left by the Malden pastor and copy out homely passages showing the old religionist's private thoughts.

Earlier direct ancestors than Joseph on the Emerson side were shadowy figures. Edward Emerson of Newbury, father of Joseph of Malden, remained for many years completely unknown, or more likely forgotten, by Ralph. Once a "Merchant in Charlestown" and, according to his gravestone, "sometime Deacon of the church in Newbury," he contributed Ralph's middle name to the family by marrying into a New England Waldo family of extremely dubious "French" origin, one of whose forebears in the direct male line was supposed to have migrated from the Netherlands to England during the reign of Elizabeth, to escape religious persecution. Edward Emerson's father was the first American Joseph, conveniently called Joseph of Mendon, from the little Massachusetts town of which he was the minister. He "barely escaped with his life when the village was destroyed by the Indians." Joseph of Mendon's second wife was Elizabeth Bulkeley, granddaughter of the first minister of Concord, and his father was Thomas, the first American Emerson.

This Thomas Emerson probably settled in Ipswich, the little frontier town of drumlins, meadows, sand dunes, and tidal marshes, in time to have Nathaniel Ward, the satirical Simple Cobbler, and Anne Bradstreet, the Tenth Muse, as his neighbors. The earlier history of Thomas always remained in doubt. One theory was that he came with his wife and family from Bishop Stortford, Hertfordshire, about thirty miles from London. He was known as a baker, and presumably was one, in spite of some slight reason that could be offered to the contrary. But he may have had both property and pride of ancestry. The rude heraldic device on the tombstone of his son Nathaniel, now renovated and still to be seen in the Old Burying Ground at Ipswich, is one bit of the uncertain evidence linking Thomas the baker with the prolific Emersons of the County of Durham who had similar arms. Whether or not Ralph had yet heard of the baker or the English Emersons he very likely knew and admired his own father's bookplate with its three lions passant on a bend and, atop the shield, a fourth lion grasping a battle-axe in the dexter forepaw; and what the bookplate displayed was only a more conventional version of the same device that marked Nathaniel Emerson's grave.

But whatever his antecedents and associations, Thomas Emerson was only one of Ralph's sixty-four ancestors of that generation, and nearly all the rest remained quite obscure. At best the boy's known ancestry was hardly more than a picture gallery from which he could eventually select a few prized canvasses to hang in his own house. These few chosen ancestors, though the physical and mental characteristics that had come down to him in the bewildering shuffle of genes and chromosomes were impossible to trace to any individuals among them, would always be important to him as makers of his private myth and legend. But, for the most part, he soon came to despise pedigree: "I was educated to prize it," he confessed. "The kind Aunt whose cares instructed my youth (and whom may God reward), told me oft the virtues of her and mine ancestors. . . . the piety of all and the eloquence of many is yet praised in the Churches. But the dead sleep in their moonless night; my business is with the living."

The Concord of his boyhood, known best to Ralph Emerson in the winter of 1814 and the spring of the following year, contained the living as well as the dead. And folkways, in this rural community, linked past and present. Such social occasions as husking bees, apple bees, quiltings, and raisings were already old-fashioned and dying out. Frolics of the coarser sort that had troubled preachers like Jonathan Edwards in the eighteenth century were now generally things of the past. Ralph had arrived in town in good time for a country Thanksgiving Day, with its apple, pumpkin, and minced pies for breakfast and turkey, plum pudding, and more pies for dinner. Through the winter the carrying in of the wood to the open fireplaces was a job fit for a boy. If the boy was skillful, he could also be trusted to see that the large, tough backlog and forelog were in place to contain the more combustible wood piled between them. At night the coals had to be raked up on the backlog and the whole covered with ashes. A heavy snowstorm was the signal for the turning out of citizens with ox teams drawing sleds upside down to force a passage along the streets and roads. The farmers drove their teams toward the center of the town, and the congregated oxen in the village square were a fine sight. Thanksgiving and Sundays and some half dozen special holidays were likely to be the only times when a boy could completely escape from the monotonous round of slates and books. But the approaching end of the war and the making of peace caused unusual excitement in Concord this winter. Once, when news came that peace was about to be concluded, the bell rang a great part of the night, and the citizens got up a subscription to pay for the powder that was fired off by the artillery.

It was not necessary to go far from the Ripley home, once Grandfather Emerson's, to find a landscape that could enrich the memory of a sensitive boy. Back of the house was the sluggish Concord River, flowing, if flowing it could be called, toward the Merrimac and the sea. Upstream a little it split into Sudbury and Assabet, and was a constant challenge to juvenile explorers, to boatmen, or to skaters—

> The same blue wonder that my infant eye
> Admired, sage doubting whence the traveller came,—
> Whence brought his sunny bubbles ere he washed
> The fragrant flag-roots in my father's fields,
> And where thereafter in the world he went.

The whole landscape, made more vivid by visits in other years no doubt, was later sublimated and sentimentalized in Ralph's dirge for his brothers Edward and Charles:

> The winding Concord gleamed below,
>   Pouring as wide a flood
> As when my brothers, long ago,
>   Came with me to the wood. . . .
>
> They took this valley for their toy,
>   They played with it in every mood;
> A cell for prayer, a hall for joy,—
>   They treated Nature as they would.
>
> They colored the horizon round;
>   Stars flamed and faded as they bade,
> All echoes hearkened for their sound,—
>   They made the woodlands glad or mad.

On November 10, shortly after the family had arrived in Concord, Ralph wrote that he was attending school there and liking it better every day. He called for a copy of an anthology of Greek writers, and in his correspondence he demonstrated his progress both in writing and in drawing. The Concord grammar school, also attended by Edward and Charles, was then kept by an Oliver Patten, a master who seems to have remained there only the one school year. It was perhaps at Patten's school that Ralph had his quarrel with Elisha Jones and Frank Barrett. Ezra Ripley, as grandfather of one culprit and as moral magistrate of the whole village, called all three boys before him and made them shake hands. Ralph accepted mediation, but was tongue-tied; and Aunt Mary, when she heard of this, reproved him sharply. "Fie on you! You should have talked about your thumbs or your toes only to say something," she told him.

In the school, no doubt, he found encouragement for the love of poetry he is said to have displayed more publicly by reciting verses from the top of the sugar barrel in Deacon White's store. On Christmas Eve he made a poem on Washington that showed he could now compose heroic couplets mechanically correct enough but exceedingly stiff and conventional in rhythm and diction. When the hated war with Britain was at last ended, he wrote with enthusiasm of "Fair Peace triumphant." Perhaps his last poetic effort during his country school days was an address to his teacher and his fellow pupils which he called "Valedictory Poem Spoken at Concord":

> This morning I have come to bid adieu
> To you my schoolmates, and, Kind Sir to you;
> For six short months my lot has here been cast,
> And oft I think how pleasantly they've past,
> In conversation with companions gay,
> The time has past like one long summer's day,
> But as I now go hence to other skies,
> Where Boston's *spires* in goodly order *rise,*
> A few short lines permit me here to say,
> Whilst Sol prolongs the cheering light of day. . . .
> To you, Respected Sir, alone I owe
> More than I now, or ever can bestow,
> Such tribute only as I have, I give,
> That is my thanks, that tribute, Sir, receive;
> A Brother too by sickness long detain'd
> From study; at his loss is pain'd.
> Another Brother small and younger too,
> New to the school, and to its studies new,
> Has here imbib'd impressions of that kind,
> To banish all its dullness from his mind.
> And now farewel my schoolmates, happy days,
> And Peace attend you in all virtuous ways,
> Farewel ye walls where Science ever shines,
> And smiling virtue opes her golden mines.

The "six short months" may have been a slight miscalculation, admissible in the arithmetic of poetry. If it was sober fact, it possibly meant that Ralph had begun school in Concord before his mother arrived in early November, 1814. More probably it meant that he continued there for a few weeks after her return to Boston about the twenty-fifth of March in the following year. She would naturally have gone alone to reconnoiter the post-war town, and there was certainly at least a brief period of indecision. But it was not long before both Ruth Emerson and her family had left the protection of the Ripley manse.

.6.

BANISHING DULLNESS FROM HIS MIND

※◉※

> If you have opportunity it may be well to impress the minds
> of your grandchildren with the importance of becoming
> *intelligent* as well as *moral* beings.
> —William Emerson of Boston to his mother, January 11, 1810

THOUGH the danger of war was past, there was no escape from the reality of poverty. Probably Ruth Emerson accepted the offer of the Haskinses to provide shelter, but in spite of its vestiges of modest grandeur the old homestead in Rainsford's Lane could be no place of rest for her. Doubling up with the Haskinses meant, so their offer had specified, that she must take them as her boarders. The distressed widow, with her dependents, may have remained in Rainsford's Lane as late as the middle of the summer, when she received at least one paying guest from outside the Haskins family, and may still have been there in the early autumn, when the merchant Daniel P. Parker and his family became her boarders.

But by late October, when Parker sailed alone for London, both his family and hers were probably installed in his Beacon Street home, with Ruth Emerson in charge and free to invite paying guests. Her boarders there apparently included Lemuel Shaw, future chief justice of Massachusetts, but no amount of respectability in them could reconcile her to being housekeeper to the public. In a letter to her Maine relatives she explained that she looked upon her undertaking "with fear & trembling" and added that "sister Mary cheers & consoles me with the idea that our toils & sorrows will soon be ended in the peaceful grave." Aunt Mary seemed pleased with the place in Beacon Street because the windows afforded "a full view of the granary burying Yard." The dooryard would serve as a pen for the cow, fetched from Concord when she was fresh. Grandfather Ripley warned that she must be fed under the eyes of the Emersons lest the children and pig belonging to the poor man who tended her should devour her Indian meal. Ralph had to drive her along Boston Common to pasture.

The neighborhood could not have been entirely ugly. Near by was the State House as Bulfinch had designed it, and not far away stood the colonial mansion John Hancock had lived in and the much newer house built by the John Phillips who was destined to be the first mayor of Boston. But poverty was an uncomfortable slough from which to view prosperity, and the family, however grateful, could not have been entirely happy over gifts sent by well-to-do friends—silk for a gown and muslin for a cap, five dollars in cash, a cheese, twenty dollars in cash, or cheese and sugar and tea worth ten dollars.

Aid toward the education of the boys could be accepted with the least compunction. Young William, already in college, now received the annual grant of the First Church's income from the Penn legacy. This had formerly amounted to as much as £10 and was presumably still important. Yet Ruth Emerson had to bear the brunt of the fight against poverty, while every boy in the family felt its effects. His anxious search in the fallen poplar leaves for a dollar bill he had lost when he was sent out to buy himself a pair of shoes was for Ralph one of the most memorable experiences of his childhood. According to family tradition he and Edward shared a coat and were greeted by schoolmates with the taunt "Whose turn is it to wear the coat today?" Once, it is said, when Aunt Ripley arrived she found the boys in a state of exaltation because they had given their last loaf to some other poor person and Aunt Mary was telling them stories of heroism to keep them from feeling hungry.

Ralph felt the cumulative effect of stern religious training quite as much as he felt the discipline of poverty. At church he was expected to digest the sermon in order that he might give text and outline when he returned home. At home on Sunday afternoons he and his brothers had hymns to learn, though he might manage to substitute original composition for memorizing. In Beacon Street he had experiences of religious terror that paralleled those of young Lydia Jackson of Plymouth, as he learned in later years. Edward Young, the graveyard poet, tinged Lydia's day and night thoughts, the doubts of the too sensitive religious poet Cowper were her own, and every flash of lightning "seemed the beginning of conflagration, and every noise in the street the crack of doom." Usually Ralph's saving sense of the ridiculous must have weakened such terrors for him. But they were commonplace in that age, when spiritual crises were "periods of as certain occurrence in some form of agitation to every mind as dentition or puberty." And the harrowing of the emotions in youth was sure to have important repercussions in later life.

If Ruth Emerson was seriously religious, her sister Fanny, frequently her counselor in family affairs, was excessively so. She gravely suspected such heresies as were hatched by the college across the Charles River and anxiously scanned the conduct of the Emersons for signs of moral and spiritual disintegration. "W^m's disposition & application," she had once written, "is encouraging . . . He has my best wishes for progress in learning & an honorable discharge from the Seminary of which he is a member— O that it were a Nursery of piety as well as human literature. It is a subject of many prayers." She had been interested in Ralph because of his "diffidence" and his "poetic effusions," and she anticipated "his future usefulness from noticing his present activity & desire to serve & please a beloved Mother." Edward seemed reasonably safe at conservative Andover, where he was soon sent. The pupils there attended preaching on Sunday and on Monday reported the sermon; and, after the evening family prayers, they joined in social prayer, the "young gentlemen" taking turns in leading it. But to make doubly sure, Aunt Fanny warned Edward that life was uncertain and that he should devote himself, soul and body alike, to religious ends. The Haskins sisters came honestly by their religious formalism. Once, it is said, when his distillery adjoining the Haskins home was afire, their father kept the children from leaving the house till he got them round the table and returned thanks according to custom. "The Lord be praised for this and all his mercies," he announced. "Now," he concluded, "you may go."

Ralph's literary activities reflected his progress in bookish learning and showed his humor as well as the family religiosity. He could discourse on Doctor Johnson's opinions of Cowley and Donne, though he conveniently fell into the Doctor's way of thinking. French phrases had begun to appear in his letters as a result of his going every Monday, Wednesday, and Friday to take lessons of a Miss Sales. In English, Ralph practiced satire and irony. He pestered his brother William with nonsense verses and took off his eleven-year-old brother Edward's humble entry into Andover, "the seat of so much learning, of the Muses, the Arts, and Sciences" with these lines:

> And now arrives the chariot of state
> That bears with regal pomp Ned, Bliss the great
> See from afar arise a dusty cloud
> And see approaching fast the gathering crowd
> See yonder rank of learned sages come
> Like reverend fathers of majestic Rome
> Down from their aged heads their hats they bend
> On either hand the bowing lines extend
> While thro' the midst with elevated mein
> Stalks "Edward Emerson the great" between
> Hark the loud clangor of the sounding bell
> To Andoveria's college hails thee well

At the Latin School, Benjamin Apthorp Gould, the new headmaster, won the respect of the boys and of the public. He was being driven hard and was perhaps driving his pupils hard, though he found it "necessary for the preservation of health and elasticity of mind," as he put it, that a reasonable portion of time be allowed for relaxation. The town's sub-committeemen who supervised the Latin School could soon boast, and not without some justification, that "from the course of instruction and discipline in the same, it is now one of the best seminaries in New England for preparing children for College."

Gould had, besides energy and good sense, literary taste and cared for the liberal arts. Ralph, who used to be excessively fond of declaiming such passages as that on Warsaw's last champion in Campbell's *The Pleasures of Hope*, was fortunate to have a headmaster who valued good speaking and devoted Saturday morning to practicing the boys in it. Gould even provided at his own expense some medals inscribed "Palma Eloquentiae," though Ralph had to see these go to other aspirants. There were lines of verse to be memorized, and even a dead language was not allowed to remain a mere graveyard for grammarians to pilfer. After some sixty years Ralph testified in honor of the Latin School that "the only . . . Greek lines I ever learned to repeat & can still repeat I learned there." Doubtless the new bookish interest Gould's efforts inspired acted as a stimulus in English composition.

The instruction in essay-writing was effective according to the taste of the time. It seems to have been in September of 1815 that Ralph Emerson handed in what was pretty obviously the best prose he could write on the subject "Love of Praise." Struggling not quite successfully for mechanical correctness but balancing conflicting views with admirable fairness, he told his readers that the desire for praise was powerful and sometimes resulted in good deeds, sometimes in bad. He learnedly cited an instance from Xenophon and both strengthened and adorned his thesis with a Latin sentence from Cicero.

By the master's favor he several times got a coveted chance to read his rhymes on exhibition programs. "An English Poem, 'Independence,' " on the program in August of 1815, was his. On such an occasion he may well have been picked as one of the boys thought most likely to shine, whether or not they were the top scholars. Once, in the following year, shortly before the annual visitation, he had the satisfaction of a poetical tribute from an usher at the school. "Aug 16," he noted down on a sheet of paper still preserved, "Mr G. Bradford today paid a very handsome compliment by writing at the bottom of my Solitude—

Musae—Welcome to Apollo's hill
Bend freely to our hallowed rill
And claim the right the God to Genius gave,
To sip divine Castalia's *consecrated wave.*

They were original but the subject did not deserve them," the youthful poet modestly commented. But whether or not he deserved the praise of Bradford's muses, it was the kind of encouragement that would confirm his literary ambition.

For some reason he switched from solitude to eloquence, but when the great occasion of the annual exhibition actually arrived, he was on the program and could hardly have felt that his audience was either unfit or few, for the school committeemen and selectmen were accompanied on their rounds by the governor of the state, the council, the sheriff, the secretary and treasurer of the commonwealth, the judges of federal and state and county and town courts, the clergy, the president and several professors of Harvard, members of the state senate from Suffolk County, the town's representatives in the legislature, and most of the municipal officers of the various departments. Besides, there were strangers, including the consuls of foreign countries, a major general named Ripley, with his staff, and Colonel Croghan, the defender of Fort Meigs. But, as there were a number of boys on the program at the Latin School and the newspaper reports were not very specific, it is uncertain whether Ralph's English verses, more learned than inspired, drew any of the applause that frequently burst from the visitors.

A few months later, when the school was visited by a popular elocutionist, Ralph, still remembered as the author of a poem on eloquence suitable for the new occasion, was selected as one of the dozen or so boys to perform for him. What could be found of his exhibition poem was brought out again and fitted with a new ending. Ruth Emerson was among the parents who turned out for the entertainment.

Ralph was serious about his school exercises and, many years afterwards, regarded the themes and poems required by Gould as his "first essays in writing." And the Latin School incited him to a variety of intellectual adventures suited to his powers. He learned there to good purpose stories of the behavior of heroes in the ancient classics. He liked his study of literature. Having reviewed Cicero and some Greek writers, he sent to his brother William for a Sallust. He began geography with Cummings's introductory text and the Latin School equipment of "2 beautiful Globes, An Orrery, and a large Atlas." Gould made places come to life by showing what each was famous for. He would answer a question about the possibility of passing over the deserts of Africa by relating incidents of Napoleon's Egyptian campaign. Ralph Emerson admired such intelligent teaching and was avid of learning while he still kept his appetite for fun. In his less serious moods he could gloat over such trivia as oddities of grammar or spelling or vocabulary. That honorificabilitudinibusque was the longest word was perhaps not a notable discovery but seemed so to him. The one subject from which he could extract little pleasure was mathematics.

Naturally most of his friends were likely to be at the Latin School. When, at the age of thirteen, he was asked by his Uncle Samuel Ripley why "all the boys dislike you and quarrel with you, whilst the grown people are fond of you," he was really not without intimates among his youthful contemporaries. At his school, besides William Furness, there was John Gardner, his neighbor on Summer Street in early childhood. In his last year at the Latin School Ralph wrote to Edward of "the *affection* existing between Curtis (the best schollar in Class) and myself" and the great affection between Leverett and the rest of the school. The whole body of pupils were a loosely knit clan, the aristocracy of the public schools, with their seventeenth-century tradition and their special studies looking toward entrance into college. In the world of copybooks and textbooks they were as much distinguished as were the members of the Ancient and Honourable Artillery Company in the Boston world of uniforms and drums. When President Monroe came to town on his national tour in 1817, the place of honor by the gunhouse on the common was assigned to the Latin School boys. There, arranged in the order of their height, all uniformed in blue coats and white trousers, and every boy wearing in his buttonhole an artificial red and white rose, they waited two or three dreary hours but were rewarded when, at length, the expected cavalcade appeared, the military fired their salute, and the President "made his first bow to our school who all took off their hats and cheered." It was the last fine gesture of the Latin School so far as Ralph Emerson, then at the age of fourteen, was concerned.

If he paused to take stock of his career since he had entered the school in 1812, he probably discovered scant grounds for personal vanity. He seems to have won none of Boston's Franklin medals for scholarship. It was already evident that, as a scholar, he was no match for his brother Edward, for Edward concealed somewhere back of his "cat's eyes" and rosy cheeks and under his thick, stiff hair an extraordinary talent for leadership in a recitation room or on a public platform and had been, Gould said, the best in his class.

But in spite of his own lack of such talent, Ralph could get from books and elsewhere much that was not taught in classes or asked for on examinations. In later life, partly, no doubt, in subconscious self-justification, he put a special value on facts and ideas that came without having to be hunted down systematically. "The regular course of studies, the years of academical and professional education have not yielded me better facts than some idle books under the bench at the Latin School," he argued. "What we do not call education is more precious than that which we call so. We form no guess, at the time of receiving a thought, of its comparative value. And education often wastes its effort in attempts to thwart and balk this natural magnetism, which is sure to select what belongs to it."

Other institutions than the Latin School had contributed to the boy's intellectual life. The family had kept his father's share in the Boston Library Society. Though the list of books charged against this share proves no actual reading by anybody, the borrowings of 1815–1817 were often such as might have appealed especially to Ralph—Tacitus, Goldsmith, Maria Edgeworth, Cicero, Shakespeare, Chateaubriand, Klopstock, Walter Scott, and Doctor Johnson. The *Arabian Nights,* various volumes of British drama, Godwin's life of Chaucer, Robertson's histories, and *The Pleasures of Hope* were all in the list, not to mention an abridged version of *The Light of Nature Pursued,* the philosophic Abraham Tucker's book with whose ethical teachings Ralph soon became well acquainted. It is not clear whether he went with the sensation-hungry public to Merchants' Hall, where the grand panorama of Gloucester Harbor showed the famed sea serpent sporting in waters only a few miles from Boston, and where one's faith in such wonders could be confirmed by a view of a young sea serpent preserved in alcohol. But he was steadily cultivating his life-long enthusiasm for science of a more sober sort. He had his private museum and foraged for curiosities; and he may have got new inspiration from visits to such places as the museum of the Linnæan Society, a collection he certainly saw by 1817.

In the meantime Ruth Emerson struggled hard to earn the necessary means for putting her boys through school and college. Her boarding house, which at best attracted too small a portion of the swelling income of commercial Boston, seldom remained long at the same address. In the autumn of 1816 she had given up her place in Beacon Street, and by late September she was in Hancock Street. This was in the same neighborhood, then the best, or nearly so, for boarding houses. But however attractive the new location may have been to boarders, it afforded only dismal quarters for the widow Emerson's children. From the basement, where he was confined during an illness, Ralph looked out upon what he described as

a dirty yard
By boards and dirt and rubbish marr'd
Pil'd up aloft a mountain steep
Of broken Chairs and beams a heap

and farther on he could see five tall chimneys, doubtless those of the antiquated County Jail in Court Street, some distance away. The grim humor of his lines on this dreary scene and on his job of scouring knives, presumably for use at the boardinghouse table, was evidence that he did not easily slump into self-pity; but it was his mother whose courage was put to the severest test.

Though she was still "kindly assisted by the Society" of the First Church, she must have looked anxiously into the not very distant future when she could expect to receive nothing more than the Penn legacy, for aid in paying college bills, and some random gifts from individual members. With Aunt Mary absent in Concord, she took stock of her affairs in a gloomy mood. She got on as well as she had expected with a family of boarders, but it was at best a melancholy life. "I pity," she said, "all who are compelled to adopt this mode of getting a living, or rather an existance, for it can hardly be called living—I try to be resigned to it because I see no other way in which I can do so well altogether for our *dear boys*— They can never know the pain it costs me to live this kind of life. . . . We have no plan yet for the future, & indeed I seem to have no time to form any plan while sister M——y is absent—but go round the same little circle again & again of petty cares—" Bulkeley was back after some years mostly spent in Maine and added his weight to her load. Though he learned his lessons in geography and grammar, he could not remember them long. William, though he was thought too young and too small to keep school yet, had lost no time during vacation, having worked in a probate office. He had held on to his job of waiter at college most of the last year and was reputed industrious and steady at his books. Ralph, according to his mother, was her "man of the house & companion in the evening" and was diligent in his studies and well spoken of by his teacher.

By May, Ruth Emerson was looking for a more convenient house, where, of course, she would get more boarders. In July the First Church assigned Ralph the Penn legacy formerly enjoyed by William and must have taken it for granted that the younger brother was about to enter college. But there were doubts and there was conflicting advice from friends, for the financial outlook was bleak. In July, it seems, Ruth Emerson made a trip to Maine, perhaps to advise with relatives.

Toward the end of August, she wrote another of her frequent appeals to the mercurial Aunt Mary. She declared she was as convinced after trial as before Aunt Mary went away that *"I cannot do without you."* Her agitation of mind was caused partly by Aunt Mary's continued absence and partly by the difficulty of managing three boys at home on vacation, "the two small ones a fortnight instead of a week as usual." Having "dismissed Hannah, & turned Cook baker & washwoman together, with preparation for W.ˢ exhibition & Waldo's examination" to look out for, she was at her wit's end.

On the first of September she made a fresh start on her long tale of woe and hope, with news of Ralph's changing prospects: "On the day of Exhibition Mr Gould called in W. room & said he had seen the President & he & himself rather advised to R. W.ˢ going in to College *this year*— The Pred.t. observed he should be his freshman, & he would try to grant him some other priviledges—Thus the path of duty seemed to be plain to let him go forward—tho' a few days before all said let him wait till next year & Ralphs mind had been brought to acquiesce in that plan & his uncle Ripley was thinking of his aiding him in his school—

"Last Thursday he walked to Cambridge & with some tremour he sat off—to be on the spot at 6 in the morning since which I have heard thro' others he passed a very good examination—He came home on saturday pleased to find he was admitted—without being admonished to study, (as was the case with many) . . ."

7.

UNDER THE TREE OF KNOWLEDGE

❋◉❋

THE Sacred *Tree* midst the fair *Orchard* grew,
    The *Phœnix Truth* did on it rest,
    And built his perfum'd Nest.
That right *Porphyrian Tree* which did true *Logick* shew,
    Each *Leaf* did learned *Notions* give,
    And th' *Apples* were *Demonstrative.* . . .
        —Cowley, "The Tree of Knowledge"

There I turn over now one Book, and then another, of
various Subjects, without method or design: one while I
meditate, another I record . . .
        —Montaigne, "Of Three Commerces,"
        translated by Charles Cotton

IT ONLY remained for Ruth Emerson to raise the funds for such of
Ralph's expenses as were not covered either by the arrangements made
with the college or by the Penn legacy. She was certain somehow to
keep the rest of her family going as usual. By about this time she had
found a new home, at No. 60 Essex Street, next door to the Boston Female
Asylum, and, though she worried about "all these expences & so small
means," she promptly engaged to take a family of four to board at seventeen dollars a week. Financial difficulties, however trying, were not
insuperable. Ralph could now safely put his mind on Harvard, where
several generations of his ancestors, most of them perhaps hardly less impecunious than he, had studied before him. He hoped to "begin with determined and ardent pursuit of real knowledge that will raise me high in the
Class while in Coll. and qualify me well for stations of future usefulness."

He would have been as much shocked as anybody could he have foreseen, by some sudden access of prophetic power, that George Ticknor, the
professor and, later, literary historian, would come back from his European
travels and studies to reveal to its governors that in the institution at Cambridge they had neither a university, as they called it, nor a respectable
high school such as they ought to have. Had Ralph Emerson understood
the real situation, he might have chosen to wait for the era of reform to
begin. But as matters stood, he was willing to accept, without delay, the

kind of higher education the New England fathers had left at his doorstep.

He had probably got his copy of the college laws bearing his own name and the President's in attestation of the validity of the formally printed *Admittatur*. He could now skip the section on entrance requirements, having already passed "a very good examination." But there were some forty pages of laws that every student promised to obey. They pictured college life as seen from the vantage point of an experienced government. Though the academic legislators did "earnestly desire" that all their youthful charges might be incited to diligence in study and to right behavior by other motives than fear of punishment, they obviously did not really expect any such millennial state of undergraduate morality.

Misdemeanors and criminal offenses were carefully placarded. A festive entertainment in the college or its vicinity, except at commencement or at an exhibition, might result in the imposition of fines. Undergraduates were not permitted to have anything to do with theatrical entertainments in Cambridge. Religious and irreligious alike must "constantly and seasonably attend prayers, each morning and evening, and publick worship on the Lord's day, on publick fasts and thanksgivings, and the annual Dudleian lecture." The Sabbath, beginning at sunset on Saturday evening, had to be kept with Puritan strictness. The dress of the boys had to conform to rule. Library privileges were severely restricted. The "books, most suitable for the use of the undergraduates, being distinguished from the rest," the students were not allowed to borrow any others "but by special license." A sudden impulse to read a radical author might easily be quite forgotten before a boy could even ask for his special license, for the library was operated only on a very limited schedule.

Ralph Emerson was compelled not only to obey the laws but to help enforce them, for he was the president's freshman, or orderly, as he had been promised he should be. But his first thoughts as a petty officer of the college could hardly have been so much for the smooth functioning of academic government as for the scant financial relief he was earning. The earnings fell far short of covering his expenses. His official position exempted him from the charge for a study, but he received bills for various equipment, supplies, and services. One bill was for the wood used in his fireplace. He was dunned quarterly for "Steward and commons," and this meant that he was eating, not in the president's house, but with his class in the freshman dining room. He was charged the usual quarterly rate for instruction. Where he could, he saved. He had no serious expenses for repairs, as many others had; no assessments for delinquencies, no fines. He avoided natural history with its special fees and spent little for books. He was not careless about returning from out of town too late for commons and so having to size a meal. By practicing frugality he could satisfy all the steward's claims by paying some fifty dollars, or at times even less, each quarter.

The room assigned to him was in the rear of Wadsworth House under the bachelor President Kirkland's study. Besides young Lothrop, a nephew of the president's who was still preparing to enter college, four upperclassmen lived under the same roof; but, though Ralph had some acquaintance with them, his subordinate status placed him outside the social circle in the president's dining room, to which they belonged.

President Kirkland, doubtless remembered by his freshman as a visitor to Summer Street in the days of the Anthology Society, seemed a friendly figure in spite of the countenance he gave to a degree of academic segregation. A person of exceptional social talent and a "really superior" man, he was, as his fellow Anthologist the late William Emerson had been, a Unitarian minister and a Federalist. Kirkland had climbed to respectability and power in defiance of poverty and the meager opportunities of the frontier region from which he had come, and in conquering himself and his private difficulties he had learned a way of putting other people at ease. Ralph took lessons in human nature as he watched him in the routine administration of academic law or saw him quelling a riot between town and gown till "a great deal of noise swearing &c" died down into the mere "muttering" of the retiring combatants.

Harvard College, or University, as it was now sometimes officially called, had been founded shortly after the Boston Public Latin School and was the oldest university on the continent north of Mexico. The yard still included the earliest grounds of 1636, though the last of its seventeenth-century relics had vanished. Along its western margin several eighteenth-century structures still stood. Flanking these to the south was Wadsworth House, the presidential residence. Three recently erected buildings sketchily completed the quadrangle formed by the bricks and stones which, in 1817, the casual passer-by called the college. The whole institution had a new air of respectability. It was Kirkland, with his strong reforming broom, who cleansed the yard of its ancient brewery and improved, at least to outward appearance, its crude sanitary facilities. Yet the president's house itself still had not only its garden but its stable, where "the man" looked after the horse and cow.

This was the little self-contained world, center of the oldest part of New England's Cambridge, upon which Ralph Emerson looked out from his room as he listened for a tap on the floor overhead. Upon such a signal he was ready to set forth, an unhurried Hermes, to carry the messages of his good-natured, celibate Zeus. For neither Kirkland nor Ralph would

have found his likeness in the lines in which the poet of the boisterous
Engine Club dramatized the doings of the same president but another
freshman:

> Then Bibo kick'd his carpet thrice;
> Which brought his Freshman in a trice.
> 'You little rascal! go and call
> 'The persons mention'd in this scroll.'
> The fellow hearing scarcely feels
> The ground, so quickly fly his heels.

Though Ralph was only fourteen, below the average age of his class,
his height and his gravity made him look older, and he seemed to bear
his delegated authority without much effort. He was "nearly as tall as
when he had reached maturity" and was "a Saxon blonde," with "pale
face, light hair, blue eyes." He was, it was observed, "calm and quiet in
his manners; and no matter how much he felt, externally he was never
moved or excited." And yet he was by no means jauntily self-confident.
Already he was remarkable for a "mingling of shyness, awkwardness, and
dignity." These were his visible characteristics. But years later he furnished
what was probably a better psychological likeness of himself about the age
of fourteen. Looking back then, no doubt mainly upon his own early self,
he described puberty as "a crisis in the life of the man worth studying,"
being "the passage from the Unconscious to the Conscious; from the sleep
of the Passions to their rage; from careless receiving to cunning providing;
from beauty to use; from omnivorous curiosity to anxious stewardship;
from faith to doubt."

Though the president's messenger boy knew many persons, he knew
few intimately. He afterwards remembered or fancied that he had been
in disfavor with the other boys at the Latin School during the latter part
of his period there and that this disfavor lasted into college. Sometimes he
spent a day or two in Boston with his mother, and his absences from the
college must have made him seem more unsocial than he was. His poetizing
may have aroused dislike. At any rate some of his later hastily drafted
verses alluded to the chilling atmosphere his muse found in college:

> I went to Cambridge when a boy
> To hear the gownsmen
> And found more sense
> In the way than in the hall
> To poet vowed to solitude
> Best society is rude

John Gardner, an old neighbor in Summer Street and a mate at the Latin School who leaned heavily on Ralph for aid during their first days in Cambridge, did not afterwards remember that the other students had "any feeling about him, but of regard & affection," though "he was not prominent in the class." Gardner added to his childhood familiarity with Ralph by taking long strolls with him about Cambridge, then a village that allowed the country to creep up close to the busy market house in Harvard Square; and his assertion that Ralph "was not talkative . . . never spoke for effect . . . had no gush . . . but there was a certain flash when he uttered any thing more than usually worthy to be remembered . . ." was at least based on no mere fleeting impression. But Gardner also had some less flattering opinions of him. He was obviously a little overpowered by Ralph's "equanimity" and thought him in need of "a few harsher traits & perhaps more Masculine vigor." Another classmate, Josiah Quincy, destined to follow in his father's footsteps and become mayor of Boston, was very little impressed. John Hill, eagerly crediting Ralph with his own first introduction to Shakespeare, Montaigne, Swift, Addison, and Sterne, went far toward building up a legend of a white-haired boy. But that Ralph actually "pored over Montaigne, and knew Shakespeare almost by heart" during his freshman year or any other year at college is at least doubtful, though he certainly did not remain ignorant of either the Frenchman or the Englishman. It may be true that some others of "the more studious members of his class began to seek him out," and, if they did, they undoubtedly "found him to be unusually thoughtful and well-read; knowing, perhaps, less than they about text-books, but far more about literature." But there were limits to his reputation and influence. Significantly there seems to be no evidence that Robert Barnwell, the brilliant South Carolinian who was the acknowledged leader of the class, repaid Ralph's admiration further than to condescend to "put his hand on the back of my head to feel for the bump of ambition" and to pronounce "that it was very, very small."

Ralph Emerson generally kept aloof from the more uproarious doings of his fellow freshmen, but he had loyalty for his class and "he keenly enjoyed scenes of merriment." In a song of his that was sung at a freshman supper following an examination, he demanded a union of friendship, reason, and pleasure to bless the close of the glad year but filled his stanzas mainly with mild witticisms about the faculty, the textbooks, and certain breaches of college discipline by the members of his class.

Study at college was much the same as at the Latin School. Memorizing and reciting were the students' two serious occupations. But here there was less liberty, it seemed. The tutors and even the professors, especially in the freshman year, were apt to be simply drillmasters and academic policemen. Ralph, who had got much of his pleasure from "idle books under the bench" at the Latin School, did not thrive on such a system. Headmaster Gould came once or twice to advise with his former pupil about difficulties with mathematics, a subject in which the boy made an "almost total failure." But before his first college year was over Ralph had hit upon the comfortable theory that it was not "necessary to understand Mathematicks & Greek thoroughly, to be a good, useful, or even *great* man." "Aunt Mary," he told his brother William, "would certainly tell you so, and I think you yourself believe it, if you did not think it a dangerous doctrine to tell a Freshman."

Well grounded in Latin by his preparatory school, Ralph continued to look for rhetorical flowers in the classics and could appreciate Professor Brazer's neat handling of such a picturesque phrase as "fatigabat alieni jam imperii deos" from Tacitus. He presumably did not take too seriously the ponderous Latin of the Dutchman Grotius on the truth of the Christian religion. Roman satire, doubtless expurgated but still racy, stood high in the esteem of the young poet, who rashly advised his too willing classmates:

> Then drink to the sprite of satirical Flaccus,
> The first we heard hymning the praises of Bacchus;
> He left us the precepts we practise tonight
> And his "Nunc est bibendum" we never should slight!

Ralph's standing in both Latin and Greek "was fair," it is said, "and his renderings in the recitations were frequently happy." With Edward Everett away in Europe, the only Greek teacher on active duty was the "taciturn, reserved, timid, gentle Dr. Popkin," a tall, square, straight figure clothed in an unvarying black suit. His sole function in life, it was believed, was to hear recitations, and he stirred from his deep mental repose only long enough to correct the mistakes of his class as they translated from the Greek. Ralph was probably less struck by the beauties of Greek than by the "immense vis inertiae" of Old Pop, forever "restlessly stroking his leg and assuring himself 'he should retire from the University and read the authors.' "

Ralph had an insatiable curiosity about history, and especially its biographical parts. He may have got something worth while from the rules of rhetoric and grammar, for these subjects were also studied in the first year; and he must have become acquainted with a few good books under the guidance of the grammarians Walker and Lowth. But such gains were more likely to be incidental to his general reading. According to one classmate, he was especially happy in the weekly exercises in declamation. Some of the fragments of florid college oratory long remained in his memory, and he lived to confess "what fools a few sounding sentences made of me and my mates at Cambridge."

The circumstance of his residence in Kirkland's house, no doubt, together with Kirkland's desire to help the Emerson family finances, brought Ralph employment as a tutor a few days after the beginning of his freshman year. Samuel Lothrop, the president's nephew, then preparing for entrance into college, went to his uncle's study to meet the young freshman. The president put things in motion. "When I presented myself," Lothrop remembered, "he gave two little taps of his foot upon the floor, and immediately I heard a movement in the room below, footsteps on the stairs, and a knock at the door." The freshman had arrived to take charge of his pupil. "As soon as we got into his room he said, with a slight diminution of the dignity and authority manifested in presence of the President, 'Lothrop—your Christian name; what is it?' I told him my name, and then made the same inquiry in regard to his; to which he replied, 'My name is Ralph,—Ralph Waldo.' "

With little delay, they got down to work on "Latin Grammar, Liber Primus, and Lacroix's Arithmetic." The pupil "enjoyed highly the ten or twelve weeks" under Ralph's instruction but made little progress in the studies assigned. The tutor was, so the pupil thought, too much a boy himself to be severe and was more inclined to talk on general topics and to read pieces of his own poetry and prose than to prod his youthful charge along the hard path of learning. Sometimes his humor got the better of him, and he would give "comic views of persons." Yet he was careful about good translations from the classics, and apparently knew reasonably well the subjects he tried to teach. Lothrop thought him a peculiar person— kind, easy, familiar, but self-sufficient, with a wall of reserve about him that no one could penetrate.

The Emerson boys habitually seized upon vacations and leaves of absence from college as opportunities to earn money by teaching while their mother kept on with her Boston boarding house, feeding relatives and strangers and staying up "till about midnight every night." William, still a mere boy though a senior in college, now spent most of the winter teaching at Kennebunk, Maine. At Waltham, where William had earlier helped his half uncle Samuel Ripley in his school, Ralph, fourteen years old, took charge of his first class during the winter vacation of his freshman year.

Knowing well enough the straitness of the Emerson economy, he was disgusted to find that his wages had to be spent for his own clothes. Following his older brother's example, he rejoiced in abnegation, catching up one corner of the family burden when he could, and was sympathetically aware of the slightest changes in his mother's financial fortunes. "I envied you," he wrote to William, "bringing your 5 Doll. Bills to mother; but Mr R said I needed a coat & sent me to the tailor's . . ." He was, however, quick to see the more hopeful aspects of affairs. "Just before I came from Boston," he reassured William, "Mr Frothingham sent Mother a note containing 20 Dolls. given him by a *common friend* for her with a promise of continuing to her 10$ Quarterly for the use of her sons in College; not stipulating the *time* of continuance   At this time this assistance was peculiarly acceptable, you know. It is in this manner, from the charity of others, Mother never *has,*—& from our future exertions I hope never *will be in want.*—It appears to me the happiest earthly moment my most sanguine hopes can picture, if it should ever arrive, to have a home, comfortable & pleasant, to offer to mother, in some feeble degree to repay her the cares & woes & inconveniences she has so often been subject to on our account alone."

As *"petty* school-master" at Waltham, Ralph found himself "surrounded," as he put it, "by my 14 disciples." He was a good enough disciplinarian to be "safe & sound as yet unmuzzled & unsnowballed" a month after his arrival, and, finding some moments free for recreation, he had by that time "learned to skate, rhymed, written & read." Though Edward seems to have come from Andover to take his turn as assistant at Waltham, Ralph was back teaching again during the spring vacation. And at the end of a third tour of duty there he returned home with a purse of $12.

In spite of an already overloaded program, he set himself for a try at the Bowdoin prize, fortunately making up his mind in advance to be philosophical about failure. He also wanted to keep his hand in as a poet. He had read unsentimental, rather sarcastic and funny verses to Lothrop. One poem, it is said, "related to his minister and his father's successor . . . whose marriage had occurred about this time." One related "to scenes and incidents at the Latin school, which he had recently left; and others to college and college life, upon which he had just entered. . . . very droll in humor, and quaint in expression." Soon after he had informed his brother Edward that "I don't write poetry when at Cambridge" and that "in this country where every one is obliged to study his profession for assistance in living & where so little encouragement is given to Poets &c it is a pretty poor trade," he gave his classmates his song taking off the persons and events of the freshman year.

He wrote his verses in spite of an ear deaf to the charms of music. It may have been in his freshman year that he had the courage to offer himself as a member of a college singing class and was advised, after attempting one note for the master, or so the story went, not to come again.

But his sensibilities were keen in other directions. The fondness he already had for what the Romantics called Nature was reflected without any exaggeration in his later verses

> How drearily in College hall
> The Doctor stretched the hours,
> But in each pause we heard the call
> Of robins out of doors.

It may have been partly for health's sake and partly from literary fashion that he acted on the theory that the air was wise and the winds thought well. But though he seems never to have had much awareness of color, he soon had a relish, if not love, for natural forms and sounds. According to a family tradition, "Sweet Auburn," as Mount Auburn, still a wild tract, was then rather sentimentally called in honor of Goldsmith's village, was "his walking-ground almost every day when he was in Cambridge."

At the beginning of their sophomore year, he and his chum Dorr found themselves in possession of No. 5 Hollis Hall, "a corner room, up one flight of stairs," and, at least as it appeared much later, "broad and low, with a huge fireplace, little closets, and wide window-seats from which one looks out upon the Cambridge Common, the old burying-ground, and, nearer by, the 'class tree,' where the seniors meet for their farewell song." In general this description was true for Emerson's time. But actually No. 5 was in those days not one but three. The principal room was shared as sleeping quarters. Its paper and paint were not more than a year old, its wainscot good, its plaster a little broken, its fireplace good, and its chimney piece perfect, said the official in charge of such matters. The two little studies adjoining were in not quite such satisfactory condition, but each of them had its quota of three book shelves, suggestive of the real business of college. The boys supplied the rest of their furniture. The atmosphere of the place was not too studious. Dorr is said to have been "a waggish fellow, who cared little for books, but was a favorite with the class on account of his wit, his genial disposition, and his undoubted talent." He promptly gained some costly notoriety by his misbehavior at public worship.

Ralph, naturally thrown more with other members of his class than he had been at the president's, saw college government in a new light. The sophomores, feeling their importance as second-year men, grew unruly. In the commons they caused a scene of such disorder that the faculty suspended a few of the ringleaders for three months. The class protested, but the government, far from yielding, made further reprisals. Within a week after the beginning of the teapot tempest many of the sophomores had left

Cambridge, and, as those who remained kept their mutual agreement not to attend chapel, they too were soon ordered home.

The Rebelliad, a contemporary undergraduate's mock epic account of the disturbances, recorded the doings of the principal actors but made no mention of Ralph Emerson. He himself wrote what was described sarcastically by his brother William as "a history of your very praiseworthy resistance to lawful authority," but this is lost. The sophomore who had not long since been the president's freshman most likely agreed with his mother that the disorders were "sad business" and yet stuck by his class out of loyalty. He is said to have "remained at home until his class came to terms with the authorities"; but probably he was among the twenty-seven, not quite half of the second-year men, who applied for reinstatement after about a week of absence from college. He must have been in good standing when, a few weeks later, he was appointed to a temporary waitership, for the faculty would have hesitated to grant even so minor an office to an unreconstructed rebel.

The rump class failed to settle down, and, though Ralph suffered no punishment as a consequence, he must have been present on more than one convivial occasion. His self-control, remarkable even at this time, helped explain his ability to keep clear of college discipline, and he was also helped by a good stomach. Then, as later, it seems, he could drink "a great deal of wine (for me)," which probably was not much by other standards, and still grow "graver with every glass." Indignation and eloquence, he said, would excite him, but wine would not. Besides, he was not ambitious to take a leading part in class carousals or conspiracies against authority. According to his own report, he was generally "a spectator rather than a fellow." His dreamy nature, his age, and in some cases his good sense, partly accounted for his lack of conspicuous leadership.

He was not the jolly, roistering undergraduate the popular clubs were looking for. He did not join the Porcellian, known as the "Pig Club," a society of robust eaters and drinkers that took Barnwell and eighteen other members of the class, or Hasty Pudding, a somewhat more intellectual fraternity that admitted eighteen of the boys of 1821, or the Order of Knights of the Square Table, a festive brotherhood that got nine of them. He would have been miserable at the musical meetings of the Pierian Sodality and would hardly have dreamed of belonging to the Engine Club, a band of reckless youths, it seems, who ran about town more often for the purpose of quenching inner fires than for the protection of the property of citizens or college, their ostensible purpose. Though he may have felt a twinge of envy when he saw many of his classmates marching in the Harvard Washington Corps, such pomp was not for him. Barnwell, Motte,

Upham, Withington, Cheney, Manigault, and Wood were elected as juniors to Phi Beta Kappa, but presumably Ralph Emerson was not seriously considered for such an honor then or in his senior year. He seems to have had no connection with the religious Wednesday Evening Society or with the Saturday Evening Religious Society, or even with Kappa Delta, though it was designed to encourage students intending to enter the ministry.

But he was a very active member of one religious circle, the old Adelphoi Theologia, and belonged to several ephemeral clubs ranging from convivial to studious. According to one story, he became in his sophomore year "the leading spirit in a little book club, of which Edward Kent, afterwards governor of Maine, Charles W. Upham, of Salem, and Dr. D. W. Gorham, of Exeter, N. H., were also members. The club purchased the English reviews, the *North American*,—then just struggling into life,—and, in general, the literature of the day which they could not find in the college library." Another club, the Conventicle, was an outgrowth of the sophomore rebellion of 1818. Alden, the wag of the class, was founder and "Kingsbury was archbishop, Alden, bishop, and John B. Hill, parson." It was made up of "a set of intimate friends, and Emerson was one of the number. Although his quiet nature kept him out of most of the convivial societies, he was always genial, fond of hearing or telling a good story, and ready to do his share towards an evening's entertainment."

He regarded his election to the Pythologian Club before the end of his sophomore year as a high honor, because, in his opinion, the Pythologian could boast "the fifteen smartest fellows in each of the two classes Junior & Soph." Its purpose was described as extemporaneous discussion; but much of his effort in its behalf went into a long poem called "Improvement." He, with seven other sophomores, instigated a nameless club for writing and extemporaneous speaking, and he was one of the faithful members who kept it alive almost to the end of their senior year. Few high-ranking students ever belonged to it, but the compositions and discussions ranged from trivialities to such serious questions as "Whether promiscuous immigration be advantageous to the United States," "Whether deep researches into abstruse metaphysical subjects be advantageous to the Student," "Whether the conduct of the United States towards the Indians can be reconciled to the principles of justice and humanity," and "Whether equality of ranks in society be best adapted to its happiness." Though some of the other members were half a dozen years his senior at a time when such a difference in age counted heavily, Ralph had a prominent part throughout. And it was evidence of his desire to be accepted as a good fellow that at the last recorded meeting he won the thanks of the club by contributing a couple of bottles of wine to encourage the spirit of the occasion.

Presumably the more social clubs he belonged to made practical use of several of the drinking songs he composed. One such piece, a parody on Tom Moore, was to be sung until "our eyes grow drunkly dim" and, in defiance of college discipline, exhorted,

> Drink brothers drink the wine flows fast
> The tutors are near and the daylight's past

but probably had no more substantial meaning for the youthful, imitative author than did the neo-medievalism, eighteenth-century sensibility, and "Inexplicable daemon" of melancholy that inspired his muse by turns. Meantime, if the faculty knew anything about either his scandalous rhymes or his innocent poetizing during his early college years, they were apparently unimpressed. His prose as well as his verse went without official recognition. He was not, it seems, assigned any exhibition part as yet and only dreamed of capturing a Bowdoin prize.

Ruth Emerson urged her children to be independent but worked strenuously to provide for them. The death of Sheriff Bradford, the Emersons' "greatest earthly benefactor," was a blow to her. But she continued to receive gifts, it seems, from the daughters of the Robert Treat Paine who signed the Declaration of Independence, as well as from an anonymous donor and from the deacons of the First Church. Her son William, now giving his whole time to teaching, was her main reliance. Once, during Ralph's sophomore year, she seems to have been unable to pay the whole rent of her house, but within a few weeks William sent $200, and she accepted it as providential. Some months later a friend of the family made it possible to pay a new instalment of the rent, and William, after having been warned that he would be expected to come to the rescue once more, was granted a respite. The death of Ralph's Grandmother Haskins in September of that year would pretty obviously mean the inheritance of a small share of the estate eventually but must have meant nothing of the sort to Ruth Emerson at the time.

Ralph was successful in cutting down a little his mother's expenses on his account. Though he faced quarterly duns from the college, he had got the Penn legacy; and in the spring of 1819 President Kirkland had been kind to his old freshman—"told me," Ralph reported, "I had grown & said he hoped *intellectually* as well as *physically* & told me (better than all) when my next bill comes out to bring it to him as I have never recieved the Saltonstall benefit promised me before I entered College." To the substantial funds he got from the Saltonstall legacy Ralph added some earnings as waiter in the junior commons, feeling mixed delight and dismay at his appointment. While he was a waiter, he was also a policeman. According to an old rule, presumably still in force, he had to make a detailed report after each meal, "of all damage done to the utensils in the hall, at said meal, and of the person or persons who did the same, or any part of it, if known." Otherwise he himself would have to pay.

During vacations he kept up his teaching for the Ripleys at Waltham, where he doubtless lived through much the same round of duties that Edward described when he took his turn in the same school. "The whole care of 17 boys devolves on me from morning to night," Edward said. "We rise as soon as we can possibly see. Then I have to hear all the morning lessons before prayers. Aunt, and I read at prayers in a Greek Testament, George Bradford in a Latin. From prayers we go to breakfast. From breakfast half-an hour for play to the boys (not to me though) Then till between one and two steadily in school. Then to dinner and then to school again till supper time, from that time to eight take care of the boys while they get their morning lessons." But there were recompenses other than the scanty pay. Being with Sarah Alden Ripley was as good for a young scholar as attending classes under his professors. "When no one is reading to her," Ralph noticed, "at leisure moments you will find her reading a German critic or something of the kind sometimes Reid on Light or Optics. As to her knowledge talk on what you will she can always give you a new idea—ask her any philosophical question, she will always enlighten you by her answer."

Ralph's mediocre record as a freshman affected his three remaining years as an undergraduate, but it was not quite true that he "gave up college studies & took to general reading" or that, as he also afterwards said, "In college, I had unpreparedness for all my tasks."

As a sophomore he was assigned the usual Greek and Latin authors, together with such texts as Blair's lectures on rhetoric, Professor Levi Hedge's *Elements of Logick,* and Locke's essays, or at least the essay on the understanding. He had exercises in declamation and composition once every two weeks. He studied algebra and worked with Legendre's geometry under the guidance of his second cousin George Emerson, the new tutor in that subject. "Mathematics I hate" was his concise comment on such subjects. He apparently passed on to physical science under his cousin's instruction. If the class got as far as astronomy he may have had a double introduction to that subject, for another Emerson, Joseph of Byfield, had recently boarded at Ruth Emerson's in Boston for some weeks while he delivered public lectures on stars and planets.

It was doubtless Levi Hedge who led the class over the stony ground of logic into the more pleasing landscape of Lockean philosophy. Logic Ralph called "notorious & important" and recklessly resolved to get his lessons verbatim. He also uttered a prayer to the "Spirit of Metaphysicks," a spirit with whom he had little acquaintance, "for preeminence among thy sons!" In rhetoric he had Willard, regularly a teacher of Hebrew. One critical theme he wrote ranked among the half dozen best, but he was soon dissatisfied with "these trite simple subjects" that were being assigned. The sophomores, perhaps by a special dispensation, studied no history.

Going on into their junior year, the boys worked at ancient classics, Greek Testament, mathematics. They finished Locke, expounder of the unforgettable doctrine that the only fountains of knowledge are sensation and reflection, passed on to the less formidable Paley and Dugald Stewart, and continued with public declamations and forensic disputes once a month and themes once a fortnight.

With his brother William's School for Young Ladies successfully established in Boston, Ralph Emerson must now have been untroubled by any doubts about financial support while he remained at college. In Hollis 15 he and his roommate, John Gourdin, a South Carolinian who was his fellow junior and fellow member of the nameless club of debaters and essayists, could settle down comfortably to textbooks and miscellaneous literary experiments. It was presumably because of William's success that Ralph could spend his winter vacation at home getting on with his dissertation for the Bowdoin prize, and Edward, a victim of chronic colds, could for the first time escape from the severe northern climate for a winter with relatives in Virginia.

Before the winter was over William's school was so full that his mother laid plans for removal to a house with a room suitable for pupils. In April she accordingly took up new quarters at 24 Franklin Place, only a short distance from Essex Street. Opposite her house was the Catholic Church of the Holy Cross, the seat of Bishop Cheverus, the same prelate, beloved of American Protestants and Catholics alike, who was later to return to France and become an archbishop and finally a cardinal. Over the Arch in Franklin Street still rested the collection of the Boston Library Society. The Rev. William Emerson had once been a trustee of the society, and his family still owned a share and drew out books.

At the college a new day was dawning. An impressive sign of it was Professor Edward Everett's return from abroad. From the start Ralph was one of the willing worshippers of the handsome idol of the undergraduates. The new professor was really superior, but he had his weaknesses and his students imitated them. If he took to heart Goethe's caution that eloquence did not teach and was out of place in the lecture room, he still had no qualms about embellishing his sermons and public addresses with flowers of rhetoric. Ralph, with a keener appetite for sermons and orations than for lectures, liked to hear such swelling phrases as "we shall stand upon the confines of another world & see creation on creation sweeping by to their doom" and "if they will not repent then *let* the passing bell wail from steeple to steeple & when you weep you will not weep alone; the angels will weep with you." He memorized these things. He could say half the sermon from which he got them on the night after he had heard it, and he knew that he was not alone in his enthusiasm for it. The Boston audience was "almost ravished" by it, and when Everett repeated it in the Capitol at Washington it was listened to in "breathless silence" and Senator Otis of Massachusetts wept bitterly.

If Ralph Emerson was dreaming of becoming a preacher and orator patterned on Everett, he also had some thought of emulating him as a professor. When he had the good fortune to hear Everett's introductory lecture on Greece, he jotted down the main points in his new journal, "The Wide World," and solemnly resolved to make himself "acquainted with the Greek language & antiquities & history with long & serious attention & study," though "always," he cautiously emended his resolution, "with the assistance of circumstances." He reminded himself that he must read Herodotus and Aristophanes and all the Greek tragedians sooner or later, and if only some relics of Egyptian literature remained he would peruse them with ardor and strange interest.

He could not soon forget the "radiant beauty of person" of a classic style that Everett possessed, the rich tones and precise utterance spoiled only by a slightly nasal quality, the talent for collecting facts and for bringing them to bear on the topic of the moment, the learned discourses on learned subjects before the green boys from Connecticut and New Hampshire and Massachusetts with their unripe Latin and Greek reading, the abstention from all ornament in the lecture room, the mixture of infantine simplicity with florid and quaint fancy used in the pulpit, the sweetly modulated manner of quoting Milton. Years after he had left college, when his enthusiasm had burned itself out, Ralph still rated Everett a culture hero, "a Manco Capac" sent to Massachusetts instead of Peru, but by that time he credited him with only *"popular profoundness."*

Ralph, though not yet fully aware of the increased strength of the faculty, promptly began to benefit from the instruction of the new Boylston Professor of Rhetorick and Oratory, Edward Tyrrel Channing, a young lawyer and journalist, fresh from the editorial table of *The North American Review*. Never a scholar or a notable writer, Channing proved to be, nevertheless, an excellent teacher of his subject. The students little guessed how fortunate his coming was. When he appeared for his inaugural, in December of 1819, they refused to form a procession in his honor. But an assembly that "embraced most of the Literati and Friends of Literature in the State" crowded the chapel in University Hall to hear his "ingenious and eloquent" attack on the old-fashioned bombastic oratory still commonly heard. He praised the oratory of ancient Greece as an "art of most finished beauty and practical application" but showed that less passion and more deliberation and reflection were needed to appeal to the modern world. Feeling and imagination were by no means to be excluded even in 1819, but they must work with the judgment. The power of an orator perfectly fitted for the age would be truly great, Channing concluded.

Whether or not Ralph Emerson heard this inaugural, he soon read it, and he must have learned much similar good sense before he graduated if the rhetorical doctrine Channing taught his classes during those first years of his professorship at all resembled that of his lectures published nearly forty years later. Channing came proclaiming the reign of law. It is not clear whether he tried, in the senior year, to impose on Ralph's compositions the kind of architectural planning he later devised for Thoreau, but undoubtedly he helped to rid them of the worst effects of Everett's intoxicating pulpit eloquence.

Meantime Channing's most gifted student continued to write on his own initiative. As early as January of 1820 he was reading about, if not in, the Greek philosophers, with an eye to a Bowdoin prize. He already knew Xenophon and Plato as the biographers of Socrates, the philosopher with whom he was mainly concerned, and he got something from Diogenes Laertius. The whole picture of Greek history and Greek thought became clearer to him. He saw Socrates as a moralist, reviewed the conflicting notions of the Socratic daemon, made what he could of the impressive drama of the philosopher's death. "A Dissertation on the Character of Socrates," presented to the faculty in July, was far from being a mature essay; but it put him on the right road and won him the second prize, $20. He was also trying for honors in public speaking, and at the end of the term he was one of some fifteen Boylston contestants whose orations were "distinguished for much correct and energetic eloquence, and appropriate action." He got what seems to have been fourth place and was awarded one of the three second prizes.

Thus he began his senior year with at least a faint halo and might count on some respect from his ambitious freshman brother, Edward. Edward roomed with him and must have inspired him to new efforts. In spite of enfeebled health, Edward had his eye on the prizes. The moment he was up in the morning his mind turned to oratory and he began trying his voice, which was often affected by hoarseness. The boys were in Hollis 9. With its inevitable pair of miniature studies, the little apartment seemed a presentable place once one got past the battle-scarred outer door. Ralph, already greedy for solitude, found his own lone chamber the best thing in college. But for him it was important for general reading and writing rather than for study. He read desultorily but with excited interest. Sometimes his enthusiasm was contagious. His classmate Warren Burton used to come to his room, saying that he did not like to read and did not remember what he read for himself but never forgot what Ralph read or quoted to him.

Textbooks and professors were, in spite of the printed "Course of Instruction," much the same in the senior as in the junior year. Edward Everett and his Greek literature were once more powerful attractions. A printed synopsis of Everett's whole course on Greek literature still among the Emerson books contains copious marginal notes whose history, however, is doubtful. But an important discovery of the senior year was George Ticknor. Ticknor, a better scholar than Everett, had arrived laden with the spoils of Europe, at the same time as the more popular Greek professor. It had taken Ralph longer to learn Ticknor's merits. But now, at the beginning of the new academic year, he listened to "an eloquent lecture" by the "elegant" Smith Professor and observed that "every soul present warmly acknowledged the force of delineation when the great deluge of the French language, sweeping down all the feeble barriers of ephemeral dialects, carried captive the languages and literature of all Europe." In his notebook he wrote a simple outline of Ticknor's lectures on what he labeled the second and third epochs of French literature, from 1515 to 1778. The orderliness of his outline suggests that he may have used a syllabus or a preliminary set of notes. Regularly, on the left-hand page he would outline the basic facts, and on the right-hand he would amplify these and add critical judgments, presumably not his own.

Two or three of his later enthusiasms were faintly foreshadowed in this notebook. Already he knew something of the proverbial friendship of Montaigne and La Boétie and he remarked upon the vast learning, the brilliant thought, and the numberless quotations in what he set down as the "most extraordinary book ever written," Montaigne's essays. His comments on Racine, a dramatist whom he later saw performed on the Paris stage, revealed his discovery that "Andromaque . . . rests on tenderness" and that "Phèdre . . . contains the Greek notion of Destiny." Molière's *Misanthrope* he labeled as too didactic but conceded that it contained "a spirit of unrivalled satire." In his notes on Pascal's *Pensées* he admired the "great force of character necessary to give a classical value to works like these."

Even if, as is possible, he was merely copying a synopsis he had not made, such things could be important to him. All these ideas were probably faint echoes of Ticknor's learning, but they may have remained in the memory of such a boy.

He jotted down in his diary, from time to time, a few choice bits from Ticknor, and, finally, on May 2, 1821, he reported that the course of lectures was finished. He added a summary of the professor's remarks that might explain his own persistent obsession in later years with the idea that the French intellect was sick: French literature, a unique phenomenon according to Ticknor, was not national and the result of "the feelings, situation, circumstances, & character of the whole people which produced it" but conformed and must continue to conform to the rules and spirit of the court of Louis XIV; and its six characteristics were conventional regularity, little religious enthusiasm and feeling, a false character in the expression of love, little deep sensibility, ambition to produce a brilliant effect, and "restriction of success to those departments which will give some kind of entertainment."

Ralph put into his journals a few hints of what he was writing for Channing. In February of 1821 he made a pertinent memorandum: "I must give Mr Channing a theme on the influence of weather & skies on mind; I have tried poetry but do not succeed as well as might be wished." He proceeded to lay out a plan, presumably a revision of an old one, for such an essay, and the concrete conclusion his thinking on the general subject led him to was that a flaming sky explained why the Hindus were "distressed & degraded by the horrors of a flimsy & cruel Superstition." Another thing he apparently intended for Channing was a set of verses headed "Castles in the air—built, in the near prospect of leaving College." But on the manuscript he wrote, "This theme is dispensed with . . . I have now closed my college list of themes . . . May 8th 1821."

Essays and themes were to him the most exciting academic exercises. But the study of philosophy, though Dugald Stewart's elementary philosophy and William Paley's moral philosophy were required texts in both junior and senior years, could stir him. He was even enthusiastic about Stewart's success in making a textbook glamorous and was struck by what he regarded as the Scot's brilliant promise of effects that were to follow from the new analysis of the human mind. It was true that President Kirkland could not understand why Ralph, the author of the Bowdoin essay on Socrates, was not a better Locke, Stewart, and Paley scholar. Yet, whether Kirkland knew it or not, the boy was learning from other advisers to feel something of the spell of philosophy.

Aunt Mary carried on a correspondence with him, inciting him to speculation with hardly more than the mere mention of such theories as the Swedenborgian one that the physical world was the basso-relievo of the moral. As some of his correspondence has been lost, it is impossible to say to what extent she was the prime mover in such speculations. As for Swedenborgianism, it was already taking hold among the students at the college. But Aunt Mary was at all events an inspiration to her nephew. She got bits of information for him about Dugald Stewart from Sarah Alden Ripley of the Waltham school. She offered him Price on morals, told him she valued his correspondence with her. In one or two letters she may have done as much for her nephew as Professor Levi Frisbie could do in weeks of teaching.

Frisbie was, however, a memorable figure as he sat at his professorial desk, his aching eyes shaded by his handkerchief; and he made his ideas felt, notwithstanding the foibles he frankly revealed in his self-portrait:

> Nice points in the schools he would settle at once;
> Who his reasons saw not, was put down for a dunce.
> Yet, ofttimes, the veriest trifle about,
> He would doubt and consider, consider and doubt;
> And at last, having acted, would fret for an hour,
> That to change but once more, was now out of his power.

Some of his doctrines were in print. In his inaugural address, delivered and published in Ralph's freshman year, he took for granted a moral sense given by nature, but insisted that it needed as much cultivation as the intellect. To him it seemed clear that imaginative literature had a great share for good or evil in that cultivation. He delightedly agreed with the indignant Edinburgh critics who had exposed the evil influence of "Moore, Swift, Goethe, and in general the German sentimentalists"; and he espoused the Edinburgh view that we must have our Cudworths and Butlers and Stewarts to take care of an inevitable Hobbes, Rousseau, or Godwin. His bad eyes doubtless hindered his writing, but he had more recently published his article about Adam Smith's observations on the moral sentiments. In it he concluded, after balancing Smith's credits and debits, that the moral sense, or rectitude as he now called it, "regulates and guides the whole system of our affections and powers . . . and conducts man to the proper end of his being."

The same theory of the innate moral control recurred in the sketchy lecture notes that remained unpublished till after his death. And in them he once more pointed out how much the simple idea of right, or sense of duty, or moral taste, needed proper development.

According to George Ripley, a sophomore during Ralph's senior year, both Frisbie and his contemporary and successor, Levi Hedge, followed Dugald Stewart and Thomas Brown in protesting against Locke and Paley, and thus opposed Andrews Norton, a Harvard professor who had to be reckoned with by his colleagues. So far as Frisbie and Hedge represented the college, its teaching was an endorsement of the Edinburgh brand of Scottish philosophy and pointed slightly in the direction of Transcendentalism. The refurbishing of what was essentially the outmoded Shaftesbury-Hutcheson theory of the moral sense was a feature that Ralph Emerson would certainly not soon forget. It was also important for him that Frisbie, earlier a professor of Latin, was a devotee of both ancient and English literature and a formidable critic of composition. After college the pupil affectionately remembered his old teacher as one of our "minds of republican strength and elegant accomplishments" and as an eloquent apostle of the beauty of virtue.

For some time at least, Ralph continued to respect Bishop Butler, one of the sober thinkers whose works were prescribed by the college catalogue for all seniors. He doubtless got the required political economy in the same year, and he read assigned essays in *The Federalist*. He seems to have studied Professor Gorham's text in chemistry, a regular part of the curriculum; but apparently he did not yet feel enough enthusiasm for exact knowledge of the physical world to wish, as he afterwards did, for leisure to go "to the college or the scientific school which offered best lectures on Geology, Chemistry, Minerals, Botany, and seek to make the alphabets of those sciences clear to me." As a boy, though he was probably seldom guilty of mere reverie, he preferred his own thoughts, and in his diary he wrote: "These soliloquies are certainly sweeter than Chemistry!" It was only toward the end of his senior year that he put his best efforts into several projects in a final and somewhat belated attempt to build up a reputation as a leading undergraduate writer and speaker, and these projects were all extracurricular.

From miscellaneous sources with which his textbooks had little to do he drew inspiration for the poem he read at what seems to have been his only appearance on a college exhibition program. He was now unwittingly rehearsing the method he was to use in much of his mature writing. What he had kept or remembered of his theme on climate and culture could have served as a useful foundation. In it he had used India and her superstitions as his chief example of the evil effects of a hot climate. He borrowed some of the verses he had written for the Pythologian Club. Possibly he recalled first-hand observations that his relative William Farnham had reported to the Emersons a few years before, upon returning from Calcutta.

He may even have had some recollection of the books relating to India that had been in his father's library.

He had once included *The Asiatic Miscellany,* by Sir William Jones and others, in a list of books he had read, and something may have come from it. Robert Southey's *The Curse of Kehama,* a mine of information on Hindu mysteries, had been referred to by Professor Edward Everett's brother John in an oration that Ralph had long since rhapsodized over. Ralph had once been enthusiastic about a passage from the Hindu classic of Menu that he had found in one of Southey's notes. And in later years, at least, both the story of *The Curse of Kehama* and its author's glosses haunted him with paralyzing terror. He was thus getting an early introduction to Hindu lore that warranted him in picturing in his own poem a "stern Bramin armed with plagues divine," a sinister figure quite unlike the religious aristocrat destined to capture his imagination.

But the slightly more than one hundred and fifty lines which he summarized in his title as "Indian Superstition" were only the green fruit of his private method of rambling literary exploration and were not appetizing fare to offer to his public. Though the poem was not a thing to be proud of, it was his one serious bid for fame as a college poet, and he urged recalcitrant Aunt Mary to be on hand for the senior exhibition, modestly assuring her that "not twenty present will know that your proud ladyship is related to the despised & ragged poet" and warning her that she "must not ask for Waldo the Poet" as he was "better known by the name of Emerson the Senior." On April 24 a throng of persons who, if they lived up to the description he had given his aunt in advance, were "the leaders of the fashion" and a "spectacle of this world's splendour" heard the poem. After the announced exercises there were probably doings of a less decorous sort with which the poet could hardly have been much concerned. Even if this exhibition night was as wild as that of the preceding October had been, "with merriment and wine, evincing or eliciting gay, fraternal feeling enough, but brutalized and defiled with excess of physical enjoyment," he doubtless came through it unscathed and outwardly unperturbed.

Some three months later he was back in the public eye on two succeeding days. His "Dissertation on the Present State of Ethical Philosophy" earned him one of the two second Bowdoin prizes. The thirty-four-page treatise seemed to one of the contestants "long and dry," but Ralph possibly impressed the faculty members by his fidelity to their own general view of philosophy. He was, at any rate, like them in having little or no traffic with the new German thinkers and was as convinced as they were that the true advance must go on under the guidance of the Scottish philosophers whose great leaders had been Reid and Stewart.

On the following morning he made a sober class poet, announcing that it was time to put away childish things.

Gambol and song and jubilee are done,
Life's motley pilgrimage must be begun . . .

he warned. He bewailed Europe's unhappy destiny, congratulated America on her noble future, and paid a parting tribute to the college. But he probably remembered his own halting lines with less pleasure than the valedictory oration that his classmate Robert Barnwell delivered at that same meeting in the chapel. Barnwell, also concerned about the perennial problem of Europe and America, declared that "The childhood of our country has past . . . We have broken from the mental thraldom, under which a foreign literature had too long confined us. . . . We will live for ourselves. . . . We will turn to our own history . . . let us unite all our powers to promote the establishment of a national literature." This was only a boy's echo of voices speaking out everywhere in America, but to an admiring classmate it might be important.

Ralph Emerson probably felt little pride in his part of these exercises, for not fewer than six other boys, it is said, had refused the honor of being class poet before he accepted it. He presumably kept his wits when his classmates got tipsy and marched through the streets of Cambridge, shouting insults as they passed faculty homes. He was probably not one of the noisiest of the crowd who showed their contempt for authority by dancing around the Rebellion Tree. With the rest of the boys he came near doing without the final honor of formal graduation exercises. Only the vote of President Kirkland prevented the faculty from canceling the whole commencement program. The faculty had had enough of the incorrigible Class of 1821.

With the aid of a final examination bearing heavily upon the allied subjects of moral philosophy, metaphysics, and theology, the seniors were able to take stock of their scholarly achievements. Ralph Emerson was "number thirty in a class of fifty-nine" and presumably would have been lower except for his record of good conduct. Yet in the practice of his own private elective system he was doing much better. He would not have served as an illustration of the educational theory expounded to the class by their tutor Caleb Cushing in his farewell speech. Cushing was sure that "The advantage of pursuing our studies in a public seminary consists not in reading certain books, but in reading them methodically, with instructers to give unity and plan to the whole course of studies, together with the stimulus of public distinction to produce competition." Ralph was doubtless reading few books methodically, but he was looking into many. Relics of them were scattered through his journals—"Wide Worlds," "Universes," and others. In a document he labeled "Catalogue—of Books read from the date December 1819—in the order of time" he seems to have tried to measure his progress by a method his professors neglected. The part of the list he apparently covered before graduation contained perhaps eighty or ninety titles and a beadroll of literary names extending from Plato to Washington Irving.

As a writer, he had won a few prizes but had done nothing worth remembering. His saving graces were his tender age and his unflagging, though, from the point of view of the faculty, misapplied, ambition and perseverance. He had got some commendation from Aunt Mary, who was usually severely critical. In the spring of his senior year she thought she had discovered a happy revolution in his style, but her discovery would have been much more firmly supported by the extant examples of his writing if it had come a few months later. He must have learned something of the art of writing from his professors, especially Channing, and was learning much more from the great books whose acquaintance he was rapidly making.

Socially, his achievement disappointed him. He had made a few close friends and a few others who were enough interested in him to be his correspondents for some months. His infatuation, in his junior and senior years, for Martin Gay, a student of his own age but two classes behind him, had no social results. Cool Gay, as he was called by his classmates, was a friend only in his admirer's journals. Ralph was struck by Gay's features and thought they showed character. He somehow became fascinated, but his fascination was not enough to prevent him from deliberately proceeding to dissection. A "dozen times a day, and as often by night" his mind reverted to the magnetic boy and he wrapped himself up in "conjectures of his character and inclinations." After months he and Gay had had only "two or three long profound stares at each other," but Ralph persisted in his silent admiration through most of his last college year, when, having heard an unfavorable tale about Gay, he decided that he would have to throw him off after all "as a cheat of fancy." The whole experience struck him chiefly as an interesting psychological problem. The problem, however, was doubtless mainly his own. He was delving slightly into his unconscious self.

He had none of the social graces that grew out of easy living. Of the less than $700 spent on his four years of college, he cyphered it out that he earned $50 by keeping school and $55 in prizes and that all but about $150 of the remainder came from the church or from charitable friends.

He was at a disadvantage with many of his mates because of the poverty of his Boston background. His mother, looking out for the best opportunities to save money, did not often remain settled for many months. In April of his senior year she had moved her family from Franklin Place to the neighboring Federal Street. As the new home was at No. 26, the Federal Street Church, built by Charles Bulfinch and now presided over by the distinguished Doctor Channing, must have been an attractive feature of the noisy neighborhood for the Emersons. Ralph's second cousin George Barrell Emerson, having quitted his Harvard tutorship, soon came to live with them, bringing his brother. In general the boarders, since the move from Franklin Place, were less troublesome, and Ralph's sick brother Bulkeley could be more conveniently cared for here. But the Emerson family home was still a boarding place; and, if Harvard friends came there, they were likely to find it filled with uncongenial people.

Whatever the total reckoning, college life came to a close in no blaze of glory for Ralph. He was just high enough in his rating to get one of the commencement parts into which the lowest students admitted to the program were unceremoniously crammed in twos and threes. He did not feel like taking part in the customary conviviality marking the end of student days. To his Aunt Ripley, the schoolmaster's sister, he wrote gloomily: "I shall not have a dinner and have not asked any body—for a conference is a stupid thing . . . if you think of coming we shall be very happy to see you; Mother and Aunt and a host of brothers will be there." As the official program for August 29 announced, he was to confer with Amos Goodwin and William Pope "On the Character of John Knox, William Penn, and John Wesley." Pope absented himself. Ralph, according to his boyhood friend Sam Bradford, had looked forward to a poem as his assignment and was so mortified at having nothing but some insignificant prosing on John Knox that even after the audience began arriving he still had to memorize his part, and when he finally spoke it he leaned heavily on the prompter.

Some of his classmates were more fortunate. George Washington Adams discoursed at length upon the influence of natural scenery on poetry, using some phrases which, though not fresh, might remain in the memory of one hearer. In the calm, lovely landscape, said young Adams, one felt a quietness, a sense of tranquillity which was itself a temporary happiness; but nature did not always smile, for she sympathized with other emotions than those of kindness and sympathy. John Hill, one of Ralph's fellow members of the nameless society of debaters and orators, tried to decide "Whether there be an ultimate standard of Taste?" and arrived at the conclusion that "It is vain to talk of taste without models." Samuel Hatch praised conservatives and warned against perpetual change. Josiah Quincy thought that the literary history of France, Britain, and all nations went to prove that "elegant literature has no other basis than that of the ancient classics" and "That to any great elevation or extension of literature a large & liberal public patronage is essential; & that . . . a republick is the only soil in which it naturally flourishes."

John Pierce, the tireless attendant upon commencement exercises, praised Upham and Barnwell for their parts. A pessimistic newspaper reporter agreed but lamented "an inferiority so obvious in the present class . . . as to induce a general expression of disappointment." Though it used to be an honor to go to college, times had changed, he grumbled. "At the present day the merest blockhead in the world is sent thither to render him wise, but it is seldom he closes his career without coming forth a greater dunce than when he began it." Ralph Emerson thought the best thing on the commencement program was an oration on genius by Sampson Reed, a graduate who had returned to Cambridge, after the prescribed three years of good behavior, to take his Master's degree. Reed's theme was the divinity of genius. The young Swedenborgian was vigorously announcing a new spiritual dawn. It is not surprising that, though his bold proclamation struck most listeners as dull and tiresome, it caught the fancy of the senior from Federal Street and he borrowed the manuscript and copied it. The somber stanzas that William Cullen Bryant, a guest poet from the Berkshires, recited at a meeting of Phi Beta Kappa on the following day rounded out the commencement season but seem to have left no lasting impression on Ralph. Perhaps, since Ralph had failed of election to the honorary fraternity, he did not attend, though the public was invited.

He wrote little, it seems, for months to come, and so left only a very incomplete record of feelings inspired by the end of his academic life. He would naturally overlook for many years some of the benefits he had got, or might have got, from academic discipline. But he had reason to remember his personal hurt when he thought of his alma mater. He "was not often highly flattered by success," he confessed, "and was every day mortified by my own ill fate or ill conduct." After a few months he went back and sentimentalized in the old haunts; but there was doubtless real bitterness as well as gay humor in his comment to a classmate: "I have darkened upon Cambridge but once since Commencement, my love for it was so wonderful, passing the love of women."

He was undoubtedly afraid that he had been on the wrong track, and he suffered some pangs of conscience. But he never fully repented of his "ill conduct" in failing to concentrate on the assigned lessons and join in the general contest for the honors awarded largely for thoroughness of preparation and accuracy of memory. Instead, within a dozen years or so, he concluded that he had been right in trusting his own instincts. "I was the true philosopher in college," he decided, "and Mr. Farrar and Mr. Hedge and Dr. Ware the false, yet what seemed then to me less probable?" By that time he was gradually transmuting his unhappy emotional experiences into a satisfying theory of the proper conduct of one's life.

8.

THE UNWILLING SCHOOLMASTER

Of studie took he moost cure and moost heede,
Noght o word spak he moore than was neede,
And that was seyd in forme and reverence,
And short and quyk, and ful of hy sentence.
Sownynge in moral vertu was his speche,
And gladly wolde he lerne . . .
    —Chaucer, prologue to *The Canterbury Tales*

BEFORE the end of his senior year Ralph Waldo Emerson had dropped his first name, and he soon insisted on being called Waldo. His mother liked the name Waldo, perhaps because it helped to distinguish him from her brother Ralph. Another reason for the change may have been that when the boy's second cousin and former tutor, George Emerson, joined Ruth Emerson's household in May of 1821 to begin some two years of residence there, he brought a brother with him. George's brother was presumably the same Ralph Emerson whom Waldo long afterwards recommended as a person "I knew . . . well in his youth."

Waldo, being inevitably doomed to the family purgatory of school-teaching, had some hope that the Latin School would give him an usher-ship. On a visit to Providence he may have looked for an opening there. He did not relish the prospect of serving under his brother William. He complained to Aunt Mary about a fatal Gehenna and a doleful day in prospect and described himself as a dull and condemned mortal. He feared that teaching girls and writing poetry might not mix. But he was soon convinced that there was no escape for him, and before the end of the year he had settled down as assistant in William's school for what the prospectus called young ladies.

William, his supervisor, was a good teacher and disciplinarian. Two years before, at eighteen, he had "offered himself as a grave & experienced professor, who had seen much of life, & was ready to give the overflow-ings of his wisdom & ripe maturity to the youth of his native city." He was quiet and amiable, but his mind was method and order and "the tap of his pencil" was sufficient to "enforce a silence & attention which spas-modic activity of other teachers cannot often command." However much the younger boy might dislike dependence on a brother, such a colleague was a godsend for the shy and unmethodical Waldo. George Emerson, now living in their home, must have been a fountain of advice for both his younger cousins. Concluding that the competitive system was wrong, he had refused an offer to stay on at Harvard as a professor, preferring to be principal of the new English Classical School in Boston, where he was promised a free hand in putting his own theories to the proof. There it soon came out that he did not believe in corporal punishment, a form of discipline still commonly used; and he told his seventy-five pupils that he would never strike a blow unless they compelled him to and would believe every word they said until they had been proved guilty of lying. He begged the boys not to try to surpass each other but only themselves and promised that the dull boy and the bright boy would get the same mark if each did his best.

In comparison with these experienced teachers, Waldo Emerson was a mere novice, and his weaknesses seemed extraordinary to him. He was terrified at entering a girls' school and was troubled by what he later called "the infirmities of my cheek," "occasional admirations of some of my pupils," and "vexation of spirit when the will of the pupils was a little too strong for the will of the teacher." Sometimes he evaded severe tests of his disciplinary powers by sending refractory pupils to his mother's room, thus compelling them to undergo a minor sort of rustication. The girls were naturally unable to resist the temptation to tease so young a teacher. At election time they made a point of asking him whether he was going to vote; and, though he was now officially "Mr Waldo," they called him Ralph among themselves. But their refraining from laughter when he tipped his chair too far and fell over backward showed their liking for him.

For compositions, he assigned such subjects as "Say not that the Former Days were Better than these" and "Has Climate Any Influence on Character?" These were topics that he had already worked over in college. He read the papers carefully and was struck by the singularly sonorous style of one and the good sense of another. He labeled "Eloquent" a theme on slavery, written by a girl whose nursery bedspread had depicted the evils of the slave trade. A manuscript of his headed "Story for September 10th 1823 Ginevra" and another marked "Stories to be written by learners" were presumably used to inspire written or oral composition and to make historical or geographical lessons palatable. When he assigned Fénelon, together with Racine, Corneille, and Bossuet, he may have been braced by his notes on Ticknor's lectures; but these would not have helped his pronunciation, and he suffered from "timidities at French."

He taught Hume's history of England and was amazed and distressed to find that one of the girls had memorized the whole of a forty-page assignment. In his classroom, it seems, the Scottish trio of Thomas Reid, Dugald Stewart, and Thomas Brown supplied most of the philosophical reading. According to one pupil, "If any one was interested in Stewarts philosophy it made him happy." The thinkers he had liked best in his college days seemed to dominate the young master still. The girls read poems to him as one of their lessons, but he was too shy to show them his own favorites. He was at the time writing down his thoughts on morals, but, as he said later, "no hint of this ever came into the school, where we clung to the safe & cold details of languages, geography, arithmetic, & chemistry."

Besides teaching in his brother's school, he seems to have given some private instruction. According to Elizabeth Peabody, he and she sat shyly together while he instructed her in Greek without charge. This seems, according to her story, to have been in 1821. But any such tutoring by Waldo could hardly have lasted long. Elizabeth Hoar remembered how she was left one day in his charge. She thought him an unusual sort of schoolmaster as "he came out to th garden where she was & holding out his hand said 'Come now, my young friend'—as if an angel spoke." But if Elizabeth Hoar was eleven at the time as she said, this must have been near the end of his schoolteaching days.

However much the shy youth may have seemed an angel in the eyes of young girls, he was a schoolmaster much against his will and looked for the quickest way out of his treadmill. In one of his verse books he jotted down the saying that

> It takes philosopher or fool
> To build a fire or keep a school.

To his classmate John Hill, then teaching in Maryland, he confessed, "I am (I wish I was otherwise) keeping a school & assisting my venerable brother lift the truncheon against the fair-haired daughters of this raw city. It is but fair that those condemned to the 'delightful task,' should have free leave to waste their wits, if they will, in decrying & abominating the same." To his journal his tone was almost as rebellious and more despondent. "But now I am," he wrote, "a hopeless Schoolmaster, just entering upon years of trade to which no distinct limit is placed; toiling through this miserable employment even without the poor satisfaction of discharging it well, for the good suspect me, and the geese dislike me."

He was not quite hopeless and had times of pleasant freedom. In the late spring, toward the end of the first year of his teaching, he was off with William on a walking tour. Northboro, some thirty miles west of Boston, was their terminal point, and there they settled down for a week in a farmhouse and were joined by their brother Edward. To the boys from the large town this region seemed idyllic. They lodged near a pond called Little Chauncey, and often crossed it and "then," Waldo said, "tied our bark to a tree on the opposite shore and plunged into the pathless woods, into forests silent since the birth of time, and lounged on the grass, with Bacon's Essays, or Milton, for hours."

Waldo was brooding over the problem of society and solitude and debating it with Aunt Mary. "I cannot tell," he wrote her, "but it seemed to me that Cambridge would be a better place to study than the woodlands. I thought I understood a little of the *intoxication,* which you have spoken of; but its tendency was directly opposed to the slightest effort of mind or body; it was a soft animal luxury, the combined result of the beauty which fed the eye; the exhilarating Paradise *air,* which fanned & dilated the sense; the novel melody, which warbled from the trees. Its first charm passed away rapidly with a longer acquaintance, but not once, during our stay, was I in any fit mood to take my pen, 'and rattle out the battles of my thoughts,' as Ben Jonson saith well. . . . Perhaps in the Autumn, which I hold to be the finest season in the year, and in a longer abode the mind might, as you term it, return upon itself; but for a year, without books it would become intolerable."

He made some progress in literary explorations even when teaching drained most of his energy. In spite of a remark that he abhorred leaving a volume half read, probably his cardinal vice was already "intellectual dissipation—sinful strolling from book to book, from care to idleness." According to his own special list of books "read," he somehow got through, or through with, at least three volumes of Sismondi on the literature of southern Europe, Hallam on the Middle Ages, a volume of Samuel Clarke's theology, Byron's tragedies, five volumes of Gibbon's Roman Empire, Erskine on revealed religion, Alexander Everett's Europe, More's *Utopia,* four volumes of Sully's memoirs, three of Lemaire's volumes on the French Revolution, the second part of Dugald Stewart's dissertation, Parts I and II of Playfair's dissertation on the progress of mathematical and physical science, Cook's voyages, a life of Burns, a volume of Milton's prose, Jeremy Taylor's *Holy Dying,* apparently some new volumes of Gibbon, Mackintosh's introductory lecture, a volume of Burke, the posthumous writings of his old teacher Professor Frisbie, two volumes of Franklin's works, two volumes of Hume's essays, Boileau's poetical works, Voltaire's Charles XII, and Molière's *Le Misanthrope.*

Presumably before the end of 1824 he had got what he cared most to get out of the whole of this list, including some books by the inevitable Walter Scott. He continued his reading of Scott much in the order of the novels as they came from the press—*The Pirate, The Fortunes of Nigel, Quentin Durward, St. Ronan's Well,* and *Redgauntlet.* He was engaged in his most extensive excursion into fiction. With *The Pirate* his enthusiasm began to cool. As for American fiction, he would not admit any comparison between *The Spy* and Scott's novels, and he was disappointed when, as he judged from some extracts he saw, the Irving of *Bracebridge Hall* "left his fine Sketchbook style, for the deplorable Dutch wit of Knickerbocker." But when *The Pioneers* was published he quickly joined in Cooper's praise.

He criticized Shakespeare because, though their greatness was clear to him, the plays seemed to fall short of the ideal on the moral side. The fact that you could cull from Shakespeare's works "a volume of poetry nearly approaching to sacred inspiration" was the very reason they had wrought "incalculable mischief," he believed. But he continued to read them and soon he was quoting them frequently. He weakened in his severely moralistic attitude, discovering a noble masterpiece in *Hamlet.* Still, as in early college days, he "thirsted to abuse the poetical character" of Wordsworth, a contemporary poet to be read with caution because "the eye always is afraid lest it should meet with something offensive at every turn." The "something offensive" was most probably to be met with in *Lyrical Ballads,* then thought by many critics to be a tasteless exhibition of contempt for the great tradition. Meantime Aunt Mary's letters suggested new views of the Hindu lore that Waldo, not long since, had stigmatized as "Indian Superstition." She quoted for him what she called "a sweet morsel of Hindu poetry." It made little difference that it was actually an imitation by the skillful Orientalist Sir William Jones. It sounded the purest mystical and pantheistical notes in the authentic religious verse of India. All was show and delusion but the divine:

> My soul absorbed one only being knows
> Of all perceptions one abundant source . . .

Though the schoolmaster had probably seen these lines in *The Asiatic Miscellany,* he was as yet hardly more than conscious of the Oriental treasures. "I am curious to read your Hindu mythologies," he wrote. Hitherto he had known only what was in the *Christian Register* about Rammohun Roy, the Hindu friend of Unitarianism who was turning the minds of many Americans toward India.

He informed his aunt, in return for her novelties, of his impression of Italian history. His admiration for Venice, the Queen of the Isles, was gone because of her disgraceful conduct. But he felt growing respect for Florence, for her councils "were uniformly marked by a high minded wise

& patriotic policy far above the spirit displayed by any other state." His reading in history made him readier to share the interest in European art that was stirring in Boston, where the plaster casts given to the Athenæum attracted the eye, he said, "from the tedious joys of writing & reading." Pale ghosts of Greece and Rome though they were, they were a revelation to him. "The beholder," he discovered, "instantly feels the spirit of the connoisseur stealing over him, &, ere he can exorcise it, rubs up his Latin & Italian lore . . ."

In January of 1822, he resumed the keeping of his neglected journals, using them mainly for discussion of religious, philosophical and literary matters, for self-examination, for a commonplace book, and for a practice book for his own literary experiments. He did not reveal the extent of his literary experiments when he wrote to his classmate John Hill early in 1823: "I keep school.—I study neither law, medicine, or divinity, and write neither poetry nor prose; nor, as you curiously imagined, have I the most vague intention of inditing Romances. I admire to hear, and aim to tell good stories . . . but that is all."

Whether seriously or not, he had long been trying to write bits of fiction, mostly moralistic or fantastically imaginative. A few months before his graduation he had, as he confessed, got deeply interested in "my Magician," was "as anxious to know the end as any other reader could be," and thought "this tale of mine might be told with powerful effect by a man of good voice and natural eloquence"—so deeply had the idea of the power of the orator taken hold of him. A fragment headed "Richards Confession" and described as a "Continuation of Magician" was so brief that it barely got an aged friar posted, in an expectant attitude, beside the death bed of King Richard. A story of Uilsa, a queen "descended from an hundred weird women fatal and feared daughters of Odin," ran through several instalments in the same blotting book and ended with Uilsa in the suffocating grip of a monstrous serpent.

There was a fragment about Omar, once the favorite of an Oriental king but now fallen from his high estate. The young romancer was inspired by Arthurian legend; or he wrote of strange happenings in the Pacific islands; or, as he sat on the margin of the River of Golden Sands in Africa, he had a vision of a slave hunt. But his obsession with a dreamlike, exotic world was already weakening as he realized that the art of fiction, after passing through an age of magicians, griffins, and metamorphoses, had come to be more effective, at least for a modern audience, by placing imaginary persons in real life.

Verse was now playing a minor part in his literary exercises. The incomplete prose tale about Richard was matched by a dozen stanzas called "King Richard's Death. A Ballad." Another ballad on an English king, a piece destined, after careful grooming and much delay, to be printed anonymously as "William Rufus and the Jew," followed, but at a distance of two years. Soon the poet was adventurous enough to experiment with irregular verse forms, even trying what he called "Prose run mad."

Meanwhile he continued his series of commentaries on the drama, curious little essays, stiffly moral. Though they might have been intended as contributions to a periodical, they had an atmosphere of unreality. Their author, though continually crying for reform, knew little of the contemporary theater that he was criticizing; and the playgoers he conjured up were ancients who had formed their taste on Aeschylus and Sophocles. He very honestly summed up the series to date for Aunt Mary by saying that "*The drama* crawls on but clamours for inspiration." Not content with theorizing, he tried his hand at a dramatic blank verse fragment in which an Indian chief eloquently defied the white men before they could cross the sea. He seemed to be trying to prove that a modern theme could be made into a play as heroic, and therefore as moral, as an early Greek tragedy.

His thoughts were also on essay-writing and he was considering proper models. He had already made up his mind that Montesquieu's Persian letters were early examples of that literary form and had tried to place them in relation to *The Spectator* papers and to *The Rambler*. Frequently his journal entries were hardly less than brief attempts at moral and philosophical essays. He tried in one of them to reason out the arguments for slavery but concluded that "No ingenious sophistry can ever reconcile the unperverted mind to the pardon of *slavery;* nothing but tremendous familiarity, and the bias of private *interest.*"

Though there was already a strong undertone of optimism in his speculations, he was still finding the problem of evil tough. He thought no elaborate argument could remove the stubborn fact of the existence of evil, and evil was the foremost difficulty in the way of belief in an omnipotent good Principle. Perhaps history would supply the answer to the question whether the place of evil in the whole scheme of things could be justified. Meantime there were the "enslaved, the sick, the disappointed, the poor, the unfortunate, the dying." Certainly "war is waged in the Universe, without truce or end, between Virtue and Vice," the nineteen-year-old philosopher conceded. There was indeed "a huge and disproportionate abundance of *evil* on earth," and the good was "but a little island of light amidst the unbounded ocean." Yet the recompense of virtue was still out of all proportion to the attractions of vice, and true philosophy saw "amid the vast disproportions of human condition a great equalization of happiness."

The death of Professor Frisbie, Waldo's former teacher, may have had something to do with a strong upsurge of interest in the problem of the moral sense. The moral sense was of divine origin and was persistent in its activity, the young schoolmaster felt sure. "It sometimes seems to sanction," he declared, "that Platonic dream, that the soul of the individual was but an emanation from the Abyss of Deity, and about to return whence it flowed." He was ready now to base even his faith in immortality on the moral sense. He composed a long treatise on "Moral Obligation." And as if he were planning a formidable essay for publication, he lengthily discussed the attributes of God.

There was good reason why his interest in religion could hardly exceed his enthusiasm for history. He was determined to search for an empirical basis of his theories, and since he himself had not the requisite experience he immersed himself in history. His historical and religious researches jointly inspired an essay. Long readings in Mosheim, Gibbon, Hallam, and Sismondi meant that he was seriously confronting the problem of the medieval church and its relation to modern Christianity. He began bringing his thoughts to a focus in the summer of 1822.

In its final form "Thoughts on the Religion of the Middle Ages" speculated on the cause of the "fact of awful interest" that nations passed through periods of decline into "semi-barbarous repose." The power of the medieval church had rested on its assumption of an authority over human conduct that annihilated the independence of society; on adherence to sanctimonious forms that affected only the surface of society, leaving the social order fundamentally unregenerate; on accumulated wealth that corrupted the clergy and the popes; and on an exercise of temporal authority that finally roused the laity against the church and spelled its ruin. The relapse of the Dark Ages was a lesson to after generations, showing the need of a pure religion, plain in doctrine and rigid in practice.

This was the gist of the young Unitarian schoolmaster's article in the opening pages of The Christian Disciple for November and December, 1822. If this was his first publication, he doubtless felt some satisfaction, though he could hardly have got much applause, for the signature "H. O. N." gave no clue to his identity. Aunt Mary had hinted in advance that she had little patience for reading what he and his master Hallam thought of the religion of the Middle Ages; and after publication, when Charles Emerson asked her opinion of the piece, she had not seen it. Outside the family Waldo relaxed his reticence enough to mention the new number of the *Disciple* to his classmate Withington and to suggest, "Please to read the first article and I will tell you who the writer is." He may have had hopes of receiving an unbiased judgment, but it is doubtful whether he got any reply, as his correspondence with Withington seems to have halted just then for many months and, indeed, all but ended. In one way the essay might have been important for him, as later events suggested. The person who gave it its place of prominence in the magazine was doubtless the editor, the younger Henry Ware. As pastor of the Second Church in Boston, Ware would naturally look over his contributors with an eye for promise of future distinction in the pulpit.

Whatever pride Waldo Emerson took in being a published if still obscure author must have been salutary. He had been little enough contented with himself. A few months earlier he had rated his social ability low and bewailed what he judged to be his coldness of nature, confessing, with some exaggeration, that the history of his heart was a blank. He had not been able to refrain from mentioning his "diseases and aches and qualms," and his pessimistic self-appraisal may have been quite as much inspired by these as by what he called his "desolate soul." His fear that his stop-gap occupation would hold him back from the ministry, surely his chosen profession, had added to his discouragement. On the near approach of his nineteenth birthday, a signal for general invoice-taking, he had discovered "a goading sense of emptiness and wasted capacity" and had soliloquized bitterly, "Well, and I am he who nourished brilliant visions of future grandeur which may well appear presumptuous and foolish now." But ambition still stirred him deeply, and he was far from giving up hope. Some ten months later, when he described himself as "hastening to put on the manly robe," the youthful author of "Thoughts on the Religion of the Middle Ages" recalled that from childhood the names of the great had always resounded in his ear and admitted frankly, if somewhat grandly, to his journal that "it is impossible that I should be indifferent to the rank which I must take in the innumerable assembly of men." For the present, however, he could only plod on with his school for young ladies.

It could hardly have been any lack of financial prosperity in the school that determined the family to leave Federal Street and Boston on May 24, 1823, one day before Waldo's twentieth birthday. They had no intention of giving up the valuable income they got from the school. Presumably the main reason why they turned their faces toward the fringe of hills visible on the southern horizon was their hope of finding better health. But they cared also for the charm of the hill country. There they had the advantage of living in an unspoiled region not too far from the large town where the two young schoolmasters did their teaching. Stones and trees became humanized and acquired such friendly and familiar names as the Study, the Cliff, and the Pine-grove. Waldo discovered that there was "an excellence in Nature which familiarity never blunts the sense of—a serene superiority to man & his art."

Aunt Mary, long used to frequent retreats into the deep solitude of Maine, commented that the family were now pleasantly translated "into what you call the Country." The part of Roxbury to which Ruth Emerson and her sons had moved was actually a temperately rough and wooded countryside later included in Franklin Park. To reach the little farmhouse in "Light Lane, Lower Canterbury," from their schoolroom it was necessary for Waldo and William to travel some two miles over the Dedham Turnpike, "a continuation of the Main St. in Boston," and then a little farther over a country lane. Their landlord was Stedman Williams, "a farmer of 30 yrs standing," who lived near by.

The neighborhood was then sometimes called Canterbury. Light Lane seems to have been only one of a number of names, some facetious, that were locally used. The Emersons' house, standing in a gravelly lawn that stretched "to an immeasureable extent on every side," was old and apparently was an attractive home only because of the surrounding landscape. But there was soon some society. Before the year was out Uncle Ralph Haskins had bought a place within a mile and a half. There was much going back and forth, and the Haskins house was particularly convenient for the residents of Light Lane because it was on the way to Boston. Sometimes the Haskinses could hear the Emerson boys making the woods resound with declamations and dialogues.

Even before the powerful Mill Corporation had built its new link to the mainland Boston had had a firm hold on little suburban Roxbury, and a stream of traffic between the two flowed over the marshy neck of the peninsula. But all was peaceful a little off the main highway. Before a year of this new life had passed, Waldo believed he had realized his "infant aspirations" to be perfectly content among rocks and woods. Roxbury seemed to him an old and pleasant home. Boston, where he earned money in order to be respectable, was the House of Pride, with no comfortable room for him. In his journal he wrote:

> Good bye, proud world, I'm going home
> Thou'rt not my friend & Im not thine
> Long I've been tossed like the salt sea foam
> All day mid weary crowds I roam
>
> Good bye to Flattery's fawning face,

To Grandeur with his wise grimace,
To upstart Wealth's averted eye,
To supple office low & high
To frozen hearts & hasting feet
To noisy Toil, to Court & Street.
To those who go & those who come
Good bye, proud world! I'm going home.

I'm going to my own hearth stone
Bosomed in yon green hills alone
Sweet summer birds are warbling there
forever mair

In spite of the somewhat exaggerated antisocial mood of these verses, the passion for nature which they expressed was sincere. Even a more secluded retreat would have pleased Waldo Emerson, at least for a time. Already, in the late summer of 1823, after but a few months of Roxbury, he had gone off, with Bacon's essays for company, on a tour, mostly pedestrian, to the Connecticut Valley, through Worcester and as far as Amherst, Northampton, and Greenfield. Such a tour gave him at once the pleasure of new landscapes and the sense of complete escape from his schoolroom.

Still heartily disliking the schoolroom and nursing his ambition to be a minister, Waldo considered the vague possibility of studying theology at Andover, presumably because of the learning of the faculty and in spite of the conservative theology taught in the Calvinist stronghold. A move in that direction would doubtless have been supported by his sometimes extremely orthodox Aunt Mary, and though his serious intention was to return to Harvard for his theology, he himself was not quite sure how far liberalism should go. "An exemplary Christian of today, and even a Minister," he told one of his old college mates, "is content to be just such a man as was a good Roman in the days of Cicero or of the imperial Antonines. . . . Presbyterianism & Calvinism at the South, at least make Christianity a more real & tangible system . . ." But this was, he thought, "the most which can be said of orthodoxy." So his doubts remained unsettled. "When I have been to Cambridge & studied Divinity," he promised, "I will tell you whether I can make out for myself any better system than Luther or Calvin, or the *liberal besoms* of modern days. I have spoken thus because I am tired & disgusted with preaching which I have been accustomed to hear."

He kept track of his young contemporaries who were outdistancing him in the race for the gown and band. He went over to Cambridge and heard

his classmate Charles Upham preach his first sermon before the divinity students and listened to Professor Andrews Norton's eulogy and critique of it. He may also have attended some of the public examinations, or exhibitions, which the divinity faculty had begun to hold in the college chapel. Meantime, though he felt a strong urge toward extreme liberalism in religious creed, he was trying to hold fast to something that would justify his going on into the ministry.

In reality Calvinism, in spite of Aunt Mary's gibe that he knew only a few bugbear words of it, had no chance with him. His admiration for a passage from one of Frothingham's sermons describing Calvinism as a doctrine which "represents man as *coming into the world girt in the poison robes of hereditary depravity & with the curses of his Maker on his head*" indicated the direction in which he was going. That he was still willing to confess publicly his faith in something less vague than pagan doctrine in the age of the Antonines was, however, made clear on the last day of May, 1823, not quite a week after his twentieth birthday, when he and his brother William signed the "Declaration of Faith subscribed by the members of the First Church of Christ in Boston," Frothingham's own church:

I. We, whose names are underwritten, declare our Faith in the only living and true God.

II. We believe in the Lord Jesus Christ, that he was sanctified of the Father, and sent into the world, that he might "redeem us from all iniquity; and purify to himself a peculiar people zealous of good works."

III. We believe in that gospel, which was ratified by the death and resurrection of its author; and solemnly promise to make it the only rule of our faith and practice.

United by the ties of one Lord, one common Faith, and one Baptism, we promise to live in Christian love; to watch over each other as members of the same body; to counsel and assist, whenever there shall be occasion; to be faithful to our master, and faithful to each other, waiting in joyful hope of an eternal happy intercourse in the heavenly world.

The same declaration had been signed by the members of the First Church for many years past. One signature was that of Ruth Emerson. But if read in the most liberal way this creed was not too narrow for a Unitarian in 1823. Undoubtedly Waldo read it the liberal way, and, so read, it marked a point from which one dimension of his future growth as a thinker might be measured.

Within a few months he had fallen into the long procession of disciples of William Ellery Channing. He walked into Boston almost every Sunday to hear the preacher who, in spite of his frail body, his dislike of controversy, and his horror of any kind of orthodoxy, even the Unitarian kind, was now taking the lead among Unitarians. Channing seemed to prove that one could be nominally a minister and yet be almost free of creeds. Still, even he held to a belief in the unique importance of Jesus, in the historicity of the gospel story, and therefore in miracles, with some exceptions. For him the Bible, if not inspired, was at least a record of inspiration.

But whatever horizons Waldo Emerson looked toward, the school for young ladies seemed to stand in the way, circumscribing his freedom of thought and action. After some two years as assistant to his brother William he was about to take over the whole responsibility. Edward, now beginning to take an important place in the family councils, had "ciphered it all out" that it would be best for both William and the family if William prepared for the ministry in Germany while Waldo and Edward himself kept the pot boiling at home. Edward would teach and study law, and when William returned from abroad the two of them would be ready to take over the family finances while Waldo took his turn at professional studies. Channing, being consulted, vainly protested, advising William to study divinity at home rather than at Göttingen. Germany, he said, was better for literature; but one who intended to preach in New England had better study his divinity there. Yet Edward Everett, an old Göttingen student, sent letters of introduction, unasked. Ticknor supplied more introductions. On December 5, 1823, William set sail for Europe.

Edward, keeping his part of the agreement, got a school of about one hundred boys and was ready to turn ten weeks of his winter college vacation into cash. He was a highly efficient intellectual engine. At college he was the great orator and quickened Waldo's love of oratory. His past record was impressive. He had ended his junior year on the exhibition program with his English oration on the encouragement of a sound literature as the duty of the patriot. The love of literature, joined with a proper regard for morals, would make America the chosen theater of God's mighty drama, the orator had declared, and he had closed with the conventional burst of patriotic prophecy. From this time he was perfectly at home on the platform.

His great hour came in 1824, on his commencement day, the day of La Fayette's suddenly arranged visit to Harvard. For Waldo the occasion had special significance, not only because it was Edward's day, but because it was his own third academic anniversary. Though he was not a candidate, some twenty-five of his classmates, having behaved acceptably during their three years since graduation and having paid the required fee, were to receive their Master's degrees. But the prime attraction was La Fayette himself, seated conspicuously on the platform. "Never was homage so unbounded, so heartfelt, so spontaneous," said one observer. "It was as if one of the great heroes of history had been permitted to return to earth." The speakers generally made it a point to allude to the old French warrior and statesman, Washington's friend, "and so permitted the repressed rapture to burst forth." Edward Emerson's oration, "The Advancement of the Age," marked the climax of the exercises. The brilliant senior with the "beautiful countenance full of force & fire, yet of an almost feminine refinement," was "not merely the first scholar in his class but first by a long interval"; and now he had reason to do his best. According to the family tradition, when he finally began to speak the huskiness of voice that had long been his curse troubled him at first; but it cleared, and he addressed La Fayette in well-modulated tones. Waldo, sitting in the audience, felt a glow of pride and triumph strong enough to last until many years later when, with incredulous eyes, he examined Edward's manuscript and saw how juvenile the college oratory had been.

Yet even while Edward was winning his laurels in college and Charles was getting a first prize at the Latin School, Waldo tempered his elation with some second thoughts on the family's achievements. He confided to one of the Concord relatives his opinion that "Proud & poor spirits are not very far divided in this world . . . Men cheat each other & themselves with ostentatious distinctions . . . they are all the disciples & slaves, & your only true Masters & Emperors are Time & Chance." He himself was living through a daily round of commonplaces. He pursued "the labours of the school, & the cares & studies at home" with "unrelaxing industry, & perseverance," his mother remarked with more satisfaction than he felt. He re-established the School for Young Ladies in a "good new room back of Trinity church," within a stone's throw of the place in Summer Street where he had once attended the A B C class. He had to pay a rental of $150 a year and faced severe competition, but still he could count profits from his "23 or 4" pupils.

Edward, not much spoiled by his college distinctions, was prepared now to chain himself to an oar in the family galley. He had, indeed, already taken a private school for boys in Roxbury with an estimated income of $600 or $700. Within a few months there were new financial rainbows, for the Haskins brothers were going ahead, on behalf of Ruth Emerson and numerous other Haskins heirs, with the building of a hotel and stable on the family estate in Rainsford's Lane. Mortgages had to be negotiated, but there was hope of sizeable returns. The old Haskins Mansion House itself had now been repaired so as to bring a higher rental the following year, and Ruth Emerson was looking forward to receiving her small part. Waldo betrayed an unfeigned interest in the family finances, as the time of harvest in the school would be short. The girls would desert him, "for," he said, "they wax old," and not enough replacements were coming in.

If he was to study theology at Cambridge, the sooner the better. And in order to shorten what might otherwise be three years of poverty there, he was planning to enter the middle instead of the junior class. He was already taking "a hebdomadal walk," sometimes to a Mr. Cunningham, sometimes to Doctor Channing, "for the sake of saying I am studying divinity." Though Channing, already famous as a preacher, was not an unconstrained, friendly person who could easily communicate himself to individuals, he doubtless made a deep impression on the mind of his young disciple.

For the moment his doctrinal influence must have been conservative. Only a few months before, he had preached a discourse on revelation that Waldo thought unrivaled since its author's Dudleian lecture. Channing, in his discourse, had "considered God's word to be the only expounder of his works," and asserted "that Nature had always been found insufficient to teach men the great doctrines which Revelation inculcated." Revelation was "as much a part of the order of things as any other event."

Waldo got a reading list from Channing and borrowed some volumes from him. But the list of "books for a theological student" that he preserved was not striking for its originality, and its eleven titles, ranging from Taylor on holy living and dying to Miss More on practical piety, did not seem very formidable. Possibly Channing saw that this self-styled theological student lacked health for hard study, or the list may have been merely an instalment of a longer one. At any rate it was no such intellectual bill of fare as the Doctor did, on occasion, give out.

Yet if Waldo Emerson was not accomplishing much hard work, he was not drifting blindly, and in his attempt to get oriented and to chart his further course intelligently he was getting more guidance from Channing than a shelf of selected readings would have been likely to give. A few weeks before his twenty-first birthday, at the beginning of what he called his professional studies, he had followed up his deliberate dedication of himself to the church with a sober inventory of his abilities and characteristics, the basis of any hope he might have of success. It was in his diary for ready reference if he needed to think it through again: "My reasoning faculty is proportionably weak, nor can I ever hope to write a Butler's Analogy or an Essay of Hume. Nor is it strange that with this confession I should choose theology, which is from everlasting to everlasting 'debateable ground.' For, the highest species of reasoning upon divine subjects is rather the fruit of a sort of moral imagination, than of the 'Reasoning Machines,' such as Locke and Clarke and David Hume. Dr. Channing's Dudleian Lecture is the model of what I mean, and the faculty which produced this is akin to the higher flights of the fancy. I may add that the preaching most in vogue at the present day depends chiefly on imagination for its success, and asks those accomplishments which I believe are most within my grasp." He had come at the profound fact of his mental composition in this attempt at self-analysis. The "sort of moral imagination" making up for a lack of hard logic was it, as he already saw. And Channing's most important service, now or ever, was doubtless in helping him to become aware of himself.

But he also had to reckon with some "signal defect of character which," as he said, "neutralizes in great part the just influence my talents ought to have." He had been convinced of this by every comparison of himself with his mates in years past. "Whether that defect," so it was reasoned out in the diary, "be in the *address* . . . or deeper seated in an absence of common *sympathies,* or even in a levity of the understanding, I cannot tell. But its bitter fruits are a sore uneasiness in the company of most men and women, a frigid fear of offending and jealousy of disrespect, an inability to lead and an unwillingness to follow the current conversation, which contrive to make me second with all those among whom chiefly I wish to be first." He thought he lacked "that good-humoured independence and self-esteem which should mark the gentleman." He was "ill at ease, therefore, among men. I criticize," he accused himself, "with hardness; I lavishly applaud; I weakly argue; and I wonder with a 'foolish face of praise.' "

Yet, unless it also meant eloquence, his moral imagination was not, it seemed to him, the only basis of his hope to thrive in divinity. He believed he inherited his father's, or, possibly, paternal grandfather's, love of eloquence. He burned "after the *'aliquid immensum infinitumque'* which Cicero desired," and one would learn to imitate when one ardently loved. In his better hours he was the believer, or dupe, of brilliant promises and could regard himself as the possessor of powers that would "command the reason and passions of the multitude." As for the kind of success he ought to win, he thought it would be chiefly in public preaching but that private influence would be a necessary objective.

He had long since made similar attempts at frank self-appraisal, but his eyes were growing sharper and his results were now more concrete. There was no sentimentalism about his merciless introspection, as he was preparing for action. Along with his belief in compensation, and his optimism, his doctrine of self-reliance was growing partly out of his personal necessity. If he lacked self-reliance, he had to have it for success. He was already a pragmatist. "Every wise man," he believed, "aims at an entire conquest of himself." He knew that he had a long way to go before he could boast of so complete a victory, but he had at least got far in the direction of a private philosophy which would serve as a guide and, insisting on self-reliance for himself, he was at the same time discovering in it a universal validity.

In view of the profession to which he was dedicated, he was also concerned with the problem of religious faith. But here he found no satisfactory solution. Even metaphysics and ethics were superficial sciences and gave no true insight into the nature and design of being. Every system of religion might be wholly false. Pre-Darwinian ideas of evolution were in the air, and the young student of theology seemed already to have a presentiment of the shocks religion would suffer from that direction. "To glowing hope, moreover, 't is alarming," he confessed, "to see the full and regular series of animals from mites and worms up to man; yet he who has the same organization and a little more mind pretends to an insulated and extraordinary destiny to which his fellows of the stall and field are in no part admitted, nay are disdainfully excluded."

Probably few aspirants to the ministry ever showed more conscience or more imagination than he. He wanted to see his problems in their broadest meaning. He wrote a lengthy letter to Plato on "the moral and religious condition of man" for Aunt Mary to answer with a sharp reproof on Plato's behalf. Though men still commended the wisdom of Plato, he said, Christ and his apostles had won the day. Yet he saw that the Christian priesthood were hard put to it to understand their own vocation. Was it really necessary, he wanted to know, that men should have before them "the strong excitement of religion and its thrilling motives"? He himself was still a friend of Christian revelation. "But," he said, "I confess it has not for me the same exclusive and extraordinary claims it has for many. I hold Reason to be a prior Revelation, and that they do not contradict each other." No wonder that he watched with keen interest the experiment his brother William was making in Germany, where American students, traveling in the wake of Edward Everett and George Ticknor, were beginning to examine curiously the new historical criticism of religion.

William had arrived at Göttingen in March of 1824. His first reports were not alluring. After weeks of struggle with the "really appalling" difficulties of the German language, he could understand something of Eichhorn's spoken commentaries on the first three Evangelists and of another professor's translations, with commentary, of Demosthenes; but by that time he was critical of the German lecture system—"for you are aware," he wrote to Waldo, "that this recitation of the professor is the leading feature, perhaps it might be just to add the grand error of the German system of University instruction." He was also displeased with the social life of Göttingen and lived in a solitude which, he said, Aunt Mary herself might envy. He saw his fellow American Calvert frequently and now and then called on a professor. "With the students," he wrote, "I have no intercourse, and from what I see of them, am not desirous of any." Used to the paternal system of college government, he was scandalized by their lack of interest in lectures, their incredible consumption of wine and beer, their endless feuds and duels, and their frequent rebellions. Soon, however, he discovered that there was another side to the picture and his mounting enthusiasm was hard to keep within bounds. "Learn German as fast as you can," he advised Waldo, "for you must come here, even if I take to school-keeping again." He suggested some preparatory exercises. He listed helpful German books including "all of Herder you can get," hoped his brother cared for Hebrew, and advised his taking a quarter's lessons in speaking French, "the language of every educated man in Europe."

In letter after letter Waldo disowned any expectation of arriving in Göttingen. "I shall come to fairy-land as soon," he wrote. "Unless I c'd take the wings of the morning for a packet & feed on wishes instead of dollars & be clothed with imagination for raiment I must not expect to go." There were moments when he was less sure of himself. He retreated far enough to admit that he would be glad to try the new scene. He at least wanted to hear in exactly what particulars the superior advantages of Göttingen consisted. But, having listened to other arguments than William's, he wrote that it had been deemed wisest for him "to give up teaching & make haste to be taught and in the very poverty of this course to forswear Germany & go to the cheapest stall where education can be bought." "Therefore," he said, "in a few months I shall probably be at Cambridge & attempt to enter the *middle* Class, which if practicable will be an economy of time not to be despised by a hard handed American who reckons acquisitions by dollars & cents not by learning & skill. I tell you your German towns are Castles in the air to me."

The awkward timing of transatlantic mails confused the long-range debate, and it was apt to break out anew when it seemed to be all but settled. Once more Waldo weakened in his resistance to his brother's re-iterated advice. He even promised that if William thought it "in every way advisable, indisputably, absolutely important" for him to go to Göttingen and would say so distinctly, he would after all "make the sacrifice of time & take the risk of expense, immediately." He was therefore ready to yield on the question of studying German, and Hebrew. "Say particularly if

German & Hebrew be worth reading for tho' I hate to study them cordially I yet will the moment I can count my gains," he finally found courage to say. "Had I not better put on my hat & take ship for the Elbe . . .?" By this time he himself was suggesting a new reason why he should take his turn at Göttingen. This was the danger that otherwise he and William might finish together at the theological school in Cambridge, where William, it was understood, was still planning to go on with his studies. If they finished together they might be rival candidates for a pulpit.

To Waldo, the effect of German learning on his brother's religious ideas was inevitably a matter of great interest if hardly one to inquire about point-blank. In his letters home William gave little ground for suspicion that his private articles of faith were much affected by Eichhorn's higher criticism of the Bible, but he was really adhering to his plan to be a minister in the face of growing religious doubts. Having heard the last of Eichhorn's lectures, he went on a walking tour to Dresden and back, visiting Weimar on the way. This meant an opportunity to discuss his personal problem with one of Germany's wisest men, for travelers were still few and were prized as much as foreign newspapers.

Goethe, in his journal for September 19, 1824, briefly mentioned William Emerson from Boston, North America, student at Göttingen, Protestant theologian, and, apparently with some feeling of satisfaction, appended the information that the visitor waited for him. Though his own impressions of the occasion were naturally more enthusiastic, William wrote home only a vague account of their conversation "about America, and then of other subjects of the highest interest." Only less cryptic in his journal of the tour, he noted that Goethe soon got to "the state of religion in the U. S." and "thought we had nothing to do with the different systems of philosophy, but that the highest aim of life should be for each one to accommodate himself as perfectly as possible to the station in which he was placed."

So far as his letters home or his journal revealed, William made no immediate sign of revolt against such a philosophy of expediency as seemed to be implied in Goethe's remarks. Yet in a new letter to his brother he was clearly debating his own relation to such doctrine, and he was pretty obviously far from confident that an American church would receive the radical teachings he had now come to accept from his professors. The results of Eichhorn's investigations of the origins of the gospels were of great importance for an understanding of Christianity. But there was a disturbing doubt as to these results. "Are we prepared to embrace these in their fullest extent?" the youthful theologian put it. Eichhorn's findings had an effect upon the picture of the character of Jesus. "And," William told

Waldo, "in this connexion the remark occurs, that every candid theologian after careful study will find himself wide from the traditionary opinions of the bulk of his parishioners. Have you yet settled the question, whether he shall sacrifice his influence or his conscience?"

The exchange of letters across the Atlantic continued with painful slowness, and Waldo gradually got a formidable list of reasons why he should study German and come to Göttingen for a substantial part of his theology. William, making a final effort, patiently summed up all the arguments: "But what advantage shall I reap? say you. At an university—a familiarity with the German language, which you will probably not otherwise obtain —then you have in the daily lectures the results of so many centuries of struggles against superstition and ignorance; you see theology in its every branch completely developed in the state to which the learned have brought it, up to yesterday—aye, today. Out of the last arises one of no little consequence, a very great familiarity with Latin and Greek, in the former of which these literati seem almost to think.—I can get their books, perhaps you answer, and do all this at home.—You can, but you never will." Waldo, however, stayed at home.

During the last six months of William's residence in Germany things moved rapidly at home. By about the first of November the Haskins heirs had completed their thirty-five-room hotel on the home estate and had named it in honor of the French hero who had recently visited Boston. Shortly thereafter it was let. A sign was hung out that would appeal equally to the military and to civilians. The figure of La Fayette was newly painted on one side in the uniform of a general and on the other in citizen's clothes. In the expectation of increased income for the family and with the determination to go back to Cambridge with little delay, Waldo allowed the girls' school to come to an end almost with the year.

"I have closed my school. I have begun a new year," he wrote on the 4th of January, 1825. Within the next month or so he had roughly computed his earnings since he left the college as "two or three thousand dollars which have paid my debts and obligated my neighbors, so that I thank Heaven I can say none of my house is the worse for me." Presumably every dollar of his indefinite but impressive total had come from the school for young ladies. In his own opinion little but the money came of his more than three years of teaching. He had "never expected success." "My scholars," he had once put it, "are carefully instructed, my money is faithfully earned, but the instructor is little wiser, and the duties were never congenial with my disposition." He was seldom patient with factual detail, he was too shy to be a firm disciplinarian, and as he had bent over the schoolmaster's desk he had had his eye on the pulpit.

About the middle of January he sent word to William that, though he had locked up school and now affected the scholar at home, the grand schemes in process of realization were to keep the family finances on an even keel. As he explained the outlook, their mother, one of the Haskins heirs, should soon receive $200 a year from the new hotel, with reasonable prospect of more. "In hour of need," he went on, "this can be easily mortgaged for $1000. Moreover if I go to Cambridge at the end of the present vacation, as I shall, the learned & reverend have consented to admit me to the Middle Class of which measure whatever may be the moral & general expediency, the pecuniary is apparent. Next I possess in fee simple $518 at interest. Lastly Edward retains his private school of 7, or $800, though the uneasy child whispers pretty loudly of slipping his neck from the ancient noose in August. When I have added that in April we shall probably migrate in a flock to Cambridge & occupy Mr Mellen's old house for $100 or 200, you will have all the data whereon our calculations proceed."

He had expected February 8, 1825, to be his last day at the pleasant rural retreat in the Canterbury quarter of Roxbury, but he seems to have returned there before his formal admission into the theological school. On February 10 he wrote to William, "Tomorrow morn^g I enter my name Student in divinity at Cambridge, and shall expect mother there in April." He had doubtless already written his affectionate farewell to what he called "my woodland life." Being no hermit, he remembered not only the "twilight walks and midnight solitude" but also

> the glad hey-day of my household hours,
> The innocent mirth which sweetens daily bread,
> Railing in love at those who rail again,
> By mind's industry sharpening the love of life . . .

9.

THE PRIZED GOWN AND BAND

But thou art fire, sacred and hallow'd fire;
And I but earth and clay: should I presume
To wear thy habit, the severe attire
My slender compositions might consume. . . .
—George Herbert, "The Priesthood"

THE records of the theological faculty said nothing of the new student from Roxbury till the 16th of February. By a vote of that day he was formally admitted to the middle class. Probably nobody was quite certain what this action meant. Postgraduate training was still a new and dubious experiment. Though the theological faculty had recently become distinguishable from the general teaching staff of Harvard College, even now it could lay claim to but three professors, and only one of these devoted himself exclusively to the school. The infant institution, tentatively named the Theological School, hardly had a mind of its own as yet, for it remained much under the control of its sponsor, the Society for the Promotion of Theological Education in Harvard University.

Educational policy was naturally in the formative stage, but the main objectives in February of 1825 could not have differed greatly from those announced two years later. Theoretically, a student who remained for the more or less regular period of three years was expected to study Hebrew, Biblical history and criticism, natural and revealed religion, Christian theology, Christian institutions, ecclesiastical powers, and the rights, duties, and relations of the pastoral office. He was also told that he must learn to speak extempore, to write and deliver sermons, and to conduct public worship. But these requirements were only gradually becoming practicable when Waldo Emerson entered, and he himself said little about such matters. Even his movements outside the school during most of the spring and summer of 1825 were only vaguely recorded.

On April 13, some two weeks after a new academic quarter had opened, Ruth Emerson began her residence in the old Mellen house, on North Avenue, near Jarvis Field; but Waldo may not have joined her at that time. The fact that the steward of Harvard College, the official who looked out for the bills due to the Theological School, had for some time surprisingly little business with him seems understandable in the light of a laconic autobiographical note that Waldo dated March, 1825, but certainly wrote much later: "lost the use of my eye for study." It may have been about this time that he went to Andrews Norton, the professor of sacred literature, and, having explained that his eyes would not allow him to take an active part, got leave to attend the lectures without reciting.

Perhaps his eyes did not prevent his taking some notes on lectures and reading a limited amount of Biblical text. In that case, it was most likely during this spring that he wrote many of the brief comments in his interleaved copy of Wakefield's translation of the New Testament. St. Matthew and St. John received by far the greater part of his attention. Now and then he would remark on the meaning of some word in the Greek original, but usually he was concerned with a less meticulous kind of interpretation. On the forty-second verse of the tenth chapter of *Matthew* he observed: "What is the reward of virtue? Virtue. This is the sum of Christianity."

This, with much else, sounded as if it were his own. On the parables in the thirteenth chapter of the same gospel he remarked: "The parables generally apply with equal truth to the whole Christian Church and to the individual soul. The oak is but an expanded acorn. The Church but a magnified man." Reflecting on another passage in the same gospel, he decided that "Faith is *the perception of spiritual truth.* . . . And the prayer is answered in its utterance." *Luke,* XV:17, seemed to carry him back to his own journal entries on self-reverence: "v. 17. *having come to himself,*' an instructive expression! Self, then, is reason, the knowledge of the true & good. Children say in the street—'Give it me, *you know me.*' and familiar forms of speech are found among men, intimating every man's conviction that if he were fully shown to his fellowmen, he would be approved. We all draw our inmost life from the Divine Reason."

The young expositor, however original or unoriginal he may have been at other times, betrayed a debt to the Theological School when he wrote of a verse in the twelfth chapter of *John:* "Prof. Norton approves this rendering = for this cause I came; for this hour." A note on *John,* XX:28, anxiously discounting any trinitarianism that might be read into the passage, was also suggestive of the school. But quite separate from any text Waldo wrote two comments that again resembled his journal meditations: "The *kingdom of heaven,* i.e. the true or right state of the soul," and "I esteem it more to the purpose of a true exposition, more in unison with the spirit of Christ, to draw a moral, than to prove a miracle."

Aunt Mary, that summer, listed his schoolteaching "& Roxbury fasts" as the definite causes of his ailment, as if there could be no doubt. But a little later she not only confessed her ignorance of "the history rise & progress & prospects of W— eyes" but rated his defective sight a calamitous as well as unexpected blow. Though she seems to have imagined at one time that he might turn out to be a laureate of religion and a sort of second Milton, with poetry a sufficient compensation for blindness, she never allowed her vision of him as a great pulpit orator to be long obscured. Her ambition for him must have closed her own eyes to one possible key to his predicament, but family records of the time are too scanty to show whether an unconscious but positive distaste for formal theology could have had anything to do with it.

Both his journals and letters all but halted. Sometimes he wrote with great difficulty, apparently without looking at the page. He had time for recreational jaunts into the country. On the 5th of April he left a memento of a visit to the Ripleys in Concord. On a wooden panel beside the fireplace of an upper room in what came to be called the Old Manse were two inscriptions, the first written in 1780 by his father, then a youthful student, and the second, as recently as 1824 by Edward. Below these family records Waldo wrote and initialed an inscription honoring the authors of both of them: "Peace to the Soul of the blessed dead, honor to the ambition of the living." Perhaps as he honored his ambitious brother he thought of himself as a mere spectator, incapacitated for action.

It was a dark year for the ambitions of living Emersons. Late that summer Edward was forced to give up his school at Roxbury, having presumably overtaxed himself by combining legal studies with teaching. His plight was especially disheartening because of his great promise as a lawyer. Daniel Webster, an admired lawyer, had been willing to help Edward, he had explained to him, "as well on account of your own merits, & Mr Everett's wishes, as from a sincere regard for the memory of your excellent father, whom I had the pleasure, in some little degree to know, & from whom I rec'd when quite a young man, tokens of kindness." But Edward was now in no condition to stick to law or to anything. And he was not the only distressed Emerson.

While Edward was making up his mind to cross the Atlantic in search of health, his brother Charles, trying to get in trim for another brilliant year in college, was spending some vacation weeks at Concord or in travel and was taking gloomy account of his own chances of realizing soaring ambitions in the unacademic world. "There are moments of enthusiasm," he wrote, "when I feel a nascent greatness within me, & then anon comes the hour of dejection & melancholy, when I mourn over my humble capacity; at college among my classmates, I see none whom my vanity acknowledges as more intelligent than myself—but at home where they surely ought to know best, why they think but little of me. Balancing these contradictory results, I have come to the sad conclusion that I shall never blind the world with excess of light . . ."

For the moment Charles's case was the least serious. Bulkeley bore the deepest wounds, though he had the good fortune not to know how deep they were. This fall and winter he was "perfectly deranged" for months, and Waldo, trying to recover from eye strain while he taught a school for boys at Chelmsford, some ten miles north of Concord, had to take him in charge.

At Chelmsford, where he had begun his school toward the middle of September, Waldo Emerson soon received a new shock. This time it was his brother William's personal crisis that he had to share. Arriving home from Göttingen and his European travels, William, according to family tradition, went quickly to Waldo and retold his Weimar experience, making it all perfectly clear at last. Now he revealed how Goethe, encouraging him in his inclination not to disappoint his family by giving up the ministry, had "unhesitatingly told him" to "preach to the people what they wanted" since "his personal belief was no business of theirs"; William, in the opinion of the great German poet, "could be a good preacher and a good pastor and no one need ever know what he himself had for his own private views."

Waldo, undoubtedly perturbed, listened with admiration to the sequel of that episode. During a terrific storm on the homeward Atlantic passage when he was more than once "compelled," as he said, "to sit down in the cabin, and tranquilly to make up what I deemed my last accounts with this world," William had realized that he "could not go to the bottom in peace with the intention in his heart of following the advice Goethe had given him" and so had "renounced the ministry; and had come home to begin the study of law." There is no reason to suppose that Waldo himself did not fully resolve to act on the advice that Aunt Mary promptly and emphatically gave out. Though she betrayed some curiosity about his thoughts on William's change of profession, she explicitly laid it down that the younger brother was immediately to prepare to preach, with or without sight. Yet William's ordeal was hardly a thing that his brother could ever dismiss as irrelevant to himself.

At Chelmsford, Waldo found his eyes partly healed. He is said, on doubtful authority, to have worked on the farm as well as taught. Farmer or not, he lived close to the soil in such a rural community, spending a pleasant "autumn and winter among these hills and plains" and learning "where the chestnut first spread its brown harvest on a frosty morning for the boys; where the apples covered the ground with white fruit." He "saw the last fires that burned in the old limekiln" and "knew the ripples of the

Baptist Pond" and the woods that were waiting to be transformed into corn fields.

But the poetic moods encouraged by his environment were no doubt kept in check by the Chelmsford people. The farmers "were all orthodox, Calvinists, mighty in the Scriptures, had learned that life was a preparation, and 'probation,' to use their word." If they read no romances, they had sterner teachers—the pulpit, poverty and labor, the town meeting. They were themselves valuable instructors for a youth recently escaped from his theological studies.

To his Chelmsford pupils the master of the Classical School was apt to seem "very grave, quiet, and very impressive," "almost fascinating." Though he was never harsh and never punished except with words, he had complete command of the boys. He used to send them home with an assignment in some such book as Plutarch's Lives and would question them on it next day. The peculiar look in his eyes, fixed on something that seemed to be beyond the field of vision, may have been chargeable to his affliction. But bad eyes did not keep him from earning the fees he was paid.

It was during a vacation from his Chelmsford school that he reached a fortunate turning point in his struggle against blindness. An earlier operation on one eye seemed to give him no relief; but now he let Reynolds, his doctor, experiment with the other eye, and from this time he began gradually to regain his sight in spite of his having to continue teaching. Apparently on William's advice, he decided to close his school at Chelmsford on the last day of December, but only in order to accept the offer of another school. He needed the money, and neither a lameness attributed to rheumatism nor his weak eyes could daunt his resolution, "God willing," "to drive & clinch the nails of instruction into at least 30 brains" at Roxbury.

At Roxbury, a day or two after the beginning of the new year, 1826, Waldo gathered his pupils "in the second story of Octagon Hall, then known as the Norfolk Bank Building." With its Gothic windows and its tower adorned by "two white colossal figures emblematic of 'Charity and her babes,' which had formerly stood upon the Boston Almshouse," the building was quite too monumental to be suitable for the ephemeral kind of academy the new teacher had in mind. He and several scholars he had brought with him from Chelmsford boarded at the home of his Uncle Ralph Haskins's brother-in-law, a Mr. Greene. David Greene Haskins and his older brother, together with Henry Harrington and "most if not all of the other pupils" whom Edward Emerson had taught a few months earlier resumed their studies under Waldo's guidance. To the younger Haskins boy, his cousin Waldo naturally seemed friendly enough. In Harrington's opinion he was not especially successful, as his mind was really on his divinity studies, but "the intellectual portion of his duties was faithfully and adequately performed."

Certainly his mind was not confined within the limits of his school-room. A few days after the return to Roxbury he used his "mended eyes" for writing again in his journals. He speculated with his usual honesty about the fundamentals of religion he proposed to preach. Perhaps at the prompting of his own recent experience with sickness, he wrote another of his informal and tentative essays on compensation. He liked to give his sentences a universal application. "The whole of what we know is a system of compensations," he asserted. "Every defect in one manner is made up in another. Every suffering is rewarded; every sacrifice is made up; every debt is paid." His thoughts ran over other favorite topics. He tried Aunt Mary with his "old faith" in self-reverence. In a less confident mood he mocked his own ambition, seeing clearly that it was too big for its slender foundation of physical health. When he had finished with his self-castigation he restored the scales of justice to their perfect state of equilibrium by observing that, after all, fate would not permit the seed of the gods to die and, whatever our pleasure, we should not hide the world's light. In general, religion, philosophy, health, desire for achievement, and love of fame were the themes he returned to most often.

By this time he seems to have taken to heart what he had heard from William of the higher criticism of the Bible. He experienced moods of ardent loyalty as well as of skepticism. He saw, as he told Aunt Mary, that the German scholars were really shaking the foundations of Christianity. He had no notion for the present of deserting because of this theological earthquake but felt heroic in his resolve to defend "the august Founder" and "the twelve self-denying heroes of a pious renown." He was anxious to have sight enough to study theology and to get into the fray. He would not see Christianity and all its good works "pass away and become ridiculous."

After he had been at the Roxbury school for a month, he could read several hours in the twenty-four besides teaching, but he soon suffered a relapse. The rheumatic pain in his hip continued and spoiled his pleasure in walking. He thought that "few men ever suffered more genuine misery than I have suffered." Part of his misery was caused by unrealized ambition. Little was yet done, he reminded himself, "to establish my consideration among my contemporaries, and less to get a memory when I am gone. I confess the foolish ambition to be valued, with qualification. I do not want to be known by them that know me not, but where my name is mentioned I would have it respected." A chief goad of his anxiety for achievement seemed to be his feeling of defeat in early life and a fear that he might not live long. "My recollections of early life," he confessed, "are not very pleasant."

He owed some of his ambition to his brothers, never long out of his thoughts. William had taught the family by example how to conquer poverty and at the same time get university training, even abroad. Charles zealously kept up his pursuit of learning and fame. When he read the life of Milton and learned that the poet, even as a boy, used to pore over his books till midnight, the young student at once wanted to emulate him. Edward, having crossed the Atlantic, had arrived at Gibraltar in November, and his letters were now beginning to reach Cambridge. He had gone on to Marseille and was in Rome by the middle of March, giving himself up "to the admiration of Roman glory & art," visiting the sculptor Thorwaldsen, hearing the gossip of the studios, scribbling in Italian, going on to see Florence, copying both Latin and Greek inscriptions, reveling like a true scholar in these paradises of a scholar. But his most serious business was simply to keep alive.

Waldo saw no way of escape from teaching, though he was getting ready to leave his Roxbury pupils and migrate to Cambridge, where his mother, "in order to get a schoolroom" for him, now moved from the Mellen house to one owned by Professor Levi Hedge. Less than three months after he had opened his Roxbury school, Waldo closed it, and, about the first of April, began his Cambridge school. Some of the boys who attended it remembered the experience but differed in their opinions of it. Young Richard Henry Dana, used to the barbarous treatment that schoolmasters still frequently accorded to their pupils, was astonished at the gentleness of Waldo and complained that "he had not system or discipline enough to insure regular and vigorous study." Oliver Wendell Holmes's brother John thought Waldo completely self-possessed and in control of the boys: "Rather stern in his very infrequent rebukes. Not inclined to win boys by a surface amiability, but kindly in explanation or advice. Every inch a king in his dominion."

Again the schoolmaster's mind strayed from schoolbooks. His eyes now comparatively well but his limbs diseased with rheumatism, the young teacher continued to debate lofty subjects with himself. The idea of friendship seemed to stir him suddenly. "In God's name," he asked, "what is in this topic? It encourages, exhilarates, inspires me." This set him off on the subject of affections. Feeling was a high form of reality and could take the place of intellectual certainty. "I *feel* immortal. And the evidence of immortality comes better from consciousness than from reason."

Meantime Aunt Mary, after some prodding from her nephew, had made a sweeping attack on the "atheism" of the German higher critics.

She was soon warning against his too unorthodox speculations. How could he so divest himself of faith? she wanted to know. She decided to let his current heresy pass as being merely an intellectual exercise, but she was glad he had been held back from his ministerial career till his anchor should be stronger than she suspected it now was. In another letter she would to God he were not at Cambridge, though presumably his connection with the Theological School was at this time extremely tenuous. He kept light-heartedly on with his thoughts, not worrying because he could see no finality in them. "There is no thought," he was confident, "which is not seed as well as fruit. It spawns like fish."

Whether it was in this or in the preceding summer that he spent some time on his Uncle Ladd's farm at Newton and heard from the Methodist Tarbox, as they worked together in the hayfield, that men were always praying and that their prayers were answered, the most important reper-cussions of that experience came in 1826. On Sunday, June 11, he wrote in his journal:

" 'Pray without ceasing'

"It is the duty of men to judge men only by their actions. Our faculties furnish us with no means of arriving at the motive; the character, the secret self. . . ."

He had found his text and was writing out the first paragraph of his first sermon. Presenting this sermon to the Middlesex Association he won, on October 10, 1826, his approbation, or license, to preach.

As he had had little theological training and was used to harboring unorthodox opinions, it is probable that if the members of the association of ministers had examined him carefully they would not have allowed him to preach; but they had not rejected his sermon and, though unordained, he was now a preacher. Five days after his approbation he repeated the sermon on prayer for the congregation of Uncle Samuel Ripley at Wal-tham. He did not realize the rosy dream he had once had of "a pulpit Orator to whom the path of his profession is yet untried" ascending the pulpit for the first time in the solemnity and strength proper to his high mission, armed with "the tremendous eloquence which stirs men's souls," while below him are "the faces of men bent forward in the earnestness of expectation," men in such a desirable frame of mind that "the preacher may lead them whithersoever he will." But at least a few of his hearers listened with rapt attention. Aunt Mary, overjoyed that he was at last entering upon his ministry, seems to have made a special trip from Maine for the occasion. She was highly gratified with her nephew's serious, simple, dignified manner. His Aunt Sarah Alden Ripley, the preacher's correspondent and guide to learning in his early boyhood, was delighted and so were some others.

With his sense of humor, the unorthodox taster of ideas had been unable to help smiling as he had pictured himself in advance in the gown and band he had prized so highly. It was a queer life and the only mood proper to it was, he thought, quiet astonishment. It was ironical that just as he assumed his office as ⟨'the meek ambassador of the Highest" he should be tossed once more into a whirlpool of religious doubts. He was pondering the theory "that it is wrong to regard ourselves so much in a *historical* light as we do, putting Time between God & us; and that it were fitter to account every moment of the existence of the Universe as a new Creation, and *all* as a revelation proceeding each moment from the Divinity to the mind of the observer." According to this theory Christianity ought to speak merely as an expounder of the moral law known by intuition. Conscious of the changes his mind had already undergone, he decided that he would not be surprised at new revolutionary developments in his thought. Aunt Mary's oracles were needed to keep him steady if he was to remain long in the ministry he was just entering.⟩

The situation was not helped by his excitement over a Boston Swedenborgian druggist's essay called *Observations on the Growth of the Mind,* just published. Probably he had already recognized in Sampson Reed, its author, an exposer of the *"historical"* fallacy. Aunt Mary, when he confided such notions to her, made an immediate attack on the druggist, ridiculing his triteness, obscurity, and "swedenishness" and crediting his rare ideas to Wordsworth. But so far as her nephew was concerned her efforts were vain. For the moment he even imagined Reed as sitting in the late Professor Frisbie's chair of natural religion, moral philosophy, and civil polity at the college. It took nearly a dozen years to make him see his new idol as a slave of dogma entrenched in another man's mind, the victim of "this immense arrogancy & subtle bigotry of his church." Eventually he wrote an epitaph to this youthful but long-lived enthusiasm when he sharply reprimanded the

Demure apothecary
Whose early reverend genius my young eye
With wonder followed, & undoubting joy,

but who had at last become the "Sleek deacon of the New Jerusalem."

Charles went on at college with his successive Penn legacy subventions to help his finances and kept up nearly to Edward's record as a student. By the middle of September, William was getting settled in New York as an apprentice lawyer. Edward had passed the climax of his foreign tour when he had made a visit of a few days at La Grange with La Fayette. La Fayette, at table or surrounded by guests and family in a drawing room adorned with an American flag and portraits of Washington and Franklin, was an unforgettable figure. Edward went on to Waterloo, carried Dante and an Italian dictionary with him as companions on Dutch canals, was in England before the end of August, and arrived home again in October. He had suffered so many hardships that he thought his travels a great mistake so far as health was concerned. But he was well enough to go into Webster's office; and once the great man came in to look for some books and stopped to talk to him for ten minutes, informing him that it was important to understand, not to remember, Blackstone. Edward soon had other jobs, including one at the Boston Athenæum, thus making sure that he would have little chance to recover fully.

Waldo Emerson himself was now alarmed by new symptoms of disease, this time in his lungs. Toward the end of October he confessed that he had resigned his understanding into the hands of Aunt Mary, Edward, and the doctor. "I give up my school this week. I journey next I know not where. I am not sick nor very well." He closed his Cambridge school, the last he ever taught; but before traveling he preached for the third time since his approbation, using the same sermon he had started out with. This time he spoke from the pulpit of Boston's First Church, where his father's career had ended fifteen years earlier. Among his auditors were seventeen of his former pupils.

For a time his plans remained uncertain. He must still have hoped that a turn for the better in his health would let him stay on in the neighborhood of the Theological School. Divinity Hall, recently dedicated by Channing's sermon, was a new attraction for him. But his uncertainty seemed at an end when Uncle Samuel Ripley lent him $70 for a southern voyage and supplied him with letters of credit good for additional cash. Thus assured of adequate funds, Waldo set out on November 25 for Charleston. He was a passenger in the *Clematis,* a ship fit to brave the Atlantic with her 105 feet of length and one hundred of height and with her twenty-five sails. It was his first trial of the sea. "After a day or two," he wrote, "I found I could live as comfortably in this tent, tossed on the ocean, as if it were pitched on the mountains ashore."

On December 7 he was in Charleston. There, for the first time, he was on American soil outside New England. He was struck by sectional differences, particularly in manners. Manners, he was still convinced, were closely under the influence of climate. He observed that the most lowly laborers showed a surprising perfection of courtesy. He had not seen an awkward Carolinian. Foraging from his boarding house on East Bay Street, he began to find old acquaintances. Samuel Gilman, a tutor at Harvard when Waldo had entered the college, offered to accompany him to the anniversary meeting of the local New England Society, and presumably they were there on December 22. Gilman was the pastor of the Unitarian Church, and Waldo again preached his sermon on ceaseless prayer. Motte, an old college friend who had now turned Unitarian and resigned his parish, introduced him to the Charleston Library Society.

But Charleston was proving too cold for an invalid whose lungs suffered "oppressions & pangs, chiefly by night"; and Waldo Emerson even considered a voyage to the West Indies. He was "not sick . . . not well; but luke-sick," having "no symptom that any physician extant can recognize or understand." The best diagnosis he himself could put into words was "a certain stricture on the right side of the chest, which always makes itself felt when the air is cold or damp, & the attempt to preach or the like exertion of the lungs is followed by an aching." About the tenth of January he departed on the sloop *William,* bound for St. Augustine.

He turned his back, as he said,

> Upon the Northern lights, and burning Bear,
> And the cold orbs that hang by them in heaven,
> Till, star by star, they sank into the sea.

And at last he saw St. Augustine appear " 'mid orange-groves and citron blooms." As the vessel slid slowly to the fragrant shore, he saw "Saint Mark's grim bastions"

> Planting their deep foundations in the sea,

and reminding him that here had once been an outpost of Spain.

Though this was the oldest American town, the Americans had been in control for only half a dozen years. One saw here, in this ultima Thule of civilized America, the enfeebled red men, "forest families, timid and tame." In the streets were dark Minorcans as well as invalids who despaired of seeing "New England's wood-crowned hills again," the rueful poet noted. Nothing was stranger to New England eyes than the two iron cages in which the Spanish governor was said to have suspended criminals and allowed them to starve to death.

Waldo Emerson, comfortable but solitary, turned to his journal and continued his old speculations or wrote sketches of the strange, torpid town. He drove an orange along the beach, sailed in a boat, or sat in a chair. He tried to shape sermons "for an hour which may never arrive." He preached once to the St. Augustinians, not from any new manuscript, but from the now well-worn inaugural on prayer.

He made copious notes on the inhabitants and observed the low estate of the church in this poverty-stricken region. He attended a special meeting of a Bible society whose treasurer, being the marshal of the district, had awkwardly enough appointed a meeting of the society and a slave auction at the same time and place, "one being in the Government house, and the other in the adjoining yard. One ear therefore heard the glad tidings of great joy," Waldo noticed, "whilst the other was regaled with 'Going, gentlemen, going!' And almost without changing our position we might aid in sending the Scriptures into Africa, or bid for 'four children without the mother' who had been kidnapped therefrom." His eyes were not blind to evil. For the present he looked at it philosophically, considering his own private ills too. "He has seen but half the Universe," he told Aunt Mary, "who never has been shown the house of Pain. Pleasure and Peace are but indifferent teachers of what it is life to know." His intimate view of slavery aroused the reformer effectively hidden beneath the philosopher. At the moment he thought of St. Augustine as good for his bodily health. He now weighed 141½ pounds, and he talked of teaching school again on his return home.

But the most memorable result of his residence of some two and a half months in Florida was his friendship with Achille Murat, nephew of Napoleon and son of the colorful cavalry leader who became Marshal of France and King of Naples. Never before in his life had he confronted a person resembling this one. Young Murat, with his wife, a distant relative of George Washington, had come from his plantation home near Tallahassee and was on the point of setting out to visit an uncle in New Jersey when he found Waldo Emerson ready to return northward. The extremely limited shipping schedule of the port of St. Augustine made it a foregone conclusion that the two men would sail together on the old, dependable sloop *William;* and on March 28 they put to sea for Charleston, by way of St. Mary's, Georgia, as fate and bad weather determined.

"We boarded together in St Augustine," Waldo wrote, "but I did not become much acquainted with him till we went to sea. He is a philosopher, a scholar, a man of the world very sceptical but very candid & an ardent lover of truth. I blessed my stars for my fine companion & we talked incessantly." According to tradition, their conversation did not halt even during the storm, when they stayed in their berths, Waldo in the lower and Murat in the upper, invisible to each other. Waldo undoubtedly defended Christianity as interpreted by the most liberal Unitarians and won the respect of the brilliant young Frenchman. Luckily the voyage was prolonged from the usual two days to nine by weather varying from dead calm to roaring tempest.

Upon arrival at Charleston Waldo Emerson made a memorandum that would have served as rebuttal to his own complaints regarding his coldness of nature: "I have connected myself by friendship to a man who with as ardent a love of truth as that which animates me, with a mind surpassing mine in the variety of its research, and sharpened and strengthened to an energy for *action* to which I have no pretension, by advantages of birth and practical connexion with mankind beyond almost all men in the world, —is, yet, that which I had ever supposed only a creature of the imagination—a consistent Atheist,—and a disbeliever in the existence, and, of course, in the immortality of the soul. My faith in these points is strong and I trust, as I live, indestructible. Meantime I love and honour this intrepid doubter. His soul is noble, and his virtue, as the virtue of a Sadducee must always be, is sublime."

In Charleston, on the 17th of April, Murat wrote Waldo Emerson an introduction to Joseph Hopkinson in Philadelphia; and the same day the young minister was defiant in his diary, as if he had tilted unsuccessfully in a further argument with the Frenchman and had tried vainly to compete with him at some social gathering. He warned himself sharply to be content with majestic thoughts and to "forego the ambition to shine in the frivolous assemblies of men." "Yet my friend," he confessed with admiration, "is at home in both these jarring empires, and whilst he taxes my powers in his philosophic speculations, can excel the coxcombs, and that, *con amore,* in the fluency of nonsense." In a later exchange of letters Murat, perhaps affected in spirits by a recent and severe illness, admitted that the truth of atheism and that of Unitarianism now seemed to him about equally probable. But on the grounds of expediency he considered his own view preferable "in a refined state of society, although in barbarous time of obscurity and ignorance," he not too generously conceded, "your theory may be more useful." Murat, still unsatisfied, thought a first step to a solution of the problem should be an attempt to ascertain "how far we can have an *absolute* notion of truth," and he intended to write a monograph on that subject. In the meantime, however, he wanted his friend to set up as a preacher in Tallahassee and substitute reason, learning, and morality for the nonsense, ignorance, and fanaticism currently taught there; and, for the future as it turned out, he unequivocally exempted Unitarianism from his general disgust for the religious character of the Americans. On his side, Waldo Emerson continued to keep the far more radical Frenchman in his esteem, and in time of religious crisis he would hardly be unconscious of him.

At Charleston, in 1827, Waldo was less troubled by his encounter with a magnetic atheist because at the very moment he himself was resting securely in the theory of self-reliance that he had long been building up into an article of faith. "I lead a new life," he assured himself. "I occupy new ground in the world of spirits, untenanted before. . . . I doubt not I tread on the highway that leads to the Divinity." His physical tread was also more determined now, and he had at last got his weight up to 152 pounds. As late as his return to Charleston, he had not finished a new sermon since he left home; but being once more in the parish of Samuel Gilman, he managed to preach again for him.

From Charleston he went on to Baltimore, where the Unitarian Church had, he discovered, already engaged enough visiting preachers to last for weeks to come. Before the end of April he was at Alexandria, with the Ladds, his relatives. Dogged by ill luck, he again encountered unusual cold. Toward the middle of May he preached in Washington "without any pain or inconvenience," but he wrote Aunt Mary that he was "still saddled with the villain stricture & perhaps he will ride me to death." He had day dreams of other things he might do rather than preach. He would be a novelist, a poet, a painter, a scientist. But he postponed any withdrawal from his newly acquired profession. In Philadelphia he visited his school-boy friend William Furness, now established as a Unitarian minister, and aided him by preaching a couple of sermons, his whole stock. At New York he found his brother William somewhat known for his lectures on German literature but settling into the law office of Ketchum & Fessenden as an apprentice on a salary of $3 a week and escaping immediate starvation by giving private instruction to a family of girls. Waldo presumably preached himself out, for he once more used both the Waltham sermons.

Meantime the First Church in Boston had sent him word that he was wanted there for a while. Going on to Concord, where his mother was living with the Ripleys again, he made, it seems, his first experiment with a third sermon, quite uninspired. He preached it and a fourth at the Boston First Church in mid June. He began the fourth with the Biblical saying that a man shall reap what he sows, proceeded to reason out the natural tendency to property owning and to the amassing of wealth, and then swung round to his favorite theory "that a system of Compensations prevails by God's will amid all the dealings of men in common life and that in virtue of this law, no man can enrich himself by doing wrong, or impoverish himself by doing right." Next Sunday he was back with another new sermon. It was on the Crucifixion and was full of the sense of the tragic; yet it too implied compensation, for he insisted, not unmindful of a hint from Aristotle, on the purification that pity and terror could cause.

And so he kept on, at an easy pace, writing and preaching sermons, picking up old threads of thought from his journals, weaving them into more formal and usually less unorthodox patterns.

Within a few weeks after returning from the South he had taken a room in Divinity Hall, a good anchorage for an expectant candidate. Charles was at the college, winning honors as usual—too easily, Waldo thought. Edward, going on with his law, kept several irons in the fire. Not many months before, he had been reading, sometimes three hours a day, to the almost blind historian Prescott. He spent much time studying in Webster's office or taking care of the new senator's business affairs or even of his family. Refusing the offer of a tutorship in Latin at Harvard, Edward, "the uncomfortable victim of a splendid ambition," made his farewell appearance there as the orator at commencement. Waldo also attended the exercises, tardily taking his Master's degree, out of course and without a speaking part.

For Waldo residence at Divinity Hall had little to do with theology. He no longer had health or much desire for an intensive study of that subject. "My eyes are not so strong as to let me be learned," he put it. "I am curious to know what the Scriptures do in very deed say about that exalted person who died on Calvary, but I do think it at this distance of time & in the confusion of langu[ages] to be a work of weighing of phrases & hunting in dictiona[ries]." He had seven of Everett's early manuscripts by him as he tried to write sermons, but he got no inspiration. He could set out for the Connecticut Valley on a short tour of duty as a Unitarian missionary preacher, or he could spend weeks as a substitute pastor in the towns of the eastern part of his state, without breaking any ties to Cambridge.

He walked much of the way to Northampton. Arriving at the hotel and being shown to a room, he complained that it was dirty. Not dirtier than he himself was, he was told. But when Judge Lyman's wife came in her carriage for him, the travel-worn minister received profuse apologies from the innkeeper. Returning from his too strenuous mission to Northampton, Greenfield, and Deerfield, and as far west as Lenox, he had only a short visit with his mother in the sitting room of the home at Concord before he was off to keep a new engagement. At New Bedford, where he went to preach for his kinsman Orville Dewey, he made good use of Dewey's fine library, closeting himself in it the best part of each day but getting exercise by sawing wood and by walking fast over the muddy, stony town. After finishing his stipulated three weeks there, he preached in his father's first parish, at the town of Harvard, then for Uncle Samuel Ripley at Waltham, next at Watertown, then back in Boston.

He enjoyed a brief interval of quiet in Divinity Hall, where he seems to have resettled himself, some time in December, 1827, taking firm possession of No. 14, a spacious room, with two windows and a fireplace, at the northeast corner on the first floor. But he missed his old pleasure in walking and grew impatient with the sad infirmities which he bore in youth but which belonged, he protested, to "the limb & sense of age." He tried to conjure them away by writing verses and resolved,

> Please God, I'll wrap me in mine innocence
> And bid each awful Muse drive the damned harpies hence.

Late in December he left his armchair to answer a call to Concord, New Hampshire, where he preached three Sundays and Christmas Day. On Christmas Day he saw Ellen Tucker for the first time.

Her stepfather, Colonel William Austin Kent, was a benefactor of the nascent Unitarian society in the town, and Kent's son Edward had been a college classmate of Waldo's. It was a matter of course that Waldo should meet the young and attractive Ellen. He was in the mood for friendship if not for love, but he at first made some show of resisting at least the latter. He wrote on the last day of the year that he was finding his fortnight a pretty long one. His mind seemed to be on Cambridge, where he once more hoped to attend some classes at the Theological School, and on the old Concord, his home. He complained at length because he could not find the kind of friend he wanted "either in the shape of man or woman." He talked humorously about his intention of joining a sleighing party to the Shaker community at Canterbury, where he thought he might "put on the drab cowl." "Among the earliest institutions to be invented," he added, "if I read the stars-right, is a protestant monastery, a place of elegant seclusion where melancholy gentlemen & ladies may go to spend the advanced season of single life in drinking milk, walking the woods & reading the Bible & the poets."

For some weeks after his return southward he was presumably much at Cambridge, and if he still had little part in the exercises of the Theological School, it was perhaps more than usual. Even if his name was omitted from the published list of candidates, he was known as a candidate as much as he wished to be in his uncertain state of health. And he must have been favorably known, in spite of his failure to go through the regular routine of the school. For there is no reason to doubt the estimate given by the well informed Uncle Samuel Ripley to Aunt Mary in February, 1828, that "Waldo is the most popular preacher among the candidates, and all he wants is health to be fixed at once in Boston." Soon, in fact, Waldo had had several pulpits offered to him with a view to settlement, but he refused them all.

Outside the pulpit his life had to be pared down to suit his energy. In the senior class of the Theological School were the Samuel Lothrop that Waldo had tutored at President Kirkland's; George Bradford, brother of Aunt Sarah Alden Ripley; and Frederic Henry Hedge, Professor Levi Hedge's son. At least two of the three were living in Divinity Hall. Another theological student, Warren Burton, once a member of the nameless literary club in college, had lived in No. 14 Divinity Hall before Waldo moved there and perhaps still had some rights in it. But Waldo, though he knew all the seniors and probably all the rest of his neighbors, got less social life than he wanted. "I am living cautiously," he told his brother William, "yea treading on eggs to strengthen my constitution. . . . So I never write when I can walk or especially when I can laugh. But my companions are few; so, sometimes I must read . . ." He was also writing some sermons; but whatever theological "exercises" he may now have started to do with Norton were doubtless completely halted or were done under somebody else's care, for the professor was seriously ill by March and was soon away for a six months' European journey.

Some unpleasant incidents occurred as the young minister, determined to postpone the responsibilities that a regular charge would entail, went from pulpit to pulpit. It must have been his enthusiasm for Sampson Reed's writings that got him involved with the local Swedenborgians, then, it seems, on the lookout for at least a temporary pastor. There was some sort of "gregarious invitation to the New Church" which he "was agreeably disappointed" to find himself saved from. Yet he watched the Swedenborgians with no little interest; and in his copy of the first volume of *The New Jerusalem Magazine,* for 1827–1828, he wrote the names of most of the anonymous contributors.

At Concord or at Divinity Hall he could afford to risk being thought feather-brained and lazy. At the first discovery of "a silly uneasiness" he escaped, he said, "from the writing desk as from a snake" and went straight to quarter himself on the first person he could think of in Divinity Hall who could spare the time to entertain him. He preferred the jesters, for, as he explained it, "after a merry or only a gossiping hour where the talk has been mere soap bubbles I have lost all sense of the mouse in my chest, am at ease, & can take my pen or book." He thought it might be good sense to wait years, "for sound head & wind & limb & sermonbarrelful," before settling in a parish of his own.

He seemed doomed to a slow start in his profession, and delay was hard for so ambitious a young man to endure. But his optimism was put to an even more severe test. Suddenly he was struck a stunning blow that no one had foreseen. Edward, with all his brilliant intellectual powers, was suffering from some obscure emotional tangle and at last reached the limit of his strength and collapsed. As early as March of this year his journal had begun to show what might in retrospect look like danger signals. The twenty-two-year-old aspirant to the practice of law had become moodily introspective. Some weeks later, as he pondered his ill health, he was oppressed by a sense of guilt because of his worldly ambitions and began to cultivate a religious humility foreign to his nature. "Words words fail me," he confessed, "but I think I see GOD—distantly, dimly, now more, now less manifestly revealing himself . . . I tho't to find him in the hurricane of ambition—but he was not there . . . Faint & weary—I have fallen prostrate. I have made the great Sacrifice—I have sacrificed my *pride*—my *pride*." His condition changed rapidly. He believed that he was almost miraculously better. But soon he began to be "affected strangely in his mind."

One morning, in the old Concord home, he came down to breakfast and, instead of treating Doctor Ripley with the customary veneration, began to make fun of him. Then he went upstairs and made a beautiful prayer, saying that his mother and grandfather had lost their reason and asking for their restoration. He had fainting fits and delirium; but Waldo, having hurried home after hardly more than beginning a new series of Sundays at Concord, New Hampshire, saw the patient quickly "restored to his former habits of thinking which," he put it, "I cannot help saying were always perverse enough."

Doctor Jackson advised that Edward should not touch a book for a year; but Waldo knew his brother well enough to predict that "the doctor's dominion will shrink back into an advisory council, & come in, I doubt not, for a due share of contempt." It looked as if Edward would soon be in Boston and attending to business with his usual precision. Waldo returned to New Hampshire, preached a second and third week there, and came back to his headquarters in Divinity Hall, but on the last day of June word came to him that Edward was ill again and this time in a state of violent derangement. Waldo went to Concord and, with Doctor Bartlett's help, took Edward in a closed carriage to the asylum at Charlestown.

Doctor Wyman objected to having the patient placed there, seeing that this was not an ordinary case of insanity and that what Edward needed was private care. Wyman was right, for Edward soon recovered his mind. But his bodily health, undermined no doubt by tuberculosis, was broken past any complete mending.

Waldo saw Edward's calamity objectively. Not frightened, he explained to himself frankly why he had no fear that he would suffer a fate like Edward's. "I have," he reasoned it out, "so much mixture of *silliness* in my intellectual frame that I think Providence has tempered me against this. My brother lived and acted and spoke with preternatural energy. My own manner is sluggish; my speech sometimes flippant, sometimes embarrassed and ragged; my actions (if I may say so) are of a passive kind. Edward had always great power of face. I have none. I laugh; I blush; I look ill-tempered; against my will and against my interest. But all this imperfection, as it appears to me, is a *caput mortuum*, is a ballast—as things go, is a defence."

Aunt Mary, looking back over the family record, saw nothing there to blame for Edward's brief mental eclipse. "The dreadfull event," she wrote, "gives no forboding of insanity to others—tis not hereditary . . . No it is disease & over exertion that has bro't this on E. His *ancestors* on my nor his Mothers side were never tainted in the least. Some of my Cousins have been so—and an Aunt—but it was an imbecillity rather in *those* . . ."

As if in mockery, fate exalted Charles, though at the same time it gave him a mild jolt. After having contributed some essays to the college magazine, he had helped to bring it to a "happy termination," as he said. He received a first prize for a Bowdoin dissertation, he delivered the valedictory oration to his class, and he had another oration to give at commencement. But as this commencement part was only the second oration, he and his friends raised a cry of injustice that brought some severe criticism from Waldo. On the day following Charles's graduation Waldo had his own little triumph. Perhaps because he was now known as a popular pulpit candidate, he was made an honorary member of Phi Beta Kappa, seven years after he had graduated.

He was beginning to give much of his time, at $15 a Sunday, to the Second Church, where he took the place of the younger Henry Ware. He was gradually getting to be more widely known, and the peculiar quality of his sermons was becoming recognizable. Frederic Hedge, a shrewd person who must have been kept well posted by Divinity Hall gossip if not by actually hearing his friend preach, got the impression that Waldo was using "great simplicity & an unconventional, untheological style" that shocked the orthodox because it was "unsanctified" but charmed "unprejudiced & appreciative minds."

At last, in the Harvard catalogue for 1828–1829, Waldo Emerson publicly acknowledged himself a candidate for the regular ministry. The account book he was now keeping gave his irregular connection with the Theological School an air of reality that it had long lacked. From August of 1828 to April of 1829 he made three payments, totaling $82.53, to that institution. The last was marked "in full" and so presumably closed forever his account for his sketchy tutoring, if indeed it was tutoring at this time, in divinity. It seems that he at least went now and then to hear the students preach their practice sermons. He told Lothrop that he did not think he would ever try to preach such sermons as those but would attempt to strike out on some new line.

Lothrop, Hedge, and Bradford all graduated in the summer of 1828 but were still at Divinity Hall in the following year. Waldo was now reserved toward Lothrop, his former pupil, making "no effort to resume our old familiar intercourse." Hedge saw, in spite of the charming sermons, no sign of future greatness in the Divinity Hall roomer who, "though not a member of the Divinity School was understood to be a candidate for the ministry preparing himself in his own way." Waldo developed slowly, according to Hedge, and was slow in his movements and speech but already exhibited, at twenty-five, "a refinement of thought & a selectness in the use of language." He was devoted to his diary and used to go to some trouble to get an accurate record of things he thought worth preserving in it. One evening he came to Hedge's room to get the particulars of an anecdote of Professor Norton's and could not sleep till he had made a note of them all. Hedge "tried to interest him in German literature but he laughingly said that as he was entirely ignorant of the subject he would assume that it was not worth knowing." George Bradford, already a "day & night companion," was to continue his affection for Waldo through many years of friendship.

With William at work in a New York law office and teaching, lecturing, reporting, writing editorials, and translating from French and Spanish journals to make a living, and Charles studying law in Boston while he helped the family finances by teaching school, Waldo, whose opinions Charles valued "more than the best of Physicians," had to look after Edward's welfare. By early November, Edward, greatly improved in health, needed to be got out of Charlestown. Waldo wanted an engagement to preach in the country, where he could take him for convalescence.

Probably he had Concord, New Hampshire, already in mind as most desirable for his own reasons. At any rate he knew he would be welcome there. Some months earlier one of the Kents had written to the American Unitarian Association to urge that, because of the critical state of the Unitarian society in the northern Concord, the young preacher who had pleased them so well should be returned. A man "of force & popular address" was needed, and "Such a man was M.̲ Emerson." Kent explained that "the society was constantly increasing while he was here, & our meetings fully attended," and that if he would be content to return, the society would be content to have but one original sermon each Sunday, letting him read a second one "from some author, making the duties as light as possible."

It was a good time for Waldo to break off from the Second Church till its members could definitely make up their minds about inviting him to settle. Its junior pastorate would, it seemed likely, be an important office, becoming in the near future the senior, or only, pastorate, as Ware, long hampered by illness, was expected to resign and join the faculty of the Theological School. There was some polite maneuvering on both sides. But Waldo quickly took Grandfather Ripley's expert advice and made a temporary strategic withdrawal.

Arming himself for cultural purposes with a German volume probably containing some of the writings of Goethe, he set out for Concord, New Hampshire, on December 6, in company with Edward as he had planned. Whether or not Frederic Hedge's urging had had any effect on him, he had by this time doubtless read enough of Carlyle's journalistic evangelizing for German literature to make him feel that he must, after all, tackle a new foreign language and try to make his own first-hand estimate of at least one provocative writer whose native tongue it was. He traveled northward in the best of spirits, for his body was well and he had an interesting personal reason for the trip that he had not revealed in any of his letters to his family. In his account book he entered not only his own and Edward's stagecoach fare but the price he had paid for a copy of one of the popular gift books of that season, a compilation called *Forget me not,* obviously intended by its publishers for a lady's boudoir. For once he was confessedly the victim of sentiment. He described the book as "for ELT."

10.

ELLEN

Ne m'arrête pas, fantôme odieux!
Je vais épouser ma belle aux doux yeux.
—Leconte de Lisle, "Les Elfes"

(Let me pass, pale phantom I despise!
I must wed my love with the tender eyes.)

LLEN LOUISA TUCKER was only seventeen years old but had surprising dignity in spite of her youthfulness and her delicate, very feminine figure. A fine forehead and eyes gave her firmly molded oval face the appearance of intelligence as well as eagerness. She had the air of a girl that knew her own mind, and she probably knew better than Waldo Emerson what was going on in his when he arrived in the town of Concord, New Hampshire. He reasoned it out that he had arranged to preach to the local Unitarian congregation for a few Sundays in order to give his brother Edward a chance to rest in the country; but Ellen doubtless knew she was the magnet that brought him there. This was not his only visit to the northern Concord since he had met her on the last Christmas Day. What came of the sleighing party to the neighboring Shaker village of Canterbury soon after their first meeting is not clear, but they were probably together then. In the spring, when green foliage softened the severe New Hampshire landscape, he made new visits to her town, and by then any well-informed gossip in the neighborhood would probably have concluded that they were in love.

The first entry he wrote in an old album of hers made a confession that was thinly disguised under his own French and the French title of a juvenile poem of Byron's. He was not explicit, but he at least acknowledged a feeling more intense than ordinary friendship—friendship with all the fire of love though without wings. " 'L'Amitié est l'Amour sans ailes,' " he wrote, "et mon affection, ma belle reine, est une Amitié amoureuse, puisqu'elle a tout le feu de l'amour, mais elle n'a point d'ailes; pas une plume. Oh Ellen, elle ne peut pas mouvoir; c'est un rocher.—"

If this meant love that lacked only poetical expression, he supplied the needful meter in another entry. This time, though he still wrote no year, he gave the rest of the date very exactly—eight o'clock in the morning of June 10—and he ended with the salutation "Good morning to thee, Ellen." He called the poem "Dreamings," and the dream he told was pretty obviously one he had had during the past night:

> It was full pleasant—fraught with happiness,
> The dream that hath been over me! I would
> To thee, dear Ellen, it were not all dross,
> The gold that makes my treasurings—the glows
> Of fancied bliss, that are to me rich jewels,—
> Rich as the lights that pave the courts of heaven,
> Burning eternal,—would they were to thee
> Stars!—but the dream! and may I tell it to thee?
> To *thee,* who shap'd and who endued it
> With all its magical splendour and deep peace?

In the dream they were alone while the world slept. They passed silently along the margin of a large river that was noiseless, gloomy, and beautiful; and they were content.

> Then the blush of dawn
> Grew in the east, and all the jewelry
> That night had thrown upon the maidenly elms
> And princely chesnuts, caught the glance of day.
> The breeze woke up, and shook the forest heads
> With its strong power, as manhood's thought mature
> Shaketh the pearls of fancy from the mind,
> Till it shall rise refresh'd and unencumbered.
> Morn wax'd: the birds their happy carrolings
> Pour'd out upon the air, the solitude
> Was full of utterable good and life
> Was holiness. The sun rode high in heaven
> And the day pass'd above us: The cool shade
> Of evening came; still we were there, alone,
> Wrapt in a conscious happiness that knew
> Nor blight nor change.
> I may not speak of all
> The calm delights; the truth, not said, but felt.
> The quiet joy that companied our steps
> Thence,—and to pass forever, nor go forth
> From all our ways— The morning thus, so full
> Of rich deliciousness, sweet day and eventide

Went by as moments— O my soul hath liv'd,
Dream as it was,—an age of happiness
In those few vision'd moments! . . .

Now, in December, when, at least in Ellen's view of the matter, their love affair was of long standing, Waldo Emerson may actually have believed that he had got over his "blushes & wishes," as he said, before returning to "that dangerous neighborhood." But if so he was quickly disillusioned. The twenty-five-year-old philosopher made only an inglorious attempt to be philosophical about Ellen. He was clearheaded enough to see that the odds were against philosophy this time. He saw that it was hard to yoke love and wisdom. "In her magic presence," he confessed, "reason becomes ashamed of himself and wears the aspect of Pedantry or Calculation." What "if the Dæmon of the man," he wisely speculated, "should throw him into circumstances favourable to the sentiment"? Then "reason would stand on a perilous, unsteady footing." Obviously, as far as Waldo Emerson was concerned, the circumstances already favored the sentiment. And though he went through his philosophical gestures, reminding himself how hard it was for a young man to determine the inner qualities of a beautiful woman and that the chances were she did not possess the virtues the lover valued in her, he seems to have come soon to the pleasing conclusion that, in this case at least, beauty was sufficient proof of goodness. The question of Ellen Tucker was, for him, as good as decided. He could detect "Nothing but light & oxygen" in New Hampshire.

Ellen herself, though she expected to have some financial means once she came into her share of the Tucker estate, was unrestrained by any calculating selfishness and, as Waldo later said, "shamed my ambition and prudence by her generous love in our first interview." Whether she went so far at their meetings in earlier months remains uncertain. It is certain that she did now. Some conversation of the sort remained fixed in the memory of her lover. "I described my prospects," he summarized it. "She said, I do not wish to hear of your prospects." He wrote more love poems in her album. In his own journal he was soon addressing Ellen in verses which gave the lie to the legend of emotional poverty he had been trying to attach to himself. "I am enamoured of thy loveliness," he wrote, "Love-sick with thy sweet beauty."

As Waldo lived one life and not two, he was doubtless unabashed when he preached to Ellen's church a sermon he had recently written on the affections. It sounded as if it were intended for Ellen and himself. For him it served to restore the dignity of his philosophy, which had proved so unreliable in her presence. Love, he said, was a necessity; but it was not the body but the spiritual properties that we loved. The affections, he showed, with Plato's *Symposium* in mind no doubt, tended to expect perfection in the loved person, and from seeking perfection in the human friend were led to seek it in God.

By Christmas Eve he had returned to Cambridge and was announcing the successful conclusion of his private mission. To his brother William he wrote that, having been "for one week engaged to Ellen Louisa Tucker a young lady who if you will trust my account is the fairest & best of her kind," he was "now as happy as it is safe in life to be." Ellen was, he explained, "the youngest daughter of the late Beza Tucker a merchant of Boston." During the residence of the Emersons in Roxbury they had known of the family whose home they passed as they followed the Dedham Turnpike into Boston. Ellen's mother had now been "three or four years the wife of Col W. A. Kent of Concord, N. H."

Waldo did not go farther into the family history of the Tuckers, which was heavy with misfortune and boded no good for Ellen. Her father, the prosperous merchant who had once been a pew-holder in the Reverend William Emerson's First Church in Boston and was later one of the founders of the Baptist Church in Roxbury, died at the age of forty-eight. Five years later her brother, George, a young medical student with leanings toward both literature and science, traveled abroad for his health and died at Paris, doubtless of what he called "a horrid cold which has turn'd my blood to melted lead." Her sister Mary died young. Now only her sisters Margaret and Paulina and her mother, Mrs. Kent, survived. Margaret was a victim of tuberculosis. It seems unlikely that either of the lovers understood until after their engagement how seriously Ellen's life was threatened by the same disease.

Back in Massachusetts, the minister resumed his supply preaching but kept in close touch with Ellen. He had hardly returned home before he bought her a copy of a second gift book, *The Offering*, edited, it seems, by Professor Andrews Norton as a means of raising money for charity. Waldo himself had written three of the anonymous contributions, two in verse and one in prose. They were mere trifles he had salvaged from his journals and notebooks. But a book with verse of his own was a fit gift for Ellen, herself a poet.

His letters to Ellen were destroyed or are lost, but those of hers which are still preserved prove that he was a faithful correspondent. She feared she would annoy him with "the metaphorical droppings of a girl in her teens," and apparently she had the humor to laugh at her own rhetorical sentimentalizing. It became obvious that his old schoolmaster's instincts were still alive when he put her to work reading a history of the Emperor

Charles V, doubtless Robertson's, and proposed writing to her in French. She liked Charles V but had some difficulty in keeping her mind on it. The proposed French letters would have caused both the lovers some trouble. "I have been reviving some old French words in my head," she wrote; "I find want of practice has put them asleep but they walk drowsily forth and I doubt not I can catch the idea of any thing you chuse to write. If it takes more of your precious time to write in this way I would not." She loved to read his "tinkling ryhmes" but could not keep up with him in versifying. "My muse," she said, "is a disobedient lady and loves not the cold . . . But you must weary of my feebly expressed thoughts—which I am afraid are losing too much of their timidity— . . ."

The correspondence eventually ran to at least nearly forty letters on her side. She humorously acknowledged his eight years' advantage in age and wisdom by calling him Grandpa and apologizing for her own "half grown ideas." She admired his letters because they were "not unmeaning love letters—written *only for courtship.*" After a few months she was doing French exercises for him and even asking his help with her English compositions. Her illnesses sometimes made her letters pathetic, but she generally kept up her jaunty mood. She feared she was fading away and passing him by in the journey of life in spite of his earlier start. At times she was forced to put off his visits till she had better health, or she was able to send him only brief notes. She wrote him love poetry and wanted more from him.

The Emersons nearly all welcomed her. Her dislike of Andrew Jackson showed that she was politically eligible as a member of the family, but that was the least of her qualifications. When she came to old Concord for a visit, Ruth Emerson thought her "a blessing sent from heaven for Waldo" and she pleased Grandfather Ripley, "the 'Apostle of half a century.'" There were a few grumblings from Aunt Mary, who had not yet seen her but whose eyes seldom saw unmixed good.

For Waldo there was enough good fortune to make unfavorable omens look unimportant. He was about to enter upon a regular pastorate in spite of some suspicions on the part of the senior minister who still nominally held it. Henry Ware had foreseen, no doubt, that Waldo would be his colleague and successor at the Second Church in Boston and had cautioned him against unorthodox tendencies. The young preacher made no humble apology. "I have affected generally," he explained, "a mode of illustration rather bolder than the usage of our preaching warrants, on the principle that our religion is nothing limited or partial, but of universal application, & is interested in all that interests man." But Ware, whose large head gave an impression of stature belied by his puny frame, was not a serious obstacle. Though he had frigid manners and no deep enthusiasm, he was benevolent. "In calm hours and friendly company," said Waldo, "his face expanded into broad simple sunshine; and I thought *le bon Henri* a pumpkin-sweeting."

Certainly the exchange of opinions between the two men did not much affect opinion in the Second Church, which, in January, invited Waldo to become junior pastor. Out of 79 persons voting, 74 were for him. He was to receive $1200 a year, but it was agreed that after the end of Ware's connection, which would be soon, he would be advanced to the rank of pastor, with Ware's salary of $1800. Waldo hesitated only because he feared that Ellen, whom he was already nursing through a severe attack of her dangerous malady, might need to travel for her health. Having got encouragement from her doctor, he decided to accept the offer.

Ignorant of the crisis in Ellen's health, Aunt Mary exploded with disgust at what she thought her nephew's vulgar success. She saw "no romance,—all common, fat prosperity; not the poet, reckless of scholarship, glad to get his bread anyhow." She prophesied that he would "be as busy as a bee, yet as cautious as if he were a tailor making patterns." Aunt Mary gloried in her own vagabondage and poverty, and she very honestly took alarm at her nephew's prospect of marrying money. But within a few days she was contentedly setting herself up as schoolmistress to Ellen, whom she tutored by mail. She tried to prepare her to be, as she said, a lasting blessing to the man to whom it was her favored lot to be attached. She instructed her what religious books and what novels to read and ventured to hope that she did not paint or talk French.

To Waldo Emerson, now at Boston in the house of a Haskins cousin in order to be near Ellen, prosperity did not seem real. At the end of January, in "these times of tribulation," which he was spending partly in Ellen's sick room as one of her nurses, he sent his unenthusiastic acceptance to the Second Church. Ellen's ill health must have been in his thoughts as he wrote: "I come to you in weakness, and not in strength. In a short life, I have yet had abundant experience of the uncertainty of human hopes." He "cast many a lingering look around the walls" of 14 Divinity Hall, a pleasant place to live. Two members of the Second Church were ready to open their homes to him in Boston. He agreed to spend the first month of his pastorate with George Sampson on North Allen Street and afterwards to board with Abel Adams on Chardon Street, not too long a walk from the church.

On Wednesday, the 11th of March, 1829, the ordination was like a family party. Edward and Charles and their mother and Ellen's mother were witnesses. The family took pride in the new pastor's "elegant & dignified" appearance and were moved to tears by the honorable allusions made to his late father. Grandfather Ripley appeared "yet nobler in old age, like an oak that gathers in venerableness what it loses in luxuriance." No eminent preachers were present. Uncle Samuel Ripley preached the sermon; Grandfather Ripley gave the charge; Frothingham, pastor of the Rev. William Emerson's old church, gave the right hand of fellowship. Another of the ministers was Upham, Waldo's college classmate. Gannett, a graduate of the year before Waldo's, seemed endowed with prophetic vision as he addressed the members of the society, urging them to spare their pastor's strength, to respect the independence of his ministry, and, even if he proved too heterodox to suit them, to give him credit for courage at least. They were not to hinder the preacher in his duty so long as they could endure him at all; if they could not endure him, manner or doctrine, they were to tell him so frankly and let him go. "If," said Gannett, "I must choose between the condition of a slave in Algiers, & the servitude of a clergyman, who dares not speak lest he sh$\underline{d}$ startle a prejudice, give me the former."

Doubtless the ceremony was not too simple to suit Waldo. He heeded John Milton's warning that ordination had no mysterious virtue in it but was merely "the laying on of hands, an outward sign or symbol of admission," creating nothing and conferring nothing. After the ordination, the family joined the guests at the four long tables in the hall of the Hancock School, in the same street with the church. The ceremonies would hardly have been complete without some observance at the manse in Concord, and four pertinent lines on the wooden panel that had long served as a sort of Emerson album may well have been written there by Edward on this occasion:

> Holy & happy stand
> In consecrated gown
> Toil, till some angel hand
> Bring sleep & shroud & crown

To be pastor of the Second Church was an honor, and the salary substantial for a beginner. But the church, even if it was the second oldest in Boston, was no longer fashionable or wealthy. Its place of worship did not add to its attractiveness. The new junior pastor, unless he was completely preoccupied with his unaccustomed responsibilities as he walked along Hanover Street, must have marveled at the old but recently renovated edifice. It was so tall, with its three tiers of windows accenting its height, that it dwarfed the spire resting firmly but not very gracefully atop its large rectangular tower. The tower itself resembled a campanile built by mistake too close to the church. There were some unpleasant memories preserved in the stories told about the place. It had been called the Revenge Church because of its origin in a quarrel, and the Cockerel Church because the figure of a cock had been perched upon its first weather vane, in derision, it is said, of the Rev. Peter Thacher, over whose ordination there had been fierce dissension. Tradition had it "that when the cock was placed upon the spindle, a merry fellow straddled over it and crowed three times to complete the ceremony."

Whether or not the new junior pastor was troubled by such old wives' tales, he could hardly have been unmindful of some somber figures in the past or present of his society. More than a century earlier the learned Puritan preachers Increase Mather and his son Cotton had both served the Second Church for many years. When Waldo climbed into the semicircular mahogany pulpit, he must have been painfully conscious of Henry Ware, Jr., still nominally his senior colleague. But when he faced the persons actually present, the pulpit's firm wings, extending laterally to make the semicircle into something resembling the Greek letter omega, and its dominating height, emphasized by the fluted columns that buttressed its curved front, doubtless gave him a sense of security. He had a psychological advantage that seemed to nullify the numerical superiority enjoyed by his congregation, which was broken up into little platoons sheltered only by the less formidable barriers of the pew walls and doors. Yet he needed courage, for he was a young man announcing new doctrines where the much respected senior pastor had recently repeated the articles of faith commonly accepted by Unitarians.

He seemed to be defiantly answering Ware's earlier admonitions when, in the first sermon he preached after being ordained, he charted his course, declaring that he intended henceforth to use a freedom befitting the greatness of the Gospel and its application to all human concerns. His own limitations were naturally strict enough, and it would be silly, he explained, to shut himself up within still narrower bounds. He would simply appeal to Biblical example if anybody complained about the want of sanctity in his style. He was willing to admit that the Scriptures were the direct voice of God. But he declared that the business of the church was to teach right living rather than religious dogma. In a second sermon he made it clear that he did not care to be an ecclesiastical policeman. He was still willing to keep up the ordinances of the church, but in the two sermons he gave notice that time-honored precedents were in danger.

He was soon averaging five introductory pastoral visits a day, and he felt them in every bone of his body. On his second Sunday he "preached at home all day & married a couple & baptized a child & assisted in the administration of the supper." He got hard-earned confidence. "I fear nothing now," he declared, "except the preparation of sermons. The prospect of one each week, for an indefinite time to come is almost terrifick." Exchanges with other pastors helped him, but there was no shirking the job of writing fresh sermons. Ellen was in Boston, at least much of the time, but he had to spend two or three hours a morning in writing and generally the whole afternoon in visiting. Charles, then living in the city, was struck by the increasingly eloquent preaching and by the amusing spectacle of the inexperienced pastor visiting his people "without any other guide or introduction, than his own knowledge of the street wherein they live." Sometimes Waldo "made long calls, kindly & affectionate on families who had no other claim to his attentions, than that of bearing the same name with his parishioners."

Even before the ordination at the Second Church, the radical schoolmaster Amos Bronson Alcott had listed Waldo Emerson as eleventh among the lesser preachers whose acquaintance he desired to make. A more enthusiastic hearer hazarded the opinion that "That young man will make another Channing." Undoubtedly many would have agreed with the New Bedford man who admired the young preacher's voice, "indefinite charm of simplicity and wisdom," and "occasional illustrations from nature" but found "the fresh philosophical novelties" of the sermon hard to understand.

Ware more than once declared his satisfaction with what was going on in his old pulpit, but actually he was first doubtful, then deeply troubled. In answer to one of Ware's privately administered admonitions, Waldo said he was distressed "that the idea sh'd be given to my audience that I did not look to the Scriptures with the same respect as others." He had only meant to say, he explained, "that my views of a preacher's duties were very high." But the new preacher had reasoned out his course for years past and was not blundering into strange heresies. Ware was broken-hearted. The parish dwindled, he said tearfully, for the church was afflicted with skepticism.

Doubtless it was the sermon that most appealed to the young pastor, but it was only one of the nine parts of the order of exercises for both morning and afternoon as he once jotted them down: prayer, Scriptures, hymn, prayer, hymn, sermon, prayer, hymn, benediction. He halted in his prayers, ill at ease. He was fastidious in his choice of words and hated stereotyped phrases. He complained that "the necessity of saying something & not stopping abruptly led him to say what he would not have said—a kind of insincerity." The ceaseless prayer, an aspiring and an actual living toward ideals, which he had long since advised his hearers to practice was something quite different from these public exercises.

As he himself had little music in him, most of the songs sung by the

choir or congregation must have given him as much pain as the worst of
them would have given to an expert. But he was delighted by the singing
of the peripatetic choir girl Charlotte Cushman, afterwards known in opera
for her fine contralto voice and later famous as an actress. Sometimes he
was emotionally uplifted when the church was filled with voices as it was
when Charles Wesley's New Year's hymn was sung. That piece had some
resounding lines that his ear was not deaf to:

> Come, let us anew our journey pursue,
>   Roll round with the year,
> And never stand still till the Master appear!

What he cared for most in the hymns was the occasional bit of poetry he
could detect and any evidences of liberal theology. In the old collection
used in his church he was troubled by false theological views. There were,
he considered, loose notions about immortality and gross conceptions of
spiritual things. He put these opinions into a sermon and had a new hymnal
adopted.

He found it awkward to visit sick people and mourners. Tales of his
unhappy adventures among his parishioners got into circulation. Called to
the deathbed of Captain Green, a rough-and-ready old Revolutionary
officer who lived next door to the church, Waldo was diffident and embarrassed, fumbled among the clutter of things on the sick man's table,
and began to talk about glassmaking. The captain was angry and told him
that if he knew nothing to do at a deathbed but to lecture about glass
bottles, he had better go. Another story told how Waldo, getting stuck in
the middle of a prayer he was making at a funeral, took his hat and left
without further ado. The young pastor himself might have jotted down
many similar incidents of his professional life, no doubt, if he had been
quick enough to realize the value of such trivia. But people shunned to
record the circumstance which they best knew, he afterwards put it, "for
example, the clergyman . . . his pecuniary and social and amiable or
odious relations to his parish." It was only when you got far enough away
from "these employments & meannesses" that their significance loomed
larger and they appeared to be "the fit fable of which you are the moral."

In common with other preachers, Waldo Emerson was naturally discouraged when he thought of the mixed motives that brought his congregation to church. He already knew well enough, without putting it into
so many words, that "Scarcely ten came to hear his sermon. But singing,
or a new pelisse, or Cousin William, or the Sunday School, or a proprietors'
meeting after church, or the merest anility in Hanover Street, were the
beadles that brought and the bolts that hold his silent assembly in the

church." Yet he wanted the opportunity of confronting even such a congregation. They were "fools," he admitted, but "potentially divine." He hoped to stick to his pulpit till it appeared that a better platform was available to him.

A few close friends meantime made his professional worries seem unimportant. Abel Adams, to whose house in Chardon Street Waldo moved his scanty belongings from George Sampson's home, was one of the most dependable and useful friends he ever had. Adams cared little for books but knew human nature and was a trusted adviser in financial matters. He exchanged Bibles with the young minister and they called themselves brothers. But Waldo had his mind mainly on Ellen. By the first of May she had left Boston and was hopefully traveling in the Connecticut Valley. Within a few weeks she had "fled like the Phenix bird" back to new Concord, and Waldo spent nearly all the latter half of June there, a part of the time in her sick room. She was "taken sick in the old way,—very suddenly," and he concluded that "human happiness is very unstable." Back in Boston again that summer, he still hoped for her recovery and was thinking, it seems, of the possibility of settling with her in the peaceful corner of Roxbury where he had once lived.

Having returned to New Hampshire at the earliest possible moment, he set out with her on a long journey to improve her health. "Ellen & I came hither in a chaise this morng. an easy ride of 12 miles from Concord," he wrote to his brother Charles from the Shaker village of Canterbury. "Her mother followed us an hour or two later in coach with our fair & reverend baggage. Ellen bore the ride beautifully & if tomorrow shd. prove fair & she continues as well we mean to go on to Meredith bridge . . . or even possibly to Centre Harbor . . . Mother Winkley or Sister Winkley hath given Ellen & I a long & earnest sermon on the 'beauty of virginity' & striven to dissuade us from our sinful purpose of 'living after the way of manhood & of womanhood in the earth' but I parried her persuasion & her denunciation as best I might & insisted we were yoked together by Heaven to provoke each other to good works so long as we lived . . ."

Waldo, untouched by Mother Winkley's Shaker doctrines, entertained his pretty companion with a humorous rhyming journal of their progress. Her fortitude was tested by the journey. As they went on toward the White Mountains, they passed "thro much wind & some shower" and wished for a fire in August. But the open air seemed better for Ellen than her nurse and hot room at home. Waldo canceled his next Sunday's engagement with his church in Boston, and they turned westward to the Connecticut Valley before starting back to new Concord.

A few weeks later, in September, the lovers were off on another tour, this time from her home to the Merrimac River, on to Worcester, Springfield, and Hartford, and back through Worcester into New Hampshire. They carried half a dozen volumes of new novels besides some heavier reading. By day they rode in the chaise, while Mrs. Kent and her daughter Margaret came along in the carriage. At the taverns they read and scribbled. He preached a sermon or two in spite of a lame knee. They hurried northward on their return, as he wanted to get back to his own pulpit and Ellen doubtless needed to reach home a week or two before their wedding.

On the last day of the month, in her stepfather Colonel Kent's old mansion in the New Hampshire Concord, they were married. Charles, the only one of the groom's family at the wedding, had a great fondness for Waldo and did not live through "3 whole days in that big house full of women" without suffering a twinge of jealousy. Time was heavy on his hands "while W. & the fair Ellen were whispering honied words above stairs," as he said, "& I was turned over to the compulsory attentions of the stranger folk." But he managed to arouse himself to an effort at generosity. "These lovers," he explained, "are blind—purblind these lovers be—I forgive them freely." Early in October the married pair were moving into the house of a Mrs. Hannah Keating, on, or slightly off, Chardon Street, Boston, and close to the home of Abel Adams. Waldo was soon laid up in his chair, unable to walk without a cane. His sprained knee was now made worse by chronic inflammation. On Sundays he preached sitting. He rode out with Ellen every day when the weather was good.

His marriage had made him a man of some substance, or rather had given him the promise of being so. "Men call me richer," he put it, "I hope it will prove so—but shall be glad if the equipage of the king & the queen for each hath their own doth not eat up master Mammon on his quarter day." He settled down to his new way of life. He bought a pair of dumbbells, doubtless in an attempt to get exercise in spite of his lameness; deposited money in the Globe Bank; paid Chickering $300 for a piano; subscribed to the Boston Athenæum; and bought books. As his knee got no better, he quit his reputable doctors and hired a quack, who had the good luck to cure him. He offered to pay $3 a week so that Edward, now admitted to the bar and at work in New York with William, could be kept from overwork; but he did not find his own immediate financial prospects rosy. "I have a fancy," he declared, "that if you shd examine my income & outlay since my marriage you wd say I was poorer not richer, therefor. But richer I surely am by all Ellen, if she bro't no penny."

In spite of his pastorate and his absorbing connection with Ellen he was prepared, at least, to do a good deal of reading, perhaps partly for his wife's benefit. In the year of his marriage he bought copies of Montaigne, Rousseau, a Cooper novel, Scott's *Marmion,* and Combe on the constitution of man. He borrowed Herder on the philosophy of history, Marcus Aurelius, Plato, and a few other authors from the Harvard College Library. He paid some small sums to the Boston Library Society and got good returns, borrowing such books as Xenophon on Socrates, Aristotle on ethics and politics, *Plutarch's Morals,* Lucretius, Epictetus, Beaumont and Fletcher, Massinger, Bishop Berkeley, Sir William Temple, Swift's *Gulliver's Travels, Clarissa Harlowe* and another novel of Richardson's, Erasmus Darwin's *Zoonomia,* Lamb's essays, Southey's *Thalaba,* Schiller's history of the Thirty Years' War, and Goethe's memoirs. He soon began to make heavy drafts upon the library of the Boston Athenæum.

He was beginning a new and rewarding period of acquaintance with books. A few deftly turned phrases and philosophical distinctions such as he might borrow from a subtle mind like Coleridge's—talent and genius, fancy and imagination, reason and understanding—might help shape his old thoughts into a semblance of order. After years of nibbling at Coleridge, he suddenly became deeply interested in him that autumn and winter. In December he wrote Aunt Mary that he was reading *The Friend.* He was aware that she did not "speak of it with respect" but went on to inform her that "there are few or no books of pure literature so self-imprinting, that is so often remembered as Coleridge's." And a few days later he added a determined defense of his author. Early in the new year he sent William and Edward a list of books he was reading: "Coleridge's Friend—with great interest; Coleridges 'Aids to reflection' with yet deeper; Degerando Hist. Comparée des Systemes de Philosophie, I am beginning on the best recommendation. & one more book—the best Sermon I have read for some time, to wit, Combe's Constitution of Man. You see the present is too mighty for me, I cannot get away to do homage to the mighty past."

He debated books with his brothers and with Aunt Mary, an instigator or a severe critic of his thinking. Charles, by his own admission, was now "quite taken with Coleridge." Aunt Mary sometimes professed to believe that Waldo did not value her and would soon put her aside. She characteristically attacked him obliquely by addressing Charles or some other member of the family. "As to Waldo's letter," she once wrote, "say nothing to him. It is time he should leave me. His sublime negations, his non-informations, I have no right in the world to complain of." Another letter showed that she was trying to keep up with the philosophical Aunt Sarah Alden Ripley as well as with him, but not very willingly. "Coleridge—& a few relations of his idealism," she grumbled, "I pick up & sit late & rise early to question of a truth which can be of no consequence to me in the

grave. Instead of truth I might say illusion—sophistry . . ." She was bewildered. Her curiosity carried her along into new speculations, but she
looked with suspicion upon "the Kantian mania w'h has revived within
two or three years" and thought Kant and his followers as destructive of
theism as was Spinoza. She was sure she would never part with her reasonably orthodox and reliable favorite Doctor Samuel Clarke, but she saw
that the newly popular philosophical doctrines left "the good old Clarke
out of all reckoning."

Waldo bought a magnet, a frame for a view of Paestum, Boswell's life
of Johnson, a history of enthusiasm, the Boston Athenæum catalogue, a
subscription to the *Boston Daily Advertiser,* a bird, a subscription to *The
New Jerusalem Magazine,* another to *The Christian Examiner,* another to
The North American Review, and another to *The Edinburgh Review.*
Such things could probably come out of his own salary, but he undoubtedly
could not meet all his expenses from that restricted source. He sometimes
paid Mrs. Keating over $100 a month for the house, with board it seems.
In March, April, and May he had heavy expenses for travel southward
with Ellen, her sister Margaret going along with them.

By the middle of March the three of them were in the Connecticut
Valley again. At Hartford he preached three times in one Sunday. There
he managed to bring Aunt Mary, who was apt to be boarding about in
odd places, for her first sight of Ellen. Ellen, in the rhymed travel journal
which it was her turn to keep on this trip, recorded Aunt Mary's disappointment. As usual, however, Aunt Mary was not wholehearted in her
verdict. "I like her better better than I dreamt," she managed to bring
out; and she even discovered genius in the girl. But though she eventually
declared that the young wife was "the lovliest Maddona of my imajanation,"
she refused for the present to accept the usual estimate of Ellen's beauty.

On the whole the journey proved to be one more trial of endurance
for Ellen. Sailing from New Haven, she and her sister and Waldo encountered a gale that drove them into Norwalk Roads for shelter. There they
lay "pouting & snuffing the insufferable mephitis of the cabin, & hearing
the rain patter & looking at each other grimly." There were "forty stout
passengers . . . sleeping or trying to sleep in an air that wd doubtless have
put out a lamp on the floor. But morning came, the wind abated, & the
steam chimney began once more to puff." After "a noble passage up the
Sound," during which they enjoyed the "fine sun mild air, swift vessels,
beautiful shores, noble seats," they got to "this long London town" of New
York.

There Waldo took over the doggerel journal from Ellen to insert some
satirical lines on the parades of splendid "paint, lace, plumes, flowers, &

brocades" on Broadway; but at the hotel she found fit subjects for more of her own social satire. Amazed at the brazenness of the city belles, she was, as she pictured herself, the overmodest country lass, a

> wondering, eager, newcome clown
> And blushing like a country Miss
> To see the utter nakedness
> And how they cheat the legs of clothes
> While the long arms in state repose . . .

But at last, safely on board the *Thistle,* she and Waldo were skirting Staten Island, then entering the muddy Raritan, the waterway to Philadelphia.

In that city, they left the U. S. Hotel for Sarah M'Elroy's boarding house, on the corner of Chestnut and Eleventh Streets. There Ellen discovered more grist for her metrical mill, but her habitual mood was far from satirical. William Furness, Waldo's boyhood friend and now a large part of Philadelphia for the young couple, "found them on one occasion walking with arms around each other, up & down their parlor." He was impressed by Ellen's youthfulness and delicacy. The young husband, he remembered, "borrowed my Hume's Hist of England." But as Waldo was "Reluctant to inflict dry reading upon his child-wife, he said he would have her begin with the reign of Queen Eliz^{th}" He stayed over two Sundays, preached three sermons, and went with Ellen to see art treasures; but he soon became "sadly impatient" of the "petty engagements which tear time into slivers." By the first of April he was on his way home, leaving his wife with her sister Margaret in Philadelphia till, as he planned, he should return for them a few weeks later.

Before the end of May he and Ellen and Ruth Emerson were in Brookline, beginning their residence of several months in the ugly and old-fashioned but pleasant, comfortable Aspinwall house. To Charles, a frequent visitor there that summer, his mother seemed to have found a peaceful hermitage that agreed with her own serene soul. The unfortunate fact for Ellen was the cruel, inexorable chafing of the Massachusetts coast's east wind, which, she said, "blows blue & shrill." For her husband, a week of daily travel between Brookline and Boston was almost enough, but he was willing to sacrifice himself, or others, to her good. Except for a "universal benevolence," Charles observed, the young husband was "all called in & centred in Ellen." Charles, finding himself neglected, was hurt and wondered "whether t'is the invariable effect of business & marriage, to make one independent of, & therefore indifferent to old relationships & intimacies."

On Election Day in Boston, Waldo Emerson, chaplain of the state senate, sat comfortably in the pulpit and listened to Doctor Channing's "noble discourse." Waldo's selection as chaplain, in the summer of 1829, apparently had had no political significance, for the administration was Democratic Republican while he, with many other former Federalists, was presumably by that time at least nominally a National Republican. But probably he had had to acknowledge a definite affiliation with the National Republicans when, in the local election of the following December, he had been chosen to represent the fourth ward on the Boston school committee during the year 1830.

The committee meant a serious responsibility with little honor. Its twelve members were elected annually, one from each ward; and the mayor and aldermen belonged *ex officio*. The committee elected all the public-school teachers, determined salaries, and removed any teacher at discretion. Each of its regular subcommittees visited and watched over one of the city schools. Visitations, reports, quarterly meetings, special meetings, and informal conferences added up to a staggering total of hours for a conscientious member.

The young minister had been promptly assigned to the subcommittees on the Latin School and the Mayhew School. He was a graduate of the Latin School, and the Mayhew School was near his home. Except when he was out of town he seldom failed to do his part. During the year he served on a special committee to make the annual return of the Boston schools to the state, vainly tried to block changes in school regulations, wrote two quarterly reports for the subcommittee on the Mayhew School. It was discouraging business for him to generalize on hasty impressions of the work being done by the scholars. Once he reported that the subcommittee "spent the forenoon in the Reading Department . . . There was not an appearance of much diligence in the reading or spelling of this class. The first class read pretty well; had advanced a little way in grammar; & were very well acquainted with the map of the United States." Some divisions of the fourth class, he faithfully recorded, were superior to the rest. One class recited arithmetic extremely well, and there was good order in the school. Such reports were tangible but not inspiring results of many meetings and visitations. The Mayhew School was an especially troublesome assignment because of an altercation over disciplinary practices in vogue there.

In the manner of his father before him, Waldo Emerson resolved to be methodical. He wished that God would grant him "persistency enough, so soon as I leave Brookline, and come to my books, to do as I intend." He was trying to define his old theory of self-reliance more sharply with the help of the Coleridgean concept of reason, reason that was not reason but the faculty by which one intuitively turned on, in one's inner self, the current of divine will and idea. He thought he saw clearer light on the seeming contradiction between self-reliance and God-reliance. He paradoxically insisted "that the more exclusively idiosyncratic a man is, the more general and infinite he is." God, truth, shone directly into the soul, and "it is," he put it, "when a man does not listen to himself, but to others, that he is depraved and misled."

In the autumn he was back in Chardon Street among his books, but his meditations on such ideas were interrupted by some speculations on a subject unhappily pressed upon his attention by the ill health of his family. Was it "possible for religious principle to overcome the fear of death"? Bacon had listed what he thought were passions and humors which could triumph over that fear. Instances of defiance of death were familiar to everybody, but were these instances of a conquest of the fear or merely of success in setting it aside, mere want of thought? Even "spiritual men" like Doctor Johnson frequently showed great apprehension and gloom at the thought of dissolution, Waldo recalled. Later he quoted Sir Thomas Browne's *Hydriotaphia* in his journal.

News came from New York that Edward seemed as much threatened by tuberculosis as Ellen and must travel. If he would not come to Boston and let his mother and Ellen nurse him, he ought to go to Magnolia in Florida, Waldo thought, rather than to the West Indian island of Santa Cruz, a more expensive and more restricted place. Florida still had the special attraction, Waldo supposed, of being Achille Murat's residence. "For myself," he argued, "I would pay a hundred dollars to live a little while with Murat." When word came that Edward was about to sail southward alone, Ruth Emerson, having decided to make the voyage with him if he wanted her, hastily set out for New York but was delayed by head winds and arrived half an hour after he had sailed for Santa Cruz.

Ellen, taking her doctor's advice not to migrate to Cuba or elsewhere unless she was prepared to stay for ten years, decided to risk another winter in New England. If Edward's case was pathetic, Ellen's was more so and was a test of her husband's fortitude as well as of her own. The pathos came not only from her youth, her beauty, and her helplessness but also from what she and doubtless Waldo believed to be her unfulfilled promise as a poet. On blank leaves in a diary which had once been her brother George's she had written some of her most revealing prose and verse. God, she said, had given her a harp, and she thought the strings were sound, though the bridge and frets were weak and wasting. She felt that every day she "ought to get one drop . . . of clear distilled essence" from her brain, but the drop did not come. Her moods fell or soared up suddenly. "To day," she once wrote, "my heart has been riding again on the south wind . . ." Her fragile verses expressed her resignation or her constancy in a touching feminine manner:

> I sheild my bosoms inmate this sweet love
> As I would mine own babe or a wee flower . . .
> I will not stay on earth Waldo
>   Unless thy love is mine
> When all that gave it birth my love
>   And beauty must decline . . .
> Sweeter the green sod for my bones
>   The black earth for my head
> The wind than thy cold altered tones
>   Whence all of love had fled—

At the other extreme, she had written satire, and she could forget the solemnity expected of her as the wife of the minister and banter him with verses on the independence she intended to assert in the next world:

> I sha'nt keep a carriage
> My wings will be strong . . .
> I therefore shall use them
> As I may see fit
> And tea out & dine out—
> Nor mind you a bit.

But her dominant tone appeared in the painfully intense sentiment of her many serious pieces on love and religion. "Lines," beginning "Love scatters oil," and "The Violet" were among her most careful compositions and were not greatly altered for printing in *The Dial* years later. Except for a few happy moments, her wish to be a poet was frustrated. Her life was too constricted. What poetry was left in her must have been congealed by the cold storms at Boston in that final December of 1830. Two lines she had probably written long before would have served best as a farewell to her dream of poetic inspiration, lines which Waldo copied at the end of his own book of selections from her poems and which his brother Charles remembered:

> I chided the moon,—she was icy cold—
> The stars were coquettes too splendidly drest

She kept on riding out day after day, believing that the open air gave her her chance for life. Before the end of January that chance had dwindled perceptibly, though Waldo was still hopeful. "As soon as the snows melt so as to give us passage," he said, "and as soon as she recovers her diminished strength so as to ride & walk we shall set out for Philad. or Baltimore, God helping us." She lived through another week of dying. But it seemed to those who were with her that they were witnessing a religious act in which there was not much room for pathos. When she was not torpid under the influence of opiates, she was serene. On the sixth of February Charles wrote that "her spirit seems winged for its flight. . . . Waldo is bowed down under the affliction, yet he says t'is like seeing an angel go to heaven." For Waldo's mother, full of piety and of affection for Ellen, "the closing scene of her short life" had "solemn & delightful interest." The girl was, she said, "calm & undismayed at the approach of death—& in a prayerful & resigned state of mind commited herself & all her dear friends unto God —biding each of us around her Farewell." On February 8, two hours after Ellen's death, Waldo wrote to Aunt Mary:

"My angel is gone to heaven this morning & I am alone in the world & strangely happy. Her lungs shall no more be torn nor her head scalded by her blood nor her whole life suffer from the warfare between the force & delicacy of her soul & the weakness of her frame. I said this morn & I do not know but it is true that I have never known a person in the world in whose separate existence as a soul I could so readily & fully believe . . . I see it plainly that things & duties will look coarse & vulgar enough to me when I find the romance of her presence (& romance is a beggarly word) withdrawn from them all. . . ."

Henry Ware preached the funeral sermon, and the nineteen-year-old Ellen, it seems, was buried according to her own request in her father's tomb in Roxbury. She had been the wife of Waldo Emerson less than a year and a half, yet she had stirred him more than anybody else ever had done or could do. Others of the family vied with him in praising her. Charles, who had known her exceptionally well, could not be eloquent enough about her. The image of Ellen that remained in his mind was, he said, "an Ideal that, if I were a Platonist, I should believe to have been one of the Forms of Beauty in the Universal Mind. She moved ever in an atmosphere of her own, a crystal sphere, & nothing vulgar in neighboring persons & circumstances touched her." Waldo himself wrote and rewrote her elegy in verse and prose.

For long after her death he had the habit of walking every morning, it is said, from Boston to her tomb, near the Roxbury Latin School. His cousin David Greene Haskins often passed him on the road to the cemetery. Never was Waldo Emerson so settled in his belief in immortality. There were moments when he could hardly conceive of the reality of either physical or spiritual death.

> *Does* thy heart beat with mine? does thy blue eye
> Ever look northward with desire,

he asked of Ellen. In other verses he seemed half serious in his disappointment that she did not by sheer will power, as if she were some Ligeia, return to keep their secret pact to remain inseparable. An obscure unreasoning and uncontrollable impulse caused him on one of his visits to her tomb, more than a year after her death, to open her coffin.

He continued to complain of his lack of emotion, and when he went back "to the first smile of Ellen on the door-stone at Concord" and reviewed the whole history of his love affair with her, it was his own coolness, as he imagined it, that he regretted. But whatever his superficial coolness, he was aware of the passion underneath. It was chiefly the lack of harmony between the outer and the inner man that annoyed and puzzled him.

In time, however, he was able to look back upon his loss with what seemed to him to be complete acceptance of the fact. "I loved Ellen," he said, "and love her with an affection that would ask nothing but its indulgence to make me blessed. Yet when she was taken from me, the air was still sweet, the sun was not taken down from my firmament, and however sore was that particular loss, I still felt that it was particular, that the universe remained to us both . . ."

11.

THESES NAILED TO THE CHURCH DOOR

❧❀❧

It is neither safe nor prudent to do aught against conscience.
Here stand I, I cannot otherwise.
—Martin Luther, quoted in MS journal "Q,"
October 27, 1832

THOUGH his mother was there, the house in Chardon Street seemed empty to Waldo Emerson. He quickly returned to his pulpit, but the real text of his first sermon was his own sorrow. He reasoned out consolation from his belief in immortality. The Second Church kept him busy. A new vestry was finished, and he had to make an address at its dedication. He had to follow up the dedicatory address with a course of lectures explaining the Scriptures for the benefit of the young people of his congregation. He went about this business with a heavy heart.

In his opening lecture he summarized supposed facts about each of the authors of the first three Gospels. He concluded with the characteristic observation that in the three simple, poverty-stricken Jews one found an example of the power of moral truth over the human soul. In a later lecture he piled up the available evidence that the Bible was authentic, and he went back over the history of English and other versions. By the end of March he was giving his theory of the origins of the Gospels, and so he went on from one subject to another. He by no means denied the historicity of Jesus but held with Gieseler that probably, after their master's death, the disciples repeatedly went over their facts together and so made their accounts essentially agree. He showed how the Messianic tradition was wrong in certain details; how, in spite of the general authenticity of the gospels, some of the recorded miracles might need special interpretations to make them palatable; how the Sermon on the Mount was a sublime declaration promising all spiritual gain and all worldly loss.

In his sermons he still found it hard to forget Ellen. A few weeks after her death he completed and preached one on suffering. He undoubtedly had his own private loss in mind as well as his law of compensation when he told his congregation that it was only reasonable to look forward to a life compounded of good and evil fortune. "Indeed it seems to me," he said, "that in reading the lives of illustrious men the mind feels a sort of incongruity when, as sometimes though rarely happens, they chance to live in uninterrupted prosperity." He had now written over a hundred sermons. But he kept on writing new ones and showed himself orthodox and unorthodox by turns. He was struggling to stay within the limits of liberal Christian doctrine but was determined to be honest. Once he had asked his brother William to make a synopsis of the leading arguments against Christianity, for William's Göttingen training gave him some authority in such matters. He had also wanted him to mark, in the works of Eichhorn or others, the passages that would tend to destroy a candid inquirer's belief in the divine authority of the New Testament.

In his second year on the school committee he was loaded with new responsibilities. He had three schools to visit regularly. Some militant parents of the Mayhew School, of whose subcommittee he was chairman, demanded a reform of what they considered unreasonably harsh discipline. He laboriously compiled the results of his committee's investigations. The committee was extremely skeptical about a complaint "That the masters had refused permission to the boys to leave the school & go into the yard, on their necessary occasions" and found no validity in the charge "That the boys are employed to clean the inkstands & sweep the schoolrooms by way of punishment." As for the sweeping of floors, the committee was of the opinion "that the familiar usage of the other schools had better be retained in this, of giving this work to all the boys of the school in alphabetical rotation." It was true, the report said, that "each boy is required, when his inkstand is foul, to carry it out & wash it," but this rule also was upheld.

Waldo Emerson was placed on a special committee that gave halfhearted support to a proposed method of classifying the city's schools in an attempt to bring order out of a somewhat chaotic state of affairs. But troubles at the Mayhew School continued to give him his worst headaches. A former teacher himself, he must have taken some pleasure in defending the accused teachers of that school against what his brother Charles called "the deep voiced mob." Contradictory petitions were filed within a few weeks of the city election. Fifty-two persons, including some of weight in the community, blamed the subcommittee for repeatedly refusing to act and appealed directly to the whole school committee. One extremely bitter parent drafted a petition of his own, charging the headmaster with "more than savage barbarity . . . and a vindicative cruelty generally to my son for more than three months . . . so much so—that his mind & spirits seem to be, bowed down to the ground." But the strong resistance of a majority of the full committee, including Waldo Emerson and Ezra Gannett, his old college mate, defeated the malcontents. A motion for the dismissal of the master was so drastically amended that it was left a mere warning that he had "exceeded the bounds of the judicious exercise of authority." The excitement continued, but the defenders of authority stood firm. When there were threats of violence, Emerson asked the mayor for a peace officer. A motion to abolish all corporal punishment in the public schools was defeated by the votes of Waldo Emerson, Ezra Gannett, and others.

Memories of his own experiences as a teacher doubtless kept up the interest of the minister in some of the visitations he had to report. He must have cared especially about what went on in the Latin and Greek classes at the Latin School which he had once attended as a pupil. He was not indifferent to the way the boys read *Viri Romæ* or Caesar, and he was pleased with some correct translations from Horace that he was fortunate enough to hear. But he had had enough and was not gratified when he read in the newspaper in December, 1831, that he had again been nominated for a seat on the school committee. Fortunately he escaped a third term. Perhaps the still smoldering embers of the fierce quarrel over the Mayhew School flared up on election day. At any rate Waldo Emerson was one of the few National Republican candidates to be defeated.

He kept from serious involvement in partisan politics but was still decisively against Andrew Jackson and his followers. He described Jackson's as "the bad party in the country," and he dined with John Quincy Adams. He wrote to Edward in the late summer of 1831: "Sad political disclosures every day brings. Wo is me my dishonored country that such poor wretches should sit in the chairs of Washington Franklin & Adams." It seemed to him, he said, that "we shall all feel dirty if Jackson is reëlected." But if he was conservative in his choice of leaders, as a man of Federalist background would naturally have been, he was liberal in some of his social and political beliefs. He doubtless agreed with his brother Charles on the duties of American citizens toward the oppressed races. Charles was already prophesying a crisis over Negro slavery and denouncing the government for its behavior toward the Indians. Waldo had long since used slavery in his sermons when he needed examples of man's inhumanity to man. He admitted the reform agitator Samuel May, *"God's choreboy,"* to the Second Church pulpit in the spring of 1831. May's address on "Slavery in the United States" was fully reported in the press. The pastor was thus linked with the reformer.

Waldo Emerson was growing restless in his shell of a home and thought of quitting Boston for good. With Charles he revisited their old haunts in Roxbury. He remembered the rough country of western Massachusetts and formed fanciful plans for a secluded life of literature and science there.

He dreamed of establishing himself on an open hillside in one of "the mountain counties." "There," he put it in language more literary than scientific,

> will I bring my books,—my household gods,
> The reliquaries of my dead saint, and dwell
> In the sweet odor of her memory.
> Then in the uncouth solitude unlock
> My stock of art, plant dials in the grass,
> Hang in the air a bright thermometer
> And aim a telescope at the inviolate sun.

At the end of May, 1831, he set out with Charles on a northern tour of "a fortnight & a couple of days beyond." At Burlington, Vermont, where Waldo preached on Sunday, they found President Marsh of the University of Vermont, an editor and expounder of Coleridge. Approaching Lake George and Ticonderoga, the travelers entered a region honored in their family history. Grandfather Emerson had been with the American army here. Charles "picked up a bullet in the old Fort at Ti. which," he said, "I would fain believe to be of true Revolutionary memory." On the return journey the brothers spent a day at Rutland in a vain attempt to find their grandfather's grave.

Waldo was oppressed with the sense of mortality. The shocking experience of a few months earlier had left him numb. In his verses he reburied Ellen,

> who outshone all beauty, yet knew not
> That she was beautiful . . .

and, falling into Aunt Mary's chronic mood, he professed a desire to die. But he had no stomach for Aunt Mary's uncompromising realism. "I should like," he wrote,

> to lie in sweets,
> A hill's leaves for winding-sheets,
> And the searching sun to see
> That I'm laid with decency
> And the commissioned wind to sing
> His mighty psalm from fall to spring
> And annual tunes commemorate
> Of nature's child the common fate.

He had another reason than Ellen's loss to think of death. His brothers Charles and Edward were both threatened. Both had once seemed destined to make a mark in public affairs. Edward was so much in love with learning that he used to wash his mind's face each morning, as he said, with a little Euripides or a scrap of Epictetus. Now he was an exile and hardly dared to return to the New England climate. He kept alive in the West Indies, where he first tried the little Danish-owned island of Santa Cruz, or St. Croix. The beauties of St. Croix, long since praised in American verse, inspired many prose passages in his notebooks and letters. He read Robinson Crusoe's adventures, sympathetically no doubt, though his own lot was not quite so desolate as Crusoe's. For some time he had the admired Boston preacher Channing close at hand and saw other compatriots coming and going. He was blistered, dieted, exercised with "friction" twice a day. He had daily periods of horseback riding, lounging, walking, bathing, reading, chatting. He was a good observer and carefully watched the process of removing the sugar from the coolers at Concordia. One or two Negroes shoveled it from the cooler into tubs as if it were so much wet gravel. The tubs were then hoisted onto the heads of laborers and carried away to the curing house.

Moving to San Juan, on the neighboring island of Porto Rico, Edward became a clerk in the counting house of the American consul, Sidney Mason, a man well informed about this island, where he had passed a third of his life. Edward lived in the house of a Negro who spoke English and whose major domo spoke French. He made the most of the exotic aspects of Porto Rican life. He watched the friars passing along the streets, began work on the Spanish language and wrote letters home in it, walked on the ramparts and admired the climate. On St. John's day, San Juan's chief anniversary, vespers were celebrated by horsemen racing through the streets. At night there were hundreds of such riders. St. Peter's fiesta was next. Edward turned to the adventures of Don Quixote in Spanish or he listened while Colonel Flinter, an Irishman in the Spanish service, read from his manuscripts on local history. He found life in San Juan bearable, and when he heard that Charles was again threatened with a breakdown he was sure this was the place for him.

In Boston, Waldo Emerson once more settled down to his philosophical speculations. Aunt Mary, always in need of a companion in her mental adventures, sometimes capriciously passed Waldo by in favor of Charles, known as her boy. As she picked up what she called "ends & orts of Kantism," she found her German philosopher pleased with certain *a priori* proofs of a supreme mind but nevertheless turning out, she thought, to be an atheist. To her it seemed idiotic for a real or pretended idealist to deny objective proofs of God. The philosopher Berkeley, admitting reality in the cause, and the ancient Hindus, admitting nothing but divine agency, did incomparably better. Kant was insane, though amiable. Charles, lacking the speculative boldness that Aunt Mary prized in Waldo, seemed to despair of keeping up a flight with her in so thin an atmosphere and was soon trying to steer her in the direction of his philosophical brother.

Waldo was reading seven or eight lectures of Cousin in the first volume of the Frenchman's course, a sane and plain guide to the history of philosophy. Still suffering from Ellen's loss, he refused the invitation of Phi Beta Kappa to be its poet. "A few months since," he explained, "I should have received it with sincere pleasure, but I have not at present any spirit for a work of that kind, which must not be a dirge." He was not the shallow optimist he was sometimes taken for, even by one so close to him as his brother Charles. "Waldo is very well—speculates on—on—happy he!" So wrote Charles to Aunt Mary. "I said to you once, 'no anxiety, no clouds, all inquiry & good hope & quiet live & easy die'— You rebuked me, but I speak it of him more in marvel than in reproach— And perhaps I am clean wrong—perhaps all minds are racked as mine is with doubt & self accusation, but all do not pour their confessions unblushingly as I do into the ear of their friends—" Actually, Waldo was trying to use his very real doubts and suffering as materials for a philosophy of life. While Charles was making his complaint to Aunt Mary, Waldo was writing to Edward: "I am trying to learn the ethical truths that always allure me from my cradle till now & yet how slowly disclosed! That word *Compensations* is one of the watchwords of my spiritual world—& time & chance & sorrow & hope do not by their revelations abate my curiosity."

Waldo Emerson had now got hold of a theory of writing that could be a valuable discipline. No one could write well, he found, who thought there was any choice of words for him. "There is always one line that ought to be drawn, or one proportion that should be kept, and every other line or proportion is wrong, and so far wrong as it deviates from this. . . . In good writing, words become one with things." The thought of George Herbert, one of his favorite poets, had "that heat as actually to fuse the words." Elevation of soul, Emerson reasoned, would determine this power over language. If the thing was in one's mind the words were bound to come; and he put such diverse witnesses as Montaigne, Horace, Seneca, Cicero, and Burns into the box to testify to this truth.

Two of these witnesses undoubtedly helped stir up in the literary apprentice a disgust for the kind of sterile gentility that threatened to restrict him. "That's why I like Montaigne," he acknowledged. "No effeminate parlour workman is he, on an idea got at an evening lecture or a young men's debate, but roundly tells what he saw, or what he thought of when he was riding horse-back or entertaining a troup at his chateau. A gross, semisavage indecency debases his book, and ought doubtless to turn it out of doors; but the robustness of his sentiments, the generosity of his judgments, the downright truth without fear or favour, I do embrace with both arms."

Emerson was dreaming of literature as a profession but was not yet certain of financial means for even an experimental period of writing. In June of 1831 Ellen's estate remained "wholly unsettled," but he had just got "a long legal opinion" favorable to his own claims. Six months later letters of administration were about to be taken out. Cutler, the executor of Beza Tucker's estate, hazarded the guess that the settlement would not be made during Waldo's lifetime. John Ashmun, a Harvard law professor, prepared on Waldo's behalf an appeal "To the Hon the Justices of the Supreme Judicial Court—in Chancery." He recited the history of the Tucker estate, argued for the claims of plaintiff Emerson to the share Ellen would have been entitled to if she had lived to the age of twenty-one, and petitioned for a writ of subpoena directing Cutler, together with Ellen's mother and the other surviving heirs, to appear before the court "to abide such order and decree as to your Honors shall seem agreeable to equity and good conscience." A rumor got abroad that the pastor of the Second Church "had refused all compromise with his wifes friends & was gone to law with them." His comment to William was: "For ye first time I saw to my sorrow yt ye thing admitted of y^t face. The facts are y^t by a mutual advised consent we get ye Supreme Court to distribute ye estate, & I take no step without advising with Mr & Mrs Kent & Margaret Tucker; and if ever such a story shd. be quoted to you refer to those persons or to Mr Cutler." Captain Nash, Paulina Tucker's husband, might probably, Waldo explained, take a different view of the matter but had opportunity to know better.

In spite of some hope of prompt judicial action, it was actually nearly two years before any decisive progress could be made toward a settlement of the Tucker estate, and in the meantime Waldo Emerson remained uncertain of his financial status. Presumably it was helped slightly by the several persons who had rooms in the Chardon Street house he still kept. One of those who apparently stayed longest with him was Warren Burton, a college classmate who may have been worth more to him than the rental of the space he occupied, for, though his writings proved ineffectual, he seems to have been developing somewhat the same views of religion and the church as Waldo's. Another inmate was Joseph Lyman, son of the Northampton Lymans. But whatever pecuniary contributions Burton and Lyman made did not make Waldo financially easy. Late in the spring of 1832 word was sent to Edward that the Chardon Street treasury was more than exhausted and that if he wanted to purchase any goods for the Porto Rican trade he would have to supply his own funds.

Waldo managed to preach a fairly full schedule. With his usual frankness, he revealed his current thought to his congregation. If some alert deacon of the Second Church could have leafed through the little volumes of his pastor's journals covering a period of eight or ten years he would, with reasonable luck, have come upon nearly all the peculiar ideas delivered from the pulpit since Waldo Emerson became pastor. The sermons presented in a somewhat more religious garb the diarist's favorite doctrines of compensation, self-reverence, and the rest. A sermon against foolish, counterfeit pride said that "The good man reveres himself, reveres his conscience, & would rather suffer any calamity than lower himself in his own esteem." Another sermon declared that physical things were chiefly significant as symbols; another, that heaven was here and now; another, that the moral sentiment, perceiver of right and wrong and therefore the sovereign part of man's nature, existed in the mind independently of experience; another, that there was a "law of progress, that on-look of human nature, which is its distinguishing & beautiful characteristic." Others asserted freedom of the will in spite of all determination from outside, or the Quaker doctrine of the inward light with its implication that "the bible has no force but what it derives from within us." Jesus, the preacher explained, had no authority as a person. The delivery of the same truths Jesus uttered would have invested the humblest created spirit with the same authority, no more and no less.

In some of the later sermons the pastor defined more precisely ideas he had often used before. "A trust in yourself," he said in his one-hundred-and-twenty-third sermon, "is the height not of pride but of piety, an unwillingness to learn of any but God himself." If self was to be trusted *"the origin of self must be perceived."* Half a dozen sermons more and he was experimenting with new phrases to underscore self-reliance in its more obvious sense. He asserted that "what you can get of moral or intellectual excellence out of this little plot of ground you call *yourself,* by the sweat of your brow—is your portion." For his one-hundred-and-fortieth sermon he sharpened some of the old saws on friendship he had gathered from Montaigne, Goethe, and Aristotle. His experience with his own brothers may have helped him understand the difficulty of finding a real friend. "Few men communicate their highest thoughts to any person . . . because they do not find persons proper to receive them," he told his congregation.

His hearers must have been struck by his habit of regarding man as divine. His calling in witnesses to truth wherever he could find them and without caring whether they had ever been associated with the Christian

tradition had its justification in the common divinity of men. "Moses &
Socrates & Confucius & Fenelon," he said from his pulpit, "think the same
thing. Justice love purity truth are intelligible to all men, & have a friend
in the bottom of the heart of every man." If he took such liberties in the
pulpit, it was natural that in the privacy of his study he now turned more
frequently to the great writers. He became more familiar with literary contemporaries or near contemporaries, such as Wordsworth and Coleridge.
After long, intermittent stirrings of curiosity, he was awakening to Goethe.
He was getting an introduction to German literature through the anonymous articles Thomas Carlyle had long been publishing in British periodicals. He thus saw a more attractive side of German genius than the
theological scholars of Göttingen could ever have shown him. But before
he could get very seriously at either Thomas Carlyle or the Germans he
had drifted into a life-shaking crisis.

From the start he had had his doubts about the ministry, but his family
connections were mostly like anchors holding him to it—Ruth Emerson,
Aunt Mary, Doctor Ripley, Samuel Ripley were certainly so. Probably
Ellen, while she lived, was a persuasive argument for his keeping a regular
profession. But by October of 1831, some eight months after her death,
his religious doubts were beginning to be strengthened by a positive dislike
of the church. He noted in his journals "how little love is at the bottom of
these great religious shows; congregations and temples and sermons,—how
much sham!" He feared that "Calvinism stands . . . by pride and ignorance; and Unitarianism, as a sect, stands by the opposition of Calvinism.
It is cold and cheerless, the mere creature of the understanding, until controversy makes it warm with fire got from below."

Soon he was bored with the week-day Biblical lectures. He had now
finished the twenty-second since the opening of the new vestry and had
got over twenty-five chapters of *Matthew* by dint of skipping several of
them. Plans for the series called for thirty-six lectures. He had to help with
the course of Sunday evening lectures that Unitarian ministers of Boston
combined to give during the winter months. He and his college classmate
Motte commonly alternated from week to week as hosts. He did not see
how the world could get on without such institutions as the church, but
he was weary of being imprisoned in it. It was "the best part of the man,"
he sometimes thought, "that revolts most against his being a minister. His
good revolts from official goodness," he confessed with bitterness. "If he
never spoke or acted but with the full consent of his understanding, if the
whole man acted always, how powerful would be every act and every
word. . . . The difficulty is that we do not make a world of our own,
but fall into institutions already made, and have to accommodate ourselves

to them to be useful at all, and this accommodation is, I say, a loss of so much integrity and, of course, of so much power."]

✠ He began to consider seriously whether he could not really cut and run without too much loss of dignity. This was in February, nearly a year after his wife's death. Within a few weeks, Aunt Mary, alarmed, was pleading with him to remain in the ministry as his ancestors had done and so leave a name to be "enrolled with the Mathers & Sewalls of that venerable City" of Boston. Some three months later he struck Charles, back from his first voyage to the West Indies in pursuit of health, as stagnating and needing to be jolted. Charles said, "He suffers like most ministers from being too much sheltered & treading too uniform a track—there is danger of growing exclusive & fastidious & losing some faculties of action." Waldo himself would have mostly agreed with this diagnosis, though it did not go deep into his real malady. It seemed to him that a thinker desperately needed to be unfettered in order to keep up with truth. Truth, said the apothegm he copied into his journal, never is but is always becoming. By June he was more outspoken. At times it seemed to him "that, in order to be a good minister, it was necessary to leave the ministry." It could all be reasoned out convincingly in the light of his belief that truth was a living, changing thing. "The profession," he put it, "is antiquated. In an altered age, we worship in the dead forms of our forefathers. Were not a Socratic paganism better than an effete, superannuated Christianity?" He was ripe for revolt.

It was probably about this time that he wrote the Second Church a letter, now apparently lost, "stating," as the church's committee reported, "a change in his opinions concerning the ordinance of the Lord's Supper, and recommending some change in the mode of administering it." Exactly what change he asked for is not clear, but presumably he wanted to be relieved of his own responsibility as administrant of the rite. There were far more fundamental objections to the ministry on his mind; but the Lord's Supper was a public ceremony, not an abstract idea, and therefore an issue that would easily be grasped by his parishioners. Perhaps he also thought the Lord's Supper a good point at which to begin reforming because it was an old subject of controversy. Though Unitarians generally wanted to keep the sacrament as a sacred feast, they were apt to feel that in other hands than theirs it easily became a superstitious practice, and they had long been uneasy about it. Waldo Emerson's father had worried over it in his day and had once had some indefinite plan to liberalize its observance. Waldo's brother William had within the last few years had some debate with Doctor Ripley on the same subject.

A seven-man committee, which included the minister's second cousin

George Emerson and his close friend George Sampson, took his proposal under consideration, but, though extremely conciliatory, could not "regard it as the duty of the Church to consent to any change in the mode of administering the ordinance." On June 20 or the following day a meeting of the church, held at the pastor's home, unanimously voted acceptance of the report of the seven. The letter which formally notified Waldo Emerson of this action was undoubtedly sincere in expressing the hope that the report might "meet with your acquiescence, if not with your entire approbation." The door was by no means shut in his face.

His brother William's question of seven years earlier whether the pastor should sacrifice his influence rather than his conscience now loomed large. There is no reason to doubt that Waldo at once made his decision to stick by his conscience; but he presumably wanted time to make sure what conscience had to say, and he must have nursed a hope that the church would after all come round to his own view and give him leave to be as liberal as he wished. At any rate no decisive action on his part was necessary at the moment, for the church building had to be closed for six weeks while repairs were being made. In company with Charles he promptly set out for Maine. After a week with Aunt Mary at Waterford he went with her and Charles to the neighboring town of Fryeburg. There, on the shores of Lovewell's Pond, as an old ballad related, a bloody battle had been fought with the Indians in colonial times. But now there should have been deep peace among the mountain and river intervals of this secluded part of the world. Aunt Mary remained at Fryeburg while her nephews went on into the New Hampshire wilds as far as Conway. There Charles turned back, leaving Waldo "under the brow & shaggy lid of the White Mts. boarding at a comfortable little house of a private family—His health . . . improved—His spirits pretty good—"

Charles returned home with the impression that his brother might yield a little. Underestimating Waldo's stubbornness, he said that "enough has now been done, (perhaps too much) for the expression of individual opinion, & I hope his own mind will be brought to the persuasion that it is his duty to stay where he is & preach & pray as he has done & administer the ordinance as nearly as he conscientiously can, in accordance with the faith & wishes of his pious parishioners—" Doubtless this was the argument that Aunt Mary had dinned into Waldo's ears at Waterford and at Fryeburg.

In the seclusion of Conway the rebellious minister thought that among the mountains one should see the errors of men more calmly and wisely. He was going back for a second Sunday at Fryeburg and was jotting down things he might decide to say from the pulpit there: "Religion in the mind is not credulity, and in the practice is not form. It is a life. It is the order and soundness of a man. It is not something else *to be got,* to be *added,* but is a new life of those faculties you have. It is to do right. It is to love, it is to serve, it is to think, it is to be humble." He was simply grinding religion down to morals, as he now habitually did.

Some days later he was at Ethan Allen Crawford's house in the Notch of the White Mountains. Aunt Mary was apparently with him there for a time but soon wrote him a farewell letter. She seemed to be ceremoniously casting him off; but her sentences were so incoherent that even he, used as he was to her cryptic style, must have been puzzled. His mood changed, and in his preoccupation with his personal concerns he wearied of these mountains whose summits were always covered with clouds. He was left with "a circle of woods to the horizon, a peacock on the fence or in the yard, and two travellers no better contented than myself in the plain parlour of this house."

Fate managed to take the heroics out of his crises. He realized that it was at last the hour of decision. But he saw both sides too clearly to feel any exaltation. "It seems not worth while," he reflected, "for them who charge others with exalting forms above the moon to fear forms themselves with extravagant dislike." The most desperate scoundrels had been the overrefiners. Society could not exist without some accommodation. Yet Waldo Emerson had really made up his mind long ago, and there was no changing it. Through with cogitation, he was ready for a climb up Mt. Washington. He timed himself as if he were testing his strength, and his record was good. The climb he made from Crawford's to the summit usually took from four to six hours. It took him four hours and fifteen minutes.

Before the end of July he was back in Boston, doubtless with the manuscript of his sermon on the Lord's Supper all but ready to preach from. It was promptly put to use as family reading while he tried to recover from a sudden and annoying disorder. Charles explained to William that Waldo "is for this last day or two troubled with a diarrhœa which he is nursing lest a worse thing come upon him." Though the trouble was perhaps merely the result of nervous tension, there was reason to be careful. What worse disease the minister feared Charles did not say, but within a few weeks many Bostonians were seized with panic at the prospect of a cholera epidemic and an association was formed to see that the sick were not forsaken.

When the church was open again, at the beginning of August, the pastor, still sick, had to call in substitutes for three Sundays. Looking ahead, he saw that the final Sunday of the month would be the regular time for communion, and he was determined to escape that. He arranged to exchange pulpits on that day and postponed his sermon on the Lord's

Supper to September. His health might have made him unfit for the ordeal at the Second Church anyhow. On August 19 he told Aunt Mary that though he "came home stronger & fatter than for years" his complaint had "stripped" him "to bones."

His mind was already on plans for the future in case separation from the church should be final. His faith in his philosophy of life was not disturbed. "I can only do my work well," he warned Aunt Mary, "by abjuring the opinions & customs of all others & adhering strictly to the divine plan a few dim inches of whose outline I faintly discern in my breast." The prospect looked "gay & glorious" to him. "So," he said, "I will sing the hymn of hope in light or gloom for a time or forever as pleases Heaven." He was content that Ellen was "beyond misfortune" and resolved that he would "not invite any others to penury & disappointment if I am doomed." He also revealed to Aunt Mary his vague notions of how he might begin a new life devoted to literature and philosophy: "I am entering into acquaintance with Goethe who has just died. The Germans think there have been but three men of genius—Homer, Shakspear, & Goethe. If I go into the country to books, I shall know him well, & you will come & board with Mother & me, & we will try him whether he deserves his niche. S. A. R. grieved he shd. die because he & Mme de Stael were suited to this world. The Germans regard him as the restorer of Faith & Love after the desolations of Hume & the French."

In early September, Edward, home for a short time to visit and to buy merchandise to take back to Porto Rico, found Waldo gradually recovering his strength and preaching again. On the 9th the embattled pastor read the long-expected explanatory sermon to a crowded house. It was a simple, restrained statement. Upon examination of the Evangelists, it appeared that Jesus, in beginning the rite of the Lord's Supper, was merely celebrating the Passover with his disciples. His remarks at the time were nothing but the figurative language he was constantly using. St. Paul, the person really responsible for perpetuating the rite, probably labored under the mistaken notion that Jesus would shortly come a second time. Thus the modern observance of the Lord's Supper was without valid authority. It was also positively harmful. It clothed Jesus with authority he never claimed. It was unsuited to modes of Western thought. It ought not to be observed even if Jesus had enjoined it. Forms in general were essential, but to exalt particular forms and to adhere to one form a moment after it was outgrown was unreasonable. Jesus himself had sought to redeem religion from formalism.

The minister, having given these reasons against the rite, said that he would be content to let others observe it till the end of the world but that he himself was simply not interested and would therefore not go on with it. As the prevailing feeling in the church favored the rite, he would soon resign his office as minister. This was substantially all he had to say. It seemed to have some effect. Charles believed that if the parish were polled three-fourths of the votes would favor keeping the minister on his own terms, but he was sure no such poll would be taken because some of the most influential men, the authoritative core of the church, adhered to the ordinance.

By this time Waldo Emerson had written an uncontroversial letter of resignation. While he waited for an answer to this, he seems to have had some reason to think arrangements might still be made to keep him. But there was no solid ground for such speculations, and any possible arrangement could hardly have given him the freedom he found necessary. Late in September he and his mother rested for three or four days at Hopkinton Springs, in Hopkinton, Massachusetts, and he doubtless tried the effect of the three local varieties of mineral water on his ailment. While Waldo still waited for news from the authorities of the church, Edward began, on October 6, his return voyage from Boston to Porto Rico. As Edward sailed past Nantasket and on toward the cape, he wrote two farewells, a note brought back by the pilot and a poem, "The Last Farewell."

> Too soon those spires are lost,
> Too fast we leave the bay,

he wrote in what sounded like his own epitaph.

On October 21 Waldo preached once more in his old pulpit. Any of his hearers who imagined that he was going to retreat a little and so perhaps prepare the way for a refusal of the church to accept his resignation must have been completely disillusioned by the tone of this sermon. The whole discourse was simply another encomium of self-reliance. Waldo Emerson was attacking formalism and the authority of institutions and traditions.

He already knew something of Fénelon and may have been braced by the Frenchman's teaching that the soul, in the climactic experiences of the religious life, does not need the aid of form and method. He had had his mind much of late upon the Quaker George Fox and managed to quote him in this sermon without suggesting a parallel with his own case. He probably found it difficult to forgo some mention of Martin Luther, for he was also thinking of him in this crisis. Not quite a week after he preached the sermon, he wrote, with an old copy of *Fraser's Magazine* open before him, this pertinent reminder: " 'Luthers words were half battles.' At Worms to the Diet he said 'Till such time as either by proofs from Holy Scripture or by fair reason & argument I have been confuted & convicted I cannot & will not recant. It is neither safe nor prudent to do aught against conscience. Here stand I, I cannot otherwise. God assist me Amen!' " The unsigned article from which he copied these sentences had been written by Thomas Carlyle. The harassed pastor had been admiring other anonymous work of Carlyle, on whom he commented, "He gives us confidence in our principles. He assures the truth-lover everywhere of sympathy."

Kindred minds of Europe's past and present seemed to conspire to encourage the rebellious American. Coleridge, Wordsworth, and Carlyle suddenly became more substantial persons in his eyes, persons he might think of meeting in their homes. On the afternoon following the preaching of his last sermon he gave his pulpit to a clergyman named Brown, an English Unitarian planning to settle in America. The Englishman came to dinner in Chardon Street the same day, a fortunate circumstance, for he was full of British literary gossip. According to Charles, "He told about Coleridge (who *is* an opium eater) & about Carlisle the author of the Characteristics article—a German bred scholar—he had been in Wordsworth's library, a fine room . . . in its prospect of hill & lake scenery . . ." Charles, no more ignorant of the world of Goethe and Schiller than were most cultured Americans at the time, looked on with curiosity while his brother studied the Germans through Carlyle's eyes and waited for the church to take final action.

"Waldo," he commented, "has been of late very much a reader of translations from the German—Schiller & Goethe—& the articles on German literature written by Carlisle in the English magazines—some of the translations are very noble—a story from Goethe & a character of the true scholar, the man of genius, by Schiller. Goethe seems to have been a sort of Homer—a Child a Favorite of Nature—to have accomplished a vast orbit in his own intellectual & moral history, to have past through the greatest changes & come in the end to a cheerful & Christian Faith. A poor scholar whom he had been kind to said of him that 'his heart which few knew, was as noble as his genius which all knew'—"

On October 28 a meeting of the Second Church's proprietors which Abel Adams and some other good friends of the pastor refused to attend voted thirty to twenty to grant the pastor's dismission but temporarily continued his salary. It turned out that the ex-pastor got the salary for the rest of the year but had to supply the pulpit at his own expense.

A few weeks after the final act of the church, his mental crisis seemed past. He told his brother William that the severing of the strained cord was a relief and that he saw peace and freedom some distance ahead of him. His head was by this time full of projects "of action, literature, philosophy." He dreamed of establishing a successful magazine. With the help of his lawyers William and Edward, and of Charles, just now sworn in as an attorney of the Court of Common Pleas, he thought he ought to make such a scheme work. It would take a few months to get it started, he thought. Yet for the moment his obstinate diarrhoea made it impossible for him to accomplish anything. The malady became so threatening that he was advised to voyage. At first he thought of going to the West Indies to spend the winter with Edward, "but in a few hours," as he told William, "the dream changed into a purpureal vision of Naples & Italy."

After the acceptance of his resignation he ceased to preach at the Second Church. He wanted to go back to say his formal farewell, but he had frequent relapses and was "as white & thin as a ghost." He was compelled to send his last message to the members of his parish in the form of a printed letter, dated December 22, 1832. In the letter he showed no resentment yet did not fail to include a reminder of the firmness of his purpose. When his former parishioners read his declaration that he did not care to live anywhere longer than he had liberty to seek and utter truth, they must have taken it to mean that he would never be a regular minister again. He had done all that he could well do in the narrow mahogany pulpit. He needed more elbowroom.

Others could perform the routine duties of parish priest better than he, and for the present he had finished with the extraordinary religious pronouncements he had wished to make. Some of his theses would have been quite too radical for the rebellious monk and university professor Martin Luther to post on Wittenberg's church door—that what was worth while in religion was simply moral truth, that any man who could see truth was as divine as Jesus ever was, that self-reverence was God-reverence. But the most courageous doings of the pastor of the Second Church had not required any physical daring and had not been cleverly dramatized. As he had nailed up his theses one by one there had been no great commotion in Hanover Street, Boston; and he had had the bad luck to attract a crowd only when he was posting his objection to the Lord's Supper, one of his weakest efforts and one that he later remembered with disgust.

He had to be content with little more credit than his conscience could give him. In the *Evening Gazette* Miss Eliza Townsend asserted that he had been a beloved and admired pastor and bade him farewell on behalf of "all who were privileged with knowing such a signal example of devoted integrity, eloquence and disinterestedness." Probably most of the parishioners who stuck by him to the end did so more from personal liking than from any enthusiasm for his reforming notions. The comment of the town ranged from heartfelt professions of loyalty to him, there can be no doubt, to the hints of his insanity that came to the ears of his friend Frederic Hedge. Some of the citizens just then much excited over the phrenological lectures Spurzheim had recently given in Boston were presumably confident that an examination of the ex-minister's bumps of self-esteem and destructiveness would confirm their more charitable suspicions.

Of his family, to him his most important critics, William could not have failed to understand him, and toward the end Charles must have abetted what seemed to others an ill-timed exhibition of obstinacy. Grandfather Ripley seems to have been persuaded that he was really insane. Aunt Mary, with all her insistence on her own private right to perfect liberty of thought and action, had fought tooth and nail against her nephew's apostasy. She kept, underneath her frowning exterior, a strong faith that she would one day see him "rising from defeat into new ground" and that, as she said, his mazy path would end well. But she was both sad and scornful as she thought the whole crisis over. After Waldo had got well out into the Atlantic and was safe from her sharp tongue and her keen eye "that went through and through you like a needle," she relieved her feelings in a letter to Charles:

"Still I am sad while I write. It is like—it is far sader than the translation of a soul by death of the body to lose Waldo as I have lost him. And now that he is far far away I can complain. I do believe he has no fixed faith in a personal God! His letters have been confused & dark—a mixture of heathen greatness—of worse than antient good heathenism—pantheism—Swedenborgianism—hypotheisis of nature & german rationalism. And *yet yet* you talk of his being a '*reformer* & needing good health.' A reformer! and beginn at the wrong end? annuling a simple rite w'h has bound the followers of Jesus together for ages & announced his resurrection! A reformer—who on earth with his genius is less able to cope with opposition? Who with his good sense less *force* of mind—and while it invents new universes is lost in the surrounding halo . . . No, he never loved his holy offices—and it is well he has left them. . . ."

12.

A FOOL'S PARADISE

❊⊛❊

Travelling is a fool's paradise. . . . I pack my trunk,
embrace my friends, embark on the sea and at last wake up
in Naples, and there beside me is the stern fact, the sad
self, unrelenting, identical, that I fled from. . . .
—"Self-reliance"

EMERSON sailed on Christmas Day. He did not choose the day but
merely went when the ship was finally ready after several false
alarms. Some disgruntled parishioners who had heard his recent
sermons may have wondered whether his departure on that particular anniversary was not ill-omened. To the sharp eye of the realistic
and experienced Captain Cornelius Ellis of the brig *Jasper* ill omens of
another sort were plain enough. In the captain's opinion, the ex-minister
of the Second Church was too sick to survive a winter crossing of the
Atlantic. The *Jasper,* on which he had purchased passage with the help of
his mother and of his staunch friend Abel Adams, did not have comfortable
quarters for even a man in robust health. She was doubtless the same
Jasper that had earlier been used to transport mules on the West Indian
run out of Boston, and no one would have expected luxury in such a vessel.
On the present voyage she carried, besides her own scanty 236 tons, a
cargo of logwood, mahogany, tobacco, sugar, coffee, beeswax, cheese, and
other freight. Her passenger list contained the names of five persons all told.

After the second morning out, every one of the five passengers was
confined to his dreary cabin, suffering from nausea and the anticipation
of going to the bottom. In this predicament, with the pleasures of memory
as his sole remaining resource, Emerson fell back on his old favorite Milton's
"Lycidas." But when the tempest showed signs of subsiding he and some
of the other passengers came from their holes till a new blow sent them
scurrying back again. The other passengers turned out to be Silas P. Holbrook, Mrs. Holbrook, Miss Holbrook, and their friend Samuel Kettell. As
Mrs. Holbrook "never went on deck" and Miss Holbrook seems to have
been inconspicuous, the two men of their party, together with Captain
Ellis, must have supplied almost all the society Emerson enjoyed during the
long voyage.

168

Despite such meager opportunities, Emerson may have engaged in some literary conversation, for both Holbrook and Kettell were, about this time, among the hackwriters who worked the literary treadmill of the Samuel Griswold Goodrich known to youthful readers as Peter Parley. During the voyage Kettell, a clever linguist, was amusing himself principally by turning a Parley book into modern Greek. One did not easily get beyond the limits of the great Parley empire. In little Malta, where the ship was now bound, one could expect to come upon a Maltese printing of what at least purported to be a foreign language version of Parley's geography. But Kettell had other claim to distinction than that of being a translator and writer for children. Only a few years earlier he had supplied Goodrich's older readers with a three-volume anthology of verses written in America from the earliest colonial times to the date of publication. As his countrymen were now showing a national spirit in their literature, it was time, he had argued, to "look seriously into the grounds of the insinuation thrown out some years ago by our neighbors across the ocean, that there was no such thing as an American book worthy of being read." To the ex-minister thinking of turning author but still quite without literary reputation, Kettell's ideas would have been threadbare but would have promised some conversation.

By the 5th of January the brig was in warmer waters. Emerson was the only person on board who was pleased when she sauntered through a calm day at a knot or two an hour. But he read little and did nothing. When he tried one of Goldoni's numerous plays he was bored. He had brought along some of his brother William's guidebooks, and probably he had in his cabin the Italian dictionaries, as well as the mattress, that he had begged of William. If the storms recurred he cared little. In spite of Captain Ellis's gloomy prediction, the invalid of a few weeks before thanked the sea and rough weather "for a truckman's health and stomach." But he was still poet enough to feel imaginatively both the arrogant power of the tempest and the insinuating charm of the ocean's quiet moods. He could recreate vividly the times when the little ship was driving, as he said,

> with naked spars
> Before the roaring gale,
> Hemmed round with ragged clouds . . .

or the reeking cabin was cold and wet, the masts strained, the sail torn, the gale blowing fiercer as the night set in, the seaman aloft scarcely able to master his struggling reef. When a calm sea relieved the monotony of the storms, he rode as a cloud over the purple floor with mists for company, felt the warmth of the water, and far below saw the motes of light by day and the streams of fire by night.

On the night of the sixteenth day of the voyage a black hummock of land, Santa Maria, the southernmost of the Azores, loomed up through the thick weather. Ten or eleven days later the little vessel passed into the Mediterranean and had on her port side the cold summits of Spain's Sierra Nevada and, nearer, white villages rooted halfway up the slopes of snow-covered hills. For the first time the traveler stood face to face with the Old World.

Physically Emerson was a new man. According to one story, chicken pox that had been suppressed in his early childhood broke out in the form of numerous boils during the voyage and so was finally disposed of, leaving him perfectly well. The boils may have been more real than the chicken pox, but, whatever the explanation, the benefit of the voyage to the sick traveler was indubitable. A few years later he could authoritatively advise his public from the lecture platform that there was such a thing as necessity of change for the sake of health and that this was the chief use of the sea voyage, "so sanative to exhausted bodies."

Though *The Malta Government Gazette* duly announced the *Jasper's* arrival on February 2, 1833, the passengers had two more weeks' board to pay to Captain Ellis before they could leave the quarantined brig. Half a month of their precious time was thus idled away in Valetta's Marsamuscetto Harbor. But the quarantine was merely a routine matter, having nothing to do with the actual state of health of the Americans; and on the 15th they took lodgings on shore and began their exploration of the island of Malta, finding it a box of curiosities. Pleased with this first glimpse of the Old World and glad to enter at its little end, as he put it, Emerson forgot his scruples against travel and opened his eyes and ears.

Past centuries spoke from the crowded buildings clinging to the gnarled finger of stone which separated the two harbors of Valetta. The sharp contours of the city offered views of the precipitous sides of basins deep down in which floated the vessels of various nationalities. A mass of swarthy people, many of whose ancestors had lived in Malta when it was an ancient Phoenician colony, seemed about to burst the incredibly tight urban boundaries. The warm-colored interior of the Cathedral of San Giovanni seemed full of memories of the great order of the Knights of Malta, once Christendom's defenders against the Mohammedans. In the dim vault Emerson saw the tomb of the Grand Master de l'Isle Adam, the gallant warrior who had received the island from the Emperor Charles V after the knights had been driven from Rhodes by the Turks. There, too, was the tomb of Grand Master de la Valette. He had fought the Turks often and had even served as their galley slave before he turned them back from Malta and built the fortress city that bore his name. Flanking the cathedral aisles were the chapels containing monuments of both masters and knights. There the unity that had made all formidable against the enemies of the cross had finally been renounced. Each nationality now jealously kept its dead in its own particular chapel.

The American traveler, struck by the rich decoration of Maltese churches, hoped that before the end of the century New Englanders would "carve and paint and inscribe the walls" of their somber places of worship. He yielded himself easily to "the religious impression of holy texts and fine paintings." In spite of his having no ear for music, he was also pleased by the swelling cathedral organ and the chanting of the friars. But his mood changed. He had already detected over a convent gate an inscription promising full indulgence, daily and perpetual, for both the living and the dead. He comforted himself by attending services in an obscure chapel where he heard the English Bible read, Watts's dependable psalms sung, and a Protestant sermon preached.

At the governor's fancy dress ball in the old palace where the grand masters had once lived and where his admired Coleridge had served the British government of Malta, Emerson had his first glimpse of European society on parade. It seemed to him that the few beautiful women were worth going far to see. He had got his invitation to the ball from the American consul, and the ball may have resulted in his call on Mrs. Davy. Whether he went to her house merely for sociability or in the hope of getting inspiration for his study of science is not clear. At her home, at any rate, he seems also to have met her husband, a brother of Sir Humphry and himself a chemist. But meantime, for the most part, Emerson had kept close to Kettell and the Holbrooks, staying with them at Vicary's, just across the Piazza San Giorgio from the palace, during the week or so he spent in the island after being released from quarantine.

Having seen Malta, the five former passengers of the brig *Jasper* hired the little brigantine *Il Santissimo Ecce Homo* and had a swift passage to Syracuse in the island of Sicily. In that ancient city Waldo Emerson found lodgings in the tiny Via Amalfitania. The house was possibly the same where Count August von Platen, the Bavarian poet who loved Italy and Sicily better than Germany, came to die a few years later. "VENNE IN SIRACUSA E IL 5 DICEMBRE 1835 MORI IN QUESTA CASA," said the stone tablet placed there long afterwards. Emerson could see Mt. Etna from a window "& the tomb of Archimedes & the Ear of Dionysius from the house top."

Syracuse proved to be "a poor grey shabby place, the ruin of ruins," neither the capital of the Mediterranean world it once was nor the pleasant half ancient, half modern large provincial town it later became. Wars and earthquakes had changed the face of things, yet Emerson liked to be here where great men had lived. In Syracuse, if history not always separable from legend told the truth, even tyrants had had the good sense to invite such guests as the dramatist Aeschylus, the poet Pindar, and the philosopher Plato to their courts. Dion, though he had finally earned his violent death, had once been a disciple of Plato and worthy of such a master. Timoleon, coming from the mother city of Corinth to deliver Syracuse anew from a Greek tyrant and later from the Carthaginians, had lived out his life as one of the cleanest and most fortunate leaders of the ancient Greek world. The fame of such men was kept green in the writings of Plutarch and Cicero; and at length Wordsworth, a poet Emerson had much on his mind, had conferred new distinction on Dion as a lost leader. For a scholar, Syracuse, though now in its fallen state shrunken into the little island of Ortygia, was worth a long voyage.

Well outside the narrow boundaries of the city of 1833 lay the ruins of the theater and of the amphitheater. Near these were the quarries; and, far to the west, along the plateau, extended the walls of Dionysius, converging into a massive fortress. Many centuries ago the power of Athens in the ancient world ebbed away as thousands of her young men were slaughtered on the slopes of the Epipolae or were consigned as prisoners to a worse fate in the quarries. For the quarries, though later masked in shrubbery and flowers, were a living death to the Athenians herded into them without protection from sun or weather. The whole extent of ancient Syracuse was a monument to the stupidity of man quite as much as to his heroism.

Gods, too, once played here their little parts, hardly worse than tragicomic, and were worshiped in the temples. The remains of one such pagan place of worship still stood, imbedded in the walls of the Christian cathedral, to symbolize the triumph of the new religion over the old. Across the main harbor, on a hill bordering the marshes that were the bane of more than one besieging army, one saw the ruins of the temple of Olympian Zeus; and not far away the creek of Cyane was flowing from the same fountain of Cyane into which Persephone's friendly nymph was transformed as a not too harsh punishment for her interference in the love affairs of her betters. On the shore in Ortygia was the fountain of Arethusa, a nymph saved by Artemis from the long pursuit of a river god and allowed to bubble up here in peace. Her fountain was crystal-clear like Cyane's but was now gathered in a basin polluted by the washerwomen of the city.

Emerson felt the strong pull of the mythical and historical past and would have liked to be scholarly. Undoubtedly he knew the sense of unity one could get from things that had been a part of the experience of the race but had dropped out of its conscious memory. He wrote home: "I want my Virgil & Ovid. I want my history & my Plutarch. I want maps & gazetteers." He and his friends rode with the American consul into the country and explored the relics of the greater ancient city. He remembered Cicero's description when he visited the quarries. One of these had been taken over by the Capuchins and turned into a garden. The traveler grew mellow under the smiles of the friendly monks and was so struck by the peaceful air of the convent that he all but accepted the "little neat room with a few books" which the padre offered to give up to him as a home. "How good and pleasant to stop and recollect myself in this worn-out nook of the human race, to turn over its history and my own," Emerson mused. But he kept an eye open to the actual. He took a boat across the harbor and up the Anapo River, but not far enough to enter the Cyane and feel the charm of the strong, narrow current with its rank papyrus thickening and threatening to put an end to the hard upstream rowing. Having seen nothing more notable in the Anapo than "canes and bulrushes and snails, and a very little, narrow, mean puddle to be famed in song," he crossed the fields to the temple of Zeus that was "enriched with the spoils of the Carthaginians 2500 years ago" but could now boast only a few broken columns.

On the last day of February, Emerson, Kettell, and the Holbrooks started by mule and on foot a thirteen-hour journey over the forty-odd miles to Catania. In the north rose Etna. Into Etna's crater, according to one story, Empedocles of Girgenti, reputed both a democrat and a divinity, threw himself in the hope that his disappearance would be interpreted as a translation to the world of spirits. In verses of unknown date the philosophic Emerson honored Empedocles as being indeed partly divine. Round the shore of a magnificent bay the travelers straggled and stumbled with their tinkling mules and shouting drivers. One weary mule slipped into the mud and was got out with difficulty. Another fell with the litter in which the ladies were riding.

Catania, a city whose pavements, with a large part of her buildings, had come out of neighboring Etna, was, in contrast to Syracuse, thronged with people, a city of the living; yet the landmarks of antiquity could still be traced there. In such a city there were several sharply contrasting worlds, and Emerson passed abruptly from one to another. He took a letter of introduction to the rich Benedictine monastery, where he arrived in time to witness the semiweekly dole to the poor. He saw "hundreds of women and children in the yard, each receiving her loaf and passing on into a court, that none should come twice to the basket." If he visited the medieval cathedral, he also saw the ancient baths and the ancient theater. When he attended the opera he commented, "It is doubtless a vice to turn one's eyes inward too much, but I am my own comedy and tragedy."

After three days of Catania he took the road to Messina, traveling by coach with several Sicilians, Itellario, priest of the church of St. Iago in Messina, Itellario's two nephews Lorenzo and Gaetano, and the tailor Francesco Nicolozi. The great kindness of his companions could not keep his conversation with them from being a comedy. He had much overestimated his knowledge of the Italian language, and as for conversing with Sicilians in their own peculiar dialect, he concluded that he might as well be with Arabs.

In the morning, from Giardini, he saw Taormina above him, a balcony overlooking this end of Sicily. Arriving at that impressive height, the traveler was amply rewarded for his pains. There, from the Graeco-Roman theater, roofed only by the sky as its ancient architects had intended, one looked out upon the unforgettable panorama of mountain and sea dominated by Mt. Etna. The little town had a fresh surprise ready whenever the visitor passed round a corner into a piazza or climbed up a circuitous strada to a higher level, and it added to the wild landscape human warmth and color that were appealing. Emerson had half a mind to be a fisherman and draw his nets at the base of Taormina's cliffs the rest of his days.

Between Taormina and Messina, through "the most picturesque country, I judge, that for the same extent is anywhere to be found," he had his Sicilian companions again and must have heard their "O che bella veduta!" repeated many times. At Messina the earthquakes had left few antiquities for him. He drank tea with the American consul and his wife, and philosophized as he noted the bustle and noise of the populace on the Sicilian shore of the strait. Humanity was much the same everywhere to "the poor hermit who with saucer eyes" had "strayed from his study." He saw Kettell and the Holbrooks once more, it seems, and settled financial accounts with them.

Setting sail on March 6, he passed between Scylla and Charybdis. In the afternoon he saw the smoke of the volcano Stromboli and, as night fell, its faint tongue of fire. In the morning he felt the unique spell of Palermo, lying in the long voluptuous curve of shore and mountains. In the mood of a docile traveler, he saw the notable places in the city and viewed the panorama of sea and land from Monreale. He studied what this foreign culture had to offer. "Art was born in Europe," he wrote, "and will not cross the ocean, I fear." He seems to have troubled little about the political condition of Sicily. American superiority was upheld by the consul and his wife. They lived socially quite apart from the Sicilians. But in the Palermo press there had recently been news reports not calculated to increase Emerson's patriotic pride. There was trouble between South Carolina and the federal government, and there were more ominous disagreements between North and South.

The manners of the Palermitans kept the transatlantic visitor wide-eyed. A lady invited him to go with her for a ride, though the day was stormy and the coach was therefore covered. On their return the bewildered traveler accompanied her into her house but was not invited to dine, whereupon he made his obeisance, paid his half dollar to her coachman, who waylaid him on the stairs, and walked home through a drenching rain. He liked the Capuchins, the most esteemed of the Catholic clergy, but even in their convent his pleasure was less than perfect. One of the monks conducted him through the long aisles lined with hundreds of grinning skeletons of Capuchins, here an abbot, there a general of the convent, every one with his name tag hanging at his breast. The monk explained that he himself would one day take his place there among his dead brothers. Emerson, through some misunderstanding, was next conducted to an insane asylum. No wonder that the world he saw in the Palermo opera seemed unreal until what struck him as a touch of natural passion transformed the whole scene and turned his pity for "the performers in their fillets and shields and togas" into admiration. As the steamer *Re Ferdinando* sped toward Naples he lay in his berth and tried to recall the manners of the prima donna and the other singers.

During his two weeks in Naples the city was crowded with foreigners, and he was forced to live in unpleasant quarters. In vain he changed from what was doubtless some obscure garret of the magnificent Chiaia to a new room. It apparently required much reading of Goethe and perhaps of other books borrowed from a circulating library at a carlin a day, and many tours up and down the Villa Reale, to keep his mind off his "black lodging in the Croce di Malta." He was lonely and cold. Guides and thieves, he learned, were sometimes the same persons. One day he had his pockets picked twice and thereafter began to behave, he thought, with tolerable composure.

By now he had become bellicose in his resistance to the claims of places and objects that took for granted an easy triumph over every traveler. "I won't be imposed upon by a name," he resolved. But in spite of all annoyances he was teachable. Naples gave him his first opportunity "of seeing any original of the great statues of antiquity," he confessed. For him it was "more than meat & drink to see so many princely old Greek heads." There was "The picture gallery too. Five genuine Raffaelles & Guido & Titian & Spagnoletto each of which you may safely admire without risk of its being a *copy*." The former Unitarian pastor was, as in Malta, delighted by the beauty of the churches. And if San Carlo's opera was closed on account of Lent, if the temple of Venus at Baiae was a cooper's shop and asses brayed in it, and if the Lucrine Lake was "not above three times the size of Frog Pond, nor quite three times as pretty," he found other things to make up for them.

His experience on Vesuvius and in its neighborhood made a story he thought good enough to save up for a lecture audience. At Resina his party, once more including the Holbrooks and Kettell, left the coach and proceeded on donkeys but had to climb the final stretch with staves straight up through loose lava and cinders. The region of the crater was warm, and the wind blew the smoke in their faces almost to suffocation as they looked down into the red and yellow pits which were the navel of the volcano. At Herculaneum little progress had been made with the digging, but a fourth of Pompeii was already open and Emerson walked into the ancient houses and shops. Anticipating the partial reforms of later excavators, he saw how the show was spoiled by the carting away of statues and utensils to the museums and thought it "a pity they could not be left here in their place at least in a single house it would make so impressive a spectacle."

Incidents of the visit to Naples, such as his seeing the corpse of an officer "dressed out in his regimentals, powdered & pomatumed, & sitting up in the bier, going to his own funeral," fixed themselves in his memory, but he was most impressed with the slightness of the change travel caused in the traveler. In the pause before the service in the English ambassador's chapel he realized that nothing was altered with him except the place. He summed up his objections to travel, the "thousand petty annoyances," the unrealized plans for study and disappointed hopes of good society. "Still," he admitted, "though travelling is a poor profession—bad food, it may be good medicine. It is good, like seasickness, to break up a morbid habit, & I sometimes fancy it is a very wholesome shaking for me."

On March 25 he paid his fare from Naples to Rome. Riding day and night in company with two Bostonians, Warren and Grant, and a couple of English people, he crossed the Pontine Marshes without being attacked either by malaria or by robbers. As he passed the Coliseum he had his introduction to the grandeur of ancient Rome. He may have settled immediately in the Hotel di Gran Bretagna, on the Piazza di Spagna. Holy Week was at hand and people were crowding into the city to witness the pomp of the church. Emerson purchased an old copy of *Officium Heb-domadæ Sanctæ juxta Formam Missalis, et Breviarii Romani sub Urbano VIII* and was ready for the ceremonies of the eight days beginning with Palm Sunday and ending with Easter.

On Palm Sunday at the Sistine Chapel he counted twenty-one purple-robed cardinals as they filed in with their attendant priests; saw the pope enter in his scarlet robes and with his bishop's miter and the cardinals presently coming one by one to kneel before the throne and kiss the pontiff's hand; and watched the attendants replacing the robes of the cardinals with gorgeous copes of cloth of gold. The blessing of the palms and the chanting of the passion, the distribution of palms and olives, and the spectacle of the pope riding aloft in his chair of state at the end of the ceremonies were strange to the eyes and ears of a New England Unitarian in 1833.

On Wednesday afternoon he was in the Sistine Chapel again. As the plaintive and melodious strain *"Miserere mei, Deus"* came out of the silence and darkness he found it touching. Everything was in good taste, he thought, and the setting was Michelangelo's chapel. He was more struck by mere liturgical forms than he had expected to be. On Thursday he watched the learned and able Gregory XVI wash the feet of thirteen pilgrims, one from each Christian nation, the American pilgrim being from Kentucky. At night, as he heard the *Miserere* sung once more in vast St. Peter's, he was probably unaware of the presence of a young Englishman, John Henry Newman, still a member of the Church of England. Presumably at the same moment with Emerson, this future cardinal was listening with sur-prise to the beauty of the voices but disapproving in his heart what he called the degrading religion of Rome.

On Good Friday, Emerson witnessed religious processions in which the marchers, muffled in black, carried staves surmounted with death's-heads. On Easter Sunday, when the whole festival season came to an end, he heard the pope say mass in St. Peter's and was pleased to see the pic-tures and statues divested of the curtains. At noon he saw the pope in the great window over the principal door of the cathedral, giving his bene-diction. The bell tolled, the drums beat, the trumpets sounded. Then, as the pope rose and spread out his hands and blessed the people, "All knelt as one man. He repeated his action (for no words could be heard), stretch-ing his arms gracefully to the north and south and east and west, pro-nouncing a benediction on the whole world. It was a sublime spectacle."

So thought the American, keeping his extreme Protestantism quite un-harmed while he watched and listened for the unforgettably beautiful or pathetic parts of such ceremonies. To him the most pathetic sight in Rome was probably a ceremony at the church of Trinità de' Monti, wherein some nuns were taking the veil—"youth, beauty, rank, thus self-devoted to mistaken duty," he commented.

By the middle of April the reluctant traveler, though still willing to trade the most imposing city "for one man such as were fit to walk here," was obviously under the spell of the place as he listed its historical and artistic riches. "Here is the town of centuries, the capital of the ancient & of the modern world. All is large, magnificent, secular, & the treasury of the arts is evidently the contribution of the whole civilized world. I have been here three weeks & my eyes are now familiar with the objects whose forms in pictures & models & casts are familiar to all Christendom. I see almost daily the Coliseum, the Forum, the Pantheon, the Apollo, the Laocoon, the Gladiator, besides St. Peters, & the Transfiguration & the last Judgment. By degrees the topography of the old City arranges itself in my head & I learn to find not only a Church or a picture, but even a shop or a trattoria, by referring it to the Column of Trajan or the Arch of Constantine. It is a grand town, & works mightily upon the senses & upon the soul. It fashions my dreams even, & all night I visit Vaticans."

The Vatican was for him "an endless collection of all precious remains of ancient art; a quarter of a mile of statues, with branching galleries. And here too are Canova's works," he went on with his inventory of the pope's and Rome's treasures. "Upstairs one story are the chambers of Raffaelle containing his world renowned frescoes; go up another story, & you enter the picture gallery where is the Transfiguration & its rainbow companions. All this unrivalled show is thrown open twice in every week, & our due feet never fail. At the other end of the town is the Capitoline Museum & Gallery also open twice in the week. Then on common days, we may go to Thorwalsden's Studio, or to Gibson's or to Wyatt's (English sculptors) or to the Quirinal Hill, & see the reputed statues of Phidias & Praxiteles, or to any of a dozen palaces, each a picture gallery, or to some church . . . & so on & so forth, to the end of the Guide book, & the end of the year. Ah great great Rome! it is a majestic city, & satisfies this craving imagination."

He began to cultivate opinions of his own about masterpieces of art. He fell in love with Raphael and stuck to his preference for "The Transfiguration," a more triumphant discovery of man in the very act of demonstrating his divinity than the stories of Dion and Empedocles had afforded. It was the world's foremost picture, if he was to be judge, and not because of any astonishing blaze of beauty resulting from some fortunate bright combination of colors and forms, but because of "this familiar, simple, home-speaking countenance." In the Vatican he admired Raphael's rooms enough but, with a gesture in the direction of functionalism, declared that "It was a poor way of using so great a genius to set him to paint the walls of rooms that have no beauty and, as far as I see, no purpose." He would not allow even the claims of originals over copies when he thought the claims exaggerated. When he came to the "Apollo" and the "Laocoön" he remarked, " 'T is false to say that the casts give no idea of the originals. I found I knew these fine statues already by heart and had admired the casts long since much more than I ever can the originals." Starting out with little more than complete frankness to build up a theory of art, he wanted some facts to go on. He wanted to know "the place of all these works in the history of art; how this vase and that statue were designed, what the sculptor and what his patron thought of them, and the marks of the eras of progress and decline. But now," he said, "they amaze me and beget a vague curiosity which they cannot satisfy, nor can any living man."

He saw that the cafés were filled with English, French, and German sculptors and painters, but he naturally wanted to observe artists in the act of creating art, and not simply eating and drinking. He was struck by the pathos of the young beginner's lonely lodgings littered "with sketches and canvas and colour-bags." Doubtless he discussed art with the companions he found in Rome. He knew an Englishman named Kingston, Lewis Stackpole from home, Anna Bridgen and her sister from Albany, some young Livingstons of New York. The Bostonians Warren and Grant went with him to visit the Danish Thorwaldsen's studio. He may have had something to do with his countryman Nathaniel P. Willis, a facile writer of travel sketches, then in Rome. He got great pleasure from his excursions with a young John Cranch, an American art student resident in the city. He liked William Wall, of New Bedford, and perhaps had some discussions with Francis Alexander, another American. Both Wall and Alexander were painters.

For Emerson literary Rome turned out to be mainly Renaissance and modern and as much English as Italian. He ascended Monte Gianicolo to visit Tasso's tomb in the out-of-the-way church of Sant' Onofrio and saw the poet's death mask, with its "air of independence & genius," in the neighboring convent. Remembering Shakespeare, he looked for Pompey's statue at whose base Caesar fell. When he visited the church of Aracoeli he remembered, with only a little confusion of localities, the English Gibbon and his history of the Roman decline and fall. At night, as he wandered in his dreams among statues and fountains, he was introduced to the late Lord Byron, a great benefactor of Italy. Possibly he knew that in the Piazza di Spagna John Keats had died not many years before, but he doubtless knew little of Keats's verse. It was by mere accident that he found in Rome one other link with English literature. At an evening party given by a college mate he met Gustave d'Eichthal, member of a family of Jewish bankers at Paris, and next day received from him a letter to John Stuart Mill in London. The letter asked Mill to introduce Emerson to Thomas Carlyle. Meantime Emerson kept in mind Goethe's enthusiastic commentary on Rome and rated it as truth.

Ending his visit in the capital of the ancient world, where he had been, as he said, "in better health than ever since I was a boy," he set out on April 23 for Florence. With him, it seems, rode Wall, Robert M. Walsh of Philadelphia, Brantz Mayer of Baltimore, an Irish priest named O'Flan-agan, and Dracopoli, a Greek student returning home after ten years of study. The carriage required five and a half days, for the 150 miles sepa-rating Rome and Florence grew into a much greater distance along the circuitous route through Città Castellana, Terni, Foligno, Assisi, Perugia, Cortona, and Arezzo. At Foligno, long since stripped of Raphael's madonna to which the town gave its name, Emerson saw the devastation of the earthquake of the preceding year. Apparently he had no time for the memorials of St. Francis at Assisi. During a cold evening at Passignano, on the shore of Trasimeno, he had leisure to remember the ancient duel between Hannibal and Rome. He did not forget that Arezzo was the birth-place of Petrarch.

But Florence was his chief objective, and within a few days after his arrival there he was settled in the Piazza di Santa Maria Novella, ready for a long stay. He had brought with him a letter to Henry Miles, an American merchant resident in the city. Miles took some trouble to act as his adviser and companion. Emerson also had Wall for society, and it seems that Anna Bridgen and her sister turned up again.

The weather was growing hot, but the city of art and letters could still be attractive. There were retreats from the heat in the Cascine in the evenings and in the Boboli Gardens; and good streets, industrious citizens, spacious and well-furnished lodgings, and elegant and cheap cafés made life more comfortable here than elsewhere in Italy. Erminia, the flower girl, came to your café every morning. If you did not buy flowers of her she would give them to you. Flowers by day, and at night there was singing along the streets. When it was time to light the lamp in his room, Emerson could expect Giga to come and repeat with him the same courteous formula, which made only a slight draft on his small Italian vocabulary. Then she would leave him to his reading of Goethe and Sismondi and to sleep. In order to get information for use in daylight he had to study at night. "Then so inveterate," he wrote home, "is my habit of depending upon my books that I do not feel as if my day had substance in it, if I have read nothing. So I labor at German & Italian a little." He finished Manzoni's pious but charming *I Promessi sposi*. Even though at least partly fictitious, people like Fra Cristoforo went a long way to balance the "hideous anecdotes of the depravity of manners" one continually heard. Emerson, only a beginner even in the conventional bookish Italian, must have struggled through the recent novel in its original northern dialect, as the Tuscan recension was not yet published.

His daily excursions took him well over Florence and her suburbs during his month there. His patriotism and his inherited Puritanism sometimes rose in revolt. His Protestantism waxed strong as he surveyed the whole ecclesiastical world of Italy and what he called its idolatry, "producing as it does of course the other extreme of unbelief & loosest morals." He even ventured to lump politics with religion and customs in general. He wrote to a former parishioner that the way to learn to value American churches, government, and manners was to come to Italy. But the physical charm of Florence mastered all his scruples. "And wherever I go," he said in his diary, "I am surrounded by beautiful objects: the fine old towers of the city; the elegant curve of the Ponte Trinità; the rich purple line of the Apennines, broken by the bolder summit of the marble mountains of Carrara. And all, all is Italian; not a house, not a shed, not a field, that the eye can for a moment imagine to be American."

As at Rome, he delighted in both museums and churches. The old churches of Florence at first struck him as too plain to compare with those of Rome, but familiarity made them grand in his eyes. His appreciation was undoubtedly helped by the long tradition of the Tuscan city's own pride in its treasures. Santa Croce seemed to him "not a Florentine, no, nor an European church, but a church built by and for the human race," and the Duomo was "like an archangel's tent." When he tried to test the best-known works of art without respect to their fame, he decided that the judgment of the world was well founded. The Medici "Venus" was his prime favorite.

As in Rome, he wanted to see art in progress as well as of the past. American artists in Italy were old hands at welcoming travelers who might prove to be buyers. But whether or not Emerson was mistakenly regarded as a potential customer, he justified his visit to one studio when he began a long-lived friendship with the sculptor Horatio Greenough. He continued his new habit of studying the opera. Yet when he witnessed Bellini's *La Straniera,* he was more curious about who and what the prima donna was in real life than about what became of her according to the libretto, as this Greek beauty strongly resembled a lady he knew in America. He doubtless saw more than he heard. His eyes, at any rate, were so much dazzled by the light and colors that he was obliged to look at his shoes for half an hour. Remembering Goethe's plea for an impersonal evaluation of art, he tried, though in vain, to be tolerant to a ballet between acts.

He called on the astronomer and microscopist Giovanni Amici and saw the famed optical instruments. He had had a recurring ambition to be a scientist. Now, it seems, he watched while Amici performed experiments on polarized light. But in this region the living celebrity he cared most to see was the author of *Imaginary Conversations*. It was doubtless through Horatio Greenough that he got his invitation to the villa near suburban San Domenico di Fiesole. At the dinner table there he heard Landor do justice to Montaigne but, shockingly enough, refuse to praise Thomas Carlyle. At breakfast in the same villa a couple of days later Landor was again erratic. Emerson had the uncomfortable feeling that the Englishman was trying hard to escape from his proper character of intellectual in order to behave like a man of the world. "Sincerity, in the highest sense," the disillusioned Emerson concluded, "is very rare. Men of talents want simplicity & sincerity as much as others." Even Walter Savage Landor could not be allowed to say with impunity that "Socrates was a vulgar sophist."

On May 28, after writing a hasty leave-taking note to Landor, Emerson said farewell to Florence. The Holbrooks had caught up with him again, and they, together with William Wall and a Philadelphian named Thomas Stewardson, were his traveling companions on the road northward. Stewardson seems to have pumped the ex-minister's mind vigorously. He was shocked by the pantheistic notions he brought up. But presumably the conversation turned more often to Italian art than to unorthodox philosophical ideas. On the five-day journey to Venice the party passed through Bologna, Ferrara, and Padua, towns whose rich art could be a commonplace only in Italy. From Monselice, on the rim of the Euganean Hills, Emerson looked out with untroubled delight over the great plain. It was like a sea with cities for islands. Venice, with its islands that were not imaginary, was dimly recognizable on the horizon. Some years earlier the reforming poet Shelley, seeing almost the same magnificent spectacle from the hills not far from neighboring Este, had been stirred to anger at the complacently tolerated Austrian tyranny. Near Battaglia, Emerson, with his companions, left the carriage and walked to Arqua to see the house and the tomb of Petrarch. At Padua he visited the university and, in a room like a hollow inverted cone, he watched as Professor Caldani lectured on anatomy from a subject. At Mestre the travelers boarded a boat for Venice. From a certain distance Venice looked like nothing but New York, and at first the Grand Canal was simply the highway leading to a hotel, the Gran Bretagna, close to the Piazza of Saint Mark.

Emerson thought that in the full moon the piazza was a world's wonder, but he pitied the people who, though not beavers, were compelled to live here. He was in a gloomy mood. Probably he was brooding over some awkward moment he had had with Stewardson or with one of his other fellow travelers. He reflected bitterly that he had no skill to live with the generality of men and seldom found the exceptional man he was looking for. "It seems to me," he repented, "no boy makes so many blunders or says such awkward, contrary, disagreeable speeches as I do." But he dutifully accompanied his party, making the rounds of Venice during these mild, cloudy days. He saw that the paintings were glorious, that the churches surpassed all those of Florence in splendor, that the city had had its great moments. But musing over the disgraceful historical record on the walls of the Ducal Palace, he made up his mind that the rule of the Austrians was "merciful to that whose story is written here in stone and iron and mire." Cary, the translator of Dante, was just ending a visit of some two weeks with his love for the city of canals still "on the increase," and Richard Monckton Milnes was regretfully taking leave after many months in "this bright and congenial atmosphere"; but Emerson, apparently not having the good fortune to meet the Englishmen and certainly without their knowledge of Venice, was soon ready to go. The government, keeping a watchful eye on strangers, had thought it worth while to record in the *Gazzetta privilegiata* his arrival with his party on June 2 and likewise made a note of his departure with them for Milan just two days later.

Setting out from Mestre with the same trusty driver who had brought them from Florence, the Americans passed through Vicenza and Verona. The travelers were very companionable now and in a holiday mood. On the third day they had their three hours of nooning at Desenzano. Across the narrow corner of Lago di Garda, at no great distance from them, lay the little peninsula of Sermione, where the ancient Roman poet Catullus had once lived. But they gave their chief attention to the modern Desenzano villagers, who were celebrating Corpus Christi. Every house had "hung out its quilts and damask and brocade"; and at the altar of the church were the little girls made up as angels in white dresses with wings. The Italian towns were all different and all picturesque. Everywhere the people were lovers of the beautiful. The peasant wore a scarlet cloak or tied a red garter or knee-band to his leg or wore flowers in his hat or buttonhole.

By good luck the travelers saw Milan from the coach of a friendly count who was not afraid to talk and took no pains to conceal his hatred of the Austrian government, "so jealous, so rapacious, which holds Italy down by the pointed cannon." Emerson seems to have hunted up many of Milan's masterpieces of art, including "The Last Supper" of Leonardo. He praised the cathedral and, remembering Manzoni's novel, did honor to the ashes of Carlo Borromeo beneath the great Gothic building. But he was beginning to tire of architecture, concluding that it was all imitation and that none came up to his idea of real greatness. He seemed to be groping toward the theory, not unrelated to Plato's idealism, that the supreme artistic act was in the mind of the artist. It was, he said, in the soul that architecture existed, and Santa Croce and the Duomo were only poor imitations. As he had earlier demanded a philosophy of painting and sculpture, he now wanted one of architecture.

After a few days of Milan he and Wall and Stewardson, together with Anna Bridgen and her sister, with whom they had once more caught up, posted along the shore of Lago Maggiore and crossed over Napoleon's Simplon into Switzerland. The wheel of the diligence was "chained and shod with a heavy log of green wood" as they went down the northern slope to the valley of the Rhone. Emerson, having taken his place on the outside by day, was compelled to ride there through the cold night with the scant comfort of a shawl lent by one of the women inside. The road followed the shore of the Lake of Geneva, through Clarens and past the Castle of Chillon to Lausanne. There Emerson inquired his way to Gibbon's house, where the history had been finished. The steamboat brought him and his friends to Geneva; and Calvin, Rousseau, Voltaire came to mind. He went to see the château at Ferney, in spite of his dislike of "the king of the scorners." On the 17th of June the Americans left Geneva by diligence. Three days later they arrived in Paris and took lodgings in a hotel on the boulevard Montmartre. Apparently Emerson soon moved to a cheaper place close by, where he was at *pension* with a number of Americans. This place may have been what he described as the *"pension . . .* at the corner of *Rue Neuve Vivienne."* There, "directly over the entrance" of the Passage des Panoramas, he was certainly established a little later, and there he was sufficiently near the geographical and institutional center.

He was hardly in the mood to go Parisian. His old prejudice against the French was not lessened by his weariness of travel. What he had liked most about Italian cities was their totally un-American, old-world character, a new experience for him. The French metropolis was becoming modern. It was taking thought for the comfort of its some 800,000 inhabitants. In the summer of 1833 there was even talk about lighting the streets with gas; and the public prints discussed "Improvements and Embellishments," including not only better monuments but better pavements and sidewalks.

The spirit of progress was in the air, but this was not what Emerson had come to Europe for.

The determination of his traveling companions to make him admire the city did not help matters. He was impatient at not discovering men and ideas. A true memoir of his travels so far would, he decided, read thus: "A man who was no courtier, but loved men, went to Rome,—and there lived with boys. He came to France, and in Paris lives alone, and in Paris seldom speaks. If he do not see Carlyle in Edinburgh, he may go to America without saying anything in earnest, except to Cranch and to Landor." He wanted to learn to speak French but generally had to converse with English-speaking people. He unfortunately met a good many acquaintances from Boston. He found his cousin Ralph Emerson. He made a call on Oliver Wendell Holmes, a medical student. He attended a Fourth of July dinner with ninety-eight of his countrymen and saw "the grand Lafayette, but not much else."

Yet this was only a small part of the story, and in the end Paris, except for antiquities and art, gave him more to ponder than any other European city had done. He need not have regretted that he had taken his lodgings for a month. Parisian books and journals, art, drama, opera, politics, religion, scholarship, and science were ready to be examined by the intellectually curious.

If "the poorest Frenchman" could "walk in the kings garden every day" or "read if he chuse, in the kings library—wide open—the largest in the world, or in the Mazarine library, or in several more," Emerson soon found that, though a foreigner, he had the same privileges. In the libraries and in the numerous cheap, well-stocked reading rooms he could get an advantageous view of the state of civilized man, perhaps even a better perspective of America than at home. If he looked into the reviews in the *Journal des débats,* he could see through French eyes the distressing picture of his country drawn by the harsh but just Mrs. Trollope or he might learn Continental sentiments regarding his friend Murat's astonishing defense of American slavery. He might also read the new instalment of a review of Gustave de Beaumont and Alexis de Tocqueville's study of the American penitentiary system and its applicability to France, a harbinger of de Tocqueville's great book on democracy in America.

Though it was not Rome or Florence, Paris also had a variety of museums, such as the Louvre and the Luxembourg, open on certain days of every week. The Louvre had all Italy to compete with and so was at a hopeless disadvantage; but even the Italian Leonardo was best represented here, and here Emerson saw Murillo "almost for the first time."

Emerson turned zestfully to the drama and opera. "More than twenty theatres," he counted, "are blazing with light and echoing with fine music every night, from the *Académie Royale de la Musique*, which is the French Opera, down to the Children's Drama; not to mention concerts, gardens and shows innumerable." On the day of his arrival Delavigne's somewhat Shakespearean play *Les Enfants d'Édouard,* new that year, was receiving its twentieth performance at the Théâtre-Français, and the public was still eagerly crowding to see it. On the same evening, at the Porte Saint-Martin, *La Tour de Nesle,* the sensational melodrama by Dumas *père,* first produced in the preceding year, was to be given for the last time. During the American visitor's four weeks in Paris theatergoers could witness such good things as *Iphigénie en Aulide* and *Marie Stuart* and such a brilliant old comedy as *Le Mariage de Figaro.* Operas were plenty, among them being *Guillaume Tell, Robert le Diable,* and *Fra Diavolo.* Auber's very new *Gustave III,* too elaborate to be performed frequently, was repeated during this July with "all the chief personages of song and dance" participating. Emerson, witnessing a performance of it, was struck by the good taste and imposing effect of the dancing and by the brilliant scenic decoration. In *Les Enfants,* he thought Mlle Mars, though she spoke French beautifully and had the manners of a princess, hardly excelled her supporting cast.

French politics was in the air as well as in the newspapers. The citizen king Louis-Philippe had arrived at the Tuileries the day after the American traveler had reached Paris. The Chamber of Deputies had barely ended its sessions. Thiers, Arago, and M. de Broglie had taken part in the debates. But the Three Glorious Days, now three years in the past, had not been, so far as Emerson could see, the beginning of a millennium. Politics now "spoiled conversation & men in France," he complained. "Cousin has quit Plato & M. Arago his magnet & galvanic battery since those unlucky 3 days. And to such paltry purpose. The press to be sure is free & says the sauciest things every day but otherwise the government has very much the character of the old government & exiles shoots or imprisons whom it pleases."

Emerson sampled the unorthodox religious notions of the Parisians. If he was just now revolving in his mind the dim idea of an independent church with himself as pastor, he got little comfort from hearing Châtel, founder of the Église Catholique Française. This was a curious institution whose priests wore newly invented dresses and at whose services martial music was performed by a large orchestra, relieved by interludes of vocal music with piano accompaniment. Châtel, sometimes eloquent, might rate as a Unitarian but was more radical than anybody who wore that label in America. Emerson, coming to this conclusion, felt sympathy for him but already had well in mind a liberalism of his own outside any church. "I feel myself pledged," he made up his mind in Paris, "if health and opportunity be granted me, to demonstrate that all necessary truth is its own evidence; that no doctrine of God need appeal to a book; that Christianity is wrongly received by all such as take it for a system of doctrines,—its stress being upon moral truth; it is a rule of life, not a rule of faith."

In the long, low-winged and domed stone palace of the Institut de France, Emerson had the good fortune to be introduced into a séance of the class of science, and the conspicuous men were pointed out to him —Biot, Arago, Gay-Lussac, Jussieu, Thénard. One piece of business at this meeting of July 8 was the official reception of Pradier's bust of Cuvier, a timely honor to the great comparative anatomist, dead little more than a year. Emerson had only to present his passport in order to open the doors of any public institution in this hospitable city, and he seems to have made good use of his privilege at both the Sorbonne and the Collège Royal. He had hardly arrived in Paris, it seems, before he had bought their miniature semester announcements, at two sous apiece, of Papinot, the bookseller in the rue de Sorbonne. Reading "these splendid news" in the Café Procope, as he afterwards remembered, he had felt a young intellectual's delight at such invitations to knowledge and "straightway joined the troop of students of all nations, kindreds, and tongues" drawn together "to listen to the first *savans* of the world without fee." Among the lecturers listed in his printed program of the Sorbonne were Guizot on modern history and Cousin on the history of ancient philosophy; but these, and the other notables, had alternates. No less a person than the philosophic de Gérando was announced as lecturing on law at the Place du Panthéon near by. The Collège Royal offered a remarkable group of professors and courses, including Jouffroy on the Greek language and philosophy and Thénard on chemistry. Emerson certainly listened to both Jouffroy and Thénard.

At the neighboring Jardin des Plantes he found the specimens arranged as nearly as possible according to Jussieu's system. Here Gay-Lussac taught general chemistry, and there were other courses. But it was the botanical garden itself, and especially its cabinet of natural history, that gave Emerson one of the memorable experiences of his life. His mind seemed to leap forward with a new vision. The significance of the whole display seemed suddenly to gain clarity for him as if it were a hard problem that had solved itself while he slept. The "beautiful collection" made him "as calm and genial as a bridegroom." This experience was one thing he had got from his travels that the natural history society at home might care to hear about. If he looked at his subject too poetically, he could at least appeal to his fellow enthusiasts for sympathy on the ground that "we have all a presentiment of relations to external nature, which outruns the limits of actual science," and with the confidential admission that "except to Naturalists I might hesitate to speak of the feelings it excited in me."

What he said a few months later to his lecture audience, after making these preliminary apologies, simply put into prose poetry his experience at the Jardin des Plantes: "The universe is a more amazing puzzle than ever, as you look along this bewildering series of animated forms, the hazy butterflies, the carved shells, the birds, beasts, insects, snakes, fish,—& the upheaving principle of life every where incipient, in the very rock aping organized forms. Whilst I stand there I am impressed with a singular conviction that not a form so grotesque, so savage, or so beautiful, but is an expression of something in man the observer. We feel that there is an occult relation between the very worm the crawling scorpions & man. I am moved by strange sympathies. I say I will listen to this invitation. I will be a naturalist."

One would like to know whether, as Emerson examined the memorable fifteen rooms, he had any realization of the irony of fate in giving him through Cuvier's painstaking classification of skeletons an imperfect glimpse of the theory that Cuvier had so consistently opposed. Cuvier seemed to make his presence felt here. His house still stood in this garden, and he was being praised on every hand now that he was dead. In this same year a biography of him that Emerson soon knew plainly stated the great scientist's answer "to those who believe in the indefinite alteration of forms in organized beings, and who think that, with time and habits, each species might have made an exchange with another, and thus have resulted from one single species." Cuvier had defied the theorists to point out the missing links between extinct and surviving species.

And one would also like to know how much, if any, first-hand knowledge Emerson then had of "those who believe in the indefinite alteration of forms." Years earlier he had had a premonition of the havoc which "the full and regular series of animals from mites and worms up to man" might work among religious dogmas. If he had not got hold of Lamarck by 1833, he had either got from some other source an idea resembling Lamarck's or pieced together something vaguely suggestive of a Lamarckian theory out of his own observations. He may have discovered helpful hints in an English translation of Herder's outlines of the philosophy of history, a book he had once borrowed. He probably knew something of Lamarck. At any rate he was now so far advanced that he was sure to get such knowledge without undue delay. Some three years later he was to tell a lecture audience in unmistakable terms that the "system of La Marck aims to find a monad of organic life which shall be common to every animal, & which becomes an animalcule, a poplar-worm, a . . . mastiff or a man, according to circumstances. It says to the caterpillar 'How dost thou, Brother! Please God, you shall yet be a philosopher.' "

These, Emerson commented, were "extreme examples of the impatience of the human mind in the presence of a multitude of (separate) facts, & the energy with which it aims to find some mark on them according to which they can all be set in some order." But such examples did not really seem extreme to so poetical a scientist as he. The normal state of his own mind in the presence of the provoking mysteries of nature was impatience and a bold desire to solve the problem of the one and the many. That state of mind was the essential condition of his experience in the Jardin des Plantes. That he saw in the show before him something besides a hazy vision of evolution is also plainly deducible. He may have got a new sense of the old doctrine of the correspondences between physical and intellectual or spiritual. But that at least a vague acceptance of the much debated theory of evolution was also a part of the experience seems more certain.

After all, Paris had paid him good returns on his investment of four weeks of his time, and he was ready to leave the city with mental baggage noticeably weightier than he had brought out of Italy. On July 18 he and Francis Alexander, one of the American painters he had found in Rome, climbed into the diligence, a conveyance that mercilessly sacrificed its drowsing passengers to the demon of speed. After riding all night through St. Denis and Beauvais, they had breakfast at Abbeville, and reached Boulogne about sunset. At Boulogne they boarded the steamer for England. In the early light of Sunday, July 21, Emerson saw without surprise the highly cultivated fields along the Thames, then passed Greenwich, docks, arsenals, and fleets of shipping, to land at the Tower Stairs in London. As it was only about seven in the morning he and Alexander met few persons till they reached St. Paul's. With a porter to carry their things they walked through Cheapside, Newgate Street, and High Holborn, and found the lodgings at a Mrs. Fowler's, in Russell Square, to which Emerson had been directed by an American traveler of his acquaintance.

Emerson came provided with a number of introductions he had got from William Pratt, his brother Edward's college chum, and from d'Eichthal. Within a couple of days, it seems, after his arrival on English soil he carried d'Eichthal's letter to John Stuart Mill, at the India House, and Mill accordingly wrote a formal introductory note for him to present to Carlyle. But, as Emerson of course did not know, Mill also sent a separate letter directly to Carlyle, putting the responsibility for the recent introductory note squarely on d'Eichthal's shoulders. Emerson, he said, appeared to be a reader and admirer of Carlyle's writings and so might get some good from the meeting he asked for, but, after one or two conversations with him, Mill did not think his presentee a very hopeful subject. And this was just the opinion that might have been expected from Mill. For whatever the conversations were ostensibly about, his logical mind, crammed with utilitarian philosophy and a variety of economic and political theories, would naturally have provided an extremely unfortunate half hour for one who had little skill in logic, knew little of economics or politics, and had already described Utilitarianism as a "stinking philosophy."

For Emerson, the visit to Carlyle and a meeting with Coleridge were the chief unfinished business. He seems to have had little appetite for London. "Immense city, very dull city," he commented, thus establishing his own uncomfortable status as a young traveler on the mere surface of London. But there was some life in London even for so casual a visitor.

Though the theaters were at a low ebb, the American traveler might have cared to see his compatriot John Howard Payne's *Clari; or, the Maid of Milan* at the Royal Victoria. There were music and dancing. Vincenzo Bellini's operatic version of the Romeo and Juliet story, his *La Sonnambula*, and his *Norma* were all to be heard, as well as *Otello* and another piece of Rossini's. Madame Malibran was singing. Through late July and early August, Paganini, the man who, as Emerson later remarked, could "extract rapture from a catgut," kept giving additional performances on his violin. Young Fanny Elssler and her sister were still dancing at the Theatre Royal, Covent Garden, when Emerson arrived in London.

Whatever attention Emerson paid to such theatrical events, the drama that most impressed him was the funeral of Wilberforce, the popular hero of many a battle for abolition of the slave trade and the friend of parliamentary reform and Catholic emancipation. In the streets the immense crowds testified to the significance of the occasion. At Westminster Abbey there were the Lord Chancellor, the Speaker of the House of Commons, and the Duke of Gloucester, all receiving the coffin at the door; the king's boys, the Westminster School boys, and the various groups of choristers enjoying their moment of importance; the temporal peers, led by Sussex and Wellington; the clergy, led by the Archbishop of Canterbury; and Sir Robert Peel among the commoners.

Perhaps at Mill's suggestion, Emerson visited Doctor Bowring and was taken by him to Jeremy Bentham's house and shown, with veneration, the garden walk and the rooms of the Utilitarian philosopher. Emerson, though far from subscribing to Bentham's doctrine that morality consisted in being useful, was given a lock of the great man's hair and an autograph. Bentham had died hardly more than a year before. Bowring, his literary executor and editor, wanted him to be "admired & loved in America." Emerson, with an unfeigned interest in literary landmarks, "walked in the garden, on one side of which is the house in which Milton lived when he was Cromwell's Secretary." Hazlitt once "occupied it a little while, & placed a stone upon it, with the inscription *John Milton—the Prince of Poets.*" The American traveler, still caring more for Unitarianism than for Utilitarianism, promised to dine with Bowring to meet the Unitarian Lant Carpenter. He also had an introduction to a man he might have caught a glimpse of in Rome or Venice—Cary, the British Museum's assistant librarian and Dante's translator.

Lant Carpenter was not the only preacher Emerson cared about. He went to hear both the extremely liberal Unitarian W. J. Fox and the brilliant free lance Edward Irving, then near his untimely end. If Emerson was ignorant of how Irving had once been entangled in the destinies of the Carlyles, he undoubtedly knew that the Scottish preacher had propounded such heresies as the humanity of Jesus and so had been put out of the Church of Scotland. He was only one of the many strangers attracted to the private church in Newman Street, London, where Irving now entertained all comers. With "a play-book in one hand, and a Bible in the other," as William Hazlitt once aptly described him, Irving boldly walked the tightrope of popular favor. The diminutive Fox, in spite of his equally fluent speech, his more pleasing voice, and his more animated and beneficent face, could not compete with such showmanship, and doubtless only such a serious-minded traveler as Emerson would discover him. Emerson's ecclesiastical curiosity, however, took him little farther than the dissenting chapels. He admired Westminster Abbey and visited and revisited it. At St. Paul's he saw a service in progress. "Poor church," he wrote in his journal.

Yet to him the most interesting person in London or its suburbs was Samuel Taylor Coleridge, and Coleridge, though once a Unitarian, as he confessed with shame, had turned out to be a tireless advocate of the Church of England. On the morning of August 5 Emerson set out to see his hero. Arriving at Highgate, he at length found somebody who could show the way to Coleridge's retreat, the Gillman home. A note requesting permission to make a call brought the reply that the poet was still in bed but would see his visitor after twelve o'clock. Returning at one, Emerson was confronted by a short, thick old man with bright blue eyes, fine complexion, and a torrent of talk.

Coleridge began with the Americans he knew, praising the painter Washington Allston, then passing to Doctor Channing, whose Unitarianism he regretted as an "unspeakable misfortune." Picking up a book which his visitor suspected had been laid on the table for the occasion, he read with great vehemence two or three pages of manuscript notes written by himself in the flyleaves, passages that struck Emerson as being out of *Aids to Reflection.* As soon as he stopped for a second to take breath, Emerson "remarked to him that it would be cowardly in me, after this, not to inform him that I was an Unitarian, though much interested in his explanations. Yes, he said, I supposed so & continued as before." The indefatigable talker went on for nearly an hour. Much of the conversation, almost completely monopolized by the old poet, "was like so many printed paragraphs in his book, perhaps the same, not to be easily followed."

Emerson had seen his man but had found him "old and preoccupied" and unable to "bend to a new companion and think with him." If the exploration of Landor's mind at close quarters had been disappointing, the discovery of the great Coleridge's limitations must have been far more so. Lack of health had driven Emerson to travel, but, having decided to travel, he came to Europe, at least so he afterwards reasoned it out, mainly because of the attraction of "Coleridge, Wordsworth, Landor, De Quincey, and the latest and strongest contributor to the critical journals, Carlyle." "If," he added, "Goethe had been still living I might have wandered into Germany also." But Goethe was dead, and now there remained only De Quincey, Carlyle, and Wordsworth to be seen. Within a few days after his return from Highgate to London, Emerson was on his way to Scotland and the Lake Country.

He traveled rapidly. He visited Kenilworth and Warwick Castles with his relative Orville Dewey, the New Bedford pastor. It may have been next day as he passed northward that he saw "Tamworth tower and town" and remembered almost accurately some of the lines of *Marmion* that he had learned as a schoolboy. He visited Matlock, "close by the Derwent, and under the eaves of the caverns of the Peak of Derbyshire." From Sheffield he went on to York, where he must have made a hurried visit to the cathedral.

He arrived in Edinburgh on the 16th of August with a letter of introduction to some person who "was then so much engaged in professional duties, that he was unable to spare even a few hours to do the honours of the old Scottish metropolis." The too busy professional man managed, however, to persuade a friend, Alexander Ireland, as good luck would have it, to take the young American in tow.

On Sunday, Emerson was in the pulpit of the Unitarian Chapel in Young Street, Edinburgh. Ireland, pleased by the visitor's sermon, was sure "that nothing like it had ever been heard" in that chapel before. Many hearers did not know what to make of the unconventional visitor. But it was not only Emerson's original thoughts but "the consummate beauty of the language in which they were clothed, the calm dignity of his bearing, the absence of all oratorical effort, and the singular directness and simplicity of his manner, free from the least shadow of dogmatic assumption" that made a lasting impression on Alexander Ireland.

The enthusiastic guide showed his guest "the courts of law and other places of interest to a stranger," and together they ascended Blackford Hill, where, in his boyhood, Walter Scott used to lie and listen to the "murmur of the city crowd" and "Saint Giles's mingling din." The old and new towns spread out on either side of Princes Street and the gardens under the protection of the castle, with Calton Hill and Arthur's Seat as formidable outposts, were rich in interest for any visitor that cared for literature or history. Not only well-versed in Walter Scott but acquainted since college days with Dugald Stewart and the Scottish philosophical school, Emerson must have understood his Edinburgh as few other American travelers could have done.

But Scott and Stewart were of the past. Emerson had his mind on certain living British writers. In spite of the revealing encounter at Highgate, he had kept his respect for Coleridge. For Alexander Ireland's benefit he discoursed on *The Friend* and the *Biographia Literaria*. "He considered that there were single sentences in these two works, which embodied clearer ideas of some of the most subtle of human speculations than are to be met with in the pages of any other thinker." He spoke of De Quincey, but apparently did not see him. He had a strong determination to visit Carlyle and Wordsworth. "Am I," he asked, "who have hung over their works in my chamber at home, not to see these men in the flesh, and thank them, and interchange some thoughts with them, when I am passing their very doors?" In 1833 Carlyle had returned from retirement to live for a time in Edinburgh, but he had soon disappeared again from the city, and it was only after persistent inquiries made in the wrong quarters that his whereabouts were learned from the secretary of the university. The information the secretary gave made it certain that the American traveler's itinerary would next point toward Dumfriesshire, in southwestern Scotland, as its chief objective.

On August 21 Emerson sailed up the Forth from Edinburgh's port of Leith to the historic castle town of Stirling in weather so bad that he kept in the cabin and read his book. Along the rainy road from Stirling to Doune and Callander that night he saw little more than his horse's head. Early next morning he was traveling, through country made classic by Walter Scott, past Loch Vennachar and Loch Achray; but "the scenery of a shower-bath," he remarked, "must be always much the same." Before he was out of the Trossachs the skies cleared and revealed the great stretches of heather that colored the country to the hue of a rose. In boats on Loch Katrine he and his party fought against wind and wave only as far as Ellen's Isle and then took to the shore again. He and four others of the company walked fourteen miles along a winding sheep track up the shore toward the west end of the lake. Ready to leave Loch Katrine, they dried their shoes, drank whiskey, and ate oatcake. It was still five miles to Inversnaid, where they were to catch the steamboat on Loch Lomond, and there was nothing for it but to use their legs again. At Inversnaid the hut, close to the roaring cataract, was full of Gaelic-talking Highlandmen and women and peat smoke.

The voyage southward by steamer was so rough that Emerson lost overboard the black cap he had bought in Malta and was left shivering with a handkerchief on his head. He finally reached Glasgow in such condition that he was unable to object when the innkeeper assigned him a little room at the top of the house. At the university he saw the Hunterian Museum. He visited the old cathedral remembered from *Rob Roy,* and the Saltmarket. On the 24th he was at Dumfries. There, as the coach halted at the King's Arms, the guard pointed out to him a son of Robert Burns standing on the doorstep. Emerson passed the small tenement of the poet's eighty-year-old widow as he followed his guide to Burns's tomb.

Next day, having learned that Craigenputtock, the farm where Carlyle lived, was fifteen or sixteen miles distant and that no public coach passed near it, Emerson hired a gig and driver. As he penetrated into the parish of Dunscore he was struck by its desolate aspect. Doubtless the region was quite as wild then as now, with coarse grass and bracken and purple and red heather thick on the rough soil in late August. Rock cropped out near the summits of the long hills stretching row upon row to the horizon. Doubtless then as now the wildness but not the desolateness of the landscape was broken by a geometric pattern of ponderous gray stone fences, and the loneliness of the scene was only emphasized when a rabbit or a few half wild sheep would start out from clumps of bracken.

Arriving at the two-story stone house on Craigenputtock farm, Emerson found that Carlyle had already been warned of the intended visit and was insistent that he stay the night. The gig was therefore sent back to Dumfries with instructions to return for the traveler next day in time for him to catch the evening coach to the south. The intervening twenty-four hours were enough—and perhaps more would have been too much—for the beginning of a lifelong friendship. The tall, gaunt Carlyle let loose his extraordinary flood of conversation. He clung "to his northern accent with evident relish" as he told lively anecdotes "with a streaming humor which

floated every thing he looked upon." Jane Welsh Carlyle, his wife, immediately recognizable as an accomplished woman, told how the trip they
had proposed to make to Weimar had fallen through for lack of funds and
described the gifts that Goethe had sent them.

As they sat in the secluded farmhouse or walked together over miles
of hills, Emerson and Carlyle revealed themselves to each other as fully
and as frankly as they could. "The comfort of meeting a man of genius,"
Emerson happily recalled his old rule, "is that he speaks sincerely . . ."
Already a reader of Carlyle, he did not need much further proof of the
man's genius. If Landor had failed to pass the severe test of sincerity, Carlyle
did not fail. And yet inevitably something was lacking here too. "Socrates,
the glory of the Greek world," was again used as a touchstone with disappointing results. Emerson, checked by this experience, felt that he had
met with "men of far less power who had yet greater insight into religious
truth" than his new Scottish friend. Naturally the thirty-seven-year-old
Carlyle, having doubtless never so much as heard the name of his thirty-
year-old visitor until this meeting was arranged, could not fully recognize
his genius on such short notice. Fortunately, though, being hungry for conversation with the outside world, he was in the right mood, and another
favorable circumstance was that his wife at once liked the stranger. Jane
Carlyle later summarized her impressions somewhat poetically by saying
that this man descended as if out of the clouds, made one day look like
enchantment, and left her weeping that it was only one day. Carlyle agreed
with her that their guest was "a beautiful transparent soul." In simpler
English this doubtless meant one who had emotional health and balance
as well as intellectual qualities.

Though it turned out that each of the two men thus brought together
was, for the other, one of the few existing minds who could serve him
usefully as a friend, they were, in thought and in character, plainly separated by a gap that could never be bridged. From the first meeting Emerson understood that Carlyle, with all his enthusiasm for the service of God,
was a vigorous animal, somewhat resembling Montaigne, and kept close
to the earth. Carlyle, on his part, was impressed, and soon distressed, by
a certain visionary, impractical quality in Emerson. It seemed fitting to
the burly Scot not to accompany his visitor over the hill on the way back
to Dumfries but to catch the last glimpse of him as he appeared to be
vanishing into thin air at the summit.

By evening Emerson had crossed the English border. He was still congratulating himself on "A white day in my years," but was ready for a
try at his next literary man, this time a celebrity, William Wordsworth,
the greatest living poet. On the morning of the 28th he went out from

Ambleside to Wordsworth's Rydal Mount home. It was a place to write poetry in. From nearby Nab Scar one could see Rydal Water, Grasmere, and other lakes spread out as if on a great map. The poet was called in, "a plain, elderly, white-haired man, not prepossessing, and disfigured by green goggles." He enumerated his transatlantic acquaintances and "had much to say of America, the more that it gave occasion for his favorite topic,—that society is being enlightened by a superficial tuition, out of all proportion to its being restrained by moral culture." He duly recited his literary prejudices, heaping special abuse on Goethe's *Wilhelm Meister*. He had read only the first part of the book. Having found it full of all manner of fornication, he said, he had thrown it across the room in disgust; but he promised to try again since he had heard Emerson's defense of it. He thought Carlyle clever and deep but disliked his obscurity and sometimes thought him insane. In his opinion Coleridge's writings were clearer than Carlyle's but ought to be less obscure. He led the way to a walk on his grounds where many thousands of his lines were composed and offered to repeat some of his latest sonnets. There he was, "the old Wordsworth, standing apart, and reciting . . . in a garden-walk, like a school-boy declaiming." Emerson at first wanted to laugh but listened respectfully when he remembered that he had come here to see a poet and that a poet was now chanting his poems.

On the following day the traveler covered the whole distance from Kendal to Liverpool. From Manchester on he rode in a railway train, presumably for the first time, and was alive to every detail of the trip. "Strange proof," he thought, "how men become accustomed to oddest things! the laborers did not lift their umbrellas to look as we flew by them . . ." Later, in Liverpool, he saw George Stephenson's prize-winning Rocket and some of the other locomotives and got informal lectures on steam power from Jacob Perkins.

While he waited for his ship to sail he heard a few sermons. One was by James Martineau. Emerson, presenting an introduction from Henry Ware, told Martineau the story of his resignation of the ministry of the Second Church. "He was then," the English Unitarian leader put it, "in a very indeterminate state of mind about questions on religion, and I was struck with the mixture of clear decision on the subject which had led to action, and of modest suspense on topics which he had not yet fully thought out. But I made up my mind that he would not be likely to return to the ministry."

On August 30 the traveler paid Captain Hoxie of the *New-York* for his passage and purchased a Mackintosh overcoat for protection against the Atlantic. At his Liverpool hotel, the Star and Garter in Paradise Street, not far from the docks, Emerson waited wearily till September 4, when his ship finally sailed with fourteen passengers in the cabin and sixteen in the steerage.

On September 5 he "saw the last lump of England receding without the least regret," but he was not very happy over the prospect before him. As he sailed homeward he considered his future career. He liked his "book about Nature" and must already have planned it or even begun to write it out; but he was not swept away by any enthusiasm or ambition, literary or otherwise. He wished he knew where and how to live. He was glad to be on his way home, "yet not so glad as others, and my way to the bottom," he assured himself, "I could find perchance with less regret, for I think it would not hurt me,—that is, the ducking or drowning." He reviewed some of his favorite philosophical theories and decided they were still valid in the light of his European experience.

He had already begun to appraise the results of his seven months in foreign countries. First-hand acquaintance with Landor, Coleridge, Carlyle, and Wordsworth was worth thanking God for. It warranted his resolve that hereafter he would "judge more justly, less timidly, of wise men." He was also prepared to judge foreign countries more confidently and more intelligently. He could understand well enough the feeling of the uninhibited Yankee with lip curled in scorn as he passed among Europe's ducal and royal palaces. Yet he felt doubtful as well as proud when he remembered the young, self-assertive America to which he was returning. Though he had pretty definitely made up his mind to speak for himself and for his own country, he was now traveled and experienced, not ignorant of the Old World, and so not single-hearted in his patriotism. Having also read much, he was steeped in the thought and feeling of other lands and of other ages. He inevitably cared for what he judged the best that was thought and known anywhere in the world. It was therefore impossible for him to be a narrow-minded nationalist. He had gone only that far toward a solution of the much discussed problem of American cultural independence when he arrived at New York on October 7, 1833.

13.

A THINKER LET LOOSE

*I fear yet this iron yoke of outward conformity hath left
a slavish print upon our necks; the ghost of a linnen decency
yet haunts us.*

—Milton, *Areopagitica*

*The one thing not to be forgiven to intellectual persons is,
not to know their own task, or to take their ideas from others.*

—"The Fugitive Slave Law" read at New York

FOR more than a year after his return from Europe, Emerson moved from one temporary home to another. Presumably he carried out his plan to spend a few days with his friend George Sampson in Boston and then go on to suburban Newton, where his mother had been living, "for a pro tempore study." Toward the middle of December he took a room in the home of James Pelletier, a French teacher, at 276 Washington Street, Boston. His brother Charles, then struggling for a foothold in Court Street, the lawyers' swarming place, was already living at Pelletier's, and he and Waldo had "pleasant Fraternal evenings." Next spring Waldo boarded for a time with a Mrs. Palmer in Franklin Place. Late in April he was back in Newton, to remain for several months. The parlor and three bedrooms that he and his mother rented in the house of a Mrs. Allen made them a comfortable resting place in a retreat as retired as the Roxbury home had been. In this woodcock's nest, two miles or more from the station of the new railroad, they counted seven Sundays in a week.

The gossip over Emerson's resignation from the Second Church had not entirely died down but had passed its peak during his absence abroad. Once or twice at least it had got into the press. Once a writer in *The New-England Magazine* had misrepresented and exaggerated Emerson's real objections to the Lord's Supper and hinted broadly that Emersonian doctrine was the evil fruit of William Ellery Channing's liberal preaching. The former "Unitarian minister, in the north part of Boston," thus attacked along with Channing found a prompt defender in Ezra Gannett, his old college mate and fellow member of the school committee. Though Gannett differed "widely" from Emerson on the rite, he could not consent, he said, "that the opinions of one, whom I hold in admiration for his unimpeachable purity and integrity, should be misrepresented to the prejudice of his character in the estimation of the community, while he is absent from his native land."

The dust of the old controversy did not keep Emerson from going ahead with as much irregular supply preaching as he cared to do. Within a few weeks after his return from abroad he went back to the Second Church, greeted his former parishioners as a returned traveler would do, and preached a new sermon reaffirming some of his well-known unorthodox views without apology. Outside of Boston, he preached most at New Bedford, where he had several tours of duty of from three to half a dozen weeks in succession. His kinsman Orville Dewey, quitting his pastorate there, doubtless wanted him to take his place permanently. Probably some of the leading members had given their informal assent to this plan; but there is no reason to believe that the church ever issued any formal invitation to Emerson. According to Frederic Hedge, a person apt to be well informed on such matters, when Emerson wrote to a committee of the church that he would not agree to celebrate the communion service or to pray except when he was in the mood, the committee suppressed the letter and the negotiations fell through. Whatever any such negotiations amounted to, the episode of his irregular pastorate at New Bedford was important only because it brought Emerson into closer contact with the Quakers or ex-Quakers there. He was impressed by the Quaker widow Deborah Brayton, the keeper of the fashionable boarding house where he lived, and was undoubtedly much more influenced by Mary Rotch, another Quakeress, a sort of local Aunt Mary Moody Emerson. Sometimes he traveled farther from home than New Bedford. He preached at Bangor, Maine, during July, 1834, and at New York for a month in the autumn of the same year. He wrote a hymn for the ordination of Chandler Robbins, his successor at the Second Church in Boston, and was soon afterwards a guest in Robbins's pulpit. Very probably he did not want to be considered a candidate for any regular pastorate.

His new freedom was now made more secure by his new financial status. Though his European voyage seems to have cost more than a year's salary at the Second Church at a time when he was no longer drawing a salary, his affairs had taken a decisive turn for the better during his absence. His furniture, except an organ, had been sold, yielding over $900 to his credit. But far more important, the settlement of the Tucker estate had at last become a thing that could be counted on. After new complications caused by the deaths of Emerson's sister-in-law Margaret Tucker and his mother-in-law, Mrs. Kent, had been cleared up, things had moved rapidly. Within a few days of his own death, Professor Ashmun, Emer-

son's counsel, had briefly argued the case before the Supreme Judicial Court in Boston; and toward the end of the following June, when the plaintiff was still on the continent of Europe, the case of Emerson vs. Cutler, the executor of the Tucker estate, had been decided. Emerson was eventually to receive the whole of Ellen's share of the two-thirds of the estate willed to the Tucker children.

In the early months of 1834 his financial expectations began to be realized in cash and negotiable paper and he had a basis for future plans. Before the end of January he had been granted permission by the executor, in view of troublesome debts, to draw at least one small sum in advance of final settlement. A decree issued by the court in the March term specified the money and stocks that he was to have as the first of two main instalments, and before the middle of May he accordingly received 67 shares in the City Bank, 19 in the Atlantic Bank, and 31 in the Boston and Roxbury Mill Dam, together with a cash balance of between three and four thousand dollars. The estimated total value of these assets was $11,600. When he had got the whole of the inheritance in hand, Emerson would, he thought, be sure of an annual income of about $1200, an amount equal to two-thirds of his recent salary as pastor. But he would have, as it turned out, slightly over three years to wait for the payment of the second half of the funds he was counting on. On the other side of the ledger he must estimate some special expenses. It would be necessary for him to pay not only his own living expenses but at least a share of those of his mother, for her income from the Lafayette Hotel now amounted to only $80 or $90 a year, about $225 short of her actual expenses. He would also be responsible for a share of the cost of keeping his brother Bulkeley. Though his outlay on Bulkeley's account was not great, it might continue for many years. The inheritance from Ellen was, however, enough to justify the resolve he must have made to put an end to his irregular ministry as soon as he could get a modest reputation as a lecturer and a writer. He was prudent, though it is quite improbable that in any circumstance he would have kept at his preaching many years longer.

The lecture platform was a logical first step to take from the pulpit. A few weeks after his return from abroad, Waldo Emerson had begun with his lecture on "The Uses of Natural History." He was humanizing and Transcendentalizing science. The world and the mind, he told his audience, were inseparably paired. Our speech was packed with metaphors "because the whole of Nature is a metaphor or image of the human Mind," he explained. "The laws of moral nature answer to those of matter as face to face in a glass." A future botanist named Moses Curtis observed that the several hundred hearers seemed highly gratified with the lecture;

but when he himself thought it over he found it mostly intangible. He was quite unable to catch the meaning of the passage, inspired by Emerson's visit to the Jardin des Plantes, on the occult sympathy between man and the material world. There was so much dreaminess in it. But no such doubts troubled Emerson's brother Charles. In his opinion, "Waldo lectured . . . to a charm." Charles "was glad to have some of the stump lecturers see what was what & bow to the rising sun."

It was probably late in December, 1833, that the new lecturer read "On the Relation of Man to the Globe." This likewise contained echoes of his foreign travel and approximated a theory of evolution in its assertions that man was no upstart but was prophesied in nature long before he appeared and that animals were created gradually from age to age, the new varieties being suited to the contemporary condition of the earth. Narrowly interpreted, this could have meant merely the orthodox belief in special creations; but to a man of Emerson's imaginative temperament it probably meant more. As in the earlier lecture, there was also insistence upon the correspondences between the world of the senses and the world of thought. Again, in spite of lip service to the old argument from design, there was a start along a path so far little trod.

Emerson was fortunate in hitting upon science as his first inspiration for lectures. Natural history was indeed, as his brother Charles said, "the study now." Everybody was "making catalogues of birds, reading memoirs of Cuvier, hearing lectures about Crustacea, Volcanoes, entomology & the like." Emerson was busy, as usual, with provocative ideas. Even though his lecture on "Water," before the Boston Mechanic's Institution on January 17, 1834, proved to be the weakest of his series on natural history, he managed to make it underscore, faintly at least, his recognition of the ceaseless revolution going forward in nature. In his "Address" read at the annual meeting of the Boston Society of Natural History in the following May, he defended those amateur scientists who labored enthusiastically, as he did, to acquire knowledge that could only be superficial. The spell of the Jardin des Plantes was again upon him. He showed that recent discoveries pointed more and more steadily at method, at a theory; and he asserted that a visit to a natural history cabinet excited reveries about relations which one could feel without being able to comprehend or define them. Scientific studies had many virtues, and they looked to him like medicine for America's disease of European imitation. Not hopeful of achieving literary independence without a great sacrifice, he proposed the somewhat short-sighted theory that scientific progress might be made independently of other nations. The otherwise evil Jacksonian party was helping us, with its ignorance of all literature and its selfish, gross pursuits, to get free of England's cultural hegemony. "But," he suggested, "a better cure would be in the study of Natural History."

His two lectures on Italy were the most frank and detailed reports of his experience abroad that he gave a lecture audience until, long afterward, he began his book on England. He read the Italian lectures not very frequently over a period of years. At New Bedford he was at a great deal of trouble to hang up prints by way of illustration. One picture he used there, a painting of the most magnificent room in the Uffizi Gallery, was by the New Bedford artist William Wall, his companion during a part of his foreign travels. He began with a disclaimer of any ulterior purpose or any special knowledge. He simply wanted to give "a brief account of the most interesting objects of Italy as they present themselves to the notice of an American traveller." He would not venture upon an analysis of Italian politics. He modestly remarked that "A learned criticism upon works of art is a very pertinent study for an Italian traveller, but I have no learning on the subject." He made an effort at restraint on the subject of the church and admitted that perhaps "the best form of worship would adopt something of this Catholic ceremony." He was trying, in spite of the inevitable glorification of travel which the lecture implied, to preserve both his Americanism and his self-respect. He ended with a gesture of defiance even toward immortal Rome, warning his hearers against any surrender of self-reliance: "The Genius of the place seems to say in the ear of every wanderer, Why are you dazzled with the name of Caesar? A part as important, a soul as great, a name as dear to God as his—is your own." Into his second lecture on Italy, relating his impressions of the country from Rome northward, he put something of the same spirit of independence, though he took pains to do justice to the accumulated treasures of many centuries of culture.

But it was in the course on his first group of representative men— Michelangelo, Martin Luther, John Milton, George Fox, and Edmund Burke—that he unmistakably rehearsed for his future platform successes and, to the discerning, pretty fully revealed the main direction of his thinking. In these lectures and in those that soon followed, his travels, studies, and miscellaneous experiences were kneaded together. It was a symbolical act for him to write his lecture on Michelangelo in a coat he had had made in Florence. He got into the spirit of Michelangelo partly by translating from the great artist's verses. Having swung sharply round from science to biography, he became more than ever a collector of notable men, and particularly heroic men, though he did not go as far in dramatizing heroism as he thought of doing when he proposed, in January of 1835, to lecture on the deaths of Phocion, Socrates, and Sir Thomas More. When he discussed literature, he made much of its biographical implications. For him every subject naturally took on an ethical coloring, but he contented himself with basic principles, habitually avoiding limited applications of his theories. He commonly slighted material values in favor of intellectual and spiritual. Idea, spirit had for him a much more vivid existence than things.

Presumably, from the start, he read his lectures and seldom attempted any extempore speaking, though when he took part in a debate before the Concord Lyceum, contending that the French Revolution caused more good than evil, he won the decision. But even if he stuck to his manuscript he quickly learned to communicate to his audiences a sense of his eloquence and daring. For some time his lectures did not carry him farther from Boston than Concord and, in the opposite direction, Plymouth. But it was obvious that he would soon command a far larger audience.

In his more strictly literary ventures he had less success. Though he had kept up a thin stream of verse since boyhood, he could as yet seldom be at ease in metrical expression. In the Newton woods he wrote "The Rhodora," a piece appropriate to that setting. In "The Rhodora," with its defense of unutilitarian beauty, and almost of art for art's sake, he created a fragile beauty. But when he sat down to write for a Phi Beta Kappa anniversary he was disconcerted. If he manufactured, as he said, the "amusing verses" in demand on such occasions he would have to "outrage" his own "solemn nature," but if he tried poetry he would not please his audience. He elected poetry, had a hard time to keep from falling into "a sort of *fata morgana* reflecting the images of Byron, Shakspear, and the newspapers," and, in his own opinion, failed to make a successful declamation of it. His brother Charles called the poem "both good sense & good verses"; but, at best, it was hardly more than good sense.

Making slow progress toward the profession of letters, Emerson had at least a vague purpose to write an article for *The North American Review* on the Concord Fight. As late as December of 1833 he had vainly nursed along his dream of establishing a magazine or paper of his own. Yet chapters of *Nature*, his first book, were growing toward completion in his journals; and his intellectual current was gathering force, though it carried along what seemed, on the surface, to be mainly the ideas he had repeated for years, as self-reliance, compensation. He found that the distinction between reason and understanding, a distinction he credited jointly to Milton, Coleridge, and the Germans, was "a philosophy itself." "Reason," he explained in a letter to Edward, "is the highest faculty of the soul—what we mean often by the soul itself; it never *reasons*, never proves, it simply perceives; it is vision. The Understanding toils all the time, compares, contrives, adds, argues, near sighted but strong-sighted, dwelling in the present the expedient the customary. Beasts have some understanding but no Reason. Reason is potentially perfect in every man—Understanding in very different degrees of strength. . . . Religion Poetry Honor belong to the Reason; to the real the absolute. . . ."

The direction of his religious thought at this transitional period of his life was becoming more sharply defined. Both Quakers and Swedenborgians were looming larger in his estimate of values. He thought both spiritually alive, as churches in general were not. Quakers he described as "a sublime class of speculators" and "perhaps the most explicit teachers of the highest article to which human faith soars the strict union of the willing soul to God & so the souls access at all times to a verdict upon every question which the opinion of all mankind cannot shake & which the opinion of all mankind cannot confirm." In theory he insisted on the genuineness of the mystical relationship, but his own mystical flights were always apt to be kept close to earth by common sense, perhaps more accurately describable in his case as the theoretical or intellectual area in his nature which could never be quite submerged in his aesthetic or unconscious self.

With the Swedenborgians he never could go more than half way, but his sympathy with their doctrine of the primacy of the spiritual had its effect on his thought. A Swedenborgian friend esteemed himself "measureably excused for not preaching" while Emerson was in New Bedford and was "giving as much New Jerusalem doctrine as the people will bear." On the first Sunday of 1835 Emerson went so far as to visit the Swedenborgian chapel in Boston. What he heard did not excite him, but he saw signs of life there. On the same Sunday he listened to the Methodist Father Taylor, the seamen's preacher, and set Taylor's church down in the same category of the living. He was simply a seeker, ready to accept whatever ideas seemed worth while, but by no means willing to lock himself up in anybody's intellectual prison. Within a few weeks a rumor got abroad that he was a Swedenborgian, and this reverberated as far away as New York but was false.

He still kept out of the storm center of the political debates of the time but had political prejudices and did some serious political thinking, which was certain to come to the surface in his later writing. He was already able to see that his favorite doctrine of self-reverence, or self-reliance, was at the root of democracy; but, with his habit of looking critically on all sides of a truth without much worry over contradictory findings, he was also quick to see the abuses of democracy. He felt humiliated when he attended a caucus and disillusioned when obviously unfit persons were elected to office. He was frankly contemptuous of "this rank rabble party, the Jacksonism of the country," in spite of his belief that there was latent virtue there; and he wanted God to avert the failure of the Whigs. He generally kept clear of all kinds of extremists. Being a philosophical man, he had little faith in even good-intentioned enthusiasts captained by fanatics and so did not think it his business to march with the legions now ready for a frontal assault on slavery. But he nevertheless had his unfaltering opinion and would live up to it in his individualistic manner. Whatever havoc opposition to slavery might work with other American institutions, he did "not wish to live in a nation where slavery exists."

If, in this crucial period, Emerson had few friends who could guide him toward a literary career, he had already proved his capacity for friendship. He could attract such excellent, though unliterary, men as Abel Adams and George Sampson. George Sampson, a Boston merchant, was a friend whom he received with democratic understanding. Sampson, a former parishioner, would not let the action of his church sever him from his pastor and still "loved him like a brother." At the time of his premature death, in July of 1834, he was on the way to join Emerson in Maine.

It was to preach Sampson's funeral sermon that Emerson mounted the pulpit of the Second Church for the last time. He was not apologetic because the events of Sampson's life "were few & nowise remarkable" or because his friend had, as he confessed to the audience, "neither literature nor wealth nor power." Instead, he praised the greatness Sampson had expended on commonplace duties. "I should be ashamed," he said, "to express a respect for Cato & Aristides & Washington & see virtues which all ages had unanimously pointed out to me, & have no eye to discover the very same virtues when they appeared among my own acquaintance & in the performance of ordinary duties. I should then feel no security that if Cato & Aristides should reappear in the world I should have penetration enough to discover them."

At least two persons were impressed by the speaker's perfect loyalty to such a friend, for Amos Bronson Alcott and Elizabeth Peabody had come together to hear the funeral sermon. Elizabeth Peabody told her sister Mary that *"words* would vainly essay to do justice" to Emerson's "apotheosis of Sampson," and that "His expression—his tones—his prayers—his readings of Scripture—his sermon . . . will live in my soul forever & ever— And *I know that man* as well as I could have known him had I been his acquaintance on earth."

Waldo Emerson and William, Edward, and Charles had been friends as well as brothers and had often remarked on their close association. Edward had written from Porto Rico that he never read the treatises on friendship by ancient and modern writers without thinking of their family brotherhood. But now ill fortune began to overtake it. Edward, the much admired scholar and lawyer who had had "from youth the leader's look" and whose "sculptured countenance" had never been shamed by "poor beseeching glance," was the first to break the circle. He had kept as long as he could to his quiet routine as merchant's clerk and American consul's assistant at San Juan. But an accidental wetting in August, 1834, had worsened his chronic cough, and before the end of the following month pains in the chest, and then pulmonary suppuration, showed that his case was hopeless. On the first day of October he died. For some two years after Edward's death the brotherhood consisted of William, Waldo, and Charles.

Among all his friends Emerson rated Carlyle, since the European tour, as his chief symbol of the profession of letters. Carlyle's words were a gospel that the literary neophyte, no matter how self-reliant, must respect. It was important to Emerson that that gospel was less British than German. Carlyle's articles on German literature which Emerson had been reading before he crossed the Atlantic probably included the old but still exciting one on the state of German literature in 1827. That article illustrated the whole Teutonic orientation of the Scot's mind. Carlyle was as bold in praising German taste, literature, and philosophy as Mme de Staël had been. He approved Fichte and Schelling as fit for importation into Britain but gave Kant the lion's share of the praise. Significantly for a transatlantic admirer who was not apt to read far in Kant's own writings, he set down the "grand characteristic" of Kant's philosophy as the distinction between reason and understanding and was as negligent as Coleridge about giving adequate warning of the limitations of intuition upon which Kant himself had actually insisted so sternly. Carlyle exaggerated and oversimplified, but his faults could not equal his virtues in the eyes of Emerson. When Emerson spoke of Milton, Coleridge, and the Germans he was probably thinking mainly of Coleridge and of the Germans as expounded by Carlyle.

By 1834 the whole Emerson circle was stirred up by the Scottish strong man of letters. In July, before an answer had come from him to his American admirer's first letter, but pretty obviously after some instalments of "Sartor Resartus" in *Fraser's* had been read by the Emersons, Charles was explaining to Aunt Mary how Carlyle's "living words, fire-baptized," showed the iconoclastic Scot "working himself clear of disbelief & coming forth into the light of hope & God's Truth. He has," Charles added, "with whatsoever strangeness & extravagance of utterance, spoken Delphic yea higher than Delphic oracles—since they touch the great mysteries of Revelation, say rather the infinite mystery of Being. You may be revolted from him at first—we all are—but his soul is so lordly, free & pure you will love him."

In the following August, Carlyle, "now of Craigenputtock no more, but of London," wrote Waldo Emerson "a noble letter." A seal of approval on the friendship begun a year earlier, it was all the more welcome because it came just after its author had finished the most spiritual of his gospels and so had recommended himself most effectively to the budding Transcendentalist. Emerson, long since a subscriber to *Fraser's,* was doubtless familiar with the whole of "Sartor" before Carlyle's gift of the four stitched copies of the excerpted articles could reach him. In spite of its extravagant rhetoric, "Sartor" must have reminded him of his own journals. Professor Teufelsdröckh resembled his American reader in his "humour of looking at all Matter and Material things as Spirit." His method was not that of common logic but of "practical Reason, proceeding by large Intuition." He thought that nature was "what the Earth-Spirit in *Faust* names it, *the living visible Garment of God,*" and that "Matter, were it never so despicable, is Spirit, the manifestation of Spirit." He was firmly convinced that here or nowhere was the ideal, in the self. For him great men were the inspired texts of a divine book of revelations making up history. He had forsaken Byron and had banished the everlasting No, accepting in its stead the everlasting Yea. He had discovered in Goethe, as Emerson was at last doing, a prophet in whom man's life "again begins, were it but afar off, to be divine."

By January of 1835 Emerson was directing the attention of his former pupil Benjamin Hunt to the "author of the pieces 'Burns' 'Characteristics' 'Corn Law Rhymes—Review,' &c. in the Edinburgh, & of many singular papers in the Foreign Review, & Frasers Magazine,—all alive—& all true," and of "Sartor." "My friends," he added, "think I exaggerate his merit but he seems to me one of the best, & since Coleridge is dead, I think, the best thinker of the age." Inspired by Carlyle's example, Emerson was taking to the private study of German with surprising zest. It seemed time lost, he admitted, "for a grown man to be turning the leaves of a dictionary, like a boy, to learn German"; but he was convinced that he was on the right trail. Goethe became almost a refrain in his journals.

Another promising source of help, a man he had known since they were together in theological school, was Frederic Hedge, the author of some vigorous criticism of Swedenborg and Coleridge. Emerson called one of Hedge's articles "a living leaping Logos" and naturally thought of its author as a desirable helper in case his own hazily projected magazine should become a reality. Hedge tried to rescue mysticism from the low and reproachful sense in which it was generally understood. He took Swedenborg, the mystic—for so he regarded him—as his text; but he denied him any special authority, cited Kant against him, and concluded with a declaration of friendliness toward the New Church somewhat overbalanced by a frank avowal that he had no sympathy with that idolatry which could embrace a human tradition as if it were a revelation from God. All this may have been serviceable to Emerson as he developed his own ideas on Swedenborg and mysticism, though it did not comprehend those ideas. The most significant part of the lengthy review of Coleridge that Hedge printed while Emerson was on his way to visit the subject himself was a discussion of the "transcendental" philosophy of Kant, Fichte, and Schelling. Only less culpable than Carlyle in his earlier essay on the state of German literature, Hedge failed to repeat Kant's emphatic warning against too great dependence on the use of the transcendental method.

Other tutors, likewise sensitive to the new winds of doctrine blowing from over the Atlantic, were ready to begin their work for the emancipated teacher and preacher now turning lecturer and man of letters. Before sailing for Europe, Emerson had had a conversation with James Freeman Clarke on "Goethe, German Literature, Carlyle, etc." Some months after his return from abroad he and Clarke began to exchange letters at long intervals, with Goethe and the Germans still the center of interest. Emerson urged Clarke to publish an article, then in manuscript, on Goethe and Carlyle; and Clarke in turn urged Emerson to do something of the sort himself and at the same time pointed to Margaret Fuller as another discoverer of Goethe. For some months she had been seeking an opportunity of meeting Emerson; and now he seemed willing. Learning of this propitious turn of events, she masked her enthusiasm as well as she could and wrote to Frederic Hedge: "I am flattered that Mr Emerson should wish to know me. I fear it will never be but tis pleasant to know that he wished it. I cannot think I should be disappointed in him as I have been in others to whom I had hoped to look up. The sensation one experiences in the atmosphere of his thought is too decided and peculiar." At almost the same time Alcott was writing in his diary, "I wish to know Mr. R. Emerson and Mr. Hedge."

Free at last from any routine of school or church, Emerson looked about for the place where he could live with a near balance of society and solitude but with the beam down slightly on the side of solitude. He had not forgotten Concord, his ancestral town, where he had once lived for some months and had often visited. It had frequently been his mother's retreat, and Elizabeth Hoar, Charles's fiancée, was likely to draw Charles there to take a desk in her father's law office till he could find room in Boston. In late September of 1834, Emerson began preparations for the move from Newton to Concord. He asked Grandfather Ripley to arrange for a wagon and reckoned up his and his mother's baggage as a bureau, a small table, two bookcases of two shelves each, two armchairs, a trunk, two beds, and some small articles, altogether making a load not too great for a large

horse cart to carry. Some three weeks later his mother wrote in her note-
book, "Came to Concord Tuesday 14 to board with Dr. Ripley the winter."
After several intervening Sundays or Mondays of preaching in New York,
Waldo Emerson himself settled down contentedly into this rural scene.

He knew that after the loss of his place as a titular leader of Boston
Unitarianism his retreat into the country would look to the world like a
confession of defeat. People would speak of him with pity or disdain. But
he easily mustered up enough courage and pride to endure any such obloquy.
It was a fitting time for the rhymed advice he wrote for himself in an
undated passage of a verse book. He would accept both "talent & disgrace,"
leave "The marble town unwept," and nourish his virtue "in a private
place." In his diary he wrote, "Hail to the quiet fields of my fathers!" As
he set up his inkstand and prepared to begin a new life he made an ambitious resolve. "Henceforth," he announced to himself, "I design not to
utter any speech, poem or book that is not entirely and peculiarly my work.
I will say at public lectures, and the like, those things which I have meditated for their own sake, and not for the first time with a view to that
occasion." Such an ideal was impossible to realize but was a mark to shoot
at. This was not the first time he had placed it on his target; but now, in
1834, it had greater practical significance.

Pleased with his prospects, he began to feel at home in Concord, though
he was still only a boarder in the manse. In his room there—apparently the
northwest second-story room, looking out toward the battlefield and the
river—he got down to work on *Nature*, the book he had pondered on his
return voyage across the Atlantic. The ocean seemed to sound in his ears
again. The great willow tree over his roof, he wrote, "is the trumpet and
accompaniment of the storm and gives due importance to every caprice of
the gale, and the trees in the avenue announce the same facts with equal
din to the front tenants. Hoarse concert: they roar like the rigging of a
ship in a tempest."

14.

LIDIAN

❀❀❀

This lady is a person of noble character whom to see
is to respect. I find in her a quite unexpected community
of sentiment & speculation . . .

> —Letter to William Emerson, February 5, 1835

And I should think she had the rare characteristic of
genius—inexhaustible originality.

> —Elizabeth Peabody to her sister Mary,
> February 25, 1835

ONE Sunday afternoon a few years earlier, the guest preacher at
the Twelfth Congregational Church, in Chambers Street, Boston, looked down into the upturned face of a young woman
seated beside the pulpit in an attitude of rapt attention. The
young woman was Lydia Jackson, a visitor in the city, and she had presumably dropped into the Twelfth Church by chance. According to family
tradition, when Lydia first looked up at the man in the pulpit she was
simply astonished at the length of his neck. But what he was presently saying must have taken equal hold on her imagination, for when the service
was over she found herself leaning eagerly forward and so tired that she
believed she must have kept the same position throughout the sermon. Upon
inquiry she learned that the preacher was Emerson. On another Sunday
she saw him walking in front of her on the way to church, his gown fluttering in the wind. Then, in 1834, she heard him lecture in her home town
of Plymouth.

It was early in that year that he appeared on the lecture platform in
Plymouth. His old friend George Bradford seems to have arranged for the
lecture. Lydia heard it and was charmed, though she did not go with the
others to meet Emerson at Captain Russell's, where he was spending the
night. He soon returned to preach a sermon in the town, and it may have
been on that occasion that Lydia was asked by a friend how she liked
hearing her own ideas preached. If the family tradition is true in detail
as it undoubtedly is in general, Lydia soon had a premonition of what was
to happen. One day as she was going up the stairs in the Winslow House

her home, she saw a clear image of herself dressed as a bride and walking down those stairs with Emerson. She was shocked, and yet did not feel guilty, for she was not conscious that any such thought had ever entered her mind. She promptly pushed it back into the realm of the unconscious. Early in October, some seven months after his first Plymouth lecture, she was writing from Boston that she "came near having a call from Mr *Emerson* that very morng—but somehow lost it."

He had stayed in the house of Captain Russell at Plymouth, and as the captain's children were by this time good friends of both Emerson and Lydia Jackson, they may have had some part, along with George Bradford, in preparing the way for the courtship that was soon to follow if it had not already begun. Le Baron Russell doubtless reported in Plymouth his visit with Emerson in the Concord manse, a visit he long remembered as "a week of pure enjoyment such excitement as a young man would naturally have from the daily society and friendship of a man whom he delighted in above all others." It was presumably during this visit of his that young Russell and his host had a Sunday morning drive to Waltham. On such a drive, at any rate, Emerson repeated poetry to the appreciative youth, giving him his first knowledge of George Herbert. Le Baron's sister Lucia, then a schoolgirl, had found Emerson a sympathetic critic of her compositions. An older sister, Mary Howland Russell, had been Lydia Jackson's friend from babyhood.

After preaching a midweek sermon at Plymouth in the following January, Emerson returned home with "most agreeable recollections." A few days later Lydia had, it is said, a momentary vision of her lover's face, gazing at her and then suddenly vanishing; and on the next day she received his letter containing a proposal of marriage. In spite of her vision, she was utterly amazed. But she wrote him to come and talk with her on the subject, and he came at once. She closed her eyes and catechized him on the seriousness of his love. They were old enough to know their own minds. He was well over thirty-one. She was eight months his senior. Their engagement was quickly agreed on and was announced in Plymouth the following day. He gave her the diamond that had been Ellen Tucker's and had it set, as she requested, in a pin; but the jeweler, misunderstanding his instructions, made this useless to her. In his diary, however, Emerson seems to have recorded no word of his engagement except that January 30, presumably the day it occurred, was "spent at Plymouth with Lydia Jackson."

He felt no unrestrained enthusiasm and had, as he confessed to his brother William, a very different feeling from that which his first engagement had inspired. "This is a very sober joy," he admitted; and he explained his attachment by pointing to Lydia Jackson's nobility of character, to their "unexpected community of sentiment & speculation," and to the fact that in Plymouth she was "dearly prized for her love & good works." Besides, his involvement in affairs of his own left him little time for Lydia. He was beginning to deliver his new course in Boston, and, as he was writing his lectures on Michelangelo, Luther, Milton, George Fox, and Burke as he went along, he was in no position to play the role of devoted lover at Plymouth. The result was that a number of letters, some hurried and brief, and not more than a few hasty visits were the best means he had of piecing out the short courtship. He now revealed himself as rapidly as he could through the letters which, at least for the probity and good sense they showed, were not unworthy of the canonization they received at the hands of Lydia Jackson. A few days after his decisive visit in Plymouth, he wrote to her:

"Concord, 1 February—

"One of my wise masters, Edmund Burke, said, 'A wise man will speak the truth with temperance that he may speak it the longer.' In this new sentiment that you awaken in me, my Lydian Queen, what might scare others pleases me, its quietness, which I accept as a pledge of permanence. I delighted myself on Friday with my quite domesticated position & the good understanding that grew all the time, yet I went & came without one vehement word—or one passionate sign. In this was nothing of design, I merely surrendered myself to the hour & to the facts. I find a sort of grandeur in the modulated expressions of a love in which the individuals, & what might seem even reasonable personal expectations, are steadily postponed to a regard for truth & the universal love. Do not think me a metaphysical lover. I am a man & hate & suspect the over refiners, & do sympathize with the homeliest pleasures & attractions by which our good foster mother Nature draws her children together. Yet am I well pleased that between us the most permanent ties should be the first formed & thereon should grow whatever others human nature will.

"My Mother rejoices very much & asks me all manner of questions about you, many of which I cannot answer. I dont know whether you sing, or read French, or Latin, or where you have lived, & much more. So you see there is nothing for it but that you should come here & on the Battle-Ground stand the fire of her catechism.

"Under this morning's severe but beautiful light I thought dear friend that hardly should I get away from Concord. I must win you to love it. I am born a poet, of a low class without doubt yet a poet. That is my nature & vocation. My singing be sure is very 'husky,' & is for the most part in prose. Still am I a poet in the sense of a perceiver & dear lover of the harmonies that are in the soul & in matter, & specially of the correspondences between these & those. A sunset, a forest, a snow storm, a certain river-view, are more to me than many friends & do ordinarily divide my day with my books. Wherever I go therefore I guard & study my rambling propensities with a care that is ridiculous to people, but to me is the care of my high calling. Now Concord is only one of a hundred towns in which I could find these necessary objects but Plymouth I fear is not one. Plymouth is streets; I live in the wide champaign.

"Time enough for this however. If I succeed in preparing my lecture on Michel Angelo Buonaroti this week for Thursday, I will come to Plymouth on Friday. If I do not succeed—do not attain unto the Idea of that man—I shall read of Luther, Thursday & then I know not when I shall steal a visit.—

"Dearest forgive the egotism of all this letter Say they not 'The more love the more egotism.' Repay it by as much & more. Write, write to me. And please dear Lidian take that same low counsel & leave thinking for the present & let the winds of heaven blow away your dyspepsia.

"Waldo E."

Two days later, in answer to a letter of hers, he managed to write little but a promise of more self-revelation:

"I say to thee my noble Lidian that you little know to whom you are saying these fine things I have just read. . . . For loving you, if we are true to our principles I expect to love you & that you will love me better & better every hour whilst the world stands. Of these things I hope to make you surer next Friday . . . And so with this short message almost too late for the stage I must flee back to Michel Angelo only beseeching you to take care of your health & to love dearly

"Waldo Emerson for whom I hope you will be *able* to find a more affectionate name than Mr E."

In her eyes he wore the prestige of pulpit and platform as a saint wore a halo, and, as she insisted on keeping his dignity intact, she refused, in spite of his plea, to call him by a more familiar name. But he had no such inhibitions about her. At the outset he had determined, presumably for reasons of euphony, to reform her name. If she remained Lydia after her marriage, most New Englanders, with their unconscious antipathy to a hiatus between vowels, would call her Lydiar Emerson. Probably he reasoned it out that way, but at any rate he was troubled by no doubts. According to his cousin Sarah Ripley, he simply declared that those who had baptized the child Lydia had been ill-advised, for her name was Lidian.

By February 12, not quite two weeks after their engagement, he was demanding letters, as he had neither seen her nor heard from her for half a dozen days. But he found too little time for writing himself. If his letter was short, he apologized that it was this or none. Next day he was writing her again. He explained his sticking to his lectures instead of coming to Plymouth. Having spoken frankly of Ellen Tucker, he felt obliged to show Lydia that she had taken him too seriously. In order to make this matter clear, he offered to let her read his journals. He continued the debate over the location of their future home, quoting the sentiments of his inkstand in support of Concord's claims: "In fine Inkstand concludes that unless Lidian can trundle Plymouth rock a score of miles northward, she must even quit it & come & sit down by Concord Battle-Bridge. In reward of that grace, Inkstand is full of promises of verses & histories writ in & by her love." The debate was going in favor of Concord but, though Lydia had for years known that that place was, as she had once put it, "a pleasant town" with "society refined & intelligent" and that it was even "at a very convenient distance . . . from Boston, and not an unreasonable one from Plymouth," it was hard for her to shift her loyalty.

Emerson kept up his efforts, against odds, to be lover and lecturer at the same time. He was impatient of his own delay in writing to Plymouth, but he explained that "a visit time & strength-consuming to Waltham a heavy cold riding like the night mare my head & throat, & two biographies of Burke with 8 volumes of his works to read mark & inwardly digest,— quite eat up my hours & minutes." At a time when he was apparently sketching out his poem "Musketaquid," he wrote Lydia a fresh apology for Concord and its "innocent river." In the same letter he added a warning that he did not want to be addressed any longer "with that prefix *Rev.*" By March 5 the troublesome lecture on Burke was finally read in Boston. Lydia Jackson was there to hear it and thought it delightful. "In describing Burke as the noblest and kindest of human beings," she told her sister, "the lecturer seemed describing himself—so much are they alike—only I would say—'nay *better* than Burke' . . ." After the lecture there was a party at the home of Mrs. Sturgis. Two Sturgis girls, Ellen and Caroline, were precocious enough to figure as youthful bluestockings.

By means of her own share of the correspondence and a visit she got up courage to make in Concord, Lydia Jackson revealed much of her character to the Emerson family and circle. Her lover's friends and acquaintance were already doing their best to fill in the picture. It was generally agreed that she was not a beauty. Charles Emerson put the matter the shortest way when he told William that "The lady is a sort of Sybil for wisdom— She is not beautiful anywise that I know, so you look at the outside alone," but added that "Mother is pleased, & everybody."

Several feminine observers got more detailed impressions, which they promptly shared with their friends. Arriving at Mrs. Bliss's home in Boston for a first meeting with the prospective bride, Elizabeth Peabody learned that she was upstairs tardily finishing a letter to her lover. Elizabeth pleasantly busied herself by reading a letter which Emerson had received from Carlyle, and in due time Lydia descended, looking, as her visitor put it, *"very refined* but neither beautiful or elegant—and very frail—& as if her mind wore out her body—she was *unaffected* but *peculiar."* The two women sat down together and "had a beautiful talk about a variety of most intellectual & spiritual things— And I should think," Elizabeth rounded out her report, "she had the rare characteristic of genius—inexhaustible originality." A few days later Sarah Freeman Clarke, another intelligent inspector, announced that Lydia was almost equal to Emerson and as remarkable among women as he among men, was singular-looking yet beautiful, had an expression of face that showed a "beaming soul," seemed to be "a searing transcendentalist" and perhaps as independent in her thinking as was Margaret Fuller, and respected Unitarianism because without it there could be no Transcendentalism.

Widely circulated rumors about the engaged couple proved at least that Emerson already had some local celebrity. Lydia Maria Child heard the gossips affirm "that Mr. Emerson was about to marry a Swedenborgian lady, who, the first time she heard him lecture, received a very strong impression that they were spiritual partners; insomuch that, on her return home, she said to a friend, 'That man is certainly my pre-destined husband.'" Margaret Fuller, her interest in Emerson already keen, "heard much of Miss Jackson and should think her every-way calculated to make Mr Emerson happy even on his own principle that it is not the *quantity* but the *quality* of happiness that is to be taken into consideration." Emerson illustrated what struck Margaret as the rule that a man marrying a second time usually selected a wife of character and manners entirely unlike those of his first.

If she had chosen to do so, Mrs. Bliss, Lydia's girlhood friend in Plymouth and now her hostess and social mentor in Boston, could have added to these various appraisals a reasonably complete and enlightening history of the past of Lydia Jackson and her family, as Plymouth was a family-conscious town.

Lucy Cotton, Lydia's mother, was, it seems, the direct descendant of the redoubtable John Cotton who had migrated to Massachusetts Bay to be a beacon light, at first flickering but soon steady and reliable, of the Puritan church during the contentious time when not only John Winthrop, but Roger Williams and Anne Hutchinson as well, were members of that colony. Lucy, according to the family tradition, had many books and spent her days with them, as befitted one who came of so learned an ancestry. Charles Jackson, who married this Lucy Cotton in 1794, came of almost the earliest Plymouth Colony stock, it is said. He was a merchant and owner of several ships enough prized to bear picturesque figureheads, and so was naturally a Federalist and hated a Democrat. Ill health kept down his spirits, and he was apt to have an air of disapproval that made his wife sad, so their sixth child, Lydia, thought. Of the seven Jackson children only three lived beyond infancy—Lucy, born 1798; Lydia, September 20, 1802; and Charles Thomas, in 1805. These three kept much of their childhood intimacy, even after Lucy's disastrous marriage and Charles's rise to prominence as a scientist. The two sisters were destined to spend much of their lives together or as neighbors.

As a child, Lydia learned her alphabet from the somber pages of *The New-England Primer* and used to repeat its familiar assurance of all men's partnership with Adam in the original sin:

> In *Adam's* Fall
> We Sinned all.

By the time she was six she was receiving a more vivid lesson in human sorrow, for her mother then began her ten years of suffering from the tuberculosis that was to cause her death.

Before Lydia was eleven years old she and her sister were sent off to Dorchester to listen to the instructions of Mrs. Saunders and Miss Beach. At the Saunders and Beach academy young ladies were taught the substantial subjects of reading, writing, arithmetic, English grammar, the French language, composition, geography, the use of the globes and maps, and history, together with the fancy ones of drawing, painting in oils and chalks and water colors, drawing and coloring maps, embroidery, plain and ornamental needlework, tambour, painting on velvet, music, and dancing. Lydia could not master all these things during her year or so at the boarding school, but both she and her sister at least liberally sampled the curriculum. One of the several books charged against the account of the sisters was a volume that taught French according to an "infallible method." Dancing was thought important, and Lydia enjoyed it, though her Calvinist aunts gave her to understand that she was pirouetting over hell-fire. A French dancing master was thorough and encouraged her to stand in the stocks an hour or more each day. She was faithful and, in later years, believed that she owed her graceful walk to her dancing lessons.

Through a summer and autumn she wrote her stiff, meager letters home from the academy on Clifton Hill, Dorchester: "I was homesick at first, but am not much so now. Lucy is not homesick at all. Mrs Saunders and

Miss Beach are very kind to me, as are the young Ladies. . . . The summer dear mamma passes very rapidly, but I hope by *me,* not without improvement. I am too well aware of the present advantages offered me, and that I came here expressly to avail myself of them, to be idle, or careless. I have begun to paint and dance, also to take lessons on the globes. . . . Are all our acquaintance well? do any inquire for us? or are we forgotten by our young friends, if we are, I shall be sorry, but I can soon, I flatter myself be consoled, for there are a number of young Ladies here to whom we begin to be attached, and who politely return our partiality. We must be disobliging and unamiable indeed if we did not secure a portion of the esteem of our Preceptresses . . ."

She wanted to know why her father was silent and why he had not visited her. She and her sister were in good health, "but," she told him, "I begin to be fearful that the same blessing is not continued to you, as we have had no assurance of your welfare." Though she was anxious about the high cost of living, she relied on him for an answer to her questions on every subject that was inexplicable to her. To her mother she wrote again in November: "The return of composition day presents me with no task I assure you; for it gives me the happiness of writing to you dear Mother . . ." She would remain in Dorchester at Thanksgiving time, but, being, in spite of that irregularity, a loyal daughter of Plymouth, she looked forward to getting home "on the Anniversary of the landing of our Forefathers." The homecoming to her sober parents must have been a notable event in her life. According to family tradition she then received from her invalid mother the only kiss she could remember getting from her, though presumably her memory was not perfect.

Lydia kept her liking for composition for several years at least, writing solemn verses of her own and copying others into her commonplace books. Among poems she signed and dated as her own was one called "Trust in Providence Recommended." It warned of unexpected dangers and concluded, without much optimism, that Providence alone could give security. The things fixed in the memory of Lydia during childhood fitted, in general, into a similar emotional pattern. At church she pored over the hymnbook. The awful pictures of God's wrath she found there seemed unforgettable. Terror "was bred in her bones." Though she could delight in such a book as *Don Quixote,* she took with great seriousness the moralistic juvenile rhymes of Jane Taylor. Later she dreamed that she met this favorite author and was so overwhelmed with gratitude, affection, and joy that she fell at her feet and wept. Lydia and Lucy, however, were not baptized till Lydia was sixteen, when her mother, having been perhaps too shy to make a public confession, was allowed to join the church on her deathbed.

When the deaths of her father and mother occurred within hardly more than two months of each other, Lydia could feel no grief, though she tried to. She soon knew she did not face poverty. Her father had owned a block of buildings on Court Street, in the heart of Boston; and the guardians estimated that each of the children should have fourteen thousand dollars, though there was some suspicion that the heirs were being cheated by the son of Jackson's partner. Lydia was to have, a little later, an income of about six hundred dollars a year. She and Lucy were sent off to school again, this time to Mrs. M'Keige's Seminary for Young Ladies in Jamaica Plain, another Boston suburb. There the Jackson girls were offered much the same things to be had in Dorchester but with Italian added. Some of these subjects were indispensable to a cultured person's mental baggage. Others were merely decorative. To Lydia and Lucy, Mrs. M'Keige seemed admirable for her personal virtues, and, if her own account was to be believed, she was an able teacher, with her excellent English education, whatever additional culture she had acquired during a residence of several years in France, and her fluent speaking of Italian as well as French. Among her pupils the girls from Plymouth found at least one worth knowing. It was at Mrs. M'Keige's school that Lydia recruited a devoted friend in Margaret Forbes.

Next year, it seems, both Lydia and Lucy went back to Plymouth and settled down to a not very delightful routine of boarding with their aunts and uncles. Lucy's marriage, a year or so later, did not entirely interrupt the intimacy of the sisters; but when Lucy was too far away for satisfactory intercourse Lydia had her close Plymouth friends, especially Betsey Davis, Sarah Kendall, and Mary Howland Russell, to console her. The four friends, with a few other girls, formed a reading society, met from house to house, and had their own newspaper, *The Wisdom of the Nine*. It seems that young gentlemen also belonged to the reading society, and there were other cultural activities than reading. The town was rich in friendly, not unintellectual society.

At nineteen Lydia made a bad recovery from scarlet fever, and during the rest of her life she believed herself a sufferer from the aftereffects of the disease. She made herself a martyr, even as a girl, by undertaking private experiments on her health or by setting herself tests of endurance. She read of Napoleon and attempted to emulate him by getting along with four hours of sleep a night. Once, having started on a new quest for perfection, she resolved to read only religious things till eleven o'clock every morning. She tried special exercises such as skipping rope and jumping over a cricket. After the fires were taken apart by her uncle in the evening she would sit, wrapped in a shawl, reading. She read her uncle's medical books and got from them a theory of health that no doubt did much to keep her an invalid in later life. Having read about hydropathy and the importance of fresh air and loose clothing, she took cold baths, slept with open windows, and buttoned her skirts to a waist.

But she also had more pleasant methods of self-improvement. Once she took riding lessons in Boston in the same class with Ellen and Margaret Tucker, though she never knew which was which. She loved society and was no recluse. She always liked old-fashioned dancing, and as late as her twenty-second year she had instruction from a dancing master and was "daily acquiring 'Politeness & the graces,' " as she assured her sister.

She was not socially irresponsible even though she lacked regular occupation, and her religious seriousness hardly slackened. She decided that her income ought to be entirely spent every year and in such a manner as to do good to others as well as to herself. She set her poor cousins to work on sewing and embroidery with herself as paymaster. There was a sudden increase in her concern about religion. Sometime during three weeks at Woods Hole when she was twenty-three, she had a half-mystical experience. She felt that all her future was dimly shown to her, and she was prepared for what was to come. Once she refused to go on a visit because she thought a process of change was going on in her that must not be interrupted, and the climax of this episode was another semi-mystical experience.

But she was by no means done with the world and was not narrow-minded. She was quick and keen, was learning skill in repartee, and was becoming generally competent in conversation. She cared for intellectual things. She was apparently keeping up with the latest developments in her own country's literature. She thought she saw James Fenimore Cooper's virtues but was glad when a review was published that would put down his indiscriminate admirers. The general cry of approbation seemed to her a disgrace to American letters. She also shared the new urge to explore other modern literatures than English and American. When, in the winter of 1831–1832, George Bradford taught German in Plymouth, she and a few other young women made up what they called a class, meeting every Wednesday evening to recite to him. She was "exceedingly interested," seldom finding anything more pleasing than the hours she was able to spare for her reading of the hitherto strange language. Thus, after some years, her literary discoveries had grown to modest international proportions. She learned German poetry and never ceased to enjoy repeating it. The class read *Wilhelm Meister,* and she was carried away by it.

When Emerson proposed to marry her, the enthusiasms of her girlhood had mostly passed, though some had left their mark. Her liking for books, for their ideas rather than for any peculiar literary excellence, was stronger than ever. In religion she was still nominally a Unitarian but had in reality become a seeker, as Emerson himself was. She was like him in wanting a religion that insisted on a continuing revelation of truth without respect to tradition and history. She was accused, as he was, of being a Swedenborgian. Her brother denied the accusation on her behalf but warned her, a few months after her engagement. "Do you know," he asked, "that the disciples of Swedenbourg consider you & Mr Emerson among their number? Young Dr Shurtluff had a long discourse with me the other day about it & said that there was a large party in Boston who were very desirous of establishing a new *New Church* & of making Mr Emerson their pastor." But Charles Jackson "told the Dr. that although much of your ideal philosophy corresponded with their doctrines . . . you were very far from being a convert to the New Church"—and he wanted to know from her whether that was not true.

Whatever she may have replied to her brother, Lydia painstakingly, if not very clearly, explained her status to Elizabeth Peabody, evidently after Elizabeth had questioned her point-blank. She had recently thought and read much on Swedish doctrine. It seemed to her, she said, that "in all kindred speculations, I catch one ray of light,—find one little rill of truth here & there—in the works of the general race of writers—but in the writings of Swedenborg and his followers—and yet more, in the sayings of Christ and his apostles I seem to have traced the light to its source, the rill to its fountain.—Not that I am a Swedenborgian—or expect to become one —yet repeated experience of this kind, affords, to me at least, a strong presumption in favour of what the N. J. Church Christians assert of their faith." And this was probably the chief substance if not the entire sum of her Swedenborgianism. Its meaning was that she was not a strait-laced orthodox religionist and was ready to go at least a little way with her future husband into such a cloudland as Transcendentalism. They were both experimenters.

Matters of grosser nature seemed to Lydia momentarily to bar the way to their union. Her sister's husband, Charles Brown, recently a member of a firm of commission merchants at Long Wharf in Boston, had lost money and reputation together and suddenly abandoned his family and fled the country. The as yet undivided Jackson estate was involved, and the plight of Lucy and her two children was so serious that Lydia would have to assume a good deal of responsibility for them. Brown, as it turned out, was to be a thorn in the family flesh, even though he stayed on the other side of the Atlantic. For many years, from as far east as Constantinople and as far west as Ireland, he wrote his wife tales of repeated but always unsuccessful efforts to rehabilitate himself with a view to returning home. Sometimes he even sent small sums of money; but his spectacular successes were always in the future and he added to his offenses by letters preaching patience and warning against unorthodox religious views such as he could easily discover in the Emersons. Emerson, however, was not frightened by the possibility, in 1835, of any such annoyances. He promptly quieted Lydia's fears by assuring her that she might devote all her own income to Lucy and her children and, moreover, bring them to Concord to live if she wished.

On her visit to Concord to meet the Emerson family, Lydia was pleased with the mother and was much taken with Elizabeth Hoar, then engaged to Charles. But there nevertheless seems to have been some coolness in her reception. Probably the unpredictable Aunt Mary at first frowned, then smiled, and no lasting harm was done. The family tradition has it that she invited herself to Plymouth to visit her prospective niece and caused much distress by her erratic behavior, and that when Emerson came and carried her back to Concord she spent the whole time on the road in trying to persuade him to give Lydia up. However this may have been, Lydia was soon declaring to her sister her delight in the whole Emerson family, Aunt Mary included. "And," she asserted, "in Aunt Mary—I have found a congenial soul—one who understands and says she likes with all her heart every thing I tell her. We have had high and sweet communion."

The wedding had to wait till Emerson had delivered what amounted to his inaugural address as a Concordian. The town of Concord had remembered the approach of its second centennial. The town meeting duly appointed committees. September 12, it was decided, was to be celebrated by a procession and an oration. By the end of June, Emerson was engaged to prepare the oration. He spent some weeks in serious work. He borrowed the proof sheets of the local history Lemuel Shattuck was about to publish, hunted up the survivors of the Concord Fight, and took quantities of notes. He got reminiscences from Jonas Buttrick and Abel Davis, as both of them had been present at the famous fight with the British. He felt pity for Thaddeus Blood when he taxed the old man's memory for details of that event, now sixty years in the past. It was "hard to bring them up," Blood apologized; the truth, he said, would never be known.

It was probably the greatest effort Emerson ever made at gathering and checking facts in the manner of a scholar, with the possible exception of his more deliberate preparation for the writing of his book on England many years later. When Shattuck became nervous over the danger that things he contributed would be published in the address before his history could appear, Emerson tried to impress this benefactor with the extent of his own original investigations: "I have now on my table," Emerson explained, "the seven first volumes of the Town Records, and the Volume of Church Records; all which books I have examined with great attention; I have Johnson's Wonder Working Providence in the Historical Collections. I have here also Hubbard's Indian Wars, Mathers Magnalia, Winthrops Journal Hutchinsons History & his Collection; Minot; & Bradford; Bancroft's U. S. Peter Bulkeleys Gospel Covenant. Allens Biog. Dictionary. Dr Ripley's Half Century Sermon & History of ye Fight; Phinney; & the Lexington Sermons; Brigham's Discourse at Grafton; &c—These books are & have been before me. At Cambridge in August I made written extracts from Neal's New Eng^d; Shepards Clear Sunshine &c; Mourt; Higginson; Josselyn; Underhill; Shepards Lamentation, &c. And I believe I have several extracts which might interest you." This meant that Emerson had made a serious attack on the available sources of early New England history.

In spite of some grumbling by those who charged that the celebration was in the hands of the aristocrats, all was in smooth running order. Plans had been carefully made for the unusual pageant of groups ranging from the school children to the surviving soldiers of the Concord Fight. The town was ready for its great day. Grandfather Ripley's "old meeting house showed such a mass of heads" as had "hardly been crowded under its roof since roof it had" when the psalm was sung from the old Bay psalm book of 1640 and was " 'deaconed' out, a line at a time, after the fashion of our grandfathers, & sung by the whole congregation."

Emerson's address, lasting an hour and forty-five minutes, was what Charles Emerson called it, "a faithful historical sketch of this Town," giving due honor to "the brave company of First Settlers," to "the red men the original lords of the soil," and to the citizens of Revolutionary days, when "the quiet river" of the town's fortunes, "swollen by tributary waters, rushed over the rocky barriers that would have choked its course." It was an admirable address for the occasion. In spite of some complaint of injury to ancestral pride, few Concordians past or present could have been displeased with the orator's account of local history; and probably no other subject would have served Emerson better as a passport to the good graces of the town.

He was by this time a property owner in Concord. The house he had first selected for his intended bride turned out to be unavailable, and the wedding seemed to recede into the distance. Lydia, grieved, opened her Bible and got the comfort she wanted, for her eye fell on the text, "Furthermore I tell thee that the Lord will build thee an house." At least so goes the family tradition, and at all events the engaged couple did not have too long to wait. About the beginning of July, Emerson agreed to pay \$3,500 to John Coolidge for the house built not many years earlier for Charles Coolidge. At last, with the Coolidge House ready and the historical address over, the wedding could take place.

On the 13th of September, undeterred by his mother's notion that his match was "a Petruchio sort of affair," Emerson set out in a chaise on his way to Plymouth; but he kept his joy well within the limits of dignity, and on his way out of Concord he stopped at the stable to have the new bright yellow reins that had been furnished him changed for green ones. He explained that he discarded the yellow reins "lest people should think he had been weaving them of golden-rod." Next day he rode on from Boston, where he had stopped for the night. The weather was rainy, but to the great relief of Lydia Jackson, a person who habitually noticed portents, the Plymouth skies cleared in the evening. Emerson did not arrive at the Winslow House, the old Jackson family home, till about four o'clock; and afterwards he sat talking with the bride so long that there was hardly time for her to dress. Then she was so slow in dressing that he started upstairs to inquire for her. They met on the landing, and, as she had foreseen in her vision months before, they walked downstairs together to be married. In the morning Emerson and Lydia, henceforth Lidian so far as he was concerned, set out in the chaise for Concord; and late that afternoon she saw for the first time the house that was to be her home from that moment till the day of her death, over fifty-seven years later.

The house, not quite half a mile from the center of the village of Concord, stood near the point where the Cambridge Turnpike branched off from Lexington Road, the stagecoach route to Boston. Long, undulating Revolutionary Ridge, rising a little distance to the north beyond but closely bordering Lexington Road, seemed like a protecting wall against the winter winds but was too distant to be completely effective in that capacity. The whole of the slightly more than two Coolidge acres was low-lying land, extending down to the Mill Brook, and so was at some disadvantage in a town where rivers and marshes were as prominent topographical features as ridges and hills. In 1835 the main part of the two-story house was L-shaped. The kitchen and servants' quarters, stretching out to the south toward the garden and the brook, made the L more emphatic. The building was unsatisfactory as it stood, but it was said to be firmly constructed. Emerson started with the conviction that the outside of it could not be fine until trees and flowers gave it a character of its own, but he had already resolved to "crowd so many books & papers, &, if possible, wise friends, into it that it shall have as much wit as it can carry."

As Ruth Emerson was going for a long visit in New York, Lidian set about getting the Coolidge House, or Coolidge Castle, as the Emersons sometimes called it, into proper running order according to her own ideas. Keeping the Emersons' maid and adding one of her own, she quickly established a domestic regime that her husband, a lover of quiet and simple life, doubtless thought unnecessarily elaborate.

Her letters to her sister showed her in a happy and determined mood. She had made a day's work of the parlor carpet, "though Nancy as well as Mr E. helped me where they could." The house and grounds were even better than she had at first thought. All was bright and peaceful, and she did not expect any event or trial that would be beyond her power to bear easily with the strength which, she said, had so wonderfully sustained her: "I look at all through which I have been conducted at the mercies which have been granted to me *so unworthy*—in deep gratitude—in calm amazement." She was soon speaking of her happiness with an almost religious exaltation and wanted her sister to come and see for herself. Lidian was delighted with the "calm holy prayers of the morning and evening the beautiful portion of scripture." She marveled at the devotion her husband showed her and thought that he and she would "surely make each others happiness. Little did they know Waldo Emerson who believed he could be content to pass through life without domestic happiness," she explained to her sister. "He was formed for it as perhaps few are. And not only to enjoy but to impart, all the warmer charities of social and domestic life."

Economy, it soon appeared, was necessary, though the financial difficulties were by no means insuperable. Expenses were piling up, and though Emerson now had $11,500 at interest, the single item of taxes, town and county and ministerial, was over seventy dollars. William Sohier, the lawyer, was doing what he could to make the second half of the Tucker inheritance available but had to overcome the inertia of others concerned in the settlement. Some of the heirs seemed, as Charles put it, to have adopted Emerson's own philosophy that one had eternity to do one's business in. Waldo Emerson himself gave an impressive example of economy by persisting in wearing a couple of old coats, "rags and all," much to his wife's astonishment. Finances became a subject of family conferences. "Mr E & myself," Lidian told her sister after some two weeks of marriage, "had the other day another sober 'Darby and Joan' calculation of both his income & mine—and find that we have plenty with careful management and renouncing of superfluities of all kinds, but without it—must go behind hand." She announced her acceptance of the new economic theory. "But," she added her reservation, "we do not intend to retrench so far as to be any less hospitable to the transcendentals & other friends than we have all along planned I promise Mr E. that I will be contented if he will be

—to give our many visitors only things comfortable dispensing wholly with luxury & show Company will be but small additional expense if we keep but the same decent table that we hope to afford at all times."

The routine of the household was getting established. For her sister's benefit Lidian described a typical day: "We have prayers in the morning a little before 7— —breakfast at 7—then I hold a consultation with Nancy about dinner and can go to my work reading or writing without further care. We dine exactly at one—Mr E & myself then set about writing letters if there are any to write or finish—for the mail at 3—then I take my nap—and then my walk with Mr E. or to see Aunt Mary—or she comes here—or I sit down alone to my occupations. Tomorrow I mean to undertake the most hopeful of the old coats to keep me busy. We drink tea at six—half an hour before which Mr E. issues forth from his sanctum to sit the blind-man's-holiday with me. In the evening he brings down his work and I take mine and after talking a bit we 'make a mum' and keep it till 9 o'clock when we call the girls and have prayers— Then we talk a while, or I read to my blind man.—Charles E did sleep here but he found it less convennt than to remain at his room; he eats with us and *talks*, too, which is better still. Sometimes it comes over me as *so* strange that I should be housed with these two wonderful beings—turning out coffee for them and helping them to pie! Consulting also about the keeping of pigs & hens—and telling Waldo to be sure to stop at the grocers in his morning expedition, and tell him to send home some eggs & ginger; —and to inquire the price of molasses & rinsing-tubs. All which he dutifully promises to do."

Lidian and her husband soon succeeded in accustoming themselves to a domesticity that proved a lasting bond between them, and it seemed probable that their common interest in ideas was destined to contribute quite as much to their mutual happiness. One anonymous resident of Plymouth had looked upon their approaching marriage as "the conjunction of the two planets" and as a kind of festival of the Transcendentalists. Lidian, fixed in her ways, had, it is true, struck this same observer as having, on the eve of her wedding day, rather the appearance of "one of the vestals . . . who in a fit of forgetfulness had let her lamp go out and was preparing herself for the living burial, than that of a maiden about to be united to Waldo Emerson." Nevertheless, her union with such a man as Emerson had still seemed sure to be "a tale of spirituality & idealism."

The marriage was always successful in most ways; but, as time went on, Lidian's strong ties to more conventional religious teachings restrained her, and she found his progress into untrammeled freedom of thought too rapid for her to keep pace with. The nickname of Asia that he sometimes gave her seemed suitable not only because no other New Englander he knew possessed such a depth of feeling continually called out on trivial occasions but also because it symbolized Christianity and even religious conservatism. Palestine, another of his names for her, expressed the latter meaning even more emphatically. In their Concord home the prayers and domestic devotions were soon omitted, to her deep regret. At first she was saddened. Later she turned upon Transcendental doctrine a stream of clever satire, good-natured but penetrating.

The family tradition that for five years Lidian felt herself more and more married but that this growth in felicity was checked noticeably when what she called the "Transcendental Times" gave her a different view of her husband, is undoubtedly correct. But Lidian herself was at first reckoned one of the new lights and worked loyally with her husband in ushering in those "Times" that later proved so distressing to her. In the autumn of 1835 she and he waited together in an attitude of pleased expectation, for their fellow Transcendentalists were already knocking at the gate of Coolidge Castle.

15.

PAN AND OTHER GODS

> *Socrates.* Should we not offer up a prayer first of all
> to the local deities?
> *Phaedrus.* By all means.
> *Socrates.* Beloved Pan, and all ye other gods who haunt
> this place, give me beauty in the inward soul; and may the
> outward and inward man be at one. May I reckon the wise
> to be the wealthy, and may I have such a quantity of gold
> as a temperate man and he only can bear and carry.—Any-
> thing more? The prayer, I think, is enough for me.
> —Plato's *Phaedrus,* translated by Benjamin Jowett

CONCORD was from two to three hours from the city of Boston
if one measured the distance by the lumbering stages that traveled
the Lexington Road past Emerson's house. The whole town contained only some two thousand inhabitants, and, if the near future
could be predicted from the recent past, its annual increase was not likely
to be more than five or ten persons. The village itself, with only a part of
the town's population, promised to be, as its name originally suggested, the
abode of peace, or of as much peace as one could reasonably expect to
find in an America stirred with bitter political strife.

Even in Concord one noticed signs of that strife. The antimasonic faction had made an impressive showing in the last congressional election
against even so honored a man as Samuel Hoar, Charles Emerson's prospective father-in-law; and less than a year later one of the local papers had
claimed that all Middlesex County was redeemed from Whiggism, the
curse of all curses. The reformers were stirring on all sides. Josiah Bartlett,
destined to be the Emersons' family doctor, had accepted the presidency of
the Concord Temperance Society. The recently founded Middlesex Anti-
Slavery Society had already held its first quarterly meeting at Grandfather
Ripley's church in Concord. George Thompson, the English abolitionist,
had spoken with extemporaneous eloquence to a spellbound audience. The
rising tide of antislavery propaganda threatened to engulf Coolidge Castle,
though its master had hitherto kept clear of organized reform. At the dining
table there sat his brother Charles, the clever talker who had not long since
declared himself an abolitionist and announced that he was going to make

a public address on the dangerous subject of slavery. Shortly after his marriage Waldo Emerson, much to his surprise, had been brought face to face at his own breakfast table with the redoubtable Thompson. Aunt Mary had happened to be boarding in the town at the time and had engineered this meeting with the abolitionist without asking her nephew's advice. A few days later a Boston mob stripped William Lloyd Garrison of "a large portion" of his clothing, and Thompson was soon forced to take ship secretly for England in order to save his life.

Concord was caught in the grip of America's destiny, yet here one could at least retreat into the woods on pleasant days and calm one's soul. After some months of his trial of rural life Emerson was delighted with it. "I love the mighty PAN," he assured himself.

He had set himself apart from the outside world as effectively as he could afford to do, and now doubtless most of the villagers and farmers felt that he was a person apart from them too. From the first his rare visits to the grocery store, where the country wits clustered about the stove, must have chilled the genial current of mind that flowed there. He was a scholar among plain but clever people. Though he firmly believed in the democratic scheme of government, he was hardly at home in the town meetings, where others with less knowledge of books than he had knew far better how to make the machinery of politics move. In the spring of 1836 he suffered the usual fate of the newly married man by being elected a hog-reeve, but his duty of assessing fines against the owners of marauding swine was presumably only nominal. A month later the town, this time taking his special fitness into consideration, elected him to the school committee after he had served by appointment to fill a vacancy on it. Citizens had been dissatisfied with the board, and he was its only former member whom they allowed to remain active. He was quickly made its chairman, and its secretary as well. But long before he came to Concord, he had learned from experience what burdensome detail such honors might load him with. He demonstrated how briefly the secretarial records might be kept; and when he was delegated to draw up the official return of the town schools, he paid the full fee to a deputy and had him do the actual work. By this time, some half year after his election, he had resigned his office.

In spite of his need for more uninterrupted quiet in his own study, he did not entirely shut himself up from the rest of the community. His wife and his brother Charles were links to life outside the home. His mother, returning some eight months after his marriage to make her permanent residence with him, must have done what she could to keep him connected with the local Unitarian society. In his early Concord years he seems to have been not only a pew-holder but a loyal attendant at Grandfather

Ripley's church. He joined the Concord Social Library and was at once chosen a member of its three-man standing committee, and later he was elected president. For half a dozen years he served the library, and after a period of freedom he was back in harness again just before the institution was taken over by the town. To the sermons he sometimes preached for his grandfather's church he added occasional lectures for the local lyceum. He was still doing more than his part as a citizen of the town; but naturally, though Aunt Mary was now becoming estranged, his close associates were his relatives and a few writers who either came to live near him or were his visitors.

Aunt Mary's defection and her half-hearted attempt at reconciliation could have been predicted on both temperamental and intellectual grounds. Though she at first took delight in Lidian, Mary Moody Emerson soon found it impossible to keep up her unwonted sweetness of temper. The demon of her satirical wit possessed her in an evil hour at her nephew's dinner table. With Charles present as a witness, she set off an explosion of tempers. Angry and ashamed, she vowed she would never again spend an hour in Waldo Emerson's house unless she were brought there on a litter. On second thought she also ruled out the litter. She regretted "two or three jokes" she had made but was otherwise determined, for a time, to be unrepentant. Yet she did not renounce, as she explained to Waldo, "my early admiration of your genius—which I love to hover over as like to some admirable sculptor—like to some vision of nature w'h haunted me in youth." And in a fit of generosity she shouldered much of the blame for their estrangement, professing her own unworthiness to be his friend. It looked for the moment as if their quarrel might be patched up.

But Aunt Mary knew that the real conflict between them was over ideas and was fundamental. She had been the most determined foe of Waldo Emerson's incipient Transcendentalism, and she was sticking to her guns. After inciting him in his childhood to think daringly, she had finally lost him in what she called "the chaos of modern speculation," where she could not feel at home. Now she looked back over their wordy battles with a sense of bewilderment. "I knew not," she admitted, "on what ground you did any thing—nor where to find your principles—they were an enigma." With a sigh of relief she explained, "I do not regret the tedious history. . . . But . . . 'tis truth to say our usual intercourse is ended." And, as it turned out, she was right about the end of their old intercourse.

Aunt Mary, with all her bewilderment over the behavior of her nephew, had seen with remarkable clarity the outlines of the chief development of New England thought in that generation. She had warned against the "humanitarians," deniers of Christ's divinity, among whom she placed him and, with some hesitation, William Ellery Channing. She thought she saw through Channing's "deep poetic sentiment, and pious enthusiasm." What had his high-strained thought accomplished in the last twenty years? What had humanitarianism done to abolish slavery? Nothing. Instead, it had chilled faith. With its supernatural character taken away, Christianity was a straw before the tempest. No matter how high man was raised by high-flown language like Channing's, after a few efforts his waxen wings would fall. Thus she had warned, adding that though Calvinism had dug a dark ravine, it was Unitarianism that had filled it with victims. In her eyes the vindictive creed of the Calvinist had at least the virtue of making sin appear in its odious reality. But she had leveled her scorn at the half-baked humanitarians because they had left out the Judgment Day and the "consummation of this passing world" from their careless reckonings. Soon she had begun to identify Transcendentalism with the worst in humanitarianism. By the time of her nephew's second marriage she had become a sworn enemy of Transcendentalism and it was too late to hope to convert her. Whatever influence she had was henceforth a check upon extreme development of the new doctrines.

But, for Emerson, Aunt Mary's estrangement was far less distressing than another misfortune which his family circle was about to suffer. In 1835, Charles had taken over Samuel Hoar's law office in Concord, and he now looked forward to settling down with Elizabeth Hoar, the lawyer's daughter, in the two new rooms that Waldo planned to build into the L of his house. Charles had good reason, if the high opinions of his friends were just, to expect a great career in both law and politics. But though his life had been all promise, twenty-seven years of zero accomplishment was his own summary of it when he saw his end close at hand. The end came more quickly than any of the family could have believed. There were unmistakable symptoms of the advanced stages of tuberculosis. Alarmed, Waldo Emerson took Charles to New York by easy stages in the last weeks of April and left him in William's care. For a few days, the stricken young man seemed to improve, but by the 9th of May he was dead. Emerson returned, bringing Elizabeth Hoar, but they were too late to see him alive. The strain of this loss, after so many losses, was heavy for Waldo Emerson. With his nerves tense to the breaking point as he stood at his brother's grave, he let "compressed nature," according to one observer, break through his restraint "*in a laugh*—and an ejaculation 'dear boy.' " He gloomily commented, " 'When one has never had but little society—and *all that society* is taken away—what is there worth living for?' "

Emerson had, as he said, lost a soul "so costly & so rare that few persons were capable of knowing its price." Concord seemed colorless without

Charles's "immense promise" and Emerson felt "not only unfastened there and adrift but a sort of shame at living at all." Others could not have known how Charles had kept critically aloof from his brother's thinking and might have proved a salutary influence on it had he lived longer. But praises came from all sides for him. Oliver Wendell Holmes, a college classmate of his, pictured the "calm, chaste scholar" in a poem read at the Phi Beta Kappa anniversary that year. Harriet Martineau remembered her indebtedness. "At the time of the hubbub against me in Boston," she later explained it, "Charles Emerson stood alone in a large company in defence of the right of free thought and speech, and declared that he had rather see Boston in ashes than that I, or anybody, should be debarred in any way from perfectly free speech."

Demands came from several of Charles's friends that a selection of posthumous writings, introduced by a memoir, should be published. Waldo Emerson had begun almost immediately after his brother's death to look over the papers left to his care, but he found much narrower limitations than he had expected. It was hard enough for him to understand why his brother's journal should have so bitter a strain of penitence and depreciation. Then came his more depressing discovery that, after all, Charles had not had notable literary talent. "I mourn that in losing him," he regretfully concluded, "I have lost his all, for he was born an orator, not a writer." Though he kept the question of publication open for a long time, he finally printed only a few brief selections from Charles's manuscripts in *The Dial.*

Yet Charles had really been an extraordinary person. Waldo Emerson did not exaggerate his own estimate when he declared, "In Charles, I found society that indemnified me for almost total seclusion from all other. He was my philosopher, my poet, my hero, my Christian. Of so creative a mind that (tho' he wrote no verse) yet his conversation made Shakspear more conceivable to me; such an adorer of truth that he awed us, and a spirit of so much hilarity & elegancy that he actualized the heroic life to our eyes . . ." So severe was the loss that Emerson found the whole structure of his own philosophy momentarily shaken. Trying to fit his loss into it, he could "gather no hint from this terrible experience," and only groped "in greater darkness." The best exegesis he could make of this obscure text was that "Night rests on all sides upon the *facts* of our being, tho', we must own, our upper nature lies always in Day."

Lucy Brown, Lidian's sister, helped to enliven the household for weeks at a time but could not make up for the great loss it had suffered. It was the fortunate birth of Emerson's first child, Waldo, in October, 1836, a few months after Charles's death, that restored the foundations of optimism.

Emerson fell an easy convert to the cult of childhood after a mere pretense of keeping a philosophical aloofness. "The stimulated curiosity of the father," he tried to explain, "sees the graces and instincts which exist indeed in every babe, but unnoticed in others; the right to see all, know all, to examine nearly, distinguishes the relation, and endears this sweet child." At first he saw nothing of his own in the child and was "no conscious party to any feature, any function, any perfection I behold in it." "I seem," he confessed, "to be merely a brute occasion of its being, and nowise attaining to the dignity even of a second cause, no more than I taught it to suck the breast." But after giving the matter another thought, he observed, "Now am I Pygmalion."

Outside his home he gradually formed other social ties. After less than a year in his rural retreat he dreamed of a choice social circle there. "I will tell you," he wrote to Frederic Hedge, "what society would please me; that you should be the minister of Concord & George P. B its school master & Carlyle a resident whilst he lectured in Boston and Mrs Ripley & Mr Alcott should be visiters." Hedge was never minister of Emerson's town. Carlyle, though he frequently hinted at a transatlantic venture, never saw America. But George Bradford was later a schoolmaster in Concord, Amos Bronson Alcott was by turns a visitor and a resident, and Sarah Alden Ripley eventually settled down in the Old Manse. Alcott, however, was the only one of them to become a frequent companion of Emerson's over a long period of years.

Emerson had heard of Alcott through George Bradford as early as the summer of 1835, and within a few days thereafter he had met the clock-maker, farmer, and pedlar who was by this time a radical schoolmaster in Boston. A few more days and he was acquainted with Elizabeth Peabody's "beautiful book." This *Record of a School* revealed to an amazed public what philosophical discussions Alcott had been carrying on with his pupils at the temple. In the following October, George Bradford brought Alcott to Concord. Alcott and Emerson were already known to each other as "spiritualists," or idealists, and now, during a week-end visit, they became aware of their agreement on a broad area of speculation. Alcott assured himself that he had found no man in whose whole mind he felt more sympathy. Emerson briefly limned Alcott: "A wise man, simple, superior to display . . ." And he jotted down the heads of Alcott's conversation. At the end of November Alcott was back again for two or three more days of talk. His words were so hypnotizing that one hardly saw the person who uttered them. "The wise man who talks with you," Emerson observed, "seems of no particular size, but, like the sun and moon, quite vague and indeterminate." Alcott, for his part, was deeply stirred by what

Emerson managed to say; and he resolved to seek this new friend's "face and favor as a precious delight of life."

That winter Emerson undertook, with many misgivings, the delicate task of suggesting revisions in the manuscript of Alcott's "Breath of Childhood," as it seems first to have been called, or "Psyche," as it was soon rechristened. Alcott had got the stuff of his book by patiently observing the mental and moral growth of his infant daughters and trying to fathom the relation of childhood to spirit. "Psyche" chanted as its refrain the superiority and priority of spirit even in a world of matter, a doctrine long dear to Emerson; and it confided the guidance of the head to the heart. Emerson, already a lover of Wordsworth's ode in praise of childhood, admired and detested Alcott's manuscript. He saw its sincerity; but he also saw that as a piece of writing it was shapeless, lacked variety of thought and illustration, and was too dogmatic. He listed a number of passages that he believed ought to be rescued from the dross and made into a book; and he gave Alcott a sheaf of suggested corrections. Alcott, never having received any such aid before, was grateful. He tried to follow directions and within a few months brought the manuscript back for fresh criticism. Some two years later Emerson twice reread it. "If the book were mine," he advised the distressed author, "I would on no account print it; and the book being yours, I do not know but it behoves you to print it in defiance of all the critics." Though Emerson offered, against his own judgment, to try to find a publisher, Alcott took the unfavorable verdict to heart.

But the sharp critic of "Psyche" sat and listened with admiration as its author, presiding at his desk, exercised the minds of his young pupils upon questions of "taste and truth." When *Conversations with Children on the Gospels* was published, Emerson tried to defend Alcott from the vicious attacks of prudish enemies. He paid for the tuition of his late friend George Sampson's son at the ill-starred Temple School. There were visits back and forth between Concord and Boston, where Alcott lived, but Concord was the preferred meeting place. Emerson was not slow to discover Alcott's weaknesses. He must have approved every line of the younger William Ellery Channing's verses addressing the impractical idealist as

> thou Don Quixote of the soul;
> Thou bee without a sting,
> Thou ball that will not roll,
> Thou rose without a thorn,
> Thou stalk without its corn,
> Thou everlasting talker,
> Thou essential sleep-walker,
> Alcott my gossip fine . . .

Yet he stubbornly held to his own high estimate of the rare intellectual qualities of his friend.

Emerson would doubtless have included Margaret Fuller when he listed his select spirits had he known her then as he began to do on the following day. She was quite as important an entrant into the widening Concord circle as Alcott. At the age of twenty-six, she was slight, tense, clever, uncommonly intelligent, and ambitious. Though she was by no means beautiful, once she got well into a conversation, she could set up an intellectual current of surprising power. She was a talker, a feminine and more scholarly Alcott come to rescue the quiet, self-contained Emerson from his too great mental isolation. She was also a lover of action, as Alcott was not. Just now she was reaching out, pleased to find masters who could give her a sense of direction, and she had long had her eye on Emerson as one such master.

Doubtless Harriet Martineau had, as she claimed, encouraged some preliminary steps toward the new friendship. But Margaret could scarcely have made any real progress till the summer of 1836, and it was probably Elizabeth Peabody who got the somewhat grimly determined young woman an invitation to Concord at that time. According to her own story, Elizabeth told Emerson she wished him to "know Margaret better" and explained how she herself had felt at first, as he now felt, a strong but unjustifiable prejudice against her. This testimony, it seems, together with Lidian's urging, overcame his objections.

Margaret's first visit lengthened out to three weeks, and her host's praise of his guest did not grow fainter the longer she stayed. She was "quite an extraordinary person," Emerson made up his mind after more than two weeks of her. "It is always a great refreshment to see a very intelligent person," he said. "It is like being set in a large place. You stretch your limbs & dilate to your utmost size." He had at once discovered exactly what Margaret could do for him. As she herself knew, she always carried her magic with her, and it had little to do with her femininity or with her wardrobe. Her "faded calico frock," she honestly told her sister Ellen, did not prevent her from "exciting respect and interest" at Concord. Her magic lay in her quick, sympathetic mentality and in her ability to get the best ideas out of her companions.

Before the visit was ended she had completed her conquest of both the Emersons. "We like her—she likes us," Lidian confided the family opinion to Elizabeth Peabody. "I speak in this way—because you know we came together almost strangers—all to one another and the result of the experiment—as Miss F. herself said in her letter to you on the subject of a nearer acquaintance with us—was doubtful—the tendencies of all three being strong

& decided—and possibly not such as could harmonize." It had turned out as Lidian had expected from the first in spite of some unfavorable rumors she had heard about Margaret. "I ought not to speak," she said, "as if I had myself had much doubt that I should enjoy Miss F's society—I had heard from the best authority that she was sound at *heart*—and I could imagine no peculiarities of intellect or character, that cou[ld] revolt me or repel my regard—if that [w]as true of her."

The advent of two such highly individual intellectuals as Alcott and Margaret Fuller in the Emerson circle within less than a year of each other was significant. However much Emerson wished detachment from anything resembling a concerted movement, his own influence as a leader thus greatly increased at the critical moment when the Transcendentalists were beginning to distinguish one another from the heterogeneous mass of New England liberals. The inevitable founding of a brotherhood of Transcendentalists for mutual encouragement and enlightenment was, whether he liked it or not, already under way. His friend Frederic Hedge, the scholarly young minister who had learned the idiom of German speech and thought in his school days, partly at the famous Schulpforta, seems to have been the prime instigator of an association. As early as 1835 a scheme had been proposed for the founding of a journal to serve as a rallying point. Hedge was at first slated to be editor of what was to be called the *The Transcendentalist,* or *The Spiritual Inquirer,* or the like. But when he was about to remove from the neighborhood of Boston to the backwoods of Maine, he suggested that Carlyle be persuaded to assume the editorial direction. Carlyle actually considered coming to America about this time, but not very seriously. Emerson planned that if the Scot would come, the journal should be his main dependence for a living. The whole project for a magazine, it turned out, had to be postponed for years. But some sort of association of the like-minded could be formed without much delay, and Hedge was still the chief mover. He would be able to attend it when he came down from Maine from time to time.

When, in June of 1836, Emerson received a proposal that he join such an association, he was dubious. For him a debating club, though the subject to be discussed was nothing less expansive than the general state of the world, might not be profitable. Suspecting that not all of even so select a company would prove to be intuitionalists, he waited a month before announcing his "hearty good will to the project." He knew his mind accurately. It was his mental habit to see a kind of vision of truth that he could only report as he saw it and would not attempt to argue. "The men of strong understanding," he said, "are a menacing rapid trenchant race —they cut me short—they drive me into a corner—I must not suggest, I

must define—& they hold me responsible for a demonstration of every sentiment I endorse. Whilst therefore I cannot sufficiently give thanks for the
existence of this class, without whom there could not be either porridge or
politics I do, for my particular, thoroughly avoid & defy them."

He had "never found that uplifting & enlargement from the conversation of many" which he found "in the society of one faithful person." But
he conceded that the experiment proposed by Hedge had never been fairly
tried, he hoped pure pleasure from it, he suggested a time for the first
meeting which proved to be too early, and he recommended Alcott as a
prospective member. Hedge's plan called for an assembly of ministers.
Emerson could hardly say enough for Alcott, though conceding that there
were some serious faults in him. "You must admit Mr Alcott over the professional limits, for he is a God-made priest," he insisted. The projected
club, however, needed a couple of months more of gestation before it
could be born.

Meantime, Emerson, though he continued to preach irregularly for a
few years longer. had written what was probably his last sermon. Yet he
still spent his eyes in reading religious literature. He had his Swedenborgian
magazine, and he had his notes on the obscure Swedenborgian Oegger.
Oegger's doctrine of the dependence of language upon natural objects and
of the special service nature did man by illustrating concretely man's moral
conceptions which would otherwise remain pale abstractions was nothing
new to Emerson, but in Oegger it was both emphatic and plain. Oegger,
however, offended by insisting on the special divinity of Jesus and on the
indisputable authority of the Bible. Swedenborgian Sampson Reed's prestige was not quite ended. Emerson had for some time been curious about
Böhme, the mystic; but it is by no means certain that any work of Böhme's
ever became his "favourite book," as Elizabeth Peabody believed. He had
extended his explorations of Oriental philosophy to the writings of Confucius.

But his serious studies generally took a more literary turn. Doubtless
for a time he and Lidian spurred each other to the study of German. One
of his prenuptial gifts to her had been an anthology of Richter. Already
Emerson had laboriously covered many pages of his journals with his own
translations of Goethe. He was struck by Goethe's theories of beauty and
by his espousal of the old idea that all existing things are to be found in
some measure in every existing thing, that each bears some resemblance
to all others. He quickly conquered his distrust of the German Olympian
on the score of morals and set out to explore the many small volumes of
the Stuttgart and Tübingen edition. In the summer of 1836 he discovered
that a Boston bookstore would sell him fifteen, the only copies available,
of the posthumous volumes then in course of publication. It was bliss to be

alive in this new intellectual dawn. Emerson found it easy to turn a deaf ear to Aunt Mary's admonition, ostensibly aimed at Lidian, to "Abandon Goethe—cleave to his antipode the Saviour of men." A few weeks after his purchase of the fifteen posthumous volumes he was sure that Goethe was "the high priest of the age" and "the truest of all writers."

Goethe's chief British admirer, Thomas Carlyle, was stirring up numerous American admirers, not only of Goethe but of himself. Among the latter, Emerson, having visited Carlyle and being his correspondent, was conspicuous. The rumor had got abroad that he had received as many as fifty copies of "Sartor Resartus," still only an improvised pamphlet. Though other persons already planning an American edition preferred to wait until there were better prospects of success, Le Baron Russell, Emerson's Plymouth friend, vigorously seized upon the project and persuaded Emerson himself to write the preface. Encouraged by a modest number of subscribers, Russell published five hundred copies. By April of 1836 Emerson had proudly sent one of these to the author but was not hopeful of a good sale, as he often heard well founded objections to the extraordinary style.

While he was borrowing and spreading the ideas of others Emerson was putting his own into order for the lecture platform or the press. His peculiar habits of thought made special difficulties for the prospective hearer or reader. The stability and unity of his philosophy was undermined by his conviction that truth grew and changed. In his opinion, the truest state of mind became false if one rested in it. He liked the flash of truth that showed intuition at work. Yet he also practiced a kind of inductive method. He affirmed the value of observation and observed commonplace facts. He not only drew much upon experiences recorded in history, in confessions, in biographies, in poetry, and in the bibles of various peoples, but he relied upon his own firsthand studies of the behavior of men. He did not expect his Transcendental theories to be valid despite all human experience. Still, when driven into a corner, he was apt to be stubbornly confident that a little later on, if not now, they would be justified by a wise interpretation of experience.

Charles Emerson had suspected him of caressing ideas and hoarding them because of their appeal to the aesthetic sense rather than valuing them as aids in shaping conduct. Though Charles had carried his complaints to Aunt Mary in vain, he had continued to take the matter to heart. Only a few months before his death he had tried to decide in his fragmentary journal why Waldo's thoughts seemed unsubstantial. "I think," he had answered the question, "because he sits among them as the epicure at his long table who would send away no dish untasted. Not that Thoughts are with him things of manufacture of mere merchantable value, no, but works of art, in the finish & perfection of which he is interested as the painter in his landscape or the sculptor in his statue— But I want my thoughts rather as bread of life—& God who gives me daily bread, supplies to me reason whereby I apprehend those which are necessary to me." Charles must have given this comment almost immediately to Waldo, and Waldo's prompt record of it in his own journal may have confirmed Charles's judgment. According to Charles, so Waldo had summed up the criticism, perhaps all truth was merely occasional, not designed to be stored for contemplation, but alive only in action. This was a bit of pragmatism that he remembered. He had, however, undoubtedly accepted Charles's dictum, not as a complete and final statement, but as mirroring one of the conflicting aspects of truth.

He held a far more favorable opinion than Charles's of the substantiality of his thoughts. He had already found that the audiences in lecture halls did not demand that the idealist dismount from his winged horse. He had already learned how to hold his audience, whether in the country lyceum or in the city. In spite of what must have seemed to some a certain rusticity of appearance, the tall, lanky Concordian could display more urbanity of mind than almost any other American lecturer. He knew the English language better than most. He had the advantage of an excellent voice, said to have been at its best when he entered his thirties.

Even before his historical address at Concord he had been in some demand for occasional lectures. In August of 1835 he had addressed the American Institute of Instruction, in Boston, on "The Best Mode of Inspiring a Correct Taste in English Literature." In November of that year, he had begun his course of ten lectures on English literature for the Society for the Diffusion of Useful Knowledge, at the Masonic Temple in the same city; and after the first evening he had believed he would never again distrust men's appetites for the abstractest speculation. Charles's comment to William, "But you & I know how the pill is gilt & sugared," had testified to the practical rhetorical skill of the lecturer as well as to the simplicity of his manner.

The ten manuscripts of the course of 1835–1836 were carefully preserved, though for Emerson their only value must have been as a record of progress. They showed how he had viewed the pageant of English authors, his chief models; they summarized his thinking at the moment when he was about to finish his own first book; and in later years they proved that the drift of his thinking had already found its permanent direction before he was known as an author.

In these lectures Chaucer was a text for comment on sources and orig-

inality and illustrated the national mind, but writers from Shakespeare to
Byron were tested mainly by ethical and philosophical standards. George
Herbert, a great favorite, was defended for his temperate use of a "style
chiefly marked by the elaborate decomposition to which every object is
subjected" and by a delight in discovering abstruse relationships. But the
most significant thing in Herbert was his power to excite the feeling of
the moral sublime. The whole course might have been very frankly entitled
"A Transcendentalist Looks at British Literature." Such writers as could
not be made to march in review under some fold of the Transcendental
banner suffered serious deductions from their fame.

Locke and Coleridge were the most unmistakable representatives of two
irreconcilable groups of thinkers much discussed in the lectures. John Locke
would "be always respectable," but his epoch, said Emerson, marked "the
decline & not the rise of a just philosophy. With him disappeared the class
of laborious philosophers who had studied Man with Plato in the belief
that Man existed in connexion with the Divine Mind . . ." Locke's reputation and example "gave leave to a crowd of Essayists who referred the
unfathomable mysteries of human knowledge thought & action, the impression of heaven & continual creation upon our plastic clay to the low
sources of sensation." But Coleridge seemed to surpass all other modern
British writers. His genius was rich exactly where Locke's had been poor.
"He was of that class of philosophers called Platonists, that is, of the most
Universal school; of that class that take the most enlarged & reverent views
of man's nature. His eye was fixed upon Man's Reason as the faculty in
which the very Godhead manifested itself or the Word was anew made
flesh. His reverence for the Divine Reason was truly philosophical & made
him regard every man as the most sacred object in the Universe, the Temple
of Deity." Naturally, *Biographia Literaria* was ranked as "undoubtedly
the best body of criticism in the English language." Now that Coleridge
was dead, his true character and greatness had begun to appear. "Already,"
Emerson declared, "he quits the throng of his contemporaries & takes his
lofty station in that circle of sages whom he loved."

Emerson had received a fee of $200 for the ten lectures, delivered in
as many weeks; and even while he had read the lectures in Boston he had
repeated some of them elsewhere and so, by a little travel, greatly increased
their market value. The not very distant town of Lowell had paid him
$96 at almost the same time he had got his $200 from Boston. He had also
been earning a modest sum by the sermons he had preached, usually twice
a week, during his Boston lecture course. A little later he received not quite
$150 from Salem for some half dozen lectures. Thus, though his financial

returns were not impressive, there was no longer any reason why he should doubt his ability to command a hearing. He was now prepared to issue his challenge more boldly, in the shape of a book.

Nature, his first book, had grown slowly out of his journals, letters, sermons, and lectures. It had seemed nearly ready for the printer by the end of June, 1836; but it was not till the 9th of September that the little volume of ninety-five pages was advertised for sale in Boston. If its title page bore no name, a name was hardly needed, so characteristic of Emerson were the bold thought, checked now and then by admirable restraint, and the poetic but quite functional style of this extraordinary essay.

In it a thinker with none of the conventional timidities of his time and place pleaded for "an original relation to the universe." It was true that at present we saw God and nature only through the eyes of foregoing generations, who had beheld them face to face. But we too might see for ourselves. Surprising vistas were to be opened up. Nature, not the poor material thing she had been supposed to be, held the key. Though separate from spirit, she consistently pointed to spirit as her source and justification. It was because of her relation to spirit that she could always, even in her humblest manifestations, fill the susceptible mind with a wild delight. In a fortunate moment she could lead her devotee into what amounted to a mystical religious experience and hinted at pantheism: "In the woods we return to reason and faith. . . . Standing on the bare ground,—my head bathed by the blithe air and uplifted into infinite space,—all mean egotism vanishes. I become a transparent eyeball; I am nothing; I see all; the currents of the Universal Being circulate through me; I am part or parcel of God." Plotinus, an avowed mystic, had said somewhat the same thing.

But Emerson, having finished this daring flight, quickly made sure that his feet were on the ground again. There was, after all, he warned, a degree of illusion in such experiences. It was "necessary to use these pleasures with great temperance." After his customary manner, Emerson was showing both sides experimentally and was looking for the middle way. In a completely sober chapter he even listed the commonplace practical uses of nature. But, well aware that material values were in no danger of being underestimated, he returned to his immaterial realm. Even beauty in nature, he reiterated Plato's doctrine, was at best only preliminary, "the herald of inward and eternal beauty." And so he repeatedly alternated other-worldliness with matter-of-factness.

The real purpose of the book was to find a scheme of unity into which God, the soul, and nature—the solid world of trees and stones and human bone and flesh—could be fitted. Emerson did not go about this business in a logical way but obviously had somehow to deal with several time-honored theories of unity. The theory of materialism, in Transcendental eyes, solved the problem of unity only by destroying God and the soul and was therefore unthinkable. The religious mystic believed that the soul could enjoy brief moments of perfect union with God and was sure that his experience, however incommunicable it was, proved him right. Emerson, even if he could not claim to speak from a very high order of experience, seems to have accepted at once this theory of unity as a partial answer to his quest. But mystical union, however exalted and real it might be, could not endure beyond brief moments, and nature, though she might be a helpful guide, had no essential part in it. The pantheist whose spiritual God made the soul and the world out of his own divine stuff achieved a far more pleasing unity. Emerson accepted this unity; and yet he was not long content to accept it, because it submerged too completely both nature and the soul. The extreme idealist's exciting theory that nature existed only in the mind, or the soul, pointed in the right direction but did not seem entirely satisfying or convincing to one who loved nature. In this first book Emerson approved mysticism, pantheism, idealism, in varying degrees, by turns. He was not satisfied with any of them, but he leaned most toward idealism. Mainly, though, his idealism was moderate. He was, it seemed, looking for a compromise.

Obviously there was now no complete unity. But in the future there might be. In a chapter on prospects, ending the book, Emerson insisted on looking into the future through intuition rather than through empirical science. He ended, therefore, not with the testimony of a scientist but with "some traditions of man and nature" sung to him by "a certain poet" who was plainly a convinced idealist. Not matter but spirit, sang this Orphic poet, was the foundation of man. Man was now a god in ruins, fallen because he had lost his innocence. But a happy revolution in both man and nature would attend a new influx of spirit.

The Orphic poet, whoever he was, was sponsored by Emerson; but the interesting doubt remained whether he was merely a figure of speech. If Emerson needed a Diotima or an Er, he had as much right to invent one as Plato had had. But it may have pleased his fancy to metamorphose the Transcendental schoolmaster Alcott into "my poet." If so, there was doubtless some significance in the fact that Alcott, his admired friend, his tireless instructor in extreme idealism through many long conversations, and the author of a manuscript book glorifying childhood as a revelation of the spiritual nature of man, gave him "some majestic discourse" just before the latter part of *Nature* was written.

What was important, however, was that Emerson chose to give his poet's song the most commanding place in *Nature*. The whole book was a prose poem with interpolated passages of stark realism. But the Orphic poet's song was a kind of final defiance to untranscendental critics and gave the whole composition an air of exaggerated idealism. |

Both Transcendental and untranscendental critics were soon vocal. Alcott, already familiar with parts of the book, read it within a day or two of publication and thought it "a gem." Carlyle rightly saw in *Nature* "the Foundation and Ground-plan" of his friend's future writing, though actually the future writing proved to be somewhat less extreme than the blueprint demanded. Within a month five hundred copies "were gone." The book had a few hundred readers at least. Reviews added to its modest fame or to its notoriety. The Unitarian *Christian Register* called it a work of genius and justly characterized it as poetical, philosophical, moral, and religious without the forms of poetry, philosophy, ethics, or theology. In *The Western Messenger,* a Unitarian and Transcendental magazine published in the Ohio Valley, Samuel Osgood, still in his Unitarian phase, complained of the obscurity of the Orphic poet's chants but warned the many who would call the book dreamy that its dreams were at least visions of eternal realities.

In January of 1837, Francis Bowen, a young instructor in philosophy at Harvard, gave the little volume what was perhaps its most unfriendly reception. In *The Christian Examiner,* another Unitarian magazine, he mercilessly exposed the weaknesses of the Transcendental mind as they would appear to any unimaginative disciple of John Locke. He did not pretend to understand the chapters on "Spirit" and "Prospects"; but he thought he saw well enough that he and other orthodox expounders of philosophy were cavalierly dismissed as vulgar minds. He saw that the Transcendentalists were really reviving, in their essential doctrines, "the Old Platonic school"; but he nevertheless credited the main inspiration of their philosophy to the Germans, whose language, he remarked, had a genius for novelty and vagueness. In his eagerness to discredit intuition he betrayed a narrow and unscientific conception of the experimental method. Before he finished, he lost his temper and revealed that he had discovered in Emerson and the Transcendentalists "arrogance and self-sufficiency" that were "no less absurd in philosophy, than criminal in morals." But, in spite of some blundering, Bowen may have done a service to the author of *Nature*. For, though in later writings Emerson was frequently carried away by an excess of faith in intuition, he paid, in general, increasing respect to the observation of actual life.

Other reviews of *Nature* were mostly either enthusiastic or sharply antagonistic. A critic in *The United States Magazine, and Democratic Review,* a little more than a year after Bowen had delivered his indictment, was delighted with the book and wanted to "call all those together who have feared that the spirit of poetry was dead, to rejoice that such a *poem* as 'Nature' is written." Various sects made ammunition of the little volume for their own private wars. An English Swedenborgian believed he had discovered an admirable bit of sectarian propaganda by some unknown member of the New Church in America or at least someone who had "read the writings of Swedenborg" and whose mind was "imbued with their truths." Not until another unwary Briton had gone so far as to reprint *Nature* for the use of young Swedenborgians did the distressing revelation come from a keen-eyed American New Church editor and one of his contributors that their fellow religionists had been hoaxed. *Nature,* it had to be explained, had much in it that was familiar to a reader of Swedenborg yet was, in its general meaning, not only an un-Swedenborgian and unchristian book but "infidel and insidious poison."

Whatever the reviewers thought of it, *Nature* was fortunately timed. Not two weeks after its publication, there was held in Boston the preliminary meeting of "Hedge's club," or the Symposium, as its originators sometimes called it in honor of Plato, though outsiders soon dubbed it the Transcendental Club and that name stuck. Emerson, the author of the book that would have served better than any other as the manifesto of the Transcendentalists, was one of the first of the not entirely like-minded to arrive at the home of George Ripley, in Bedford Place, on September 19. The other persons present during the course of the afternoon were Ripley, Hedge, Alcott, Convers Francis, James Freeman Clarke, and Orestes Brownson. The conversation, Emerson thought after some hours of it, was "earnest and hopeful."

The conversers were a group of young and hopeful men. Francis, the oldest, was not quite forty-one; Clarke, the youngest, was twenty-six. The rest were in their thirties. Everyone was a scholar in his own way, but Hedge was remarkable for his grasp of German philosophy, and Ripley was *The Christian Examiner's* writer on foreign thinkers. Brownson was the most formidable controversialist and was quick to catch at new religious and social ideas. He had left the Presbyterian Church to become a Universalist minister and then gone on into the Unitarian ministry but had not yet taken his final plunge into Catholicism.

It was suggested that the rule of admission into the group be that no man should be received whose presence would exclude any topic, but this was doubtless an ideal that could hardly be lived up to. Ripley and his guests, planning their next meeting, agreed on inviting Channing, the veteran leader of American Unitarianism in its long advance into liberalism.

It was also decided that invitations should be sent to James Walker, Unitarian minister at Charlestown; Nathaniel Frothingham, the Unitarian pastor of the old First Church, where Emerson's father had once served for many years; John Sullivan Dwight, fresh from the divinity school at Cambridge and on the lookout for a Unitarian pulpit; Cyrus Bartol, out of the same school a year earlier and likewise waiting for a pulpit; Doctor Channing's nephew William Henry Channing, another recent theological graduate from Cambridge; and the public-spirited Jonathan Phillips, once one of Doctor Channing's atheistical college mates but afterwards one of his deacons, and "one of the intuitive men," as the great preacher said, "whom I take delight in much more than in the merely logical."

Almost the first remark Emerson had made at the preliminary meeting was "that 't was pity that in this Titanic continent, where nature is so grand, genius should be so tame." He had pointed out that there was "Not one unchallengeable reputation" and had cited Allston, Bryant, Greenough, and Doctor Channing by way of illustration. When the second meeting was held, early in October, at Alcott's house, in Boston, this provocative indictment of Emerson's was the topic of conversation. All who attended the preliminary gathering were there, but the only new member present was Bartol. Channing, who cared for few friends and had to conserve his strength, kept aloof. Some recruits came later. One of these, Theodore Parker, must have strengthened the logical fiber of the group's discussions. Meetings continued to be held at irregular times and places. Emerson seems frequently to have found himself not too much oppressed by better logicians and more ready talkers.

If the Symposium was an amorphous club with no dues to collect and no regular members, the persons taking part in its discussions were nevertheless easily identified and their intellectual orientation gradually came to be understood. If these persons were, as was commonly reported, the Transcendentalists, then the Transcendentalists appeared to be mostly extremely liberal Unitarian ministers who were quite as much interested in literature, philosophy, or even social reform as in the church. Most of them were seekers after new truth and were impatient of restraint by any creed. Some were on their way out of the church, or even out of Christianity itself. Though they would not let God be human, they tended to make man divine; and their incipiently divine man had it as one of his duties to get his own most important revelations without depending on a middleman between himself and God. Yet they were not too insistent on original intuitions to realize their deep indebtedness to many minds and doctrines. They had the fervor and conscience of the seventeenth-century Puritan, and they were still getting some nourishment from the dry stalks of Unitarianism. Their intellectual horizons were broadened by the rationalism of the eighteenth century and by the new theories of the natural scientists. They felt the liberalizing pull of political democracy and the expansiveness of the Romantic movement in literature. But they also drew much from the potent essences of various idealisms, mysticisms, pantheisms, and Platonisms. They levied at will upon ancient and modern philosophies and religions. They had the conviction that the world was their province, and they foraged through it for spiritual and mental food. They were not, however, in so much danger of overindulgence as one might have supposed. Even if Transcendentalism sometimes seemed to be the saturnalia of faith, the members of the Transcendental Club were, after all, mostly intellectuals who exercised a good deal of judgment and self-restraint.

Early in December, 1836, Emerson, strengthened, no doubt, by his new ties with fellow Transcendentalists as well as by his newly-won repute as an author, was back on the lyceum platform with a course of no fewer than twelve lectures announced as "Philosophy of History." He saw that the number of lecturers advertising in the newspapers "bore a pretty large proportion to the number of ears in Boston." But, having drawn good audiences the preceding winter, he had made up his mind to be his own manager and was taking the whole financial risk. He went sensibly about his business as manager. Though he had to accept undesirable days in order to get the Masonic Temple again, he was determined to have it. Facing the common on Tremont Street, it was known and accessible to everybody. Its two Gothic towers, rising nearly a hundred feet from the ground and overshadowing the chaste Ionic-columned portico of neighboring St. Paul's, seemed admirable symbols of the aspiration for culture and for the good life that stirred many a lyceum audience in the mid-nineteenth century. It was in this building that Alcott's ultra-liberal Temple School fittingly had its home. On the second floor was the large, oddly-shaped lecture room, "with circular seats upon a spherical floor." Theoretically, a thousand persons, arriving by way of the winding stairways in the towers, were accommodated at a lecture. During this winter Emerson usually found about 350 in his audience.

Though lecturing was for him a necessary means of money-getting, he managed to take it light-heartedly. He did not mean to let his subject cramp him, as he explained to his brother William. "But so much lecturing & now a little printing," he said, "has bronzed me & I am become very dogmatic; and I mean to insist that whatsoever elements of humanity have been the subjects of my studies, constitute the indisputable core of Modern History! To such lengths of madness trot we when we have not the fear of criticism before our eyes: and the literary man in this country has no critic." He needed room to draw his big circles. His announcements seemed to vie, he admitted, with Puck's brag that the earth would be girdled in forty minutes. Each of his lectures took only about ten minutes longer than that.

His dozen lectures brought no carefully elaborated inductive reasoning or logical process of any kind to bear upon the problem of the one and the many. They were twelve cantos on the beauty of that same unity which he had sought to discover in his recent book. Now he tried other exploratory paths. History was defined as the unfolding of the universal mind. The individual, unable to read the lesson of unity in his own life because he was too close to it, had to turn to history. The idea of a spiritual, or intellectual, unity was dominant everywhere. An important aid to the understanding of the unity of history was science, for science, as in Lamarck's evolutionary theory, moved toward central truths. Art, literature, politics, religion, society, trades and professions, manners, ethics were different aspects of history; but as each was singled out and examined it seemed only to add to one's sense of universal unity. "We learn," the lecturer summarized when he faced his audience for the last time, "that there is one Soul . . ." But he seems immediately to have substituted mind for soul. The two things seemed to be the same, and he was in a lecture hall, where the greater realistic force of an unpretentious expression counted.

Exciting passages abounded in the lectures. Doubtless the audience listened anxiously for the sharp comments upon current questions of public interest. A discussion of politics brought the radical thinker momentarily into the conservative camp, where, however, he was ill at ease. In this last winter of Andrew Jackson's administration, Emerson was in no mood to applaud the retiring President. Both political parties, though, had serious faults, he saw; the radicals were not often wisely led, and the conservatives opposed both good and bad measures of their opponents. Yet no matter what the strife, he concluded philosophically, humanity was always the gainer. Amid the harsh discords of politics citizens tended to improve and to become independent of the mutations of parties and states. If Emerson was a conservative, he was one of a new stripe. He was plainly already turning over in his mind his theory that the true function of government was to prepare the way for the self-reliant individual.

The lectures repeated Emerson's habitual glorification of the individual. The individual, sharing in the light and power generated by the universal mind, had a share in divinity. "The walls," Emerson said, "are taken away; we lie open on one side to all the deeps of spiritual nature; to all the attributes of God." He quoted from Oriental philosophy and scripture "examples of the class of sentences, which make us feel the exceeding greatness of our moral sentiment," and he saw moral sentiment as the sure guide of the individual mind. He decried organized reform movements as destructive of individualism. He praised heroic individualism as the heart of good manners. Problems of original sin, the origin of evil, predestination, and the like were merely the childish diseases of the soul. The central arch of ethics was the self-reliance of the single man. Yet there was no narrow egotism in such self-reliance. "The sincere man," the lecturer declared, "who does without second thought that which he is prompted to do . . . is not an individual so much as he is the hands & the tongue of Nature itself." In his manuscript he added a sentence but put it in brackets which may have indicated some doubt as to the wisdom of reading it in public. The gist of it was that if a man could be completely obedient to the inner promptings he would be omnipotent, for his will would be one with the divine will.

At times, in this series on "Philosophy of History," Emerson seemed to be bringing his characteristic ideas into a new harmony. But he stopped far short of suggesting anything resembling a complete philosophical system. His ideas were too poetical to submit to logic. He was content to remain a poet who, whatever shaping power of imagination he lacked, was really inspired by a vision of the unity of things.

Many hearers were pleased with the bold lecturer. Alcott, though he credited a remarkable voice and an effective trick of transition from vulgar to sublime subjects with part of the magic of Emerson, was convinced that his friend was destined to be the great literary man of his age. If Convers Francis was troubled by the abrupt transitions and by his own difficulty in remembering the best things that were said, he nevertheless came away with the conviction that there were passages of unequaled precision and beauty. He believed that the Emersonian charm resulted from hearty truthfulness, simplicity, purity, and vision. William Ellery Channing, deaf in one ear and delicate in health, avoided the lyceum; but he seems to have followed Emerson's lectures with the aid of his daughter Mary. She, with other former pupils of Elizabeth Peabody, delightedly listened, and she "often borrowed the manuscripts to read to him." Elizabeth Peabody "never heard him express anything but pleasure and essential agreement."

Horace Mann, likewise barely outside Emerson's circle of friends and disciples, was enthralled by the orator's magnificent generalizations. The opening lecture of the course, he thought, "was to human life what Newton's 'Principia' was to mathematics." Emerson seemed to him to succeed in his attempts to impose unity on all things: "As a man stationed in the sun would see all the planets moving round it in one direction and in perfect harmony, while to an eye on the earth their motions are full of crossings and retrogradations; so he, from his central position in the spiritual world, discovers harmony and order when others can discern only confusion and irregularity." It was one of the most splendid manifestations of the truth-seeking and truth-developing mind that Mann had ever heard. He was aware, however, that the person sitting next to him was less well pleased—Walter Channing, dean of the Harvard Medical School, complained of a headache. In spite of Emerson's transparent language, "it was almost impossible," Horace Mann explained, "to catch the great beauty and proportions of one truth before another was presented."

16.

THIS AGE, THIS COUNTRY, ONESELF

> ... I stand in my place, with my own day, here.
> —Walt Whitman, "Starting from Paumanok"

ONCE through with his lecture season, Emerson sank back into the rural life he had chosen and was still contented with. Between spells of work in his study he schemed improvements in his house and grounds. The shadow of ill health fell suddenly, threatening him with exile. Late in the spring of 1837 he was suffering from "a slight but somewhat increased inflammation on the lungs." He told his brother William, "I am in feeble health at this moment & shall perhaps need to make a long journey or a voyage," and he had Doctor Ripley write him a letter of introduction stating that the "late pastor of the second church in Boston" was "travelling in hope of regaining his health." But the danger was soon past, and he did not travel.

At home, both architecture and landscaping challenged him with discouraging problems. It did not seem easy to make his house and its not very expansive grounds into the kind of home he had wanted. Gardening, as he later decided, could never be expected to give grandeur to a house in a fen. He would never be able to make over almost the entire south side of his house into one great window for the advantage of the winter sun. As yet he could not dream of building a marbled bath, or a turret such as Montaigne had for a library, or a cave for summer study such as delighted William Harvey, the discoverer of the circulation of the blood. The improvements he had so far made were modest ones. He had carried out his plan to square the L of his house by adding two new rooms. Within a few months after his marriage he had begun planting trees. In the spring of 1836 he had hired Cyrus Warren to set out 15 apple trees, 3 pears, 1 plum, and 1 peach. Before June was over he had paid his subscription to the Tree Society. He got the first of two notebooks that he devoted to records of his plantings and to miscellaneous horticultural lore. Pines, hemlocks, maples, elms, chestnuts, oaks were to be set out from year to year, for he was a lover of trees.

By the summer of 1837 he was pleased with his garden and liked to work in it. It seemed to be the road to health. "Yesterday afternoon," he congratulated himself, "I stirred the earth about my shrubs and trees and quarrelled with the pipergrass, and now I have slept, and no longer am morose nor feel twitchings in the muscles of my face when a visitor is by." When he had the good luck of two excellent days, he weeded corn and strawberries. He was intent on becoming fat and gave up his studies. The birds entertained him as he gardened. The Maryland yellowthroat seemed to chant to him all day long, "Extacy! Extacy!" He pitied city dwellers. "The striped fly that eats our squash and melon vines, the rosebug, the corn worm, the red old leaf of the vines that entices the eye to new search for the lurking strawberry, the thicket and little bowers of the pea-vine, the signs of ripeness and all the hints of the garden, these grave city writers never knew," he boasted. He managed his garden with the help of a neighbor. Early next year he proudly told Carlyle that he had recently set out, on the west side of the house, "forty young pine trees to protect me or my son from the wind of January." Soon he was lamenting the dearth of gardens in America. He saw that his fellow countrymen had no experience of such as were common in Europe. Here, without the musky English gardens, the verses of Tennyson could not have been written, he declared; and from the days of his Italian travels he recalled the Villa d'Este as "a memorable poem in my life."

He added a little farming to his gardening. Doubtless few of his American ancestors during two centuries had failed to dabble in farming, whatever their chief occupations were. He soon fell into the thrifty habit of buying a pig and, in due time, sending for one of his townsmen to kill the fatted hog. In 1838 he began the expansion of his miniature domain by purchasing from Peter Howe the "heater piece," a triangle of slightly more than 127 rods that lay like a wedge driven into the crotch of the Lexington Road and the Cambridge Turnpike. His new land got its name because its shape suggested the piece of cast iron that was heated and placed inside a hollow flatiron.

He was now fairly well braced against the financial crisis of President Van Buren's administration. Even before he received the final instalment of his share of the Tucker estate, he was enjoying, not only the dividends from the half he had long since got, but $500 a year from that still in the hands of Pliny Cutler. At the end of July, 1837, he learned from his lawyer that it was only necessary to sign a receipt in order to bring to a close the long negotiations over the estate and to receive his second instalment. This instalment, consisting of shares in the City, Atlantic, and Massachusetts Banks of Boston, made him richer by $11,674.50. He was also to have a reversionary interest in one-third of $3,750 held back for the purpose of making annuities. He was able to keep most of his stock intact, while some thousands of dollars that he soon lent to his brother William would be an equally dependable source of income. Within a year or so the improved state of his finances was making itself apparent in the Concord assessors' books, where the true value of his stocks and money at interest was recorded as $19,400 and that of his house, barn, and land as $3,450. Besides, Lidian had her own smaller inheritance; and though for some time devoted to the aid of her sister, it at least made the future of the Emersons look brighter. Unfortunately Lidian's property was already confided to the hands of her dishonest cousin Abraham Jackson, who was eventually detected and punished but only after a long career as an embezzler.

Emerson soon found that his accounts with publishers added little to his financial prospects. His earned income, almost entirely from his lectures, was still dwarfed by his receipts from securities. But when he pondered the question of whether his "accidental freedom by means of a permanent income" was really the decisive thing that was shaping his career, his answer was No. And in the light of the history of his thought and character he was justified in his conclusion. He saw the moral implications of the question, but he believed that, as he put it, "my direction of thought is so strong that I should do the same things,—should contrive to spend the best part of my time in the same way as now, rich or poor. If I did not think so," he reflected, "I should never dare to urge the doctrines of human culture on young men."

His income from all sources was hardly more than enough to turn the wheels of the domestic machinery that Lidian quickly built up. Before she had been three years in the house she required "2 middle aged women besides Hepsy" as household aids. Her husband congratulated himself because he had a wife with "an angel's heart," delighted in his child Waldo, and liked being entangled even in commonplace domestic affairs. Within a year or two he had to reform his schedule in order to save time for writing. He tried rising at six o'clock, taking his coffee in his study, and keeping aloof from the family till twelve o'clock or one. Yet he almost rivaled Alcott in his nursery studies. In spite of his dislike of religious ceremonial he carefully recorded in his diary the fact that his boy, dressed "in the self-same robe in which, twenty-seven years ago, my brother Charles was baptized," was taken to the village church for the conventional christening at the hands of Doctor Ripley. "I feel," Lidian told her sister, "as if a volume might be filled before one could duly set forth all that this child is to him, both as possession and hope . . ." His growing affection made him consider whether, in case of disaster to his family, his philosophy would hold together. But he assured himself that it would. In February of 1839 the domestic pattern was further complicated by the birth of a daughter.

Lidian Emerson insisted that the child should be called Ellen, after the first wife.

From his edge of the village it was so short a way to the woods and Walden Pond that Emerson could quickly pass from society to solitude. It was true that he sometimes found the woods too full of mosquitoes; and he picked the crude blackberries at the risk of splintering his hand. But, as there was an endless variety of landscape and sky, he seldom came home unrewarded. As he strode through the woods one September day he heard a pattering like rain, and, looking up, "beheld the air over and about the trees full of insects (the winged ant) in violent motion and gyrations, and some of them continually dropping out of the flying or fighting swarm, and causing the rain-like sound as they fell upon the oak leaves." On a June night he left his journal and walked in moonlight that made amber of the world. "The meadows," he noticed, "sent up the rank smells of all their ferns and grasses and folded flowers into a nocturnal fragrance. The little harlot flies of the lowlands sparkled in the grass and in the air." His capacity for enjoyment of the summer was immense. At noon, when the mercury stood at ninety in the shade, he reveled in the "circumambient sea" of heat.

He incessantly reverted from outdoor nature to human nature. People stirred his curiosity. He wanted society and did not want it. He refused invitations to evening parties "chiefly because," he said, "besides the time spent, commonly ill, in the party, the hours preceding and succeeding the visit are lost for any solid use, as I am put out of tune for writing or reading." It was a triumph for him to become a valued member of a club. Within five years after settling in Concord he was elected to the town's Social Circle. The circle had twenty-odd farmers and villagers, men of character and of some reading, capable of teaching him the hard reality of life close to the soil. When he turned to more ambitious excursions into friendship, he was apt to be disappointed. "We are armed all over," he told Margaret Fuller, "with these subtle antagonisms which as soon as we meet begin to play, & translate all poetry into such stale prose!" Yet he got along well enough with the philosophical Alcott and loyally championed him throughout the crisis that ended in the closing of the Temple School in Boston. And Margaret Fuller herself was invaluable to him.

Margaret Fuller was a gadfly who stung people to action. When she was a visitor in his home in the spring of 1837 she managed to give Emerson five or six lessons in German pronunciation. Though his attempts to learn to speak the language proved abortive, she at least made him read it with more determination. As she had earlier assisted Alcott in his Temple School and had now begun as a teacher at Providence, she had an interest in educational theory and, doubtless, persuaded Emerson to shape his ideas on that subject into an address. She also helped him toward a critical theory of art. Thus she always paid her way and was a welcome guest. Unable to find a house in Concord to take as her own, she made frequent use of Emerson's, "this mansion of peace," as she called it. Elizabeth Hoar saw how she succeeded in making Emerson talk his best. "He is a ray of white light," the admiring Elizabeth told Aunt Mary, "& she a prism— If not so pure & *calm,* yet she has all the elements of the ray in her varied being." Margaret Fuller was in a state of contentment. "I know not," she confided to Charles Newcomb, "when I was most happy in the many hours of meditation I passed in the tangled wood-walks, or those of conversation with my friend whose serene and elevated nature I never came so near appreciating as now." But though the house was full of company, with the lawyer William Emerson and his wife there from New York to add an element of practical common sense to the discussions, the host would not be diverted too much from his regular hours of work. He shut himself in his study during the morning, postponing the pleasures of conversation and of reading aloud until the afternoon.

Margaret, not content to stretch Emerson's intellectual horizons with such ambitious projects as her ill-starred life of Goethe and her five annual series of conversations in Boston, also looked after his social improvement. She not only insisted on threshing out the theory of friendship but vigorously practiced the art at the same time. Quiet persons like Elizabeth Hoar marveled that Margaret knew "so many beautiful people"; and certainly Margaret was not content to wear them "like a diamond chain about her neck." She kept her beautiful people circulating and took care that the best of them got to Concord. One of the most prized was the very youthful and vivacious Caroline Sturgis, already known to the Emersons but really introduced into the Concord circle by Margaret. By June of 1838 Caroline was visiting at Coolidge Castle, borrowing manuscripts, and starting a long-lived correspondence with Emerson. A year later Emerson was asking Margaret Fuller for an introduction to Anna Barker, "your Recamier." Anna's right to the appellation was proved by social triumphs on both sides of the Atlantic. Margaret, the intellectual prodigy, saw in Anna, a New Orleans beauty, the unrealized half of what she herself wished to be. On first acquaintance with Anna, Emerson objected that she had less intellect than feeling, "and of course," he complained, "she is not of my class, does not resemble the women whom I have most admired and loved." But after a few months he shared an untroubled admiration of her with a number of his friends. Within a year Anna became the wife of one of these, Samuel Gray Ward, a Bostonian of much charm.

Ward came to Emerson in 1838, also by way of Margaret Fuller. He could not escape the broker's career he was born to, but during his student days he had had the good fortune to meet not only Anna Barker but Margaret Fuller. From Margaret, seven years his senior in years and far more in culture, he got his mental awakening. Having traveled abroad, part of the time with so scholarly a person as George Ticknor in Italy and in Germany, he had acquired some literary and artistic theories that Emerson respected. Emerson added him to his list of hopeful young men and was his correspondent for many years. Ward and, later, Margaret were sponsors of the poetical nephew and namesake of the famous preacher William Ellery Channing. Emerson and Ward both toiled over Ellery's manuscripts in the hope of getting the somewhat clumsy poet on his literary feet. Ellery, wayward and willful, went beyond the bounds of poetic license and was the victim of whimsical spells of inaction. He caused fresh anxiety among his friends when his furtive wooing of Margaret Fuller's sister Ellen came to light; and Margaret soon found herself his surprised and, at first, unwilling sister-in-law. Ellery, though never fully subdued, became in a short time a resident of Concord and was Emerson's companion on many walks.

Emerson had a habit of discovering promising young men, and a few of them lived up to expectations. It may have been Lucy Brown, his sister-in-law, who first brought him and Henry Thoreau together, and the time may have been as early as 1836. At any rate, she had probably begun her brief residence in the Thoreau home by then. The following year Emerson tried to get a suitable subvention for the stubborn senior who had offended the college authorities by his revolt against the competitive system of study. It seems to have been his inquiry "Do you keep a journal?" that inspired Thoreau to write the first of his thousands of diary entries in October, 1837. By the following winter he and Thoreau were exploring the Concord countryside together, and Emerson was speaking of his independent and unprepossessing companion as of a favorite. "Montaigne," he observed, "is spiced throughout with rebellion, as much as . . . my young Henry Thoreau."

However rebellious, Thoreau must have owed more to their friendship than Emerson did, but he had repaid much of the debt within a few years. When he stated eloquently the objections of the poor youth of genius against what looked like a foreclosure of his rights in nature by the proprietors of the land, Emerson jotted down some notes in his journal for future use. Emerson was pleased when the "protester" suddenly "broke out into good poetry & better prose." Word eventually got around among the bright young men of the Boston area that Thoreau, though rated by James Russell Lowell as "the most inimitable of all imitators" had become in the eyes of Emerson "one of the wonders of the age" and was being indirectly quoted by the same "Great Original" in lectures. Thoreau's verses on "Sympathy" struck Emerson at once as "The purest strain, and the loftiest, I think, that has yet pealed from this unpoetic American forest." Foreseeing that the new journal the Transcendentalists were planning would offer an opportunity for Henry, Emerson was for that reason more favorable to its founding. "My Henry Thoreau," he announced, "will be a great poet for such a company, & one of these days for all companies."

When James Russell Lowell joined with boyish enthusiasm in the conservatives' hue and cry against the rising Concord literary group he had not only heard Emerson lecture but had known him as a friend. Suspended in his senior year and sent to Concord by the Harvard College authorities, he had carried letters of introduction and had been in time to be invited to a Fourth of July party at the Emersons', and to make the sixth undergraduate guest at dinner and tea. The memory of such hospitality did not dull his satirical thrusts at Emerson in a juvenile class poem, but he was soon remorseful, wrote an apology, and received in reply one of his former host's masterpieces of courtesy. For Emerson, the whole episode was simply the exploratory beginning of another long-lasting friendship.

Visitors now came to Concord in increasing numbers, and according to Lidian everyone was welcomed. She enjoyed the delight her husband took in his guests, and she turned away regretfully, as she said, "from high discourse to Martha-like care of wine & custards." Edward Taylor, the pastor of Seamen's Bethel in Boston whom Emerson had long admired, came to spend a night with him after treating an audience in the old village church to a sample of his appealing oratory. Channing, a more polished preacher, was another guest. But after one of his visits Emerson commented: "Once Dr. Channing filled our sky. Now we become so conscious of his limits and of the difficulty attending any effort to show him our point of view that we doubt if it be worth while." The doctor's nephew William H. Channing, a radical young minister, also came.

A youthful Cambridge tutor named Jones Very, a practicing mystic recently discovered by Elizabeth Peabody, was welcomed but found Emerson too selfish and too earthy to breathe in the highest spiritual altitudes. Jones Very might be in the borderland between sanity and insanity, but, being admirable for his selflessness and unworldliness, could be forgiven much eccentricity. Professor Felton came the same day with him; and Thoreau, Rockwood Hoar, and Barzillai Frost, the local minister, were invited in to meet the guests. Though Jones Very could not be happy in so large a company, he impressed Emerson.

Within a few months it was noised abroad that Emerson was puffing him up into a saint and philosopher; and at the same time rumors were rife that Very had become quite insane, imagining himself another Christ, divinely commissioned. Very came back to Concord for a visit of several days, and Emerson, unperturbed by the disapproval of the gossips, studied this pathological case in the hope of learning a little wisdom as well as psychology. He saw that the gentle mystic distrusted him as being too intellectual. "He thinks me covetous in my hold of truth, of seeing truth separate, and of receiving or taking it, instead of merely obeying," Emerson observed but nevertheless turned hopefully to a couple of essays the young man had written and to some sonnets he had printed in a Salem paper.

Next year, 1839, after Emerson had circulated "a roll" of the extraordinary sonnets in manuscript and a number of them had been printed in a Western magazine, he had Jones Very at Concord again for a few days. Before the end of that summer he had selected "Out of two hundred poems . . . sixty six that really possess rare merit." Sixty-five of these he published, with Very's essays on Shakespeare and epic poetry, in a neat, slender volume.

A register of visitors to Coolidge Castle during these early Concord years of Emerson's would have served as a directory of New England's Transcendentalists, social reformers, and liberal-minded or radical-minded scholars, with a few other miscellaneous persons. Hedge came, a man notable for his philosophical and linguistic talent. So did Sarah Alden Ripley, a human mill, grinding German, Italian, Greek, chemistry, metaphysics, or theology, utterly indifferent as to which was thrown into her hopper. Guests were as various as Horace Mann, bent on forming a county educational association; John Dwight, full of knowledge of music; Cyrus Bartol, starting out on his career as minister and author; and Aunt Fanny Haskins, "a remarkable specimen of still life." There were visitors of many ideas and visitors of one idea. Emerson found it necessary to "treat the men and women of one idea, the Abolitionist, the Phrenologist, the Swedenborgian, as insane persons with a continual tenderness and special reference in every remark and action to their known state."

Among his fellow Concordians Emerson soon came to be respected, if not marveled at, but was hardly esteemed an equal. Years later the popular opinion was expressed by Sam Staples, a fellow townsman who had in his time been bar-tender, clerk, constable and jailer, deputy sheriff, representative in the General Court, auctioneer, real-estate agent, and gentleman farmer. "Well," Staples summed it up, "I suppose there's a great many things that Mr. Emerson knows that I could n't understand; but I *know* that there's a damn sight of things that I know that he don't know anything about."

As there was no effective international copyright, Emerson shielded Carlyle as well as he could from American pirating. Acting as Carlyle's agent meant petty business details and annoyances. Emerson got his first serious experience of the sort when he looked after the American edition of *The French Revolution.* He prepared a prospectus, collected the names of subscribers, and was responsible for some of the press notices. Without much hope of acceptance, he wrote a review and sent it to editor James Walker. Walker printed only a mutilated version of it in *The Christian Examiner.* The reviewer, resolved to salvage his rejected paragraphs, remembered that Orestes Brownson had asked for a "notice" to put into his new journal, *The Boston Quarterly;* but the extensive criticism of the *Revolution* that tardily appeared there seemed not to have any Emersonian flavor. In spite of all his anxiety about his now famous British friend's success, however, Emerson was independent in his judgment. Rereading the book, or at least most of it, he felt "astonishment and unabated curiosity and pleasure" but condemned its "perpetual levity." A few months later he published the first two of the four volumes of Carlyle's *Critical and Miscellaneous Essays.*

Emerson, though he was being gibed at by superficial critics as a follower and imitator of Carlyle, did not labor without some return. Carlyle was stirring up a few new friends for him in England. The young intellectual John Sterling had found *Nature,* it seems, on Carlyle's table and had "fallen overhead in love" with its author. Emerson sent some things he had printed, and so began the correspondence that covered the few remaining years of Sterling's life, though the two men never met. By the spring of 1839, Richard Monckton Milnes, a member of Parliament and, according to his friend Carlyle, "a beautiful little Tory dilettante poet and politician," had begun collecting Emerson's writings in order to review them in a British journal.

Though Emerson had none of Carlyle's fierce determination to save the political and economic world from its stupidity, he was by no means oblivious to the need of such salvation. He wanted to deal with men as individuals, not in masses, but he felt contradictory emotions. In one of its aspects, the age seemed to him the age of trade, when everything gave way to avarice. In another aspect, he saw it as a social era, the age of associations and the age in which people believed that such economic fundamentals as trade and production could be altered by law. He did not clearly foresee the social upheaval that industrialism would cause. In the spring of 1837 he was "gay as a canary bird" because he had learned that the destiny of New England was to be the manufacturing country of America and he would therefore have to worry no longer out of morbid sympathy for the farmer.

He was pleased that his line of duty kept him clear of the debate over the serious financial distress of the late 1830s. A visit from his brother William, a lawyer in Wall Street, must have made him sufficiently aware, if he had not already been so, of the panicky condition of the country as banks in New York and Boston began to suspend specie payments. His own modest wealth must have been endangered. But he refused to believe that the universe was tumbling to ruin. "The humble-bee," he philosophized, "and the pine-warbler seem to me the proper objects of attention in these disastrous times." At the moment he was very probably composing a preliminary version of his lines to the bumblebee. He wrote them mainly in a mood suggestive of anything but the fear sweeping over financial America. As he defied bodily disease and was resolved not to "sail for Porto Rique" to escape it as his ill-fated brothers had done, so he defied the threatening economic storm. He defied it by ignoring it. Following the flight of the bee, he had a vision of

> sunny hours,
> Long days, and solid banks of flowers;
> Of gulfs of sweetness without bound
> In Indian wildernesses found;
> Of Syrian peace, immortal leisure,
> Firmest cheer, and bird-like pleasure.

Yet in the end he made his poem only less poignant in its recognition of human sorrow than was Keats's much more somber ode to the nightingale. Emerson's bee was a philosopher wiser than human seer because he managed to make ridiculous, so far as he was concerned, the

> Want and woe, which torture us.

But obviously want and woe remained very real to us.

Discussing the financial crisis in plain prose, Emerson observed that the black times had great scientific value and were an epoch that a critical philosopher would not miss. "What was, ever since my memory, solid continent, now yawns apart and discloses its composition and genesis," he commented. The crisis he thought interesting to watch, not fatal. He saw the resources of the vast continent, and the blight of trade and manufactures seemed to him only a momentary mischance.

He must have imbibed, perhaps unconsciously, some more or less radical views from George Bancroft, the Democrat. He read the second volume of Bancroft's history of the United States that year. He had long since discovered for himself that his own favorite doctrine of self-reverence was "root and seed of democracy." To a lecture audience in 1838 he announced that the encroachment of the democratic element on the monarchial was one of the first fruits of reflection in our modern age. It may have been the same year that his wife told a correspondent that Emerson never used the term lower classes and that it was wholly objectionable to him. For days at a time he would receive Edward Palmer as a guest. Palmer, "a gentle, faithful, sensible, well-balanced man for an enthusiast," had solved the current specie problem by renouncing the use of money entirely and accordingly did not pay for his lodging. Instead he was apt to leave behind him a free copy of the *Herald of Holiness,* the little paper he printed on the Bowery in New York. Palmer seems to have been not so much an extreme democrat as the mildest and most inoffensive of communists. Aunt Mary thought him crazy, but Emerson was willing, as usual, to hear both sides. And even when he failed to see how it would help matters to take money out of circulation, he was glad to have his guest demonstrate how the invincible me could still exist in contentment after everything had been stripped from it.

In 1839 Emerson was probably near the peak of his sympathy with the Democrats as a party. Not long before, it was true, he had felt bitter as he passed by the shop where "the dictator of our rural Jacobins" was instructing his political pupils and counting the votes they would cast in the next election. Emerson detested the radical politician who valued chiefly "persons who are nothing but persons." But he would doubtless have felt much the same way about a Whig politician of the same order. Now, at any rate, he seemed to be about to announce himself publicly as a Democrat, or, more radical than the general run of Democrats, a Locofoco. The political-minded in his audience had taut nerves as he read his first lecture in the course of 1839–1840. In that lecture he seemed to them to be talking plainly when he classed all men as either of the party of the past or of that of the future, found the colleges and all monied foundations of learning or religion on the side of tradition, but saw the party of movement daily and steadily gaining and himself welcomed the future.

Theodore Parker was delighted and wrote to Convers Francis: "It was *democratic-loco-foco* throughout; and very much in the spirit of Brownson's article on 'Democracy and Reform' in the last *Quarterly.* . . . Bancroft was in extasies,—he was rapt beyond vision at the *loco-focoism* of the lecture, and said to me the next evening,—'It is a great thing to say such things before any audience, however small . . . but let him come with *us* before the 'Bay State' and we will give him 3000 listeners.' " A "grave, whig-looking gentleman" who heard the lecture said he could account for it only on the supposition that Emerson "wished to get a place in the Custom House under George Bancroft." Bancroft, an admirer of intellectuals and himself one of the most cultured of the Democratic officeholders, shortly afterwards invited Emerson to dinner. Though the dinner looked unpolitical, it may be that Bancroft had some hope of bringing him onto the political platform.

Meantime, Emerson, in spite of his distrust of fanatical reformers, was becoming more dissatisfied with the uneasy truce over slavery. Lidian, one of the delighted hostesses of the Southern Grimké sisters when they came to plead the antislavery cause in Concord, must have encouraged him in the direction of action. Some two months after the Grimkés had left, he read an address on slavery in a Concord church; and when Lovejoy, the antislavery editor, was killed by an Illinois mob, Emerson felt outraged. He saw clearly that the history of the Negro race to date had been a tragedy that did not easily fit into even a Transcendentalist's great circles. Negroes, he wrote in his journal, in 1838, were more pitiable when rich than when poor. "Of what use are riches to them? They never go out without being insulted. Yesterday I saw a family of negroes riding in a coach. How pathetic!" But he was in no shouting mood. He had his unswerving belief that if Transcendental doctrine, demanding that all men be treated as gods, won acceptance by individuals it would spell the end of such evils as slavery. And though the subject of abolition even became poetic in Whittier's hands, he did not think that it was his own calling to deal with it.

He turned back to his books. He read Oriental lore again and sampled Ripley's specimens of foreign literature. He was pleased with new readings in Tennyson. He no longer cared much for novels. It took public opinion to drive him to read *Oliver Twist*. He thought Dickens remarkable for his sharp eye for exteriors but not for insight into character. In some of George Sand's books, discovered with Margaret Fuller's help, he found, however, "authentic revelations of what passes in man & in woman." Before the end of 1838 he had bought a copy of Kant's *Critick of Pure Reason,* an unsatisfactory translation published by Pickering at London. Possibly it was his hand that marked a passage on pages 431 and 432; but if it was, he failed to take its caution to heart. His own highly intuitive philosophy was not strictly "transcendental" but was dangerously *"transcendent"* according to Kant's definition.

Emerson himself saw, however, that the idea of spirit was evanescent and really out of reason as well as out of sensuous experience. He saw both sides, weak and strong, of his philosophy. He had sharply contradictory moods. He could write a prose poem on the divinity of man: ". . . I grow in God. I am only a form of him. He is the soul of me. I can even with a mountainous aspiring say, *I am God* . . ." Then, before he laid down his pen, he could confess: "A believer in Unity, a seer of Unity, I yet behold two." What he was writing might have served as an epilogue to his first book, a confession of his failure in it to discover real unity. "Whilst I feel myself in sympathy with nature, and rejoice with greatly beating heart in the course of Justice and Benevolence overpowering me," he went on, "I yet find little access to this me of me. I fear what shall befal: I am not enough a party to the great order to be tranquil. I hope and I fear. I do not see. At one time, I am a Doer. . . . but presently I return to the habitual attitude of suffering." Thus, at times, he became conscious that at the end of his whole quest for truth there could be only the tragedy of futility so far as any final static results were concerned. But to him this did not mean that it was futile to observe diligently the changing aspects of truth that would perhaps, after all, have to be accepted as the ultimate realities. Meantime he was, as always, simply a seeker, looking for any semblance of unity wherever he could find it. It sometimes occurred to him that the unity for which he longed was discoverable in his relations with minds in past centuries. He was amazed when he considered how near the seventeenth-century minds of Marvell and the "metaphysical poets" Donne and Cowley were to his own.

In his home there was agreement as yet on the grand law of compensation, though experience often seemed to count heavily against it. Lidian, sick and sometimes despondent, still made her "weak & most fearful nature" hold to this faith and so "endure the thought of the evil that is in the world." As late as 1839 she told Elizabeth Peabody, "My Understanding fails to show me how things can be so—yet my Reason when I will listen —steadfastly affirms— All must be for the Best . . . All despondency *is* founded on delusion;—with me, and I think with most, it originates in bodily disease—or fatigue at least— It is in the nerves,—the soul disowns it." Emerson, according to Lidian, had no easier time than she in keeping up faith. He was at the very moment, she said, preparing to lecture on human misery. In theory, he made light of it. "But in fact—I scarce ever saw the person upon whom the suffering of *others* made so real impression," she added.

In the series of lectures he continued to read in Boston, Emerson stubbornly stood his Transcendental ground. Though he skillfully varied his ideological rhythms, the real contents of the lectures changed little more than did the general titles which he gave to the courses. Instead of the ten lectures on "Human Culture" delivered at the Masonic Temple in the winter of 1837–1838, he offered ten lectures on "Human Life" at the Masonic Temple in 1838–1839. In 1839–1840 his ten lectures, once more at the Masonic Temple, were announced as on "The Present Age."

He held the attention of the liberals and radicals, and for a long time there was little diminution in his audiences. At the opening lecture in December of 1838 Alcott found the audience "choice," including every hopeful and devout person of his acquaintance. According to Samuel Ripley, the house was fuller each night as that season advanced, the audience being "composed mostly of young men and women of the higher and more intelligent classes." Undoubtedly many came because of the recent attacks on Emerson as a dangerous radical, attacks which he had at first mistakenly feared might end his usefulness as a lecturer. His own excitement was great, so great for a time that he could not sleep at night and had to postpone one lecture till he got back on his feet. At home Lidian was delighted with the lecture on "Love"—"to me the most glorious *poem* I ever heard—celestial—holy."

The Boston course still yielded the main part of what Emerson earned by his lectures. In the winter of 1837–1838 the average attendance was 439, the total receipts were $796, the cost of the lecture hall was $130, and other expenses, including those for advertising, tickets, and travel, were $95. Emerson therefore found that he had earned a net profit of $571 on ten weekly lectures. In spite of the financial depression, his profits were more than one-third greater than in the preceding winter. It was true that in the critical season of 1838–1839 at the temple the gross receipts from ticket sales seemed to drop a little, but they still amounted to over $700. Next winter the average attendance was estimated at about 400, and probably the ticket sales were about the same.

But if, during the years 1837–1839, the Boston lectures brought the largest cash returns, a couple of addresses delivered in Cambridge, across the Charles River, were destined to reverberate longest in the ears of the world.

The first of these, a Phi Beta Kappa oration, was a stopgap, for Emerson was asked to prepare it on short notice after the Rev. Dr. Wainwright had finally made up his mind to decline the honor. Yet the address had actually been in preparation for many years. From his own college days, when the faculty had rated him as only average, Emerson had had something ready to say on the subject of scholarship and its relation to the culture of the individual. As early as 1835 he had half resolved to put together a paper on the duty and discipline of the scholar. It was perhaps in the same year that he pondered the foreign sneer at the dearth of literary production in America but warned himself against cultural nationalism. He cautioned himself not to "read American," for, he reflected, "Thought is of no country." By May of 1836 he was definitely planning to make a "sermon to Literary Men."

Now, more than a year later, he was asked to be the orator of the Harvard chapter of the national scholarly literary society that had been founded at the College of William and Mary, in Virginia, during the American Revolution. Its regular members were the winners, from year to year, of an educational marathon that Emerson wished to reform. But he himself had long been an honorary member, the conservative-minded society was a conspicuous symbol of scholarship, and the occasion of its anniversary gave him the hearing he wanted for his own liberal ideas.

Precisely at noon on August 31, 1837, two hundred and fifteen members of Phi Beta Kappa marched into the meetinghouse near Harvard Yard and joined the guests already gathered there. The Rev. William Parsons Lunt was there with a "finished" poem. A band played, and a minister offered a prayer. It took Emerson one hour and fifteen minutes to read his oration to an audience that was partly hostile, partly friendly. John Pierce timed him and listened impatiently. He was struck by Emerson's "misty, dreamy, unintelligible style" and credited it to "Swedenborg, Coleridge, and Carlyle." Alcott was delighted but would never forget "the mixed confusion, consternation, surprise, and wonder" of some who were present. Frederic Hedge, Caleb Stetson, George Bradford, and others of the orator's "most devoted literary friends" drank it all in, fully satisfied. "What crowded and breathless aisles, what windows clustering with eager heads, what enthusiasm of approval, what grim silence of foregone dissent!" So Lowell long afterwards summarized the conflicting moods of the listeners. To him the address seemed a classic, "our Yankee version of a lecture by Abelard." Oliver Wendell Holmes, though he probably cared little for its esoteric passages at the time, would one day think it worthy to be called "our intellectual Declaration of Independence."

Friends must have realized that the address was mostly what they had often heard Emerson say before but never express so well. This time he had polished his manuscript to the last phrase, and he was confident. He felt, as he put it, that he was playing on his listeners "as on an organ." But his manner was as much the trained athlete's as the musician's. His sentences were quick, powerful jabs, and almost every stroke opened the way for another.

In the past Phi Beta Kappa's anniversary had been little more than "a friendly sign of the survival of the love of letters amongst a people too busy to give to letters any more." But the time had come for a change. "Our day of dependence," the orator announced, "our long apprenticeship to the learning of other lands, draws to a close." This was more a hope than a boast, and he went on to show what would have to happen if it were to be realized. The scholar would have to transform himself from a narrow specialist, "the delegated intellect," into a man of broad culture participating in the world of ideas and action, *"Man Thinking."* He had nature, books, and his own action as tutors to give him efficient aid in bringing about his desired transformation and to be his working partners afterwards. Once this narrow specialist had turned into man thinking, he would find that his duties were all comprised in self-trust. Trusting himself, this thinker who had allied himself with broad humanity would find his own age and his own country fit to work in and himself fit to do the work. If he was an American he was especially fortunate. The spirit of the age became every day more democratic, more individualistic, magnifying the importance of the single man. Let the American no longer be timid, imitative, too deferential to European precedent. Instead let him be self-reliant and individual. Let "the single man plant himself indomitably on his instincts, and there abide." Then "the huge world," Emerson assured his audience in his peroration, "will come round to him." This was the sum of what the Phi Beta Kappa orator said.

As he had already published his essay on nature, little was needed on that subject. But books, representing the mind of the past, were a challenge he had never fully met before. No one knew better than he that books could be precious lamps at which the flame of thought was rekindled in hours of darkness. But everybody else knew that too. What most needed to be taught now was the necessity of liberating imitative minds from slavery to authority. The true scholar-thinker must not be subdued by his instruments. Books were for idle times. "Meek young men," Emerson warned, "grow up in libraries, believing it their duty to accept the views which Cicero, which Locke, which Bacon, have given; forgetful that Cicero, Locke, and Bacon were only young men in libraries when they wrote these books."

Bent on providing his timid scholar with intellectual muscles as well as backbone, Emerson insisted, more vigorously than ever before, on the importance of action. The Concord villager who lived in quiet retirement may well have been answering the gibes of "practical" men whose target he had been. He challenged the practical value of the doer who was no thinker as well as of the thinker who was no doer. "The so-called 'practical men,' " he said, "sneer at speculative men, as if, because they speculate or *see,* they could do nothing." Then, for the benefit of the scholar, he read what might have served as a prospectus of William James and John Dewey: "Action is with the scholar subordinate, but it is essential.

Without it he is not yet man. Without it thought can never ripen into truth. . . . Only so much do I know, as I have lived. Instantly we know whose words are loaded with life, and whose not." Only action could complete thought. William James, many years later, marked this passage in his copy of Emerson.

Self-trust, self-realization, was the core of the address. Mainly the appeal was completely understandable to the most untranscendental minds. Its broad basis in common sense made this one of Emerson's most powerful writings. It was alive with rhetoric that went home to the hearer. The scholar's duty not to defer to the popular cry even if respectable leaders of society joined it came out as "Let him not quit his belief that a popgun is a popgun, though the ancient and honorable of the earth affirm it to be the crack of doom." But Emerson the Transcendentalist was not completely hidden. He was determined to keep this discourse intelligible to both his immediate audience and a much larger one beyond the walls of the meetinghouse and would not run any serious risks. Yet he ventured for a moment or two to reveal, back of the single, self-reliant man, the "one soul which animates all men." This was a sufficient hint to the imaginative.

As for the literal-minded, they vastly exaggerated Emerson's doctrine of American cultural independence. The nationalistic note in the address, though often taken as the dominant one, was not dominant. Self-trust for the individual, no matter of what nationality, was the dominant note. The problem of self-trust merely happened to have a special meaning for America, an adolescent country that feared to grow up intellectually. Emerson announced the special American aspect of the problem in his opening paragraph and then pushed it aside. Only as he neared the end of his address did he halt his long commentary upon "this abstraction of the Scholar"—the timeless scholar, unlimited by nationality—and turn to matters "of nearer reference to the time and to this country." Even then he was mainly concerned with the characteristics of the age, and, in spite of his renunciation of what he called "the romantic," he saw them for the most part in terms of European Romanticism. Only in his final paragraph did he get round to what he had to say of his own country. He was no narrow-minded nationalist.

At dinner in commons, after the program in the meetinghouse, Oliver Wendell Holmes enlivened the occasion with a song, and there were "witty toasts and speeches from all parts of the Hall." A certain Warren from Plymouth, having evidently understood the importance of the orator's brief allusion to the one soul back of every individual, gave a toast that pleased Emerson. "Mr. President," he said, "I suppose all know where the orator comes from; and I suppose all know what he has said; I give you

The Spirit of Concord; it makes us all of One Mind." Governor Edward Everett, after replying to a toast in his own honor, heaped flattery upon the Phi Beta Kappa orator and delivered a little eulogy of the late Edward and Charles Emerson, both high honor students during their years at the college.

Waldo Emerson and Lidian returned to Concord with Margaret Fuller and, presumably, other company. A festive spirit must already have pervaded Coolidge Castle, where, on the following day, fourteen members of the Transcendental Club gathered for an all-day party, with Margaret Fuller, Elizabeth Hoar, Sarah Alden Ripley, and doubtless Lidian Emerson admitted into the inner circle pro tempore. The Transcendentalists, it appeared, required as much space and as great a variety of substantial foods as even devotees of Locke's sensual philosophy could have reasonably demanded. "They filled every seat at a table the whole length of the dining-room"; and Lidian fed them, as she put it, "beef . . . a noble great piece for the Spiritualists—(with which mine husband was especially pleased)—a boild leg of mutton with caper sauce and for side dishes ham and tongue . . . corn—beans tomatoes macaroni cucumbers lettuce & *applesauce* and . . . puddings . . ." An "array of soft custards graced the board," and there were "pears raisins & nuts for dessert." What the fourteen had to say about the Phi Beta Kappa oration Lidian did not record, but she left no doubt about her own views. Though she disagreed with the opinion that the audience had looked "particularly edified," she was so certain that the orator's words had been "God's truth—fitly spoken" that she would "have cared little—but for their own sakes—if the hearers generally had hissed the speech."

Within a month a first printing of five hundred copies of *An Oration,* later to be known as *The American Scholar,* was sold out, and Emerson was more in the public eye than he had ever been before. It was doubtless partly for rest that he deserted his study. He rested by doing some farming and gardening. But visitors, as Lidian explained to her sister, also "prevented Mr. E from resuming his old studious ways." When at last he was "full of zeal to begin writing either a book or a course of lectures" —he had "not yet decided which"—Lidian's preference for lectures may have affected his decision in their favor. It would, however, have been difficult for him to remain in retirement now that he had got a reputation as an orator. By April of 1838, when the ten lectures of his Boston course were over, Concord needed his help in championing the cause of the Cherokee Indians, then being pushed out of Georgia and across the Mississippi in accordance with what the government called a treaty. At the town's meeting of protest he spoke, "very unwillingly," as his wife said, "preferring individual action." This propagandizing by mass demonstration was, as he put it, "like dead cats around one's neck," but it was one of the "holy hurrahs" that he could not escape. In spite of his strong feeling about the mistreatment of the Indians, it was hardly less distasteful for him to write his individual protest to President Van Buren in an indignant letter dated the day after the meeting and soon broadcast to the nation by the newspapers. This too was an act done for an occasion and therefore not quite his own. "I hate myself when I go out of my sphere," he told John Pierpont, "but a man must have bowels sometimes . . ." He could play the role of the happy warrior only when his act grew naturally out of his own past experience and thought, as did the divinity school address of the following summer.

He had unwittingly begun to write the divinity school address years before he was invited to deliver it. Three years before he delivered it he had gone back to Divinity Hall at Harvard and had witnessed "the best performance" with a heavy heart. A little later he had tried to list the defects of Jesus—no cheerfulness, no love of natural science, no kindness for art, nothing of Socrates, of Laplace, of Shakespeare. A perfect man ought to recognize the intellectual nature as well as the moral. "Do you ask me," Emerson had written in his journal, "if I would rather resemble Jesus than any other man? If I should say Yes, I should suspect myself of superstition." He had nevertheless continued to preach irregularly through most of 1837. Then his pace had slackened and he had nearly stopped early the following year. Meantime he had been visibly wearying of churchgoing and other conventional religious acts. After attending church one Sunday in March of 1838, he had been all but ready to say that he would go no more. "I ought to sit and think," he had said to himself, "and then write a discourse to the American Clergy, showing them the ugliness and unprofitableness of theology and churches at this day, and the glory and sweetness of the moral nature out of whose pale they are almost wholly shut." But he could hardly have suspected how near he was to carrying out this half-formed purpose.

Three days later he received a letter from several persons who spoke for what they somewhat pompously called the "Senior Class of Divinity College Cambridge." They asked him to deliver "the customary discourse, on occasion of their entering upon the active Christian ministry." The graduating class numbered only about half a dozen young men; but the occasion offered him a platform from which he could speak to Unitarian ministers, if not laymen, everywhere. At the Phi Beta Kappa anniversary he had bearded the scholars in their own stronghold. Now he could come to grips with the preachers in theirs.

His formal acceptance written on the 27th of March revealed nothing about his intentions. But as he was called to Cambridge soon afterwards for a discussion of theism with "The Divinity School youths" and may have seen more of them before July 15, there is room for doubt as to how ignorant they were of the nature of his discourse when he began to read it to them on that day. Anyhow students of theological schools of the more liberal sort seem to have been able to take a generous dose of radicalism without flinching, though the ministry, having to beware of offending laymen of more conservative opinion, could easily be alarmed.

The little chapel on the second floor of Divinity Hall had been altered some seven years earlier so that the pulpit no longer stood awkwardly against the windowed wall and faced an auditorium about twice as wide as it was deep. Instead, the pulpit was now at the north end and the speaker might easily command the attention of the hundred or so listeners who could find seats. The room "was very much crowded" and the audience paid "profound attention" as Emerson spoke.

He began with a soothing description of the charm of nature in "this refulgent summer." The world was indeed a marvel of perfection. But when the mind revealed the universal laws, then the great world shrank at once into a mere illustration and fable of this mind. The perfection of these laws suggested that only one will, one mind, was everywhere active. This was the supreme law, and the perception of it awakened in the individual the religious sentiment, divine and deifying. This sentiment, though it created all forms of worship, was an intuition only and could not be received at second hand. Jesus understood the intuitive faculty of man and the divine and deifying religious sentiment in which it resulted. In the jubilee of sublime emotion he said, "I am divine. Through me, God acts; through me, speaks." But his doctrine was distorted by the understanding of men, it being only to be taught by the reason. The understanding, man's lesser faculty, caught the high chant from the lips of the poet Jesus and said after a lapse of time, "This was Jehovah come down out of heaven. I will kill you, if you say he was a man." Christianity became a myth.

Thus historical Christianity, Emerson went on to explain, became not the doctrine of the soul but an exaggeration of the personal, the positive, the ritual. "It has dwelt, it dwells," he said, "with noxious exaggeration about the *person* of Jesus." The soul knew no personal preference and invited every man to expand to full circle. But Christianity had built up an absolute monarchy, and Jesus had become a demigod like Osiris or Apollo. This was intolerable. It would be vain, however, Emerson cautioned, to attempt to establish a new cult, with rites and forms. Better breathe new life into the old. Yet the only real remedy was to dare to love

God without mediator and to cleave to the spiritual, rejecting the formal religion.

Elizabeth Peabody long afterward believed she remembered seeing in the manuscript a passage that "would have saved many a weak brother and sister Transcendentalist from going into the extreme of *ego-theism*" had Emerson not omitted it in reading for lack of time and had he not later refused to print it because he had not read it and did not want to be unfair to the critics who were talking about the spoken address. "It was a warning," she said, "against making the new truth a fanaticism." But as her memory often deceived her in old age the omitted passage may have been imaginary.

In July of 1838 she and the rest of the elect were, it was said, enraptured. Theodore Parker, having found this address a warrant for a liberal reform of theology, immediately noted in his diary that Emerson had "surpassed *himself* as much as he surpasses others in the general way. . . . So beautiful, & just, so true . . . & this week I shall write the long-meditated sermns. on the state of the church, & the duties of these times." But in general the most liberal wing of the New England ministry, the Unitarian preachers, were shocked. Dean Palfrey of the theological school was said to be much hurt.

Some of the more intellectual college boys, such as James Russell Lowell and his circle, began by ridiculing the address but gradually swung round to a favorable view of it. Nathan Hale, Jr., was glad he had not heard it, but he had heard enough about it and wanted to kick every one of the divinities he saw, as he thought it insulting in them to choose Emerson for their orator. Lowell, watching from his Concord retreat, pitied persons who pinned themselves to Emerson's coat tails and were so blinded by the dust that they thought they had got above this poor little earth; and in his verses intended for the commencement week festivities he prophesied woe to religion when a man who had the title of Reverend preached what an atheist like Abner Kneeland would have been proud to emulate and what, by Judge Thacher's standards, would doom the offender to the county jail. But when his friend George Loring cautioned him against prejudice and a too hasty judgment, Lowell himself began to feel uncertain. Loring presently reported that for his own part he had begun to read Emerson and liked him.

The members of the class in divinity that had stirred up this storm of controversy hesitated but finally decided to print, not publish, three hundred copies of the address. Emerson probably made some insignificant changes in the manuscript or proof sheets. To an admonition from Henry Ware, Jr., now of the divinity faculty but once his colleague at the Second

Church, he replied that as his conviction of the substantial truth of the doctrine he had expressed was perfect he felt it very important that it be spoken out; yet he would "revise with greater care" before he published.

For the most part Emerson's family stood on his side at this crisis. Even one of the two preachers among them was more friendly than critical. Uncle Samuel Ripley, fearing that his nephew would be "classed with Kneeland, Paine &c, bespattered & belied," pleaded with him not to allow the offending discourse to go to press, but, once it was printed, urged him to come to Waltham and speak from Ripley's own pulpit. Though Grandfather Ripley, the venerable Concord pastor, was "a good deal disturbed at Waldo's sentiments" and considered his example "a hindrance to the progress of professed religion in Concord," Uncle Samuel, even if he did not pretend to understand everything in the address, declared his entire sympathy with Emerson and was obviously delighted to see him stand "firm and unmoved," no more minding what was said of him "than he does the whistling of the wind." And though Aunt Mary was long afterwards to recall the "lecture to the di^y school" as a thing "w'h should be oblivion's, as under the influence of some malign demon," William Emerson, in New York, was "no way shocked at your heresies," so he told his brother. Lidian was as loyal to her husband's views as she had been at the time of the Phi Beta Kappa address. "But you want to know," she wrote to her sister, "how much of a cloud these mists of prejudice have formed over his light— Why, none at all. I do not know that he has felt a moment's uneasiness on his own account . . . For my own part I sympathize with his calmness entirely. If I am moved at all it is only with joy at his having had the moral courage to encounter so much obloquy. . . . Were I but worthy of him—neither sickness or care would prevent my being one of the happiest of women."

Emerson himself felt that his aloofness, his position as "merely an observer, a dispassionate reporter," not a partisan, would guarantee him the scholar's perfect freedom. "The young people," he observed, "and the mature hint at odium, and aversion of faces to be presently encountered in society. I say, No: I fear it not. No scholar need fear it."

The controversy raged for some time in the press, and the name of Abner Kneeland, the "blasphemer," was again linked with Emerson's. Perhaps Emerson, no atheist, was known as a signer, with Doctor Channing and other tolerant persons, of the petition asking pardon for Kneeland. He acknowledged the polemical skill of his former teacher Andrews Norton, "the old tyrant of the Cambridge Parnassus," but thought him an illustration of the low state of religion. Henry Ware, Jr., went far toward exonerating the divinity teachers and students from any blame for Transcendental heresy by preaching a sermon, *The Personality of the Deity,* and publishing it *"at the Request of the Members of the Divinity School."* Ware sent a copy of this to Emerson with a letter, hopeful of prodding him into an argument. Emerson labored over a private reply, carefully grooming and canceling phrases. But the gist of it all was that he simply refused, as usual, to argue. Instead he merely reaffirmed his long-time loyalty to his own highly individualistic and intuitional method of truth-hunting.

Of the religious reviews, the most friendly were only lukewarm in his support. *The Western Messenger,* a Unitarian and, in the main, Transcendental magazine published in the Ohio Valley, was a wavering ally but did not want to desert him till it became clearer just what the war was about. *The Boston Quarterly Review,* Orestes Brownson's new and vigorous journal, thought the address "somewhat arrogant" and reproved its spirit as "quite too censorious and desponding, its philosophy as indigested, and its reasoning as inconclusive," but contended that the large amount of error in it could be dismissed, while the good it did would live after it. The influence of Emerson's "free spirit, and free utterance" would, said Brownson's review, have a lasting effect on American literature.

There were powerful enemies who were ready with decisive condemnation. In November *The Christian Examiner,* the chief Unitarian periodical, assured the public that the notions advanced in the address, "so far as they are intelligible, are utterly distasteful to the instructers of the School, and to Unitarian ministers generally, by whom they are esteemed to be neither good divinity nor good sense" and passed on disdainfully to praise Ware's rejoinder in *The Personality of the Deity.* An extremely conservative Presbyterian journal, *The Biblical Repertory and Princeton Review,* discoursed long and by no means unlearnedly upon the German philosophy, its evil works and its Oriental connections; dismissed Cousin, the French adapter of that philosophy, as superficial and conceited to the last degree; and finally passed on to a brief denunciation of the "nonsense and impiety" of Emerson's address. The address was "obviously in imitation of Thomas Carlyle" though based on principles like those of Cousin. Nothing of it was from the Bible. The author was clearly "an infidel and an atheist."

A pamphlet war followed before the excitement died down. Andrews Norton, "the hard-headed Unitarian Pope" whose St. Peter's was once little Divinity Hall, had announced at his inaugural, twenty years earlier, that "our religious faith rests for its main support on what we believe the declarations of God, communicated by Jesus Christ"; and he had not changed his mind. Now he printed an address delivered *"at the Request of the 'Association of the Alumni of the Cambridge Theological School'"* under the suggestive title of *A Discourse on the Latest Form of Infidelity.* If this was not a frontal attack on the Transcendentalists, it was at least a determined attempt to cut the German ground out from under their feet. Answers naturally came thick and fast on behalf of the New School. George Ripley wrote a long one that betrayed surprising bitterness but came near achieving his purpose of crushing Norton under the weight of German learning. He was in high spirits about the business.

Aunt Mary, who sided with Norton, reported that her nephew said nothing about the controversy. He knew that the "sour faces" of which he wrote in his journal were not merely imaginary. "The whole band of clergymen," so Samuel Ripley commented on the plight of his nephew, "have raised their voice against him, with a very few exceptions; and the common people, even women, look solemn and sad, and roll up their eyes . . . 'Oh, he is a dangerous man; the church is in danger; Unitarianism is disgraced; the party is broken up' . . ." Doubtless many strictly conservative Boston families, like one Convers Francis knew, were taught "to abhor & abominate R. W. Emerson as a sort of mad dog." But neither the sourness of Boston conservatives nor the dislike of the divinity faculty or of the clergy in general caused Emerson great distress. "The taunts and cries of hatred and anger, the very epithets you bestow on me," he could imagine himself saying, "are so familiar long ago in my reading that they sound to me ridiculously old and stale. . . . I, whilst I see this, that you must have been shocked and must cry out at what I have said, I see too that we cannot easily be reconciled, for I have a great deal more to say that will shock you out of all patience." He seems to have turned the matter over calmly in his mind, warning himself against acquiring a persecution complex.

If, as seems probable, his poem "Uriel," apparently not written till some years after the event, was a sublimation of the crisis caused by the divinity address, it exaggerated the reality as poetic license entitled it to do. Perhaps Emerson, not without a sense of humor, was touching up Horace Mann's portrait of him as "a man stationed in the sun," for he quite possibly knew that portrait.

He seemed, in his poem, to become Milton's sharp-sighted archangel Uriel, looking out over the universe from his vantage point in the sun, seeing the true motions of the planets, and understanding the laws that remained obscure to observers standing on the earth. The young deities overheard discussing what subsisted and what only seemed might have been the audacious young members of the Transcendental Club, and Uriel's speech that caused a shudder round the sky was perhaps a poetic version of the divinity school address. Well informed readers may have guessed the identity of the actors who shook their heads behind the masks of the old war gods, and of those who played the parts of the friendlier seraphs frowning from myrtle beds. Uriel's depressing eclipse may have resembled what the author of the divinity address had at first mistakenly expected to experience.

> A sad self-knowledge, withering, fell
> On the beauty of Uriel;
> In heaven once eminent, the god
> Withdrew, that hour, into his cloud;
> Whether doomed to long gyration
> In the sea of generation,
> Or by knowledge grown too bright
> To hit the nerve of feebler sight. . . .

And Emerson felt something of the archangel's defiant mood, though he was not bellicose and though his severest indictments of the orthodox were not uttered in a "voice of cherub scorn."

As Hedge remembered in his declining years, he heard Emerson read the poem aloud long before its publication and got the idea that it was to be interpreted ironically, the archangel typifying the radical vagaries of the day. It seems more likely that Emerson was really dramatizing himself in that character, but with some subtle irony.

The only Emerson who suffered serious eclipse after the divinity address was Emerson the preacher. He preached twice on Wednesday, August 15, at Watertown, and on two Sundays in the following January at Concord. According to his own carefully kept record, his sermon at Concord on January 20, 1839, was his last. He had narrowed down his profession to that of author and lecturer; but for some time he published nothing more that reached, then or later, so many readers as the Phi Beta Kappa oration and the divinity address had. His oration at Dartmouth College, read some days after he had stirred up the hornet's nest at Cambridge, was published in September. It was on the subject of literary ethics, was a poor relation of the Phi Beta Kappa oration of the year before, caused hardly a ripple of excitement, and was promptly forgotten by all but a few. In February, April, and July of 1839 *The Western Messenger,* edited by Emerson's friend James Freeman Clarke, published new and old verses called "Each in All," "To the Humble-bee," "Good-bye, Proud World!" and "The Rhodora."

Meantime, however, a few weeks before the resounding Phi Beta Kappa oration had been spoken, Emerson had done his part for a local patriotic celebration by contributing a few stanzas that could be set to familiar music. The famous fight with the redcoats had taken place almost under the shadow of Concord's manse, an Emerson family home. Grandfather Ripley, now the master of house and land, had given the town a slice of his little field on condition that the grant should be fenced with heavy stone and that a monument commemorating April 19, 1775, should be erected on the ground by July 4, 1837. The cornerstone was laid late in 1836, but the monument, though it bore that date, was not dedicated till the following Fourth of July. On the afternoon of that day a "great concourse of people" assembled beside the shaft to hear prayers from their pastors and an address by their congressman, Samuel Hoar. But when the original hymn by a "citizen of Concord" was read by Ripley and "beautifully sung" by a choir to the tune of Old Hundred, the author was not there to hear, being absent on a visit to Plymouth.

The "assembled multitude" was "highly gratified and deeply impressed" by the day's exercises and may have approved the local paper's judgment that the hymn spoke for itself and that it at once excited ideas of originality, poetic genius, and judicious adaptation; but probably few persons clearly perceived at the moment the fitness and the assured vitality of the simple phrases packed into the first stanza:

> By the rude bridge that arched the flood,
> Their flag to April's breeze unfurled,
> Here, once, the embattled farmers stood,
> And fired the shot heard round the world.

The "Concord Hymn," as it was later called, was at once taken up by the newspapers, though it was some thirty-eight years before its opening lines were cut in stone on the farther side of the river.

But though it was to become a part of the American tradition and deserved immortality, the "Concord Hymn" offered Emerson no pattern for his future verse. The not very new pieces he published in *The Western Messenger* of 1839 showed, however, more subtlety of perception and a more indirect and a freer style than he had used in early years. There were also other signs that he was escaping completely from the conventional themes and rhythms that he had practiced during his youthful apprenticeship. By 1839 he was insisting on a theory of poetic liberty. He wanted "not tinkling rhyme, but grand Pindaric strokes" and "such rhymes as shall not suggest a restraint, but contrariwise the wildest freedom."

Yet in spite of his belief that a single stanza of poetry could outweigh a book of prose, his progress as a poet was necessarily impeded by his too great occupation with prose. He continued to write poetic prose and, as it turned out, was often called upon to act as critic and editor of miscellaneous amateur writers.

17

THE DIAL AND THE ESSAYS

Was unterscheidet	(What distinguishes
Götter von Menschen? . . .	Gods from us men? . . .
Ein kleiner Ring	A narrow circle
Begränzt unser Leben,	Contains our life,
Und viele Geschlechter	And our generations
Reihen sich dauernd	Are helplessly fastened,
An ihres Daseyns	As so many links,
Unendliche Kette.	In the great chain of being.)

—Goethe, "Gränzen der Menschheit"

Edel sey der Mensch . . .	(Man should aim high . . .
Nur allein der Mensch	It is only man
Vermag das Unmögliche . . .	Can do the impossible . . .)

—Goethe, "Das Göttliche"

IN March of 1835 William Ellery Channing lost a night's sleep over the rumor that some young men proposed to found a Transcendental journal. A little more than four years later the same young men, now members of the Transcendental Club, were talking the journal out of dream into reality. At a meeting of the club in September, 1839, Theodore Parker was convinced that the three persons competent to take charge were Emerson, Margaret Fuller, and Frederic Hedge. Presently he narrowed down his choice to Emerson as editor. Margaret, Hedge, and humbler spirits, he thought, should be assistants. But Emerson had no intention of trading his freedom for an editorial chair, and by early November the election had lighted on Margaret, "George Ripley having promised to undertake all the business part of it for her."

Margaret meditated a number for the following April, though she preferred to wait till autumn, "which," said Emerson, "looks like a century in such affairs." When she began her appeal for contributors, she discovered that the solidarity of the Transcendentalists was far from perfect. She leaned heavily on Emerson. He wrote to her in December, "I believe we all feel much alike in regard to this Journal; we all wish it to be, but do not wish to be in any way personally responsible for it." Hedge, in what seemed a perverse mood, reminded her that he himself could once have been the editor and warned her that though he was as much interested in the journal as ever, she was not to count on him for any help. He blew hot and cold. Within a few weeks he frankly confessed that he was afraid to identify himself publicly with the Transcendentalists lest he be taken for an atheist in disguise. And he explicitly announced that he did not agree with the ideas of Emerson and Alcott.

Emerson thought Hedge's view "quite worthless" but cautioned Margaret that her ill health was a real danger and that she ought not to go ahead with the journal unless she felt confident of quick improvement. As she wanted to go ahead, he suggested contributors. Besides more obvious persons, he named Samuel Gray Ward, Henry Thoreau, Caroline Sturgis, Sarah Freeman Clarke, Christopher Pearse Cranch, and young Ellery Channing; and, as it turned out, all of them sent in acceptable manuscripts. He helped George Ripley negotiate with publishers. Confident that the journal would succeed, he backed up Ripley's demand "that *they* shd take all the risk & should give us half the profits."

He got the promise of a paper from Alcott. He asked Ellery Channing for verses. He collaborated so extensively with Margaret Fuller on the introductory address, "The Editors to the Reader," that he wrote only his own name at its head in his copy of the first volume of the magazine. The not very dependable firm of Weeks, Jordan, and Company published *The Dial*, No. 1, on the first of July, 1840.

Running through the pages of a copy that Alcott had brought him from Boston on the day of publication must have seemed to Emerson like leafing through the family album and the guest book. Besides his introductory address, modestly commending the infant quarterly to those conscious of a new "strong current of thought and feeling," there were two of his own poems, "To Eva" and "The Problem." "A Short Essay on Critics," with its classification of members of the literary bench and bar as subjective, apprehensive, and comprehensive, was signed F. and was Margaret's. "Notes from the Journal of a Scholar" consisted of scraps that Emerson had intelligently selected from the notebooks of his brother Charles. In one of these scraps, perhaps the most poetical thing he ever wrote, Charles, tentatively exploring the boundaries of the unconscious, identified himself with others in a manner suggestive of later passages in Melville and Whitman: "The reason, why Homer is to me like dewy morning, is because I too lived while Troy was, and sailed in the hollow ships of the Grecians . . . And Shakspeare in King John does but recall to me myself in the dress of another age, the sport of new accidents. I, who am Charles, was sometime Romeo. In Hamlet, I pondered and doubted." "The Last Farewell" was Emerson's brother Edward's poetical valedictory to life. The verses called "Sympathy" were by Emerson's young townsman and protégé

Henry Thoreau. So was the not very remarkable prose on Persius. The "Lines" beginning "Love scatters oil" were by Ellen Tucker and made a slender column in her memory. The youthful Samuel Gray Ward's love of art found expression in some verses.

Alcott was here with fifty rather abstruse and not very poetic apothegms, a first instalment of the "Orphic Sayings" that delighted satirists of *The Dial*. Some ideas resembling Emerson's echoed rather hollowly among abstractions labeled with Roman numerals. "Your first duty is self-culture, self-exaltation: you may not violate this high trust. . . . Men shall become Gods. . . . The voice of the private, not popular heart, is alone authentic. . . . All things are instinct with spirit." Alcott, lacking the power to make poetry of such ideas, had, as Emerson said, left them "cold vague generalities." Yet Emerson himself insisted that they be printed, and soon after their publication he decided that they were "of great importance to the Journal inasmuch as otherwise, as far as I have read, there is little that might not appear in any other journal."

Wearying of the first number, he dreamed of making *The Dial* less literary in order that economic, political, and other questions of the time might get some attention. He could not have been surprised when Carlyle promptly reported that *The Dial* was too ethereal for him. In the opening article of the second number Emerson drew heavily upon his recent lecture on literature. He also printed a first instalment of his own poem "Woodnotes"; and in a lengthy article called "New Poetry" he introduced the public to the verses of the dreamy, gentle Ellery Channing. Carlyle, though he saw improvement over the first *Dial,* warned that there was still too much soul. But the Transcendental quality of the magazine remained strong. Its reputation for intelligibility was not helped by the printing of "The Sphinx" in the third number. The popular opinion regarding writers for the periodical was a little later expressed without great exaggeration in some unfortunately dull satirical verses that the usually vivacious and clever Oliver Wendell Holmes recited at a Phi Beta Kappa anniversary. According to Holmes, the deluded infants who talked in Dialese addressed the world as if they had resolved all its mysteries and doubts.

In April of 1841 the fourth number seemed to promise something more substantial. Robust Theodore Parker dealt with the problem of labor and not without a glance now and then at reality as understood by the workingman. In his lecture "Man the Reformer," contributed to the same number, Emerson tried characteristically to trace social and economic conflict to its root in private character, discovering that the greatest of all reforms would be effected by substituting love for selfishness. To Volume II of *The Dial* he was a laggard contributor. Aside from a second instalment of "Woodnotes," there were some minor verses of his and not much prose. He seems to have helped Ripley transfer *The Dial* from Jordan of the bankrupt Weeks, Jordan, and Company to Elizabeth Peabody, bookseller and publisher to the Transcendentalists.

Meantime his boyhood dream of writing a volume of essays had been realized. On New Year's Day of 1841, it seems, he had sent the manuscript to the printer. Wishing to acknowledge the debt the book owed to the Concord woods he thought he might call it *Forest Essays* but dropped the first half of that title. *Essays* was published a little past the middle of March.

Both literal-minded and too hasty readers might have been saved much distress if Emerson had explained in a prefatory note that he habitually looked sympathetically at both sides of his subject though not always in the same essay. For the benefit of these classes of readers he might also have said to begin with what he chose to reserve for the tenth essay: "But lest I should mislead any . . . let me remind the reader that I am only an experimenter. . . . I unsettle all things. No facts are to me sacred; none are profane; I simply experiment, an endless seeker with no Past at my back." But the title he had given his book was itself a warning.

A book written by an essayist highly conscious of Plutarch, Montaigne, and Bacon was apt to be one of almost unlimited freedom. Emerson's essays, it is true, were not so miscellaneous as theirs. All of his were tied somehow to the main threads of his philosophy. But their arrangement in the volume did not often suggest their particular interrelationships. As the essay on nature was not finished in time to be included, there could be no trilogy of Over-soul, self, and nature if Emerson considered such a grouping. He did not attempt to emulate even the modest degree of orderliness he had achieved some five years earlier in his "Philosophy of History," though a few of the essays were closely related to that course of lectures.

But it may have been his satisfaction with the lectures which caused him to give the essay on history first place in his new book. History, rather than nature, now appeared to be the best expositor of the divine mind; and the essay showed how the divine mind was the chief actor in the annals of mankind and worked its will through individual selves. This idea was, in its simplest form, as old as religion. Recently it had got new dignity from Hegel's lectures on the philosophy of history and from Cousin's introduction to the history of philosophy. Emerson knew Cousin's book, and Cousin had known Hegel himself as well as his published writings. But Emerson worked out his theory in what was unmistakably his own way and made it a fit, if very incomplete, introduction to *Essays*.

Within each essay unity was only partial. Perhaps most passages could have been transferred from one paragraph to another or from one essay to another without harm. Only the sentences were indisputably units, but they were admirable. Many of them were arrows which Emerson had so often practiced with that he could drive them into the bull's-eye with consummate skill. One such sentence often seemed worth an essay by any contemporary writer. The ideas were explosive, the diction bold and picturesque. Sometimes there were new words of the author's own coinage, sometimes obsolete or obsolescent ones that emanated an aura of quaintness. As if to afford still more variety, Emerson would occasionally include a poetic or Scriptural archaism. But generally his words were undated and much alive; and on the whole his English was as clear and as strictly correct as almost any written in England or America.

For a reader who knew *Nature* and the published addresses and had a fair acquaintance with the lectures, the leading ideas of the essays already had a degree of familiarity. But such familiarity only gave the essays the advantage of being more easily understood and of seeming more credible. Freshness of phrase, generous illustrations of the meaning, and added polish of form made them superior to the lectures. They were a new imaginative creation; and this was true in spite of the fact that every idea of Emerson's, as of any other poet, had close relations with what had been said by some earlier thinker.

Emerson was able to compress his thoughts best on subjects about which he had thought most. "Self-reliance," the essay that had been longest in his mind, bristled with challenging epigrams: "To believe your own thought, to believe that what is true for you in your private heart is true for all men, —that is genius. . . . In every work of genius we recognize our own rejected thoughts; they come back to us with a certain alienated majesty. . . . Trust thyself: every heart vibrates to that iron string. . . . Society everywhere is in conspiracy against the manhood of every one of its members. . . . Whoso would be a man, must be a nonconformist. . . .Nothing is at last sacred but the integrity of your own mind. . . . I do not wish to expiate, but to live. . . . A foolish consistency is the hobgoblin of little minds . . . An institution is the lengthened shadow of one man . . . Travelling is a fool's paradise. . . . Insist on yourself; never imitate. . . . Society never advances. It recedes as fast on one side as it gains on the other. . . . Society acquires new arts and loses old instincts. . . . The civilized man has built a coach, but has lost the use of his feet. . . . A political victory, a rise of rents, the recovery of your sick or the return of your absent friend, or some other favorable event raises your spirits, and you think good days are preparing for you. Do not believe it. Nothing can bring you peace but yourself."

In some respects "Self-reliance," expounding the key doctrine of Transcendentalism, was one of the most untranscendental of the essays. Its theme was very old. "All that depends on another gives pain; all that depends on himself gives pleasure . . ." said the ancient Hindu law. In ancient Europe the same doctrine had been taught by others than the Stoics. In sixteenth-century France, Montaigne had been sure that "though we could become learned by other Mens Reading," yet "a Man can never be wise but by his own Wisdom." In England the poetic glorification of the individual had risen to a climax at the beginning of the nineteenth century. In Germany one found it in Goethe's "Prometheus" and in his much more sober doctrine of self-culture. Pioneer life in the New World had insistently taught self-reliance of the practical sort of which Franklin, with his own notable stock of epigrams, was a favorite apostle. The author of *Essays* himself had collected numerous scraps of folk wisdom on the subject. Doubtless many a practical-minded reader got happily through "Self-reliance" without being much perturbed by more than a few surprising paradoxes and bold plunges beneath the surface of common sense. That was pretty obviously what Emerson wanted to happen. Some weeks before publication he betrayed his impatient desire to avoid overrefinement in this essay when he commented, "My page about 'Consistency' would be better written thus: Damn Consistency!" As in his address on the American scholar, he was determined to speak to a large audience and was loath to explain a mystery because "all that we say is the far-off remembering of the intuition."

But characteristic intuitive, idealistic, mystical doctrine, though he had almost hidden it, was really an indispensable part of "Self-reliance." For the initiated, he made it clear that the foundation of the self-trust he was teaching was an aboriginal Self. The "ultimate fact" was "the resolution of all into the ever-blessed ONE." It was as if the essayist had suddenly left the world of the *Boston Daily Advertiser* and the *New York Journal of Commerce* and got lost in conversation with a friendly circle of Neo-platonists on the left bank of the ancient Tiber or were seated beside the Ganges with some swarthy yogi who had fortunately escaped from the deadly formalism and superstition of the Brahmans.

"Compensation" was harder than "Self-reliance" to fit into a practical-minded man's reading. But it was understandable to the most unimaginative as an attempt to refute the doctrine, then, as Emerson believed, commonly taught in churches, "that judgment is not executed in this world; that the wicked are successful; that the good are miserable." After all, what thinking man could really make sense of the theory that God remained all but dead to the present world but came alive, both omnipotent and just, the moment the curtain was rung down on it? To Emerson himself "Compensation" had important personal significance. As his struggle in early life for self-trust was finally rounded out by his essay "Self-reliance," so his incessant endeavor to adjust himself to the tragedy of his own losses came to a fitting climax in "Compensation."

His long record of buffetings by death and disease seemed to make him immune to the taunt that he was a mere dreamer filled with the easy eloquence of ignorance. Certainly he was not deceived about the magnitude of the problem he was attacking in the essay and did not expect complete success. He only hoped "to record some facts that indicate the path of the law of Compensation; happy beyond my expectation if I shall truly draw the smallest arc of this circle." Probably many of his readers condemned him too hastily because they failed to understand how limited his objectives were. He was not attempting to deny evil. He was attempting, at the most, only to balance good and evil and expected the result of any such balance to be not perfection but justice.

He did not succeed any better than he had expected. It was good sense but not convincing argument to cite polarity in every part of nature—darkness and light, heat and cold, the ebb and flow of waters, male and female. One might agree that for every grain of wit there was a grain of folly and yet be skeptical when the proposition was reversed. It was easy to show that the haves were going to lose something but not so easy to prove that the havenots were going to get their share. In the end the mystery of suffering and of evil remained about as Job had left it when he confessed that there were "things too wonderful for me, which I knew not." Probably the final appeal that Emerson addressed to his practical-minded reader was the one he himself felt most keenly: "We cannot stay amid the ruins." And in that he was right. No man kept on living without faith and hope however much he might profess himself a complete pessimist. The professed pessimist, Emerson might have defended himself, was a sentimentalist, luxuriating in a feeling which he had no intention of matching with action. But as the author of "Compensation" Emerson obviously had his chief success in fighting a rear-guard engagement. He could do little more than beat an orderly retreat in the face of overwhelming odds. In "Spiritual Laws," the following essay, he soon got onto more tenable ground with his theory of evil: "All loss, all pain, is particular; the universe remains to the heart unhurt."

"Love" was one of the most pleasing and was the most Platonic of all the writings of Emerson, lover of Plato. The *Phaedrus* and the *Symposium*, whose exotic homosexual elements were conveniently ignored, together accounted for essential parts of this essay. But it owed much to the sharp observations Emerson had made on life. The glorification of the passion of love, undertaken with sudden access of fervor such as Socrates himself experienced when he had fully made up his mind to do justice to this fit subject for a philosopher-poet, was followed by a sublimation of physical passion into spiritual. Emerson climbed, with Plato's Socrates, the ladder of love, asserting that by physical love we are "put in training for a love which knows not sex, nor person, nor partiality, but which seeks virtue and wisdom everywhere, to the end of increasing virtue and wisdom."

"Friendship" also had some relation to Emerson's reading but had firmer roots in his experience and in the favorite ideas nurtured through many years in his journals. If Emerson looked again into Bacon and Montaigne, he made no effort to match either the worldly wisdom or the orderly style of Bacon and laid claim to no such success in the art of friendship as Montaigne had had, but must have seen that he could surpass both writers in the depth and philosophical acumen of his thought. One so widely acquainted with authors must have heard faint echoes of many familiar voices as he wrote, voices at least as distant in antiquity as Aristotle's, but he had his private resources. On this subject of friendship he was a conscious experimenter and observer, as his letters to such friends as Margaret Fuller, Sam Ward, and Caroline Sturgis showed. Henry Thoreau was another of the many persons who helped prepare him. But in spite of any aid he got from either friends or books the essay was very much his own. "Friendship" proved to be a new chapter on his old theme of self-reliance.

The glow of enthusiasm with which he began the essay soon faded. He seemed to think of only the kind of friendship in which, according to Montaigne's caution, one should walk with bridle in hand and with prudence and circumspection. He came near to agreeing with the classical admonition Montaigne had quoted, *"O my Friends, there is no Friend."* If Emerson's genuine friend existed, he was an epitome of the virtue of self-reliance. "Let me be alone to the end of the world," Emerson put it, "rather than that my friend should overstep, by a word or a look, his real sympathy. . . . Let him not cease an instant to be himself." He had to admit in the end that he had seemed to do a kind of treachery to his subject, for "The essence of friendship is entireness, a total magnanimity and trust." Yet when he warned his friend, "Unhand me: I will be dependent no more," he was trying to prepare the way for a reunion on a higher platform. He was like the Stoics in limiting friendship to the wise and good. Whether those he admitted into his select company were friends or merely a select company remained, on his own showing in "Friendship," doubtful.

"Prudence," "Heroism," and "The Over-soul" made a disparate trio.

In "Prudence," an essay on "the virtue of the senses" or "the art of securing a present well-being," Emerson came nearest to by-passing his high doctrines but discovered in the end that all the other virtues were friendly to prudence. In "Heroism" he expounded self-reliance only thinly disguised. In "The Over-soul" the self-reliant mood of the most highly individualized self appeared once more in its true light. So far as the individual's relation to the divine mind was concerned, self-reliance was shown to be something akin to wise passiveness. The soul rested in the arms of Unity, or the Over-soul, as the earth rested in the arms of the soft atmosphere. From this surrounding presence the soul received light, truth; and of these it somehow became, in turn, the revealer. But Emerson, the theorizer of mysticism, found the actual revelations of the Over-soul as incommunicable and indescribable as the practicing mystic usually found his experiences to be. The windmill of mysticism was a noble one, no mere grinder of corn, but Emerson broke his lances against it in vain.

"Circles," "Intellect," and "Art" rounded out his book. He pictured truth under what was for him the absolutely perfect figure of concentric circles. No act, no truth was final. A bigger circle would include the one just drawn. There would always be a later and broader generalization that could be made, and it was foolish to hate expanding truth. Closed minds needed to stand clear of it. They needed to "Beware when the great God lets loose a thinker on this planet." Once, when he was preparing the *Essays* for the press, Emerson dreamed that as he was floating at will in the ether he saw the world not far off, "diminished to the size of an apple"; and that, in obedience to an angel, he ate it. But it is doubtful whether he ever, in any moment of consciousness, thought of truth as a thing so definitely limited or so completely attainable. "Intellect" recommended a saving mixture of will and intuition, as well as freedom of thought and self-reliance. But intuition and passivity were again triumphant. In the last essay Emerson denied that art was imitation. It was rather inspiration. The Over-soul was at work once more, this time guiding the hand of the artist. And if there was one universal artist back of all artists, then all art was akin. The distinction between the fine and the useful arts ought to be forgotten, Emerson assured his reader as he had assured his audience in the lecture hall long before.

The first series of *Essays* completed its author's ruin in some eyes but made his reputation in others. After reading "Self-reliance," Aunt Mary, with her fiery temperament only slightly cooled by her sixty-six years, had a bad night. She wanted to know whether "this strange medly of atheism and false independence" was "the real sane work of that man whom I idolised as a boy, so mild, candid modest obliging." If her brother William had only lived, she was sure, his son would never have committed these offenses against Christian decency. She regretted that Waldo Emerson "had not gone to the tomb amidst his early honors" instead of living on to be disgraced by his *Essays*. She blamed his wife and Sarah Ripley for not interfering before it was too late to save him. Sarah Ripley appeared to be the guiltier one, for she had been "one means of early infecting him with infidelity." Aunt Mary now tried an appeal to Elizabeth Hoar but feared that Elizabeth's faith had also been shaken. Aunt Mary's world seemed to be falling away from beneath her feet. But she was still determined to cling to her old-fashioned faith. "If," she pleaded, "my joys and hopes are delusive oh wake me not . . ."

The leonine Orestes Brownson, laying his hand on a copy of the *Essays*, proclaimed to the patrons of a Boston bookstore that anyone who wished to know what sound Transcendentalism was should read that book. Brownson regarded himself as one of the three profoundest men in America and was at least capable of recognizing Transcendentalism. Felton, the jolly Greek professor, belied his reputation for good humor when he reviewed *Essays*. "It is idle to argue against these old, but ever-recurring errors," he groaned. With his knowledge of literature, he could not fail to see that this book was written by a master of English and contained "many single thoughts of dazzling brilliancy; much exquisite writing, and a copious vein of poetical illustration." But he was certain that the Emersonian doctrine of self-reliance and intuition, "if acted upon, would overturn society, and resolve the world into chaos." Edward Everett wrote home from England that he hoped his nephew and namesake, Edward Everett Hale, would keep away from Transcendentalism if Emerson's *Essays* was a sample of it. He found it hard to believe that such a clear thinker and beautiful writer as he had known Emerson to be a few years earlier could have printed such conceited and laborious nonsense as this book now introduced to the British public by Carlyle.

The little London edition of the essays sponsored by Carlyle was not a complete surprise to the British public. A year before its appearance, Richard Monckton Milnes had formally introduced Emerson's earlier publications to its prospective readers. Milnes, a Tory writer described by his friend Carlyle as a bland-smiling, high-bred, Italianized little man with long olive-blond hair, had deftly sketched for *The London and Westminster Review* the normal well-informed conservative opinion of the American Transcendentalist. Emerson, according to the *Westminster* article, was a sort of lesser, transatlantic Carlyle. He wrote in a vigorous and eloquent style, faithfully represented the idealism that could be detected below the surface of American life, and announced doctrines that were naturally attractive to assertors of democratic principles but failed to pause and consider what a bedlam of egoists would be turned loose on the world "if this indiscriminate self-reliance was generally adopted as the sole regulating principle of life." Presumably this Emerson of Milnes's was approximately what many Britons expected to find when they picked up the *Essays* in the bookshops.

Carlyle did much in his lengthy but restrained preface to the English edition to attract intellectuals and frighten others away. This first English edition quickly made what he called an appropriate sensation, and there were many reviews, striking all notes, he reported. He himself felt that Emerson had strained not quite successfully to catch the universe in his net. Harriet Martineau wrote to America to prophesy a thousand years of life for the book. Britons wanted enough copies of it to make it profitable for a piratical British publisher to reprint the volume within two or three years. Milnes was so well pleased with it that he was anxious to get back into critical harness for the sake of the American author. John Sterling wrote Emerson that in Britain, where the social prestige of church orthodoxy was powerful, there were probably not a hundred persons outside London who could appreciate the essays; but for his own part he was delighted. "You are," he said, "the only man in the world with whom, though unseen, I feel any sort of nearness . . ." Recommending the essays to Caroline Fox, he advised her "to devote three months entirely to the study of this one little volume."

Emerson resolved that "I shall one day write something better than those poor cramp arid 'Essays' which I almost hate the sight of." And if he got little pleasure from the volume, he got quite as little financial return from it. In order to bolster up his finances he would have to get a high interest on his money investments or continue the lecturing from which he had got brief respite.

His lyceum itineraries had burst their tightly circumscribed bounds in 1840 when he had carried his lectures out of New England for the first time to read three of them at the Mercantile Library in New York. But he had made the long journey unwillingly. Lonesome, even at the home of his brother on Staten Island, he had comforted himself with the marine spectacle at the Narrows more than with the table talk of such persons as his kinsman Orville Dewey, a minister, and the poet and editor Bryant, doubtless full of politics in that year of a Presidential election. On his way home he had managed, with his half dozen lectures at Providence, to stir up local curiosity about Transcendentalism. The deeply religious Charles King Newcomb, "a slight, dark young man, with a hesitant manner and a nervous laugh" and "a heavy mass of tangled dark hair which was always slipping over his eyes and being flipped back with an impatient gesture," had seemed to be almost ready to declare himself a disciple. But the lecturer had disappointed "all the young persons" by failing to devote an evening to a forthright exposition of the new doctrines. Each day it had been expected that he would break out with the New Light in the next discourse. He had been glad to retreat toward Concord, congratulating himself on the $300 he had earned during his travels, but had learned on passing through Boston that he would lose over $200 because of the failure of the Atlantic Bank to pay its dividend.

In the summer of 1841, with his new book well out of the way, he tried halfheartedly to prepare an oration for a college commencement while he contemplated the sea at Nantasket Beach. He had earned his vacation, and Nantasket, then unspoiled, was the right place for it. He loved "this vastness & roar—the rubbing of the sea on the land so ancient & pleasant a sound," and "the color & the curve" of the ocean. He had pleasant memories of Malta and Sicily and his other Mediterranean experiences. But the oration, "The Method of Nature," did not prosper. The dreamy mood of Nantasket that had got into it could hardly appeal to the students and their friends who celebrated their academic festival that August at the little backwoods town of Waterville in Maine. According to the local newspaper, an honest farmer probably expressed the opinion of the generality when he remarked, "It is quite likely that the oration contained a great deal of *science;* but even if it did not, no one could know the fact."

The City Bank failing to pay a dividend in the autumn of 1841, Emerson was forced to prepare manuscripts for another series of winter evenings at the Masonic Temple. Of his eight lectures "On the Times," it was doubtless "The Transcendentalist," the manifesto his Providence audience had expected in vain, that aroused the greatest interest in Boston. Though he denied that there was a Transcendental party or even a single pure Transcendentalist, he found Transcendentalism real enough. It was, as he described it, a slightly more than moderate idealism and strong intuitionalism running, in its extreme form, into mystical ecstasy. Though it might be a saturnalia of faith, it was really excessive only because its devotees failed, through imperfect obedience, to live up to it. Even the strong among them were dissatisfied with their experience, but they kept on their way unperturbed by ridicule. If they were rank individualists and too solitary to be good members of society, it might still appear that society owed much to them. So Emerson explained the newness and its apostles to the Bostonians, as objectively as he could. Afterwards he warned Aunt Mary not to make more of his role in the lecture than that of mere observer. He had been only a biographer, he told her, "describing a class of young persons whom I have seen— I hope it is not confession and that, past all hope, I am confounded with my compassionated heroes & heroines." And yet, in spite of his characteristic effort to keep his individuality intact, his account of the composite Transcendentalist was a picture in which his own features were not missing.

The financial results of his course were not encouraging in this year when he was compelled, as often, to look narrowly at his finances. Though he had once received an average of $57, he now had but $40 a lecture. His Boston market was slipping. He repeated five of the eight lectures at Providence but "found a small company & a trivial reward." He was forced to look again in the direction of New York, where he spent the first weeks of March, 1842, repeating a selected half dozen of the Boston lectures. He had a friendly enough reception there. Though *The Evening Post,* William Cullen Bryant's paper, complained of some incoherence in his thought, it declared that "More than almost any other public speaker, he makes an intelligent hearer think for himself." William Emerson saw that his brother had "produced a marked sensation in the best part of our community" and had won "many lovers & admirers." Yet the lecturer was earning only some $200 above expenses.

But, fortunately, at New York he was receiving other pay than money. As an observer of the full tide of life in the crowded metropolis he was learning timely lessons. Here the reformers daunted him with their precise and determined plans for saving the world. One could not escape the tireless enthusiasms of men like the tall, pale-haired Horace Greeley, the New Hampshire and Vermont farm boy who had arrived in the city some ten years before as a youthful journeyman printer dressed in comical garb but was now the editor of his own paper, the successful *New-York Daily Tribune.* Greeley loved the tingling life of the great town and knew the poverty and distress of its unclean masses. He was a born reformer, and at the moment he was full of the doctrine of Fourier. Fourier's principle of attractive industry was declared to be comparable in the social realm to the law of gravitation in the physical world. Men could be brought together in communities where they could forget their old inhibitions and find their proper emotional and cultural development and their proper destiny. Fourier was a pre-Freudian psychoanalyst of parts. Albert Brisbane, the chief American expounder of this new gospel that he had brought back from Europe, later struck Henry Thoreau as looking like a man who had lived in a cellar, far gone in consumption. But he was really a person of great force. He had digested the contents of his master Fourier's works and offered them to the public in a book called *Social Destiny of Man.* And now he had captured Greeley and his *Tribune.* Emerson had been in town only a few days when Brisbane's daily articles on Fourierism began to appear on the *Tribune's* front page.

The lecture platform, as well as the press, was a strategic hilltop the propagandists wanted to seize. But from the moment when Emerson confronted Brisbane and Greeley together at their Graham boarding house he knew that he could not satisfy them. "They are bent on popular action: I am in all my theory, ethics, & politics a poet and of no more use in their New York than a rainbow or a firefly," he wrote home. Greeley complicated matters by declaring himself a fellow Transcendentalist. Emerson had hardly got lodged in the Globe Hotel before Brisbane was there with the first full instalment of his plea for the new system. "He wishes me," Emerson reported to Lidian, " 'with all my party,' to come in directly & join him. What palaces! What concerts! What pictures lectures poetry & flowers. Constantinople it seems Fourier showed was the natural capital of the World, & when the Earth is planted & gardened & templed all over with 'Groups' & 'Communities' each of 2000 men & 6000 acres, Constantinople is to be the metropolis & we poets & Miscellaneous transcendental persons who are too great for your Concords & New Yorks will gravitate to that point for music & architecture & society such as wit cannot paint nowadays."

Emerson also found in Manhattan a few acquaintances very different from Greeley and Brisbane. He discovered one "William Greene a devout man who seems to read nothing but Boehmen & Madame Guion," and Greene took him to see "a devout woman, Mrs Black, of the same stamp." Both mystics were simple, unpretentious souls. Rebecca Black made her living by slopwork for the tailors. Henry James, "a very manlike thorough seeing person," then a rebel against Calvinism drifting toward Swedenborgianism, came to Emerson's hotel for a visit, and so began a friendship that lasted many years. Emerson thought him "the best apple on the tree thus far." In James's home he saw *The Dial* lying on the table, and in the nursery he may have seen the two-months-old son, William. Possibly, as tradition has it, Emerson climbed the stairs to give his blessing to the infant philosopher. But whether or not William James received the blessing, his Pragmatism doubtless owed something to the incipient Pragmatism which he found, many years later, in the writings of the Transcendentalist.

Lidian's guess that one result of the New York trip would be the addition of some "very respectable lions" to "the transcendental menagerie" was, however, not quite accurate. A chief virtue of this experience for Emerson was that it tested his individualism and love of solitude. The city itself left him first hot, then cold. The endless crowds made him feel more keenly the value of his own particular class, but he had his moments of enthusiasm. "For a national, for an imperial prosperity, everything here seems irrevocably destined," he told Margaret Fuller. "What a Bay! what a River! what climate! what men! What ample ample interior domain, lake mountain & forest! What manners, what histories & poetry shall rapidly arise & for how long, and, it seems, endless date! Me my cabin fits better, yet very likely from a certain poorness of spirit; but in my next transmigration, I think I should choose New York."

Events conspired to make the individualist face the sorry problems with which society was concerned. The Fourierism that confronted him in New York was much like the associationism he had seen at George Ripley's Brook Farm. In the summer of 1840 there had been some half serious talk between Emerson and Alcott of founding a sort of informal Transcendental university, possibly at Concord. George Ripley and Margaret Fuller had joined the discussion later, it seems. But in the following October, George and Sophia Ripley, Margaret, and Alcott had met at Emerson's home to consider plans for the founding of Brook Farm in the Boston suburb of West Roxbury. The blueprint of Brook Farm had called for not only an educational establishment but an ideal community where intellectuals could work a little with their hands and learn a way to escape any share in the evils of industrialism. But the bare suggestion of anything resembling a communal scheme had chilled Emerson the individualist. "And," he had written in his diary, "not once could I be inflamed, but sat aloof and thoughtless; my voice faltered and fell. . . . I do not wish to remove from my present prison to a prison a little larger." After the meeting he had wanted to keep an open mind and had explained in detail his sympathy and his objections; but the upshot of the matter was that he decided against Brook Farm.

Yet by now the general excitement over economic and social reform had stirred him deeply. He desired at least to experiment with some limited reform completely under his own control. Nothing came of a plan of his to receive into his home the needy Alcotts that they might join him and Lidian in a one-year program of "labor & plain living." And the scheme to have the maid and the cook eat at the Emerson family table quickly proved impractical. Louisa, the maid, though she at first accepted it for the sake of the general social betterment of the household, rejected it when Lydia, the cook, firmly refused to budge from the kitchen. Thus the plans for "Mr Alcott, Liberty, Equality, & a common table" all went by the board.

A somewhat similar plan of Emerson's was more fortunate. It was arranged that, since the Alcotts would not come, Henry Thoreau should. For one year he was "to have his board &c for what labor he chooses to do." At the age of twenty-four Thoreau was "an indefatigable & a very skilful laborer," and Emerson, having been a skeleton all that spring of 1841 until he was ashamed, worked with him and at his direction. Emerson now had hopes of robust health; and, at the same time, he felt virtuous because he was aiding genius and was taking at least a minor part in the social experimentation that the reformers were continually dinning into his ears. In the summer the social experiment in his home was made more complex by the presence there of young Mary Russell as teacher in the nursery. Marston Watson, who afterwards became her husband, "always heard" and believed that she was Thoreau's "Maiden in the East."

Thoreau demonstrated remarkable versatility. He rowed Emerson on the Concord at night, introducing him to the "shadowy, starlit, moonlit stream, a lovely new world," Emerson said. "Through one field only we went to the boat and then left all time, all science, all history, behind us, and entered into Nature with one stroke of a paddle." A realist in the garden and a poet on the river, Henry was ready anywhere to play the philosopher and indulge in a discussion of Transcendental doctrines. "I said to him what I often feel," Emerson commented, "I only know three persons who seem to me fully to see this law of reciprocity or compensation,—himself, Alcott, and myself: and 't is odd that we should all be neighbors . . ."

Though Emerson could tire of Transcendental theory and once testily commented that he was familiar with all Henry's thoughts, "my own quite originally drest," he usually rated Henry as one of the most original of men, an incarnation of self-reliance. If Henry Thoreau appeared to Hawthorne quite unsophisticated except in his own way and ugly as sin, with his long nose and queer mouth, he was nevertheless a healthy and wholesome person to know, and his ugliness was of an honest kind that became him better than beauty. Thoreau could show the tenderness of a woman as he sat beside his dying brother but could often be crabbed enough. Hawthorne's impression that Emerson had suffered inconvenience from such an inmate was undoubtedly correct. But as Thoreau's stay at his friend's house extended far beyond the original estimate of a year, amicable relations must have prevailed. Henry himself afterwards told Emerson of his appreciation of the complete freedom he had been allowed to enjoy as "your pensioner." Lidian found the young man admirable, and in several letters he later wrote her from Staten Island, where he lived in William Emerson's family as a tutor, he showed a warm affection for this motherly woman who was nearly fifteen years his senior and, at times, idealized her till his admiration became a kind of Transcendental Mariolatry. Emerson remembered with some amusement one incident that resulted from those "two or three letters to my wife" from Thoreau: "She spoke of them to his family, who eagerly wished to see them. She consented, but said, 'She was almost ashamed to show them, because Henry had exalted her by very undeserved praise.'—'O yes,' said his Mother, 'Henry is very tolerant.' "

Meantime Emerson watched the progress of Brook Farm. After all, if what he heard was true, the numerous experimental communities that were now being established might really transform American society. At the end of Brook Farm's first year a shrewd merchant named Clapp told him that it must happen soon that these communities would change and control the price of bread as the manufacturing and commercial associations had done the price of cotton and farmers would be driven into associations in self-defense. Emerson visited West Roxbury and observed the experiment there at first hand. He could even take his part in one of the farm's charming sylvan fetes. Once, on a September day in 1841, when a birthday picnic party was in progress in the woods and the festive farmers were sporting in colorful costumes, Hawthorne, lying under the trees in his favorite role of observer, saw Emerson and Margaret Fuller emerge into the little glade which was the center of the gay throng. But Emerson's later description of Brook Farm as "a perpetual picnic, a French Revolution in small, an Age of Reason in a patty-pan" both simplified and exaggerated what he actually saw there. George William Curtis, a resident for some two years beginning in 1842, remembered that Emerson used to come as an interested spectator, enamored of the spirit of the enterprise but not of the actual community, "in which he saw very plainly all the unconscious drolleries."

Emerson may have been drawn to West Roxbury as much by his friends as by the novel social scheme of the place. On some visit he might see George Bradford, still plying his old profession of teaching, and Charles King Newcomb, vaguely drifting somewhere between Transcendentalism and Catholicism. Before Newcomb left the community, he loved it so well that he dreamed of erecting a shrine, to be called, perhaps, Our Lady of Brook Farm or the Holy Cross of West Roxbury. Lidian's nephew Frank Brown was there for a time. Various friends of Emerson's appeared on occasion.

But in spite of the good things he was later to say of the experiment, Emerson himself was persuaded that it was a mistake. Such an association would hardly invite intuitions, he must have been sure. After its first two years, he was of the opinion that it would show a few noble victims and that the rest of the members would shirk their duty. Hawthorne boasted that he had lived in the community during its heroic age. According to

Emerson's observation the virtue of Brook Farm was simply that it showed the possibility and convenience of good neighborhood, but that virtue could be borrowed and the rest left.

Yet the need of much mending of the social structure seemed patent. The evils of the cutthroat labor market could not be concealed even behind Walden Woods. In the winter of 1842 the projected railroad through Concord began to look real. But before there was any railroad to build, the region was flooded with poor Irish laborers. Edmund Hosmer, the farmer who used to work out Emerson's road tax for him, threatened to sell out and go to the West because the Irish undersold him in the labor market. Hosmer, a person who always looked "respectable and excellent to you in his old shabby cap and blue frock bedaubed with the slime of the marsh," represented an invaluable stratum of Concord society. He was not a mere Napoleon with sixty battles to his credit but had won six thousand, on as many hard-fought summer or winter days. Society could hardly afford to let such a man go down to defeat in this miserable economic confusion. Soon their employers were driving the poor Irish themselves as if they were Negroes.

Emerson saw these things happening. Across the Mill Brook he had the perpetual reminder of the red charity house on the poor farm. For many years Nancy Barron, the mad woman who was one of its inmates, had screamed herself hoarse, as if she were quite unaware that Concord was an idyllic retreat where poverty and other ills of the bustling world had no business to come. Emerson could hear her when he had a window open. He was not a snob. He objected to class distinctions, saw the human values in the poor, liked the unrestrained attitudes and manners of men and women in Prince Street, Charter Street, Ann Street, and the other haunts of poverty in Boston's North End, and discovered more picturesqueness in people at work than in persons consciously posed. But in the face of any organized reform heralded as for the benefit of the workers he was apt to be the convinced individualist. He wanted a more fundamental reform.

The temperance movement was gaining great momentum. In June of 1841 the Middlesex County Temperance Society held its annual meeting at Ripley's church. There were 226 delegates present as against only 30 at the annual meeting of the preceding year—"another evidence," said *The Republican,* a Concord newspaper, "of the wonderful interest that is now taken in the progress of temperance principles." On the day of the meeting Emerson paid $3 to the Cold Water Army. But within a few months he paid more for several bottles of Madeira without any exercise of his prized right of scorning consistency. When he yielded, a year or two later, to a challenge to deliver a temperance speech at the village of

Harvard, it was temperate living, not merely temperate drinking, that he praised. Temperance pledges, he warned, would not win the victory. Souls were not saved in bundles, he was sure. If he bowed for the moment to organized reform, it was only to reissue his declaration of self-reliance.

Wars of liberation were, according to him, for individuals to fight against their own weaker natures. His part, outside his private war, was to teach that fact. As late as 1841 he thought of the Negroes, in their misery, as, in the most profound sense, slaves of themselves. A movement to reform religion nearly stirred him into action. At the first convention of the Friends of Universal Reform, it is true, he finally made up his mind to speak, but by then the meeting was at an end. He attended, but only as a much interested spectator, the succeeding conventions in Chardon Street and their sequel, the Bible Convention of 1842. He was fascinated by the spectacle of fanaticism in all its colors and shades. "As a historian of the Times," he remarked, "one would certainly wish to be there."

The one religious organization to which he continued steadily to give financial aid was the Unitarian church in his village. Though he otherwise had little or no connection with it, he did not wish to offend his neighbors and he had his family's interests to consider. Hawthorne was amused when Emerson kept him and Hillard under cover until the good Concordians had safely got to church. Only then could the three set out on a Sunday walk to Walden. In private Emerson would sometimes express himself without any inhibition on the subject of religious dogma. He marveled that "these physicians, metaphysicians, mathematicians, critics, and merchants, believed this Jewish apologue of the poor Jewish boy," and he wondered "how they contrived to attach that accidental history to the religious idea, and this famous dogma of the Triune God, etc., etc." Preaching was cursed, and the better it was, the worse, he said. "A preacher is a bully: I who have preached so much,—by the help of God will never preach more." He had presumably not preached since January of 1839. But he kept on paying pew rent as well as taxes for the support of the church. He would also pay an odd dollar to the impecunious Methodists, and he could even go back to the pulpit of the Second Church when the old building was about to be torn down and very honestly tell his former parishioners how little his ideas had really changed since youth. He seemed to be confessing in the pulpit that he ought never to have been in the Christian ministry.

His study and books, his garden, the fields, his family, his friends made a rich tapestry against which life could be placed and admired; but nothing remained the same. Doctor Ripley had only remarked, after a spell of apoplexy and palsy, that he believed he had had a bad turn. Next year, May 2, 1841, the day after he was ninety, he preached the last of his farewell sermons. This extemporaneous effort was esteemed, said the church scribe, "the most impressive and eloquent sermon he ever delivered." But in September he died, and for Emerson the Puritan world receded farther into the past. On November 22 of the same year the family gained a new and firm hold on life by the birth of Edith, Emerson's second daughter. But toward the end of the following January, Waldo, his five-year-old son, was suddenly stricken with scarlatina. When Louisa May Alcott, only some three years the boy's senior, went to inquire how he was, she knew the answer at once from the tragic face of his father. Elizabeth Hoar's brother Rockwood was never more impressed with a human expression of agony than by that of Emerson leading the way into the room where little Waldo lay dead.

Emerson gradually attained a mood of acceptance and, in his letters and journals, wrote down hints that slowly grew into "Threnody," an ode which was almost a pastoral, in honor both of the boy and of nature. But at first he thought he could comprehend nothing of his loss but its bitterness. His philosophy was put to a severe test. To Samuel Ripley it seemed obvious enough that, since young Waldo's death, Emerson could never be the same again. Lidian, having suffered an incurable wound, brooded over unanswerable questions, and, apparently, turned for comfort to more orthodox doctrines than Transcendentalism.

Yet there were some compensations for Emerson. Concord began to look more like his dream of a center of intellectuals when Hawthorne, in July of 1842, brought Sophia Peabody, as his bride, to the manse, the house to whose name he soon gave literary eminence. But Sophia's enthusiasm for Emerson and Transcendentalism and Hawthorne's cool habit of analysis were not quite reconciled in the pair's later relations with the Concord sage. Hawthorne confessed that there had been times in his life when he might have asked this "prophet" for the key to the riddle of the universe; but now, as he explained it, "being happy, I felt as if there were no question to be put, and therefore admired Emerson as a poet of deep beauty and austere tenderness, but sought nothing from him as a philosopher." Emerson himself found it as hard to capture Hawthorne the man as to make anything of Hawthorne the storyteller.

Margaret Fuller never realized her vague idea of starting a school in Concord, but with her class in mythology at Boston she was often Lidian's schoolmistress and sometimes Emerson's. She by no means gave Emerson his first introduction to the ballet, but she helped revive his interest in it when she went with him to see Fanny Elssler in *Nathalie*. The two spectators may well have debated whether this was poetry or religion. Yet Emerson was not quite at ease as he pondered the philosophy of the ballet.

He admired as much as anyone the extreme grace of Fanny Elssler, "the winning fun and spirit of all her little coquetries, the beautiful erectness of her body, and the freedom and determination which she can so easily assume"; but he felt some doubts when he thought of the college boys who "left metaphysics, conic sections, or Tacitus" to watch her tripping satin slippers. Characteristically, he decided that "the morals, as it is called," lay "wholly with the spectator."

In the spring of 1842 he paid a new instalment of his debt to Margaret by aiding her escape from the foundering Transcendental magazine, *The Dial*. By about the middle of March her mind was made up that the April number would be her last. She could no longer afford to sacrifice health and labor, "with such a bankrupt's return," and she was ready to put either Theodore Parker or Emerson into the editorial chair. On first learning the fact, Emerson thought that he might promise to take responsibility only for the July number. But he soon decided to accept the editorship without reservation, in order to keep it out of strange hands. There was little hope of financial success. It was estimated that not more than three hundred subscribers could be relied on and that these might pay about $750 above commissions to the agents. Some $700 of this would be eaten up by the cost of publishing.

Emerson was already ominously admitting "that I rely on one expedient to make it valuable namely a liberal selection of good matter from old or from foreign books when dull papers are offered & rejected"; but he also urged his friends to contribute. He persuaded Hedge to supply a translation of Schelling's introductory lecture at Berlin but got little else from him. He asked help of Parker, though he did not wish to see him in the editor's chair, and the result was some profound scholarly articles on current religious controversy. Margaret Fuller gave weight to both his volumes of *The Dial* with her essay on Romaic and Rhine ballads and her crusade for women's rights. Alcott collected manuscripts and news in England.

After a severe struggle with the oddities of Charles Newcomb's style, Emerson managed to get the first of "The Two Dolons" into print, undoubtedly to the discouragement of subscribers. Jones Very was allotted a few pages but was unhappy when he saw them. "I found my Poem the 'Evening Choir' altered considerably from what I had written," he complained, and he said firmly that he preferred his own lines. Emerson's poet Ellery Channing had his day in the sun. Thoreau, serving sometimes as an assistant to the editor, suddenly became a leading contributor. The youthful Charles Stearns Wheeler sent letters of literary gossip from Germany. A few articles about current social problems fortunately came in. Benjamin Peter Hunt's travel sketches also served to give an air of reality to the too spectral magazine. Young James Elliot Cabot tackled Kant boldly. Emerson himself supplied many notices of books. His poetry during his editorship fell below the level of what Margaret Fuller had got from him. For substantial filler for his two volumes he had to fall back on several of his lectures.

By March of 1843 *The Dial* no longer so much as paid expenses; but Emerson, hating on his own account to end it and remembering Margaret Fuller's sacrifice for it, made up his mind to prolong the agony another year. It now had only 220 subscribers and was nearly hopeless. In the following October, Emerson, though he was already running into debt because of it, considered the desperate expedient of turning the editorial responsibility over to his impecunious and unsteady townsman Ellery Channing. But the number for April, 1844, was the last. George Curtis did not exaggerate more than most writers of epitaphs when he described *The Dial* as going out like a star from its unique place in American literature and its contributors as clothed in white garments. And yet many of *The Dial's* contributors, changing their white robes for darker and more practical garb, continued to bear an important part in the country's intellectual life.

During the last years of *The Dial,* Emerson, as usual, found no escape from lecturing. Before the City Bank resumed payment of even meager dividends in October, 1842, it had been unfruitful for eighteen months, causing him a deficit of $900, an important sum in his tight economy. Thus he was persuaded "to go peddling again." Seeing that lyceum goers were now becoming conscious of the New England cultural revolution of which he was a part, he gathered his commentaries on the characteristics of his region into a series of lectures. With these lectures he set out for Baltimore, Philadelphia, New York, Brooklyn, and Newark early in the new year, 1843.

At Baltimore, the mother city of the church of Rome in English-speaking America, the cathedral's pictured walls and chanting priests reminded him of the Old World. At both Baltimore and Philadelphia he saw what he could of the fine arts, also reminiscent of the Old World. At Philadelphia he praised the Quakers, revealing his sympathy with some of their "spiritual views." He visited Lucretia Mott, the Quaker reformer just back from her antislavery address before a Washington audience whom no man would have dared to speak to as she did. She warned Emerson that he was living too much out of the world and may thus have helped to inspire his speech on West Indian emancipation a year later.

He visited Washington. He heard Calhoun and Benton speak in the Senate. One night, in the rotunda of the Capitol, he watched, with Calhoun and others, while Horatio Greenough unsuccessfully experimented with the lighting of his statue of George Washington. He found the room in the Capitol which contained the newly invented electric telegraph, and at the Patent Office he saw the treasures Wilkes's expedition had brought back after years of exploration that had carried the American fleet into strange seas and put its commander's name on the map of the Antarctic Continent. It was also at Washington that he made a new friend in Giles Waldo, a young man whose ardent discipleship and copious stream of letters soon grew to be somewhat overpowering. In New York, where Emerson made a false start with his lectures on New England under the management of a feeble committee and had to make a new beginning at the Society Library, he saw Henry James again and discovered the inevitable new friend and disciple in William Tappan, "a lonely beautiful brooding youth who sits at a desk six hours of the day in some brokerage or other." But after two months of travel Emerson wanted to be at home again with his children, "sprawling on the floor as victim & playmate of the noisy pair"; and he was back in Concord with Ellen and Edith on the ninth of March.

At home, some weeks later, he observed the beginnings of Fruitlands, another utopian community. Alcott, one of its founders, had for several years tenanted a cottage and an acre of ground in Concord. Though dis-trustful of his spade as a means of getting a living, he had settled down, well pleased with himself. His long-suffering wife had been pleased too and, for the first time in years, had gone singing about the house. Then, one day, he had felt an irresistible urge to go to England. Emerson, once more summoned to the aid of his perennially impecunious friend, had had to raise the necessary funds for the voyage. As Alcott would not willingly shake hands with a merchant, being above all trade and tradesmen, raising subscriptions had been difficult. But Emerson had succeeded in begging $50 for him and had supplied $325 more, it seems, from his own pocket. The thankful Alcott had wanted to include a miniature of Emerson in his bag-gage and had loyally read his copy of the *Essays,* conjuring up memories of home, while approaching the English shore in the last days of May, 1842. In July, after having charmed many hearers, though not Carlyle, he had presided triumphantly over a meeting of the friends of human progress at Alcott House School, Ham, Surrey.

When Emerson had learned that Alcott intended to bring back Charles Lane and Henry Wright, two of his English followers, he had sent him a letter to read to them, warning them that though their new American friend was trustworthy as to theory he was not so as to facts. But Lane and Wright had paid no heed to the warning, and the three enthusiasts had embarked themselves, with a remarkable library of mystical, occult, and miscellaneous books, and crossed the Atlantic to found Fruitlands. Emerson watched with some sympathy but no faith as the impractical men prepared to cultivate their scenic, unproductive acres on a hillside near the village of Harvard. It was in June of 1843, the year in which the Millerites were preparing for the end of the world, that the Alcotts and their reforming friends began their new world hopefully in spite of austere economies. Labor on their farm was almost entirely manual, for they respected the rights of their fellow animals. The table presented a barren aspect, as not even the hens or the bees could be robbed of the fruits of their toil. Emerson, visiting the farm in July, found all well but commented, "We will see them in December." The winter of 1843–1844 was unfortunately marked by terrible cold, and by the middle of January the Fruitlands community, perhaps never strong enough to have survived even a mild winter, was broken up. Alcott lost no money of his own, but the blow was nevertheless overwhelming to him and he wanted to die, though he did not. Emerson continued in later years to raise small funds for Alcott's support and even looked after Charles Lane's business affairs while Fruitlands was being slowly liquidated.

However cool and restrained his theory of friendship was, Emerson actually spent a good deal of time and money on his friends. He helped Margaret Fuller by negotiating on her behalf for the publication of her *Summer on the Lakes*. He still tried hard to establish closer relations with Hawthorne, though Hawthorne gave him little encouragement. Once they got off together for a two days' excursion on foot to the town of Harvard, where they visited the Shakers. Once at least, with Henry Thoreau dancing and leaping ahead of them, they skated on the Concord River. Sophia Hawthorne observed that while her husband glided over the ice as stately and grave as a Greek statue, Emerson pitched along, head foremost, half lying on the air. In financial matters it was another story. Emerson helped out the impecunious storyteller by buying barrels of his apples. Though he could hardly read most of Hawthorne's somber fiction, he was pleased with "The Celestial Railroad," a satirical parody of *The Pilgrim's Progress* in which the German-born Giant Transcendentalist was described as resembling "a heap of fog and duskiness."

He gave many hours to the poet Ellery Channing, now settled in a little red house as his nearest neighbor on the Cambridge Turnpike. He had long walks and conversations with him, found publishers for his poems, and reviewed his volume of 1843 in *The United States Magazine, and Democratic Review*. Somewhat blinded by his loyalty to the man, he greatly overestimated the value of Ellery's verses. He wrote to Sterling, in England, that Channing was, "though young, the best poet we have." He paid his poet for chopping wood and, against all precedent it seems, for papers contributed to *The Dial*. When, toward the end of 1844, Channing went to New York for an ill-fated experiment as a writer on Horace Greeley's *Tribune,* Emerson once more anxiously sponsored him.

For a time, it seems, Emerson was almost persuaded that he himself ought to quit Concord. Margaret Fuller once warned him that the town was too peaceful to be a fit home for a lyric poet or orator, and Caroline Sturgis thought it a great marsh where he ought not to spend all his life. The question of leaving its "tame landscape" and moving to "a more picturesque country, perhaps to Berkshire perhaps to the sea" was "often agitated," as Emerson afterwards recalled; but he concluded that changing his home would not change him enough to repay him for the trouble. Gradually he settled himself more comfortably where he was. He did what he could to make Concord winters more endurable. By about the middle 1840s, it seems, he had installed airtight stoves and given up the regular use of his drafty fireplaces. In summer Hugh Whelan, now his hired man, took responsibility for the garden. The birth of Emerson's second son, Edward Waldo, on July 10, 1844, was a new and persuasive reason for contentment. Life was expanding again and getting a firmer root.

Emerson did his part to increase the cultural facilities of his village and was hopeful about its future. He was one of the original directors of the Concord Atheneum, founded in 1842, and contributed to its slender collection. If the "city facility and polish" he wanted his children to have along with "rural strength and religion" were not easily procurable in a place so secluded as Concord, he saw that Concord would not always be so secluded. He had already paid the first of his many assessments on the local railroad stock. The trains began running between the village and the city in June, 1844. The locomotives dashed past Walden Pond, crying at the top of their iron lungs, "Ho for Boston!" In September of the same year Emerson bought a little more Concord land, the Wyman field, on the north shore of Walden Pond.

Though he still held fundamentally to his old philosophical ideas, he was gradually becoming somewhat less otherworldly. He speculated, when he read "The Borderers," whether Wordsworth had not some time seriously asked himself if a brave sin might not stimulate his intellect and pay its way. He could not have known that Wordsworth had had a French daughter, but he was probing realistically into psychology. He read in the pagan mystic Proclus, he said, "as I would take opium." He found much pleasure in Chinese lore, notoriously more realistic than Western philosophy. But his interests were wide. He had an opinion of Browning's *Paracelsus* and he watched sympathetically the rising star of Tennyson and was enough known as an admirer to be asked to furnish an introduction to an American edition of that poet. Months after he had written his poem

on Saadi in *The Dial,* it seems, he began his reading of *The Gulistan.*

Spurred on by Margaret Fuller's skepticism as to his knowledge of Dante's *Vita nuova,* he translated the whole of the little Bible of love and got Ellery Channing to try his hand at putting at least some of the metrical passages into verse. The thirty-six sheets of Emerson's holograph manuscript that have now come to light testify to the correctness, in general, of his description of his work as "the ruggedest grammar English that can be, keeping lock step with the original." Naturally in such a *tour de force* his lock steps were sometimes missteps, but he managed to keep much of the fragile beauty of the book. His success in this latter respect was perhaps greatest in his rendering of the final lines, where Dante, as if he had not already idealized Beatrice beyond credibility, promised that if God would give him some years of life he would attempt "to say of her that which was never said of any one." It may possibly have been another and an improved version of this translation that Emerson suggested some four years later as printable "in two parts" in *The Massachusetts Quarterly Review,* or it may be that he had by that time forgotten the actual state of his manuscript. As late as a year after he had finished his first version he reprimanded Caroline Sturgis for copying out what he called his precious blot to send about for others to see. He asked her only to imagine herself turning Milton into French as a school exercise and then having this exercise printed as the new translation of that poet. If he was hardly just to *The Divine Comedy,* he knew the value of the lesser book in spite of its far remove from modernity.

In the winter of 1843–1844 he gave no lecture course but devoted himself to the preparation of a new volume of essays. On October 9 of the following year he signed his final agreement with James Munroe & Company. They were to sell the two thousand copies to the trade at a ten percent discount from the retail price of one dollar and were themselves allowed a commission of thirty percent, the author, as usual, keeping the control of his book in his own hands. Before the end of the month the second series of *Essays* was published. Emerson had already sent off sheets of the book to the English publisher Chapman, and by the end of the year he received a copy with London imprint and Carlyle's prefatory notice warning off prospective pirates.

In both form and ideas the book had strong Emersonian characteristics. The nine essays were arranged in hardly more than haphazard order. "Nature," chiefly notable, in comparison with the book of that name, for its plainer hints at the theory of evolution, was there because it had needed much altering and so had failed to get into the first series. "Gifts" was a revision of the essay of that title already printed in *The Dial.* "The Poet," destined to bring occasional sharp cries of dissent from Herman

Melville, along with approval for the nobility of certain passages, was a fresh proclamation of its author's old theory of the artist, master of liberating symbols, as spokesman for universal nature and universal mind. It was also an admirable example of the myth-making of which Emerson had become enamored in his reading from Plato. The passage on the winged soul of the poet with his immortal progeny was a charming prose poem. But the demand for a poet who "knew the value of our incomparable materials, and saw, in the barbarism and materialism of the times, another carnival of the same gods whose picture he so much admires in Homer" showed Emerson on the road to an untranscendental sort of realism.

These essays of 1844 were mostly less militantly Transcendental than the first series and leaned less on theory and more on experience. "Manners" showed more knowledge of the actual world and made more concessions to it than "Love" or "Friendship" had done. Its gentleman could not only outpray saints in chapel but give the law wherever he was and be good company for pirates as well as for academicians. Emerson was in this volume even more willing than ever before to see all sides. In "Nominalist and Realist" he spoke with a sincerity seldom surpassed by any author when he confessed, "I am always insincere, as always knowing there are other moods."

The frankest confessions might therefore be expected in the essay which afforded the severest test of his willingness to confront theory with fact, the essay "Experience," first tentatively called "Lords of Life." He was in the same predicament with most philosophers and religionists and theorists of various stripes—he had tried out his theories long enough to know that they were far from matching experience at every point.

But, though he was much more honest than most, he was loath to make any fundamental concession. Even now when he came to grips with the problem of experience as never before, it was a foregone conclusion that no foundation stone of his Transcendental theories was going to be rejected. He had not given up his belief that in deep moments of faith the appeal to experience was really invalid and vain. He had long since had the conviction that experience, even of suffering, could be an inferior order of reality. When put to a cruel test by the death of his son, he had confessed, "I chiefly grieve that I cannot grieve; that this fact takes no more deep hold than other facts, is as dreamlike as they; a lambent flame that will not burn playing on the surface of my river." It was true that the tragic experience did not fade out so soon or so harmlessly as he then thought it would, but he had nevertheless only exaggerated a fact of his nature and of his philosophy which he stated again, with like exaggeration, in the essay "Experience." It looked, as he got into his essay, as if he would produce simply another poetic exaltation of the spiritual over the physical,

a sort of hymn to Maya, illusion. Experience hardly seemed to be a subject for one who had declared that his life was "optical, not practical."

Dream delivered us to dream, he complained. Change of moods and
objects was a necessity of our nature. Life itself was a bubble and a
skepticism, a sleep within a sleep. Though Emerson could not renounce his
belief that there was "that in us which changes not and which ranks all
sensations and states of mind," he was willing to admit that "the new
philosophy" must absorb skepticisms. Somehow all this unreality of experience must be made part of a triumphant experience of the self. Illusion,
temperament, succession, surface, surprise, reality, subjectiveness were all
lords of life, and none could be by-passed. Perhaps even this was not the
complete picture. Emerson admitted that he was still too young by some
ages to compile a universal code and that he was only gossiping about
the politics of eternity.

And yet if he could not know all, he knew how to accept good-
humoredly what he had got. Life had been a wonderful experience, though
nothing more than receiving, without having anything in the end. One
played, it seemed, an exciting game with experience, but not for keeps. All
the hankering after practical effect really seemed to Emerson to come from
a mistaken conception of life. Learning a little truth was enough reward.
In his ears he always seemed to hear the law of destiny "that every soul
which had acquired any truth, should be safe from harm until another
period."

In his essay "Politics," an excellent test of his ability to confront the
kind of reality so confidently expounded by the keeper of the village
grocery store, Emerson spoke partly from theory, partly from experience.
He knew something of ancient and modern works on politics and much
more of history and biography. He saw that his own favorite theory of self-
reliance was the taproot of democracy, but his sympathies were broad. He
had had some experience of the American political scene. As a Federalist
by inheritance, he had naturally become a National Republican, or at
least he had been more than once a National Republican candidate for an
unwanted office. Later he had presumably voted with the Whigs, but only
because he had thought their candidates the best, and with increasing dis-
satisfaction.

He undoubtedly had the feeling that property was safer with the Whigs
than with the Democrats, yet his own modest possessions did not blind him
to the rights of the unpropertied. Sometimes, at least, he keenly felt the
evils of industrialism. His sharpest arrow aimed at the camp of the indus-
trialists may have been one that he left unshot, a set of verses, not earlier
than the 1840s, which he called "New England Capitalist." The capital-

ist's machines, he said, were only manikins modeled on the capitalist himself and served as weapons for his conquering will. The squirming victim
of Emerson's wrath behaved shamefully enough:

> He built his mills, &, by his politics, made
> The arms of millions turn them.
>   Stalwart New Hampshire, mother of men,
>   Sea-dented Maine, reluctant Carolina,
>   Must drag his coach, & by arts of peace
>   He, in the plenitude of love & honor,
>   Eats up the poor,—poor citizen poor state.

Emerson, as he said, understood poverty much better than riches. Coming
to know more well-to-do merchants, he found virtues in them; but he could
think of a rich friend as only accidentally so and suited by character for
poverty.

As for slavery, his sudden leap into the political arena in aid of the
abolitionists had occurred only a few weeks before the publication of the
second *Essays*. Then, in his address on emancipation in the West Indies
he had seemed to at least one observer to be a new man—not cold, clear,
and intellectual but genial and benevolent, smiling as if to defy world,
flesh, and devil. What his essay "Politics" might have been had it come
late enough to reflect this outburst of assured enthusiasm for reform can
only be guessed at, but it could easily have been less philosophical and
academic than it was. Almost at the moment the second *Essays* came from
the press, it seems, he was visiting the extremist William Lloyd Garrison in
his dingy office and, at last, respecting him without reservation. But if his
surprising fraternization with the radical abolitionists came too late to
affect "Politics," the earlier history of his political theory and practice was
the significant background of that essay.

"Politics" was inevitably a delicately balanced essay. To a partisan
filled with a sense of the necessity of immediate decision it could only be a
disappointment. Emerson took the detached view that the form of government, rapidly changing, was only a memorandum of national standards
of culture, also rapidly changing. Property would always have its share of
power, legally or illegally; but there was an instinctive feeling, still inarticulate, that the whole constitution of property at present was injurious
and degrading to persons and that truly the only interest for the consideration of the state was persons and their culture. As for basic political patterns, democracy was best for Americans because the religious sentiment
of the present time accorded best with it. There was no decisive superiority
in either of the great political parties of the hour. "The philosopher, the

poet, or the religious man," Emerson said, "will of course wish to cast his vote with the democrat, for free-trade, for wide suffrage, for the abolition of legal cruelties in the penal code, and for facilitating in every manner the access of the young and the poor to the sources of wealth and power. But he can rarely accept the persons whom the so-called popular party propose to him as representatives of these liberalities. . . . On the other side, the conservative party, composed of the most moderate, able and cultivated part of the population, is timid, and merely defensive of property." The basic trouble was that all public ends looked vague and quixotic beside private ones; and, accordingly, the antidote to the abuse of power by the government was the influence of private character, the growth of the individual. The state existed to educate the wise man, and once he appeared the state would expire. No perfection of organized authority, it was clear, but the perfection of individuals was the supreme end in view. Government, politics could at best be only incidental aids.

Essays, second series, aroused the usual dissonant voices of praise and blame. Lydia Maria Child, an ardent abolitionist who used both her hands to "row the boat of practical endeavor," complained that these essays took away her strength, as they harped too much on the unreal, elusive quality of things. Margaret Fuller found the new series far more adequate than the first, with more glow and more fusion. She promised to make it her companion through life. Frederic Hedge made amends for the earlier hostility of *The Christian Examiner* by printing there an admiring review which, however, betrayed his anxiety to reform Emerson and make at least half a Christian of him. In *The United States Magazine, and Democratic Review* an anonymous critic of both series of essays delighted in the bold reduction of the "apparent contradictions" of the universe to unity. The essays, he found, were the purest and most poetic expression of that philosophy of identity, Transcendentalism, from which the mind derived at the same time inspiration and repose. As for the historical background of Emerson, it looked German enough; but, said this by no means blind disciple, "Plotinus and Proclus, Plutarch and Marcus Antoninus are evidently greater favorites with him than Schelling and Hegel," and it was only by superficial observers that he was classed with Carlyle, a thinker manifestly lacking "this all harmonizing sense of the unity of being." Carlyle himself admired the "real *word*" the new *Essays* spoke and, as usual, hinted broadly at the too much theory and too little practicality. Instead of looking for the philosophy of unity, he studied the book's rhetoric with a practiced eye, looking for rhetorical unity. He found the new *Essays* genuine Saxon, strong and simple but somewhat incoherent, a bag of duckshot, he said.

18.

LEAPING AND PIERCING MELODIES

❀❀❀

The songs, thus flying immortal from their mortal parent,
are pursued by clamorous flights of censures, which swarm
in far greater numbers and threaten to devour them; but
these last are not winged. At the end of a very short leap
they fall plump down and rot, having received from the
souls out of which they came no beautiful wings. But the
melodies of the poet ascend and leap and pierce into the
deeps of infinite time.

—"The Poet"

SINCE boyhood Emerson had wanted to be a poet, but he had lived
more than half his life before he made up his mind to publish a
volume of his verses. Rufus Griswold had collected a few of them
in an anthology, but Griswold habitually welcomed the worst poets
as well as the best. Edgar Allan Poe, a highly gifted but erratic critic, had
once conceded that Emerson's "love of the obscure does not prevent him
. . . from the composition of occasional poems in which beauty is apparent *by flashes*." But after having bestowed that more restrained than
discriminating praise, Poe resumed, from time to time, his somewhat monotonous ridicule of *The Dial* and the Transcendentalists. Emerson was
still reluctant to make serious claims for his own poems because he saw
the discrepancy between them and his idea of poetry. He might not have
decided to publish them if his friends had not already put them into circulation. Even when he had come to a decision he moved slowly. For more
than two years after the appearance of his second series of essays his main
business was to prepare his poems for the press, yet he concerned himself
mostly with quite different things, thus living up to William James's much
later dictum that poetry "ought to be the overflowing of a life rich in other
ways."

For Emerson life was rich in variety but usually quiet. The numerous
works and days he found enumerated in the old copy of John Evelyn's
Kalendarium Hortense: or, the Gard'ner's Almanac given him by Alcott
suggested very inadequately the variety of events and responsibilities that
demanded his time. The garden was merely the most pleasant of his avoca-
tions, and his study, only his principal workshop.

While he continued to look after his friends who could not take care of themselves, he became more deeply involved in the struggle over slavery. Early in January of 1845 Samuel May, brother of Alcott's wife, and Samuel Sewall, her cousin, bought Hillside, on the Lexington Road, for the Alcott home, keeping the land in their own names for safety's sake. Emerson, presumably acting as agent for May and Sewall, paid the money to the grantor. But at the same time he himself took title to eight acres just across the road to the south, and these were also for Alcott's use. He paid $500 for these additional acres. Before January was over he had had some part in the Concord meeting to protest the expulsion of Elizabeth Hoar's father, an agent of Massachusetts, from South Carolina. The Hoar incident increased the growing tension over slavery. About the same time Emerson was urging the Concord Lyceum to admit Wendell Phillips, the antislavery agitator, to its forum. He went to Boston to hear the debates in the Texas Convention and was disappointed at the Whig speeches favoring moderation; but his philosophy calmed him within a few weeks and he concluded that the world spirit would not be defeated even by the annexation of Texas.

His curiosity about revolutionary social schemes still unjaded, he turned back to Fourier with a determination to read him. He would be willing, he said, to enlist under Fourier's banner for five years if experiments were permitted, but there was an immense presumption against every experiment in morals. He thought Fourier would not go far outside France. Soon he was attacking Fourier as a charter to libertines; and, perhaps about the same time, he was listening to his friend Sam Ward's conservative talk and becoming, as he said, "much warped from my own perpendicular & grown avaricious overnight of money & lands & buildings." He let each mood have its way momentarily for the sake of the experience and to avoid getting into a mental rut.

Diving into a very different world of ideas he found new reason to admire Proclus. He read with eagerness of "arrested development" in that nine-days wonder, *Vestiges of the Natural History of Creation,* a book he liked except for its timid theological ideas, though many thought it dangerous. He took a new interest in the *Bhagavadgita,* a charming confusion of Hindu speculations in which an indescribable blend of pantheism and mysticism with practical teachings regarding acceptance of commonplace duties principally impressed the reader. Emerson had hitherto known only fragments of this song, itself merely a small fragment of a massive poem. Now, with a copy of the English version, presumably placed in his hands by his new friend James Elliot Cabot, he became an enthusiastic reader of the book and took pains to find more readers for it.

Ellery Channing, shy but quick-witted and full of the same tang of New England soil that one found in people around Concord, was back from his New York misadventure and was looking for a farm. Henry Thoreau was building his hut on Emerson's land at Walden Pond, where he began to live on July 4, 1845. Sam Ward finally published his edition of Goethe's essays on art. Caroline Sturgis talked frankly about the poems Emerson was accumulating. They pleased her better the more she read them. Sometimes she saw that the words full of meaning but not images made a melody. Now and then, she found, a line darted forth like a tongue of flame and others moved harmoniously about it; but sometimes these little flames seemed to hiss and sputter as if cold water had been thrown upon the coals. She wanted the poems put into a book, but she warned the poet against abstractions. She advised him to make saw-dust pies with his little daughter Edith rather than continue to question the invisible; and she offered to take him into the mountains to hunt rattlesnakes, an occupation likely to school him in concrete realities. Hawthorne, Caroline Sturgis's host during at least part of her visit in Concord, was having trouble in keeping up his rent, not having paid a cent to Samuel Ripley for the use of the Old Manse through more than half of the year 1845. Emerson, as well as Ellery Channing, was anxious to keep this rarity in Concord, and he urged Caroline Sturgis to come back to the manse as a boarder and so help clear up the financial tangle there. In October of that year Hawthorne gave up the Old Manse and left Concord for some years.

Having already poured a good deal of money into Alcott, the bottomless pail, Emerson remembered him in a will he made out in September. One section of the will directed that Emerson's eight acres of the Hillside land should be administered by Lidian for the benefit of Alcott during the latter's lifetime and should thereafter become the property of Alcott's heirs. The property was thus to benefit Alcott and his family but "be free from all claims of his creditors." The same will also named Henry Thoreau as heir to the Walden Pond land on which he had built his hut, a provision naturally canceled after Thoreau had finally left Walden.

Away from home, Emerson the radical and friend of radicals had minor adventures among the conservative-minded and saw the country. At Middlebury College, in Vermont, the "prejudices entertained . . . with regard to the peculiar views of the Transcendentalists" were at the time impressive enough to be noticed in the public prints; and it was probably the address he made there this summer of 1845 that brought down on him the prompt rebuke of a ministerial prayer asking one special favor: "We beseech Thee, O Lord, to deliver us from ever hearing any more such transcendental nonsense as we have just listened to from this sacred desk." Yet he was "listened to with an intensity of interest and pleasure, rarely observed on such an occasion." At Wesleyan University, Middletown, Connecticut, some heresy was detected in him, and afterwards he was warned that unless some passages of his address were altered publication of it might give offense to the patrons of the college, mostly religious people unaccustomed to speculation. He did not publish it, probably because he had read much the same thing at Middlebury and it was already reported in the newspapers. Coming home by New York, he revisited William Tappan, for whose benefit he praised Caroline Sturgis; and he ended the southern part of his tour by voyaging up the Hudson in a rainstorm.

In Concord the new house he was building for Lucy Brown, Lidian's sister, on a lot he had recently purchased near his own home, was being completed. Thoreau, author of verses for Lucy, came in from his Walden hermitage to do some of the work. Emerson put over a thousand dollars into the house. It would help keep a good entertainer near Lidian. Meantime, when Emerson could shut himself up in his study, he went on with his reading under the guidance of Elliot Cabot, but he vainly tried to catch Cabot's enthusiasm for Schelling and Spinoza. He was naturally repelled by what seemed to him harsh mathematical logic. He was more interested in the success of his friend than in propagating the doctrines of Schelling when he later made an unsuccessful effort to find a publisher for Cabot's translation of the essay on freedom. Out of his study again, he directed some clear-eyed glances at the national political scene. He was growing disgusted with the "boyish" policy of the Whig Party, an opportunist party that was, he saw, trying to "disembarrass itself of the abolitionists" while he was beginning to respect them. Whiggism, he made up his mind, was "a feast of shells." Even the Whigs' admirable Daniel Webster, "the great cannon loaded to the lips," was now hardly audible to Emerson's ears. Emerson was present and possibly spoke at the September convention of anti-Texas agitators at Concord. He arrived belatedly in Cambridge to join some twenty persons at the adjourned meeting of a few weeks later. That autumn he hated the narrowness of the Native American Party, and further showed his liberality by paying for the use of the vestry when Robert Owen appeared in Concord. At the home of Alcott, a proper place of entertainment for the founder of the long since defunct community at New Harmony, Indiana, he seems to have heard the latest social theories of the old reformer. In the same month he refused to lecture at New Bedford because the lyceum there had excluded Negroes from regular membership.

While he emulated other villagers by adding to his few scattered plots of land, acquiring a little from the Town of Concord and putting over twelve hundred dollars into a new purchase of more than forty acres of woodland near Walden Pond, he became more and more a literary man. Urgent requests kept coming to him to help fill up projected or real literary journals, or to provide publishers with new books. In the spring of 1845 he had refused to make any serious promise of aid when the "transcendental bookseller" John Chapman, London publisher of his essays, wanted to found "a *new* Dial." But he had informed the Englishman that "I am really bent now on collecting a volume of poems from the pieces I have scattered in the Dial & elsewhere with some MSS of that kind which may seem fit to print, and of this book I mean to send you a timely transcript." When the New York literary adviser Evert Duyckinck made a vigorous attempt to get prose from him for Wiley and Putnam's Library of Choice Reading, Emerson once more turned the discussion to his poems. These, Duyckinck thought, would fit nicely into Wiley and Putnam's Library of American Books as a companion "volume" to "a small collection by Mr Poe including some remarkable juvenile poems." But, though Wiley & Putnam published *The Raven and Other Poems* before the end of the year, Emerson rejected their proposal to put his own pieces into such a flimsy pamphlet, priced at thirty-one cents and yielding a royalty of six cents a copy. He had to push his verses aside on account of lectures, and a misunderstanding with the same New York firm over their handling of one of Carlyle's books soon left his plans for publication in this country as vague as ever.

He returned to the lyceum platform unwillingly. It seemed too bad to grind down Transcendental ideas for popular consumption. His lectures, it occurred to him, were "a kind of Peter Parley's story of Uncle Plato" and "a puppet show of Eleusinian Mysteries." But by December, 1845, he was reading a course of seven for the Boston Lyceum. The subjects were reminiscent of his early lectures on biography but caused him much more labor in his own and other libraries. After his introductory lecture on the uses of great men, he got onto dangerous ground. In Plato, Swedenborg, Montaigne, Napoleon, Shakespeare, and Goethe he had formidable minds to cope with. He prepared for a serious study of Plato by buying Charles Lane's copy of Sydenham and Taylor's very imperfect translation. The poet Longfellow's fine library yielded some books on Shakespeare. Further help came from the Boston Athenæum. While Emerson worked hard to finish the manuscripts of the course, Caroline Sturgis, a guest at his house, found the days long and quiet but the evenings social. Caroline alternated between exaltation and a feeling of frustration in this thin intellectual atmosphere. The prospect of seeing some Transcendental guests eat plum pudding amused and relieved her. She wanted to dance the tarantella and dance herself to death. But the seven lectures, whatever Caroline may have thought of their lack of reality, brought Emerson $350 from the Boston Lyceum, and this meant only a few dollars less for each lecture than he had made above all expenses in his most successful privately managed course, eight years earlier. He got only half as much for repeating the course on representative men in neighboring Lowell, though Lowell paid better than other towns where he read some of the same lectures.

In the following February, after the Boston course was ended, he was raising funds for Ellery Channing, for Ellery was now obsessed with the notion that, being a poet, he must go to Europe, the homeland of poetry and art, and go quickly. Ellery had calculated that he could make his voyage and spend a year in Italy for not more than $300. Emerson agreed to pay $75 himself, and he probably got $50 more from Sam Ward. Caroline Sturgis was to give $75, and another well-wisher was to add $100. Early in March, Ellery sailed for Marseille. He went on as far as Rome but was back in New York Harbor almost exactly four months after he had left it. A few weeks after Ellery's return Emerson was writing a letter for Margaret Fuller to carry to Carlyle. Margaret, having broken away from New England, had already run through her New York period and was now hopeful of absorbing the essence of Europe.

During much of the spring and summer of 1846 Emerson worked at his book of poems. He was sensitive to literary patterns that he was discovering in an un-English and un-European past. For several years he had known something, perhaps not much, of the Persian poet Hafiz. By October of 1843 he had "had the Gulistan of Saadi," on whom he had earlier written verses in *The Dial*. Now, one fortunate April day, he bought at Elizabeth Peabody's bookstore the two volumes of Joseph von Hammer's German translation of the *Diwan* of Hafiz. He soon felt, it seems, the moral ambivalence of the poems in this collection. It was easy for him to see that they were not mere sensuality. Sooner or later he made numerous notations in the German volumes, and his many manuscript and printed translations testified to his delight. Even in 1846 the somewhat extravagant figures and not very coherent ideas of the brief, clever, exotic pieces were not too late to leave their mark on the verse he was still getting ready for the press. At the end of July he told Elizabeth Hoar that he had lately written "Mithridates," "Merlin," and "Alphonso of Castile."

While he wrote or collected poems he was not oblivious of political and military doings. Once he burst out with the angry declaration that democracy became "a government of bullies tempered by editors." As the Mexican War began he prophesied that the Americans would conquer but that Mexico would be the poison that would bring them down at last.

Both he and Thoreau found 1846 a bitter year. Henry Thoreau, the protester who did not want to be a partner in the business his government was carrying on, had long refused to pay his poll tax; and now, when he came into the village from his Walden hut to get a mended shoe, he was seized and spent a night in jail.

Emerson, used to doing his own protesting on the lecture platform or on the printed page, felt no enthusiasm over Thoreau's behavior. The prison was, he thought, one step to suicide and did not reach the evil so nearly as other possible methods would do. The scholar knew very well that no government would ever please him. "Why should he poorly pound on some one string of discord, when all is jangle?" Emerson told Alcott that Thoreau's conduct was mean and skulking. Almost at the same moment, however, he was full of admiration for the manuscript of *A Week on the Concord and Merrimack Rivers*. Under an oak tree on the bank of the Concord River he listened one afternoon as Thoreau read his "seven days' voyage in as many chapters." Emerson called it "pastoral as Isaak Walton, spicy as flagroot, broad & deep as Menu" and was ready to help find a publisher for it.

The domestic economy of the Emersons underwent a revolution during that summer, when they tried the novel experiment of living in their own house as the boarders of a Mrs. Marston Goodwin, who was allowed to bring in other boarders, as well as her four children. Lidian was in feeble health and had to be relieved of the care of housekeeping, but the sixteen months of Mrs. Goodwin's stay, when there were sixteen or eighteen persons in the house much of the time, could not have been easy for her or for Emerson. Yet the experiment, lasting apparently from May, 1846, to September, 1847, left Lidian with the conviction that Mrs. Goodwin was "born for the blessing of others" and was "thoroughly tender & self sacrificing."

About the same time, whether through Mrs. Goodwin's beneficent influence or not, the family seems to have got more into the spirit of play. Thereafter family picnics and other outings in the Concord woods were occasions memorable to the children. Blueberrying parties would start out immediately after dinner. Emerson, says family tradition, would drive the carryall with Grandmother Emerson and perhaps Aunt Lucy and others aboard, while Thoreau drove the hayrack loaded with the children and their mothers and the servants. Emerson himself seldom picked berries but strolled about or sat in the shade with his mother and with Aunt Lucy. Henry Thoreau explored the terrain, finding the best places for the pickers to work. At home, outdoor life received a new impetus early in 1847, when Emerson loosened the tight boundaries of his farm, hardly more than garden and orchard, by purchasing Warren's little field just to the east.

Meanwhile, never free from his literary occupation for long at a time, he had lectured as far away from home as Bangor, Maine, and, what was more important, had struck a bargain with his old publishers, James Munroe & Company of Boston, for the printing of his poems. Keeping control of the book in his own hands, he bore all the expense of manufacture and had the publishers account to him at thirty percent discount for the copies they sold. The first edition presumably consisted of fifteen hundred copies, stereotyped; and he was charged $373.37 for the printing. At the same time he got a similar agreement for publication of a smaller number of copies of the second series of Ellery Channing's poems. Aware of the danger of losing his foreign market to pirates, he had already sent the manuscript for the London edition of his own book to John Chapman. Publication in Boston occurred on Christmas Day, or, at latest, December 26, 1846, though the date of the imprint was 1847.

The little volume, called simply *Poems,* began defiantly with "The Sphinx." Many prospective purchasers at the bookstores must have been too dismayed to read farther. "Each and All," "The Problem," "To Rhea," "The Visit," and "Uriel," the poems immediately following "The Sphinx," did not suggest easy holiday reading. Simpler pieces, such as "The Rhodora," "The Humble-bee," and "The Snow-storm," were well concealed; and the "Concord Hymn" was held back to the end of the book. The common man, with his common emotions, so much celebrated in the popular poetry of the day, had given place in this volume to the introspective thinker whose idiom was highly intellectualized and sometimes marked by metaphors as violently wrenched out of nature as were those of Donne and Cowley in the seventeenth century. The lines were often firmly spun but were not apt to fall into broadly woven rhythmic patterns. Frequently the thought had to stand alone and make its way without much metrical aid. The lines were usually short and sharp, stinging the mind to action and not pleasing the senses. Perfection of rhyme was patently undervalued. The dome of many-colored glass was missing. The light that shone through the poems was generally the white light of intellect if not of eternity. The reader was like a traveler suddenly set down in an arctic landscape, immensely impressed if he could properly adjust his vision, but perhaps chilled. If the senses were chilled, the mind got vigorous exercise in interpreting the frequently cryptic style. But the by now rather familiar Transcendental ideas kept emerging as the meaning cleared up.

If "The Sphinx," reprinted from *The Dial,* was not already famous for its obscurity, it was soon to be so. Even Henry Thoreau, after filling thirteen pages in an attempt to explain it stanza by stanza, confessed that he now saw "the great advantage of verse over prose—and how all commentaries must be finite, but a text is infinite." He suspected that his commentary might prove "as enigmatical as the Sphinx's riddle. Indeed," he exonerated himself, "I doubt if she could solve it herself." So far as an extant rough draft shows, the struggle Emerson had with the poem before he printed it had nothing to do with clarification of its meaning. It was only artistically a gain to get rid of such lines as

> Bring Sphinx a pair of spectacles
> Her muddy eyes to clear

and to substitute

> She melted into purple cloud,
> She silvered in the moon;

for

> She hopped into the baby's eyes
> She hopped into the moon . . .

and it was not until many years later that he tried to put the meaning of the whole poem into two prose sentences: "The perception of identity," he summarized, "unites all things and explains one by another, and the most rare and strange is equally facile as the most common. But if the mind live only in particulars, and see only differences (wanting the power to see the whole—all in each), then the world addresses to this mind a question it cannot answer, and each new fact tears it in pieces, and it is vanquished by the distracting variety."

But this was oversimplified, and did not fully recognize the contradictory elements in the thought of the poem. These were left for the reader to put into proper logical relation. The diagnosis of man's ills which the Sphinx, or man's inquiring spirit, made in the first half of the poem was almost exactly balanced by the reply of "a poet" in which one might reasonably have expected to find a proposed cure. The inquiring spirit had a clear vision of the unity of nature but discovered man standing strangely aloof, the sole discord in the otherwise universal harmony. Even the child was bathed in the general joy of identity with the world soul. But man was not. Something had poisoned him, and he himself was poisoning the ground he walked on. What was the reason for man's evil fate? But instead of dealing with cause and cure, "a poet," as confident in his optimism as the Orphic poet of Emerson's first book, simply accused the Sphinx of blindness and denied the existence of any real disease.

It was one of Emerson's most Emersonian ideas that only the "perception of identity" was lacking. His poet, answering the dull Sphinx, supplied that perception. The answer she got in several charming stanzas was really a defense of man, and of the justice of his lot, on the ground that what troubled him was only his inquiring spirit and his insatiable thirst for perfection. However black his condition had looked when the Sphinx, with mother Nature chiming in, had ended the superficial diagnosis, it now took on a rosy hue. The bard, rejoicing in sharper vision than the philosopher could boast, easily discovered love, the unifying force, operating, plain enough to all good eyes, just below the surface. Fortunately there was no need of any drastic change, it seemed. The moral of the first part of the poem now appeared to be pointless, for the evil of the world had dissolved before the penetrating glance of the poet seer.

With her mission obviously at an end, the inquiring spirit, now reverting to genuine Sphinxhood, wrapped herself up in the altered garment of the ancient myth and faded away, becoming indistinguishable from the most pleasing aspects of nature:

> Uprose the merry Sphinx,
>   And crouched no more in stone;
> She melted into purple cloud,
>   She silvered in the moon;
> She spired into a yellow flame;
>   She flowered in blossoms red;
> She flowed into a foaming wave:
>   She stood Monadnoc's head.

Harmony not only continued to reign throughout the universe, but at last it was harmony visible and perceived, and man had sufficient reason to be happy, being freed by truth from the very real curse of illusion.

Probably few readers of the book saw that the next poem, "Each and All," was simply an earlier and less involved poetic experiment on the same theme. The third piece, "The Problem," was perhaps Emerson's most magnificent glorification of the religious spirit but was weakened by his too equivocal dislike, in the opening lines and at the end, of religious formalism. Yet the somewhat feeble beginning on church and churchman may have caught the attention of the reader taught to look for shocking unorthodoxy in the author, and there was little delay in getting at the surprisingly rich array of epigrammatic couplets. The epigrammatic couplets enumerated evidences of the genuineness and power of the religious impulse. This impulse, being the flow of the Over-soul through men's minds, was also equivalent to inspiration and genius, and might result in art:

> Not from a vain or shallow thought
> His awful Jove young Phidias brought;

Never from lips of cunning fell
The thrilling Delphic oracle;
Out from the heart of nature rolled
The burdens of the Bible old;
The litanies of nations came,
Like the volcano's tongue of flame,
Up from the burning core below,—
The canticles of love and woe:
The hand that rounded Peter's dome
And groined the aisles of Christian Rome
Wrought in a sad sincerity;
Himself from God he could not free;
He builded better than he knew;—
The conscious stone to beauty grew. . . .
Such and so grew these holy piles,
Whilst love and terror laid the tiles.
Earth proudly wears the Parthenon,
As the best gem upon her zone,
And Morning opes with haste her lids
To gaze upon the Pyramids;
O'er England's abbeys bends the sky,
As on its friends, with kindred eye . . .
These temples grew as grows the grass;
Art might obey, but not surpass.
The passive Master lent his hand
To the vast soul that o'er him planned . . .

"To Rhea" and "The Visit," other reprints from *The Dial,* were poetic companion pieces to the essays on love and friendship. In "Alphonso of Castile" Emerson succeeded in dramatic monologue with something of the same irony of tone and vigor of expression that Browning had frequently used. Emerson's Alphonso advised the "celestial fellows" mostly in language that even a peasant would have understood. The ruthless king, seeing all things on earth deteriorating, called upon the gods for drastic reforms, including the doing away with nine-tenths of the miserable inhabitants:

Earth, crowded, cries, 'Too many men!'
My counsel is, kill nine in ten,
And bestow the shares of all
On the remnant decimal.
Add their nine lives to this cat;
Stuff their nine brains in one hat . .

> So shall ye have a man of the sphere
> Fit to grace the solar year.

"Mithridates" had the same assertive, masculine, untranscendental tone. The vigorous hater of the Romans, somewhat transformed from his historical character, might have been an American Transcendentalist, weary of his restraints and off for a vacation in the unspiritual world of money-getters, eaters, drinkers, sinners:

> Too long shut in strait and few,
> Thinly dieted on dew,
> I will use the world, and sift it,
> To a thousand humors shift it,
> As you spin a cherry.

With a Faustian zest for the long-delayed feast of life he cried,

> Hither! take me, use me, fill me,
> Vein and artery, though ye kill me!

Perhaps Emerson wished only to honor the daring intellect curious to know and experience the world. If so, he succeeded in making the mental drama concrete.

If he seldom got any poetic inspiration from the potent wine of sexual love, he now and then struck off passages that betrayed acquaintance with passion, as in "Fate," or "Destiny" as it was later called:

> Thy beauty, if it lack the fire
> Which drives me mad with sweet desire,
> What boots it?

There was no lack of dramatic quality in "Hamatreya," an adaptation of a passage in *The Vishnu Purana*. Though the Concord names and the simple vernacular speech must have disappointed a reader expecting the traditional poetic manner, there were not only passages of simple farmer's talk about clay, lime, gravel, a granite-ledge, and a misty lowland to go to for peat, but also the consciously rhetorical

> Earth laughs in flowers, to see her boastful boys
> Earth-proud, proud of the earth which is not theirs;

and the stark, cool comments of the poet before the beginning and after the close of the Earth-song:

> Ah, the hot owner sees not Death, who adds
> Him to his land, a lump of mould the more.
> Hear what the Earth says . . .
>> When I heard the Earth-song
>> I was no longer brave;
>> My avarice cooled
>> Like lust in the chill of the grave.

"The Rhodora" was pure simplicity and charm. In it and in "The Humble-bee" Emerson, rejecting the economist's philosophy, surrendered himself as fully as he could to a childlike enjoyment of nature. "Woodnotes" was a more elaborate hymn to nature. Much of it was slightly Wordsworthian but was also from as close observation as Wordsworth himself used; and the forest seer, perhaps mainly created in the image of Thoreau, was at least as real as the boy of Winander.

> And such I knew, a forest seer,
> A minstrel of the natural year . . .
> He saw the partridge drum in the woods;
> He heard the woodcock's evening hymn;
> He found the tawny thrushes' broods;
> And the shy hawk did wait for him;
> What others did at distance hear,
> And guessed within the thicket's gloom,
> Was shown to this philosopher,
> And at his bidding seemed to come.

In the second part of "Woodnotes" the pine tree diagnosed man's ills much as the Sphinx had done:

> The wood and wave each other know
> Not unrelated, unaffied,
> But to each thought and thing allied,
> Is perfect Nature's every part,
> Rooted in the mighty Heart.
> But thou, poor child! unbound, unrhymed,
> Whence camest thou, misplaced, mistimed,
> Whence, O thou orphan and defrauded?

And before it finished it was murmuring pantheistic praise of "the eternal Pan" and the unity of all things with an accent reminiscent of India:

> Thou seek'st in globe and galaxy,
> He hides in pure transparency;

> Thou askest in fountains and in fires,
> He is the essence that inquires.
> He is the axis of the star;
> He is the sparkle of the spar;
> He is the heart of every creature;
> He is the meaning of each feature;
> And his mind is the sky.
> Than all it holds more deep, more high.

"Monadnoc" showed Emerson faltering in his faith that nature really had the transforming power which had made the forest seer admirable. He was momentarily as much disillusioned with the dwellers about Monadnock as Coleridge had been skeptical of Wordsworth's noble hill people with diction peculiarly fit for poetry. But, loath to believe that "the brave old mould" was broken, he did what he could to discover minor virtues in his mountaineers. With their ploughs and carts and household arts they were praiseworthy or even heroic. They were admirable masters of language for their own purposes. They wielded masterfully their fourscore or a hundred words, displaying power that a cultured man like the poet might envy in them as much as in Montaigne.

> Rude poets of the tavern hearth,
> Squandering your unquoted mirth,
> Which keeps the ground and never soars,
> While Jake retorts and Reuben roars;
> Scoff of yeoman strong and stark,
> Goes like bullet to its mark;
> While the solid curse and jeer
> Never balk the waiting ear.

It was one of Emerson's triumphs to escape the ignorance of the educated, or at least their biased judgment, and revel in the display of vigor on no matter what intellectual plane. But a moment later he would be worlds away from his rude mountain dwellers, singing the superior reality of mind and spirit.

As if to prove his versatility beyond any doubt, Emerson wrote, in his "Ode Inscribed to W. H. Channing," a stinging rebuke to the sordid politics of the era when "the famous States" were "Harrying Mexico" but at the same time attached an apology for his own isolation from political squabbles. Things were in the saddle and rode mankind, and something would have to be done; but for himself he fell back on his own doctrine of individualism. Let one live one's own life. The state would follow the best it could. "Astræa," in spite of its title, was another of Emerson's many tributes to Emersonian self-reliance; "Étienne de la Boéce" honored self-reliance in friendship.

The "Ode to Beauty," the first of a group of love poems or poems about love, was justly excepted by Thoreau from his general admiration of Emerson's verse because, among other reasons, its lines sloped too quickly to the rhyme and because it sounded like parody. It was, said Thoreau, as if the poet had used a hatchet on his verses as they came out, chopping some short and some long. But the same criticism might have been made of many other poems of Emerson's. "Give all to Love" had somewhat the same faults but more vigor. It opened with one of Emerson's most uninhibited recommendations of love but ended with the cool advice that stoical self-reliance be kept alive underneath the passion, ready to play its part in case of need, and with the equally assured declaration of faith in compensation should the beloved be lost:

> Leave all for love;
> Yet, hear me, yet . .
> Keep thee to-day,
> To-morrow, forever,
> Free as an Arab
> Of thy beloved.
>
> Cling with life to the maid;
> But when the surprise,
> First vague shadow of surmise
> Flits across her bosom young,
> Of a joy apart from thee,
> Free be she, fancy-free . . .
> Heartily know,
> When half-gods go,
> The gods arrive.

The volume also contained a few of the poems that had been written for Ellen Tucker and the not very graceful "Initial, Dæmonic and Celestial Love." The latter recalled the essay "Love" with its modern Platonism. Its three parts were no more satisfying than Spenser's four hymns on love and beauty and heavenly love and heavenly beauty, but the last of the three struck fire more than once in the course of its long, irregular progress. Emerson was at home in his mystical vision

> where all form
> In one only form dissolves;
> In a region where the wheel
> On which all beings ride
> Visibly revolves;

and for short periods he was as capable as Dante of religious exaltation. He knew what the Italian poet meant by an "increate perpetual thirst" that could draw one toward "the realm of God's own form." But the concreteness and the intensely personal quality of Dante's visions were impossible to him, and his emotion quickly took on an intellectual paleness.

This intellectual pallor and the brevity and irregularity of lines and meter were the faults that impressed one most in this book. Yet there was hardly a poem that did not have some rare excellence. The poems on love were followed by poems on the art of poetry. In "Merlin" Emerson was really defending his own irregular meter. "The kingly bard," according to the poetic of "Merlin,"

> Must smite the chords rudely and hard,
> As with hammer or with mace;

Emerson boldly asserted that it was not the bard's business to encumber his brain with the coil of rhythm and number but to climb for his rhyme, passing into the upper chamber without taking the trouble to count the "compartments of the floors,"—mounting to paradise by the stairway of surprise, he called it. "Bacchus," praising the wine of poetic inspiration,

> wine which never grew
> In the belly of the grape,

was not wanting in what it extolled and had many vigorous lines. "The House," with its more coherent imagery and simpler structure, was a satisfying poem in spite of the excessive substitution of irregular feet that turned the virtue of variety into a minor vice. For once the muse showed herself an architect with a plan, and the result was a house built to music and yet firm on its foundation.

> She lays her beams in music,
> In music every one,
> To the cadence of the whirling world
> Which dances round the sun—

"Musketaquid," fortunately moving in an almost sluggish blank verse, keeping pace with the river's current and suiting the contentment and restfulness of the Concord landscape, was followed by three elegies at the end of the book. The Concord landscape appeared again in the "Dirge" Emerson had written chiefly to commemorate his brothers Edward and Charles. Another Concord poem was the long but charming "Threnody," inspired by the death of his son Waldo,

> The hyacinthine boy, for whom
> Morn well might break and April bloom,
> The gracious boy, who did adorn
> The world whereinto he was born,
> And by his countenance repay
> The favor of the loving Day . . .

Emerson, too firmly and contentedly fixed in the universal laws, and so grieving that he could not grieve, collected rich epithets and scattered them through a poem which, if it was not grief, was a nearly perfect philosopher's substitute. A book which owed so much to Concord woods, fields, and river ended, naturally enough, with what later came to be known as the "Concord Hymn," turning back in memory to the town's embattled farmers of 1775.

With all the virtues and faults that helped to unfit it for popularity among the general reading public, the volume seemed to some of its author's friends to be his passport to the poetic hall of fame. To others it was hardly poetry at all but philosophy. Longfellow had it read to him all evening and late into the night of December 26. To him many of the pieces were Sphinx-like, many exquisite. He saw that the poems were more intellectual than emotional; and, not without insight into the art of a poet so extremely different from himself, he called Emerson a singer of ideas. Alcott, though he said "many fine things" about the volume, repaid Emerson for some of his own criticism by asserting that "the sentiment was moral and the expression seemed the reverse." Oliver Wendell Holmes, confessing that he had read Emerson's poems in *The Dial* more for their faults than for their virtues, was now willing to look for virtues. He still complained of unreasonable obscurity, a tendency to old-fashioned conceits, and disdain of old-fashioned artistic proprieties. He frankly disliked the vague and mystical things even though they might be the most excellent in the volume. But in the poems he liked best he found more of the wild strawberry flavor than in anything else that American soil had produced. Horace Greeley, no qualified judge of such matters himself but well informed, asserted that the poems had pleased everybody but the most stubbornly bull-headed.

Aunt Mary, at last in a relenting mood, tardily announced that if only

Waldo were fixed in the Christian faith he would be capable of writing a *Paradise Lost* without the tiresome parts. Caroline Sturgis, an unconventional young woman who was weary of statuesque human beings and wished she had red hair and eyes like a comet, told him, much as she had done long before, what she believed was the simple truth about his poems. Their thoughts pleased her, but she expected more emotion in poetry. Philosophy was philosophy still, though delivered in rhymes by Alphonso the Wise. Carlyle, with his habitual dislike of poetry, wished, when he read *Poems,* that Emerson would be concrete and would stick to prose. In spite of difficulties, he imagined he gained a real satisfaction from the book; but he preferred floods of sunlight to what he described as these thin, piercing radiances, like starlight.

Probably Margaret Fuller's criticism, based on a fairly up-to-date knowledge of the poems but published a little before they were put into book form, expressed nearly the average opinion of Emerson's friends who were qualified to judge. Some would not have agreed with her in admiring the melody of the poems, but most must have approved her praise of "subtle beauty of thought and expression" as well as her chief strictures. "But his poems," she had said, "are mostly philosophical, which is not the truest kind of poetry. They want the simple force of nature and passion, and . . . fail to wake far-off echoes in the heart. The imagery wears a symbolical air, and serves rather as illustration, than to delight us by fresh and glowing forms of life." What her critical comments on Emerson the poet amounted to but did not say was that while he harked back to Johnson's "metaphysical poets" of the seventeenth century, he was moving, as was Edgar Allan Poe, in the direction of what later came to be called the symbolists. And this was true.

Before *Poems* had been out of the press long enough to justify the date on the title page, the reviewers were at work. On December 29 the *Boston Courier* justly called it "one of the most peculiar and original volumes of poetry ever published in the United States," and discovered in it not only harshness of diction and obscurity of thought but "exceeding refinement" of sentiment and "piercing subtlety" of imagination. Cyrus Bartol, in *The Christian Examiner* of some weeks later, conceded that no modern writings were superior to those of Emerson in original merit, and that no one had a finer eye than he for detecting the lines of correspondence that united all things. But Emerson, if Bartol was to be judge, had more height than breadth, was the poet of a class rather than the poet of a race. And then Bartol ventured to stir up the old ashes of religious controversy, blaming Emerson for recognizing nowhere the Christian faith and for appearing to acknowledge no distinction between man and the deity. The Protestant critic, though gentler, was, on that point, not far from agreement with Orestes Brownson, now a Catholic. Brownson, in his quarterly, declared that Emerson's poems were "not sacred chants" but "hymns to the devil" and could be relished "only by devil-worshipers."

Cornelius Mathews, reviewer for *The Literary World* of New York, agreed with the *Examiner* at many points and seemed to echo several of Bartol's judgments. But he was unworried by the religious issue, reported that he had observed what looked like an increasing friendliness toward Emerson, and pointed a finger of scorn at the die-hard critics. Mathews had some sharp comments for Emerson too. He was wide awake, even if too unsympathetic with the seventeenth-century men, when he quoted Johnson's reproof for their violent yoking of heterogeneous ideas. But the upshot of his whole commentary was that Americans had in Emerson "one of the finest, as he is certainly one of the most singular, poetical spirits of the time." In "the torpid and respectable North American Review," recognized by Mathews as one of Emerson's implacable foes, Francis Bowen, still contemptuous, condemned Emerson along with eight other poets, including Ellery Channing. He remembered Emerson's earlier "offensive opinions" but asserted that this volume of poems contained "the most prosaic and unintelligible stuff that it has ever been our fortune to encounter." "Is the man sane," he asked, "who can deliberately commit to print this fantastic nonsense?" James Russell Lowell's censures, published more than a year later in *A Fable for Critics,* had wings, as Bowen's did not, though they were the fledgling witticisms of a youthful critic. And if Lowell looked only in Emerson's prose for the "grand verse," he found something deep in the poems; if he was struck by their incoherence, he nevertheless judged that the worst of them were "mines of rich matter."

Meantime the poet's life continued to be full of other things. On Christmas Eve, 1846, as *Poems* was about to issue from the press, the Emersons sleighed to the Alcotts' and saw presents distributed. At home they had an extraordinary Christmas dinner. Pies were a staple diet there throughout the year, but on this occasion each piece inclosed a note addressed to a member of the family. Gifts were reserved for New Year's Day, still regarded by the Emersons as a more proper time for festivities than Christmas. Ellen, then not quite eight years old, recorded in her journal that on the first of January, 1847, her father gave her *The Diadem,* a parlor annual, for 1846 and for 1847. Both volumes contained poems of his. Next day he entered in his account book an item of $3 paid for music at the children's party. A few days later he entered a one-dollar subscription for a runaway slave. Within a couple of months he was busily carrying on correspondence in an attempt to help the poor Danish, or Prussian, novelist Harro Harring, for Harring thought himself abused by his publishers.

About the time his poems came from the press Emerson had received word that he was wanted in England to read lectures. Lyceums flourished there and in Scotland as in America. The English edition of *Poems,* though the difficulties of its style were not helped by the numerous printer's errors, doubtless strengthened the demand for Emerson; but the essays and addresses had been enough. For several years he had received invitations to cross the Atlantic. Now a concrete and persuasive one came from his friend Alexander Ireland, his Edinburgh guide of 1833 but by this time manager and editor of two Manchester newspapers. On December 28 Emerson wrote him a favorable, though not decisive, reply. Ireland sent more detailed information on the prospects. Confident that he could successfully publicize a lengthy British lecture tour, he offered to attend to all necessary business arrangements. Liverpool, Manchester, London would certainly listen; a circle of "Literary Institutions" in Yorkshire and Lancashire needed quantities of lectures. Lectures sometimes commanded fees of from £5 to £10, and summer was the only off season.

Emerson, still dubious whether he could collect an audience in any British city but London, listened next to Carlyle's profession of confidence in the success of the proposed tour. Carlyle praised the solidity, practicality, and sagacity of the dark, energetic Alexander Ireland, and he held out the unique bait of a London audience of British aristocrats. According to Carlyle, Emerson was an aristocrat himself and would like to speak to Britishers of his own class.

Before any decision could be made about British offers a new and very different proposition needed an answer. The Englishman Heraud had now decided to postpone his projected magazine, but a somewhat similar American scheme was making progress. A meeting at Emerson's home one day in April decided to publish "a successor of the Dial"; and Emerson, Theodore Parker, and Charles Sumner were instructed to choose an editor and a publisher. Emerson, experienced in Transcendental journalism and bent on his British tour, flatly refused to be a principal this time. When, in spite of his protests, he was announced as "in the Direction" of *The Massachusetts Quarterly Review,* he was provoked. But he could not escape entirely. With good grace he supplied an address to the public for the initial number.

Neither the prospect of transatlantic lectures nor the business of founding a new magazine seriously interfered with the calendar of his fields and orchards. Fruit trees were purchased in quantity at Plymouth. The varieties of pears that were to grow to formidable numbers began arriving. Napoleon, Beurre Diel, and Urbaniste were only a few of those to be set out at once along with young apple trees. Henry Thoreau surveyed the two acres and sixty-six rods of the newly acquired Warren lot. John Hosmer, John Garrison, and Anthony Colombe put out seventy trees there and in the heater piece. On the first of June, Emerson made an inventory of his trees, naming nearly all of the 128, tree by tree. The distinct sections of his orchard now made an impressive showing—west of the arbor and south of the path, west of the arbor and north of the path, old orchard strip in the east garden, west garden, heater piece east fence.

Soon after the great tree planting, Thoreau relocated two firs, perhaps ten years old, to make them fit better into the new scheme; and next day, with the help of Anthony Colombe, he laid tribute on the Wyman lot and Walden Woods, bringing back forty-two white pines from one to five feet high, one pitch pine, and eleven hemlocks for the adornment of the arbor. On the following day he brought seventeen savins from Flint's Pond and set them out by the arbor. Some five weeks later Emerson, Alcott, and Thoreau took the road to Walden to cut hemlocks for columns to the curious summer house now planned for the further ornament of Emerson's grounds. Alcott, sometimes with Thoreau's help, kept at his pleasing labors as architect and builder by day, while at night he had happy dreams in which he continued his day-time occupation. As for the gibes of the townspeople at what he described as the sylvan and serpentine style, he considered that Michelangelo's finest work might well have provoked similar remarks. At the end of August, Emerson was surprised that the little house he expected to call Tumbledown Hall had not yet fallen.

By late July the English visit had been decided upon, with the first of October set as the approximate date of sailing. Alexander Ireland had stirred up enthusiasm in the proper quarters. James Hudson of the Central Committee of the Yorkshire Union of Mechanics' Institutes had put in his oar, "I can engage for the north and south of England that we should hail with delight the great transatlantic Essayist and our Lecture Halls would be crowded with men who have already learned to love and now only wait to *see* the American poet." He offered seventy-five guineas for fifteen nights at institutes in his neighborhood and thought he could promise other engagements once he was sure Emerson would come. Ireland and Hudson together seemed to make the scheme foolproof. Before time to sail Emerson got word from Mary Howitt. She wanted to advertise him by publishing a memoir of him about the time he arrived in England. But he begged off. With a view to revisiting France, he hired a Doctor Arnoult to give him twenty-four lessons in French conversation, and went to Boston for them every Tuesday and Friday. He discovered another French instructor in the *Courrier des Etats-Unis* and subscribed for it.

Emerson, now about to face the Old World as the representative of American culture, was in his forty-fifth year and had conquered the serious physical ills that had beset him in early life. The thinness of his body, accentuated by his nearly six feet of height, would make him look fragile in comparison with the solidly built Britons, and their vitality would awaken his envy. But in spite of the narrow and sharply sloping shoulders on which it was set, his head gave the impression of firmness. His shock of brown hair, now darker than in his youth, and his short, unobtrusive side whiskers partly framed a face with rugged features and penetrating blue eyes. Sometimes, perhaps commonly, his face had a luminous, friendly expression revealing an unusual combination of sensitiveness and self-control.

Probably his expression never approximated that of the obviously idealized crayon portrait of *"about* 1846." His more serious mood may have been caught with some fidelity by the 1846 daguerreotype made for Carlyle's benefit, and by David Scott's somber painting of 1848, liked by both Alcott and Sanborn. The Scott portrait showed Emerson the lecturer, mildly stern, watching his audience intently. The worried, tense face of the Pirsson daguerreotype of 1848 was not convincing. Though the English artists were doubtless prejudiced by their notions of what a native American should look like, they were right in discovering the Indian type in Emerson's features. If Alcott was in an attitude of worship not conducive to the clearest vision when he saw ideal and classic beauty and Olympian contour of figure in Emerson, he was not deceived as to the dignity and force with which the lecturer could impress his audiences.

Through his books and through a few friends and acquaintances Emerson was already known to a number of Europeans. Carlyle was the most powerful of his British friends. But there were lesser ones. The perhaps two thousand or more copies of an English reprint of his lecture "Man the Reformer" had helped make him attractive to readers who cared more for the problems of their own day than for the timeless ideas of his essays and poems. His religious liberalism frightened many readers. A brilliant woman, a friend of Carlyle's, dared to confess only in a whisper that she had spent a day on the essays and found them full of truth. She did not dare to recommend them to anybody else. Yet a few of the religious but unorthodox might even have endorsed Elizabeth Hoar's opinion that the teachers of the nations at this time were Jesus, Goethe, Carlyle, and Emerson. John Heraud believed that *The Monthly Magazine,* under his own brief term of editorship, had helped secure a wide acceptance of Transcendentalism, or an English version of it. In the English universities there were a few young men of great promise who were ready to receive the Emersonian doctrine. Such were the Oxonians Arthur Hugh Clough and his young friend Matthew Arnold, though it is hard to believe that there was not some cool skepticism mixed with their enthusiasm from the start. It was only a few years later that Arnold put his unsteady faith into his sonnet "Written in Emerson's Essays." As he challenged the dead, unprofitable world to listen to this new, oracular voice, he saw with sorrow that man after man, full of bitter knowledge, smiled incredulously and passed by unmoved. He himself repeated his mentor's golden text and waited for an answer:

> Yet the will is free:
> Strong is the Soul, and wise, and beautiful:
> The seeds of godlike power are in us still:
> Gods are we, Bards, Saints, Heroes, if we will.—
> Dumb judges, answer, truth or mockery?

Emerson was not unaware that he had enthusiastic readers in France, where he planned to visit before returning from his British tour. Margaret Fuller had written him soon after her visit in Paris that the Polish poet Adam Mickiewicz had first made the *Essays* known there. Margaret, baiting the elusive, mystical Pole with a copy of Emerson's poems, had "found in him," as she reported, "the man I had long wished to see, with the intellect and passions in due proportion for a full and healthy human being, with a soul constantly inspiring." This much of the story, at least, Emerson knew; but there was much more of it.

Is seems that Mickiewicz, discovering Emerson in 1838, had promptly communicated his enthusiasm to his friend Edgar Quinet. By 1842 the Collège de France was the center of the new excitement over the American Transcendentalist. During his last two years as professor of Slavonic languages and literature there, Mickiewicz managed to introduce Emerson to his students. By 1844, when Mickiewicz gave up his professorial chair, Quinet, a professor of Southern European literature, was parading Emerson before his students in company with Vico, Condorcet, Herder, and Hegel and was praising him without much restraint. In a lecture of 1845 he declared that in the same North America which was pictured as so materialistic he had found the most idealistic writer of the age. The historian Jules Michelet, a member, with Mickiewicz and Quinet, of a remarkable triumvirate at the *collège,* is reputed to have shared their admiration for

Emerson. Politics was playing no small part in the teaching of the trium-virate, and Emerson and America were expendable ammunition for the liberal movement soon to result in the Revolution of 1848.

It was Philarète Chasles, also of the Collège de France, who, in August of 1844, brought Emerson out into the full light of publicity. In the *Revue des deux mondes* his notable article on literary tendencies in England and America was sure of reaching the intellectuals of more countries than France. Chasles imagined, as any other specialist in Germanic languages and literatures would have been apt to do, that Carlyle was the master of Emerson. But he placed both high. In America, he discovered, Emerson was the one puissant original just as Carlyle was in England. He saw the fundamental democratic tendency of Emerson and the broad streak of conservatism in Carlyle. But the significant thing was that he had made Emerson a literary figure in French eyes. From the professors the Emer-sonian contagion spread to the Comtesse d'Agoult, another political radical, and to Émile Montégut, a youthful but scholarly writer not unlike Emerson in freedom of thought and mystical leanings. Meantime somebody had made French of the critical chapter on Emerson and other American writers in Margaret Fuller's recent *Papers on Literature and Art.*

Comtesse d'Agoult's article in *La Revue indépendante,* July 25, 1846, was presumably the first to be devoted to Emerson alone by any critical journal in France, and it was intelligent as well as weighty. The countess remembered hearing Mickiewicz mention Emerson in a lecture. "But," she said, "mentioned thus casually and without any precise significance attached to it, the name of Emerson did not awaken the curiosity of an audience with more pressing matters to worry about, and surely no one except me in that assembly tense with political passions dreamed of remembering it." At all events she remembered. Finding no copy of Emerson's writings in Paris, she sent to London for Carlyle's English edition of the first *Essays.* Reading that book, she made up her mind that its author was no literary man, no political theorist, no philosopher, hardly even a moralist, but some-thing better than all these—a wise man acting in conformity with his own nature. She quickly got a firm hold on his key ideas and cast his horoscope. She was persuaded that the union in his superior mind of the spirit of Protestant individualism with the spirit of pantheism provided a new medium out of which a native, original American art might grow. She looked upon him as the personification of the American genius, a genius impatient of all authority and disdainful of tradition.

In August of the following year, when Emerson was preparing to cross the Atlantic in person, he unwittingly received a second formal and im-pressive introduction to the French, this time through Émile Montégut, soon to be influential as Frenchmen's handy guide to American, English, and German literature. With the *Revue des deux mondes* for his platform, Montégut spoke with much assurance and no doubt made some converts. It was true, he found, that in Emerson the philosopher tended to become a moralist, and that was a bad augury, for the moralist flourished only in an age of doubt and indecision. And yet, at home in the company of Montaigne, Charron, and Shakespeare, Emerson was a sage, having originality, spontaneity, wisdom as an observer, a nice analytical sense, critical ability, and freedom from dogmatism. The self-reliance which, Montégut recognized, was the key to Emerson's thought made life no immolation, as Puritanism had done, but perpetual heroism. In the new American philosophy the individual attracted the universe to himself, as in other philosophies he was absorbed by it. Montégut, in common with other French admirers, saw in Emerson a thinker whose ideas could be used for bullets in the political war then raging in France; but he was looking for arguments against extreme leveling democracy. He saw how it could be argued that Emerson declared for the individual in order to protect character and genius against the intolerant mob. But he showed his sense of values when he abruptly turned his back on the political turmoil of the moment and ended with an eloquent plea for Emerson's thought as timeless truth.

On the whole, to a well-informed transatlantic observer, it might have seemed that Emerson could hardly have chosen a more appropriate time for his voyage to Europe. England was probably then in a more receptive mood for such doctrine as his than ever before. In France the growing political crisis seemed to offer the largest scope to the French democrats who had felt the inspiration of his writings. However vaguely conscious he himself was of the fitness of the time, he was going. On October 5, 1847, having paid up his debts and written Alexander Ireland the latest version of his plans, he boarded the packet ship *Washington Irving* in Boston Harbor.

19.

NOT A WORLD TO HIDE VIRTUES IN

※❀※

> But England is anchored at the side of Europe, and right in the heart of the modern world. ... .
>
> —*English Traits*

LIDIAN, Henry Thoreau, and the Alcotts saw Emerson off for England. Probably Ruth Emerson, though now in her seventy-ninth year, was also at the wharf to bid her son farewell. Mrs. Alcott wept. Thoreau, chosen to be the protector and man of all work for Lidian and her children, looked with a critical eye on the packet ship *Washington Irving,* a sailing vessel in an age when steamers were already the efficient passenger-carriers of the Atlantic, and discovered reasons why a voyage in her would not be desirable. The stateroom Emerson was assigned "was like a carpeted dark closet, about six feet square, with a large keyhole for a window." The skylight over his head was "the size of an oblong doughnut, and about as opaque." And instead of walking in Walden Woods he would have to promenade on deck, "where the few trees, you know, are stripped of their bark." The ship, already shorn of romance in Thoreau's eyes, was towed ingloriously out to sea by a steam tug "without a rag of sail being raised."

Three days later the little ship, weighing some 1500 tons freight and all, had made only 134 miles and was creeping through a forest of logs, boards, and chips spewed into the sea by the rivers of Maine and of New Brunswick. Seven men, three women, and ten children had the run of the quarter-deck and made, with the voluble Captain Caldwell, the society of the ship. The sick were selfish and those not sick too lacking in energy to inquire about the sixty-five persons in the steerage or to help amuse the children. Dickens, Dumas, and Captain Marryat were in the library for the comfort of the literary. Emerson had the diary of his great-grandfather Joseph of Malden in his cabin for his private reading. A whale passed, deliberately showing his whole length. There were schools of mackerel and blackfish. Schools of porpoises swam by the bowsprit, throwing themselves out of the water. The land birds failed to turn back soon enough, and Emerson saw one of them drowning in the sea. Astern, the waves broke into the most delicious green. Eleven days out, the ship came one night into an area of phosphorescence so bright that one could read the dial of a watch by the weird light. This was the passage Emerson long remembered for gales that made the overjoyed Malay cook cry, "Blow! me do tell you, blow!" But the gales of October, 1847, whatever they amounted to, were presumably blowing in the right direction, for on the 21st the coast of Cork was visible and next day the mountains loomed on the opposite side of St. George's Channel.

There, on the starboard, lay Britain, a great ship anchored at the side of Europe, in the heart of the mid-nineteenth-century world. Never a ship of fools, she sometimes had the aspect of a man-of-war; sometimes, of a merchantman. Emerson knew Britain's great achievements in the past and her great names. It is doubtful whether, even after some hints from Carlyle, now rapidly entering into a period of profound pessimism, he had an adequate understanding of the unrest and bitterness rife among her score or so millions of people at the moment of his arrival. The Reform Bill of fifteen years earlier had been only a palliative. Recriminations over the wealth and political power of the few and the poverty and political impotence of the many were shrill and insistent. The peace of Britain was made less secure by neighboring Continental countries which were powder kegs ready to be touched off by the flame of revolution. A few more months and, as the ultra-conservative political thinker Thomas Carlyle put it, "we had the year 1848, one of the most singular, disastrous, amazing, and, on the whole, humiliating years the European world ever saw. . . . Everywhere immeasurable Democracy rose monstrous, loud, blatant, inarticulate as the voice of Chaos." Emerson was certainly aiding the growth of democratic thought, but the extreme European reformers, eager to remake the world by violence, were hardly capable of understanding this unbellicose philosopher.

The *Washington Irving* moved up past the coast of Wales and into the Mersey on October 22. It was after dark when she arrived; but Emerson, with three other passengers and the captain, climbed into a dangerous-looking little boat and, first by oars and then by sail, got to the Liverpool water front. Emerson experienced some confusion and delay because Alexander Ireland, kept back by his duties in the newspaper office, failed to meet him, and because Carlyle's letter marked for delivery to him "on the instant when he lands in England" was not delivered till after he had been ashore for a couple of days. But on the 25th he went from Liverpool to Manchester; and there Ireland promptly began to prove himself "the king of all friends & helpful agents, the most active unweariable & imperturbable." And on the same day Emerson, finding that his lectures would not begin for a week, decided to accept Carlyle's pressing invitation and was quickly on his way to London.

At ten o'clock that night Jane Carlyle opened the door to him and he saw the redoubtable Scot himself behind her with a lamp in the entry. He was their guest for several days, but it took only a moment to loosen the floodgates of Carlyle's talk. It was long past midnight when the conversation recessed till breakfast next morning. "At noon or later," Emerson wrote home, "we went together, C. & I—to Hyde Park and the palaces (about two miles from here) to the National Gallery and into the 'Strand' to Chapman's shop Carlyle melting all Westminster & London down into his talk & laughter as he walked." If Carlyle had not changed much during the fourteen years since Emerson had visited him at Craigenputtock, Emerson saw him now in a new light, felt that he had not come to know him very well before, and was surprised at his rude vigor and range.

Emerson now saw the chasm between himself and this man who was "not mainly a scholar, like the most of my acquaintances," he wrote to Lidian, "but a very practical Scotchman, such as you would find in any sadler's or iron dealer's shop, and then only accidentally and by a surprising addition the admirable scholar & writer he is." Emerson was reminded of the Irish gardener at home. "If you wish to know precisely how he talks, just suppose that Hugh Whelan had had leisure enough, in addition to all his daily work, to read Plato, & Shakspeare, & Calvin, and, remaining Hugh Whelan all the time, should talk scornfully of all this nonsense of books that he had been bothered with,—and you shall have just the tone & talk & laughter of Carlyle." Carlyle's uninhibited conversation revealed "a very unhappy man, profoundly solitary, displeased & hindered by all men & things about him, & plainly biding his time."

An accidental meeting at the National Gallery with Mrs. Bancroft, Lidian's girlhood friend and now the wife of the American minister, soon resulted for Emerson in an introduction to Samuel Rogers. In the house that till recently stood on an extension of St. James's Place, with its trios of curving windows looking out on Green Park in the rear, the eighty-four-year-old poet received Emerson, Mrs. Bancroft, and a few others with indiscriminate politeness and went through his routine of showing pictures and manuscripts and telling anecdotes of the great. After a few more preliminary glimpses of London society Emerson returned to Liverpool on the 29th.

As his lecture season was to begin with concurrent courses in Manchester and Liverpool, he engaged lodgings in both cities. He had in each place "a handsome furnished parlor & bedroom," with fire, lighting, and service. At Liverpool he lodged at a Mrs. Hill's. At Manchester, his chief headquarters during the autumn and winter, he lived in a simple house in suburban Fenny Street, Higher Broughton. His landlady there, Mrs. Massey, bought his provisions for him and made them go as far as she could, carried his letters to the post office and his boots to the cobbler. He usually took his meals at home, and in solitude except when he had invited guests. But he was soon being asked to friendly houses. At Liverpool the British Unitarian leader, James Martineau, an acquaintance of 1833, now got "an indelible impression of the depth and greatness of his nature." It appeared that *The Dial* was "absurdly well known" in these parts and served as an introduction to its former editor.

His lectures for both the Manchester Athenaeum and the Liverpool Mechanics Institution were drawn from his old course called "Representative Men." But after a few days he started to give concurrently a miscellaneous course consisting of "Eloquence," "Domestic Life," "Reading," "The Superlative in Manners and Literature," and, it seems, "The Humanity of Science." At the end of November he revisited Liverpool to lecture for a new branch of the Roscoe Club.

The success of his British tour now seemed endangered only by a number of resentful religionists who were trying to shut him up. He was preached against even by some in the Church of England, but they were not his most violent enemies. Though his lecture on Swedenborg in the course on "Representative Men" was objected to by the general public only as "a misty subject, mistily treated," the Swedenborgians were deeply offended. The Rev. J. H. Smithson, a New Jerusalem pastor apparently influential in the Manchester Athenaeum, sent a letter of protest to the American and promptly carried his quarrel into his pulpit. A "crowded congregation" heard his assertions that Emerson was wrong in calling Swedenborg a mystic at all, wrong in considering Swedenborg's theologic interpretation of everything a vice, and wrong in saying that evil should be shunned as evil rather than as a sin against God. Smithson vigorously defended his own belief in demons and evil spirits and lashed out against Emerson's somewhat startling claim that man, even in brothels, in jails, or on gibbets, was on his way upward toward God. To Emerson's advice that "Every ardent and contemplative young man at eighteen or twenty ought once to read the theological books of Swedenborg and then throw them aside for ever," Smithson replied confidently that if the ardent and contemplative young man obeyed the first half of this admonition he would be in no danger of carrying out the rest of it. Emerson, cautious about overoptimism, wrote home that "my reception here is rather dubious & by no means so favorable as Henry pleases to fancy."

Generally he was thought a good platform speaker. If there was at first some complaint that his voice was nasal, it was conceded that at times he spoke with musical richness and depth. Some disliked the evenness of his rhythm and the sameness of expression in his face. Doubtless many were struck by a certain stiffness in his manner, his "bolt upright" posture, his behavior on the platform "as if he were a great overgrown school-boy, saying his task," and his "downright plain" way of reading his manuscript. "Now and then," said George Phillips, "his face lighted up, and his strange mystic eyes flashed as with the Delphic fire, but it was a momentary ebullition, and the statue was itself again." Yet praise soon outweighed blame. "His voice, his delivery, his very carelessness of his audience, his indifference as to whether they understand him or no, seem," another observer put it, "to become endeared to one as forming part of the individual Emerson, whose thoughtful pathway lies alone through the mental world."

Many would have lionized the transatlantic visitor had he been willing to be the lion. But if he had to refuse to dine with the mayor of Manchester, he skillfully played his part in Free Trade Hall at the soirée of the Manchester Athenaeum, chief sponsor of his lectures. The throng must have been dominated by John Bright, though he only sat silent at the high table, and by Richard Cobden, his great ally who had returned a few weeks earlier from a triumphal Continental tour. But Emerson, when it came his turn to speak, was immediately in his own proper element. He remarked that he had known the British cultural and political leaders before he came over. "When I was at home," he said, "they were as near to me as they are to you." The arguments of the Anti-Corn-Law League and its leaders were, he said, known to all friends of free trade. He also remembered what was expected of him as a specialist in ethics. He spoke of "the moral peculiarity of the Saxon race,—its commanding sense of right and wrong, the love and devotion to that."

Once his Manchester and Liverpool courses were over, Emerson was ready to make diligent use of Bradshaw's monthly railway guide. He was impressed by the superior mechanical might of the English in the swift trains, for he rode everywhere "as on a cannonball." In December he began the lecturing his agents had arranged for him in widely scattered towns. He first went north to Preston. But he at once doubled back to Manchester and soon got as far south as Nottingham. Then, after a week of consolidated effort with travel only between Nottingham and its near neighbor Derby, he went north to Preston again, but only to turn around and hurry to Birmingham, a new farthest south for the tour. With almost equal perversity his schedule sent him, once more, north of Manchester to Huddersfield, and thereupon, instead of sending him to Chesterfield and Leicester, reversed that desirable order. With little regard to any feeling of futility he may well have had by this time, it next hustled him off to Birmingham again. He was like a tennis ball batted back and forth among these northern towns. He went from Birmingham to his old lodgings in Manchester to spend Christmas Day.

On Christmas Day he had Alexander Ireland and John Cameron as guests at his Manchester lodgings. But before the end of December he was in Worcester, from whose cathedral tower he saw the Severn and the Malvern Hills. He lectured several times at Leeds, where he dined with the mayor but was warned by the president of the mechanics institution to reconsider some passages in his lectures that were likely to be construed as attacks on Christianity. Between Leeds lectures he appeared at Halifax and Ripon. He was several times at Sheffield and once at York, where the minster was "beautiful beyond belief." He continued his Yorkshire campaign till the 21st of January, leaning heavily on "Napoleon," "Domestic Life," and "Shakespeare."

He had soon fallen into the habit, new to him, of accepting invitations to private homes instead of going to the hotels. His correspondence had grown inconveniently large, especially with young men, in England and Scotland, and even in Ireland, where the poet William Allingham volunteered his friendship. He was asked if he would not remove to England. In Manchester late in January for two weeks of comparative quiet, Emerson had insistent calls from organizations whose desire to use him testified to his popularity. "Peace; Thomas Paine anniversaries; Roscoe Club Soirees; Infant Athenaeums that hold bazaars, all beckon & solicit the attention of the new come lecturer," he wrote home. "My Societies are to the full as droll as Pickwick's." He paid for his own ticket to the great Free Trade banquet, where he was delighted to hear Cobden again. Long a student of the art of public speaking, he watched his man carefully. Cobden spoke calmly, surely, and factually. His dogma of free trade had given him an effective education. But for Emerson the memorable event of his fortnight of freedom from timetables was his own private banquet, a farewell symposium of the friends and disciples he had won by his books and lectures in Lancashire and its neighboring counties.

Some notable persons he had met in this region were not present at his Manchester lodgings on January 29. Perhaps Philip Bailey, author of the then popular *Festus,* was not invited. The admired George Stephenson, builder of the first effective locomotive, could hardly have been expected in this last year of his life. Though Herbert Spencer later tried vainly to kindle Emerson's interest in synthetic philosophy, he did not come from Derby in January, 1848.

But those who actually arrived for the festivities showed to what a variety of minds Emerson could appeal. Two came from Nottingham. Joseph Neuberg, the German merchant, had been Emerson's host there. Later he became an extremely useful friend of Carlyle's. Henry Sutton, "the pride of Nottingham," was a marked man in even this gathering. He was a timorous, spiritual young man and had nearly got rid of his body. According to report, he contemptuously fed it on roots and water. In his recent book, *The Evangel of Love,* he had impatiently announced his devotion by displaying on the title page a quotation from Emerson, but he had found the courage to tell his new master privately that he liked Alcott "much better than I do you." George Dawson was a lecturer and at times announced the same subjects Emerson did. Thomas Ballantyne was a Manchester editor. William Maccall, an ex-Unitarian minister "full of metaphysics and poetry," seems also to have been among the guests.

Doctor W. B. Hodgson, later professor of political economy at the University of Edinburgh but at this time a schoolmaster in the Manchester area, not only attended at Emerson's lodgings but opened his own house to the guests. Alexander Ireland was naturally present, and his associate Francis Espinasse, a clever journalist. Espinasse was known as a follower of Carlyle but was sharply reproved by Jane Carlyle for showing signs of deserting to the Emersonian camp. He was an obviously fit guest. John Cameron, from Wakefield, was, according to Emerson, a "most erect & superior mind" but, like many others, too greatly in debt to Carlyle. Thomas Hornblower Gill, a "wonderful six feet of brain and nerves" but thin and ungainly with his "small Puritan head, which was more than half *forehead,*" was the hymn-writer and poet Emerson had first seen and admired at Birmingham. George Phillips, an "erratic genius," had "marched from the far moors of Yorkshire, and crossed the steep and rocky summit of Stanedge" on a "boisterous winter's day" to be present on this occasion.

The somewhat malicious Phillips told the story of the symposium with most detail and made Emerson's guests look like a menagerie. "A more motley, dissimilar, heterogeneous mass of persons never before, perhaps, met together at the table of a philosopher," he said. Espinasse classified them as "mystics, poets, prose-rhapsodists, editors, schoolmasters, ex-Unitarian ministers, and cultivated manufacturers" and asserted that their only bond of union was "a common regard and respect for Emerson." There were some unconventional happenings. Gill insisted on reading "a fine passage in Plato" and, having read it, commenced a long dissertation upon it. But Emerson, pleased, like the rest, "sat silent and listening, with that calm pale face of his." Gill had his triumph in spite of his spectacular accidents with food and wine at table, but Henry Sutton sat at the right hand of Emerson, being, it seemed, the master's apostle St. John. After dinner, the company listened to "a reading by Emerson—at urgent request —of his paper on Plato." A few remained for breakfast next morning. Alexander Ireland was little troubled by the amusing incidents of the occasion, and Emerson himself looked upon his guests with a sympathetic and friendly eye and wrote home to Lidian, "These are all men of merit, & of various virtues & ingenuities." He was no snob.

After his two weeks' respite from lecturing, he left Manchester for Edinburgh. On his way north he stopped a few times for sightseeing or for lectures. Near Barnard Castle he explored the region of Scott's *Rokeby*. From Barnard Castle to Darlington he passed, during the whole of an afternoon, through the great domain of the Duke of Cleveland and met the duke himself in the highway, returning with his dogs from the hunt. Emerson thus got his democratic eyes accustomed to one aspect of British aristocracy. Presently, in a counting room at the Gateshead Iron Works, he was studying a very different symbol of British society in a George Crawshay who had, Emerson understood, "refused the tests at Cambridge, after reading my Essays." Through Crawshay's misinformation Emerson lost the proper train to Edinburgh but, after some telegraphic explanations, arrived to find his audience still waiting for him, "really a brilliant assembly," fit to listen to his new lecture, "Natural Aristocracy."

Yet Scotland, still a stronghold of orthodox Presbyterianism in spite of the ominous "Disruption" of some five years earlier, looked like dangerous ground for Transcendental lecturing. The country had already been alerted. In *Tait's Edinburgh Magazine,* George Gilfillan, a wobbler in his later estimates of Emerson, welcomed him as the *"Coming Man,"* but warned him against repeating offenses of which he had been guilty in England. There, Emerson had "mesmerized" or "mystified" his audiences and had uttered "imprudent, and even outrageous" things. Such "escapades" were "certain to be misunderstood," and, Gilfillan sternly announced, "in Scotland they will not be endured." The judgment of *Blackwood's Edinburgh Magazine* that, though the lecturer was pre-eminent among Americans for original genius, he was guilty of obscurity and incoherence was a much less serious matter; but in an article in *Macphail's Edinburgh Ecclesiastical Journal and Literary Review,* nicely timed for his arrival in Scotland, some generous praise of his innocuous qualities masked a defense of orthodoxy against any attacks he might make on it. And the rumblings of the Edinburgh journals were only a prelude.

At Edinburgh and Glasgow Emerson had somewhat the same interlocking lecture schedules that he had had at Manchester and Liverpool, but the courses were shorter, and Glasgow got only half as many nights as Edinburgh. At Edinburgh, after his initial lecture, he read the apparently very old "Genius of the Age," "Shakespeare," and "Eloquence." Meantime Glasgow citizens, presumably judged less literary than those of the old capital, were hearing the much worn but reliable "Napoleon" and "Domestic Life."

The criticism Emerson now got was not entirely one-sided. According to a self-styled student, though the visitor indeed horrified the orthodox, he stirred the hearts of the liberal. But the common opinion was unfavorable. A pamphlet called *Emerson's Orations to the Modern Athenians; or, Pantheism* summed up this "Chimera of the Oracle of the Woods" as a brilliant and dangerous though visionary propagandist of the skepticism of which France had afforded an appalling example. The urbane Edinburgh Philosophical Institution could take four lectures and survive public opinion, but several of the directors of the Glasgow Athenaeum were panic-stricken.

In Edinburgh, Emerson was pleasantly settled in the bachelor apartments of a correspondent and admirer, Doctor Samuel Brown. In recent years Brown had entertained Margaret Fuller and had learned what he could of Emerson from her and other traveling Americans. He was a friend of Carlyle and also knew Edinburgh and the Scottish pantheon. An imaginative scientist, he was unsubdued by the discipline of his laboratory; and Carlyle aptly described him as "that kind of a man, that if God Almighty wished to hang a new constellation in the sky, he would give him an estimate for the same." At Brown's, Emerson found David Scott, "a sort of Bronson Alcott with easel & brushes," and Craig, Brown's Siamese twin, "sharer of all his chemistry or alchemy." It was from this retreat among the unorthodox that the American guest sallied forth to explore and to read lectures.

What Emerson wrote home at the time showed that his Scottish tour was really a memorable experience. The day after his arrival he saw John Wilson ("Christopher North"), Mrs. Jeffrey, Mrs. Crowe, "and looked all round this most picturesque of cities . . . and in the evening met Mr Robert Chambers (author of the Vestiges of Creation) by appointment at Mr Ireland's (father of Alexander I.) at supper. The next day at 12," he went on, "I visited by appointment Lord Jeffrey . . . then went to church, & heard John Bruce preach, and then to Mrs Crowes at 5.30, to dine with De Quincey, and David Scott, & Dr Brown. De Quincey is a small old man of 70 years, with a very handsome face, and a face too expressing the highest refinement, a very gentle old man, speaking with the greatest deliberation & softness, and so refined in speech & manners as to make quite indifferent his extremely plain & poor dress. For the old man summoned by message on Saturday by Mrs Crowe to this dinner had walked on this stormy muddy Sunday ten miles from Lass Wade, where his cottage is, and was not yet dry . . . He has a childish facility, and has also relation to Ellery Channing, & to George Bradford, say George's amiableness raised to the tenth power. . . . He invited me to dine with him . . . & I accepted."

There was no respite. "The next day," Emerson wrote, "I breakfasted with David Scott, who insists on sittings for a portrait & sat to him for an hour or two. . . . At 1 o'clock, I went to Glasgow, and read my story there to an assembly of 2 or 3000 people in a vast lighted cavern called the City Hall, that will hold 5000 people. . . . Next day, I dined at Edinburgh with Robert Chambers . . . This day I went to the University to see Professor Wilson & to hear him lecture (on moral philosophy) to his class. . . . His lecture . . . was on the association of ideas, & was a very dull sermon without a text, but pronounced with great bodily energy, sometimes his mouth all foam, he reading, the class writing, and I at last waiting a little impatiently for it to be over. No trait was there of Christopher North; not a ray."

Emerson stretched out his letter to extraordinary length, for he was full of his Scotch news. "Afterwards," he said, "we went to Sir Wm Hamilton's Lecture on Logic— He is the great man of the college . . . but now suffering lately from palsy. We went over the Old Parliament House, saw all the judges, & heard a little of the pleadings of the barristers, under the guidance of Francis Russell, Esq. who, you may remember, visited us from Dr Brown. . . . I saw George Combe, who had called on me & had invited me to breakfast . . . Combe talked well & sensibly about America. But, for the most part, there is no elasticity about Scotch sense it is calculating & precise, but has no future. Then to Glasgow & spent the night at Professor Nichol's observatory . . . I saw next day the Saut Market and O plenty of women (fishwives & others) & children, *barefooted,* barelegged, on this cold 18th of February in the streets. . . . At Edinburgh again . . . visited Lord Jeffrey . . . Jeffrey as always very talkative, very disputatious, very French . . . I should like to see him put on his merits . . . but here he is the chief man, has it all his own way, and is a mere Polonius. . . . The next day, I dined with De Quincey & his pleasing daughters . . . We carried our host back with us to Edinb. in the carriage to Mrs Crowe's, & to my lecture!"

Thus Emerson in his own words put an end to any suspicion that he suffered from a lack of hospitality in Scotland. There were many, including a few notable persons, willing to give the lecturer a clean bill of health. David Scott at first found him "severe, and dry, and hard" in appearance but gradually discovered that he was "elevated, simple, kind, and truthful" in character. Scott managed to suggest all of these qualities in the portrait he painted in oils. De Quincey, saved at length from bailiffs and opium but not from his shyness and his fear of old Edinburgh specters, must, however habitual his amiability, have been warmed a little by the American visitor. At any rate he recommended him in a letter to Derwent Coleridge as a distinguished author of fascinating books and as one who "knew your illustrious father personally, and honored him"; and then he actually came, with Doctor Samuel Brown, to the railroad station to see the "foreigner" off to Dundee. In the provincial town Emerson learned that even defenders of Scottish religion had friendly moments. "On Monday," he continued his long letter, "I left Edinb. & came to Dundee & lodged last night with Mr Gilfillan, who wrote Gallery of Portraits, & who is minister of the Free Church there. This day I have come to Perth and tomorrow I return to Dundee & Gilfillan. On Friday to Paisley, & on Saturday I leave Scotland . . ."

Having finished his Scotch lectures at Dundee, Perth, and Paisley, Emerson returned to England in the last days of February. On his way southward he took advantage of Harriet Martineau's invitation in order to be near Wordsworth. It was his first opportunity since 1833 and would be his last.

An hour and a half with Wordsworth, now within some two years of his death, was time well spent in spite of the old man's tiresome prejudices. These he poured out volubly, once he was completely awakened from his afternoon nap. Emerson found him "full of talk on French news, bitter old Englishman he is, on Scotchmen whom he contemns; on Gibbon, who cannot write English; on Carlyle, who is a pest to the English tongue, on Tennyson, whom he thinks a right poetic genius tho with some affectation." Emerson commented that "though he often says something I think I could easily undertake to write Table Talk for him to any extent for the newspapers, & it should cost me nothing & be quite as good . . . as any one is likely to hear from his own lips. But he is a fine healthy old man with weatherbeaten face, and I think it is a high compliment we pay to the cultivation of the English generally, when we find him not distinguished." And if Emerson turned his eyes from the man to the poet, certainly the case was altered for the better; and his astonishing dictum, apparently never retracted, that "The Ode on Immortality is the highwater mark which the intellect has reached in this age" was only one of many evidences of his great regard for Wordsworth.

During his two days as guest of Harriet Martineau, Emerson went on horseback with her and William Greg to get the best views and dined with the Arnolds at Greg's. Then, "through all these wondrous French news which all tongues & telegraphs discuss,' he set out for Manchester and from there went on almost immediately to London.

In London, Emerson settled himself in the Strand, a vantage point from which Doctor Johnson's "full tide of human existence" could be conveniently observed. He had "a good sittingroom & chamber" to himself in John Chapman's house at No. 142. That house was no dull place, with literary and other people coming and going; and Emerson, within some two weeks after his arrival, was to get a notion of what curious encounters might occur there. To his great surprise, and certainly to hers as well, Jane Carlyle, looking for one of the several bookish Chapmans in the Strand, was conducted by mistake to Emerson—deposited in his arms, as she put it. Proffered hospitality so urgently that she had no opportunity to explain her mistake, she settled down for half an hour's visit before she went on her way.

Once Emerson got outside Chapman's house, only a minute's walk would bring him to London landmarks. Within a few rods was the little island of St. Mary-le-Strand, dividing the noisy traffic into two streams; and near at hand was the great quadrangle of Somerset House, marking historic ground. Almost directly back of Somerset House one could, by paying toll, cross the Thames on John Rennie's beautiful Waterloo Bridge. In this part of London one saw more evidences of Britain's wealth and power than of her distress. London, the wealthy and powerful city, was remarkable, not only for omnibuses, steam ferries, penny post, and the rapidly growing West End, but as the city where one heard Grisi sing, Macaulay talk, and Faraday lecture; where one ate Soyer's cooking and had Rothschild for one's banker. London had the best, and so it was an economy to come here. The new Houses of Parliament, now in course of construction, symbolized the might of the kingdom and of the empire as well as the advance of British freedom. London, it was true, was a different city to different people. Hugh Whelan, the gardener, wrote to Emerson, admonishing him not to fail to see Oxford Street lighted with gas and begging him to look up the place where Hugh's uncle used to keep the sign of the Dog and Duck. Emerson himself had found only a "very dull city" here some fifteen years before. Now he went out to Chelsea and talked with Carlyle.

In March of 1848, Carlyle was full of a new enthusiasm. He was taking *The Times,* the first daily paper he had ever had, and was delighted to see the new French revolution "teaching this great swindle,

Louis Philippe, that there is a God's justice in the Universe after all." It was at Carlyle's suggestion that Emerson had a look at the Chartists. They were just then reviving after some years of quiescence and were about to work themselves up for the grand climax, or grand fiasco as it proved to be, of April 10. At the National Hall in Holborn, Emerson watched their ceremonies in honor of the deputation that had returned from carrying congratulations to the new French Republic. The "Marseillaise" was sung, but the great throng preferred the slogan "Every man a ballot and every man a musket." In the streets the unrest got out of control. Day after day a mob caused anxiety among shopkeepers by wandering about and breaking windows and stealing. Emerson pondered the place of the scholar in politics. "When we would pronounce anything truly of man," he noted, "we retreat instantly on the individual." And yet when he heard there was to be a Chartist revolution on Monday and an Irish revolution the following week, it occurred to him that the right scholar would feel these things a challenge and a test of his genius.

But in London the titled aristocracy and the intellectuals soon began to demand what time Emerson could spare from his reading and writing hours. His notebook was well filled with appointments with interesting people of these more fortunate classes. Within a week after his return to London he had a long visit from the entertaining Milnes, and he was to see much more of him. Milnes, having once reviewed Emerson in a London journal, felt a kind of proprietary interest in him. This future Lord Houghton was now the symbol of aristocratic sympathy with democratic reform. Thackeray, making merry in *Punch* over an imaginary English revolution inspired by events in France, headed his cabinet list with "Minister of Foreign Affairs, President of the Council, and Poet Laureate, Citizen Monckton Milnes." But Emerson noticed that, though people jestingly addressed his friend as Citoyen Milnes, they spoke of him "between jest & earnest" as "really one who might play one day a part of Lamartine in England."

By the end of March, Emerson was writing to Lidian: "At Mr Bancroft's I dined with Macaulay, Bunsen, Lord Morpeth, Milman, Milnes, & others. Carlyle, Mr & Mrs Lyell, Mrs Butler, & others came in the evening. At Mr Milman's I breakfasted with Macaulay Hallam, Lord Morpeth . . . At Mr Procter's (Barry Cornwall,) I dined with Forster of the Examiner, Kinglake (Eothen) & others. At Mrs Drummond's I found Mr Cobden & Lord Monteagle . . . Carlyle carried me to Lady Harriet Baring . . . Macaulay is the king of diners-out. I do not know when I have seen such wonderful vivacity. . . ." And he went on to tell how he found Lord and Lady Ashburton, Lord Auckland, Carlyle, Milnes, Thackeray, Lord and Lady Castlereagh, the Bishop of Oxford, and others at Baring's.

He heard incessant talk of the French revolution. "Besides the intrinsic interest of the spectacle and the intimate acquaintance which all these people have with all the eminent persons in France, there is evidently a certain anxiety," he put it, "to know whether *our* days also are not numbered, and whether the splendid privileges of these English palaces, to which, they plainly see, that the world never had any thing that could compare, are not in too dreadful contrast to famine & ignorance at the door, to last." He had a good opportunity to hear Carlyle dispensing jeremiads to aristocratic company, but he observed that these prophecies of woe were not taken as gospel in even this company where many were the Scot's friends. "The aristocrats say," he informed Lidian, " 'Put that man in the House of Commons & you will hear no more of him.' "

Some of his new friends marveled that an American could look so human and be so inoffensive. The Bishop of Oxford observed after Bingham Baring's dinner that "Emerson is very little Yankee, tall, thin, with no atrabilious look" . . . Crabb Robinson, the experienced tuft-hunter, was astonished at his civilized condition. "It was," he confessed, "with a feeling of predetermined dislike that I had the curiosity to look at Emerson at Northampton's, a fortnight ago; when, in an instant, all my dislike vanished. He has one of the most interesting countenances I ever beheld —a combination of intelligence and sweetness that quite disarmed me." The stranger looked as if he might be a worthy addition to one's collection, and Crabb Robinson did not run away. "I was introduced to him," he commented with evident satisfaction.

Emerson's election for the term of his English visit to honorary membership in the Athenæum was a sign that he had been accepted by intellectuals and aristocrats. Scientists, artists, and literary men, together with "liberal Patrons," made up the regular membership of the club, or so the book of rules and regulations boasted; and the honorary members were "Foreign Ambassadors and Ministers Plenipotentiary, Foreign Members of the Royal Society, and such other Foreigners of distinction for Science, Literature, or the Arts, (not exceeding Ten of the latter at one time,) as the Committee may deem it advisable to name." His unanimous election to the Reform Club was evidence that Emerson was acceptable to liberal political leaders. In general he easily disarmed the prejudiced in all ranks of society. Thomas Cooper, the Chartist, skeptic, and poet, after attending Garth Wilkinson's party in honor of "the illustrious American" at Hampstead, walked back with him into London and found his talk "gentle and good" but managed to keep his own national prejudice nearly intact by declaring, "He was the only American in whose company I ever felt real enjoyment." Quickest of all to accept Emerson were the literary aspirants, usually young men, but sometimes women. The enthusiasm that Eliza Maria Gillies showed for him seemed to belie her protestation that she had no notion of playing Bettina to a new Goethe. Matthew Arnold, an aspirant with a better claim to attention, did not forget him during London's spasm of political excitement that spring. In what the much younger man described as "a very pleasant interview," they discussed Carlyle, Wordsworth, and Harriet Martineau, neighbor of Arnold's family in the Wordsworth country.

In London, Emerson nearly always accepted the invitations he got, no matter from what quarter. He went to the home of Lord Palmerston, the experienced minister of foreign affairs and future prime minister, and saw "a quite illustrious collection,"' or to the home of Lady Morgan, "a sort of fashionable or London edition of Aunt Mary, the vivacity the wit, the admirable preservation of social powers, being retained,—but the high moral genius being left out." He wanted to "know how that 'other half' of the world lives, though," he said, "I cannot & would not live with them." He impartially appraised virtues and vices. If he liked the aristocrats for their simplicity of speech and manners he noticed that they suffered from want of thought just as fashionable circles at home did.

He went to Oxford on invitation of Arthur Clough, a fellow of Oriel College, and Charles Daubeny, a professor of botany. "I was housed," he wrote home, "close upon Oriel, though not within it, but I lived altogether on college hospitalities, dining one day with Mr Stanley, of University College, & his Fellows; the next day, breakfasting with Jacobson, & some Deans & Doctors; dining at Exeter College, with Palgrave, Froude, & other Fellows, & breakfasting, next morning, at Oriel, with Clough, Dr Daubeny; &c   They all showed me the kindest attentions; showed me their college buildings, the Bodleian Library, &c, not forgetting the Randolph Gallery; but, much more, they showed me themselves, who are many of them very earnest, faithful, affectionate; some of them highly gifted men; some of them, too, prepared & decided to make great sacrifices for conscience sake. . . . They seemed to think I had come to stay a good while, & marvelled much at my rapid departure at the end of 48 hours."

Oxford, though an aristocratic symbol of the past, was, Emerson knew, a battleground where new ideas were fighting the old. In this somber dark-timbered hall of Oriel, where Gothic windows, bearing colorful coats of arms, blurred the feeble daylight, Arthur Clough was more troubled by

the new ideas than one might have guessed who saw him step forward
to the upper table at commons to repeat the Latin grace,

> Benedictus benedicat,
> Benedicitur benedicatur.

Yet it seemed clear to Emerson that the boldest minds here were painfully
restrained. He was soon truly "fond of these monks of Oxford." But he
got no new illumination when Froude, a young scholar he much admired,
pointed out Pusey's window to him and declared reverently, "From that
window came all our light"; and he realized how impossible it would be
for him to breathe this atmosphere year after year as the fellows were
doing. His large reservation from total praise of Oxford was that here "you
may hold what opinion you please so that you hold your tongue." Apparently he took his own counsel and held his tongue during his visit, stirring
up no public debate. "Everybody liked him," Clough testified, "and as the
orthodox mostly had never heard of him, they did not suspect him . . ."

Emerson saw other British institutions, often with the help of the best-
qualified guides or when the best performers were on. At the British
Museum Sir Charles Fellows instructed him on Greek remains and Coventry Patmore showed him prints. At the theater he saw Mrs. Butler as
Cordelia and Macready as Lear. At Covent Garden he heard Grisi and
Alboni sing. Richard Owen provided a ticket to his own lectures at the
Royal College of Surgeons, and Emerson took care to hear as many of
them as possible. Fortunately Owen also showed the Hunterian Museum,
a thing he could very well do, as he had prepared the catalogue of its collections. Emerson, in the lecture room, watched intently; saw that Owen's
vinous face was a powerful weapon and that his surgical smile and air of
virility penetrated the audience; admired the scientist's perfect self-com-
mand.

With Robert Hutton, Emerson attended a meeting of the Geological
Society of London, presumably at Somerset House, and had the good fortune to hear what he called "the best debate I have heard in England,
the House of Commons & the Manchester Banquet not excepted." The
Scottish geologist Andrew Crombie Ramsay, one of the members present,
also thought it a good night and "was glad of this," he said, "for Emerson,
the American, was there." Among the speakers was Charles Lyell, a geologist whose discoveries had helped pre-Darwinian evolutionary theories.
Frequent subsequent meetings with him may have added something to
Emerson's enthusiasm for science. Early in April, Emerson was back with
the Geological Society after dining with the Geological Club, its inner circle.

He saw Kew Gardens under the guidance of Sir William Hooker, the director. Crabb Robinson, now assured of his harmlessness, took him to what was considered a highly successful anniversary meeting of the Society of Antiquaries in the Freemasons' Tavern. All the members enthusiastically drank the health of Emerson and got a response from him. At table he discussed Shakespeare's sonnets with John Payne Collier. Collier's Shakespearean forgeries had not yet been exposed.

Just at the moment when Emerson was getting comfortably acquainted with Dickens and more comfortably with Tennyson, a Hawthorne minus Hawthorne's bashfulness, he decided to cross the English Channel without further delay. Tennyson warned him against going yet and refused to go along. Instead, he offered to go with him to Italy. But the boulevards seemed to have grown calm enough since the flight of Louis-Philippe, and Emerson, with an effort, stuck to his own plan. Presumably he had by now carried out his intention to file his French tongue further in London and had got some preparation by attending the French theater there. On May 6 he crossed to Boulogne and next day took temporary lodgings at a hotel, the Montmorency, No. 20, boulevard des Italiens, in Paris.

After a couple of days there, he moved to the left bank. The radical Goodwyn Barmby, once a listener to Alcott's teachings in Surrey and later an enthusiastic Emersonian, said that Emerson "took up his abode in the lovely little apartment which I had not long before occupied, in a hotel in the Rue des Beaux Arts, which I think I recommended to him." According to Emerson's own account, his comfortable rooms were at 15, rue des Petits Augustins (a street later renamed Bonaparte). But the arrangement of streets in that quarter was such that the two addresses might conceivably have been the same. It seems, at any rate, that when Emerson arrived he was not surprised to find his English friends already at his hotel—the Rawdon Quaker W. E. Forster, Carlyle's friend and Emerson's host a few months earlier; the Paulets, Emerson's Liverpool friends; and the Manchester novelist Geraldine Jewsbury, Jane Carlyle's intimate, known less formally at Cheyne Row as Miss Gooseberry. Emerson engaged his apartment for a month. He was thus settled in the heart of the capital, close to the Ile de la Cité.

He took to dining at a table d'hôte on the right bank where there were usually five hundred Frenchmen, he estimated, demonstrating how the language should be spoken. But as Clough, his Oxford friend, had reached France before him and remained there longer than he did, the two dined together "daily" during Emerson's whole stay. Though there were a good many Americans in Paris at the moment and very few English, Emerson kept mainly with his British friends, presumably because his business abroad was chiefly with Britain. Clough was, to a slight extent, a compromise. He

had spent several years of his childhood in America but had proudly flourished his British flag there and always remained, in spite of a later residence in America, as English as his very English face. Besides Clough,
Emerson often had the Paulets as dinner companions until they left Paris;
and he saw something of Forster and Miss Jewsbury. One morning he
brought Hugh Doherty to breakfast. Doherty was an Irish socialist who
had found England too hot.

What Emerson most wanted was acquaintance with Frenchmen of
information. But Clough was doubtless the next best thing. Clough was
full of "interest in life and realities, in the state of woman, and the questions so rife in Paris through Communism, and through the old loose and
easy conventions of that city for travellers" and talked "so considerately
of the grisette estate," that Emerson found him "the best *pièce de resistance,*
and tough adherence, that one could desire." Presumably the two men had
some uninhibited conversation on the subject of the grisettes. Possibly, too,
Clough carried some jesting on the subject too far to please Emerson. On
May 13, at any rate, Emerson wrote in his Paris diary what could most
readily be interpreted as a reply to something of that kind. "What," he
asked, "can the brave and strong genius of C. himself avail? What can
his praise, what can his blame avail me, when I know that if I fall or
if I rise, there still awaits me the inevitable joke? . . . But when I balance
the attractions of good and evil, when I consider what facilities, what
talents a little vice would furnish, then rise before me not these laughers,
but the dear and comely forms of honour and genius and piety in my
distant home, and they touch me with chaste palms moist and cold, and
say to me, You are ours." In London Emerson had had some conversation
with Carlyle and Dickens on chastity; but whether the C. of the Paris
entry meant Carlyle or Clough, Emerson was obviously not marked for
conquest by the grisettes.

He nevertheless saw as much of Parisian life as he could. If he was
not at the French Academy on May 19 for the reception to the literary
historian Ampère which Philarète Chasles, Emerson's own critic of some
years earlier, reported in the *Journal des débats,* he found enough less
dignified Parisian experiences open to him. He seems to have attended the
theater at least half a dozen times. The plays he saw included the classic
Phèdre and *Mithridate.* He saw Rachel in both the Racine plays and heard
her sing the "Marseillaise." The slight woman seemed to him to grow paler
with passion as she chanted the words of the song and shook the tricolor
banner in her hand. It was probably for her acting that he saw François
Ponsard's *Lucrèce,* though that play had some significance of its own,
having marked, a few years earlier, the reaction against romantic Dumas

and Hugo on the Paris stage. He bought a ticket to a ball, presumably for the opportunity of observing another side of Parisian life. He also bought a ticket to the Winter Garden. He went to the Louvre and jotted down some notes on the Spanish school. Velasquez and Spagnoletto he took for strong, swarthy men, "good soldiers or brigands at a pinch." He imagined that these Spaniards painted with a certain ferocity.

On the boulevards politics grew tenser. Emerson calmly speculated whether the revolution of February would prove to be worth the loss of the trees cut down to make the barricades, but soon he realized that there were plenty of radicals who thought that revolution had been too mild and were looking forward to a new one. He had the good fortune to see the radicals' ringleaders Blanqui and Barbès in action before the explosion occurred. He and Forster and Mrs. Paulet failed in their first attempt to find the Barbès club and attended the first sitting of a free trade club instead. But the next evening, the evening of May 10, they saw from a side box the Barbès club in such an uproar that even Emerson's equanimity was disturbed. On the 13th, probably in the company of Dionysius Lardner, a popular scientific writer who had once been professor of natural philosophy and astronomy at University College, London, Emerson visited Blanqui's club. Blanqui, if a Paris newspaper reported the meeting accurately, told his faithful to boycott the national demonstration prematurely set for the following day. "But wait," he counseled, "wait five or six weeks, and then the winds and the tides will be in our favor . . ."

Emerson was back at Blanqui's club the next evening with Forster and so witnessed its last sitting under its formidable leader. Blanqui, in spite of Clough's notion that he had "a certain hang-dog conspirator aspect," was a memorable sight. And his Rights of Man Club, as it was called, was a first-rate as well as very timely attraction. At one of its meetings, Emerson recorded, an orator in a blouse advised the rich not to worry about their property. "We shall guard it," he assured them, "with the utmost care, in the belief that it will soon be our own." Emerson seems to have witnessed also the curious human drama in progress at the Women's Club. The dignified and sensible leader had to be constantly on her guard against the masculine part of the audience, for they were quick to find opportunities to make the proceedings ridiculous.

On May 15, the day after Emerson's second visit to Blanqui's club, suddenly came the *émeute,* or, as the Parisians seemed to prefer to call it, the *échauffourée.* Though it may have looked a few days later like nothing more than a scuffle, it threatened at the moment to be more serious than a riot. Early in the afternoon a crowd, soon swollen to several thousands, invaded the National Assembly on the pretext of presenting a petition in favor of Poland. The members of the clubs had appeared in force, ready for violence. Barbès was bawling his demand that they be allowed to come in and submit their petition. But the National Guard arrived in time. The conspirators, ejected from the Assembly, retreated to the Hôtel de Ville. There they proclaimed a new government, but they could hold their ground only a short time before they were captured.

Emerson was not at the center of the melee but "saw," as he said, "the sudden & immense display of arms when the rappel was beaten . . . the streets full of bayonets, and the furious driving of the horses dragging cannon towards the National Assembly; the rapid succession of proclamations proceeding from the Government, & pasted on the walls at the corners of all streets, eagerly read by crowds of people;—and, not waiting for this, the rapid passage of messengers with proclamations in their hands which they read to knots of people, & then ran on to another knot & so on, down a street . . ." The former orator of the peace society in Boston was thrilled by the martial drama and its colorful setting. Lidian commented from Concord, "Only think of your having been caught in a Revolution as one might be in a shower . . ."

The "scuffle" was the grand climax of French political action so far as Emerson was concerned, but his role of observer was not quite ended. On the twenty-first he witnessed the elaborate fete of Concord, Peace, and Labor. Clough, who got out early to the Place de la Concorde that gloriously bright Sunday morning and watched the arriving contingents from various parts of France, from Poland, from Italy, and from Germany, and even a green-flagged Irish Club consisting, as he said, of "about three of our fellow-subjects of the sister-island," was inclined to look with condescension on the whole affair. But Emerson was pleased when, later in the day, he observed the estimated 1,200,000 people standing in the Champ-de-Mars "like an immense family the perfect good humour & fellowship is so habitual to them all"; and that night he thought "the illumination in the Champs Elysées was delicious." Perhaps he remembered miniature Brook Farm. "It was easy," he said, "to see that France is far nearer to Socialism than England & it would be a short step to convert Paris into a phalanstery." With the ticket George Bancroft had got for him from American minister Rush, he went to the Assembly to hear Lamartine's "*great* speech" on Poland, a speech so long that it had to be delivered in two instalments with a recess of twenty-five minutes between them. Emerson was struck by the "manly handsome greyhaired gentleman with nothing of the rust of the man of letters." The chamber seemed to him "an honest country representation." He was glad of the defeat of the extremists at the hands of the February revolutionists, the shopkeepers, as he called them.

He wanted to supplement his unexpected political and martial experiences with some first-hand knowledge of French society. As late as May 17, though he had had the promise of an introduction to some French ladies, his concierge and the concierge's wife had been his only domestic acquaintance. He was at length received in the home of Alexis de Tocqueville, but this Frenchman had an English wife and was famous for a book on American democracy. Milnes, now gibed at in London as Citizen Milnes, was in Paris and had arranged the meeting. Before the end of the month Emerson added his critic the Comtesse d'Agoult to his list but had seen almost no other private society in Paris. Under more favorable circumstances, doubtless de Tocqueville and the countess could have introduced him to a brilliant French social circle and he might have got some notion of the part he had played in the growth of French political thought. But as it was, his experience of French intellectuals was unsatisfying.

George Sand had turned journalist to aid the extremist faction and had briefly burned with political ardor, but she had now gone back to the country in disgust. The copy of Emerson's *Poems* Margaret Fuller had given her bore no fruit that the poet could taste. He saw Leverrier working out algebraic formulas on the blackboard for his class, "quite heedless of politics and revolutions." He heard Michelet lecture on Indian philosophy and lost some of his respect for him. The "creed of the Indian Buddhists," he commented, "was not meant for a Frenchman to analyze and crack his joke and make his grimace upon." Perhaps he did not know that Michelet had been one of his admirers and Michelet did not know that Emerson was in his lecture room. Quinet, another of the old circle of Emersonians at the Collège de France, had long since grown too radical to keep his professorial chair. But Emerson, though his enthusiasm for Quinet as a literary man was not great, seems to have missed him and Lamennais only because he could not wait long enough for them in Paris. Mickiewicz, presumably the first to make Emerson known in France, had gone off to Italy and had raised a Polish legion to fight in the ill-starred revolution there. The clever Comtesse d'Agoult was thus, as it turned out, the only Emersonian with whom Emerson had any satisfactory meeting in Paris. He recorded with restrained enthusiasm his "one very pleasant hour" with her. She recorded her meeting with "the moralist" with no more emotion but felt at least enough of her earlier admiration to have a crayon sketch made of him by Charles Lehmann, who rediscovered the Indian type in Emerson's head.

Sometime before Emerson turned back across the Channel he sat for the crayon sketch by Oswald Murray that came eventually into the possession of Alexander Ireland. The Murrays apparently knew little of Emerson and were undisturbed by any rumors of his notoriety or fame. Mrs. Murray used to let him hold the baby while he sat to her husband and she prepared tea. His serious business, however, was not with artists and not with any but Frenchmen. He stayed on in Paris until within four days of his first London lecture. Along with experiences that he could compound with the usual Anglo-American prejudices in a lecture on France, he was getting some pleasing impressions. "All winter I have been admiring the English and disparaging the French," he wrote home. "Now in these weeks I have been correcting my prejudice & the French rise many entire degrees." He liked the "universal good breeding" of Parisians and their apparent abolition of the British and American superstitious reverence for broadcloth. They seemed "the most joyous race." In Paris the river was an ornament, in London the Thames was out of sight. Paris had magnificent gardens and palaces worthy of the name. London did not. For enjoyment, for independence, Paris was best of all cities. Leaving Paris on the second day of June, Emerson spent the night at Folkestone, then took the express for London.

He had decided upon his London lectures only after a long period of doubt. The need of money had made him consider them seriously, though he had thought the time unfavorable. Alternatives to a London course had seemed at first to be a return to the Liverpool platform, an experiment in Bristol, and continued silence. Alexander Ireland had made the additional suggestion of "private classes" at Manchester; but by that time John Chapman, publisher and landlord, had busied himself, with some other friends of Emerson, about a London course. Still Emerson had almost decided not to lecture. According to Espinasse's story, before he would budge his friends had found it necessary to get up a petition. At any rate a formal petition had been got up as early as April. One copy had been signed by Carlyle, Dickens, and a few other celebrities. Whether or not this petition had had any serious effect, final arrangements had soon been made for a course of six lectures "on the Mind and Manners of the Nineteenth Century" to be read at the Literary and Scientific Institution in Edwards Street, Portman Square, from June 6 to 17. And now Emerson, back in London on June 3 and properly equipped, no doubt, with his new Parisian frock coat and waistcoat, was ready to begin. The subjects he announced in *The Times* were "Powers and Laws of Thought," "Relation of Intellect to Natural Science," "Tendencies and Duties of Men of Thought," "Politics and Socialism," "Poetry and Eloquence," and "Natural Aristocracy."

He was fearful, he seems to have told his audience, of the Englishman's "hard eyes" that were used to looking for practical things. He tried to give his first lecture a practical and timely air. He kept abreast of the latest news by making an example of Lamartine. But his usual idealistic tone soon reasserted itself. Instead of honoring the literary man who had abandoned his own craft for politics, he found the general praise of Lamartine's act a sign of the prevalent lack of respect for the office of the intellectual man. And he repeated, in the same lecture, his habitual dislike of naturalism in literature. Much of the recent philosophy of poetry had been pathology, he said; and the laws of the intellect had been transformed into the laws of disease. The effect of a fine natural gift ought to be to exhilarate; and beauty, not ugliness, was, he declared, the flowering of virtue. He still spoke from his customary mountain peak.

Behind the scenes Alexander Ireland, his guest at Chapman's during the course at Edwards Street, noticed that he wasted little time. Between appearances on the platform Emerson "generally devoted many hours a day to study, retiring to his room immediately after breakfast, and extending the forenoon to three o'clock." He also had social engagements. With Ireland, he visited Leigh Hunt and was delighted; and with Ireland he went to the home of the wealthy social reformer and associationist John Minter Morgan. He was much amused as Morgan explained to his guests, mostly socialists, a huge colored revolving view of future social life according to the reformer's dreams. Emerson even found time for the theater and once heard Jenny Lind.

But at precisely four o'clock on lecture afternoons he would suddenly appear before his audience at the Literary and Scientific Institution. He would stand there silent for a moment, producing an effect "at first somewhat startling, and then nobly impressive," said a British reporter. With his manuscript on the desk before him he "turned over the first leaf, whispering at the same time, 'Gentlemen and ladies.' The initial sentences were next pronounced in a low tone, a few words at a time, hesitatingly . . ." The audience smiled a little at "certain nervous twitches and angular movements of the hand and arms" but were more impressed by his "eminent bonhomie, earnestness, and sincerity, which bespoke sympathy and respect, —nay, more, secured veneration." He made no attempt to play the lion. "The moment he finished," Alexander Ireland observed, "he took up his MS. and quietly glided away,—disappearing before his audience could give vent to their applause."

But Emerson, an experienced lecturer, was by no means oblivious of his audience, and while they studied him he studied them. It was, as he wrote home, "a curious company that came to hear the Massachusetts Indian." He was doubtless right in judging that some came to see others, "for, besides our high Duchess of Sutherland & her sister, Lord Morpeth & the Duke of Argyle & Lord Lovelace came, & other aristocratic people,

& as there could be no prediction what might be said to & therefore what must be heard by them, & in the presence of Carlyle & Monckton Milnes, &c. there might be fun: who knew?" Carlyle was himself a prime attraction and did his duty by making "loud Scottish Covenanter gruntings of laudation, or, at least, of consideration," edifying those in his vicinity. Other persons who came were Procter ("Barry Cornwall"); Charles Lyell, the geologist; William Spence, the entomologist; Mrs. Jameson, the popular writer; Thackeray, about to publish the final instalment of *Vanity Fair* and fast becoming famous on account of that novel; John Forster, editor of *The Examiner,* a powerful journal; Douglas Jerrold, playwright, humorist, and journalist; and William and Mary Howitt, a literary as well as domestic team, tireless producers of wholesome verse and prose, original or translated.

In spite of the high average intelligence of such an audience, the old complaint of obscurity was heard again. Miss Hennell asked Carlyle whether he thought they would understand better if they stood on their heads. Actually Carlyle himself, according to Espinasse, could say nothing better about the lectures than that they were very Emersonian and, when he talked more freely, summed them up as "Moonshine" and "intellectual sonatas." Carlyle, no idealist, was interested in the immediate business of saving the economic and political world. Emerson wrote to Lidian that he had no better persons at his lectures "than Jane Carlyle & Mrs Bancroft who honestly come." Probably the "certain wife-like jealousy" which, Espinasse judged, made Jane Carlyle look on Emerson as "a sort of rival of her husband" was no very serious matter. Lord Morpeth, appearing at Edwards Street on the last day of the course, took alarm at the dynamite he discovered in "Natural Aristocracy." Calling on the lecturer at Chapman's, he begged him not to repeat the passage asking who could blame the peasant for burning the barns of the idle rich. Many years later Emerson remembered this with the somewhat exaggerated comment that "Aristocracy is always timid."

Meantime, in London, he was wined and dined by Morpeth and other aristocrats. The Duchess of Sutherland had him to lunch at her magnificent Stafford House. Her son-in-law, the Duke of Argyll, got the impression there, as in the lecture hall, that Emerson was charming but somewhat cloying, wanting bone and gristle. For his own part Emerson, the aristocratic democrat, observed the titled aristocrats with much interest as he faced them across their dinner tables. He made the most of his opportunity to study what was for him a new variety of humanity.

Though his "guinea-paying" audience at Edwards Street had grown larger day by day, the price of admission was too high for what he called "*my public,*" and he received only £80 net instead of the £200 predicted. Though he hated lending himself even to innocuous propaganda, he needed money so much that he agreed to lecture, during the last days of June, under the management of the Metropolitan Early Closing Association. For a fee of thirty-five guineas he was to read his old manuscripts "Napoleon," "Domestic Life," and "Shakespeare" in what he called "the Cave of the Winds of Exeter Hall." The reticent lecturer, used to escaping from the village of Concord to the Walden Woods, was unhappy, he wrote to Lidian, when he saw "the advertising Vans that go up & down the Strand announcing to all millions in huge red letters that R W E is to speak."

In the more popular lecture hall there was less glamour than at Edwards Street, but some notable persons appeared. Chopin, already known to the unmusical Emerson, had sent him a ticket to a *matinée musicale,* "his first London Concert," given on the same day with Emerson's opening lecture. But as the lecture was read at night, the composer may have heard it in spite of his busy day. William Michael Rossetti, a fervent admirer of the essay "Self-reliance" and a member of a set who praised Emerson's poetry "for its august seer-like qualities, notwithstanding some rustiness on the hinges of verse," heard "Napoleon" on that first night of the course and remembered the lecturer's "upright figure, clear-cut physiognomy, clear elocution . . . resolved self-possession." Crabb Robinson, having attended at least part of the earlier course, heard "Domestic Life" and thought it probably the most liberal lecture ever delivered in Exeter Hall. Carlyle came the same evening and "was seated by the joyful committee," Emerson said, "directly behind me, as I spoke, a thing odious to me."

On the last night at Exeter Hall, Monckton Milnes, the chairman, made some well-intentioned remarks on the visitor from over seas. The audience did their part "by rising *en masse,* hearty cheering, and waving of hats, &c." Emerson did his by coming forward to testify to "the unbroken kindness he had received from a large number of Englishmen and Englishwomen during his stay here—he had not been aware there was so much kindness in the world." He declared "that increased knowledge had increased his respect for the English character." Between the first and second lectures at Exeter Hall, he had gone back to Edwards Street with "The Superlative in Manners and Literature" in order to get ten more guineas towards his passage home. But it was his speech in response to Milnes's compliments at Exeter Hall that actually ended his long, much interrupted British lecture season. It had been almost eight months since his first lecture in Manchester.

The day after the Exeter Hall course ended had been set aside by publisher John Chapman for a kind of final celebration. Doubtless the Carlyles came, as they had promised to do, along with other friends who were to bid Emerson farewell. But Emerson had now postponed his sailing from the 8th of July to the 15th, and Carlyle and he had already planned a trip together to Stonehenge as their own private farewell party. On the 5th of July, Emerson made the rounds of Windsor, Eton, Stoke Poges "& so forth" with some friends, and he spent the 6th at Cambridge. Next day he and Carlyle took the train to Salisbury, discussing the British and the Americans and other subjects along the road. From Salisbury they went by carriage to Amesbury and then on foot to Salisbury Plain. Emerson was struck by the drama of this meeting of "the two talkers one from America one from Scotland" beside this old ark of the race, which had guarded these downs "in a long solitude of millenniums." While larks were soaring and singing overhead in the windy sky, the two friends "counted and measured by paces the biggest stones" and philosophized.

In the preceding October, in Cheyne Row, Emerson had spoken sharply in reply to some talk of Carlyle's about Cromwell. He had informed his friend "that he must not expect that people as old as I could look at Cromwell as he did." Carlyle had "turned quite fiercely" upon him. Emerson told George Phillips, or at least so Phillips said, that Carlyle "rose like a great Norse giant from his chair—and, drawing a line with his finger across the table, said, with terrible fierceness: Then, sir, there is a line of separation between you and me as wide as that, and as deep as the pit." In London, the following spring, Emerson had discovered that his friend was "no idealist in opinions, but a protectionist in political economy, aristocrat in politics, epicure in diet" and that he went for "murder, money, punishment by death, slavery, and all the pretty abominations, tempering them with epigrams." He was obviously a little scornful of this "covenanter-philosophe" and "sans-culotte-aristocrat." Carlyle's scorn for certain opinions and qualities of Emerson was as obvious. It required a great fundamental mutual respect to hold the two men together in spite of the gulf between them; and Mary Ann Evans, the future George Eliot, was not being merely sentimental when she "shed some quite delicious tears" over certain eulogistic remarks of Carlyle's on Emerson and averred that "This is a world worth abiding in while one man can thus venerate and love another."

At Stonehenge old quarrels seemed forgotten and mutual respect, if not love, was strong. Carlyle was "subdued and gentle." He was apologetic about his incorrigible pessimism. "I plant cypresses wherever I go," he said, "and if I am in search of pain, I cannot go wrong." Doubtless the two men felt their impotence in a place that reminded them of the passing of ages and the succession of religions. In the morning they returned to the mound in company with the local antiquary and heard his explanations.

On the way back to Salisbury they visited Wilton and Wilton Hall, "renowned seat of the Earls of Pembroke, a house known to Shakspeare and Massinger, the frequent home of Sir Philip Sidney, where he wrote the Arcadia." They had a brief look at Salisbury Cathedral. At Bishopstoke they were joined by the "omniscient" Arthur Helps whom Emerson had seen in London, and they went on with him to his house at Bishop's Waltham.

It was a rainy Sunday at Bishop's Waltham, with plenty of time for conversation. The Americans were discussed again, and Emerson amused himself by arguing the doctrine of non-government and non-resistance with his companions. Along the road to Winchester there were further questions about America. Emerson hedged and put off his friends as best he could. He felt a stubborn loyalty to America but was conscious of her human immaturity. There, in America, lay Nature, "sleeping, overgrowing, almost conscious, too much by half for man in the picture, and so giving a certain *tristesse*, like the rank vegetation of swamps and forests seen at night, steeped in dews and rains." In the high Allegheny pastures still slept "the great mother, long since driven away from the trim hedge-rows and over-cultivated garden of England."

After the Stonehenge excursion Emerson visited Coventry and a few other towns on his way to the steamer at Liverpool. The Coventry visit of July 12 was for the sake of Charles Bray, author of a book on necessity which Emerson liked and an enthusiastic reader of both Carlyle and Emerson. Mrs. Bray, with scant warning, hastened to get the best room ready, and "the great spirit" was duly entertained at Rosehill with adoring attentions, "though only for a few hours." Mary Ann Evans arrived to honor the author of the essays that had been her friends in the loneliness of Birdgrove. She was delighted with him. He was, she wrote to her friend Sara Hennell, "the first *man* I have ever seen." The conversation at Rosehill was cut short by the coming of Edward Flower, a friend of Americans as he had spent some boyhood years in Illinois. Flower insisted on carrying the Brays, Miss Evans, and Emerson back to Stratford-on-Avon with him. Finally, after returning to Coventry for tea, Emerson got off in the direction of Liverpool. Probably none of the Coventry or Stratford Emersonians remembered him more vividly than did the sharp-eyed Mary Ann Evans. A dozen years later, as she read one of his lectures, she confessed that her heart went out "with venerating gratitude to that mild face." But when she became famous as George Eliot, Emerson was blind to the virtues of her novels.

Near Liverpool, at the Paulets', there was a farewell gathering of many friends, apparently from all parts of the country. July 15 was the day of sailing. Clough, one of the party at the Paulets', stayed with Emerson to the last, even accompanying him aboard the new Royal Mail steamer *Europa*. As they paced the deck, Clough, it is said, complained that with the American's departure the young men of England would be left leader-less, for Carlyle had only led them into the desert and left them there. Emerson agreed, it seems. But his agreement was at least half in jest if, as the story goes, he ended by placing his hand on the head of Clough, declar-ing him thereby ordained bishop of all England and admonishing him to go up and down the country to gather the straying youth together and to shepherd them into the promised land. The story Clough wrote next day to a friend was merely that he left Emerson on the deck of the steamer and saw him pass rapidly down the Mersey on his way home.

Clough's farewell, doubtless a hearty one whatever the circumstances, must have been echoed by many young men in England. Clough's friend Matthew Arnold must have been one of these well-wishers. Some sixteen years later he wrote Emerson that "I look back with great satisfaction to having made your personal acquaintance when you were here . . . and I can never forget the refreshing and quickening effect your writings had upon me at a critical time of my life."

Others certainly welcomed the lecturer's departure with a sigh of relief. The conservative guardians of English church and state had little reason to regret his going, and soon, from some quarters, ripples of satiric laughter were heard at the expense of his young disciples. Even the novelist Charles Kingsley, in spite of his conservative churchman's prejudices a radical sympathizer with the wrongs of the working class, made Alton Locke's brief enthusiasm for the American Mr. Windrush and his "Emersonian Sermon" on "the all-embracing benevolence of the Deity" a warning plain to all: "Socrates and Plato were noble . . . but what were they but the exclusive mystagogues of an enlightened few, like our own Emersons and Strausses, to compare great with small? What gospel have they, or Strauss, or Emerson, for the poor, the suffering, the oppressed? The People's Friend? Where will you find him, but in Jesus of Nazareth?"

For his own part, Emerson had more gains than losses to count. Of the three most important persons he had sought out on his first transatlantic journey—Carlyle, Wordsworth, and Coleridge—two survived, and he had talked with both of them again. To that short list he now added a remark-able number of British, and a few French, intellectuals with whom he had had some first-hand acquaintance. His observations of Britain and France in political and economic turmoil had given him a better understanding of the kind of world in which most persons lived, if it had not fully warranted the jubilant Aunt Mary's judgment, based on reports from abroad, that he was getting "beyond the mists & rainbow visions of transcendental philosophy" and was once more mingling "with the woes & cares of *practical* life." Actually, however, it was not apparent that he had lost any of his old, fundamental beliefs.

In spite of what he thought an admirable steamer and, since the witty Tom Appleton was aboard, an admirable ship's company, Emerson was glad to be nearing home at the rate of nearly twelve knots an hour and was by this time in a mood to resolve never to travel again "until my children force me to." He made a very incomplete inventory of the stock in trade with which he had done the best he could in Europe: "Weak eyes, that will only serve a few hours daily; *no animal spirits,* an immense & fatal negative with our Anglican race. No Greek, no mathematics, no politics,—How the deuce man do you contrive to live & talk with this nervous exigent race? Alas, I know not how they have borne with me so long—, and the oddity & ridicule of it all, is,—given me a literary reputation too, which I make dangerous drafts upon, every day I live." At Concord he might feel less painfully the limitations that had troubled him abroad.

At Concord, Lidian had been unhappy. Perhaps her almost chronic ill health was the result of a serious sickness in her early years, as she believed, or of the harsh "health" disciplines of her girlhood. Perhaps it was partly her unconscious protest against a philosophy that she was unable to live up to. The long absence of her husband and his habitually restrained expression of his regard for her might also conceivably have helped to explain the chest of select homeopathic remedies that Lidian kept at hand. During the last winter she had spent weeks in bed, the doctor coming every day. She had sent word to her husband in England and had put an end to his plan to invite Margaret Fuller to live with them when Margaret should return from Italy. He had written Lidian enough letters, but she had asked in vain for wha: he called "that unwritten letter always due, it seems, always unwritten." He had apologized to her that a photometer could not be a stove. A little later, apparently, she had read over the letters of Ellen Tucker that he had preserved and had praised them. Her feeling about the "precious file" was "just & noble," he had assured her. Even with her children, young Henry Thoreau, and, much of the time, her sister Lucy in the house, she had been lonely, as her letters had let him know.

But he must have known from past experience that her distress was mainly over imaginary ills and that, at the worst, it would cause no break in the love and respect which had from the beginning made their marriage a successful partnership. He had carried her picture with him abroad and had once shown it to friends with the comment that "If any of our family are saved, it will be through her merits." Presumably, as the *Europa* entered Boston Harbor, he worried quite as little about his domestic affairs as about the weather or the condition of the garden.

His voyage ended at a quarter after six on the morning of July 27, 1848. He had told the Brays at Coventry that "his wife insisted on being on the shore to meet him, though they live twenty miles inland." But the early hour of his arrival may have prevented her from greeting him till he reached Concord.

20.

DOWN FROM HIS IVORY TOWER

All duties that the dullards do
In selfish, greedy mood,
The wise should also do, detached,
For universal good.

—*The Bhagavad-gita,* translated by
Arthur W. Ryder

EMERSON, on his return from Europe, was perhaps in as robust health as he had ever known. To some friends, he seemed to have found better health of mind as well as of body because he now made an effort to turn his attention more and more in the direction of "practical" things. Charles Newcomb, guiltless of any great degree of practicality himself, apparently believed that the English visit had helped in both ways. Ellery Channing, a close observer of Emerson over a long period of time, saw that by the end of the 1840s he had become less nervous and sensitive and ate more heartily and was less ideal, less abstract, more interested in men. Channing noticed that Emerson was developed in this direction by his now rapidly maturing children. "But as I have said," he wrote in his journal, "it was after his English visit that he became so much happier and more joyous . . . & also assumed a more public life & habit, as he became more & more a lecturer."

Emerson had never been more than half-hearted about his separation from society, and long before his second transatlantic voyage he had sometimes allowed social pleasures, as well as his acres and his finances, to encroach dangerously upon the time he needed for essays and poems. But now he was plainly less austere and scholarly in his habits. Having drawn heavily upon his stock of original ideas, he repeated more and so did not need to exert the same energy he had put into his earlier works. He retreated but little, or not at all, from his old doctrines but no longer felt called upon to expound them so frequently or so fully. Past middle age, and a little chilled by the temperature on his high platform, he wanted to warm his hands at the common hearth.

He even showed signs of becoming a country squire. On his expanding but still miniature woodlots and fields, the gentleman farmer enjoyed casually overseeing the business of the season. He had now got a foothold beyond the Concord line in the town of Lincoln. Captain Abel Moore's estate yielded up a *"saw-mill-lot"* of nine acres and some rods in 1849; and next year this piece grew by the addition of more than two acres bought from Cyrus and Nathan Stowe. One autumn Emerson agreed to buy half of Cyrus Warren's four-acre lot with an option on the other half, and the next spring he had all of it in his possession.

In the garden and orchard he kept close watch and even performed some of the labor. He took his hoe and water pail and fell upon his sleepy pear trees, determined to make them produce. He broke up the soil, pulled out the weeds and grass, manured and mellowed, watered, pruned, and washed; killed every slug on every leaf; detected and killed the detestable pear worm. His pears and apples pleased him till he went for a look at Edmund Hosmer's trees, three stories high and loaded with fruit. In his diary he wrote a few weeks later:

"August 15. Apricot Plums.

"September 7. We are so late this year that I picked the first musk-melons to-day,—four;—to-day the first ripe tomato: and all the Bartlett pears to ripen in the house. The whole product of my Bartlett at the corner of the garden might count forty-five pears.

"The Green Gages yield every day a supply, and the two purple plum trees.

"To-day, too, we dig seven bushels of excellent Chenangoes.

"12th. To-day tomatoes for the first time on table.

"September is the month of melons: melons last with us till 15th October."

He was an amateur in the original sense of the term. His daughter Edith long remembered how, when she was eight or nine years old, he took her to the orchard and introduced all the trees to her by name. But he soon got something more than poetry from his orchard. In 1851 he paid Edmund Hosmer $3 to carry six barrels of apples to market. By 1855 he had a yield of apples estimated at seventy barrels.

As a practical horticulturist he could not compete with Ephraim Bull. A little way down the Lexington Road the new Concord grape, with its dark oval berries covered with a "thick blue bloom," was by this time being exhibited to curious visitors from all over the United States and was destined to win medals from European royalty. But Emerson was a thrifty farmer. Year after year he sold his little cranberry crop. His fatted hog weighed perhaps 276 pounds at butchering time and the new shoat he bought to feed weighed less than a hundred pounds. He purchased first one cow and then another. The barn, occasionally used to house such human beings as the French-Canadian Colombe and his family, was now put to its proper use. The brindled cow had to be sent to Tuttle's bull and the heifer to Wheeler's. The time came when a "Native" was exhibited in the fourth class of heifers at the local Cattle Show. Horses began to move through the pages of Emerson's account books, bringing with them their accessory bridles and saddles and harnesses, together with chaises, buggy wagons, carryalls, sleighs, and buffalo robes. It was necessary to hire the services of a James Burke or a John Sullivan to help care for all these things.

Abel Adams of Boston still advised about a miscellany of financial details but could not relieve Emerson of much of the responsibility. Scattered family properties or investments were often unproductive or otherwise troublesome. When some complicated transactions in connection with the settlement of the Haskins estate brought Emerson eleven hundred dollars that his mother had owed him, Uncle Ralph Haskins "was very unwilling to see so much good money fall into such bad hands." Emerson went back to Uncle Ralph's counting room "to hear his various proposals" and to agree on an investment that would be convenient to his uncle as well as to himself. He had to pay $25 as the third and fourth assessments on his share of the Northern Telegraph Company. As agent for Charles Lane, his English friend once of Fruitlands, he collected over nine hundred dollars as full payment of a mortgage and bought £195 to send to England.

On the advice of Abel Adams he made unfortunate investments in shares of the Vermont & Canada Railroad and of an Ohio road and anxiously debated the merits of the business with his brother William, and with Adams and Sam Ward. Adams eventually made good the loss by paying the expenses of Emerson's son through college; and the shares at length revived and became saleable. A Fitchburg Rail Road engine had set fire to the timber on the *"island lot,"* and Emerson wanted $50 as damages. The company finally agreed to cut the wood and pay him as much for it as it was worth before the fire. He paid assessments on new shares in the railroad and got dividends on old ones. In 1853 he sold his twelve shares.

Ellery Channing's opinion that Emerson was drawn out of his philosopher's corner by his children was correct. When they carried a May basket to Mr. Minott, a neighbor they habitually consulted about the weather on festival occasions, Emerson contributed the accompanying poetical address describing the flowers and not omitting some mention of the prowess of the weather prophet. His administration of household discipline was indirect and frequently humorous but extremely effective. He used to follow his children through the nursery door and would croon them an improvised lulling song that was fanciful or absurd. He usually began it with "Goodnight to Mr Minot's cow, Goodnight to Mr Minot's barn." His youthfulness and his poetic moods impressed his children. Edith remembered that she "entirely recognized Father as a poet," and connected his blue eyes and fresh appearance with Concord's skies, woods, and Walden Pond. She "had an idea that Waldo & Walden had some relation to each other." Emerson brought home fireworks from Boston for the Fourth of July. When Ellen, then fourteen years old, was sent off to boarding school at the western Massachusetts town of Lenox, he was her correspondent and adviser on educational matters. He helped Edith and Edward with their Latin lessons. Sometimes he enlivened such studies by repeating choice passages of poetry. Doubtless the trouble he had with his eyes helped to turn him often from his books to the children, though it was not till 1852 that he bought his first pair of glasses.

Lidian, still unflagging in her interest in domestic matters, had outlived her earlier enthusiasm for philosophical speculation dear to the heart of her husband. She joined his mother in support of the Christianity that had been superseded by Transcendentalism in his study. When she had described herself during her husband's British lecture tour as "a Christian" and "a Swedenborgian," she had certainly been serious about at least the first epithet. She exhorted her elder daughter to be a Christian and so enjoy the inner peace she herself had in spite of many infirmities. She was doing her best to transform Emerson himself into a practical man, though she found him hard to budge from his old ways. As for the church, he took formal legal action in the early 1850s to separate himself even from the parish. Yet he went on paying what he pleased toward the support of the minister, and Lidian's efforts to tame him and make him an acceptable member of society were not without some slight success.

He used to come "every day to sit for a while with his mother." She was never reconciled to his heresy and used to walk with others of the household to the Unitarian Church "every Sunday morning," or she would have the communion service read to her at home and would ask that her grandchildren be present. Yet she had lived in his house contentedly almost the whole time since his marriage. Even after she broke her hip in 1851 she would sometimes quietly appear among the family. Arthur Clough, beginning his New England residence of some months with a visit to Concord, found "Old Mrs. Emerson, called 'Madam' . . . sitting in the room —a small, benevolent-looking, large-eyed old lady, the original of Ralph Waldo." But she kept to her own room more than ever and needed more attention than her nurse, Charlotte Haskins, could give her. Emerson did his part for her with exemplary loyalty until November, 1853, when she had "lived eighty four years, yet not a day too long, & died suddenly &

unexpectedly, at the last." He told his brother William that there was now "one less room to go to for sure society in the house."

He was more often with William, in New York or at Concord, and the regular flow of correspondence between the two on business and on family matters continued year after year. Once the brothers went on a journey to Cape Cod, and Emerson carried home some botanical specimens. "Henry Thoreau," he said, "could hardly suppress his indignation that I should bring him a berry he had not seen." Bulkeley still required looking after as he was moved from place to place. Aunt Mary kept mainly on the outskirts of the family but sometimes had to have financial advice. She was still apt to lose control of her temper, and once, when she had made a descent upon William's household, she "outraged all feeling and propriety." She would rediscover some old writing of Waldo's and praise it. She singled out an article of his in *The Dial* because it was marked "by the spear of Uriel." Aunt Sarah Alden Ripley, now a widow living in Concord, must have had claims on his time. He more than once came to the aid of Lidian's brother, Doctor Charles Jackson, and was always a firm believer in Jackson's right to the honor of being the discoverer of the surgical use of sulphuric ether, the first widely used anesthetic. When Jackson, a scientist with more than one specialty, had to fight politicians in order to keep his place as geological surveyor of United States mineral lands in Michigan, Emerson turned to his own political friends for help and found his time "sadly occupied for a fortnight" with the affair.

Nathaniel Hawthorne, purchasing Hillside in 1852, partly of Emerson, returned to Concord for a year or so. But as far as Emerson was concerned the chief event connected with Hawthorne during this second and briefest period of his residence was the farewell dinner given to him in Boston before he set sail for Liverpool to be the American consul there. Thoreau, too, was less profitable than in earlier days. To Emerson, unable to discover positive results of Thoreau's devoted study of nature, he sometimes seemed "like the wood-god who solicits the wandering poet and draws him into antres vast and desarts idle, and bereaves him of his memory, and leaves him naked, plaiting vines and with twigs in his hand." "As for taking Thoreau's arm," Emerson declared, "I should as soon take the arm of an elm tree." When Thoreau's first book, long since written, was finally published, he refused to review it, excusing himself on the ground that he and Thoreau were of the same clan and parish. Yet he continued to prize the man who gave him "in flesh and blood and pertinacious Saxon belief," as he said, "my own ethics." Even if Thoreau, lacking ambition, sometimes seemed most successful as captain of a huckleberry party, he had unique values. By the early summer of 1855 the Emersons were alarmed by the increasing feebleness of his health and urged him to spend a week in their home.

Alcott, though not now living in Concord, was a frequent visitor there and absorbed untold days of Emerson's time in conversation. According to Emerson, though his good nature seemed to invite rats and mice to make their nests in him, Alcott was "the most refined and the most advanced soul" in New England and made Plato seem real. He would listen to the reading of the introductory chapter to *Representative Men,* then still in manuscript, or would discuss the chapters on Plato, Goethe, and Swedenborg. On a fair day he and Emerson might walk and talk as far as Walden Pond. On a rainy day they merely talked, ideas pouring inside the house, rain pouring outside. Emerson followed the fortunes of the public "conversations," or, more properly, monologues, that Alcott delightedly gave, and in October of 1853 he helped him plan his first Western tour and even paid his fare as far as Cincinnati. In 1855 he blocked Alcott's plans for a return to England "in search of his pedigree" and persuaded him to accept a subscription for the support of the Alcott family instead of passage money. Emerson managed the subscription and paid a part of it out of his own pocket.

Within a few weeks after coming back from his foreign travels, Emerson was, as he said, going over Concord twice a week with Ellery Channing. Channing, rather than Thoreau, was now and for years his chief companion on long walks. The peripatetic conversations contributed to Ellery's manuscript "Country Walking." Emerson encouraged the writing of this with a promise, it seems, of $20 for each of five monthly parts if no publisher would buy them, and no publisher did.

Meantime, in March of 1849, Emerson had met with twenty-nine other men at the Alcott home in Boston to plan the promotion of general sociability in eastern Massachusetts through a large and loose-jointed Town and Country Club. In a few weeks there were 120 members, partly because of his zeal. Though he soon wanted either to reduce the membership or to form a new and smaller club, he at first saw no reason why there should not be five or six hundred. He prodded his friends, reminding them of their duty to attend the meetings. A projected *Town and Country Magazine,* informally connected with the club, was to have Lowell as its editor and Emerson, Lowell, and Hawthorne as contributors—or so Alcott dreamed —but nothing came of it. What did come out of the short-lived club was doubtless, for Emerson, a marked access of sociability and some practice in the conventional gestures that went along with it. It seems to have been about this time of his first enthusiasm over clubs that, in his determination to be sociable, he took to smoking cigars. Now and later he smoked them very temperately and in a kind of tentative manner; but a philosopher, and particularly a Transcendentalist, with a cigar in his mouth was to some persons a disturbing spectacle. Henry James, the novelist's father, was horrified and seems to have labored under the mistaken notion that Emerson was a helpless innocent astray in a bad world.

Politics helped draw Emerson out of philosophic retirement. The "dismal" election of 1848 brought the Whigs, "*first-rate* in opposition, but not so good in government," into power under President Zachary Taylor. They had elected him in spite of their dislike of him. Nothing was settled. Emerson obviously had no political panacea in mind, but he was drifting toward the Free Soil Party if he had not already joined it at the polls. Though he soon had moments of admiration for even the extremist William Lloyd Garrison, he was not blind to the man's narrowness and imperviousness to other ideas than his own. Garrison neighed like a horse when any new view was suggested to him, Emerson said, "as when I told him that the *fate*-element in the negro question he had never considered." But when the Compromise of 1850 gave slavery a long push forward, Emerson found himself nearer Garrison's camp.

He was disgusted at the letter of commendation sent to Daniel Webster with eight hundred signatures collected in Boston. March 7, the day of Webster's speech for the Union, a speech that seemed an insult to the antislavery men, was to be kept at the Emerson home as an anniversary of infamy. With the final enactment of the Fugitive Slave Law, an effective implementing of the right of the South to get back its runaway slaves from the North, Emerson lost his respect for the authority of his government. He was soon one of the implacables on the side of Charles Sumner. He even made tentative attempts to give literary aid to the extremists. A couple of days before the Fugitive Slave Law was passed, he told Edmund Quincy, now an antislavery propagandist, that he was "never more at a loss than when asked to send a scrap for an annual." Some two weeks later Quincy suggested to him that the new law might prove a tonic to the muse. It did, and Emerson sent several contributions in time for printing in *The Liberty Bell.*

During the following year his temperature rose. He was more bitter than Whittier. Though the Quaker poet had promptly pronounced Webster fallen and lost and dishonored, he had also asked in "Ichabod" that the reverence of old days be paid to the great orator's dead fame. Emerson was full of reproaches. "The word *liberty* in the mouth of Mr. Webster," he said, "sounds like the word *love* in the mouth of a courtezan." He turned more sharply than ever before upon Edward Everett. Everett, he said, "advises pathetically a reverence for the Union." For his own part, he was convinced that there could never be peace and a real Union while this devilish slavery, seed of war, was in American soil. "Root it out," he wrote in his journal, "burn it up, pay for the damage, and let us have done with it."

This was his mood when, on May 3, 1851, he addressed the citizens of Concord on the Fugitive Slave Law. In both geography and patriotism, his address was narrowed down almost to Massachusetts. It put the South aside as essentially a separate nation. What it lacked in liberality, it made up for in intensity. Infamy was in the air, Emerson warned his fellow townsmen. Who could have believed that a hundred guns would be fired in Boston to celebrate the passage of the Fugitive Slave Law? There had been a political betrayal, and Webster was the arch betrayer. "All the drops of his blood," Emerson declared, "have eyes that look downward." But again there was a note of wisdom. As for action, the principal thing to do was to follow the example of the British in the West Indies and buy the slaves. There must have been by this time a good deal of loose talk about the expense of such a move, and estimates were evidently going up by leaps and bounds. But the increasing cost did not daunt Emerson. If it was going to be two thousand million dollars, as was now said, it would be paid more enthusiastically than any other contribution had ever been, he was confident. A chimney tax would be paid. People would give up their coaches and wine and watches, and the churches would melt their plate. Everybody would help "to dig away this accursed mountain of sorrow once and forever out of the world."

Emerson took to the campaign platform, repeating the speech at various places in Middlesex County in support of John Palfrey, once the divinity dean at Harvard but now out for election as congressman on the Free Soil ticket. At Cambridge "students from Harvard College did what they could to disturb the audience and insult the speaker, by hisses and groans, interspersed with cheers for Webster, Clay, Fillmore, Everett, and 'Old Harvard.' " But whether the disturbers were Southerners and their Northern sympathizers, as was asserted and denied, or were mere rowdies conveniently pretending to espouse the cause of the South, Emerson stood with perfect composure till the hubbub died down and then resumed where he had left off, as if nothing had happened. The interruption gave added weight to his words.

In his journal he called the Fugitive Slave Law a "filthy enactment" and swore, "I will not obey it, by God." He gave a little money for a fugitive slave sponsored by Henry Thoreau's mother, it seems. In November he wrote to Anna Barker Ward that he made it a point of conscience to cast his vote on the second Monday of that month whenever it came round. This November he even received one stray vote in the Concord election as undeclared candidate for representative in the General Court, but Sam Staples was triumphantly elected. Emerson began to be urged to enter more fully into the campaign. His friend Furness and Lucretia Mott, the tireless Quaker, were on a committee that asked him in vain to be a lecturer in the antislavery course at Philadelphia. Wendell Phillips and the Vigilance Committee of Boston hoped he would make an address at Tremont Temple on the anniversary of the celebrated Sims's forced return to slavery under the authority of the Fugitive Slave Law.

Emerson bought some of the one-dollar Hungarian bonds when, in the spring of 1852, Kossuth, the leader in the fight for Hungary's liberty, came to Concord. Concord put her best foot forward. Townsman Wheildon's Gobelin tapestry of "Fame" was placed against the wall over the platform in the Town Hall. Emerson, with all his family present to encourage him, was there to make the address of welcome. He warned the visitor of the danger of his growing popularity, since "everything great and excellent in the world is in minorities," but welcomed him as the man of fate, as the first soldier of freedom in that age, and as a republican better entitled to interpret George Washington than were "those who live idly in the city called after his name." He had some difficulty understanding Kossuth's speech. When the Hungarian appealed to him for the English word for Österreich, he suggested ostrich; but Kossuth cried, "No, no!" and somebody realized it was Austria that was wanted.

A few months later Emerson was waking at night and bemoaning the smallness of his part in the antislavery fight. He seemed to be almost at the point of deserting what he had religiously guarded as the special sphere of a scholar and thinker. "But then," he wrote, "in hours of sanity, I recover myself . . . I have quite other slaves to free than those negroes, to wit, imprisoned spirits, imprisoned thoughts . . . which, important to the republic of Man, have no watchman, or lover, or defender, but I."

On October 24 he was at Plymouth, looking across the hazy water toward Marshfield and thinking that Webster must have died. Webster had died at three o'clock that morning. Emerson, again in a relenting mood, thought that "Nature had not in our days, or not since Napoleon, cut out such a masterpiece." He must have promptly refused the Boston petition signed by friends who wanted to hear him speak on the character of Webster. He was already starting out on a long lecture tour through the state of New York and the West when Lucretia Mott and others again begged him for an address at the Pennsylvania Anti-Slavery Fair in December. Even if he wished to accept this invitation, he could not. Periodically the lyceum platform almost isolated him from political controversy. Though he had read by early August the circular letter his friend Arthur Helps had written on *Uncle Tom's Cabin,* he apparently did not get seriously into Mrs. Stowe's book till some five or six months later. But his views on the slavery question had been spoken in no uncertain terms. Near the end of 1852, Arthur Clough, a fresh observer of the American scene, wrote home to England that Emerson favored purchasing the slaves and was politically a Free Soiler, "which only means that you won't have any new Slave States." This was true as far as it went but understated Emerson's abolitionism.

The Kansas-Nebraska Bill of 1854, annulling the long-established safeguards of the Missouri Compromise, was hardly before the Senate when Emerson began to denounce it privately. But his chief public effort during the long debate on the new bill was his New York address on the Fugitive Slave Law. The occasion was the fourth anniversary of Webster's seventh of March speech, a momentous plea for the adoption of Henry Clay's truce with slavery. The speech in which Emerson now measured his political wits against Webster's last great effort was not of the fighting kind he had made at Concord, but more philosophical and calm. He began with an apology for leaving a scholar's business for politics. He did not fail to remind his hearers that self-reliance was the true salvation. But his speech was mainly a call to political action through organization. In a burst of optimism, he predicted a general rush to join the Anti-slavery Society.

At home the following June, he was paying the printer for "Nebraska" posters, presumably already used in protest against the hated bill that had now become law. On the Fourth of July, Lidian, having heard that there was to be a celebration that day, wanted her family's disapproval known, and, with her husband's consent, draped the gates as if for a funeral. It was presumably about this time that Emerson began to be active, with Samuel Hoar and others, in the Concord committee of correspondence. He was thus helping prepare the way for a new Republican Party, a party to be formed for the avowed purpose of putting an end to the extension of slavery. He continued sporadically to hit hard at slavery from the platform, but he would have agreed with Convers Francis that he had little popular success as a political speaker. His antislavery discourses were, he told William Furness, the worst in the country—only less bad than slavery. He seemed to lose his strength when he abandoned his customary post as a detached observer.

While black slaves wanted freedom, white women were fighting for their own rights and were enlisting on their side every prominent male they could persuade. In 1850, some two years after the feminine declaration of independence was made at Seneca Falls in the neighboring state of New York, the women of Massachusetts tried to prod Emerson into supporting their convention at Worcester. They must have remembered that in *The Dial* under his editorship Margaret Fuller had first published the plea that grew into her book called *Woman in the Nineteenth Century*. But the truth was that he saw the contradictory aspects of feminism. He had made an English translation of the *Vita nuova* and had written an essay on love. He did not care to see the old courtly and romantic ideals of womanhood hastily abandoned for a dubious modern substitute. His imagination balked when he pictured women with masculine aggressiveness wrangling in public. Yet he would not oppose any striving for human liberty and equality.

He wrote Paulina Davis, one of the Worcester convention leaders: "If women feel wronged, then they are wronged. But the mode of obtaining a redress, namely, a public convention called by women is not very agreeable to me, and the things to be agitated for do not seem to me the best. Perhaps I am superstitious & traditional, but whilst I should vote for every franchise for women,—vote that they should hold property, and vote, yes & be eligible to all offices as men—whilst I should vote thus, if women asked, or if men denied . . . these things, I should not wish women to wish political functions, nor, if granted assume them." The following year he begged off again. In 1853 Wendell Phillips urged him in vain to appear as one of the first signers of a petition demanding action on women's rights by the Massachusetts constitutional convention. In future years he weakened in his already half-hearted resistance to the feminine crusaders. But in 1855, when he read his lecture "Woman" before the Woman's Rights Convention in Boston, he still hoped that women would not after all wish an equal share with men in public affairs.

He was open-minded about schemes for reform but distrusted organized reformers. His dislike of propaganda, as well as his ignorance of naval discipline, might have explained his apparent refusal of an invitation to lecture on flogging a few weeks after Herman Melville had published illuminating comments on that subject in *White Jacket*. He was not entirely ignorant of new and ominous theories of class struggle. By late 1852 he had some acquaintance with the early writings of Karl Marx, who was already sending articles from London to Horace Greeley's paper in New York and had other means of reaching the English-speaking world. In a brief passage credited in his journals to Marx, Emerson found the inspiration for two lines at the end of a detached quatrain. He seemed to contrast the self-reliant individual with the supine classes or races of men who were the easy victims of fate:

WITH the key of the secret he marches faster,
From strength to strength, and for night brings day;
While classes or tribes, too weak to master
The flowing conditions of life, give way.

Emerson was obviously not the poet laureate of the new social revolution. He had long observed various theories of communism in action, and, though they mostly went no more than halfway, his individualism had revolted against them. He probably did not know much of Karl Marx's doctrines. If he did, he was still a rank individualist. Marching in lock step would have been intolerable to him. He was also an idealist, not a materialist. Certainly he earned no future laurels as even the most unbellicose of fellow travelers.

In these years he felt some steady literary loyalties but also had a good many disenchantments. His eyes probably limited him more now than they had done since the early days of his Concord life, but he often had other eyes to use. During her long stay in his home in 1851–1852 his cousin Charlotte Haskins read "quite a number of books" to him "while he would sit with his back to the light," making "pithy and pleasing comments." He had already declared himself uninterested in Germany since Goethe's death; and soon he would not read Fichte, Kant, Schelling, and Hegel, for they had failed, he was convinced, as purveyors of truth. But while he more and more lost patience with the imposing logic of Western thought, his affection for the ejaculatory, intuitive Oriental philosophies grew. When his *Bhagavadgita* was worn out by the many friends he lent it to, he refused to sponsor an American edition of it, because the old Hindu song seemed too sacred to offer to unprepared readers.

The contemporary English and American literary scene did not move him greatly until Walt Whitman appeared. He was soon weary of *Vanity Fair* and must have agreed with Elizabeth Hoar in putting Thackeray down as a man who despaired of the heart and accepted London. It was true that he took much pleasure in Charlotte Brontë's *Shirley*. In his journal he neatly summarized Tennyson's *In Memoriam* as "the commonplaces of condolence among good Unitarians in the first week of mourning." He thought Browning ingenious, yet Browning seemed to make him return with some satisfaction to Tennyson. Tennyson, he said, was "the more public soul" and walked "on the ecliptic." He had a growing affection for Longfellow as a person but not as poet or novelist, though he managed to bring up for him the astonishing opinion that *Kavanagh* was the best sketch so far in the direction of the American novel. He more understandably thought that in *The Song of Hiawatha* Longfellow had not done his whole duty by the unintellectual Indians, for they required that the poet should find them brains in order to make them worth while. His chief enthusiasm was for a very different book of the same year, 1855—Whitman's *Leaves of Grass*.

Emerson probably had his gift copy of *Leaves of Grass* by about the Fourth of July, the date of publication. The thin paper-bound quarto must at first glance have struck him as likely to turn out to be another cheap bundle of verses, as feeble as the many he had wearily examined year after year in his vain search for the American poet. But on July 10 he wrote to his friend Sam Ward that it was "so extraordinary for its oriental largeness of generalization, an American Buddh,—that I must send it to you, & pray you to look it over." The prose preface resembled a little some of the college orations Emerson had heard on the future greatness of America and her literature, but this was different because of its sustained intensity. Some of its ideas closely resembled those of his own essays. He must have read with complete recognition many a line in the long initial poem:

> I loafe and invite my soul . . .
> Apart from the pulling and hauling stands what I am . . .
> I know I am august,
> I do not trouble my spirit to vindicate itself or be understood,
> I see that the elementary laws never apologize . . .
> Magnifying and applying come I,
> Outbidding at the start the old cautious hucksters . . .
> Taking myself the exact dimensions of Jehovah and laying them away,
> Lithographing Kronos and Zeus his son, and Hercules his grandson . . .
> Honestly taking them all for what they are worth, and not a cent more,
> Admitting they were alive and did the work of their day . . .

Whitman, emulating the ideal poet of his preface, professed to love all forms of human life; allowed many "long dumb voices," of slaves, of prostitutes, of deformed persons, to speak through his fresh rhythms. When he identified himself with the hounded slave, flagging in the race and leaning against the fence, blowing and covered with sweat mingled with blood, he was pronouncing in verse his own address on the Fugitive Slave Law. As for God, he declared that words could not say "how much I am at peace about God and about death." Emerson must at once have recognized a kindred spirit in the poet of *Leaves of Grass,* an oracular and ejaculatory writer, a seer, and, in some respects, a Transcendentalist. But he must also have seen that if Whitman was a Transcendentalist he was one who had turned half realist and was the poet of both body and soul.

Emerson was delighted, and on July 21 he wrote a letter calling the book America's "most extraordinary piece of wit & wisdom," greeting its author "at the beginning of a great career," and declaring a desire to see him. Charles Norton thought the new book partly superbly graphic, partly intolerably coarse, but told Lowell that it was no wonder Emerson liked it. Its author, he much too simply explained it, had read *The Dial* and *Nature* and was a combination of Concord philosopher and New York fireman. At the end of September, Emerson informed his friend Cabot that "the strange" Whitman seemed "a Mirabeau of a man, with such insight & equal expression, but hurt by hard life & too animal experience." He still thought *Leaves of Grass* "the American poem." He asked Furness, his old schoolmate, whether he had read "that wonderful book—with all its formlessness & faults." He sent out more inquiries and more praise. His letters and his talk with friends were perhaps chiefly responsible for the movement of a thin column of the curious in the direction of New York.

But though readers did not object violently to *Leaves of Grass* because of its magnificent glorification of self-reliance, of the virtues of universal brotherhood, and of a future democratic America, complaints soon began to reach Emerson about the frank, fleshly passages. People marveled at his sponsoring a book so well stocked with repulsively honest verses on sex. A Philadelphia intellectual who had examined the "profane & obscene" *Leaves of Grass* and made up his mind that the author was a pretentious ass without decency, was amazed to be confronted with a newspaper clipping containing what purported to be a letter of respect and gratitude to that same author over the name of one whom, of all American thinkers, he most revered. He wanted Emerson to back him up in his indignant refusal to believe that the letter in question could be more than a malignant jest. But it was no jest. As Emerson had told Samuel Longfellow, Whitman had "done a strange rude thing in printing in the Tribune . . . my letter of thanks for his book." By now the letter was no doubt available in all corners of the country. To help it along, Whitman had it printed as a leaflet. He was, as he saw it, doing his part in the legitimate fight of a book for the world. In the second edition of *Leaves of Grass* he again printed the letter, much to Emerson's astonishment. He even had a telling excerpt stamped on the back of the volume.

The strong medicine of *Leaves of Grass* did not much upset such liberals as Alcott and Thoreau, and they soon visited Whitman. Moncure Conway, a young radical just then in his Emersonian phase, had, according to one story, taken fire when Emerson had first spoken to him of the book, had read it on his way to New York next day, had called on Whitman in Brooklyn, and had come away delighted. But even Emerson experienced moments of regret. After receiving complaints from friends who had tried reading the poems aloud in the presence of ladies, he told Conway that if he had known his letter would be printed he might have made some deductions from his praise; and he confessed that "There are parts of the book where I hold my nose as I read. One must not be too squeamish," he commented, "when a chemist brings him to a mass of filth and says, 'See, the great laws are at work here also;' but it is a fine art if he can deodorize his illustration. However, I do not fear that any man who has eyes in his head will fail to see the genius in these poems."

It may have been on December 11, 1855, that Emerson first had Whitman to dinner at a New York hotel. He seems to have been only mildly surprised when his poet shouted for a tin mug for his beer. Later, Whitman took him to "a noisy fire-engine society," a new experience for the Concord man. But the friendship, uneasy as it was, lasted for many years. Whatever halfway retractions he might make in old age, Emerson had, after a long search, found his American poet. Whitman, however varied his stories of his relation to Emerson might be, respected the essayist whose influence on him was important when the first *Leaves of Grass* was about to take form. That influence was most convincingly described in Whitman's statement to John Trowbridge in 1860, "I was simmering, simmering, simmering; Emerson brought me to a boil."

During the seven years following his return from England, Emerson published little but some lectures and essays that had been long known to his listening or reading public and some biographical writing he had done in collaboration with friends. The small miscellany called *Nature; Addresses, and Lectures,* appearing in September of 1849, set the pedestrian pace of his achievement for this heptad of years. A new edition of the second series of *Essays* followed, and a book he now printed for the first time, *Representative Men,* a series of lectures already well known in the United States and in Britain. Though these lectures were old, he had held them back for revision. Cutting down the mechanical work as much as possible now, he had had an amanuensis make a fair copy. In the last days of December a few friends began to receive copies of the volume and by the first of January it was on sale. The title page bore the date 1850.

At the outset Emerson made it clear that he was attempting to institute no cult of heroes but was using great men simply as convenient representatives of things and ideas. Significantly, he went on to underscore the self-reliance that was God-reliance. The great might be helpful in saving us from our contemporaries but could not substitute their genius for ours. Emerson must have consciously rebelled against Carlyle's less democratic view of great men in the lectures *On Heroes*. He honored the great man for standing firm on legs of iron but honored him more when he could abolish himself by letting in the element of reason, the universal mind.

Plato, conveniently representing philosophy and connecting Asia and Europe, posed in his person the always unresolved contradiction between unity, the Oriental conception of the world, and diversity, the Occidental conception. Plato was what the American lecturer must have known he himself was—"a balanced soul" and "a man who could see two sides of a thing." Emerson also found in Plato a companion believer in the doctrine of inspiration—the Over-soul was once more on the march. The Yankee Transcendentalist endowed the Greek philosopher with a degree of mysticism much like his own. He excused Plato's indignation against popular government as expressing "personal exasperation." He conceded that Plato had the fault of being always literary and without the vital authority which the screams of the prophets possessed, and that another of his weaknesses was his lack of system. "He attempted a theory of the universe, and his theory is not complete or self-evident." No one could ever exactly tell what Platonism was. Plato had undoubtedly failed. The enigma of existence still remained. Yet all these detractions sounded as much like an apology for Emerson himself as for Plato, and Emerson could easily forgive the faults he listed. Many writers might have produced a more scholarly and accurate treatise on Plato, but few could have absorbed his spirit so completely as Emerson had done.

In print the lecture on Swedenborg still unhesitatingly classed the great religionist as a mystic, still praised his vision of the universality of every natural law and of its correspondence to spiritual law, but still lamented his "theological bias." That bias was pervasive in the thought of Swedenborg and "fatally narrowed his interpretation of nature." It ended by making him ridiculous in spite of his great genius.

Emerson was not happy about this chapter. He had felt that Jesus was the representative mystic he ought to sketch, and later he envied Renan his subject. Had he chosen Jesus, he would undoubtedly have had, in his view, a purer mystic than Swedenborg, with less of the tough wrapping of theological determination to cut away. But his interpretation of Jesus, he knew from experience, would have aroused antagonisms for which he would have been bracing himself as he wrote. Such a sketch of Jesus as he would have wished to make would have required, as he said, "great gifts,—steadiest insight and perfect temper; else, the consciousness of want of sympathy in the audience would make one petulant or sore, in spite of himself."

Placing the lecture on Montaigne alongside that on Swedenborg, Emerson managed to show himself in these contrasting lights. He stood halfway between the Swedish religionist and the French skeptic, but to the skeptical Montaigne he felt an older and more settled loyalty. He remembered his first acquaintance with him and the delight he had had in the discovery of so much wisdom. "It seemed to me," he said, "as if I had myself written the book, in some former life, so sincerely it spoke to my thought and experience." His liking for the essays had not greatly changed since his youth. He still found Montaigne's frankness and honesty irresistible and was obviously troubled by no doubts regarding the Frenchman's sincerity, even in the extraordinary apology of Raimond de Sebonde. The theory of skepticism challenged the Transcendental sayer of Yes, for he was aware how important skepticism had been in his own intellectual growth. When he wrote on Montaigne as its exemplar, he quickly branched off into a treatise of his own on it. But though he made the most liberal allowances for its function he came back in the end to a strong affirmation of his private faith. Skepticism was lost, at last, he said, "in the moral sentiment, which never forfeits its supremacy."

Though Emerson took it for granted that Shakespeare was the greatest of all his representative men, he had the least success in judging him by Transcendental standards. He saw more clearly than Carlyle that Shakespeare triumphed in not being original at all in the narrow sense; and he seems to have understood better the great Elizabethan's place in the development of English drama. But at one point his difference from Carlyle was more significant. Carlyle thought it better that Shakespeare, "everyway an unconscious man, was *conscious* of no Heavenly message." Emerson dissented, declaring that Shakespeare had ended as a mere master of the revels to mankind—"never took the step which seemed inevitable to such genius, namely to explore the virtue which resides in these symbols and imparts this power." It was an old complaint. "The world," Emerson made his final reservation, "still wants its poet-priest . . ." He meant that Shakespeare lacked a full measure of the great Transcendental faculty of reason, spiritual intuition. Yet he saw that this poet possessed in superlative measure its supposedly attendant faculty of genius. Shakespeare was puzzling.

Both Napoleon and Goethe suffered from somewhat the same deficiency as Shakespeare's but with more disastrous results. The downfall of Napoleon was remembered as an exciting event of boyhood days. His nephew Murat had been Emerson's friend. The great emperor had always seemed to possess a kind of magic. But now he was put down as "no hero, in the high sense," useful as the brilliant, thoroughly modern representative of successful mediocrity and as showing what the powers of intellect could do divorced from conscience. Goethe, though his magnitude suffered less diminution in this new scale of values, was, in some respects, Napoleon's counterpart in the literary world. Equally modern, equally successful, he also spoke for the spirit of the age. While he represented well in his own mind the German tendency to introspection and the study of the inner life, he failed to ascend to the highest grounds of genius, for he had not worshiped the highest unity. He preached the doctrine that man existed for culture. But, though a lawgiver of art, he was not an artist. He was fragmentary, a writer of occasional poems and an encyclopedia of sentences. Yet both he and Napoleon, two stern realists, effectively set the ax of modernity to the root of the decaying tree of cant and pretense.

Representative Men supplied little new incitement to the controversy over Emerson. He was now commonly thought to be past the peak of his performance. From now on he heard the refrain that his latest book, whatever it was, had "less vigor and originality than the others." "The fate of my books," he jested, "is like the impression of my face. My acquaintances, as long back as I can remember, have always said, 'Seems to me you look a little thinner than when I saw you last.' " J. J. Garth Wilkinson, the Swedenborgian scholar, admitted that it would require "some tough work at long arts and sciences" to refute the lecture on Swedenborg. But Froude, a man Emerson had admired at Oxford, was sharp in the not very intelligent comment he wrote for *The Eclectic Review.* He wanted Emerson to keep more to his own side of the Atlantic and thought "he would be doing us in Europe more real good by a great deal, if he would tell us something of the backwoodsmen in Kentucky and Ohio." The book was quickly pirated and put on sale at railroad stations in England at a shilling, and its name circulated through the papers as an appropriate household word, Carlyle reported. Carlyle himself thought the lectures excellent line engravings. As he read each lecture, he gave warm assent till he neared the end of it, when he usually had to dissent. He did not need to say why. At the end of an essay or lecture of Emerson's one generally found the most optimistic, Transcendental generalizations.

In France, Montégut, still firmly fixed in his prejudice against a leveling kind of democracy, welcomed Emerson again as a hater of the vulgar and a lover of individual greatness. He now discovered in him both the mystic and the skeptic. He saw the contrast between Carlyle's violent and angry rebellion against things as they were and Emerson's imperturbable confidence in the eternal order. But Montégut deserted Emerson for Carlyle when he compared the ideas of the two regarding great men. Emerson's great man, in contrast with Carlyle's, was the man of easy grandeur. But easy grandeur was hardly admissible since Christianity had recognized suffering and the virtue of sacrifice.

As co-author and co-editor of the *Memoirs of Margaret Fuller Ossoli*, Emerson was qualified by acquaintance, understanding, and sympathy. Margaret had been a familiar figure in Concord, where she had continued "for years," as he said, to come "once in three or four months, to spend a week or a fortnight with us." Toward the end of her life he was in correspondence with her across the Atlantic and was offering to help her find a publisher for her history of the ill-fated Roman revolution she had witnessed. In July of 1850, when the *Elizabeth* ended her homeward voyage from Italy on the beach of Fire Island, Emerson sent Thoreau to the scene of the wreck, supplying him with funds. Thoreau, in turn, shared the funds with Ellery Channing, who went out from New York. The "flame tormented by the wind," as Emerson aptly called Margaret, was quenched in salt water as the storm lashed Fire Island and the Long Island shore. Thoreau returned to Concord to read his notes to the assembled Emersons and Elizabeth Hoar. Lidian's faith was shaken when she tried to understand how a tender Providence could have ordered the loss of a whole family, for Margaret's husband and child had died with her.

Emerson's first decision was that Margaret had not been an important enough figure to require a detailed memoir. But Horace Greeley, editor of the paper on which she had worked in New York, and William H. Channing, an early friend of hers, insisted that something be done and that Emerson must do it. Channing went so far as to name both the author and the book. According to him the title was to be *Margaret and her Friends*. Channing and Emerson came together for consultation; then Sam Ward, important in the early life of Margaret, was drawn in temporarily, only to drop out after a few weeks. Though Emerson was soon busy collecting Margaret's correspondence and other papers, he was still doubtful whether he would go on with the memoir. Many personalities were involved, and Margaret had been personal. Emerson must have suspected that he had long underestimated the appeal of her personality. Now, or soon, a story was being told of how the poet Mickiewicz had wanted a divorce in order to marry Margaret and how Mazzini had offered to marry her. When Emerson expressed surprise at these things and at the tale that "Ossoli a young nobleman prosecuted his suit against all denial, & married her," Elizabeth Hoar replied, "It is not at all wonderful. Any one of those fine girls of sixteen she had known here, would have married her, if she had been a man. For she understood them." New light was sought abroad, but misfortune dogged Emerson's attempts to get reminiscences from Browning and Mazzini. Within a year or so, however, the project had been definitely decided upon. It had been settled finally that the memoir should have a triumvirate of authors and editors—Emerson, William H. Channing, and James Freeman Clarke—together with various informal collaborators.

The two volumes of the Boston edition of *Memoirs of Margaret Fuller Ossoli* were out early in February, 1852. It was true, as Emerson told George Bradford, that the *Boston Post* and the *Boston Daily Advertiser* actually professed admiration. The *Post* "never saw a production in which there was less tawdriness or fulsomeness of praise" and thought the collaborators succeeded in giving a clear and just idea of Margaret. This was intelligent criticism. If the book made little attempt to tell a connected story of Margaret's life, it gave the reader a rich confusion of excerpts from her letters and journals and from other pertinent documents, together with frank and incisive comments, principally by Emerson, on her character and thought. It could not clear up the history of such matters as Margaret's clandestine love affair with Ossoli and her marital relations with him, but it made an effort at completeness in essentials and at honesty and fairness such as had seldom been seen in American biography. Even the Fullers seemed to be satisfied; and next year they vainly offered to pay Emerson for an introductory essay to a volume of Margaret's writings.

During the seven years following the British lecture tour Emerson continued to collect facts and anecdotes for the character study of the English nation he had begun even before his return to America; and he wrote much of this book before the end of 1855. But the chief literary business of his seven years was reading lectures. He could now go almost anywhere he pleased and expect to find an audience. Financial need drove him to exploit his reputation.

In the last months of 1848, shortly after his return from abroad, he was busy in New England lyceums. It struck the Rhode Islanders, at Newport, that he could not say enough in praise of England in his lecture there early in December. "He laid it on pretty thick, I assure you," one listener reported. "Why England is England," "England," and "London" were some of the new titles, not always for different lectures, that began to appear in the press notices and lyceum records. Before the winter of 1849–1850 was over the lecturer was once more on the road. Now he struck farther away from home ground, where most of his manuscripts had grown familiar. Before the end of January he was in New York. There, Nathaniel Willis asserted, "England" and "Spirit of the Time" brought out as intellectually picked an audience as he had ever seen. "From the great miscellany of New York they come selectively out," Willis said, "like steel filings out of a handfull of sand to a magnet." About the middle of March, Emerson was back again. "Natural Aristocracy," first heard by an Edinburgh audience, struck *The Evening Post* as remarkable for "originality, insight, varied learning, quaint and racy expression, and thorough absence of logic." The last lecture of the course brought out the largest audience. One hearer was Martin Van Buren, the ex-President. Three of the New York subjects were repeated in Brooklyn, and half a dozen lectures had to be read in Philadelphia before Emerson could go home. By then it was about the middle of April. From New York, Brooklyn, Newark, Paterson, and Philadelphia together he had got a total of some $630 above all expenses.

But for Emerson the lecture campaign of the year was the one that took him for the first time beyond the Ohio and, though only for exploration, as far west as the Mississippi. He had long been preaching national as well as personal self-reliance, but though he had visited the Old World twice he had never penetrated very deeply into his own country till now. In the West he traded his lectures not only for fees but for an education in American culture, supposed to be simon-pure only at this safe distance from Europe. In Cincinnati a hundred men had signed a petition that he should come and lecture. Early in May he still balanced the claims of Cincinnati against those of his library and garden. But the chance to see Niagara and the new West outweighed his melons and books.

His visit to Niagara Falls was only the beginning of his adventures. He was a passenger in the steamer *America* when she caught fire on the way from Buffalo to Cleveland but reached the latter port in time to avoid destruction. After reading a lecture in Cleveland he had "a rough pleasant ride over the lake to Sandusky," and then set out by railroad southward. "Beautiful road, grand old forest, beeches, immense black walnuts, oaks, rock maples, buckeyes (horse chestnuts) in bloom, cornels in white flower, & red buds—a forest tree whose bloom is precisely the colour of the peach-blossom,—made all the miles rich with beauty . . ."

At Cincinnati, Emerson was a pleasing surprise according to a local critic—"so far, in his intellectual and oratorical lineaments, from resembling the newspaper portraits above which we have at various times seen his name written, that we half incline to think the wrong man has come along, and attempted to play off a hoax upon us backwoods people." This was a first impression, immediately after the critic had heard "Natural Aristocracy." The attendance seems to have kept up well till the five lectures that had been announced were completed. But when Emerson yielded to the entreaties of friends and gave an additional three his luck changed.

He was eager to see the new country. He visited Fort Ancient, "one of those primeval remains, for which Ohio is famed," with a party including, it seems, Rutherford B. Hayes, a future President. Having got as far

west as Cincinnati, he wanted to go farther. The Cincinnatians easily persuaded him to make an expedition to the Mammoth Cave of Kentucky, and
with a company of sixteen men and women he set out by steamer for
Louisville. There, as neither the mail coach to Mammoth Cave nor available horses or carriages could accommodate so many, the party had to
take to the rivers again—182 miles down the Ohio to Evansville, 150 miles
up the Green River and by Barren River to Bowling Green. In the Green
River, deepened by its locks, they passed through a primitive forest, the
trees marked far from the ground by the latest floods. Ducks clambered
up the shores with their broods, and wild turkeys flew before the steamer
from tree to tree. In the wider stretches of the river were great masses of
dry leaves matted together which, when stirred with a pole, would emit
dangerously inflammable gas. On the morning of the third day out from
Louisville the holiday-makers were at Bowling Green. That night they
arrived in coaches at the cave, and early next morning they made the chilly
descent. With their lamps, Roman candles, and Bengal lights, they were
prepared for an exciting fourteen hours of subterranean exploration that
took them through magnificent chambers and galleries and across rivers,
over the eighteen miles to Serena's Arbor and back, a hard journey. When
they came once more into the open air they learned that a violent thunder-
storm, of which they had had no hint, had passed above them. Next day
they made a visit of four hours "to new parts of the cavern—to the 'Gothic
Chapel,' to the 'Star Chamber,' and to 'Gorin's Dome.'" In the Star
Chamber the illusion was perfect when the guide collected and hid all the
lamps. Emerson lay on his back for a quarter of an hour while the more
musical members of the party sang "Night and Love."

By stage and by steamer he got to Paducah, and there he took passage in the *General Washington* down the broad Ohio, past the once
grand dream city of Cairo. The almost transparent green of the Ohio
poured into the vast muddy current of the Mississippi. The Mississippi, a
lonely river, was flanked by monotonous green wildernesses. There were
"no towns, no houses, no dents in the forest, no boats almost." But sometimes one could see "a flat wood boat lying under the shore," and the
steamer would blow her whistle, ring her bell, and near the land. Then
"out of some log-shed appear black or white men, & hastily put out their
boat, a large mud-scow, loaded with corded wood."

Among his fellow passengers Emerson saw some from the Eastern
states. Captain Mervine, of the U. S. Navy, introduced his daughter, Mrs.
Drury, of Canandaigua, New York. "Then there were planters travelling,"
Emerson noticed, "one with his family of slaves, (6 blacks;) peaceable
looking farmer like men who when they stretch themselves in the pauses

of conversation disclose the butts of their pistols in their breast-pockets. Then a knot of gamblers playing quite ostentatiously on the cabin-tables, & large sums changing owners rapidly, and, as we Yankees fancied, with some glances of hope aimed at us that we should sit down with these amiable gentlemen who professed to be entire strangers to each other, &, if asked any question respecting the river, 'had never been on these waters before.' "

At St. Louis, "the Metropolis of the West, & on the frontier, the starting point for Santa Fe & California, and for the Upper Missisippi," Emerson hesitated. The rivers were getting low, and he did not wish to be caught on a sand bar. But when, after three days in company with cholera and death in his hotel, he was ready to take the risk, he encountered not sand bars but more cholera and death aboard the steamboat *Excelsior* between St. Louis and Galena. He meant to go as far north as the Falls of St. Anthony and see the Indians; but, learning that the council between the Sioux and Chippewas and the territorial dignitaries was ended, and finding no companions for the northern journey, he took the stage from Galena, "across nearly the whole state of Illinois one measureless prairie" to Elgin, and thence came to Chicago by railroad. After crossing Lake Michigan he climbed aboard a Michigan Central train to find John Murray Forbes, president of the road, as a companion for the remainder of the trip to Boston. Niagara River, Lewiston, and Lake Ontario were markers along the route home. It had been an exploring expedition rather than a lecture tour; but the $471.71 Emerson had received for the Cincinnati lectures was more than double the amount of his expenses during the whole journey.

From this time his lecture territory was as narrow or as wide as he chose to make it. He began the regular season of 1850–1851 with, it seems, only scattering appointments in New England. But in February he was as far west as Buffalo. He was now carrying some of his new manuscripts on the general topic of "Conduct of Life." By late March he was in Pittsburgh, worn-out after two nights in the cars and a third "on the floor of a canal-boat, where," he said, "the cushion allowed me for a bed was crossed at the knees by another tier of sleepers as long limbed as I." His course, half a dozen nights long, marked, said a local paper, "something of an era in the history of the Iron City, whose fame has hitherto been acquired chiefly by the products of her manufactories." The lecturer from the East was recognized as a missionary of culture. Next winter he made a few alterations in the course and repeated it in Boston, where he was also a missionary of culture. He made a vigorous attempt to head off newspaper reports. They were often annoyingly imperfect but accurate enough to make his lectures too well known in towns where he had hoped to read them later. The fuller the newspaper reports, the more they cut into his fees.

At Montreal, in the following April, he reached his farthest north on the American continent. He arrived in the Canadian city by crossing the St. Lawrence on foot only two days before "the ice *shoved*, as they call it, &," he wrote home, "I stood on the quay & saw acres & acres of ice rolling swiftly down stream, & presently my *road* came floating down with the rest, the well beaten black straight road I had traversed." Most of the active business men were natives of England or Scotland, and it was a piece of good luck that the American visitor began with his lecture "England" instead of starting at once with his course on the "Conduct of Life." He helped Anglo-American relations still more by a speech at the dinner of the St. George's Society. Everybody, it seems, was pleased. A newspaper critic called the lectures eloquent and had never known anything of the kind to be so popular in Montreal.

Next winter, after some preliminary lecturing mainly in the state of New York, Emerson was off again to the West. Cincinnati was his first main objective, and he gave lectures there once more. He again saw Ormsby Mitchel, the astronomer. After some acquaintance with the wine-making Longworths, he made up his mind that they were "the most remarkable people here," but he had other reasons for liking Cincinnati and would "almost feel compelled to go thither again" if the same persons should ask him. After a slow river voyage he arrived at St. Louis on Christmas Day. As the citizens were just then feting Thomas Meagher, recently escaped from exile in Van Diemen's Land to the American lecture platform, he agreed to attend a dinner in the rebellious Irishman's honor. In St. Louis he found "kind adventurous people" but apparently saw as yet no sign of the surprising excitement over the German philosophy of Hegel that he witnessed there a few years later. Though he had nothing but admiration for Eliot, the Unitarian minister and "the Saint of the West," he believed "no thinking or even reading man" was to be found "in the 95000 souls." By the seventh of January he had, however, given St. Louis his six or seven lectures, principally drawn from his newest course, the "Conduct of Life"; and he was prepared to try his luck, for the first time, on the lecture platforms of the thirty-four-year-old state of Illinois.

At Springfield he was "in the deep mud of the prairie." "In the prairie," he wrote to Lidian, "it rains, & thaws incessantly, &, if we step off the short street, we go up to the shoulders, perhaps, in mud. My chamber is a cabin. My fellow boarders are legislators, but of Illinois, or the big bog. Two or three Governors or ex-Governors live in the house.—But in the prairie, we

are all new men, just come, & must not stand for trifles." In the raw
little town that had vainly tried for more than a dozen years to look like
a state capital Emerson was naturally not on the lookout for one of the
world's greatest living men and so may excusably have given only a passing glance to the law office of Abraham Lincoln. In spite of the bad weather
and a local paper's warning that this master of wonderful style and thought
was not a lecturer in the usual sense but a monologist, talking rather to
himself than to his audience, many people came to Representatives Hall
to hear the visiting lecturer. He read them, it seems, "The Anglo-Saxon,"
"Power," and "Culture."

Through with Springfield on January 12, he was lecturing in Jacksonville the following day; but his next appointment was in Cleveland, Ohio.
He raced back to St. Louis, thence down the Mississippi and up the Ohio
by steamboat, and overland by train to Cleveland. Financially the Western
tour had been a success. Cincinnati, St. Louis, Springfield, and Jacksonville
had, together, paid him slightly over a thousand dollars. He went home
with a growing respect for the potentialities of the new country. His impressions of its cultural condition were not very flattering, but he was hopeful. He saw both sides and included both in his "Anglo-American" lecture.

"Your western romance," he said in the "Anglo-American," "fades into
reality of some grimness. Every thing wears a raw & ordinary aspect. You
find much coarseness in manners; much meanness in politics; much swagger
& vaporing & low filibusterism; the men have not shed their canine teeth.
Well; don't be disgusted . . ." These were poor country people and lived
hard. But their sense of freedom and equality was never interrupted. The
people were all kings, and the scepter was a cattle dealer's driving whip. The
condition of the Western states today had been the condition of all the
states fifty or a hundred years ago. Here was practical democracy, Emerson
saw with his usual freedom from snobbishness.

The West and the South needed, in this time of national unrest, to
be drawn into a closer cultural relation with New England and with
New York and the other Middle Atlantic states, where he now lectured
year after year. There seems to be only the evidence of a partly canceled
rough draft of a letter to show that he had an invitation in 1853 to
read lectures, presumably a course of eight or ten, in New Orleans; and
one can only conjecture the reasons back of such an invitation and the
reasons why it proved abortive. What is clear is that the failure of Emerson
to give such lectures was part of the fateful failure of the American lyceum
to bring North and South together in a common forum of ideas. Early
in the following year, however, he set out on another tour of the West.
This time Detroit, Chicago, and Milwaukee marked the main line of his

penetration. When the railroad was out of commission, he traveled some sixty-five miles in a sleigh along the shore of Lake Michigan. He was getting a vivid impression of the vast geography of the region of the Great Lakes. In Concord that spring Henry Thoreau and others petitioned him for a reading of as many of the lectures he had delivered in other places during the past winter as might be convenient for him to give, "though," said their letter, plainly the work of Thoreau, "they promise to repay him only with an eager attention." Concord promptly got a couple of lectures.

During these years Emerson made a few addresses outside the lyceum circuits. With his oration at Williams College in August of 1854 he unwittingly stirred young James A. Garfield, later a President of the United States. Garfield once declared that, though he could remember only a sentence of the address, he dated his real intellectual life from the hour when he sat under the high pulpit in the old parish church at Williamstown and was dazed by the new vision Emerson opened before him. In January of 1855 Emerson thought his engagement to speak before the Massachusetts Anti-slavery Society was "like Hamlet's task imposed on so unfit an agent as Hamlet." To him "the mountains of cotton & sugar" seemed as "unpersuadeable by any words as Sebastopol to a herald's oration." At Amherst College in August of 1855, he appeared as substitute orator. In the following month he spoke at the dedication of the Concord cemetery, Sleepy Hollow.

Meantime the old treadmill of lectures for village and city lyceums had to be kept turning through each lecture season. Once a tour was decided upon, an extensive correspondence settled the details. Requests came in from dozens of towns. A tentative schedule for only two weeks of the winter of 1855 included nine towns in the state of New York and one in Canada —Rochester, February 15; Syracuse, 16; Rome, 17; Oneida, 19; Vernon, 20; Rochester again, 21; Lockport, 22; Hamilton, Ontario, 23; Syracuse again, 24; Canandaigua, 26; Watertown, 28; Cazenovia, March 1. This meant twelve lectures, and every one required a tiresome journey. But for Emerson, perennially in need of funds, it was a very familiar sort of business.

Near the end of December, 1855, he paused at the Tremont House in Chicago, bound for Iowa. "I rode incessantly," he informed Lidian, "from Salem Mass where I took the cars on Thursday morning two days & two nights & was here at nine yesterday A. M. Tonight at eleven or else tomorrow at seven A. M. I go again to the Missisippi & across it to Davenport & then to Rock Island But it is a little doubtful still as there is no arrival from that quarter whether snow & wind will allow me to reach the river As for the crossing, once there, there is now no difficulty, for it is frozen." On the next day, the last day of the year, he lectured in Davenport, Iowa; and in his diary he noted that he had three times crossed the Mississippi on foot.

If hard travel taught him something of the unbookish world, his lectures not only made it possible for him to give months of every year to writing but helped spread the reputation of his books. With his lectures on England ready for use as a part of *English Traits* and with those on the "Conduct of Life" written and read from lyceum platforms, Emerson's distinctive achievement was not far from complete. But as the ecliptic of his career slanted downward a little, his literary reputation continued to grow. Émile Montégut's translation, *Essais de philosophie américaine,* published in 1851, helped to establish more firmly the Emersonian bridgehead in France. For Americans the basis of Emerson's increasing fame was ably surveyed by the learned and radical religious controversialist Theodore Parker in *The Massachusetts Quarterly Review.* Moncure Conway doubted whether Parker ever comprehended Emerson. It was true that Parker was in some respects at the opposite pole of Transcendentalism from the Concord man, but he understood him well enough.

On the whole he placed him very high, among geniuses of the first order. He called him the most American as well as the most cosmopolitan among all American writers. But he also listed the glaring faults of his hero —lack of any exact scholarship, lack of exact mental discipline, lack of any systematic training in the sciences to which he appealed so often, lack of proper esteem for the logical, demonstrative, and historical understanding and consequently too much dependence on intuition, too much inclination to be the complete mystic. Emerson, he found, discouraged hard and continuous thought, conscious argument, and discipline, though the Emersonidae were more guilty on this score than was their master. But in spite of the fact that Emerson demonstrated nothing, Parker said, he assumed his position far in advance of his time. Not a pantheist, so Parker thought, Emerson did not sink God in nature though he sometimes made man identical with God. Not creative as Goethe and Shakespeare were, he exhibited a body of writing of remarkable consistency, and his life and writings together formed a consistent whole that might challenge the world. Parker saw Emerson as the child of Christianity and of American political idealism and yet outside the church and outside the state. He was unrelenting in his attack on the want of logic of which Emerson was certainly guilty but nevertheless ended by raising him up to the highest place among writers of English since the time of Milton. He even thought that Milton had not added so many thoughts to the treasury of the race or created so much loveliness.

In comparison with such astonishing praise, it was a small matter that

Emerson attracted to Concord a minor foreign literary figure like Fredrika Bremer, the Swede, or the sculptor Horatio Greenough, "grandest of democrats" if not of sculptors; or that he, though no Baconian, found himself cast in the role of friend and aider of Delia Bacon when she was trying to shift Shakespeare's laurels to the head of the Elizabethan Francis Bacon; or that he continued to show his old power over youth, exercising it in these years on such new friends and disciples as Moncure Conway and Frank Sanborn; or that he drew to America for a time his English friend Arthur Clough.

Emerson now had all the praise he needed. There were other judgments hardly less flattering to him than Theodore Parker's. Clough, after some months of American residence, called him "the only profound man in this country" but later modified this estimate so that it was less unjust to the country though scarcely less favorable to Emerson. "I more and more recognise his superiority to everybody I have seen," he wrote home to England. But acceptance and success, instead of spurring Emerson on to new achievement, seemed to make him more content, in the latter half of his life, to abandon his lonely tower in order to regain his hold on what Hawthorne called "the magnetic chain of humanity."

21.

THINGS IN THE SADDLE

If I refuse
My study for their politique,
Which at the best is trick,
The angry Muse
Puts confusion in my brain. . . .
'T is the day of the chattel,
Web to weave, and corn to grind;
Things are in the saddle,
And ride mankind.
                    —"Ode Inscribed to W. H. Channing"

BY 1856 the dangerous rivalry between North and South had at last got out of hand. The two greedy economic systems could not be reconciled however much one might depend upon the other. The social cleavage was fast becoming even more fundamental than the economic. While the South angrily resisted the harsh Northern industrial hegemony, she was aroused by the growing threat to her social order, an order founded on the absolute supremacy of whites over blacks. The North, though equally guilty with the South in introducing slavery into the country, had found her soil and climate unsuited to it. She had at length freed her Negroes and, having only a small population of ex-slaves, felt no danger from their presence and could afford some generous gestures toward them. Out of the ancient trap, she prided herself on having got abreast once more of European opinion on the sanctity of human freedom. The South, caught fast in the old system, had to resist any change. Thoroughly alarmed at the aggressiveness of the North, she was making a final effort to arm herself with political power and was at the same time considering the alternative of secession. The hotheads on both sides were loud in their demands. Even ethical idealists could behave with fatal unwisdom. The moral indignation of the impatient antislavery reformers at the North threatened to end not only the slave economy but the Union itself and was, as it turned out, pushing the country toward the blood bath of a fratricidal war.

The stench of political decay was in the American air and penetrated the study of even the most retired scholar. Growth was giving way to disintegration. Optimism received a severe check. The dream of a good life on the fresh, clean soil of the New World had to be postponed or given up in favor of a more realistic view of things. The thinker, though he had little faith in victories to be won by political or military shock troops, had to quit thinking for action.

Emerson already felt himself drawn closer to friends like Theodore Parker, tireless enemy of slavery. The praise Parker had heaped upon Emerson in *The Massachusetts Quarterly Review* article of 1850 did not at all explain Emerson's growing admiration for Parker. Parker's accelerating attacks on slavery explained that. From 1851 through 1855 Emerson had been urging Parker on: "We all love & honour you here, & have come to think every drop of your blood & every moment of your life of a national value. . . . Ever new strength & victory be to you! . . . People love war too well, now, as aforetime, not to love the best soldier of these days."

Emerson became suspicious of friends who cared more for the Union than for the antislavery cause. Oliver Wendell Holmes, in a speech at New York, tried to moderate the Northern hatred of the slaveholders because it was dangerous to the welfare of the country. Emerson, though he acknowledged Holmes's disclaimer of any advocacy of slavery, drafted a sad but severe rebuke. As "for the Union with Slavery," he declared, "no manly person will suffer a day to go by without discrediting disintegrating & finally exploding it."

When Charles Sumner, the intransigent foe of the Southern bloc in the Senate, was brutally assaulted as he sat at his desk in the Senate chamber, Emerson was carried away by anger. To him the shame of Sumner's assailant seemed to be shared by the whole South, and Sumner was "the whitest soul I ever knew." In the free states, he told his fellow townsmen, life was "adorned with education, with skilful labor, with arts, with long prospective interests, with sacred family ties, with honor and justice." But in the slave states, he rounded out his contrast, life was a fever and man was "an animal, given to pleasure, frivolous, irritable, spending his days in hunting and practising with deadly weapons to defend himself against his slaves and against his companions brought up in the same idle and dangerous way."

With such a speech, though it was spoken only to his Concord neighbors, Emerson came near making himself a political figure. He received word that he had been appointed an alternate delegate to the first national nominating convention of the Republican Party, to be held at Philadelphia on June 17; and soon he was being urged by the poet Whittier, though apparently in vain, to go to Philadelphia, as ex-Governor Boutwell could not. He proclaimed uncompromising political views with more boldness. To his brother William he wrote that "If the Free States do not obtain the government next fall, which our experience does not entitle us to hope, nothing seems left, but to form at once a Northern Union, & break the old." The following winter, when Ellen Emerson visited the home of the poet Longfellow she saw a picture of her father and one of Charles Sumner linked together with a wreath.

In Concord relief for the Union men fighting to keep their hold in bloody Kansas unloosed purse strings. Emerson, one of the subscribers, proudly estimated that the well over a thousand dollars raised during a few days in June of 1856 amounted to one percent of the valuation of the town. He told a relief meeting at Cambridge that in the case of Kansas "all the right is on one side." He made his speech vivid by naming persons from Massachusetts towns who had been murdered or seized in the border war. He indicted the government of the United States as the chief culprit and made probably the most open statement he had ever made of his theory of the supremacy of the individual conscience over the authority of government. All the Emersons were delighted when schoolmaster Frank Sanborn, head of Kansas relief for Middlesex County and later for Massachusetts, came to talk to them on this favorite theme. In November, William Lloyd Garrison asked permission to include Emerson's portrait in a composite "magnificent lithographic print" along with portraits of Theodore Parker, Wendell Phillips, Joshua Giddings, Gerrit Smith, Samuel May, and other antislavery heroes.

Meantime Emerson lectured again as far west as the Mississippi Valley. This meant "plenty of night travelling and arriving at 4 in the morning, to take the last & worst bed in the tavern." In January of 1856 the mercury fell to twenty-two degrees below zero on the twelfth day of the cold snap. "Winter in Illinois," Emerson wrote home, "has a long whip. To cuddle into bed is the only refuge in these towns." During a "sleigh jaunt" on the Mississippi he caught a cold and could hardly speak. The clothing supplied him from home also made him unhappy. "One petty misfortune," he informed Lidian, "causes me a deal of trouble,—those shirts are not measured rightly, & will not button." His audiences, too, were a problem. Sometimes they seemed to him like children. But when the stout Illinois farmer walked out of the hall after a short trial of the Easterner's wares, Emerson thought the Illinoisan must be right. The committee told him that what the people wanted was a hearty laugh. But he used what spare time he could between lectures to work on his next book, *English Traits*. At Chicago he lamented that the bitter cold kept him from getting off some sheets of it to his publisher. Thoreau, appointed his agent during his absence, would, he knew, be vexed by this failure.

As Emerson moved eastward he got better press reports on "Beauty," his favorite lecture on the Western tour. In Illinois a Dixon paper had said flatly that his style was "most miserable," while a Freeport print, though conceding that for intellectual quality "Beauty" was "vastly superior to any lecture we have yet had," judged that there was in it none of the magnetism important in popular oratory. In Ohio people liked these things somewhat better, it seemed. At Cleveland they listened with profound attention, and some even liked the sober style of delivery. At Columbus the local critic regretted that a man who possessed so many graces of mind should not give some study to graces of attitude, yet he asserted that "Beauty" would long be remembered as "the finest lecture ever delivered at the Atheneum." Back in Boston the Freeman Place Chapel was the scene of a minor triumph when half a dozen lectures, including "Beauty," made a net profit of $772.36. "France," another lecture of the course, roused the ire of Doctor Oliver Wendell Holmes, once a student of medicine in Paris, because it charged his most admired professor, the famous Doctor Louis, with professional showmanship.

There was much miscellaneous business that had to be attended to. The alert red-headed and bewhiskered Boston lawyer Horatio Woodman craved the society of literary men and benevolently wished to make them wealthy. By 1856 he was arranging a small but profitable investment in Wisconsin land for Emerson. Hermann Raster, a German newspaper editor in New York, negotiated with Emerson, on behalf of the scholar and critic Doctor Karl Elze of Germany, for the inclusion of *Representative Men* in *Dürr's Collection of Standard American Authors* at Leipzig this year. A thousand new copies of each series of *Essays* were printed in Boston, and there was a reprint of the *Poems,* called the fifth edition.

There were minor adventures on the farm. Jessie the calf could not be found and had to be searched for by Emerson and his hired man, but, as it turned out, she had been lying all the time under the quince trees in the garden. On the two following days there was a great storm, the wind and rain knocked down many pears, and the floor of Ellen's closet had to be commandeered for the Flemish Beauties and other varieties thus prematurely harvested.

The family income, as Emerson recorded it day by day in his account books, made an oddly variegated picture. On October 17 he received through Phillips, Sampson, & Co. the sum of $100. This was the result of the promise made by G. Routledge of London to pay him £20 for an advance copy of *English Traits* in order to beat British pirates to the press. On the 19th he got seven cents a pound for his 700-pound cow; on the 22nd, $1.50 for apples; and on the 23rd, $20 from the Marlboro Lyceum. For the whole of the year 1856 the major items of his income would probably have amounted to a little over $1400 of dividends and rents and perhaps a little less than $1700 in lecture fees; but his expenses were heavy and he was far from rich.

His social and even convivial times were, however, growing more important; and this year they fell into a more regular pattern, with one climactic day of each month assigned to the Saturday Club. The Saturday Club, which he helped to found, was just beginning its long career as the social focus of the leading intellectuals of the Boston area. The original members, those of 1856, were Louis Agassiz, the immigrant scientist just then piecing out his meager income by serving as schoolmaster to Emerson's daughter Ellen and other pupils; the younger Richard Henry Dana, more than a successful lawyer and antislavery agitator now that his California voyage before the mast was a matter of literary history; John Sullivan Dwight, once the teacher of music at Brook Farm; Emerson; Elizabeth Hoar's brother Rockwood, the jurist; James Russell Lowell; John Lothrop Motley, now a popular author because of his recently published first book on the Dutch; Benjamin Peirce, mathematician and astronomer; Sam Ward, Emerson's friend and correspondent for years past; Edwin Percy Whipple, already adding the dignity of critic to his lesser repute as a bank clerk; and Horatio Woodman, social manager and financial adviser to his better-known friends. Longfellow and Holmes entered the club a year or so later, and were soon followed by the historian Prescott, by Whittier, and by Hawthorne. Henceforth, year after year, Emerson made his trips to Boston, commonly every month, for the meetings of the club.

Far removed from this exemplary brotherhood was the disturbing figure of Walt Whitman. As critic Whipple of the Saturday Club jested of him, "he had every leaf but the fig leaf"; and of all this New England Parnassus, Emerson alone recognized his great qualities. Emerson was untroubled by nearsightedness. Though he saw no first-rate genius in any fellow member of the Saturday Club, even in Hawthorne, he was sure he saw it in Whitman. Unfavorable judgments of *Leaves of Grass* continued to come in from friends as liberal-minded as Arthur Clough. To Clough it seemed remarkable but perhaps "rather a waste of power & observation." But Emerson, oddly bracketing "wild Whitman, with real inspiration but choked by Titanic abdomen," and the Baconian enthusiast Delia Bacon, "with genius, but mad," called them "the sole producers that America has yielded in ten years."

Herman Grimm and Gisela von Arnim, daughter of Emerson's old favorite who had once exploited with great success her correspondence with Goethe and was thenceforth familiarly known to the world as Bettina, began to write to Emerson from Europe. Grimm and Gisela seem to have been almost Emerson's first German correspondents. Grimm had read Emerson in 1855 and believed that he and his friend Joseph Joachim, the violinist, were perhaps the first in their country to know the American's writings. In the Emerson home the amusing struggle with the German script began. Success depended on the wits of Ellen, since her father read German only from the printed page. Once a particularly difficult letter from Gisela required a whole winter of intermittent labor to unriddle it. Emerson himself was unable to keep his reading up to date in Grimm's numerous volumes that came to him as gifts from year to year. One of these, a book of essays, was dedicated to him. Herman Grimm's father and uncle, already known as collectors of fairy tales, were bringing out their great German dictionary so slowly that one was dubious of their ever arriving at the latter half of the alphabet; but Emerson soon began to buy the expensive work.

To those who had heard Emerson lecture frequently since 1848, important parts of *English Traits* were likely to seem familiar when the book appeared in print. From its informal beginnings in England, it had grown to hundreds of manuscript pages some five years after his second visit there. But the "first of, say, sixteen or seventeen chapters" of it did not go to the American publisher until the autumn of 1855; and it did not reach the public till August 6, 1856. It was a success and, though Emerson refused to allow puffing advertisements, seventeen hundred copies were sold within four days.

The whole of it related in some manner to Britain, and nearly all to England. Though the more personal chapters were not well integrated with the general analysis of English character, this was Emerson's most unified and coherent book. Of all his writings it was also the most objective and had the firmest foundation in first-hand observation of men and manners. Carlyle called it such a book as did not turn up "often in the decade, in the century," and thought that Benjamin Franklin might have written such a thing, in his own way, but no one since. Franklin would certainly have made shrewder observations on trade and on government but would not have gone so deep under the surface as Emerson went. As matters stood, no other American account of England could compare with this, and seldom had any traveler made so wise an appraisal of the character of a nation.

It was true that some dissenting criticism from Hawthorne and other well-informed persons did not entirely miss the mark. Hawthorne, then the American consul at Liverpool, was "not unconscious," he admitted, "of a certain malevolence and hostility in my own breast, such as a man must necessarily feel, who lives in England without melting entirely into the mass of Englishmen." Still he had some justification for his fear that the book would "please the English only too well; for," he told Emerson, "you give them credit for the possession, in very large measure, of all the qualities that they value, or pride themselves upon; and they never will comprehend that what you deny is far greater and higher than what you concede." This view of the matter was partly confirmed when Clough wrote from England, "I think you praise us too highly—I was anxious for more rebuke—and profitable reprimand." But perhaps Carlyle saw the deeper intention of the author better than either Hawthorne or Clough did. When he first learned from an Irish newspaper that the book showed a *"medicinal* intention" he remarked, "God knows there was hardly ever such a Hospital of Lepers" and wished the doctor more power; and having seen the book, he made no complaint that it was not sufficiently medicinal. Emerson, if one saw below the surface of *English Traits,* had really succeeded in striking a balance between admiration and censure.

Doubtless praise of the Teutonic heritage of England as well as of America, a country that figured as a sort of transplanted England, was excessive. Scotland and France were used principally as convenient foils to set off the excellence of England. The Normans "came out of France into England worse men than they went into it one hundred and sixty years before," and "Twenty thousand thieves landed at Hastings" to become "founders of the House of Lords." "The Frenchman invented the ruffle; the Englishman added the shirt." Yet Emerson explained the more pervasive influence of the French on the Continent in a manner to delight a Frenchman. "What influence the English have," he unsmilingly announced, "is by brute force of wealth and power; that of the French by affinity and talent." He laughed at the islanders' pretensions abroad. He gave the chief reason for their attachment to home and home habits as merely their dullness.

If he found every islander a self-sufficient island himself and glorified the Englishman as the man who, of all the world, stood firmest in his shoes, he also noted that cold and repressive manners prevailed among the English. If he seemed to admire wealth and success along with the wealthy and successful Englishman, he was not blind to this successful man's unimaginative passion for utility and found his hero heavy at fine arts while he was adroit at the coarse. The spiritual quality that Emerson prized seemed to be lacking in most of the English literature of the time. He pictured the Church of England as the victim of artificiality. English religion was torpid. Englishmen were warned that they would have to pay a penalty for conformity. "That Chapter on the Church," Carlyle approved, "is inimitable . . . and the matter too dreadfully *true* in every part." The feudal character of the English state, Emerson went on, was getting obsolete and glared a little in contrast with democratic tendencies. And though England was the best of actual nations, the English mind was in a state of arrested development.

English Traits, within a month of publication, had sold 3,000 copies and was selling a new edition of 2,000. But the author, now read with eagerness by many who cared nothing for his earlier books, soon went back to his lecture platform. Early the following year, after going southward to Philadelphia, he set out again on a Western tour. At Rochester, where he tried to lecture between spells of darkness when the gas lights failed to burn, he learned that a literary reputation could not compete with a political one, or at least not in these times tense with political excitement. Horace Greeley, having missed an appointment of his own, sat on the platform to the too great delight of the audience. Emerson "could scarcely keep the people quiet" as "they were so furious to shout Greeley! Greeley!" At the hotel he had the misfortune to share with the restless man "a parlour with two little bed chambers opening into it." Greeley was good enough company in the evening, but in the morning "he rose at 6, lit the candles, & scribbled political paragraphs to send away to the Tribune. He is an admirable editor," Emerson wrote home, "but I had as lief travel with an Express man or with Barnum." He came upon Greeley again at the Tremont House in Chicago. At Cincinnati, on his return trip, he found that most of his lectures, as well as the Unitarian church, were under the management of his friend Moncure Conway.

At home that spring, he soon recovered from what looked like a belated attack of measles. The domestic scene was not entirely a restful one. The house echoed with the half articulate cries of Mary Martha Macaw, the parrot, a disturber of the peace destined, it seems, to stay on for years to come. It was already an old story that the children had to be got off in relays to schools, or on visits to Boston or New York. Edward brought home the latest slang from Sanborn's school, and the family, including Emerson himself, began to talk it. It was in 1857 that Emerson altered his house by making a den for his own use; but as this retreat was accessible from his study only by a roundabout route leading up two steep flights of stairs and proved to be hot in summer and cold in winter, he probably did not often use it.

The routine of domestic life was interrupted when the family escaped briefly from the summer heat of Concord. In August of 1857 Emerson seems to have signed his name for the first time in the "Island Book" at Naushon, the charming domain of his friend John Murray Forbes. Naushon, one of the Elizabeth Islands, was eight miles long; and every mile, forested or open, had its varied attractions. From a secluded spot among moss-bearded trees or rock-studded hillocks or beside a miniature lake one quickly emerged upon the shore of Vineyard Sound or of Buzzards Bay.

In Concord, Emerson could take to the roads and fields. Ellery Channing and Henry Thoreau still sometimes walked and talked with him. Both made willful, temperamental companions. On his worst days Thoreau would merely talk for victory, or he would annoyingly arrive to bring up something he had just read and then leave unceremoniously. He and Emerson, overcharged with individualism, resembled a couple of lobsters trying to be affectionate. Ellery Channing would come to Concord only occasionally now. He would hide for a fortnight in a chamber of the house he had rented to Sanborn, would emerge to walk and dine a few times with Emerson, and would then disappear perhaps for months.

In 1857 Alcott was back in Concord developing new plans for the improvement of Emerson's yard, and Emerson himself was gathering facts for a biographical sketch of Alcott for *The New American Cyclopædia*. Alcott's purchase of the Orchard House and his return that autumn to live once more in Concord marked a new advance in the social life of the village. The Alcott girls loved acting and had talent for it. Plays and entertainments were now given in the vestry of the Unitarian Church, and the Emerson children took some part in them.

The Atlantic Monthly, beginning publication with Lowell as editor and with other members of the Saturday Club as the chief contributors, was henceforth the most prized periodical in the Emerson study and parlor. Among the poems in the first number were Emerson's delicately chiseled "Days," a masterpiece in unemotional black and white, and his "Brahma," an extremely faithful transcript from Hindu scriptures. "Brahma" provoked the laughter of those who were ignorant of Hindu lore—and they must have comprised most of the readers of *The Atlantic*. Some parodies resulted. Emerson simply allowed his audience to get along the best they could in their ignorance. The poem, however, was no *tour de force* but a natural outgrowth of his now habitual Oriental reading. A year or so later, when Philip Jogut Sangooly took tea with him, Ellen was delighted "to have a real live Brahmin, brought up a priest to Kreeshna &c, knowing Sanscrit and all the Vedas and able to tell Father all he wanted to know, in our house here in America, in Concord." During many years following Sangooly's visit Emerson paid dues and assessments to the Oriental Society. Meantime he looked critically at *The Atlantic* as an instrument for the guidance of the age. As for the contributors, he remarked that only "the sentiment of freedom is the sting which all feel in common." *The Atlantic* was meant to be no mere literary magazine but also a new weapon against slavery, and its political aim made it sectional and limited.

The appearance of John Brown of Kansas at the Concord Town Hall had already effectively dramatized the slavery question for Emerson and his fellow townsmen. It seems that Emerson was introduced to John Brown by Thoreau. He admired the tough Kansan and approved the doctrine of armed resistance to the slavery men on the frontier. He asked that a subscription of $15 he had made to the Concord Lyceum be turned over to John Brown instead. It is not clear whether he yielded that year to Elihu Burritt's request that he sign the call for a national convention in support of the same compensated emancipation that he himself had publicly advocated a few years earlier. On the Fourth of July, when the Concord people gathered at a breakfast and floral exhibition for the benefit of Sleepy Hollow Cemetery, they probably sang Emerson's ode printed with the day's program, but some may have been surprised to find that it was really a call for the freeing of the slaves.

There was more lecturing of the usual unpolitical kind from New England southward to Philadelphia. In March and April of 1858 there was another course at the Freeman Place Chapel in Boston, but Convers Francis, an early admirer, was disappointed. Emerson seemed to him to make no progress in the subject. There was no opening out, no expanding of the thought; and as for the structure of the lecture it was the familiar miscellany. The truth was that the need for money pushed Emerson out into the lyceum circuit whether he had anything new to offer or not. However old his lectures seemed, Freeman Place Chapel alone could still yield him nearly $900 in fees.

Time was beginning to leave its mark on him as he completed his fifty-fifth year. The Rowse drawing, made during this period, betrayed no signs of age in him; but it did not give the impression of lifelikeness. Rowse overrefined his subject. The features were too delicately formed. Though the face perhaps properly wore an expression half humorous and half sad, it was too young. It was in March of 1858 that Louisa Dewey first saw in Emerson evidences of age. In spite of his limited physical strength he had been leading, much of each year, a strenuous life. Away from home for weeks or months at a time, he had traveled in uncomfortable trains, lived in primitive hotels, lectured in ill-ventilated and poorly lighted halls in all kinds of weather. At home, he was involved in wearisome business affairs. A lawsuit to test the validity of his title to one of the little pieces of land he had purchased near Walden Pond was finally settled but in favor of "the enemy"; and he "sat," as he said, "expectant for a fortnight," waiting for sheriffs or messengers to summon him "to pay whatever damages accrue." The case had dragged on for years. Once the jury had disagreed and had been discharged.

In July of 1858, shortly after the annoying litigation was ended, Emerson visited the Bancrofts at Newport, and by the end of August he was with the Forbeses at Naushon. The woody isolation of Naushon must have given him the solace he needed, for his poem "Waldeinsamkeit" seemed to him to suit the landscape there so well that he copied it into the island guest book. But the climax of his summer was his more than two weeks with the Adirondack Club, a sporting outgrowth of the Saturday Club.

He and his fellow members traveled, by way of Lake George and Lower Saranac Lake, to Follensby Pond and Big Tupper Lake, where the artist William J. Stillman, their captain of the hunt and chief guide, taught them how to rough it. The experience was a severe test for a philosopher accustomed to escape into privacy after brief social encounters; and it is perhaps significant that though Emerson stood, erect and apparently alert, at the center of the group painted by Stillman, he was quite apart from the two well-defined knots of his fellow campers.

Yet if he proved himself useless to the captain of the hunt, he was easily recognizable as the chief poet of the expedition. "The Adirondacs" showed what rich sensuous impressions he brought back as his share of the game. He remembered the club's flotilla passing through "gold-moth-haunted beds of pickerel-flower" and through perfumed banks of blossoms where the deer fed at night and the teal by day, the loud chorus of the dogs as they scoured the shores for game, the whipping of the rough waters for trout, the bathing, the laughter of the loon, the procession, as the boats moved past, of the pines whose images were sharpened by the low glow of twilight. Once, he recalled, he was

> In the boat's bows, a silent night-hunter
> Stealing with paddle to the feeding-grounds
> Of the red deer, to aim at a square mist.

But as he could see nothing but the mist where he was told to aim at the deer, he did not fire.

In Concord, he mounted the platform at the local agricultural fair, having been "drawn into this trap of a Cattle Show Speech, by neglecting to say *No* early enough." He suffered, as frequently, the annoyance of pursuit by newspaper reporters who were determined to publicize what he wanted to reserve for his own use in the lyceums. His speech made the farmer fit company for philosophers and poets but otherwise kept close to the soil. Convers Francis, now rebelling against the monotonous Transcendentalism of the lectures, judged that the Cattle Show speech showed Emerson just what people thought he was not—a practical man. This practicality may have been probed to the core when the Emerson family entertained the Social Circle, which included some Concord farmers.

Quite different guests were present when Alcott gave, in the Emerson house, his conversation on "Private Life." There was some general debate, but the occasion was long remembered because of a clash between Aunt Mary Moody Emerson and the equally sharp-tongued and pugnacious elder Henry James. Aunt Mary, though at last humble enough to forget her vow not to enter the home of her nephew, was still formidable; and, if the not unbiased Alcott reported truly, she administered a severe check to James and won the admiration of everybody present.

Aunt Mary, now in her eighties, was as much trouble as a course of lectures, even though she boarded outside the Emerson home. When she indignantly refused to pay her Concord landlady more than $3 a week, Emerson and Elizabeth Hoar, seeing that $5 was not too much for such a boarder, paid the difference themselves. But the spectacular scenes in which Aunt Mary was the central figure were about over. Late in October she was packed up and carried to Mrs. Cobb's in Boston, "a large part of Concord assisting"; and a few weeks later she was ready to go peaceably with Emerson to Williamsburg, Long Island, where, on what was then the margin of the metropolitan area, she was to spend most of her remaining years under the guardianship of a niece.

The trip of December, 1858, was for lectures in the New York region and Philadelphia as well as for Aunt Mary's convenience. At Philadelphia, Lucretia Mott, the Quakeress and abolitionist, found "The Law of Success" "full of gems" and knew Emerson was telling the truth when he confided to her that " 'I got some leaves out of yr. book'—addg. 'from yr New Bedford Fr^{ds}' "; but she denied his doctrine of compensation so far as it concerned morals. In morals, she put it, "wickedness works only evil & that continually & the only way . . . to destroy it is with unquench-

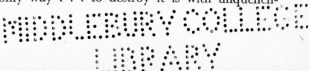

able fire." Before the end of the year Emerson was facing Canadians at Hamilton and Toronto. Emerson the lecturer now had success after success, and the financial returns from his writings were also becoming important. It must have been with satisfaction that he set down the sum of $1988 as the income from his lectures in a year when he had given fewer than usual and traveled less widely. Adding in his dividends from banks and railroads with his rentals and some minor business profits, his $215 from *The Atlantic Monthly*, and his $872 in royalties from his Boston publisher, he computed his total income for 1858 as $4162.11. Early in the new year he earned more with lectures in Baltimore, Brooklyn, and various towns along the road to the West. Then, after his speech at the Burns centenary celebration in Boston, a speech copied into British and German newspapers and praised by Burns's compatriot Carlyle, he gave in the same city a course of lectures which brought him nearly $700 above expenses.

But he felt now that his intellectual life was on the wane and asserted that he was a natural reader, not a writer. He dug in his garden, presumably with more contentment. Once when Ellen came into the Concord railroad station she met him "walking along with a spade in his hand," and looking "very rural." Events conspired to turn him toward an easier way of life. He felt a new sense of relief that spring when the heavy responsibility for Bulkeley that he had shared with his brother William for many years was at last ended. On the 27th of May, Reuben Hoar's wife came from Littleton to say that his brother Bulkeley, a boarder with her family and helper with their farm work, had died that day. Thoreau took charge of the funeral at Concord. For Bulkeley half a century of mental twilight was finished. "His face was not much changed by death," Emerson told William, "but sadly changed by life from the comely boy I can well remember."

The Saturday Club continued to school Emerson in sociability and conviviality, and he was a loyal member. He warmly advocated the election of several friends, labored hard on verses for the club's celebration of Lowell's fortieth birthday, and prepared a speech for Holmes's fiftieth birthday. He wrote a lecture on clubs and believed that their history from antiquity to the present would be an important chapter in the history of civilization. He defined the proper qualifications of members as mainly good manners and a willingness to sink trifles and know solid values, and held that companions so qualified had great worth for scholars, who did not want to be always pumping their brains but needed gossips. Yet at bottom he was still the individualist, only less radically so than he had been in the early

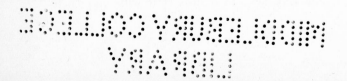

essay on friendship, and he warned that the highest results from conversation required the enforcement of the rule of one to one.

The prospects of a "vacation of independence" at Waterford in Maine, of a second outing with the Adirondack Club, and of a return to Naushon vanished on the slopes of Wachusett early in July, 1859. Since his first camping trip Emerson had had greater enthusiasm for the wilds, and here, even from the summit called Little Wachusett, he could look out over a scene that filled him with admiration. Around the horizon he could see Monadnock, the Hoosac Mountain, or what he took for it, in Berkshire County with a hint of the Catskills beyond, and, to the eastward, the tamer counties sprinkled with towns or shining with rivers or ponds. But his enthusiasm cooled when he suffered a sprain as he was making the descent. For months he was an invalid. It seemed to him that he might as well have sprained his head. After consulting no fewer than four reputable doctors and getting contradictory advice, he eventually went to Doctor Hewett, apparently the same "quack doctor Hewitt" who had cured his knee thirty years earlier; and somehow he gradually got well.

The nightmare of slavery had now grown into a horrible specter, and it seemed to shout to every house where people with consciences lived that there would be no more sleep till it was laid. This spring John Brown, the Kansas partisan, had reappeared in the Concord Town Hall, prophesying an end of all comfortable dreaming, while persons Alcott called the "best people" of the town—Emerson, Thoreau, Judge Ebenezer Rockwood Hoar, and Mrs. Alcott—had listened, some being moved to contribute to his funds without asking particulars of his plans. The old man had not yet lost his fire, though since he had first been seen in Concord a flowing beard had, as Alcott thought, given the look of an apostle to the soldierly figure. In October his long years of fanatical apostleship came to a fiery and bloody climax in his attack on Harpers Ferry. Two days later he was captured by a government force including some marines commanded by Colonel Robert E. Lee.

Emerson wrote to his brother in New York: "We are all very well, in spite of the sad Harpers Ferry business, which interests us all who had Brown for our guest twice. . . . He is a true hero, but lost his head there." Three days later he told Sarah Swain Forbes that Brown was "a hero of romance, & seems to have made this fatal blunder only to bring out his virtues. I must hope for his escape to the last moment." Many Concord people waited in tense excitement. Sanborn, too much involved in John Brown's affairs, left his school and took refuge in Canada till Emerson persuaded him to return, had to retire to Canada again, defied the authority of the United States Senate in a fracas in Concord, and soon got discharged from a merely nominal custody.

In Emerson's lecture "Courage," read in Boston on November 8, John Brown seemed already to have achieved sainthood of a superior sort. He was "The Saint, whose fate yet hangs in suspense, but whose martyrdom, if it shall be perfected, will make the gallows as glorious as the cross," or so, at any rate, the *New-York Daily Tribune* quoted the lecture as it was first given. The day before Brown's conviction of treason and of murder in the first degree Thoreau called his fellow Concordians together to hear his plea for the captain and for the slaves. In several speeches Emerson asked aid for John Brown's family and openly championed the cause of the man he thought fit to be a martyr. At the meeting in Boston on November 18 he foretold what a favorite his hero would be with history. This was six days after Edmund Clarence Stedman's ballad had been published in Greeley's *Tribune*. Stedman had warned,

> And Old Brown,
> Osawatomie Brown,
> May trouble you more than ever, when you've nailed
> his coffin down!

Possibly Emerson had already seen the New Yorker's verses, but both he and Stedman soon seemed to be good prophets. Before two years were past, John Brown's soul began its march over the battlefields of the Civil War.

Meantime, on December 2, the day of Brown's execution, a quiet meeting, planned by Thoreau, Alcott, and Emerson, was held at Concord, with the three philosophers and two other men reading verse and prose in solemn commemoration. The town, for its people were mostly present, it was said, with many others from neighboring places, sang Sanborn's dirge. Fortunately for the peace of Concord's literary circle, Hawthorne did not return from abroad for some months to come. When he eventually got round to the subject of John Brown, he could hardly believe that the newspapers had reported Emerson's Boston lecture correctly. He shrank "unutterably" from the notion "that the death of this blood-stained fanatic has 'made the Gallows as venerable as the Cross!'" and, in spite of his admiration for Brown's integrity of character, he judged that "Nobody was ever more justly hanged."

In January and February of 1860 Emerson went far into the West again with his lectures. Buffalo, Detroit, Chicago, Milwaukee, and Madison, Wisonsin, made the rough outline of his difficult tour. From Lafayette, Indiana, ₑe had to charter a special train to Michigan City in order to reach Chicago ₙ time. In Wisconsin the wells were dry and it was hard to find water ₒr the horses that were, for one whole day, the lecturer's motive power. ₒnce, in Michigan, Emerson had to ride nearly fifty miles in a buggy to ₑep an appointment. When he caught cold from wet clothing, imperfectly ₐundered in Chicago, he sucked troches and, as he told it, only awed the Wisconsin legislators with a richer orotund than he could normally boast. After the Western tour he went as far southward as New York again but ₕad to give up Philadelphia, where he was not wanted since he had got ₐ reputation as a John Brown sympathizer.

He was still keeping in touch with rebels and with revolutionary think- ₑrs and poets as well as he could. James Redpath dedicated his book *The* ᵖ*ublic Life of Capt. John Brown* "To Wendell Phillips, Ralph Waldo Emerson, and Henry D. Thoreau, Defenders of the Faithful, who, when he mob shouted, 'Madman!' said, 'Saint!' " From Indiana, Emerson had ₓritten home: "I have not yet been able to obtain Darwin's book which ₗ had depended on as a road book You must read it,—'Darwin on Species.' ₗt has not arrived in these dark lands." He had hardly returned home, it ₛeems, when he found Walt Whitman in Boston and walked with him up ₐnd down the common to discuss the sheaf of sex poems ready for insertion ₙ *Leaves of Grass.* This time, as usual, he wanted to go along with the ᵣadical but also wanted the radical to listen to reason.

Whitman keenly felt the appeal of the objections Emerson made but ₓould not let himself be budged. "During those two hours," as Whitman ₚut it many years later, "he was the talker and I the listener. . . . each ₚoint of E.'s statement was unanswerable, no judge's charge ever more com- plete or convincing, I could never hear the points better put—and then Iᵗ felt down in my soul the clear and unmistakable conviction to disobey all, and pursue my own way. 'What have you to say then to such things?' said E., pausing in conclusion. 'Only that while I can't answer them at all, I feel more settled than ever to adhere to my own theory, and exem- plify it,' was my candid response. Whereupon we went and had a good dinner at the American House." "Enfans d'Adam," as the group of sex poems was then called, duly appeared, apparently without any alterations out of deference to Emerson's judgment, in the new edition; but whether Emerson's argument had any influence or not, it was a fact that in his later writings Whitman moved in the direction of the spiritual.

That spring Emerson attended a reunion that took him back to his days as a schoolmaster. Nearly forty years had transformed the girls he

and his brother William had once ruled over in their school for young
ladies in Boston. Now he faced some twenty oldish women; but he could
decipher most of them at once, as he wrote William. He needed help to
discover Isabella Tilden under her disguise as Mrs. Brown, and Miss Bangs
was hard to recognize in the person of Mrs. Williams. Miss Norwood was
much altered. Ann Carter had kept her beauty in spite of the stoutness she
had acquired. Emerson would hardly have chosen his own transformation
but he had at least gained by getting rid of some of his shyness. He made
his speech, received rings for himself and William, and found the occasion
so "entirely pleasant" that he missed the return train to Concord.

His favorite theory of moral sentiment, as old for him as his school
teaching, had reappeared a little earlier as the subject of his lecture at the
Music Hall in Boston, where he now sometimes helped fill in the gap left
when Theodore Parker was forced out by ill health. In May, Parker died
in Italy. At the memorial meeting in Boston, Emerson reluctantly made
a brief speech. Though he desired to honor Parker as a great liberal, he felt
aloof from that logical, sledge-hammer mind. To Moncure Conway's new
magazine at Cincinnati, he sent the manuscript of his lecture on "Domestic
Life" but would promise nothing on Parker. "My relations to him," he
explained to Conway, "are quite accidental & our differences of method
& working such as really required & honored all his catholicism & mag
nanimity to forgive in me."

Emerson now found life grown more mellow. About health he was
easier than ever before. He had never been able to give, as he said, "much
reality to evil and pain." Advancing age made him care less. People now
took his distinction as an author for granted, and he had the respect of
his own village. When he kissed Anna Alcott at her wedding, her sister
Louisa thought that his kiss would make even matrimony endurable, for
he was, she said, "the god of my idolatry, and has been for years." His
dream of a Concord literary community had been realized beyond any
reasonable expectation. At the end of June, Hawthorne, Thoreau, and
Alcott ate strawberries and cream with him to celebrate Hawthorne's return
from abroad. With Hawthorne at the Wayside, the house that had in
earlier years been Alcott's Hillside, Concord once more had its full quota
of literary celebrities.

In August, twenty-three-year-old William Dean Howells arrived from
the West, by way of Boston, to look them over. Having worshiped at the
shrines of Hawthorne and Thoreau, he advanced on the Emerson house,
armed with a card of introduction procured at the Wayside. He knew the
fame of Emerson as the impossibly incomprehensible one but had himself

ead the essays published in *The Atlantic* and a few of the poems and had
ot a strong impression not only of etherealness but of force, beauty, and
visdom. Confronting the fabulous man, he was struck by the youthfulness
f his face and by the strange charm of eyes that looked at the stranger
vith a vague serenity. He was reminded of Lincoln's eyes, though Emer-
on's were pleasanter and less sad. The profile of the Concord man sug-
ested an indescribable combination of gravity, quaintness, and subtle but
indly sportiveness. But the part Emerson played in the conversation was
ardly worthy of him. He spoke of Hawthorne and pronounced *The Marble
Faun* "mere mush." He talked not very accurately or weightily about the
West. He wanted Howells to know the poems of Ellery Channing, and
when he learned that his visitor knew of them only through Poe's cruel
riticism, he dismissed Poe abruptly as *"the jingle-man."* Howells retreated
n confusion.

Politics was now the recurring, inescapable subject of debate in every
American village. The new Republican Party, a radical reform party,
eawakened hope in the antislavery men of the North. Down to the Emer-
on house on the night of October 24, some two weeks before the fateful
lection day, marched the Republican youth in their torchlight procession.
"'Close order! open order! halt! ground torches! three honest A. I. cheers
or the gentleman and his son! R. W. Emerson!' Cheers, speech, left face,
a march by . . . a march by again with hats off as each passed, a turn
again round the mile post and march on to Mr Bull's, with fife and drums."
The air was electric. On Saturday evening, the 3d of November, came
he general Republican rally for which the Wide-awakes had been prepar-
ng. On Tuesday the 6th, at the Town Hall, Alcott cast his first ballot in
any Presidential election, voting for Abraham Lincoln and the other Republican candidates. Emerson must have cast his for the same party leader,
but undoubtedly it was not his first Presidential vote. Next morning the
news was, he said, "sublime, the pronunciation of the masses of America
against Slavery."

To the superficial reader, Emerson's new book, *The Conduct of Life,*
published on the 8th of December, must have seemed strangely out of
place in the midst of the exciting events that were sweeping the nation into
war. Politics seemed perhaps a distant and unreal thing to one who could
leave it long enough to enter fully into the mind of this calm, self-possessed
observer of life under the aspect of eternity. But Charles Norton may have
come nearer the truth when he told Clough that the book could not have
appeared at a fitter time. To him it seemed that its confirmation of moral
principles based on eternal laws was what was most needed.

Carlyle, with no thought of connecting it with American issues, found it "the best of all your Books" and "read it . . . with a satisfaction," he said, "given me by the Books of no other living mortal." He was certain that Emerson had grown, not only older, but "more pungent, piercing.' He was, for once, without a word of blame to say, and he became almost ecstatic in his praise of "The finale of all, that of 'Illusions' falling on us like snow-showers, but again of 'the gods sitting steadfast on their thrones all the while,—what a *Fiat Lux* is there, into the deeps of a philosophy which the vulgar has not, which hardly three men living *have*, yet dreamt of!" Undoubtedly Carlyle liked the book partly because of its less daring tone and less bold claims for the Transcendental ideals, now implicit rather than explicit. Alcott and Thoreau did not think so much of it. Thoreau was displeased because it was moderate and wanted the fire and force of the earlier books. Emerson agreed with Carlyle in believing that this one would sell. As he still kept the control of his works in his own hands, he ordered his printers to provide six thousand copies for Ticknor & Fields, his new publishers.

The Conduct of Life had no chapter on politics or on slavery and frankly gave up any debate on the spirit of the times in favor of the eternal question, "How shall I live?" But in undertaking once more the solution of the problem of the individual way of life, Emerson seemed resolved to offend common sense as little as possible. Some of his friends regretted the low plane to which he kept in discussing fate, power, and wealth. To those who had earlier accused him of refusing to open his eyes to the evil in the world, he now seemed, at least until he had got well along in his essay on fate, to have made a complete about-face. His imagination reveled in instances of nature's cruelty. He heard too distinctly the crackle of the bones of the victim in the coils of the anaconda and visualized the slaughter house at the graceful distance of some miles from the dinner table. No use to try to whitewash Providence "or to dress up that terrific benefactor in a clean shirt and white neckcloth of a student in divinity." Great men were perceivers of the terror of life and manned themselves to face it.

In general the essay on "Power" was on a this-worldly plane. The grand principle of compensation appeared there divested of its former halo. The "belief in compensation, or that nothing is got for nothing," characterized, Emerson said, all valuable minds "and must control every effort that is made by an industrious one." In "Wealth" he seemed vaguely to make morals one with industry, fell back upon the time-honored *laissez-faire* theory of economics, and did not quite save the day for ethical idealism when he made economics one of the lower rungs in a kind of Platonic adder to climb which was the object of true thrift. The reader must have been reminded of the old Protestant—or Catholic—theory that God prospered his own and that they in turn glorified God with their gain. Even in "Worship," where, as the essayist plainly believed, he was making up for any lowness of tone in the preceding chapters, he declared that " 'T is remarkable that our faith in ecstasy consists with total inexperience of it." It was sensible enough, in the essay "Beauty," to insist on the functional theory of art, and it was not the first time he had done so; but this too looked a little in the direction of the practical, non-Transcendental ideal of life.

Yet the old Emersonian products were by no means marked down or put in the basement. It was as if a merchant had taken his most valuable stock out of the window in order that the cheaper wares might have their turn on bargain day. It took only a little looking about to discover the familiar favorites. If fate seemed to threaten to grind down the soul into despair, the individual mind and will were there to insure a sphere of liberty. If this one was true, so was that other, its contrary. Underlying all was a determined optimism, as in the unquestioning faith that evolution pointed upward. There was no moral deformity that was not simply a good passion out of place. Self-reliance held its old virtue. The moral sentiment was, as before, a thing to conjure with when evil threatened. And the law that ruled throughout existence, "Law which is not intelligent but intelligence;—not personal nor impersonal . . . dissolves persons . . . vivifies nature; yet solicits the pure in heart to draw on all its omnipotence," was hardly less than the Over-soul, now no longer known by that name. Though they seemed to have lost a little of their lonely grandeur, the old gods were still sitting on their thrones.

22.

THE FIERCE STORM OF WAR

But when the blast of war blows in our ears,
Then imitate the action of the tiger . . .
　　—Shakespeare, *Henry V*

The thinking class are looked at inquisitively in these
times by the actors, as if some counsel were expected from
them. But the thinker seldom speaks to the actor in his time,
but ever to actors in the next age. . . .
　　—*Journals*

Everything about a civil war is lamentable . . . but
nothing more so than victory itself.
　　—Cicero to Marcus Marcellus, from the Latin
　　text quoted in *Journals*

DURING the final months of President Buchanan's administration
many Southerners believed that the Confederacy would peace-
fully assume its place as an independent nation, and many Northerners did not care if it did. Harassed and weary, the honest
old statesman who had been a compromise candidate acceptable to both
Northern and Southern Democrats only wanted to hold things together
until his successor could take over the responsibility and decide upon a
definite policy. Meantime the abolitionists kept their one goal always in
sight—the end of slavery, whether the Union survived or not.

After a few lectures that took him into the state of New York in January, 1861, Emerson, now avowedly an abolitionist, appeared on the 24th
of that month as one of the speakers at the annual meeting of the Massachusetts Anti-Slavery Society at Tremont Temple in Boston. Wendell Phillips, the archabolitionist, had just stirred up pandemonium with his speech;
and though some policemen who entered the room were asked for aid,
they would not interfere with trouble-makers. When Emerson was announced the sympathetic audience raised three vigorous cheers for him,
while the mob matched these with three for the Union; and for some time
he waited for a chance to speak. After he began to talk he was more than
once interrupted by noisy persons in the gallery and by the unruly crowd
pressing in underneath, and there were hisses, groans, and cries of "Put him

out," "Dry up," "Unbutton your coat," and so forth. It was in vain that he tried to ingratiate himself with his Boston audience by recalling his Boston origin. He had a hard time even to get through a story he wanted to tell. His own summary of the experience was that "sorely against my inclination and habit, I went, and, though I had nothing to say, showed myself. If I were dumb, yet I would have gone and mowed and muttered or made signs. The mob roared whenever I attempted to speak, and after several beginnings, I withdrew."

The financial prospects of the lyceum platform looked dark in this political crisis, but Emerson still received some invitations. Even San Francisco asked him for a course, though no transcontinental railroad was ready until some years afterward. There were, as before, his lectures to Parker's old congregation at the Music Hall. And there was the class of women, friends of the Emerson family, to whom he was to read lectures privately. He could also talk as much as he cared to before audiences that paid no admission fees. The exhibition of the Concord schools in March required "Remarks" to the pupils and townsmen impressively massed at the Town Hall. Emerson had long since served his time as teacher and as school committeeman. "And yet," he said, "when I heard new recitations and exercises I was willing to feel new interest still."

Once the period of indecision was over, the war began to appear and reappear like some monstrous crimson thread crossing the warp of every American's life. Lincoln, the President-elect, had kept silent as long as he could on questions of policy involving force but had managed, when he did speak, to rouse the dislike of the abolitionists by his reiterated promises to look to the Union, leaving slavery untouched wherever it already existed. In his inaugural address, on the 4th of March, he quoted himself, "I have no purpose, directly or indirectly, to interfere with the institution of slavery in the States where it exists." He made it plain that he would obey the Constitution in its provision that fugitives from service or labor should be delivered up on demand, and this meant in plain English that fugitive slaves would be returned to their owners. He insisted that Southerners and Northerners were not enemies but friends and that the "mystic chords of memory, stretching from every battle-field and patriot grave to every living heart and hearthstone" would yet "swell the chorus of the Union." There was nothing in all this to give much comfort to an abolitionist. Lincoln, no matter what happened, was obviously going to continue to put the salvation of the Union above emancipation. Emancipation could wait till it was an essential means to the preservation of the Union.

The test of the President's ability to keep the loyalty of his people came when the first cannon was fired against the flag of the Union at Fort Sumter. The whole North was electrified, and Lincoln became, in the people's eyes, the leader of a divinely sponsored crusade. Those who wanted to regard it as simply for the preservation of the Union were at liberty to do so, as that was the official view. But the old reformers, the irreconcilables like Garrison, and Phillips, and Emerson's friend Charles Sumner, were determined that the chief end should be the destruction of slavery.

Many years earlier Emerson had pleaded the cause of peace and had believed that war might be finally abolished once the individual citizen acquired the proper degree of mental and spiritual culture; but he had also cautioned the members of the peace society that "A wise man will never impawn his future being and action, and decide beforehand what he shall do in a given extreme event." Now he used his reserved right to become warlike. At the same time he cursed the unbearable evils that pushed him into this position. However consistent with his oration on peace, this new position he was forced to take was essentially false to his character and philosophy. He tried to be philosophic still. To Clough he wrote of "our mad war,—the most wanton piece of mischief that bad boys ever devised." Remembering the inflexible spiritual laws, he added, "But of shallow things the causes are not shallow . . ."

Two days before the anniversary of historic April 19, broadsides were shouting in capital letters through Concord village, "WAR! WAR! WAR!" and calling, "TO ARMS!!" One exhorted everybody to leave the farm and the workshop, the counting room and the office, and come to the Town Hall and prove that Concordians were not the degenerate sons of brave sires. The other demanded volunteers to fill up the ranks of the company about to march from the Old North Bridge. Within five days another handbill was repeating, "WAR! WAR! WAR!" and asking for volunteers, good men and true who would be ready for any emergency at a moment's notice. These were to be the modern minute men. Emerson had caught the enthusiasm by the 19th. On that day, as he told his daughter Edith, "our village was all alive . . . with the departure of our braves. Judge Hoar made a speech to them at the Depot, Mr Reynolds made a prayer . . . the cannon which was close by us making musical beats every minute to his prayer. And when the whistle of the train was heard, & George Prescott (the commander) who was an image of manly beauty, ordered his men to march, his wife stopped him & put down his sword to kiss him, & grief & pride ruled the hour. All the families were there. They left Concord 45 men, but on the way recruits implored to join them, &, when they reached Boston, they were 64."

Emerson had just begun a course of half a dozen lectures in Boston when the war broke. On the first day of his course, April 9, he had remarked that the critical times invited rather than repelled his themes; it would be wholesome to turn one's eyes from the alarms that threatened the fall of a character-destroying civilization to what was pure and permanent. But he soon had a change of heart. After discoursing on genius and on art, he explained that he had intended to offer next some illustrations of a law which had great importance in science, literature, and daily life, but that the tumult of the time made that lecture impertinent. Instead, he had something prepared for the occasion—"Civilization at a Pinch." This was on April 23, after the Concord company had marched away.

His thoughts were on the war. The war, he said, was giving the country a chance at last to stay honest in the eyes of Europe. Now the conspiracy had been forced out of doors. There was a hardy refreshment about war. He called for sacrifices. The South was well officered and, with some right, despised the peaceful North. Who knew the future of this war? Who knew whether a separation would not be the best issue, "a separation for the time"? He was drifting into a plainer, less poetic style, appealing more surely to the average intelligence of his audience. His daughter Ellen, watching him in action before a Boston audience some two weeks later, sat in a daze of pride and fear, sorry that she understood everything. She did not want to believe that his lectures were less intellectual now than they used to be. She "couldn't bear to have Father come down at all from his pinnacle."

On or off the lecture platform, he was out to help win the war. When he found that the drill club his son, Edward, belonged to lacked arms, he went to the adjutant-general of Massachusetts, got an order for thirty muskets from the Cambridge arsenal, and came home triumphant. He visited the warship *Minnesota* in Boston Harbor, delighted in her numerous crew and large cannon, and saw that guns of all kinds were arriving while he was aboard. At the Charlestown navy yard he felt the indefinable thrill that was a recognition of the terror and immense pretension of warlike adventure. "Ah! sometimes gunpowder smells good," he confessed.

He seemed to feel an upsurge of vitality. Thoreau, in his last, long illness, was ready to start to the upper Mississippi Valley to try, in vain, a change of climate. Emerson, once inferior to him in physical stamina, had husbanded his resources better. Emerson still looked to the future. He paid $500 for the Minott field on his western boundary line, thus rounding out his grounds. Early in July he accepted the offer made by Abel Adams to pay Edward's way through college. Edward, only seventeen that month, was excited over the war and was anxious to join the army but not strong enough.

The war was continually returning to trouble Emerson. He had a subscription of $50 to pay to the Concord Volunteer Relief Committee. He lamented the undemocratic dependence of the country on a few generals and cabinet officers. He painfully explained the causes of the war to his friend Herman Grimm in Germany. Sometimes he thought it was a war of manners, the difference being accounted for by climate and slavery; but he also saw that Northern industry had encroached daily on the planters, getting the balance of political power. He thought that the military effort would be short, since the North had overwhelming advantages, but that the period of adjustment would be hard. Confident of Northern success and glad that the crisis had been reached in the national disease, he wrote to Aunt Mary that "The shame of living seems taken away, & to mature & old age the love of life will return, as we did not anticipate." From Clough he got light on the English sentiment about the war. If it was true, as Clough said, that people in England were "brutally ignorant & unfeeling" about the American war, trouble might come from that quarter, given the right political complications.

At Bull Run on July 21 the North was rudely shocked from its hundred days of dreaming of a quick victory over the South. The bewildered Union soldiers Emerson's friend Mrs. Drury saw dragging themselves back into Washington seemed to tell a different story. The South, equally guilty of overconfidence, had to wait longer for its awakening to realities. The North felt a painful consciousness of divided purpose. Ellen put the crisis truly though too simply. The only grief, she declared, was that the Northerners had not yet made up their minds what they were fighting for. Emerson, conceding to Elliot Cabot that the war had now assumed such huge proportions that it threatened to engulf everybody—"no preoccupation can exclude it, & no hermitage hide us"—still thought it better than "what we lately called the integrity of the Republic, as amputation is better than cancer." He still believed in ultimate victory, but he poured out his wrath upon the Southerners with little restraint and saw the crisis so grave that he mentally put himself into the line of battle, declaring his hope "that 'scholar' & 'hermit' will no longer be exempts, neither by the country's permission nor their own, from the public duty." He confided to his journal, apparently somewhat later, that though "practically nothing is so improbable or perhaps impossible a contingency for me," he did not wish "to abdicate so extreme a privilege as the use of the sword or the bullet."

But his life continued to be largely that of the quiet literary man and unpretentious country squire. By early August he had taken to riding horseback a little with his daughters. The Concord Cattle Show was still a great social event, and his family received no fewer than ninety-nine guests. He and his daughters went in the carryall with his exhibit of fruit. As there was slight competition that year, he was for once a successful competitor, receiving two prizes totaling $3.00. Toward the end of every month the Saturday Club was apt to draw him to Boston. He dined with the brilliant and liberal Prince Napoleon, a remarkable replica of the great emperor. The prince, the second of the great Napoleon's nephews that Emerson had known, stuck to his French and Emerson to his English.

The Concord Soldiers Aid Society doubtless had much to do with the activities of Emerson's family. The women of the house were members. Presumably the three of them plied their knitting needles while Emerson read from Shakespeare, or tried to read, in spite of an inflammation that made him "very musical." He liked the sympathetic Frenchman Count Gasparin's book on the United States in 1861, a thing related directly to the present crisis. His own books, he told his brother, had had no sale this year and his winter lectures would mostly omit their dividends. These losses were serious, for he was now used to counting on a return of $500 or $600 a year from his books alone. His bank stock and other investments also began to yield less.

In his "American Nationality," read at the Music Hall in November, he painstakingly searched out benefits accruing from the war. He was pleased by the complete awakening of the country from mental torpor and by what he thought wholesale destruction of shams and counterfeits. He now endorsed the administration's determination to win back its lost territory, and he remembered with admiration the fine military energy President Jackson had once shown in thwarting South Carolina's defiance of the government. However vacillating the administration might be, he had no fear that half measures would succeed. Hawthorne reported with little exaggeration to his English friend Henry Bright that Emerson, "like the rest of us," was breathing slaughter. The partisan had almost swallowed up the philosopher.

While the Emersons were busy "knitting socks & mittens for soldiers, writing patriotic lectures, & economizing with all our mights," their familiar world seemed more unstable than ever. Alcott, in January of 1862, seemed a symbol of immortal leisure as he ended a spell of writing on "The Countryman in his Garden" and made the rounds of his friends' houses, taking apples and cider to Hawthorne, Emerson, Channing, and Thoreau. But Thoreau was consciously nearing his end, and Hawthorne, with two years more to live, was somber and apathetic. News of Clough's premature death had come from overseas. William Emerson's son William, now an invalid, had gone off to Curaçao, as his uncles Edward and Charles had gone off to the West Indies a generation earlier. Aunt Mary, at last growing senile, had asked and received assurance that her body would be brought back to

Concord for burial. Many years earlier she had begun wooing and expecting death, but this time she would not have long to wait. Emerson's son, Edward, trying to rebuild his health, had been working as a surveyor in Mount Auburn Cemetery at Cambridge and was now chopping a little every day in the woods. He had heard of a land journey to California that looked like the right road to health and so to a commission in the cavalry such as his friend William Forbes had.

Called to Washington at the end of January, 1862, to lecture at the Smithsonian Institution, Emerson studied the wartime leaders. Doubtless Charles Sumner, his chief guide during one busy day, indoctrinated him rapidly in Washington politics. From Sumner he must have got confirmation of his own strong feeling against any retreat from extreme abolitionist doctrine. From Seward, the secretary of state, his principal mentor on the following day, he could have had an antidote to this radicalism of Sumner's. Yet Sumner, chairman of the Senate's committee on foreign relations, exerted a steadying influence on the administration's foreign policy. He showed some of his British correspondence to Emerson. He was resolved that there should be no war with Britain. Seward had not long since suggested a European war as the best means of uniting North and South. Whether either of these political leaders was rational or not depended on the subject under discussion. Emerson struck up an acquaintance with the secretaries of war, navy, and treasury, and with the attorney general. He was twice taken to see the President, first by Sumner and later by Seward.

He saw when Sumner introduced him to Lincoln that the President, for all his lengthy awkwardness and uncouthness of movement, was quick on the trigger. "Oh, Mr. Emerson," said Lincoln, "I once heard you say in a lecture, that a Kentuckian seems to say by his air and manners, 'Here am I; if you don't like me, the worse for you.' " Emerson already knew the kind of culture that gossip had derisively pictured as Lincoln's. He had seen it in the West—possibly this same specimen of it, for Lincoln had very probably come to hear him lecture there. Though he was not pleased by its rawness, he could admire its force. The meeting with Lincoln made him more certain of substantial virtues under an unprepossessing exterior and minimized his fears. Already accustomed to the uncouthness of even such literary geniuses as Thoreau and Whitman, he was not blinded by prejudice. He saw that the Westerner was a "frank, sincere, well-meaning man, with a lawyer's habit of mind, good clear statement of his fact; correct enough, not vulgar, as described, but with a sort of boyish cheerfulness."

He listened while Lincoln "argued to Sumner the whole case of Gordon, the slave-trader, point by point, and added that he was not quite satisfied yet, and meant to refresh his memory by looking again at the evidence."

All this argument seemed to Emerson to show "fidelity and conscientiousness." Seward insisted on taking the unwilling Emerson to "the English Church" on Sunday and tutoring him through the unfamiliar service but afterward brought him to Lincoln for a second visit. Emerson observed statecraft in action as the President and his secretary of state discussed the dangerous *Trent* affair and the critical relations between the United States and Britain.

At Coolidge Castle, or Bush, as the family had begun to call it by about this time, life was becoming less retired than ever. Aunt Susan Emerson, William's wife, from New York, was a boarder for some months, and two of her sons were with her a part of the time. Ellen's protégée, Edith Davidson, later nicknamed "Ellen's daughter," came for long periods of residence. The privacy of Bush was threatened still farther by the neighborhood travel through the pasture and alongside the house. Emerson took up his private bridge over the Mill Brook to halt this encroachment, but for some unexplained reason he put it back again within a few months. On Sunday nights visitors swarmed into the house. On weekdays Aunt Susan would ride horseback to meet the mail. The whole family was eager for news from Edward. Equipped with a new fund supplied by Abel Adams, a friend whose benefactions to the Emersons did not cease until after his death, Edward was now on his way to California. As Aunt Susan approached the house, waving a letter in her outstretched hand, her nieces would be waiting, together with their father, back from his morning inspection of the pears.

Emerson, as in earlier years, entertained the family by reading such a boyhood favorite of his as *Childe Harold's Pilgrimage,* still a favorite with him. Thanks to his traveler's and club man's habits, he had come to enjoy a cigar in his study, where books were no longer the sole attraction; but Edith, a lover of air unmixed with tobacco, might descend on him, open his windows, and finally drive him outdoors. He got into the habit of going out, even before breakfast, to visit the beehive, new this year. After breakfast he would again observe the bees and would entertain his daughters with remarks about them.

But outside Bush, Concord lost much of its worth this year. Henry Thoreau had loved Walt Whitman with a love which, Emerson thought, might have grown out of a taste "for wild nature, for an otter, a woodchuck, or a loon," but had "hated Alcott," "hated a sum that would not prove." Now he ended his long search for basic realities. Sam Staples, his former jailer, "Never saw a man dying with so much pleasure and peace." At the funeral Emerson read his prose address, but he had left it to Ellery Channing to compose the ode that was "plaintively sung," as other odes for special occasions had been sung before in Concord. Alcott read selections from Thoreau's first book and one of Thoreau's poems.

For Emerson the muse remained dumb, but Channing wrote many verses in honor of their former companion on country roads and in the fields. Channing described the gnarled and unsocial Henry as a "sweet man of Nature" and associated him lovingly with White Pond and its dark, familiar grove, and

> deep green shadows, clefts of pasture ground;
> Mayhap a distant bleat the single sound,
> One distant cloud, the sailor of the sky,
> One voice, to which my inmost thoughts reply.

Emerson sorted over his memories of Thoreau, found them satisfying, began reading the voluminous manuscript journals, prophesied that if they were published they would sow a new crop of naturalists, and considered setting about their publication himself. He read a lecture on Henry at the Music Hall in Boston. A few years later he published the first edition of Thoreau's letters and refuted the charge, frequently made, that as a writer Thoreau was a mere imitator of Emerson.

The war was dragging on with no end in sight, though sometimes Northerners indulged in empty dreams of a brilliant military coup. One day in June of 1862 Emerson, hearing cannon fired in Boston, wondered whether Richmond had fallen. But the much puffed young Union general proved a disappointment. "Strange," Emerson disgustedly wrote in his war journal, "that some strongminded president of the Woman's Rights Convention should not offer to lead the Army of the Potomac. She could not do worse than General Maclellan."

Emerson wanted no peace so long as slavery existed. "If it costs ten years of war," he declared, "and ten to recover the general prosperity, the destruction of Slavery is worth so much." But now even emancipation would not be enough, he thought. In August of this year he feared that if Lincoln delayed much longer the South might adopt emancipation before the North could and so appear before the world as the champion of freedom, gain recognition from France and England, and put the North in a false and disastrous position. He was in agreement with Sumner but was also swinging towards Lincoln's doctrine of the importance of the Union, it seemed.

Though he remained more in Sumner's camp than in Lincoln's, the preliminary Emancipation Proclamation, issued in September, caused him to make an almost complete recantation of his distrust of Lincoln. Lincoln had "been permitted to do more for America than any other American man," he publicly admitted. He was willing to forget "all that we thought shortcomings, every mistake, every delay." Yet even this recantation contained a note of warning. Lincoln must not fail to live up to his promise and make emancipation an accomplished fact. In the privacy of his journal Emerson commented that the President thought emancipation almost morally wrong and resorted to it only as a desperate measure. It was true that Lincoln, the supposed temporizer, had kept from the start his single-minded devotion to the cause of Union. Only a few weeks before his preliminary proclamation he had written to Greeley: "If I could save the Union without freeing any slave, I would do it; and if I could save it by freeing all the slaves, I would do it; and if I could save it by freeing some and leaving others alone, I would also do that."

Edward, after some five months of travel, was home again with the story of his severe hardships: At Omaha he joined a train of goldseekers and emigrants, mostly farm people from Minnesota who went on horseback or on foot beside their mule teams. He bought a roan mustang for his own mount, and she nearly broke his neck after five minutes of acquaintance. But for the next two months he rode her across the prairies and the plains. There was never a settlement in sight and only here and there a band of Pawnees or Sioux. The Indians were dangerous till the travelers reached Fort Laramie. There the westward-bound column halted till enough recruits had joined it to make a total of some eighty men or boys bearing arms. At the Great Divide many of the company turned north to look for gold in Montana But Edward and some others followed the California Trail, and in August they arrived in Salt Lake City. Thence, with a single companion, Edward pushed on through the desert nearly forty miles a day till they had the good luck to sell their animals and equipment and took the overland stage. His companion bade him farewell and settled in Nevada. But after four days and nights of miserable bumping across the Sierra, Edward arrived in Sacramento, and early in September he was at San Francisco. Before the end of that month he was at Panama, ready to cross the isthmus from the Pacific to the Caribbean Sea. Early in October he reached New York and quickly came to Concord, where the family set to work to put some flesh on his bones. His heroic efforts to prepare himself for a soldier's life had failed. Wanting health for the army, he obeyed his father's wishes and went back to his studies. The family were his classmates through Harvard. In his freshman year they were indignant about hazing. Next year, when they heard of sophomore exploits, they were sophomores.

On the 1st of January, 1863, with Lincoln's new proclamation, the provisions of the preliminary one took full effect, and emancipation was a fact. A jubilee was held in Boston on that day. Fearful lest his part, "a string of verses, a sort of Boston Hymn," as he said, should not be ready for the occasion, Emerson had refused to let his name appear on the program. But at the last minute he whipped the recalcitrant verses into form, and his was actually the opening gun in the sputtering fusillade of thanksgiving and congratulation at the Music Hall. The poem, though it had really been begun several years earlier, seemed made for the occasion and was quite as devout and almost as militant a composition as Julia Ward Howe's battle hymn. In it God addressed his admonitions not only to the Pilgrims but to their successors and to all Americans of the year 1863. This "Boston Hymn," as Emerson ended by calling it, showed that he had now reversed his ante-bellum plea for the purchase of the blacks from their white masters. One of his quatrains rang out like a bugle call:

> Pay ransom to the owner
> And fill the bag to the brim.
> Who is the owner? The slave is owner,
> And ever was. Pay him.

It was a fine burst of moral indignation. So far as the slave was concerned, it was just; but it added to the general feeling of bitterness toward the white Southerners, bitterness that later begot the madness of the reconstruction era and disgraced the conquering North. Meantime, though the "Boston Hymn" was without the popular appeal of the familiar army songs, to such Negro soldiers as could understand it, it was as good as a ration of powder and bullets. A surgeon who read it to Thomas Wentworth Higginson's black regiment on a South Carolina island thought that "Emerson would have trembled for joy to see how much the men drank in the religion of his poem." The black regiment's opportunist chaplain promptly took the poem for his text. Emerson, putting his own preachments into practice, spoke at a meeting in Boston for the support of Shaw's Negro regiment and paid a subscription to the regiment fund.

Meantime, during the winter, he was back in the lyceum groove. With the help of a friendly but either inefficient or unfortunate Western agent, he made a tour that took him as far from home as Chicago and Milwaukee. At Niagara Falls, in the only hotel then open, he was aroused at three o'clock in the morning by the cry of fire. Gathering up some of his personal belongings, he escaped through a cloud of smoke and cinders. The house was thoroughly burned out, and he had managed in the confusion to lose his ticket from Buffalo to Chicago. But having walked the two miles to the Suspension Bridge, he came opportunely upon Reuben Rice, once co-director with him of the Concord Atheneum. Rice was now superintendent of the Michigan Central Railroad, and, as if posted at the bridge by special act of providence, he insisted on giving Emerson a pass from Detroit to Chicago, thus saving him a large part of the expense of replacing the lost ticket.

At Indianapolis, on the way back, Emerson heard the pianist Gottschalk and the prima donna Carlotta Patti mainly because he had to wait several days for them to vacate Masonic Hall. Lawyers and college professors were brought to see him while he waited. He attended an examination of the classes at the asylum for the blind, made a brief speech there, and recited a ballad of Walter Scott's. When he finally lectured he seemed to get small honor. According to one local reporter his delivery was just good enough to get out an idea but could not keep it on its feet. What the reporter admired was Emerson's trick, doubtless unconscious, of "seeming to forget the last word or two, always significant . . . and stumbling upon them unexpectedly with an effect that the most elaborate declamation could not produce."

At Pittsburgh, having more days of enforced idleness, Emerson made the most of his opportunities. At one forge he saw the casting of a fifteen-inch cannon, "the sublime in mechanics." He was struck by the show of power and beauty. "The look into the furnace," he said, "is like looking at the sun, and, after the eye is a little used to it, you begin to see the white iron thawing into drops & rivulets, like thawing glaciers, until presently you see floating islands, all white, in the white sea. We stayed a couple of hours: at last the ore was ready in the two great furnaces; the great clay spouts, one from each, were heated by burning chips, &c. and the rosy iron brooks rushed out along these channels, say 40 feet long each, into the mould, which is sunk into a perpendicular pit 18 or 20 ft deep Tis a wonderful spectacle, & one comes to look at every one in the crowd of workmen with vast respect." In February he was as far north as Montreal.

Emerson pondered the war again and tried to convince himself that it had its good points. In Boston he joined the Union Club, which symbolized devotion to the ideal of a united country. He watched Lincoln closely. The President, he thought, "should remember that humanity in a ruler does not consist in running hither and thither in a cab to stop the execution of a deserter." He believed that the results of universal suffrage ought to be accepted and that there was no use in pretending that fine gentlemen could be elected who would please the English or the French. Lincoln's taste could not be refined. But citizens ought to hug themselves if they had got "good nature, honest meaning, and fidelity to public interest, with bad manners,—instead of an elegant *roué* and malignant self-seeker."

Emerson complained of the British government's winking at the building in British ports of ships of war for the Confederates. He wrote English friends letters of introduction for Moncure Conway and William Evarts, Northern agents sent to England to try to influence English opinion. Sometimes he retreated into his naturally pacific Transcendental mood. He confessed "that this mad war has made us all mad; that there was no minority to stand fast for eternal truth, and say, Cannons and bayonets for such as already knew nothing stronger; but we are here for immortal resistance to wrong; we resist it by disobedience to every evil command, and by incessant furtherance of every right cause."

His mind was carried away from the war and back to his boyhood years. Aunt Mary Moody Emerson, having lived into her late eighties in spite of her early desire for death, died at last on May 1, 1863. Her body was brought back to her native Concord, where Emerson, Lidian, Ellen, Edith, and a few others followed it to Sleepy Hollow. Emerson brought friends home with him and offered to "produce all the memorabilia of the Sibyl," but they failed to ask for any. "The present," he acknowledged, "is ever too strong for the past, & in so many late years she has been only a wreck, & in all years could so readily be repulsive, that few know or care for her genius." He seemed to be the only one who cared. "Her genius," he said, "was the purest and though I have learned to discriminate & drop what a huge alloy of theology & metaphysics, her letters & journals charm me still as thirty years ago, & honor the American air."

One of the oddest events of the Civil War, or so it must have seemed to him at first thought, was his appointment as member of a committee of visitation to West Point. But he was known personally to Stanton, the secretary of war, and to others at Washington, and the obvious effect of choosing him was to give a certain moral dignity to the doings of the War Department and brace the loyalty of citizens who cared for such a thing as morality even in wartime. He did not learn until after his arrival at West Point that his committee was expected to remain there for some two weeks, a thing he had no intention of doing. But while he stayed he picked up a few ideas for future use. He heard an examination in the scientific classes. He went into the barracks, admired the perfect order, saw the mattress on the iron bed rolled up into a scroll, talked with a cadet: " 'Who makes your bed?' 'I do.' 'Who brings you water?' 'I do.' 'Who blacks your boots?' 'I do.' " This was a lesson in self-help worth using in the address Emerson was to make at Waterville College a few weeks later. He saw flying artillery drill, watched a mortar practice with eight- to ten-inch shells, witnessed a siege battery in action against a target over five thousand yards away. He was, it seems, one of the most attentive members of the board.

John Burroughs, a budding naturalist who was teaching a country school near by and was much at West Point, learned to his surprise that a committeeman he had taken to be an eager and inquisitive farmer was Ralph Waldo Emerson. After a sleepless night because of his discovery, Burroughs got Myron Benton, a "rural philosopher and poet," to introduce him and start him off on his first conversation with the Transcendentalist. Both Benton and Donald Mitchell, known by his pen name of Ik Marvel, were with Burroughs; and the three, filled with a sense of the importance of coming upon Emerson much as if they had discovered Socrates on the banks of the Hudson, carried his shiny black oilcloth bag as they trudged beside him to the landing. They listened to his talk as he bought his ticket, boarded the ferry, and started across the river, for he was still talking as he moved out into the stream. He had come to examine and report on an army establishment, but his true character had got the better of the pretended military inspector when he had been challenged by Burroughs and his friends. The committee, in making their report, confessed "some embarrassment from the fact that all were inexperienced in the special duties here assigned them" but commented resignedly that such, they learned, had been the history of former boards.

Lectures at Dartmouth and Waterville Colleges were incidents of that summer of 1863. At Waterville, and perhaps at Dartmouth, Emerson lashed out angrily at England. He declared that the war had been a revelation, had shown that it was not because of slavery that England disliked the United States. England's deeper interest was not in freedom but in trade and in her superiority of all kinds. As her dominant role had been threatened by the Americans her joy was great in seeing this nation broken. Her interest in the success of the rebellion was now undisguised. England had great merits, Emerson wrote more calmly in his journal, but had failed when the occasion for magnanimity, the Olympian hour, had arrived. Yet he took care to exempt some persons in England from the general blame. He set Carlyle, culpable as he was in his political opinions, safe to one side on a high pedestal, for, as he decided, his friend's errors were nothing compared with the merit of his manly attitude. He carefully excepted all of "the truly cultivated class" of England. That class of persons, whether in England, in France, in Germany, or in America, existed for each other "across all possible nationalities." Having excepted these, he seemed willing to condemn the rest, though he thought the proper American answer was not war but contempt. He had never been so bitter against any nation.

His aroused fighting spirit had more than once flared up in verses written in wartime. It had flamed high in what served as a dirge for Colonel Robert Shaw and his slain followers of the Negro regiment later memorialized in bronze relief by Augustus Saint-Gaudens. He had quickly forgotten the minor key of his opening verses,

> Low and mournful be the strain,
> Haughty thought be far from me;
> Tones of penitence and pain,
> Moanings of the tropic sea;

and had drifted into a denunciation of the statesmen who failed to end slavery. It was in this poem that he made his appeal to the heroism of the young soldiers:

> So nigh is grandeur to our dust,
> So near is God to man,
> When Duty whispers low, *Thou must,*
> The youth replies, *I can.*

To Emerson, Colonel E. N. Hallowell's letter of a few weeks later must have made these lines seem ironical. Hallowell wanted permission to ask Emerson's son, Edward, to join up. The colonel explained that his regiment would soon have a vacancy among its second lieutenants, and he mercilessly reminded Emerson that younger men than Edward had died to establish freedom. Hallowell's regiment was the same Fifty-fourth that Shaw had commanded. As for Edward, he would gladly have risked his life if he could have found anybody who would pass him on the score of health and let him into the army.

Wartime was a hard time for a philosopher, yet there were moments when Emerson dropped his newspaper and calmed himself with the belief that the universe was not going to blow up. "On the whole," he reflected, "I know that the cosmic results will be the same, whatever the daily events may be."

In such a mood, perhaps, he turned to the manuscript journals left by Henry Thoreau. He saw, as he helped arrange selected pages and advised about the contract with the publisher or read again in the manuscripts with growing admiration, that Thoreau had been more a man of action in some respects than he himself. He saw that the much younger man had been more practical in carrying out ideas the two had had in common. But it was he, Emerson, who had really been the pioneer, it seemed to him. As he reviewed Thoreau's life he could imagine himself a mere spectator in a gymnasium where youths were leaping, climbing, and swinging with unapproachable force, yet he reflected that "their feats are only continuations of my initial grapplings and jumps."

He was back on the lecture platform in December with "The Fortune of the Republic," fighting his war once more, gathering up his accumulated indictments of England and flinging them at her with what must have been telling effect on his audience. He did not want a British war, but he had to ease his mind. As for the republic, he was full of hope, seeing the light breaking in all directions. Why should he not have faith in America? For America, he told his listeners, existed for the regeneration of the world by bringing social and political institutions to the ideal standard. That winter he carried the same lecture through the New England towns and to Brooklyn.

To his fame as a literary man was added his repute as a loyal and influential citizen. He wrote his share of suggestions regarding promotions and appointments. He had, it seems, been chiefly responsible for Charles Sumner's election to the Saturday Club, the first election that the thoroughgoing abolitionist had ever received to anything in Boston. He had also used his acquaintance with Washington officials in an attempt to further the fortunes of the picturesque Walt Whitman. The New York poet, having wandered "through camp and battle scenes," had fetched up in Washington, as he himself put it, "in harsh and superb plight" and so found it "necessary for me to fall for the time in the wise old way, to push my fortune, to be brazen, and get employment, and have an income." Whitman had unblushingly provided Emerson with a model form of recommendation, presumably of no use. In writing to Chase, the secretary of the treasury, Emerson had acknowledged that his friend was not without "marked eccentricities" but had loyally pointed out his "great powers and valuable traits of character." "If his writings," he had explained, "are in certain points open to criticism, they show extraordinary power and are more deeply American, democratic and in the interest of political liberty than those of any other poet." But when Whitman eventually got his government job it was not under Chase.

In Concord, Emerson had war matters and town and domestic matters to look after. He spoke at the Concord fair for the benefit of Negro orphans. The fair was a part of the local war effort. The town meeting elected him chairman of the school committee. If he was reformer and educator, he was also gentleman farmer. He had long since become an authority on horticulture. George Bancroft had asked him for advice about pears and had been given a list of fifteen varieties recommended "with much confidence" as suitable for filling the season. In 1864, the master of Bush scored again at the Cattle Show, taking a third prize for pears. Even at this late period the social life of Bush and the numerous cares of house and farm could be too much for him. At times, it seems, he went off to a hotel in order to write without interruption.

One of the most hopeful signs of the survival of a civilization diseased with war was the Saturday Club's celebration of the tercentenary of Shakespeare's birth. Emerson, with his fellow committeemen, Holmes and Lowell, labored with might and main to gather in guests from the Boston and New York areas. He also wrote a speech for the occasion, as the extant manuscript proves, though it is possible that, for some unexplained reason, he did not give it. Elliot Cabot, a member of the club, said he remembered Emerson at the dinner, getting up to speak, "looking about him tranquilly for a minute or two, and then sitting down; serene and unabashed, but unable to say a word upon a subject so familiar to his thoughts from boyhood." Yet Emerson's later silence and the silence, apparently, of all but Cabot throw doubt upon the accuracy of Cabot's memory. Almost exactly two years later, it would seem, Emerson was referring to this speech as "My speech at the Shakspeare festival," as he would hardly have done had he failed to deliver it.

Hawthorne, too weak to attend the Shakespeare dinner, died within a few weeks. With other members of the Saturday Club, Emerson walked beside the coffin up the hill to Sleepy Hollow in "a pomp of sunshine and verdure, and gentle winds." As he thought back over his late neighbor's Concord days and over the somber tales and novels, or such of them as he knew, he was struck by "the painful solitude of the man, which, I suppose," he said, "could not longer be endured, and he died of it." As Emerson had failed to discover the highest excellence of the tales and novels, so, doubtless, he left out of account the part Sophia Hawthorne had played in her husband's life. But he had long vainly waited on Hawthorne's moods in the hope of conquering a friendship for himself. "Now," he said, "it appears that I waited too long."

With both Thoreau and Hawthorne dead, Alcott made a larger part than ever of Emerson's literary society; and, unfortunately, he spoiled conversation by insisting too much on his theory of the nature of God—"personality," or "personalism"—while Emerson still held to his own belief in the "profound need of distinguishing the First Cause as superpersonal." The "thesis of personality" was hardly more than Alcott's peculiar version of a religious opinion held by much of Concord and Massachusetts, including all the Emerson family, it seems, except Emerson himself. Much to the surprise of some Bostonians, it came out that in their home village both Emerson's daughters taught in Sunday school and, in spite of their immense pride in their father, not only admired but emulated their mother's more conventional religious faith. Edith Emerson was even persuaded that if her mother had not brought them up as Christians her father would have done so himself. Thus Alcott's retreat in the direction of religious orthodoxy could not have completely upset his neighbor at Bush but might easily have bored him as a too frequent subject of conversation.

Yet Alcott had values that were still prized, as he himself knew. He seems to have suspected that Emerson came to him "to feed on him." Emerson read his own mind differently, being convinced that he talked with Alcott "not so much to get his thoughts as to watch myself under his influence. He excites me," Emerson explained it, "and I think freely." Whatever reward Emerson had expected, he had cared enough about it to go on raising what he called his Alcott Fund. During some eight years this had grown at the rate of slightly less than $100 a year, the approximate amount of the contribution he himself had once made to it, but had also decreased at times by reason of payments made to the beneficiary.

Emerson was more and more widely accepted. In 1864 he was elected a fellow of the American Academy of Arts and Sciences and neatly pigeon-holed, in imitation of the French manner, in Class III (Moral and Political Sciences), section 4 (Literature and the Fine Arts). He was also to have been a member of the National Academy of Literature and Art, being one of the twenty persons named in the bill of incorporation that his friend Sumner introduced in the Senate this year but never got through Congress. Walt Whitman, obviously unacceptable to Congressional critics, was not on the roll, nor was Herman Melville. If Congress could have understood Emerson it might have eliminated his name; but, as matters stood, public opposition to the Concord liberal was about dead. Alcott began to lecture admiringly on "Mr Emison," much to Emerson's apparent disgust; and the elder Henry James, a less merciful critic, entertained his own lecture audience with a dissection of the man he had studied with such voracious curiosity. Matthew Arnold, rising to important stature as a critic, wrote Emerson a generous letter of recognition from England.

The war still overshadowed everything else. Edward, now twenty years old, was insistent again on quitting college and entering the army. Emerson and Lidian began by giving him leave to enlist for garrison duty only. Then Edward made up his mind to see active service, and they would not command him to desist. But Edith wrote him a plea on behalf of their father. She could not help asking Edward, "Which seems to you of most value to your country—the services of one private for a month or so or Father's life and work?" She thought "that Father must break down; his public life must cease with your going for he has neither heart nor health for work." Edward, undersized and frail, tried to enlist before the war was over but never saw active service and carried his bitter regret to the end of his days.

Emerson meantime faced international and national political problems with great anxiety. He thought the British all squinted when they looked across the Atlantic—"lords, ladies, statesmen, scholars, poets . . . *Edinburgh, Quarterly, Saturday Review,* Gladstone, Russell, Palmerston, Brougham, nay, Tennyson; Carlyle,—I blush to say it; Arnold. . . . No Milton, no Bacon, no Berkeley, no Montesquieu, no Adam Smith was there to hail a new dawn of hope and culture for men . . ." He wrote to Carlyle that a visit to America "would have made it impossible that your name should be cited for one moment on the side of the enemies of mankind." He welcomed Edward Lyulph Stanley, later the fourth Baron Stanley, who, though he arrived with an introduction from Carlyle, was "on *our* side in politics." Emerson had him in Concord in company with Agassiz, Channing, Alcott, and Wendell Phillips. When Goldwin Smith came over with an introduction from Matthew Arnold, Emerson did more missionary work for the Northern cause. He went with this English guest to Naushon to show him John M. Forbes, Emerson's admired "only 'Squire' in Massachusetts," an effective friend of the Union.

At the Bryant festival in New York, Emerson made a graceful speech more fit for times when culture was nurtured than for wartime. But a few days later came the national election. According to Alcott, Emerson distrusted Lincoln, though less than Alcott himself did. But certainly voting the Republican ticket seemed the best available means of saving the country, and probably Alcott did not understand how far Emerson had now gone in accepting the President. Emerson seemed a determined supporter of Lincoln when he congratulated George Bradford on the results of the election. "Seldom in history," he said, "was so much staked on a popular vote.—I suppose never in history." He made his sentiments clearer still when he began the opening lecture of his course at the Melodeon, in Boston, late in the same month. At last he spoke with something resembling Lincoln's enthusiasm for the Union, but he did not go the whole way. The election, to his mind, decided that a nation was no casual combination to be dissolved lightly, or by stealth, or by violence; but he thought it did not decide that no separation should take place in an orderly fashion and by a solemn act of both parties if either party, because of geographic necessities or irreconcilable interests of production and trade, desired it.

The course on "American Life," as it was called, proved a great breadwinner, Emerson's daughter Ellen said. Requests came in from five or six cities for repetitions of all the half dozen lectures, and from weaker lyceums there were calls for at least one of them. Emerson was soon on the road, doing his best to supply the demand. Even before finishing in Boston, he had begun in the lesser New England towns, and by the middle of January he was well on his way to the West, where his principal engagements were at Chicago and Milwaukee. In February and March he used the Boston lectures once more at Worcester, Massachusetts.

The red tide of war was rapidly running out. When Lee surrendered, at the little Virginia village of Appomattox Court House that April, Emerson felt the full emotional impact of the great "event. It was, he wrote, "a joyful day . . . & proud to Alleghany ranges, Northern Lakes, Missisippi rivers & all lands & men between the two Oceans, between morning & evening stars." "Mankind," he said, "has appeared just now in its best attitude around Mr Lincoln—in these recent experiences—& will aid him to use sanely the immense power with which the hour clothes him." But he was troubled by the fear that Grant's terms were too easy; and, worried over the problem of reconstruction, he was once more tending in the direction of the extremists and away from Lincoln's policy. "If we let the Southern States into Congress," he predicted, "the Northern Democrats will join them in thwarting the will of the Government. And the obvious remedy is to give the negro his vote."

A few days after the surrender, Lincoln's death and the national pageant of the funeral, a prophecy of the War President's place in history, stirred men's feelings up again to a high pitch. Across the land, night and day, as Whitman wrote, journeyed a coffin, and in remotest villages where the news was known honor was done to the dead. In Concord, where they had celebrated Lee's surrender with a social dance in the Town Hall, people were asked to suspend all labor and business between 11 and 2 o'clock on April 19, the day usually kept as the chief local historic anniversary. The people gathered in the Unitarian Church to join the rest of the country in solemn funeral services. The order of services included music and selections from the Scriptures and prayers, together with what the printed program called addresses by R. W. Emerson and others. It was clear from what Emerson said to his neighbors on that day that he saw Lincoln now without any prejudice and acknowledged his virtues justly and fully: his soundness, tenderness, good humor, great ability as a writer, fitness to represent his people, fitness as leader in the great crisis. He conceded every point at last. Many passages in the President's letters, messages, and speeches, Emerson saw, were destined to wide fame. "His brief speech at Gettysburg will not easily be surpassed by words on any recorded occasion," he said. Lincoln's election to the Presidency was "a triumph of the good sense of mankind, and of the public conscience. . . . Rarely was man so fitted to the event. . . . Only Washington can compare with him in fortune."

Lincoln had at least been more fortunate than most Americans in the Civil War. If he had gone through the most terrible ordeal, he had had the satisfaction of sticking to his principles from first to last, the Union he had been determined to save seemed to be saved, and his wish that all men might be free from physical slavery was nearer realization. And if he had finally suffered death at the hands of an assassin, he was a martyr in the eyes of the world. Such fortune seemed to be the best that could have been expected.

Others concerned with the war were less fortunate. Emerson's scholar, the thinker, had, as Emerson had foreseen, been unable to speak very effectively in such an emotional crisis. He had inevitably been forced to be as much a man of action as he could, and the kind of action required had not given reality to his thought but had only made it seem less real. Giving rein to his feelings of loyalty and patriotism, he had felt a pleasing exhilaration. He had won ready acceptance as a loyal citizen and had therefore gained social prestige. But his real occupation was now nearly gone. He had had to retreat too far from his prized position as a philosophical observer. And this was true of the Transcendental thinker even more than of any other.

Emerson himself was a conspicuous example of this plight. For him, an idealist, the war had been a disease in his own system as well as in the body politic. He found it hard to get the poison of hate out of his blood. At the end of the conflict he could not refrain from writing down privately a list of the atrocities he charged against the South. His thinking did not thrive so well as before. He no longer enjoyed a sphere of almost limitless intellectual liberty. For him the idea of liberty had become too much constricted in the symbol of the manumitted slave. It was hard even for so puissant a liberal as Emerson to free himself from the narrowing boundaries of his postwar world.

23.

THE FIRMAMENT SHRINKS TO A TENT

> The god of bounds,
> Who sets to seas a shore,
> Came to me in his fatal rounds,
> And said: 'No more!
> No farther shoot
> Thy broad ambitious branches, and thy root.
> Fancy departs: no more invent;
> Contract thy firmament
> To compass of a tent.'
>
> —"Terminus"

FOR years Emerson nursed the idea of writing a *History of Liberty*. He planned that it should come down from the earliest times, and he presumably intended to make the Civil War his climactic chapter. In his commemoration speech at Harvard, where, perhaps because of his loyal support of the Northern cause, he had once more become acceptable, he held that war was "within the highest right" and was a "marked benefactor in the hands of the Divine Providence." He thanked the soldiers for "a new era, worth to mankind all the treasure and all the lives it has cost; yes, worth to the world the lives of all this generation of American men, if they had been demanded."

It was hard for him to face disillusionment now that he had felt a keen sense of triumph. It was not long before he realized that something had gone wrong, but he adjusted himself to the facts slowly and painfully. Everybody, it seemed to him, was back at his shop again and cared little about patriotism any more, even when thieves were stealing the public gold as well as the newly won rights of the slaves. After all, he saw, the war had left wounds that were not clean and would not heal quickly. He could already write with great tenderness to his old classmate and late enemy Robert Barnwell, a South Carolinian who had been a senator of the Confederacy. "But I wish you to know," he told Barnwell, "that distance, politics, war, even, at last, have not been able to efface in any manner the high affectionate exceptional regard in which I, in common I believe with all your old contemporaries of 1817–21, have firmly held you as our avowed chief, in days when boys, as we then were, give a tender & romantic value to that distinction, which they cannot later give again." Yet he was intent mainly on upholding the newly won rights of the Negroes, and he shared the average Northerner's ignorance of how criminal the reconstruction policy was proving in practice and how dangerous it was to the future welfare of both white and black races. He distrusted President Andrew Johnson's attempt to continue Lincoln's policy of generosity. With many other Northerners he regarded Johnson as a victim to the blandishments of the Southern planters and as a traitor to the cause of liberty.

He gradually moved out of the shadow of the national tragedy and put his mind on other matters. Soon after the close of the war, he visited several of the smaller New England college towns. He read lectures at Ripley Female College in Vermont and at Williamstown and Amherst in Massachusetts. At Williamstown he left an indelible impression on Charles Woodbury. Woodbury, seizing what scant opportunity he could find, attempted in a much less than half-hearted manner the hopeless task of being Emerson's Boswell. He was also one of the many enthusiastic students who put up notices, rang the college and church bells, and collected both undergraduates and faculty in the meetinghouse to hear Emerson.

In Concord, at what was officially called the seventy-first annual exhibition and cattle show of the Middlesex Agricultural Society but was locally known as the Cattle Show, Emerson made a speech on the governor's appointment of a commission to inquire into the means of replanting the Concord and Merrimac Rivers with fish. Besides the speaking in the Town Hall, there were a plowing match, a trial of strength and discipline of working oxen, and a procession of officials and others escorted by the West Cambridge Band. Various classes of livestock and farm produce were exhibited—stallions, breeding mares, colts, farm horses, family and matched horses, roadsters, bulls, milch cows, blood stock, milch heifers, working oxen, fat cattle, swine, poultry, grain, fruits, vegetables, flowers. Ephraim Bull, originator of the Concord grape, was naturally chairman of the committee on grapes. Being by this time a veteran exhibitor of pears, Emerson served as a member of the committee on pears. He and his fellow committeemen required competitors to make full reports in writing on their modes of cultivation and their methods of keeping and ripening pears.

At Bush the most important day was when young Colonel William Forbes, the son of Emerson's friend of Milton and Naushon Island, was married to twenty-three-year-old Edith before the long window in the parlor, with the Unitarian minister conducting the ceremony. After the wedding the bride made the final preparations for the "wedding-tour" of a week at Pigeon Cove, "kissed all her family and went down the front stairs." Her father and Ellen, looking out the front entry window into the bright October sunshine, saw Will Forbes, the handsome ex-cavalry officer, standing beside the team of horses and the buggy; "and," as Ellen put it, "down the walk went little Edith Emerson in her brown hat and dress, away from her father's house for evermore and gave her hand to her bridegroom at the gate and he put her into her seat, tucked the shawls all round her, walked round and got in the other side, and they whirled away." Girls from the neighborhood's literary families had their less important parts in the occasion still to complete. Una Hawthorne, now "certainly become one of the family at last," helped pack the presents. May Alcott, Louisa's sister, packed up Edith's books.

Emerson, extremely fond of his daughter, began to make his daily comments on his loss: "There are several very agreeable circumstances about that child's going away, but there is one sad one and that is that she is gone. . . . Yes she was an idle minx, but she has gone and she troubles me." In his new son-in-law, however, he had a financial adviser to relieve him of many of his old troubles. Now that he could not hope to continue his lectures many seasons longer, he saw that the family resources needed to be husbanded carefully. Within a few years Will Forbes had arranged better investments for Emerson's money stocks and had looked into contracts with publishers and spurred payment of royalties. Cousin Abraham Jackson, the dishonest manager of Lidian's real estate, was eventually brought to justice and to jail.

But meantime, the need of funds drove Emerson in December of 1865 as far south as Brooklyn, where he read half a dozen lectures and had the comfort of Charlotte Lynch Botta's hospitality in New York. In the following January and February the same need of money sent him westward over the long road to the Mississippi Valley. With the aid of a friendly Detroiter as his lyceum agent he had linked up towns in New York, Pennsylvania, Ohio, Michigan, Indiana, Illinois, Wisconsin, and Iowa in defiance of time and space.

The prospect of completing the three-year term of service on the school committee to which he had been elected in 1864 could not have pleased so experienced a man as he. And when he was called upon to assist Superintendent Bronson Alcott in examining teachers and pupils, he must have been convinced that he could not go on with such time-consuming duties. He quickly resigned, being succeeded in office by his brother William, a resident of Concord since he had tentatively retired from his law practice in New York. Emerson, however, continued his service as library committeeman as long as he lived, obviously finding it congenial and only a slight drain on his strength.

When he was home from his lectures he needed liberty for the recreation which his daughter Ellen urged him to take. Ellen might praise the spring weather and summon him to a long walk as early as the first days of April. He would wear his Illinois coat, hunch up his shoulders, and mutter abuse of the wind, the sky, and the earth. He would praise the fine trees and lament that they must fall. At Ripple Pond he would be enchanted with the ripples. They were, he said, the Aeolian harp of the eye. Or at home he might be discovered reading the *Odyssey* with one of the girls visiting at Bush, or he would delve into the old family papers and entertain all comers with them. Another day he would be at Milton with his daughter Edith Forbes, listening to an opera mostly improvised by her husband and her brother from old songs.

His Boston lectures in the spring of 1866 were a kind of festival occasion. The audience was much the same from year to year, so that the family knew almost everybody and enjoyed a lecture as if it were a party. The financial results were, as Emerson must have known in advance they would be, flattering enough. His publishers, Ticknor & Fields, had managed the course ably. In June a trip to Monadnock, where Emerson displayed surprising bodily vigor, was a different kind of family party, only a few days before Edward, still fighting hard for health, set out for some months in Iowa. Just as Edward was about to depart, Emerson had a message from the Forbeses at Milton. His voice broke as he read of the birth of his first grandchild, Ralph Emerson Forbes, Edith's son.

But honors did not come singly to the sixty-three-year-old poet and essayist. A week later he received the degree of Doctor of Laws from Harvard. He knew nothing of it till a neighbor came to Bush with the news in the evening after the ceremony. Next day it was announced in the Boston paper that he had been proclaimed " 'jucundissimum poëtam et hominem multarum literarum' . . . delightful poet and man of letters." President Hill's letter of notification explained that he had got the degree because he had cultivated literature and philosophy with distinguished success and had thus reflected honor upon his alma mater.

By the end of the following January, he had lectured his way for the first time as far as Minnesota. He discovered that Minneapolis was the "town of greatest promise in all the Northwest . . . the Falls of St Anthony being the waterpower, & all behind & around it a land of wheat & lumber." The Sautel Sioux warriors had been rounded up to the best of the white man's ability, and removed elsewhere; but at Faribault an old chief still presided over an encampment of miscellaneous old women, girls, young men, and dogs. Jean Baptiste Faribault, the French-Canadian fur trader who was their patron, conducted Emerson from tent to tent. In one, Emerson found a family all asquat and ready to devour their supper from a board placed on the ground in lieu of table. In another he and his party interrupted girls singing Indian psalms by the light, not of birch bark or pine knot, but of a kerosene lamp. Farther down the Mississippi River the same winter Emerson had a warm reception among the members of the St. Louis Philosophical Society, founded little more than a year earlier and already the chief American center of Hegelian thought. He could only admire, not understand, the tireless talk of William Harris and his nineteen or so philosophers and propagandists. Harris and his men were glad enough to have him as their guest lecturer but were bursting with their own version of the gospel according to Hegel. His curiosity was deeply stirred again when, a little later, he received the opening numbers of *The Journal of Speculative Philosophy,* the St. Louis society's remarkable publication that seemed to make the Missouri town for the moment the capital of all American philosophical studies. His long lecture tour had taken him to a new farthest west in Kansas. But he was growing weary of grueling journeys nearly half way across the continent and was prematurely resolved never to come to the West again.

On Concord's April 19 he was presumably escorted to the Town Hall, as the handbills promised he would be, by the Concord Artillery and by Gilmore's full band. As orator at the dedication of Soldiers' Monument on that day, he did his best to list the virtues of war and alluded to reconstruction in a tone little softened by two years of peace. But his tone was appealing as he recalled incidents of the conflict, with the families of the soldiers as his most interested hearers. A special section of the hall had been reserved for relatives of the dead named on the monument. Some of the incidents retold by the orator were drawn from the experience of the Concord boys. It was a number of months later that he wrote, with the inconsistency he shared with many wise men, that "Science shall not be abused to make guns" and that "The poet shall bring out the blazing truth that he who kills his brother commits suicide."

When the first bound copy of Emerson's *May-day and Other Pieces* reached Bush on April 28, only the format was still to be looked at critically by the family; and Ellen's opinion that, though the binding was pleasing, the print was "mean and cold and ugly" in spite of "all the fuss, the critical comparing of every sort of type, the visits to Mr Fields, and all the trumpeting I have heard" seemed a final judgment on that matter. As for the contents, these poems had been read in the family circle and doubtless greeted with an insistent demand for clarity; and there had been plenty of time for polishing. It was true that, though almost all of them had been written after the appearance of the first and heretofore only volume of his verse, a number had been printed during the twenty years since that book, and so were familiar and could hardly be changed. But except for "Brahma," which had by now an established reputation for impenetrability, there was little that would annoy the uninitiated reader.

Emerson may already have had in mind the program for modern American poetry which he soon wrote in his journal, a program calling upon the poet to let old times go and write on tariff, on universal suffrage, on woman suffrage, against war, against monopolistic greed, for freedom of communication, for laws made for the common and not the particular and selfish good. But if he was thinking it, he was not following it. Nor did his theory that science was dimming and extinguishing much that had been called poetry in the past—a theory he later explained to Mrs. Botta— leave any deep trace in his new volume. The long title piece, remarkable for its unflagging pleasure in the simple charm of nature, was such a confession as might have been expected from one who had haunted Concord woods and ponds half a lifetime. Memorabilia besides "Brahma" were "The Romany Girl," "Days," and "Terminus." Though not his last verse, the book was, as Emerson seemed to say in "Terminus," a valedictory to his muse. "Terminus," however, said much more than that. It was early to say so much, but the poem also announced Emerson's admirably restrained acceptance of the physical and mental decline that could not be long postponed.

But if Emerson accepted the inevitable in advance, he did not, like most aging men, turn conservative in his thinking. If his remarks at the meeting for organizing the Free Religious Association raised no new ripples on the surface of liberal thought, they showed no retreat from the divinity school address of nearly thirty years earlier. Some two years later he assured the same association that he rejected, not Christian doctrine, but the Christian claim of a miraculous dispensation, and he repeated his time-honored belief that "the moral sentiment speaks to every man the law after which the Universe was made." It was no accident that Emerson was the chief speaker at what seems to have been the first meeting of the Radical Club. He continued as unorthodox as ever. His English friend Lady Amberley, visiting Concord about this time, remarked that he never went to church, though his children went and Ellen taught in the Unitarian Sunday school.

In general the most orthodox had decided to forget his heresies, but now and then somebody belatedly discovered them and complained. "A man of wondrous mind, of most lovable nature," wrote a kindly critic after hearing Emerson lecture at Oberlin, Ohio, "his philosophy fails beside the faith of thousands of illiterate believing souls." A less tolerant Boston preacher told his congregation "that Mr. R. W. Emerson was 'a specimen of miserable, mutilated morality.' " Others reminded the veteran Transcendentalist of the Last Judgment and offered to pray for him.

Even in his own family, Emerson was still occasionally reproved for his freethinking. Lidian, as Lord Amberley said, was decided in her Christian belief and did not understand her husband's mind. Confirmed in her opposition by her daughters' liking for her mild orthodoxy, she enjoyed exercising her skill in debate. Emerson's skill in such an encounter was mainly in sidestepping troublesome arguments without yielding. With the passing of years the debate always remained unsettled. "Enchanting scene at dinner," Ellen once recorded, "Mother burning for theological controversy, hoping to reduce Father to a sense of the error of his ways. But each charge ran itself out in vain the smiling man had shifted his position."

The divinity school at Harvard was not yet in a relenting mood, but the university, having recently made him a Doctor of Laws, sealed its approval at the annual commencement of 1867 by electing him an overseer. And almost at the same moment he appeared for the second time as the orator of Phi Beta Kappa. It had been nearly thirty years since his address on the American scholar, and the second Phi Beta Kappa address was like a historical supplement to the first. It seemed to prove his prophecy of 1837 correct. It also suggested new advances for liberalism. It openly upheld women's claim to suffrage and cited "the search for just rules affecting labor" as another evidence of progress. It made much of science as a force of progress. It glorified the cultured minority. Self-reliance and the moral sentiment came to the surface once more. But it was far from true that in this address Emerson reached "the highest mark of his power as a writer"; and the solid but not extraordinary virtues it possessed were, moreover, obscured by the accident of the orator's physical distress when he read it. Ill health dogged Emerson that year, and on that day, for the first time in Ellen's memory, his eyes refused to serve him. He could hardly read.

But he continued with his lectures. He culled pages from old ones and carried them about New England and New York and even to the West. In December, 1867, he was off to Chicago and lectured there after appearing at scattered lyceums as far west as Des Moines. At St. Louis he stirred up his friends the Hegelians. But to his journal he confessed that Hegel was, to him, a bore.

Next spring he was as far south as Brooklyn. The New York journey, commonplace to him, got new animation from Ellen, now frequently his traveling companion and general assistant. Traveling was still an adventure for her. "Father came," her pen fairly sang to her sister, Edith, "and oh! the grandeur of starting to go to New York! The new-varnished car with

the exciting inscription 'New York & BRISTOL STEAMBOAT Line,' the
stateroom tickets in Father's pocket, the consciousness that there was a
new trunk with a canvass-cover (who would ever have thought of my
arriving at that dignity?) all full of new clothes, and a red flannel dress-
ing-gown, was enough to puff up anybody. I finished Father's new watch-
guard and presented it on the way, and Father read me all the poems in
the Transcript. . . . We were having a beautiful time when the boat became so very unsteady that I went to bed." In the morning, she said, "the
anxious Papa was up and dressed and begging for me at twenty minutes
past six."

In New York came the first test of Emerson's supposed familiarity with
the surroundings still strange to Ellen, in spite of her visits there. Ellen, not
much impressed by his performance, told Edith the whole story: "I never
had thought that Father wouldn't know the way, but he did not in the
least. So I told him Uncle William said Canal Street; down Broadway;
and Fulton St. and we walked along securely, but oh! so slowly that when
we reached Broadway I was tired. So we went to Trinity Church and sat
there and enjoyed the window till it was time for Brooklyn, and easily then
found our way to my much-desired haven."

In Brooklyn they found Henry Ward Beecher's church almost empty,
but it filled fast. Ellen must have watched her father for signs of panic, for
she knew too well his fear of being caught and indoctrinated with orthodoxy. But he "was intent on the people's faces, and said there were few
Calvinists here, one woman, that just came in, was, and one or two men
but most of them were no such thing, it always made its mark on people's
faces. he could always tell them by sight, or Methodists either, Methodists
were very different, but equally marked." Having been persuaded to go
to church with his daughter to hear the famous preacher, Emerson now
faced a new test of endurance. Some one was speaking, and Ellen looked
round. "There was Mr Beecher making the first prayer. I was pleased to
see that Father was so much interested at discovering him," she wrote, "that
there could be no doubt he had come willingly, for I had from the beginning made such a point of coming that I had given him no smallest chance
to be recusant, and had feared secretly that it was wholly a self-sacrifice
for my benefit. Dear Mr Beecher, you are just as good as you were . . . I
could not wish that Father should see you to better advantage than he does
at this minute. . . . Mr Beecher stopped to read some notices. . . . finally
he began to praise Mr Emerson, and to tell the congregation that he was
to lecture in Brooklyn this week, and when & where. Then . . . he . . .
preached about joining the church. There was nothing for it, but to forget
poor Papa as entirely as I could and devote myself to Mr Beecher on my

own account. . . . Father of course enjoyed the loud and cheerful uproar of the singing . . ."

They went out by a side door but soon found themselves entirely blocked. Emerson "caught a word from the winds," as Ellen told Edith, "and said 'Why! it is General Grant!' and hastened to push forward." The poet, still young at heart, caught his daughter's youthful enthusiasm and surrendered completely to it. "Father and I," Ellen said, "joined madly in this pursuit, and ran along, now in the street, now out, like little boys beside the trainers, and one way & another succeeded in seeing his head & shoulders, and, now and then, an interrupted glimpse of his face. . . . as we walked down the ferry-street, we saw the procession and its outrunners turning into it from a side-street nearer the boat than we, and immediately it was 'Up steam! and after them O my Soul!' . . . Then Father, saying 'We have nabbed him now; he can't get to the boat without our seeing him,' manned the small gate, and posted me in an advantageous position behind him. But we were outwitted. General Grant went in at the horse-gate. Father quickly discovering his intention rushed to the gate and saw him very well, so did I. He had an army-hat, but was dressed in old—Father wanted to say shabby—clothes with nothing in the least military about him. We could see just how tall & just how broad he was, and Father remembered and re-sented Edward's saying he was as large as Mr Geo. Brooks, declaring he was larger."

Emerson was insatiably curious about the man who had, people said, won the war. "All the trouble about squeezing in," Ellen wrote, "and the fact that we were all gazing at the General & not at the boat resulted in the boat's going off without us, so we had a long opportunity of staring. Our victim stood with his eyes cast down a little, as motionless as possible. Now arrived the boat from New York and instantly the news spread to all her passengers who crowded with all their might to get their share of the show. Poor Gen. Grant hastened onto the boat and into the ladies' cabin, his grateful country's people close at his heels or running in front as before. In the cabin he was cornered, every one formed in circles round him and then they began shaking his hand. Father & I as well as every one else watching his every movement, and Father approved, in my ear, the line of his nose, his 'resemblance to Michael Burke,' (which I do not see) his eye, and called my attention to the shape of his head. The moment he left the boat, we tumultuously followed and surrounded him, till he made his escape into a horse-car, and Father told me as we walked up that he had been much pleased with his manner and was glad there was nothing distinguished in his look."

After these adventures the Concord villagers arrived safely at the house of the literary lioness Mrs. Botta, whose guests they were to be; but Emerson was hardly in trim for his Brooklyn lectures. Mrs. Botta saw that heroic measures were necessary and promptly took charge of him. His cold, as Ellen told the story on the following day, "grew much worse, and last night she sent for Dr Knczsoffski a hydropathic doctor who packed Father's throat and came again at six this morning and packed him all over. Then at noon she introduced a rubbing-doctor who rubbed his throat, and he is just barely able to speak (in public) now, and has gone over to Brooklyn in a hack."

In July, Emerson persuaded Lidian, who was seldom farther from home than Boston, to go with him for a few days in Newport, the Rhode Island resort. In August a lecture at Middlebury, Vermont, was an excuse for him and Ellen to climb Mt. Mansfield from Underhill. The voice of the mountain was hard to hear in the uproar made by a party of players at the top, "filling the house, too, all night with violent fun." Though balked in their enjoyment of what Emerson called their "religious visits to the crags," he and Ellen had made up in advance for their loss by spending a day on the banks of the Winooski River at Essex Junction. Some days later he was guarding Bush alone against the danger of the night robberies from which Concord was suffering.

Deserting his sentinel's post, he got away to the Boston banquet for the Chinese embassy. There, as a lover of Oriental lore, he fittingly honored Confucius and his wisdom along with gunpowder and printing and the patient labor and stoical economy of the Chinese immigrants of California. His speech was brief, and, if William Clapp's story was accurate, was delivered without benefit of manuscript but in a form similar to the extant printed version. After the banquet Clapp asked for the copy he had been promised for the press. Emerson, pursued even to the cloakroom, rummaged in vain in his old-style carpetbag and concluded that he must have left the manuscript in Concord. But the press, still not willing to be put off though it was now past midnight, insisted that he write out the speech from memory; and, after a persuasive word from Charles Sumner, he agreed. Though he was taken to a brilliantly lighted room to do the writing, he wanted still more light, and candles were accordingly brought. From time to time he stopped to ask Sumner's confirmation of some passage. It was perhaps one o'clock in the morning when he finished. Next day he called at the newspaper office and made a few corrections.

In the space of a couple of years he suffered serious losses from the ranks of his friends and family. In a single month of 1867 had occurred the deaths of both Sarah Alden Ripley, the aunt who had spurred him up some of the lower rounds of the ladder of learning, and Abel Adams, his faithful financial adviser. A bequest of $2000 to Emerson, with $1000 to each of the three children, showed how Adams had kept his respect for his former pastor. Lucy Brown, Lidian's sister, a familiar figure in Concord; Susan Haven Emerson, William's wife, a resident of the village; and William himself all died in 1868. William returned to New York after his wife's death, but on a day in September, only a few hours after Emerson's arrival at his bedside, he was dead. He was the last of Emerson's brothers, and his death was a great loss. His probity had shone "in all his face and demeanour" and had been easily legible in the voluminous correspondence that had passed between New York and Concord over a long period of years. The two brothers had never been far apart even in the matter of religious opinion. When William's funeral was held in Concord, Ellen was troubled because pastor Grindall Reynolds read the usual service. At many funerals it had seemed to her to be appropriate, but she was sure that here it jarred on the minds of all who knew that neither Emerson nor his brother, nor his brother's sons, had accepted the creed it implied. Emerson, now sixty-five years old, walked with his two nephews behind their father's hearse.

In the autumn, when he lectured again in Boston, Emerson drew an audience that was a fit symbol of the regard which the cultured persons of that city had finally agreed was his due. Lowell was spokesman for Boston and for much more of America when he published in *The Nation* his homage to Emerson the lecturer. To Lowell, Emerson seemed to merit Ben Jonson's praise of Bacon as the one noble speaker of his time, full of gravity and nobly censorious in his language and so pithy in his thought that his hearers could not cough or look aside from him without loss. This was the judgment of a friend and did not describe the Emerson of the present so much as of the past. Leslie Stephen, listening to the first lecture of 1868 in a more critical mood, thought it rambling and incoherent. Certainly the purchasers of tickets who made, as Emerson said, "all my net receipts, as I read it $1655.75, which is by much the largest sum I ever received for work of this kind," did not hear so strong a voice as had been heard in earlier years.

The course was hardly over before his son-in-law, William Forbes, suggested that "a private class of young men," William Forbes's own friends and acquaintances, should be summoned "for readings of poetry or prose, & conversation." Emerson was delighted. James Thayer and others were brought into the directorate and agreed on a plan of readings to a limited group of both men and women, a friendly circle in which the lecturer could feel perfectly at ease. "I know what books I have found unforgetable," Emerson assured Thayer, "& what passages in books. . . .

I should like, in poetry, especially, to mark certain authors & certain passages which I prize, & to state on what grounds I prize them; & to distinguish good poetry from what passes for good." He thought that he could give some vogue to Oriental poetry and other "unfrequented sources" which he admired.

Measured in financial terms the readings were by no means so profitable as the lectures of a few weeks earlier, but in other respects they were perhaps as successful. The class was private and sharply restricted. The meetings, probably lasting not quite two hours, required ten successive Saturdays, or kept as near to that schedule as possible. A ticket for the course, so it was rumored, cost ten dollars. It came out through one member of the class that the readings were so quiet and leisurely that they gave one the sense of repose. Emerson struck Annie Fields as "extremely natural and easy" in manners and speech. Once he shut his eyes as he endeavored to recall a passage from Ben Jonson. Gradually, from week to week, he picked his way among his old favorites, and by the end of the course had covered "the great circle of English poetry from Chaucer to Walt Whitman." There was a difference of opinion as to whether he read too little and commented too much or commented too little and read too much. A reliable account of what he said on Walt Whitman might be among the most interesting of lost Emersoniana. But Ellen, often her father's faithful reporter, had sailed away in the autumn for a visit of some months to Fayal in the Azores; and if anybody else wrote an adequate account of the Boston readings of this winter, it has not yet come to light.

Numerous lecture appointments took Emerson out of town and even a few hundred miles westward before his Boston readings were ended. During the same eleven or twelve weeks he managed to give a whole course of lectures at Providence, where he soon afterwards added a couple of readings similar to those he had given in Boston. He gave private readings for friends or for clubs, and he lectured here and there through the season. Making a speech at the Humboldt centennial celebration in Boston and seeing the two volumes of *The Prose Works* through the press were for him lesser events of the year 1869.

One of his important days this year was the 26th of May, when he spoke before the New England Woman Suffrage Association and, to confirm the liberalism of his speech, allowed the women to elect him a vice-president. As late as 1867 he had shown signs of continued resistance to the feminists. When Alcott had gladly agreed to sign Lucy Stone's appeal for suffrage rights Emerson had refused. But now he said what was equivalent to signing that appeal. The suffrage movement, no whim but an organic impulse generated in the progress of civilization, was right, he declared, and the question might now well be put to the vote. Woman's claim to the ballot was sure to be granted eventually; and when it was, he believed, voting would be reformed, would be clean and honest and even polite. He indulged in poetical fancies regarding that happy future and conjured up palaces for voting booths instead of the taverns and corner groceries. It was obvious that he was not going to stand in the way of the new movement, yet the women did not escape without a few familiar words on special feminine virtues and graces. He was still restrained, and some two years later, in a family tea-table debate on the same subject, he drew fire from both the radical and conservative sides. "Father," Ellen put it, "won't speak one word till particularly requested he gives his views and as a reward has directly the fury of all his household levelled at them."

He was conscientious about his responsibility as an overseer of Harvard. He agreed with many other persons that the university needed reform; and he was presumably one of the majority of the overseers voting to approve the selection of Charles Eliot as the new, reforming president, for he was on the overseers' committee of notification. When hazing was discussed, he looked for counsel to Frederic Hedge, a person acquainted in his boyhood with conditions in Germany; but what action he took as a result is not clear. For years the question of compulsory chapel troubled him as well as the university authorities in general. There was much debate, and in the meantime the students had to go to prayers.

As Emerson was soon enthusiastic about President Eliot, he was doubtless on the side of the innovators when the overseers endorsed the new elective system early in 1870 and recommended its extension. He attended the overseers' meeting that voted to ask the corporation not to permit the granting of any degree in the academic department without an examination, as "under the present system a degree is hardly more than a certificate of residence at the University for a specified time and is of comparatively little value." The corporation placed him on a committee to present a new plan for the granting of Master's degrees. The plan recommended that an end be put to the old system of offering a Master's degree, for a small fee, to any well-behaved graduate of the college a few years after his graduation. Emerson often served on overseers' committees that visited the various departments of the college. He aided the Harvard College Library by steering into it the books Carlyle had collected for the writing of his history of Frederick the Great and wished to give to some library as a peace offering to New England. The gift of these books was Carlyle's apology for his earlier bitterness toward the New England antislavery reformers.

In October of 1869 Emerson carried the first four chapters of his "so-called new book" to his friend James Fields, the publisher; and in March of 1870 he was in print once more. The title *Society and Solitude* signified a long and still undecided contest between imponderable forces in his own experience. But except for its use in the first essay of this new series, it was merely a convenience, a roof under which he now stored old lumber from his workshop of earlier years. The book sold faster than its predecessors, but he saw that its popularity was mainly due to his fame. "Your name," he said, "has been seen so often that your book must be worth buying." This was doubtless the right explanation, though Carlyle averred that Emerson was here his old self and something more and judged the style "inimitable, best—Emersonian throughout." But Carlyle still looked in vain for the full recognition of evil he had repeatedly demanded. "How you go," he complained, "as if altogether on the 'Over-Soul,' the Ideal, the Perfect or Universal and Eternal in this life of ours; and take so little heed of the frightful quantities of *friction* and perverse *impediment* there everywhere are; the reflections upon which in my own poor life made me now and then very sad, as I read you."

By the autumn of 1869, after a period of incubation, the University Lectures, pointing vaguely in the direction of a graduate school, were entering upon their brief and unhappy existence at Harvard. Emerson, temporarily a member of the faculty, found himself advertised to give a series, not of half a dozen loosely connected or unconnected discourses such as he was used to reading on the lyceum platform, but of eighteen lectures theoretically forming a unit and concentrated on his calendar between April 26 and June 3. Instead of being a free lance, he was a component part of an omnibus course in philosophy. Francis Bowen, more than once his severe critic, led off with the philosophy of the seventeenth century, with John Fiske on Positivism and C. S. Peirce on the British logicians following. Emerson's friends Cabot and Hedge came next with roughly concurrent lectures. Cabot's were on Kant. Hedge's were on theism, pantheism, and atheism. Emerson's own part of the course was announced as "Natural History of the Intellect." George Fisher on Stoicism was last.

Now, at close range, Emerson did not find his new duties attractive. He knew that any such systematic study as the university expected was not for him. He still could not take formal philosophy with determined seriousness. He could not, he admitted, "read Hegel, or Schelling, or find interest in what is told me from them." It was a foregone conclusion that he would, for the most part, persist in his own very informal method. What attempts he did, nevertheless, make this year to arrange his thoughts more conventionally were painful.

On April 26 he began his instruction on schedule. Francis G. Peabody, one of the mere handful of registrants in University Lectures, scribbled a few catch words and captured a few characteristically Emersonian turns of thought and speech. According to Peabody the Concord philosopher denied any attempt at a system and wanted only to dot a little curve of personal observation. System-makers were gnats straining at the universe. The note-taking grew erratic after the opening weeks. Peabody got some idealistic and pantheistic ideas out of the fourth lecture. He recorded that mind made the world and matter was dead mind. He seems to have failed to attend the sixth and eleventh meetings. Frequently he ended his version of some Emersonian dictum with an exclamation point, presumably a tribute to boldness or originality. He noted in his clipped college jargon that XIV was cut by F. G. P. and XV by R. W. E. The truth was that Emerson stayed at home because he could not get the fifteenth lecture ready. He said he had the remaining ones pretty well mapped out, and the people at Bush heard him boast that "If the Divine Providence will carry me through this next lecture I'm not afraid of the rest." But Fisher, the last man in the composite course, was to supplant him the following Friday, and Emerson had to, or was glad to, cut his schedule two meetings short. Peabody ended with fewer pages of notes on Emerson than on any other teacher in the course except Cabot, though this did not necessarily mean that Emerson was either one of the worst or one of the best of the seven expounders of philosophy. His was, according to Peabody, the only one of the seven series of lectures which was not rounded out by an examination.

Emerson had seldom been more unhappy than in those spring weeks when his college duties were "eating him all up." Ellen thought that "he never was so hardworked & hurried before, and of course he never was less able to bear it." It is doubtful whether his spirits were much affected by the scant attendance. At any rate, his colleagues could have been little better off, and he himself might perhaps have had the greatest number of disciples if the university had granted the petition of the divinity school boys who wanted to attend his class without paying the fee. But the experiment in university teaching not only came too late in his life but could never have been congenial to him. He complained to Carlyle that "it made me a prisoner, took away all rights of friendship, honor, and justice, and held me to such frantic devotion to my work as must spoil *that* also." He was paid $8.75 for each of his sixteen lectures.

To W. H. Channing, a guest at Bush a few weeks after the lectures ended, it seemed that Emerson needed no other medicine than the routine of domestic life. Emerson walked with his guest in the woods to show his favorite hemlocks, oaks, pines, and wild flowers; talked of Thoreau as they passed the crossed tree trunk that marked the site of the Walden hut; read passages from his English journal of 1847–1848; discussed philosophy from the Hindus to Hegel; volunteered some criticism of contemporary authors;

commented keenly on the latest scientific investigation as showing the unity of life through the whole universe. But what most impressed the impressionable Channing was the charm of the family life and the pride Emerson took in his children. He seemed more genial than Channing had known him before. He was teaching his children entire independence of his own personal faith, though Elizabeth Hoar declared that to her he was the most profoundly religious person she had ever known. Ellen, now in the foreground, read Homer, the Greek dramatists, and Dante under Elizabeth Hoar's guidance; or she filed her father's correspondence and put his manuscripts and journals in order or helped her mother manage the household.

But all was not so well as Channing thought. The Forbeses, better informed than he, schemed vacations from Bush for the sake of Emerson's health. A couple of fine days with Ellen at the then fashionable Nantasket Beach, where Emerson observed with great interest "the belles, Grecian bend and all," could not cure his weariness. Not even the news of the quick Prussian victories in the opening days of the Franco-Prussian War was sufficiently strong medicine, though he apparently associated the Prussians with the prestige of German philosophy and of Goethe. He was distressed by the conviction that he must write but could not. The chief trouble was that the English publisher Hotten had threatened to collect and reprint old pieces Emerson wanted to revise or forget. Tiresome negotiations had to be carried on through Moncure Conway and Alexander Ireland. Conway and Ireland, having at first innocently abetted the scheme of the publisher, now persuaded him to wait on condition that a new volume of Emerson's own collecting and editing would be furnished—a volume that turned out, after years of worry on the part of its author, to be *Letters and Social Aims.* For Emerson the obligation to get the promised book into shape was like a suspended sentence of life imprisonment.

There was also the introduction he had promised to write for an American edition of *Plutarch's Morals,* the old translation by "Several Hands" that William Goodwin was revising. Intermittently, from January to the late summer or autumn of 1870, Emerson toiled at it. But this was a labor of love, for since early youth the book had been "like my conscience," Emerson told his readers. The actual work must have consisted largely in a search through his old journals and essays and a joining together of the fragments he brought up from the depths. When the reader came suddenly upon such a declaration as "The central fact is the superhuman intelligence, pouring into us from its unknown fountain, to be received with religious awe, and defended from any mixture of our will" he might as well have been leafing through some essay of Emerson's published nearly thirty years earlier, though the passage was not even at this late date a misstatement of its author's still firm Transcendental faith.

Yet even such a labor of love as the introduction could distress an old man. According to Ellen the "wicked Plutarch" hung on her father "with a heavy weight." She noticed that he read both old and new translations and bought for the occasion a Greek Plutarch and compared the English "all along, with that." "Besides," she told Edith, "he has collected all the authors who have written about Plutarch, and he has had a really delightful time reading the whole. But alas! he hasn't yet begun to write and doesn't feel quite able to." Doubtless Ellen overestimated the amount of reading he did in the Greek text; but he took his task seriously, somehow pieced together a charming essay on Plutarch, and earned all of the $500 the publishers paid him.

During the first days of September, while both the Hotten book and the introduction to Plutarch were still on his conscience, he was persuaded to go with Edward to Maine and New Hampshire on the plea that he must show his son Aunt Mary's old haunts. He led the way to Elm Vale, where twilight and clouds did not wholly obscure "the gleam of the lake and the fine mountain terrace and elms in the lowland," and "looked with the eyes of old times at Aunt Mary's Window." In the White Mountains he and Edward came upon James Bryce, future author of the classic British analysis of the American state. As it chanced, Bryce had letters of introduction to Emerson in his pocket. Bryce and Edward, rambling off into a wilder region, came upon Stillman, the artist of the Adirondack Club of years past.

Lecturing slackened in the following winter. Emerson went to New York to speak at the annual reunion and dinner of the New England Society in late December. In January he visited a few lyceums in New England towns and went as far west as Buffalo and Detroit. Home again, he made his brief speech at the meeting for the organization of the museum of fine arts in Boston. Then he faced once more, with waning courage, the Harvard course; for, though a failure at first trial, it had been granted another year of life and he had somehow allowed himself to be put into the galling harness a second time. He yielded too easily to requests for his time that were coming in from all directions and was soon, as Ellen said, "all snarled up in many engagements which the great cloud of lectures renders embarrassing." He altered his Harvard schedule of 1870, substituting a few manuscripts not used then for those he wanted to omit. But he had lost his sureness of touch and every responsibility was a mountain. His promise to publisher Hotten made even the distant future look black.

Suddenly, before he could finish the eighteen lectures at the university, he got an offer of relief, an invitation from John M. Forbes, Edith's father-in-law, to join the Forbes party in a journey, mainly by private Pullman car, to the Pacific coast. California, the wonderful country, lay on his horizon as dreamlike as Japan or Tahiti. Lidian, Ellen, and Edward were unanimous in favoring the journey, and the doctor joined in their appeal. Emerson was convinced that he could take care of Hotten on his return, he was willing to cut his Harvard lectures short once more, and he sent in his resignation as chairman of the overseers' committee on foreign languages. On the afternoon of April 11, the day when he was to have read the next to the last of his lectures in Boylston Hall, he was on his way to California.

The party, once they had assembled in Chicago, where George Pullman himself saw them off, were nine persons. Edith and William Forbes were Emerson's special aides. James Thayer, the husband of one of Uncle Samuel Ripley's daughters, was the chief reporter of table and Pullman car talk and historian of the expedition. He described the meeting, in Utah, with Brigham Young, whose secretary, better informed than the president of the Latter-Day Saints himself about literary reputations, recognized the essayist and inquired, "Is this the justly celebrated Ralph Waldo Emerson?" Thayer got a few vivid impressions of the vast desert region farther west. At a little station in Nevada the air was invigorating in the early morning, a lone meadow lark was singing, two or three Chinamen were standing near a hut, and a white dog was jumping and playing about them. During the day the travelers saw many Indians, "short and dirty creatures,—Utes and Shoshones," owners of the wigwams, "all smoky at the open top," that were visible here and there on the plains. On the following morning it was impossible for the passengers in the palace car "Huron" to see enough of the beautifully forested Sierra Nevada as the train passed through mile after mile of sheds that protected it against the snows still deep on these mountains. Thayer also recorded that in San Francisco the party observed Chinatown's night life in theater, gambling houses, opium dens, restaurants, and joss houses; and he put down Emerson's mild comment on the opium dens —that there was "not much aspiration there,—or inspiration." Emerson noted in his own memorandum book that on the 13th he arrived in Chicago, that on the 19th he called on Brigham Young in Salt Lake City, and that on the 22d he was watching the sea lions on the shore of the Pacific. The next day, Sunday, in San Francisco, he read, it seems, "Immortality," a lecture he commonly reserved for Sundays. On the 26th, doing what he could to meet further demands without any special effort, he began to read a short series of lectures in Doctor Stebbins's Unitarian church.

The San Franciscans were curious about the Transcendentalist. To a writer for the *Daily Evening Bulletin* he seemed "tall, straight, well formed, with a head constructed on the utility rather than the ornamental principle." He was refreshing to see in spite of his black garb. His audience, having gathered after only a few hours' notice, doubtless listened to his first lecture at Stebbins's church in a mood of determined appreciation. He accidentally upset a vase in the pulpit, and when he descended and gathered up the flowers he was applauded. His style was thought "entirely colloquial," but people listened "with rapt attention." He apparently made no effort to impress his hearers. According to a local critic who heard the second lecture, they "would not dream that he had said anything during the whole evening which he thought particularly worthy of being said." The manner of the lecturer was much what many of his audiences had observed in recent years. "His notes lie before him—a bulky mass of manuscript," the San Francisco critic put it. "On commencing his discourse he fingers them over backwards and forwards, as if at a loss whether to commence in the first page or the middle; and finally selecting a good starting point, he begins in a conventional tone of voice to read. He is so familiar with them that he does not confine himself closely to them. . . . Sandwiched in between his selections from his manuscript are interpolations improvised for the occasion. . . . But the difference between hearing him read his works and reading them one's self is certainly in favor of the latter." In a third lecture he was full of anecdote and ended with a tribute to the resources of California.

His further lecturing at San Francisco and an engagement at Oakland were postponed till he could visit some of the natural wonders of the state. Even before he had seen these marvels he had fallen in love with California. He wrote home that "if we were all young,—as some of us are not,—we might each of us claim his quarter-section of the Government, & plant grapes & oranges, & never come back to your east winds & cold summers." Nine or ten days among the mountains and trees of the Yosemite and Mariposa regions left him aghast with admiration, and there was no lack of Californians willing to encourage him to remain in that mood.

Hearing that Emerson was in the Yosemite Valley but about to leave it, the young Scotch-American naturalist and explorer John Muir protested. "Do not thus drift away with the mob while the spirits of these rocks & waters hail you after long waiting as their kinsman & persuade you to closer communion," he admonished, and urged Emerson to join him "in a months worship with Nature in the high temples of the great Sierra Crown beyond our holy Yosemite." He assured Emerson that it would cost him "nothing save the time & very little of that for you will be mostly in Eternity." Muir, a kind of ecstatic Thoreau devoted to giant trees, mountains, and glaciers instead of hills, ponds, and marshes, managed to see

Emerson several times and tried hard to convert him to the religion of the outdoor life. The thirty-three-year-old Muir, apparently unimpressed by any signs of age in his new friend, was disappointed but persistent. He was sure his man was a spiritual kinsman.

He was right about the spiritual kinship, and, though without Muir's exuberance, Emerson was sufficiently impressed by his month in California to write from Truckee on his way home: "There is an awe & terror lying over this new garden—all empty as yet of any adequate people, yet with this assured future in American hands,—unequalled in climate & production. Chicago & St Louis are toys to it in its assured felicity. I should think no young man would come back from it." Early in July, when Emerson had been home for some weeks, Muir wrote him a new prose poem on California. Muir was about to "start for the high Sierra East of Yosemite" and "would willingly," he said, "walk all the way to your Concord if so I could have you for a companion." Some correspondence passed between the two men, but the Californian probably did not know how much honor the Concord man did him. Emerson began a new list of what he called *"My Men"* with Thomas Carlyle and ended it with John Muir.

In October, California, in the person, not of John Muir, but of Bret Harte, arrived in Concord. Ellery Channing "positively refused to have any part in his reception, guidance, or dinner"; but the Emersons and others offered their hospitality, and Harte came to Bush. At the preliminary skirmish which ensued, Emerson stuck to his guns when Harte told him that the passage in *Society and Solitude* about learning and religion entering the frontiersman's hut along with the piano was false. Harte averred that "It is the gamblers who bring in the music to California. It is the prostitute who brings in the New York fashions of dress there, and so throughout." Emerson retorted that he spoke also "from Pilgrim experience, and knew on good grounds the resistless culture that religion effects."

Early the following month Bret Harte was back at Bush again. A striking figure with his blue eyes, his long nose, and his black hair just turning gray, he sat in the green rocking chair before the blazing fireplace as he filled out Emerson's imperfect reminiscences of California with his own abundant information and gave his withering judgment of Joaquin Miller. Ellen, though quickly convinced that Bret Harte was attractive except for his detestable habit of smoking, waited hopefully, no doubt, for some illumination on his writings. A faint illumination came before dinner was over but reached her only through her sister, as she explained: "I did not hear, but Edith did, when Mother said, 'Mr Harte I wanted to ask you if you have really witnessed the instances of disinterested feeling, which you describe, in rough people, or rather whether you know that such have been by personal experience?' There! wasn't that the test question of a radical in search of fact? Edith says his answer was non-committal, she thus reports it. 'Of course it must be there, if I said it was.' I, Ellen, however call that a clear admission that he has never seen it, has created his tales out of the whole cloth."

What Bret Harte made most of among his impressions of Emerson was a "self-indulgence" quite out of character in one reputed remote from sublunary commonplaces. He burlesqued the Concord sage's invitation to a " 'wet night' with him, over a glass of sherry," an invitation that had been hospitably emphasized with a gesture of the sage's cigar. Harte failed to understand that both the sherry and the cigar had served mainly to cover up his host's troublesome shyness. But Emerson had explained to James Thayer a few months earlier. He rarely cared to finish a cigar alone, "But in company . . . To one who found it difficult to meet people, as he did, the effect of a cigar was agreeable; one who is smoking may be as silent as he likes, and yet be good company."

Emerson was literary man of all work. Ellery Channing's colloquial poem *The Wanderer*, momentarily expected from the press at the time of Bret Harte's visit to Bush in early November, had cost him trouble and money, though he had been surprised by the untamed poet's docility about metrical changes. He still gave some lectures and addresses, and the rest of the family waited anxiously for news of his success or failure. In August he had made his brief address on Walter Scott at the Massachusetts Historical Society's centenary celebration. Late in November he set off to the West, disconsolate at the thought of spending Thanksgiving away from home. Chicago, in spite of her great fire, wanted him. Ellen implored him "to write his lecture large and to give up turning over & skipping." At Chicago he was greeted, it was said, with mild applause by a "coldly-intellectual" audience. At least one of the audience was impressed by the quaintness of the lecturer's appearance. Dressed in clerical garb and wearing his hair long and "combed closely to his head," the celebrity from the East had a platform manner "slightly stiff and awkward but that of the true gentleman."

There were a few more lectures or readings in Illinois and Iowa. Later in the winter Emerson kept his engagements in Baltimore and Washington and in at least one or two other towns outside New England. Coming down from Washington to Baltimore to hear him, Walt Whitman and John Burroughs, once his enthusiastic disciples, found that he had lost much of his old appeal. They agreed that his lectures showed no progress in many years and were irrelevant to the problems of 1872. A little later, as Emerson was boarding his train in Washington, Burroughs found out from him, he said, what was the matter between him and Whitman. Emerson wanted Walt's friends to quarrel a little more with Walt and make him pay more attention to the requirements of artistic taste. Whitman doubtless needed such advice, but it made his loyal admirer boil. Burroughs had, indeed, not quite cooled since hearing, a little earlier, that Emerson had warned Whitman, through a mutual acquaintance, to write the songs of a nation and not simply make inventories.

At Washington, Emerson visited Charles Sumner, whose invitation Whitman had carried to Baltimore. With Baird of the Smithsonian Institution he discussed "present aspects of science, Darwin, Agassiz." Undoubtedly he was already well aware of the sharp rift between Darwin and Agassiz. At the Saturday Club he must have heard Agassiz state his own side of the quarrel. He had long owned a copy of *Contributions to the Natural History of the United States,* a book in which Agassiz had repeated his belief that the "branches in the animal kingdom are founded upon different plans of structure, and for that very reason have embraced from the beginning representatives between which there could be no community of origin." In the same work Agassiz had declared plainly enough that "the arguments presented by Darwin in favor of a universal derivation, from one primary form, of all the peculiarities existing now among living beings, have not made the slightest impression on my mind." Emerson himself made no sign, it seems, of sympathy with his friend Agassiz in this debate; if he was unable to make the Darwinian doctrines do his own philosophy much service, he was not at all likely to be frightened by them. *The Descent of Man* was stirring up a storm of indignation among the orthodox, but Emerson had absorbed Lamarck's theories many years before even Darwin's work *On the Origin of Species* had appeared, and now there was no reason why he should be disturbed.

He did more than his scheduled lecturing in Washington, where there were many things to remind him of the war years and their results. He lectured in the G. A. R. course. He was not only taken to see the Negro students in Howard University but "compelled by an artifice to speak to them." He hated to be taken by surprise and hated extempore speaking. "Nevertheless," he told Lidian, "I survived." The speech, at least partly extempore, it seems, and an extremely poor one in his opinion, was reported pretty fully in the press, much against his will. He quickly began to receive letters of congratulation. His subject had been "What Books to Read," and his very natural inclusion of his favorite George Herbert's poems among his choice titles seems to have caused a run on that book in shops as far away from the capital as Boston.

At the Concord Lyceum he was announced long in advance to lecture, especially for the occasion, "upon local matters of interest to all citizens of Concord." But when the 7th of February arrived he read his essay "Immortality." Alcott noticed the eager interest of the Concord audience, and there were other evidences of the appeal of this charming commentary on death and life. A few weeks later, when Mrs. Thoreau was taken seriously ill, Lidian hastened to see her. "True to their instincts," Ellen told her sister Edith, "they began patting with velvet paws but with a sharp claw out enough to scratch, and had quite a terrific skirmish, till at last the stern joy of finding themselves well matched reconciled them, and they ended with a love-feast & a beautiful time. Mrs Thoreau repeated Cato's Soliloquy with enthusiasm, and said she rejoiced in dying, and Mother sent her a jar of honey dropping from the comb, & certain sheets from Father's 'Immortality,' and Miss Thoreau said she enjoyed them to the utmost." On the 12th Mrs. Thoreau, stoical as her son Henry had been, died after remarking to her daughter, "It has been a pleasant sickness, hasn't it Sophia?"

The annoying Hotten book made some progress. And *Parnassus,* the collection of favorite poems from many authors with which Edith had for years helped her father, had seemed almost ready in the fall of 1871; but Osgood had decided that, before he published, he wanted a commentary to connect the selections and to secure the copyright. This connecting commentary was destined to be a mere publisher's dream; but the book was held up and, in the following February, Osgood, still unsatisfied, offered $500 on the day of publication and a royalty of 5 percent on the retail price if Emerson would provide a critical introduction to each division. This scheme also was destined to fail, but there was further delay.

James Fields wanted another series of "literary conversations" for April and May, and Emerson agreed. In the meantime Mrs. Fields, apparently persuaded that a sort of preliminary, restricted showing of her lion would be wise, had him read "Amita," his account of Aunt Mary. Nearly forty persons Mrs. Fields had invited to her home for the occasion were edified by what she called "an extraordinary picture of a strange stoical noble character." As the character of the amazing aunt unfolded, Doctor Holmes, a mixer of medicine with fiction, and young Harry James, later known for novels that were sometimes as much psychological studies as fiction, listened with interest.

The new Fields scheme for six Monday afternoon lectures, informal enough to be called "conversations," became a reality at Mechanics' Hall, Boston, in the middle of April, 1872. The collections Emerson had made for *Parnassus* were handy source material, and he had his numerous other manuscripts to draw upon for much of his substance. Doubtless it was mainly because of his age and his too hasty preparation that he often failed to establish the connection between text and commentary. He made astonishing leaps from piece to piece in his readings. He promised Ellen that he would avoid such errors in the future, but at the next lecture she would find that he had not reformed. "He won't read the lecture to me before he goes," she complained, "nor give me any chances to know what poems & how so I can't be of the least use except in telling him whether he speaks loud enough. He says he hasn't time to spend on reading a word of it aloud, he must work every minute by himself."

There was no privacy at Mechanics' Hall, and Ellen was tense with worry, though she got nothing from others of "the usual friendly audience of best people" or from the newspapers that was unfavorable. On the 16th, the day after the opening, she wrote in desperation to Edward that she had sat at the lecture "in about as great a fear as I was able to bear, lest there should be some terrific crash, for I hadn't heard it beforehand as I ought, and his memory is entirely gone, so that he blithely read the same page twice over . . ." His memory could not have been entirely gone, but it was weakening and she had reason to be fearful. Several times she came home feeling blue because she had not been able to hear. Emerson was aware that her heart died within her every Monday; but he himself was unworried by his mistakes, because, he said, he knew and everybody knew that he was worn out and passed by and that only his old friends came to hear him and they only for friendship's sake. Ellen sometimes suspected that she was having a case of nerves. "But I care," she wrote to her sister. "I cant bear that he should show diminished lustre."

People who listened to the Boston lectures that spring had paid at least $1400 into the private account of the lecturer, which was greatly helped almost at the same time by the $2000 he and Lidian received when they sold the Winslow House at Plymouth. But there were also some strokes of ill fortune. Only a few days before the Boston course ended, the Emerson family pride suffered by the burning of the woodlot on the shore of Walden Pond toward the village. News came that the planted lot was all burned and that the grove where Thoreau's hut had stood was badly hurt. Emerson, exploring the desolation, could only comfort himself with the belief that some trees in the grove were not fatally injured. In the following summer came a far more severe disaster at Bush.

Early in the morning of the 24th of July, 1872, Emerson was awakened by the sound of fire. At first he took it to be the sound of the rain coming into his room. When he understood what was happening he brought water. But he could not reach the fire, as it seemed to be inside the walls. He tried to get above it but found the garret full of stifling smoke. When he called to Lidian she was so much alarmed by his voice that she was relieved to find that it was only the house on fire. As Ellen was not at home, the responsibility fell on him, and he had to make quick decisions and act. He rushed out into the yard, calling to the neighbors, "Fire! Whitcomb, Staples, Fire!" Going back, he got the manuscripts of the nightmare Hotten book and of *Parnassus* safely out. Staples and Whitcomb came in a few minutes. Whitcomb stood at the gate and sent the first passing wagons to give the alarm. Other men began to arrive, and presently most of the village, men and women, were at work, pulling out whatever could be saved.

Almost everything was saved from complete destruction. With great difficulty, holes were hacked in the slate roof, and smoke became flame. The most remarkable sight was one-armed Ephraim Bull, son of the originator of the Concord grape. He was managing the hose on the roof. But even invalids who never came out were out this time. One housekeeper saw that flour and sugar were sheltered from the rain, another received all the clothing and organized a band of helpers to get it to safety. Ellen's piano was moved to the Staples parlor. Dishes and carpet were got out before the roof fell in, smothering the fire, on which the engines were already playing. Louisa May Alcott and her sister May looked after scattered manuscripts. Some of these were charred about the edges, but all, or nearly all, were saved, with nearly all the books. This was approximately the story that could be pieced together from the testimony of various eyewitnesses. Emerson, in his memorandum book under July 24, told it in three words: "Our house burned."

Ellen, returning home from Beverly, found all four lower rooms "safe," as she optimistically expressed it. She and her father and mother were at once installed as boarders in the Old Manse, and her father hired a room in the Court House for his study. There most of his books were soon getting back into order, but a few had strayed. Four volumes of *Goethe's nachgelassene Werke* were not recovered from a local barber till some months later. It was estimated that the $2500 of insurance would nearly pay for rebuilding, but it would have been difficult to stop the flow of gifts intended to pay for a new house and for a vacation of travel. Caroline Sturgis, now William Tappan's wife, wrote to offer $5000 to rebuild the house. Judge Hoar made his own account at the bank available to Emerson. Francis Lowell, a college classmate, arrived and left a letter which, he said, was to be given to Emerson later. When it was opened, it proved to contain a check for $5000, the gift of several friends. This money was for the rebuilding of the house or for any other purpose Emerson might prefer.

A sudden change for the worse in Emerson's health alarmed the family, and William Forbes, without consulting Emerson, wrote to Hotten and

Alexander Ireland that his father-in-law must be released from his agreement about the book. A trip to Europe began to be thought imperative. Next, the friendly machinations of Le Baron Russell and others came to light in Concord when Judge Hoar announced himself the messenger of an association that had chosen Emerson its treasurer. Hoar explained that the purpose of the association would be attained when Emerson had spent its funds, consisting of ten thousand dollars deposited to Emerson's credit in the Concord National Bank; but he advised that part of the money be used for a trip to Europe. Preparations for putting the new funds to work soon got under way. William Ralph Emerson of Boston, a distant relative, offered to serve as architect. John Keyes, whose daughter Annie became engaged to Edward Emerson about this time, was to superintend the rebuilding. But Emerson could not at once make up his mind to travel abroad.

Little more than a week after the fire he had to speak at the Boston dinner to the Japanese envoys, though he tried to beg off. Doubtless he had given no effective answer—if, indeed, he had given any answer at all —to last February's request from the Japanese legation in Washington for advice regarding an educational program for the mikado's subjects. Now, however deep his interest in the Orient, he could do little about it. He mustered up enthusiasm enough to discover the romantic aspect of the late emergence of Japan from national privacy and praised "the enlightened policy of President Fillmore" that "sent Commodore Perry to that country." Later in August he attempted to work himself into a vacation mood by going with Ellen for some days to the New Hampshire coast and to Maine. He was trying to recover from a general decline of health, and she was nursing her sprained ankle. As they discussed the proposed voyage to Europe, he agreed that he would never again be so free. He wanted to see not only his transatlantic friends but his son, for Edward had sailed for Europe nearly a year earlier in the hope of carrying on the medical studies he had begun at Harvard. It came out that the real reasons why Emerson did not want to go were his weak and uncertain health and his unfortunately changed appearance. He would hate to meet Ruskin, Huxley, Tennyson, and the rest in his present condition. "When nature indicates that it is time," he put it, "it is more graceful to retire at once, not to seek the world." Ellen then proposed that he make the voyage incognito and meet only Edward. He liked that plan.

Though he was very gay much of the time, he seemed to return to the thought that this was possibly the end. He gave directions about the disposal of his manuscripts. Edward, if only he were "a scholar by profession," could make use of them; otherwise, Emerson thought, they would be worthless. He mentioned Hedge and Cabot as men who might be trusted with them. He was sure that all the early manuscript books ought to be burned and likewise all the sermons, for he considered that what was good in them had been extracted for use in the essays and other writings. He enumerated many manuscript journals by name and assessed their particular values. He had meant to cross out in all the manuscript books the passages he had published, but he had been very negligent about doing that. He did not want the records of his interviews with Carlyle and Tennyson used in their lifetime. He thought he had materials for beautiful lives of Ellery Channing and Alcott and said it would be a pity if they outlived him, for the world would miss two very good chapters. But he spoke as if nothing could be done about these things. Meantime he struggled for words to express his thoughts.

He worried over the endless Hotten book, and could not bear to think of letting his old things be reprinted as they were. He kept talking as he and Ellen walked through the woods, and she could hear him bursting out with "Hotten will say 'I shall lose a thousand pounds.' "

"And I shall lose my life, you might answer," Ellen put in.

He wouldn't listen to the suggestion that it would be well for him to go to England and see to the publishing of the book there. That would spoil his plan to have Osgood bring it out in Boston and send the sheets to Hotten and so run no risk of mistakes in the English edition. Ellen, fearing that he would never be able to see any book through the press again, remembered that Elliot Cabot was the one man he was always returning to as fit to care for his manuscripts. Cabot was a dear friend and had an understanding of philosophy. Possibly he would correct the proofs when they were ready. At the first opportunity Ellen led on to the suggestion that Cabot should be taken into partnership, but her father, though seeming to consider the possibility for a moment, said decisively, "No, *nobody* could do it."

In September he spent some days resting at Naushon, but his health needed prolonged relaxation. Even before the fire his appearance had strikingly altered. By the spring of this year his hair had been reduced to a "mere outline." His mind was as much changed as his body. His memory was less certain. It was especially unreliable when he searched for the exact word, but it made a variety of troubles for him.

On the first day of September, after his return from New Hampshire and Maine, Ellen sketched his case for Doctor Edward Clarke when she asked for medical advice: "Memory went first. He used to be remarkable for never forgetting errands &c. It must be 5 or 6 years since that faculty failed, and now for as much as 3 years he has been unable to remember that he was asked to do things, even when reminded of details of asking.

Not always, but very commonly. And now in giving him errands I often see that he is trying to attend and cannot possibly so I write it. His work on books and lectures has been very difficult to him for several years. . . . I just took his proofs to read for him. He said 'I get an impression in reading them that they talk too much about the same thing, but I cannot find out.' There were 27 pages. One sentence slightly varied came in four times, another twice word for word. In the spring he was able to set such things right. Since the fire he cannot. . . . In ordinary conversation about facts he cannot remember words or names at all. (There's no such difficulty in talking with people who are interested, on his own ground.) It is painful to him of course in company. Alone with us he plays with it, and is very witty in his stumbles. Sometimes having got through a short sentence straight, tho' evidently jumping in the dark for his words, he laughs and says 'It is a triumph to remember any word.' All this is very much increased this last month but it is not wholly new, there has been all too much before, and it has been coming on very gradually." The decline had undoubtedly been gradual, but the downward curve dipped sharply in this, his seventieth year.

George Bancroft sent $1000 to add to the funds raised for Emerson by his friends after the fire. By the middle of October the total seems to have been at least some seventeen or eighteen thousand dollars. With ample funds collecting and with work on Bush already beginning, Europe loomed larger. The funds could easily have increased to much greater proportions. Friends as far away as England promptly offered their aid, but since it was not needed it was refused. As the money poured in, Ellen commented, "No one ever saw such an outburst of sympathy and kindness as our fire has drawn from the world—or rather we seem to be another Chicago." By the end of September, William Forbes was writing to engage transatlantic passage for Ellen and her father. Presents on account of the fire had hardly ceased before presents for the voyage began coming in. The not very definite plan was that Emerson and Ellen should find Edward. After cutting short his medical studies in Germany and abandoning plans for some work in Austria, Edward had gone to England and remained there in order to continue his studies at St. Thomas' Hospital in Lambeth; but there was already doubt whether his health would let him stay on.

The plan that Emerson should travel incognito seems to have been still at least half-heartedly adhered to, but when he had written to Charles Norton and to Moncure Conway, who were both abroad, he had failed to warn them to remain silent. Edward tried in vain to preserve secrecy. When Norton spread the news, Edward had to explain to Carlyle and others that Emerson wished to mend his health in the Mediterranean before he saw his English friends. But for Emerson there was no hope of remaining private. He could not even refuse to make a special trip to New York in the middle of October and speak at a banquet for Froude, for he himself had helped to make Froude's American lecture tour possible.

If his French and German fame spread slowly, he was widely honored in Britain, where he could hardly come privately. In returning to England in 1872, he could expect to do nothing to further the doctrines he had taught there a quarter of a century earlier; but he could expect to find that those doctrines had not been forgotten. Besides a few of the older intellectuals, such as Carlyle, there were younger men risen to some importance since Emerson had last crossed the Atlantic who were now his friends or disciples. A small stream of English peers and commoners had long since been flowing through Concord. Max Müller had already begun sending his books there. Matthew Arnold, whom Emerson credited with "the true critical perception and feeling of style" and ranked as high in England as he ranked Sainte-Beuve in France, had, it seemed, discovered more lasting value in Emerson than in Carlyle. Emerson had maintained his reason, Arnold thought, while Carlyle had not; and Emerson's popularity would grow with the growth of reason in human affairs. Though Emerson once asserted that he generally felt himself repelled by physicists and did not know even their names, John Tyndall, perhaps the last transatlantic visitor he had had at the Old Manse, had expended no small amount of enthusiasm on the writings of Emerson. He had marked his copy of *Nature,* so he said, "Purchased by inspiration." He exaggerated his debt to its author by declaring that "Whatever I have done, the world owes to him." Tyndall and the other friends from Carlyle down to youthful disciples made it certain that Emerson would be welcomed again in Britain.

But the plan of foreign travel had quickly expanded. Britain covered only a small part of the map on which Emerson marked his course as he set out on his third eastward voyage across the Atlantic. He looked beyond the British Isles to France, Italy, and Egypt. In a more favorable time Greece, still unvisited, would doubtless have proved the strongest magnet for him, but that country could hardly have been inviting in winter, or in any season so long as Greek brigands ran loose. As the goal of an old scholar's winter travels, Egypt was best.

Egypt had strong attractions for Emerson. Her long valley, closely hemmed in by deserts and covered with mild and cloudless winter skies, was a pleasing dream for a sixty-nine-year-old veteran of nearly that many New England winters. On the banks of her river stood pyramids that were the world's most magnificent commentaries on the vanity of human greed and pride, ruined temples that were memorials of man's ancient search for answers to his deepest riddles, and sphinxes that were symbols of the inscrutable wisdom that refused to reveal the answers. These affecting monuments marking the painfully narrow boundaries of human wisdom were worthy of a pilgrimage by a student of philosophy and religion.

Somehow Emerson had vaguely focused his interest in these things on the figure of Osiris, the most attractive member of the vast Egyptian pantheon, and had got the notion that, in spite of many contradictory stories, Philae was the final resting place of the much abused earthly body of that divine being. In one of his notebooks he wrote, "Who is he that sleeps at Philae?" and answered, "Osiris." When Egypt had first been suggested as the ultimate objective of his voyage, he had said, "Yes, I should like to see the tomb of 'him who sleeps at Phylæ.' "

And so it happened that Emerson and his daughter Ellen set out, by way of New York, on a long and much interrupted voyage whose most distant port of call was to be the little island far up the Nile.

24.

VOYAGE TO THE ISLAND OF PHILAE

> To be rich is to have a ticket of admission to the master-
> works and chief men of each race. It is to have the sea, by
> voyaging; to visit the mountains, Niagara, the Nile, the
> desert, Rome, Paris . . .
>   —"Wealth"

THE *Wyoming* steamed out of New York Harbor on October 23,
as scheduled. As she passed Staten Island in the gray but calm
and pleasant weather, two missionaries bound for India sang
"We're out on the ocean sailing" and "America." The *Helvetia*
was astern, sailing for London. Ellen and her father were "as happy as
clams" till, in the evening, they passed Fire Island Light and thought of
Margaret Fuller, who had been lost off this shore more than twenty years
ago. Next day they ran into stormy weather. Seasickness prevailed. But
Emerson did not suffer, and the following day was "warm & blue & still."

The steamer, one gradually became aware, was alive with missionaries.
Many of them were on their way to India. The editor of a religious paper
was going to visit Egypt, Sinai, the Holy Land, and Greece and would take
St. Paul's voyage before paying special attention to Germany. One minister and his wife had left a Presbyterian church in Wisconsin in order to
establish Protestantism in Italy. A Quaker woman, though she apparently
possessed no tongue but her native English one, had got the conviction that
since the Franco-Prussian War there would be a great opening for the
gospel in the south of France. She was therefore on her way to the south
of France. There were Baptist missionaries and Methodist missionaries. On
Sunday an Episcopal clergyman, brother of the late President James
Buchanan, helped lead the choir. At table, Emerson was at first flanked
on one side by a speechless young Mormon woman from Utah with an
untidily stuffed head of reddish hair; but she soon disappeared, to return
no more, leaving unsaid whatever may have been in her mind. Emerson
wrote home to Lidian: "My well known orthodoxy, you will be glad to
know, is walled round by whole families of missionaries, & I heard two
sermons, & the English service, & many hymns on Sunday. But the liberal
ocean sings louder, & makes us all of one church." Lidian commented that

459

he was probably glad to escape with his philosophy—Transcendental, was it?—unharmed, if, indeed, he was so lucky.

As his cabin mate Emerson had a young Belfast man, a violent sympathizer with the South, and so had to turn in some other direction for comfort. But he found little. It was only after getting cozily settled in conversation with the editor of the religious paper that he discovered that person's profession. Since his usual dread of publicity had now only grown stronger, he resolved to beware of the dangerous man in the future. But even with the greatest care he could not avoid publicity. Soon there was nothing for it but that he must gratify the desire of the ship's passengers, "for most of whom it was the single opportunity of a lifetime to hear him." Ellen, negotiating on his part, compromised and settled for a reading, explaining that her father never did anything extempore. He accordingly read miscellaneous poems. Some of these pleased everybody, though many of the company were suspected of not being quite up to poetry. Next evening the poet had to yield to the demand that he read from his own poems, but he was not so successful as before.

On November 3 the *Wyoming* was at Liverpool, and next day he and Ellen, reunited with Edward, were in Chester. Emerson, taking his son with him, called on the Bishop of Chester, an old friend. On the 5th the three Americans breakfasted with the bishop. Emerson wore his cowl, as he did again in the evening when, upon urgent request, he went with Edward to attend the meeting of the Archaeologic, Architectural and Historic Society. At the meeting he was much noticed, and when the customary motion was made to thank the presiding officer, who happened to be the bishop once more, Emerson was called upon to second it "that we may have the opportunity of just hearing his voice"; and so he did, speaking beautifully, according to Edward.

In London, Emerson was installed, with Ellen, in the Down Street rooms Lowell had used earlier. Elizabeth Hoar, the most recent occupant of the apartment, had just left it when its new American tenants arrived. From Down Street, Emerson sallied out next day to Chelsea, where his "two or three hours with Carlyle in his study" must have been the high point of the brief English visit of this year. Carlyle "opened his arms & embraced me after seriously gazing for a time, 'I am glad to see you once more in the flesh,'—& we sat down . . . & had a steady outpouring for two hours & more on persons, events, & opinions," Emerson wrote home.

The Atlantic voyage had given the traveler more vigor, it seemed, and he could better meet the people who, according to Edward's account, began "to throng Fathers doors." But he kept quietly in his rooms whenever he could, and when some amusement or business was suggested he would retort that "Old age loves leisure." When Dean Stanley and Lady Augusta asked him to dinner "with the most learned men in England and the Queen of Holland at a small round table," he refused, his real reason being, it seems, that Ellen was not invited. And he refused for the same reason, so Ellen believed, when he was invited to "a great dinner" at the Inner Temple. Such familiar friends as Norton, Conway, Allingham, Charles Newcomb, and W. H. Channing felt free to come to Down Street. Carlyle, most privileged of all, came too; and though Ellen could not understand his burr-ridden conversation, it kept her father laughing.

On November 13, when Edward was on his way home across the Atlantic, Emerson obeyed Ellen's summons to move on to Canterbury. But he was usually opposed to moving at all. At Canterbury he insisted that he was dragged away from London and wanted to go back, but his protests to his daughter were interspersed with suggestions that they settle down in Canterbury for good. As Una Hawthorne had observed in London, Ellen was inexorable about hurrying on to Egypt and the Sahara. Now that her father cared mainly for rest, she was his conscience.

But in France even Ellen began to weaken. When she and her father arrived in the lodgings reserved for them by Lowell in the Hôtel de Lorraine in Paris, Emerson was thankful that he had reached a place where he could "stay today, & tomorrow, & the next day, & longer." Ellen, finding that she could easily make herself understood in French, decided to agree with him. "I hate Egypt, it won't let us stop anywhere," she complained. Here in Paris, in the same hotel with Lowell and his wife and with John Holmes, the Autocrat's brother, the travelers found difficulties at a minimum. These American friends answered all the troublesome questions, and Lowell went with Emerson to the banker's and on miscellaneous errands.

Le Figaro was telling the story of the great Boston fire that had broken out in the street where Emerson was born, and the American colony was too much upset by the news to think of going on with plans for its banquet to celebrate General Grant's re-election. The Parisians, just recovering from their own catastrophic Prussian war and its sequel, were hailing the first performances of Pailleron's *Hélène* at the Comédie-Française. But the Emersons must have stirred out very little. Once they and the Lowells were at dinner with the Laugels, but the Laugels had tried in vain to gather a distinguished company to greet their guests. The Renans were traveling, Elizabeth Laugel apologized, while Montégut, Emerson's early admirer, was in the country; the Lasteyries and Prince and Princess Orloff were likewise out of reach; Ivan Tourguéneff was in bed with the gout; and Mme Viardot, though depended upon to sing, failed to appear.

Ellen summarized the rest of the brief Paris visit for her sister in a few sentences: "In Paris from Friday Nov 15$\underline{th}$ *soir* till the following Thursday we had a warm snug home, a capital table d'hôte, where one side of the table was our friends & selves the other all French   'It is a legitimist hotel, and very respectable people come here,' said Mr Lowell. Two or three members of the Chamber of Deputies, among them the Marquis de Grammont grandson tell Mother of that beloved sister Rosalie of our friend Mme de Montagu, Mme Lafayette's sister. . . . They talked politics daily. 'Twas as good as a play to see, & Mr Lowell highly enjoyed the privilege of hearing, no one else could. Imagine my alarm when on the fourth day one of the deputies took to looking at me on ending his remarks, and as I strove to mind the rule of manners the Storers discovered & to put on an intelligent expression, he wasn't slow in going a step farther and addressing various remarks to M$\underline{lle}$ There was no help for it, I struggled hard, understood, composed my reply in the expectant silence of the whole table, and brought it out, whereupon there was . . . applause on the French side of the table . . . Monsieur was encouraged and talked to me more, and next spoke to Father who finds it harder to understand than I do, and there is no subject ancient or modern that we didn't hobble painfully through. One was delightful. The language of America. They all supposed it of course was the American Indian speech, and that the higher classes learned a little English. . . . On Sunday we went to church—for a whole month Father never missed going to church on Sunday!—to the Chapelle Évangelique de l'Étoile, M. le Pasteur Bersier, a handsome man whose speaking charmed Father . . . Mr Lowell . . . devoted himself to Father very much and was his guide about the city   Harry James came several times, and once took Father to the Louvre and Father came home enchanted."

On November 21 Emerson and Ellen, accompanied by Curnex, a traveling servant, left Paris and began the "endless journey" to Marseille. Emerson was determined to be uncomfortable, but on the second day, tired as he was, he was delighted and advised Ellen that "if you want to do the greatest kindness possible to anyone send him from Lyons to Marseilles." They saw Avignon before darkness fell, and then, according to Ellen, "there was nothing but weariness & hunger till we at last saw the beautiful lights of Marseilles." The next afternoon they left Marseille for Nice. Ellen, remembering her voyage to the Azores, was in ecstasies through southern France and in Italy. Emerson condensed all experiences in Nice and as far as Florence into three sentences: "Nice charmed us with gardens palm-trees, pepper trees, & . . . the Mediterranean washing the picturesque shore, on our Sunday, &, the next morning being beautiful weather we took the steamer for Genoa having heard bad news of the roads on account of the great rains. The whole day on the Mediterranean was full of beauty, as we were passing ever in sight of castles towns & villages on the shore. It was night by the time we reached Genoa & we were hindered from paying our respects to the memory of Columbus, by being put on board a steamer bound to Leghorn instantly to paddle all night, & find Pisa in the grey morning."

On the 26th they installed themselves for three or four days in the Hôtel du Nord at Florence. The city was quiet, with no greater excitements than a few plays, such operas as *Lucia di Lammermoor* and *Norma*, and the arrival of Prince Hassan Pasha for a few days on his way to Rome and Cairo. *La Nazione*, though it lacked room for a list of all the notable foreigners who were just then descending on Florence, announced that Emerson, "one of the most distinguished poets and philosophers of America," had arrived there on his way to the Orient. Though he seems to have done little at Florence but visit the Uffizi Gallery and view some places and manuscripts out of love for Dante and a few other great spirits, he had not lost all his youthful enthusiasm. After she had visited Santa Croce, Ellen was amused to see that he felt as much elated as if she had met Galileo, Michelangelo, Alfieri, and Machiavelli in person. He seemed to respect her as if she had been in exalted society.

He even had zest for linguistic adventures. Neither he nor Ellen could speak Italian without great effort, but on the train between Florence and Rome they made use of the ample opportunity to test what skill they had. After they had succeeded in putting a sentence together by their joint labors, he enunciated it with fine clarity. The joyful Italian to whom it was addressed believed for a moment that they understood his tongue but had to content himself with the simplest exclamations until they got out their dictionaries and guide books and used their fingers and a combination of French and English with Italian.

At Rome they settled first at a Madame Tellenbach's pension in the same Piazza di Spagna where Emerson had lived nearly forty years before, saw St. Peter's and some historic ruins and art galleries, and found old friends. Rumors of cholera up the Nile made their itinerary doubtful, and they thought of giving up Egypt entirely. Ellen seemed ready to settle down to reading Tacitus, but Emerson excused himself from any part in that plan. Soon, however, they had better prospects.

Baron von Hoffmann, son-in-law of Emerson's friend Sam Ward, came daily to call or to leave flowers, and the Concord villagers were guests at his and his wife Lily Ward's Villa Celimontana during their last ten days in Rome. By that time there had been, according to Ellen, "numberless dinners & teas," and Curnex, the traveling servant, had delightedly collected sheaves of cards from callers. Such dignitaries as the American and

French ministers came to pay their respects, as Curnex must have noted with satisfaction. If Emerson did not receive the extraordinary attentions that the chief foreign and Roman families had recently lavished upon Ernest Renan, it was partly because he did not want them. Probably he did not appear at the reception in the Capitoline Museum for the members of the first Italian Juridical Congress, though he had an invitation through George Marsh, the American minister.

At the Villa Celimontana, he and Ellen lived "in great glory" such as had never been known in Concord. Though without much of the leisure he had longed for, he seemed content. Ellen summarized the usual day: "Then I go to breakfast with Father in his study and after breakfast comes the Baron to arrange the pleasures of the day. . . . then away with the Baron in a carriage we go to see churches, gardens or galleries. Come home to lunch at one with Lily who is lovely, and then at 2.30 away we go again. Company to dine finishes the day." After it was all over, Ellen wrote home: "The hospitality of Villa Celimontana 'ran fine to the last.' Father said to the Baron in parting from him 'You are one of the knights of King Arthur's Round Table' . . . You see it is the longest visit Father ever made, and he never took so kindly to visiting before."

On the 18th Emerson and Ellen, together with an American family named Whitwell and a Scottish Miss Farquhar, went from Rome to Naples, where the great Boston fire was still being discussed along with the San Carlo Opera. There, on the 21st, they boarded the steamer *Nil* of the French line connecting Marseille and Alexandria. Two days of the passage were rough, and Ellen got out her Bible and read the story of St. Paul's voyage in "a ship of Alexandria sailing into Italy." The *Nil's* berths were built across the boat instead of lengthwise, and forty-eight hours of rolling meant that a passenger spent that time largely in shooting back and forth between the head and foot of a berth. In the mood of dejection induced by such exercises a passenger might have pondered the question whether this unfriendly steamer, named for the great river toward which she was sailing, was not an inauspicious omen. There to the south the river rose almost erect, a monstrous serpent with his tail planted on the equator and his jaws opened wide in a gesture of defiance toward Europe. But our travelers were doubtless troubled by no such sinister fancies when, on Christmas Day, they landed in Alexandria and were for the first time on Egyptian soil.

Curnex proved an able bodyguard, scolding "like any ten Americans" as he fended off the wolves that preyed upon tourists. Emerson trudged off through the mud to see Pompey's Pillar and Cleopatra's Needle, but to Western eyes the whole city was a curiosity. Along the streets euphorbias were ablaze with scarlet leaves, loaded camels reluctantly submitted to their masters' whims, tailors sat crosslegged on their window seats as they sewed, and merchants of all kinds sat crosslegged in their gorgeous costumes at the doors of dark little dens full of merchandise. It was the gateway to the Orient. The local French paper, *Le Nil,* duly recorded the arrival of "the celebrated American author" and his departure for Cairo on the following day.

All the way through the delta to Cairo, Emerson turned a dismal stream of wit against the country. It was a hopeless marsh and nothing could argue a wilder insanity than to leave America to see the barrenness and mud of such a place. He pointed out some water around which a crowd of people had collected—to drown themselves, he explained. The weather, though it should have been warm, was still hazy and cold in Cairo, and the travelers faced the same fifty-eight degrees of temperature that had dogged them from Boston onward through Europe.

But the thought of going southward up the Nile was pleasing, and Ellen quickly began to point out the picturesque features of the country. She had only to sit on her donkey and every time she turned her head she saw "greater fun, more beauty" and did not know how to express her joy in Africa. She even lost her prejudice against color and declared that brown was far handsomer than white. Her father joined her in exclamations of admiration when a *sais,* perhaps a native of Nubia or Abyssinia, dressed "in white, except the black or green Zouave jacket without sleeves, embroidered with gold, and the long scarf wound five or six times round his waist below it," ran beautifully ahead to clear a passage for some carriage in the narrow streets and demonstrated with his roaring voice the utterly unimpaired strength of his lungs. Amusing old men, large and tall, with solemn faces framed in white beards, rode by on donkeys the size of a rocking horse. The donkeys were so small that their riders' feet were barely lifted off the ground. What was neither charming nor amusing was at least memorable. Ellen got the impression that the children had only one eye each or else had bad eyes covered with flies and were dirty. The women were ugly in indigo-dyed cotton and vied with the children in filthiness. Many a baby less than a year old rode calmly astride his mother's left shoulder, holding on by her head without the least attention from her.

But Emerson, grown cheerful enough since reaching Cairo, had his usual luck and soon found entertainment of a different sort. George Bancroft, now the American minister to Berlin, had just returned from upper Egypt and had by some kind providence taken quarters, a day before the Emersons, at the khedive's own New Hotel. During his several remaining days in Cairo, Bancroft looked after Emerson much of the time. It was Bancroft who got him the opportunity to see the great Museum of Egyptian Antiquities under the guidance of no less an Egyptologist than its founder, Mariette. It was Bancroft who got him an invitation to breakfast at the khedive's, Bancroft who took him there in a carriage, Bancroft who sat next to the khedive. The General Stone on whose behalf Emerson had once written a plea to Charles Sumner and who was now the head of the Egyptian military establishment went along to the breakfast and turned out to be another dependable companion for Emerson in Cairo. At the breakfast Prince Hassan, home from Oxford, regaled the American essayist with college talk, including much about boating and little about Pusey or Ruskin. Having moved from the New Hotel to Shepheard's, the Emersons found there the entertaining Charles Leland preparing to write his Egyptian sketchbook. It seems to have been "in the shadow of the pyramids" that Emerson came upon a man he could hardly have remembered from a much earlier meeting—Leland's friend George Boker, the Philadelphia poet who was then American minister to Turkey and, fortunately, a friend of the khedive. But the excitements of Cairo and its environs could not make the travelers forget old Concord customs. Ellen saw to it that there was a miniature private New Year's celebration, with gifts and rhymes, at the same hour as the customary observance at home, as nearly as it could be calculated.

By now there were favorable reports of conditions upstream. Many voyagers whose fears of quarantine had kept them in Cairo were beginning their exodus southward. The Emersons and their party of Whitwells —Mr. and Mrs. Whitwell and their daughters May and Bessie—and Miss Farquhar had engaged their dragoman and their dahabeah, the *Aurora*, and the date of sailing was tentatively set for the 6th of January. Besides the dragoman, they were to have a captain and his mate, ten oarsmen, two cooks, a factotum boy, and two waiters. Emerson, it is true, was talking of home again and might have been willing to start in that direction with no further ado, saving out only time enough for a fortnight with Lowell in Paris and for visits with Tennyson, Ruskin, and Browning in England. But Ellen steadied him, and by the 7th the *Aurora* was on her way. The goal was now conservatively set as Thebes, or Luxor, some days short of Assuan and Philae. Doubtless the recent excitement over the cholera had had much to do with this temporizing and indecisive cutting down of the itinerary.

For Emerson the dahabeah was not an ideal home but had strong attractions. There was no place where he could sit with Ellen apart from the others; but it was good for him to be all day on the deck, a kind of parlor without walls or ceiling. There, with the temperature still hovering around sixty degrees Fahrenheit after nearly a week of sailing southward, the passengers were apt to sit on their sofas, wrapped in blankets. Though they wanted ten degrees more of heat, they were comfortable in the sunshine and liked to stay on to talk through the brilliant moonlight evenings. Every day was "nothing less than heavenly." If the river was often like a muddy pond, there were great groves of palms and a variety of life along the shores, where, almost every day, the passengers had an opportunity to stretch their legs for an hour. If the travelers led too lazy an existence, with the dragoman ready to attend to any difficulty for them, they nevertheless got some lessons in Arabic from the delighted waiters and had, daily, two hours of reading on Egypt. As most of the company refused any initiative, Ellen took command, said "now read, now stop, now go ashore," and established "manners and customs."

By the time they reached Luxor they had got their extra ten degrees of heat and Emerson was obviously prospering in health as he sat all day long in "the broadest sweetest sunshine that the heart of man can conceive of," with a subsequent ten-hour night in which to recover from any excess of this curative regimen. At times he fell into the gloomy frame of mind which he styled Doctor Crump. It was true that he had few of his customary amusements, had never since Cairo found anyone who enlivened him, and had read out his little library except Martial, whose works he now kept at for hours daily. Besides, the whole journey was, he felt, "a perpetual humiliation, satirizing and whipping our ignorance. The people," he said, "despise us because we are helpless babies who cannot speak or understand a word they say; the sphinxes scorn dunces; the obelisks, the temple walls, defy us with their histories which we cannot spell." But this was not the whole story. The possibility of meeting Sam Ward and his party farther up the river was exciting. Philae was still unvisited. Emerson was already in treaty with Bedowy, the dragoman, to extend the voyage to Philae, as he had originally intended.

Three or four days in the region of ancient Thebes helped put him in better spirits. Luxor, the modern town, was a mere speck in this impressive world of sun and sky and sand and stones where the traveler who came there really lived. Emerson proposed settling down and never going home. The vast temple of Karnak and several lesser ones lay mainly in the rich plain which the Nile would invade at flood water. Beyond the river and out of its reach, the tombs of the kings, high and dry, honeycombed the barren cliffs. The ancient Roman gods, Jesus, and Mohammed had left their marks. Decaying temples of early Egyptian deities had been adapted to the worship of their successors. But the ancient Egyptian culture dominated both the valley and the hills. There were bewildering arrays of gigantic stone columns crowned with stone papyrus and lotus, avenues of sphinxes, monotonously repeated designs and figures and hieroglyphs, bas-reliefs of triumphant kings and gods in profusion. The inner walls of some of the tombs were adorned with colorful scenes from ancient Egyptian life —sowing, reaping, bread-making, hunting, sailing, fighting, the activities of wild or domestic animals. All these were the enduring memorials of the love of life and the fear of death and oblivion. This region was the nearest thing to the Egypt of antiquity.

Though the travelers were not so fortunate here in finding expert instructors as they had been at Cairo, they had the luck to come upon Georg Ebers, the German Egyptologist, in Tomb 35. He was, said Ellen, "a charming man who showed us what everything meant." There were quite enough guides and advisers of a more political sort. Mustapha Agar, the British consul, vied with his enemy, Ali Fendi Murrad, the American consul, in showering friendly attentions upon Emerson and his party. The two consuls alternated in visiting the travelers. The British consul sent his Arabian horse, with circus housings of blue velvet and gold and tassels and ornamental bridle so that Emerson could ride to the great temple of Karnak mounted in state more befitting an ancient Pharaoh than a modern poet. The American consul, hearing of the lavish generosity of his rival, hastened to outdo him by inviting the whole dahabeah party to come and spend a month at his house.

But the *Aurora* passed on southward, propelled by her oarsmen or by the wind in her two lateen sails. Each sail was "the shadow of a pyramid," as the pyramid itself was "the simplest copy of a mountain, or of the form which a pile of sand or earth takes when dropped from a cart," Emerson noted. Every day was enchanting with its cloudless blue sky and reviving sun, every night the stars were "in full glory" and the weather was "warm enough," Ellen wrote, "to allow us to lie on deck and watch them." And so the *Aurora* sailed on, her passengers living hardly more than a dream, till, in the last week of January, she came to Assuan. There the first cataract marked the limit of her progress.

Arriving at Assuan, the Emersons got the disappointing news that, as the quarantine had been removed, Sam Ward, with his party, had set out a few days earlier on their way southward to the second cataract. A reunion with such a friend would have been, as Ellen read her father's mind, an event of prime importance in any part of the world. But for Emerson there remained Philae, the original goal, and now the end, of his long outward journey.

In some later notes on his travels he wrote that great men of the ancient Greek world felt the attraction of Egypt and "pined to visit the temple-tomb of 'him who lies at Philae,' that is, of Osiris" and that he himself "did not rest" till he saw the famed places of the lower Nile Valley and came "to Philae, & to the temple of him who sleeps there." The British consul at Luxor had given him a letter of introduction to a friend at Assuan. The consul's friend, apparently notified in advance, promptly called when the American dahabeah arrived, and next morning he sent donkeys for the trip to Philae.

Ellen seems not to have traveled those final half dozen miles, and presumably what Emerson's visit to Philae mainly lacked was this enthusiastic historian. For though she had yet found no Egyptian temple that pleased her, Ellen could hardly have failed to admire had she seen this little garden of beauty at the meeting place of the Libyan, Arabian, and Nubian Deserts. The Assuan Dam would one day use the pylon towers of the highest temples as measuring rods for the waters it impounded in the winter season, but in 1873 the dam was decades in the future and Philae was still the Pearl of Egypt. "Nothing," said the Frenchman Laurent Laporte in his book on the Nile voyage, "can be more ravishingly beautiful than this island. A lovely vision, it rises suddenly before you, brilliant and airily fantastic as a dream. It is a strange and wonderful mirage . . . that seems just to have emerged from the sleep of centuries, or from the waves of the Nile; a city of temples, palaces, sculptured pylones . . ."

In the region of Assuan, Emerson first came upon the Englishman George Owen. Owen confessed that Emerson "had been his idol and his guide from his earliest youth," heaped incense on his idol's shrine, brought over "the book he valued most in the world, his Shakespeare," asking that Emerson write his name in it, and also brought a *Religio Medici* with an inscription as a present to him. The river was now alive with travelers, and Emerson was inevitably cast in the role of a venerated idol, a symbol of his own past.

On the way downstream, Edfu, though hardly more than a temple, proved delightful even to Ellen. There the great temple built by Ptolemy III and his successors, and recently cleansed by Mariette of its fungus growth of Arab houses and incumbering heaps of rubbish, stood in a marvelous state of preservation, barring the discoloration and the defacement of reliefs by the Christians. At the beginning of February, in summer weather, Emerson and Ellen resumed the exploration of Luxor for a few days. He "liked donkeys nearly as much as I," she reported, and "he usually seemed very gay while mounted, though sometimes he had a slow donkey, and he had apparently an ambition to be at the head of the caravan." On excursions Curnex went along, carrying the chocolate bag, a little tumbler, Murray's guide, and the opera glasses. George Owen, the Englishman whose dahabeah had parted from the *Aurora* at Assuan with a salute of firearms on both sides, had now turned up again in the Luxor region, and Emerson got much comfort from him. Calling on his friends the consuls at Luxor, the American expounder of plain living and high thinking came away embarrassingly loaded with stone monuments, wooden statues, and yards of mummy cloth, all of which their rival generosity had forced upon him.

Four other dahabeahs became friendly with the *Aurora,* and there were gay social hours. The combined parties, including the Roosevelts of New York, with their "Enchanting children, healthy, natural, well-brought-up, and with beautiful manners," made a total of some twenty-five persons, mostly Americans. One of the enchanting children was a future President of the United States but was then, at the age of fourteen, busily collecting Egyptian birds. The New Yorkers asked their new friends to luncheon. "Almost before we were ready," Ellen wrote home, "the pretty little light boat the Roosevelt children used was waiting alongside, and we were rowed over to the Abou Erdan, by Theodore whose round red cheeks, honest blue eyes, and perfectly brilliant teeth make him a handsome boy, though plain . . ." The boy "rowed with a pair of sculls, and a sailor behind him with another, talking to us," Ellen said, as she hoped her nephew Ralph Forbes would talk when he was three years older, "and as big as Theodore." Ellen cared less for the ruins of empires than for "that visit!" "I approved," she reported, "all I saw, I felt the comfort of a family, I had the delight of seeing children again, and we agreed together, and could talk endlessly. It came to an end all too soon, and we saw them no more."

By this time the boats were through with their visits to Dendera and, presumably, Abydos. At Abydos, a city where Osiris was once much honored, the Emersons, by happy chance, found the German Egyptologist Heinrich Brugsch, who "told us what the chapels were for who were the personages on the walls, what the pictures meant." There they saw the famed tablet recording the succession of Egyptian kings. Then, after descending the river a little farther, partly with the help of oarsmen, Emerson, Ellen, and Miss Farquhar, fearful of losing their steamer from Alexandria to Naples, abandoned the *Aurora* and took the train for Cairo.

At Cairo there was much hurrying about in preparation for sailing. Emerson had to miss a reunion with Richard Owen, the scientist, his acquaintance of 1848. On the 19th of February, after some days of delay till storms subsided, the Emersons were "actually on board of the Rubattino Line steamer for Messina & Naples." As he waited in Alexandria Harbor, Emerson looked back upon the Nile journey with more affection. The whole voyage up and down now seemed to him "full of agreeable incidents." He was "not so blind or dependent," he wrote to William Forbes, his son-in-law, "but that I could wake to the wonders of this strange old land." He remembered the "colossal temples scattered over hundreds of miles" as being, like the Greek and Gothic temples, a challenge to his own century —"something you cannot do, & must respect." His lazy habits and the mild Egyptian winter weather had been the medicines he needed, and he enjoyed a surprising immunity from worry over the writing of books or even of correspondence. He would hardly write a line and was pleased to think how many "useless letters" he had managed to escape by leaving home.

With only eight other passengers, all Pennsylvanians, he and Ellen found plenty of room on the *Egitto,* their steamer. They saw Crete, "which," Ellen said, "principally interested Father because Jupiter was born there, but its wonderful beauty of course held him longer." They were missing Malta, Emerson's first place of landing in the Old World forty years before, and making for Naples by the shortest route. Ahead of them now and on their left they saw the precipitous cliffs and promontories of Sicily, with the imposing mass of Etna not far back from the shore. Ellen, at her father's direction, stayed on deck now. Farther north they had more intimate views of the land on either side. "Calabria on one side," wrote Ellen, "& Sicily on the other are just in their early spring . . . It is very pretty & touching to see spring—after Egypt."

Her youthful enthusiasm was a tonic to her father. She was exactly thirty-four years old on the day when she sailed into the Strait of Messina, and she declared that whether she looked at past, present, or future, she could only exclaim "how broad how bright how full" her life was. She had vitality enough to defy time and the devil even when she was seasick. She doubtless managed the Pennsylvanians as well as her father. "I didn't feel strong enough to land at Messina," she wrote home, "nor Father." But the Emersons and the rest of the *Egitto's* passengers had not only a "very sick" but a "most sociable & affectionate" six days together. His new friends "all knew how to make the most of Father," Ellen said, "and we had readings & much talk."

The Emersons were once more at their Hôtel de Russie in Naples on the 25th. Soon they were in Rome again. Young Henry James turned up in the ancient capital and was a prime favorite with them. But Emerson was kept busy by many persons. For some two weeks he lived through a steady succession of lunches, dinners, and calls. He seemed strengthened by his travels and had so much zest for society that he put off leaving Rome. The cloud that Sarah Clarke had seen hovering over him a couple of months earlier was gone, she perhaps too optimistically discovered.

Elizabeth Hoar, an artist named Tilton, the sculptress Margaret Foley, the artist William Wetmore Story and his wife, diplomat Marsh, Lady Ashburton, the von Hoffmanns, and at least one duke and a princess were among the people, mostly not Roman, whom he was meeting. One evening, at Mrs. Sumner's, he read "In State," doubtless the piece by Forceythe Willson that eventually appeared in *Parnassus*. More was wanted and he read "Timrod & Wm. Strode." This probably meant that he read Henry Timrod's "Ode" sung on the occasion of decorating the graves of the Confederate dead, at Magnolia Cemetery, in Charleston, and the seventeenth-century Englishman William Strode's "Music." These pieces and Tom Taylor's apologetic poem in *Punch* on the death of Abraham Lincoln, another thing he read at Mrs. Sumner's, were all published a little later in his *Parnassus*. When, on March 10, he and Ellen ended their Roman visit, not even the early hour of departure could discourage the artist Tilton from taking them to the train in his carriage or Baron von Hoffmann from being at the station to open the carriage door for them.

During their four or five days in Florence on their way northward they made the usual visits to the art galleries, had a meeting with Bayard Taylor, and saw, for the first time, their German correspondents Herman Grimm and Gisela, his wife. As Emerson could speak no German, he learned with much satisfaction that Grimm talked plain English. He left Ellen to struggle with the German language for the benefit of Gisela. Grimm professed surprise at finding a man who, in contrast to his pictures, looked fifty instead of seventy and had "such bright colouring." Ellen herself was almost persuaded that the miracle had happened, though her father's hair was only longer, not thicker, than in Egypt, and was brown only at the top of his head. But within a few days she was dubious again about any improvement in either his memory or his general bodily health. She and her father "gave up all Italy," Ellen exaggerated, "and Venice & Milan," because they were "not young energetic curious travellers, but old & lazy."

Leaving Florence just before the middle of March, they were in Paris, at the Hôtel de Lorraine once more, after two days of continuous travel. Curnex, having served out his time as valet, guide, and factotum, spending his master's funds and disbursing fees with a lavish hand, was allowed to go. Emerson, dependent as he had grown, was willing to be Ellen's guide to the Louvre and to the botanical garden, his old favorite. He had already revisited the garden with his nephew Charles Emerson and had returned there repeatedly alone. He and Ellen went to the theater a few times "with great joy." One evening, with the Lowells, at the Théâtre-Français, they were delighted with Molière's *Le Malade imaginaire* and the Medieval farcical masterpiece *Pathelin*. Every day Emerson went somewhere with his nephew or with Lowell.

There were some social hours with Frenchmen. The Laugels, undaunted by their failure to rally their literary and artistic friends in Emerson's honor in November, had better luck now with their invitations for the 27th of March. Emerson dined with Taine and Tourguéneff and had some conversation with Renan at last and with the geologist Élie de Beaumont. Remembering that Emerson had read only part of the not very recent history of English literature, Taine next day sent a note to Elizabeth Laugel with an inscribed copy of that book for him.

During this Parisian visit Emerson got much pleasure, it seems, from James Cotter Morison, the Positivist, a knower and lover of things French. After a couple of dinners, Morison came and spent an evening in Emerson's room. At the hotel, the Lowells and John Holmes were, as in November, the chief entertainers. Evenings were usually spent in Lowell's parlor, where Emerson and Lowell smoked their cigars together. But at table there was a Polish Count Savinsky who, with the aid of a bottle of Burgundy, got an introduction; and it seems that there were also a couple of other Poles, a minor French writer, and Ellen's favorite, the Marquis de Grammont.

On April 5 Ellen returned with her father to London, and soon she was busily recording their adventures: "We arrived Saturday night, and Sunday while I was at church, Mr Froude and Max Müller came Lord & Lady Amberly a little later. . . . Monday Lady Stanley of Alderly, Tuesday Mr Edw. Dicey Wednesday Mr Froude, Thursday Lady Amberley. Mr Hughes & Mr Newcomb & Mr Conway have also called, small hope for letters & sightseeing. Father bold as a lion (for him) about all this going out. Is said to be much improved." Next day Emerson was "in the full tide of dinners & calls, busy every moment." He liked this life better than usual, though he had moments of homesickness when he proposed "to take the Fitchburg train."

He was having occasional lapses of memory. Words escaped him. But he was apparently not greatly annoyed as yet. Sometimes he put his fancy to work when he was caught in errors. Ellen, seeing that he made no tragedy of his misfortune, found him simply amusing when he wanted to "take an obelisk" instead of an omnibus. Places, less surprisingly, were jumbled in his mental map of London. "Then," Ellen wrote home, "when we went to Westminster the other day, he expected to go to Charing + first and then turn, whereas the driver took us across the top of Green Park . . . he sat still and didn't interfere with the course of the cab, but he took it out in talking . . . said he was expecting the driver to come to his senses every moment, but the repentance must now be so late as inevitably to lose our dinner for us." When Ellen pointed out the towers of the abbey before them, he had to accept the facts but offered an explanation of his own: "Well, the case was urgent and required a miracle, and the Abbey has pirouetted and settled in the other end of London. Happily the fairies are our friends and see to it that at all costs *we* come out right." Presumably he was at his best when he faced strangers or at least made his most determined efforts then.

With all his invitations to eat and drink and converse, it was hard to find time for any serious conversation. He got rather far, however, with George Howard, the future Earl of Carlisle; with Lecky, already the author of a history of European rationalism; with Stanley, the liberal dean of Westminster; and with Froude. He took a special liking to Howard as well as to the Duke of Argyll. Argyll had more than a political reputation, being long since known for his attempt to reconcile religion with science.

Emerson was still finding his proper place in the company of liberal thinkers. It was no accident that Max Müller, the student of comparative religion, was one of his most attentive friends during this last English visit. This was the year of Max Müller's appearance as a lecturer on the science of religion in Westminster Abbey at Dean Stanley's invitation, an occasion without precedent in the history of the abbey. Moncure Conway, an American liberal settled in England, hovered about the compatriot by whom his thinking had been shaped in earlier years. The English writers Emerson now had to do with were, most of them, likewise unmistakably liberal. John Stuart Mill, the vigorous leader mourned a few weeks later by British intellectuals; George Henry Lewes; George Eliot; and Robert Browning were all of that stripe. Carlyle was also a liberal so far as religion was concerned. Of the political leaders with whom Emerson now became acquainted, Gladstone was at the moment the most conspicuous; and, though only gradually outgrowing his conservatism, he was, as prime minister, the titular head of the Liberal Party.

Ellen, if not her father's secretary, was at least his social historian; and her letters home, though hastily written and sometimes confused in sequence of events because of the speed at which she was moving, bristled with personalities. "Father dined," she wrote, "at Mrs Grenfell's with Prof. Müller and Dow: Lady Stanley of Alderley. . . . Father went with the gentlemen to the Cosmopolitan Club . . . Mr Conway . . . told us of an invitation through him from Mrs Rob: Crawshay of Cyfartha Castle, Merthyr Tydvil in Wales to make her a visit. . . . we called on Mr W. H. Channing . . . Mrs Edwin Arnold was there. . . . Father went to dine at Mr Dicey's . . . When I came in from shopping I found Mrs Paulet, Miss Newton & Miss Jewsbury calling on Father. . . . Father . . . lunched with Mrs Grenfell, called on Sir Henry Holland . . . When he came back he went to the Nortons, lunched with them, and Mrs Baird Smith, DeQuincey's daughter . . . At 7 we dined at Mr Froude's, Mr Stevens

& Mr Carlyle were the other guests . . . Miss Norton called on me . . . Mr Carlyle also came. . . . That evening we dined at Lady Amberley's. . . . The other guests were Mr J. S. Mill, his step-daughter Miss Taylor & Prof. Frazer. The talk was chiefly on Goethe. . . . Father stayed and was introduced to a Mr Leckie whom he liked particularly. . . . Father went off with the Amberleys. . . . They had found Earl Russell . . . We recd. notes, from Lord Houghton inviting us to visit him in Yorkshire . . . from Mr Geo Howard . . . inviting us to dine, and from Prof. Max Müller inviting us to make him a visit in Oxford. This Father accepted with joy. Lord Houghton's was for a time when we couldn't go . . . Easter . . . After breakfast as I recounted our invitations, and among them Lady Augusta's to go to church with her, at the Abbey, Father suddenly resolved on going. He wished to see the Abbey and to hear the Dean. . . . Happily there was some history in the sermon, and that interested Father . . . After church we called on Mr Carlyle. I have seen no house yet that seemed to me quite so interesting and pleasant. . . . Mr C. . . . was in a more amiable and cheerful humour than he had been a few days before when Father walked with him, and Father has been very happy in the remembrance of this call. He said things about W. S. Landor that relieved Papa's mind moreover, giving him a hope that the sins of his hero were not so great as he had supposed. . . . Mr Conway came and stayed till we went out to dine at the Deanery. Dean Liddell of Christ Church, Oxford, was there, and Mr & Mrs Leckie, and Dean Church of St Paul's with his wife, and the Duke & Duchess of Argyll. . . . Deans Stanley & Liddell . . . talked of Egypt. Why and how has Egypt such a hold upon me? No other subject seems to interest me to the same degree, and the memory of it is so lovely. . . . Dr Hinton came . . . author of Man & his Dwelling Place. . . . Father went to Lady Amberley's where he met Mr Browning and was well pleased. They disagreed about poetry. Mr Browning praised Shelley. . . . Wednesday Apr 16 Today breakfast at Argyll Lodge and a beautiful time. . . . Then went with Mr Geo. Howard to his house, perfectly beautiful. . . ." These were some of the details that Ellen jotted down from the experiences of the ten days from April 6 to 16.

She presently picked up the thread of the narrative in a new report to Concord, continuing her day by day account. "The next day we dined at the Norton's . . . Mr Lewes who wrote the Life of Goethe & married Miss Evans was there, and was skillful in telling stories. . . . April 18th we went to breakfast with Mrs Smalley. . . . Friday . . . we dined with the Howards. Mr Howard is a young gentleman who loves Father as all the Stanley family seem to . . . The other guests were Sir Arthur Helps,

Mr Browning, Mr Froude, the Duke & Duchess of Argyle . . . Saturday
. . . we dined in the P. M. at Kensington Museum and looked it over
with Mr Allingham host and Mr Browning. We had very good talk and
I saw Raphael's Cartoons . . . Sunday to church. Then to lunch with
Dr Carpenter, then to St Paul's to hear Dr Liddon . . . Monday I went
to Seven Oaks . . . and Father the House of Commons, the Duke of Bedford & Mr Playfair seemed to be the people who talked with him most.
. . . he went with Mr Hughes to the Workingmen's College. Tuesday we
breakfasted with dear Sir Henry Holland, perfect bliss. Then at 11 o'clock
went to Eton & Windsor with Miss Stanley and Mr Howard, lunched with
Mrs Ponsonby in the Castle, and saw all my soul desired . . . came home
and dined with the Hugheses and W. E. Forsters . . . Wednesday breakfasted at Mr Cyrus W. Field's with Mr Gladstone, Duke of Argyle, Mr
Hughes Mr Norton, Mr Smalley. . . . lunched with Mr Tyndall, Mr
Huxley & Mr Hurst being the other guests . . . Mr Allingham took us at
three to see Guild Hall . . . we dined with Lady Airlie, the company was
the Duke & Duchess of Cleveland, D & D Argyle, Mr Campbell, Mr Howard
Lady Stanley, Mr Browning & Mr Cowper who was once in Concord. . . .
Thursday . . . Father after breakfast with Mr Gladstone spent the fore-
noon with Mr Carlyle with real comfort, bade him goodbye and then went
to the Howard's & lunched with Mrs Lewes. We dined at Sir Frederick
Pollock's . . . Friday calls all day lunch at Mrs E. Arnold's with Mr
W. H. Channing, dined at the Conways' . . . Saturday packed & went
Sunday to Tintern Abbey & Raven'scroft—stayed with the Amberleys . . .
Monday to Cyfarthfa & luxury & the kindest hostess. Mr Conway also, for
2 days. Then to Oxford."

Before he had got through the hurried round of London dinner tables
and drawing rooms, Emerson was tired and, according to Ellen, could not
remember "half as well as when he came" but "rejoiced so much in seeing
Mr Gladstone, and Earl Russell, and the Howards that I am sure he will
look back on it with pleasure."

His one attempt at a speech on this English visit, it seems, was at the
Working-Men's College in London; and his address there was extemporaneous and therefore doubtless brief. Conway, present on that occasion,
remarked that when Emerson "spoke of the 'pathetically noble' effort of
English scholars to educate their humbler brethren, there was before us
another 'pathetically noble' sight in the figure of the white-haired sage
beaming his last farewell, and uttering his last animating word to the class
that received him as prophet at the dawn of a closing generation."

Emerson showed courage and wisdom in refusing urgent invitations from
Max Müller, seconded by the vice-chancellor of the university, to appear

as a lecturer, as the French critic Taine had done before him, for the Taylor Institution at Oxford. "If I were at Oxford with any leisure, & could believe that I could interest young men there," he told Max Müller, "I should willingly read something to them, but certainly not for a fee. I go to see & to hear, & so pray you to secure me a corner in your Lecture-room & Ruskin's." Being informed that Max Müller would probably lecture on the origin of language on May 1, that Ruskin would lecture next day, and that Ruskin, Jowett, and others were being asked to a dinner in honor of the expected guest, Emerson went to Oxford at the appointed time.

The Two Paths had somehow struck his fancy decisively, he had long wanted to know its author, and so did, as he had written ahead, "rejoice like a boy in these expectations." The lectures were duly heard and the dinner was eaten, but Emerson got more than enough "doleful opinions of modern society" from Ruskin when they had retired to the lecturer's chambers. Yet Ellen could attend both lectures and also hear Ruskin's pessimistic conversation and still come away with unabated enthusiasm. She longed for time to tell not only of "Prince Leopold's coming to lunch with us and our going to tea with him and his showing me the pictures of his family" but of "Mr Ruskin whom I fell in love with," and the "seriousness of his talk, the sweetness of his ways, the interest of his rooms and the things he showed us." She also had pleasing memories of "dear Mr Max Müller" and of "a hundred things that come and go all unrecorded."

If the youth of Oxford had no chance to hear Emerson's voice, the youth of England seemed still to be readers of his books and had no intention of letting him depart in peace. "That class," Ellen put it, "which Father calls 'very young persons' have discovered that he is in England and he has letters asking him to arrange an interview anywhere, anyhow, only not to refuse. Some he answers and often he has to let them go." His time was too short and his strength too slight to allow him to act as father confessor as he had done in 1847 and 1848, and he appointed no new bishop to succeed Arthur Clough.

From Oxford he and Ellen went on to Warwick, where his friend Flower met them and showed them the castle before carrying them home with him to Stratford-on-Avon. At Stratford, church was attended for the sake of Shakespeare. Beside his tomb the clerk seated the Americans and their friends. Afterwards Emerson returned, as Ellen said, "to take a better look at the tomb, and see how Miss Bacon probably would have planned to disturb those mysterious bones." In the evening he entertained his hosts, the Flowers, by reading aloud to them.

By the 6th of May he and Ellen were in Durham and on the next day arrived in Edinburgh, where he "met a large party of notabilities" at the home of Fraser, a professor of logic and metaphysics in the university. He was entertained at dinner by William Smith, the translator of Fichte. Smith had heard him preach in Edinburgh in 1833 and had listened to his lectures in 1848. Emerson and Ellen hurried on southward again through Keswick. At Bowdon, a few miles from Manchester, Alexander Ireland, chief instigator of the lecture tour of 1847–1848, was their host for a couple of days; and, at Ireland's, Emerson had a final interview with "many of his old friends and hearers" of that earlier time. At Liverpool, R. C. Hall, also known to him since the years of the second visit to Britain, saw him off on the Cunarder *Olympus* when she sailed on May 15.

As the Emersons had expected, they found their American friends Charles Norton and his family among the passengers on the crowded ship. Norton talked little to anybody but Emerson and took care to preserve notes of their conversations. Sometimes the two would smoke their cigars together in the daytime, and at night they would have a couple of hours of talk before the lights were extinguished in the saloon. Norton discovered that though Emerson talked to everybody, was the greatest talker on the *Olympus*, he was fresh and ready for more at night.

What struck Norton most in the aging man were the limits of his mind, his firm closing of other avenues of truth in favor of his own optimistic philosophy. Norton undoubtedly got an exaggerated idea of these weaknesses, but he was not so much wrong as unfortunate. He was getting his most intimate view of Emerson when Emerson was in one of his weakest phases. He was even persuaded that Emersonian optimism was degenerating "into fatalistic indifference to moral considerations, and to personal responsibilities" and was "at the root of much of the irrational sentimentalism in our American politics, of much of our national disregard of honour in our public men." During the whole voyage he hardly caught a glimpse of the real Emerson of other days. Yet he saw through the distorting medium of old age some of the sage's faults and virtues. He detected a good deal of inconsistency and much caprice in literary tastes and judgments. Emerson was handicapped by imperfect sympathies. Extraordinary dicta like the statement, made, at Norton's dinner, to Lewes, Goethe's biographer, that *Faust* was a bad book were now seasoned with a minimum of the familiar Emersonian charm of phrase. Yet during the voyage Emerson read and reread Omar Khayyám, forgetting that he had condemned it six months before. He surprised Norton by admitting that he had just now, for the first time, heard of the Finnish epic, the *Kalewala*. He had happened to meet its French translator at the table d'hôte of the Hôtel de Lorraine in Paris. He also struck Norton as absolutely without conceit. He "blushed like a youth one day," Norton said, "when I spoke to him of his influence on the men of my generation." He was so insistent on the joy of living that Norton quite logically took him up when he bewailed his seventieth birthday, which fell during the voyage, as the close of his youth. But Norton, surprisingly enough, failed to realize that he was dealing with a man whose faculties were far from what they had been. He wrote him some birthday verses, assuring him that he would be a youth till he died.

On May 26, when the bitter cold of the voyage was changing to warmth, the travelers saw the American shore set off with the fresh green of spring. Boston, though recently scarred by the great fire, seemed, in the fiery halo of the best sunset "since we were in Egypt," to be "beautiful & imposing." After remaining on the *Olympus* over night, Emerson and Ellen were delayed many more hours before they could start for Concord with Edward Emerson and William Forbes. Ellen, writing letters while she waited, explained that she was "spending the day in the depot as they haven't got the house in order at home yet and hoped we shouldn't arrive till afternoon." Meantime her father was "going about to attend to business and see friends in the city."

The returning travelers were kept ignorant of the fact that the little village of Concord had been preparing an elaborate reception for them. A committee had purchased lumber and green cloth and accessories; had kept a workman busy for two days erecting an arch of welcome near Bush; and, at an additional expense of nearly thirty dollars, had hired a band that included baritone, alto, and bass horns. The committee was hampered by uncertainty. It was planned, possibly for the benefit of the schools, that Emerson should be brought home in an afternoon train; but even the day of his arrival was uncertain. A system of signals was arranged. As soon as the *Olympus* arrived in Boston Harbor the Concord bells would ring for fifteen minutes. Notice of the train on which Emerson was to reach Concord would be given by striking the bell twelve times for the noon train, three for the three o'clock train, five for the five o'clock train, six for the six o'clock train, or seven for the seven o'clock train.

The bells first announced arrival by the noon train, but a telegram changed the hour, or was intended to change it, to 3:30. In the mild state of confusion Concord telegraphed to the president of the railroad and arranged for the engineer of Emerson's train to give timely notice that Emerson was aboard. Accordingly the engine of his train whistled all the way from Walden Woods to the station so that no such noise was ever heard before in the village.

At the station the whole town, it seemed to Ellen, had assembled "Just as they always did in the war to see the Company off or receive it back, just as they do on Decoration Day, or any great town occasion, a sight always festal." As Emerson faced the crowd Sam Hoar ran to his side and demanded and got three cheers for him. When the train started off, the people in the cars threw up the windows and added a cheer of their own. The school children may have been at the station to honor Ellen as well as her father, for during her absence she had been re-elected to the school committee. Some of them had come even from the outer districts, three and four miles distant.

The band played while people in wagons and carryalls and people on foot moved down Main Street and Lexington Road, all managing to reach the arch of welcome before the returning travelers in order to greet them again as they entered Bush. The school children sang "Home, Sweet Home." Emerson and Ellen, with others of the family already in their party, found Lidian at the east door and walked through the newly restored house to the front to look out on the crowd. Emerson went to the gate to express his thanks, and the crowd dispersed only after some more cheering.

Alcott was one of the most interested spectators. He had come to Bush the evening before to bring a copy of his *Concord Days*, "bound in flexible covers, with illustrated title page, and photograph," a gift for Emerson's seventieth birthday. To him it seemed that both this spectacle in honor of his neighbor and his neighbor's response were charming. "Whatever doubts," he wrote in his journal, "any may have had respecting its agreeableness to him, were instantly dissipated by the hearty response and cheer with which he returned this expression of his townsmen's regards. It was a surprise to him. 'What meant this gathering? Was it a public day?' . . . I did not hear his speech distinctly, but trust someone gifted with a faithful memory will preserve it." Edward Emerson thought he remembered, many years later, that his father had only said, "My friends! I know that this is not a tribute to an old man and his daughter returned to their house, but to the common blood of us all—one family—in Concord!"

Alcott, perhaps in a wistful mood, thought it "a novelty in the history of this our historic revolutionary village, this honoring scholars publicly" and believed that it stirred "the latent patriotism which has slumbered unfelt perhaps in the old citizens, descendants of the patriots of 19th of April, and now rekindled at the fame of their townsman." Whatever patriotism it stirred, such a pleasing festival in honor of a village's own poet, essayist, and seer was doubtless never witnessed before or since in America, unless in fiction. To a reader of Hawthorne, the late storyteller of the village, this gathering of 1873 might, however, have recalled the final scene in "The Great Stone Face," a story which, Moncure Conway asserted, was inspired by Emerson.

25.

TERMINUS

❊❀❊

Oh, but the play is not yet at an end, there are but
three Acts yet acted of it? thou hast well said: for
in matter of life, three Acts is the whole Play.
—*Marcus Aurelius . . . Meditations,*
translated by Meric Casaubon

BUSH had been restored at an expense of more than $6500 drawn
from the cash paid by the insurance company and from the funds
given by friends after the fire, and though still unpretentious it
was a comfortable home. The bay windows in the dining room
and nursery, the large garret provided by the square roof, and especially
the well-lighted and spacious bathroom instead of the old dark, cramped
ones, made the house more pleasant than before. After establishing the
ritual of the daily bath in the 1850s Emerson had for eighteen years, winter and summer, proudly taken his cold-water morning plunge, his "invariable," in a hat tub. The modern bathroom was a symbol of progress. The
whole of the reconstructed building, when it was shown at a great reception, with committees of the Emersons' friends acting as guides to the guests,
seemed to warrant the hope of a new and more prosperous era in the life
of the master of Bush.

He was well and lighthearted and imagined he was making progress
on the book long since promised to the English publisher. It was now
thought certain that Egypt had given him renewed life and health. His
enthusiasm for the beauty of his restored house and the comfort of his study
did not tire. The burning and restoration seemed to the whole family like
events in a novel, and day after day they surveyed their rooms and possessions "with a feeling of romantic interest." The lemon stick Emerson had
bought in Naples and its successor, the boxwood cane, must have given
him all the help he needed to get rapidly about over his favorite roads and
fields.

But in spite of all, he was growing old. In 1875 the Gutekunst photographs of "The Three Boys"—Emerson, William Furness, and Sam Bradford—recorded admirably his changing moods. Dejection, chastened self-
confidence, restrained humor revealed themselves in his face. His long hair

was thin though still much darker than Furness's or Bradford's. His short side whiskers were gray. Possibly the meeting with him in Beacon Street, Boston, that Robert Collyer remembered occurred about this time. Collyer, struck by his sadness, asked him about a friend. " 'He is growing old,' Mr. Emerson replied sorrowfully. I asked for another. 'He is growing old,' still more sadly. 'You are looking well, though, Mr. Emerson,' I said. 'Yes, I am well enough,' he returned, 'but I am growing old too.' "

The most unmistakable sign of age was his loss of memory. The mind of the intuitive philosopher seemed to be failing much as the mind of the masterfully logical philosopher Kant had failed. By 1874 Alcott, Emerson's senior, saw the marked change in his friend. "It must be mortifying," he commented, "to one of his accurate habits of thought and speech and his former tenacity of memory to find himself wanting in his once ready command of imagery to match his thought instantly. I remember when the least hesitancy in another was painful to him in the extreme, so facile was his genius, his rhetoric so fit and so brilliant."

But even now, it seemed, much of the old fire could flare up again. Within a few months Alcott was chiefly troubled by the persistent opposition Emerson kept up against the Alcottian theories. It was only Emerson's skeptical attitude that seemed to him to make their conversation drag. "Was I still the visionary enthusiast, whom he must check by his moderated sense and less hopeful mood? Or was he in the subjunctive?" Alcott asked himself. "Yet my friend," he remembered, "complains of growing old, says that his memory is gone, and that his Diary has few entrances in these late days. Does he exaggerate, as the rhetorician must? I have known not a single scholarly acquaintance whose memory of words was ready and retentive like his." But, as Alcott observed, Emerson very cleverly covered up failures of memory by circumlocution. Another thing that made it harder to catch him in his lapses of memory was the habit he now had of falling into subdued tones in his conversation.

Fortunately he had no longer any need to worry over finances. In 1873, when his income from lectures was very low, he could expect $2,000 from his $28,000 in railroad bonds now prospering under the skillful management of the Forbeses. Apparently the money given him on account of the fire was not exhausted by the rebuilding of the house or by travel. In 1874 the sale of the Jackson estate in Boston's strategic Court Street brought the heirs, according to Emerson's account book, over $63,000, and of this Lidian was expected to receive $20,000. In 1875 the Concord assessor reported that Emerson then had $20,000 in stocks and bonds and Lidian $16,000, that their buildings and 51½ acres of land were worth $7,500, and that they had two cows, a horse, and two carriages. In the middle

1870s Emerson usually kept a checking account of around $1700 in the Atlantic National Bank of Boston. The outlay for domestic servants and for his man John Clahan had to be remembered, but at least the farm and garden paid him something for their keep. If his beloved pears—the Bartletts, the Napoleons, the Golden Beurres, the large greenish yellow and russet Flemish Beauties, the juicy and rich Louise Bonne de Jerseys colored pale green with a dark blush, the high-flavored Seckels, and the rest—brought him but scant honor at the Cattle Show and but little cash at the market, his orchard made other contributions to the family economy, and the strawberry crop he sent to market in the summer of 1873 alone amounted to at least some twenty-four hundred boxes.

With Lidian and Ellen in his house, Emerson must have found domestic life entertaining. Ellen was full of enthusiasms. And both she and her father considered Lidian in action a first-rate spectacle, though the imaginary "calamities" that marked her course "from day to day" aroused pity. Lidian had been, as Ellen saw her, "so innocent, so pathetic, and so funny." "I don't think," Ellen had summed her up, "any family before has ever contained so curious, and interesting a character as she is. I contemplate her all the time with increasing pleasure, and find her innocence unfathomable. I wonder if she could have got into a family more unlike her than the Emersons who are hardly born innocent, and cannot stay so."

But Lidian had at last entered a happy period of transformation. She was no longer the pallid invalid that the Amberleys had visited in 1867. She had begun to abandon what Ellen called her double emotional life and to give up her perpetual brooding on the evils of the world. She had now proved her prowess as a talker at the club May Alcott had founded. People had noticed the delight which Emerson, who also attended the club, took in these exhibitions of his wife's unsuspected abilities. For the most part, the little world that Lidian knew had not seemed to put the highest value on her. But Ellen had at last had her own eyes opened to a certain beauty in her mother and had come to appreciate her courage and high-mindedness and the excellence of even her amusing traits. Now in her middle seventies, Lidian was constantly being invited out and had, in Ellen's eyes, become a belle. With social life, her spirits rose and she hardly noticed her husband's gradual decline. She took to playing whist with the Alcotts.

In 1874, Edward married Annie Keyes. Recently graduated from the medical school at Harvard, he settled down in Concord as partner of Doctor Bartlett, the Emerson family doctor. Edith, though she had long since become Edith Forbes and had her growing family to care for, kept in close touch with her Concord relatives and incited them to visit her at

Milton and at Naushon Island. Naushon drew Emerson almost every year, usually in August.

He now left the family circle much less frequently than he had used to do. When, in 1874, he went with Ellen to the house of Caroline Sturgis Tappan, a friend since early Transcendental days, he found Doctor Oliver Wendell Holmes and William James among the guests there. He had not ceased to go to the Saturday Club and was still successful in getting friends into it. He urged the election of Doctor Asa Gray, the botanist, an expounder of Darwinism with a difference partly due to Gray's religious orthodoxy, and was delegated to inform him that he had been chosen. He still valued the Concord Social Circle. When its meeting was held at Bush in 1875 there was an extraordinary feast, perhaps because of his son Edward's admission as a member.

He kept going through at least the formalities of his office of Harvard overseer as faithfully as he could. He had been re-elected in 1873 for a term of six years. He had long since helped collect funds for the memorial to Harvard's dead soldiers, had even looked over the plans for the curious Memorial Hall approvingly, and had proudly witnessed the laying of the cornerstone. He had solicited donations to the college when it was poverty-stricken. He had long served, and now still served, on the Greek committee and other visiting committees of the overseers as well as on their special committees.

Though he did not attend all the meetings at which the overseers continued to debate the old rule of compulsory attendance on prayers in the college chapel, his interest in the subject must have been keen. The corporation, the overseers, and the faculty debated and resolved. Opinion seesawed. The sentiments of individual overseers were seldom recorded in the official minutes. Whatever sentiments Emerson expressed on the subject of prayers were not even hinted at. Yet some rumors of his attitude got abroad. In 1874, when the debate over prayers seemed critical, *The Commonwealth,* a Boston paper, reported that he had favored keeping attendance compulsory. Since prayer was the highest act of the human mind, he was supposed to have argued, it would be wrong either to take it away from young men or to permit them to deprive themselves of it.

If this report was correct, Emerson was for the moment not Emerson. It is true that he had once preached ceaseless prayer and had apparently never renounced it, but the ceaseless prayer he had advocated was a state of spiritual health rather than a ceremonial and had nothing to do with praying formally on schedule. It was also true that since his days as a schoolmaster and as a school committeeman in Boston he had been inclined to favor strict discipline for schoolboys. But this bias of his was not enough to make the argument reported by *The Commonwealth* sound Emersonian. If Emerson actually argued and voted as rumor had it, Cabot's comment on the rumor was probably the best explanation: "The truth was, he was simply dwelling in his early associations." The aging man, Cabot doubtless meant, was a boy again, sitting in chapel, and did not want his boyhood memories disturbed.

Writing now meant collaboration, Emerson found. He helped his children, and, before long, his friend Cabot, hunt out publishable passages from old lectures or journals and fit them together. Ellen, naturally most with her father, was the court of first appeal and remained the general manager of literary collaboration till Cabot became supreme. It was a severe test for her. As late as 1868, when she was in her thirtieth year, she had read, she told Gisela Grimm, very little of her father's writings except his poems. But she must have become far better acquainted with both his books and his manuscripts in the half dozen years following. Her close association with her father had been her best preparation. But she needed all the breadth of vision she had got from her formal education under Sanborn at Concord, at the Sedgwick school in Lenox, and under the direction of Agassiz at Cambridge as well as the liberalizing she had got from her travels alone to the Azores and with her father in Europe and Africa. She was completely loyal to her father, and yet she was unsympathetic with his more radical doctrines. She was clever herself at writing, but in a style quite different from his. Mainly she could help him by suggesting what ought to be kept as likely to appeal to readers, what deleted, and what made more clear. She found that he could still be stubborn in defense of his own taste.

Edith's pleasure in hearing her father read verse had, more than anything else, kept alive the project for an anthology of his favorite poems by miscellaneous authors. It had early been decided that it should be called *Parnassus,* and that title had survived through many years while the editing had languished or progressed slowly. During his travels of 1872–1873 Emerson had occasionally entertained his friends by reading from a tentative notebook collection. Changes and additions were discussed at family conferences and in much family correspondence. As late as November 17, 1874, on the verge of publication, "God Save the King" was deleted from the proof sheets in favor of "Bonnie Dundee." On the 18th of December, William Forbes "came home proud as a peacock bearing the first copy of *Parnassus*" to Edith.

The collection was by no means representative of Emerson's own best literary judgment, which he had outlived. It was never meant to be limited to great pieces of poetry. It contained much homely humorous and sentimental verse as well as some masterpieces of imaginative writing. The extraordinary mistakes chargeable to editing were numerous enough to cause much anguish. George Hillard complained that the text failed to keep abreast of changes made by the authors. James Clarke objected that he had been credited with what was not his. Stirling, the Scottish philosopher, was perturbed, as many others must have been, by the deliberate omission of Shelley. The greatest American poets were completely ignored—Poe, Whitman, and Emerson himself. Poe was dead, but Whitman had good reason to be displeased. William Rolfe, already editing Shakespeare, sent in notes on miscellaneous errors. There were complaints from a poet who was included but not credited with his own verses. But the book was a financial success. As Alcott was told, it was the best venture its editor had made and had earned $1000 within some nine months after publication.

By the late summer of 1875, when *Letters and Social Aims* seemed about to take final form but before Cabot took hold, Ellen was fully initiated as managing collaborator. She found the work "interesting & painful" and kept her sister fully informed about it. "I find it easier than three years ago for two reasons," she told her, "I am better acquainted with it so feel less blind & helpless, and I have now not the least scruple about showing Father things, while then I couldn't bear to, because it was the beginning, and I hated to shock him with the sense that his memory was failing him. But as fast as one hill of difficulty with this book is ascended I come in sight of another twice as appalling, so my spirits are seldom high about the business. Father's, however, rose as soon as he began to feel the cable draw and perceived that I was really helping him along. He is evidently more cheerful ever since, and often sings praises, and proposes writing to the Advertiser that a partnership has been formed. He doesn't like to summon Mr C. to this, but I foresee that 'twill be necessary." Hotten, the original instigator of the book, was dead; but his successors, Chatto & Windus, wanted it still. A few articles long ago printed in magazines were to be used as chapters; but the contents of the volume were mostly being sifted out of the literary stock piles at Bush, approved, and somehow arranged and unified.

Within a few weeks Cabot had come to join Ellen and her father in their extraordinary literary adventure. A publishable passage was boldly wrenched from its old context and made to do service wherever Cabot and Ellen thought it could. "In this way," Cabot confessed, "it happened sometimes that writing of very different dates was brought together: *e. g.* the essay on Immortality, which has been cited as showing what were his latest opinions on that subject, contains passages written fifty years apart from each other." Emerson himself could do little but take part in the search for materials. Though the new method of compilation was not unlike the method he himself had used when he had worked alone, he now had little or nothing to do with the actual synthesis of the scraps gleaned in the search. As Cabot candidly explained after publication, it was "open to any one to say that he never really decided upon publishing them, and, if he had been left to himself, never would have published them."

According to Ellen, her father was at first frightened at the spectacle of a new hand holding his pen; and, according to Mrs. Cabot, Cabot was frightened at being that new hand. But soon things were going smoothly enough. It is impossible to determine the exact extent of each collaborator's work. Cabot bore a heavy responsibility. To him Emerson "always spoke . . . of the volume as 'your book.' " It seems at first to have been Ellen's idea, if not Cabot's, that the collaboration should be kept secret, doubtless to avoid wounding Emerson's pride; and the book, christened *Letters and Social Aims,* appeared in the middle of December, 1875, without any word of apology. But Cabot eventually made a very frank confession to the reading public. *Letters and Social Aims* was almost posthumous, and its compilation raised much the same ethical question as was faced by the editors of Hegel when they had to bring order out of the confused manuscripts relating to, rather than giving, his lectures on the philosophy of history.

If the book, even in its hitherto unprinted parts, was mostly an old story, so were the papers Emerson infrequently read in public. Sometimes, however, an audience might be surprised with something particularly suited to the occasion. The address at the opening of the Concord Free Public Library in October of 1873 had a local flavor, with its references to Concord literary worthies, Thoreau being given the place of honor. Yet the manuscript seems to have been prepared with little help. Ellen, fearful of the outcome, witnessed what seemed almost a miracle of delivery, a miracle possible, no doubt, only to a veteran lecturer. The easy mastery Emerson had used to feel was suddenly restored to him. "I was proud of Father's voice," Ellen assured Edith, "proud of his skill, and more thankful for it than can be told, for I had read the address in part and was dismayed at its fragmentary nature. But when he came to deliver it he neatly connected it extempore in a manner no one would suspect. . . . When he came to the end, the end was either left at home or shuffled, Wasn't it a pity? But again he happily covered it up. No one knew but he & I."

He seemed to enjoy venturing out to read a poem or even a lecture at a place like the Fields home in Boston, and he could sometimes be persuaded to face large audiences. In 1874 he turned up at the New England Women's Club "poetical picnic." There he, William Lloyd Garrison, and others read original poems.

Few cared to debar him in his old age in spite of his unrepented religious liberalism. Even the divinity faculty at last ended its embargo of thirty-six years. As late as June, 1873, that faculty had refused to grant the petition of the senior class to have him appointed as commencement preacher, and a few months later had locked the door against him by inciting the Harvard overseers to forbid the divinity students to elect any graduating-class preacher other than an instructor of the university. But on May 12, 1874, he stood once more in the old chapel. Professors as well as students were there to hear him. Emerson had told his friend Charles Norton of the intended address and had fittingly asked that he might spend the night at the Norton home on that occasion. Norton was the son of the man who had so vehemently attacked the divinity school address of 1838. There were thus gestures of reconciliation on every hand.

Charles Norton, and doubtless many others, had privately wondered what Emerson could possibly add now to his masterpiece of 1838. He really had nothing to add. But the students at least, according to their scribe, were delighted with what he gave them in 1874. After the dean had introduced him with some eulogistic remarks, Emerson arose, said the scribe, "and for more than an hour gave the audience such a treat, intellectually and morally, as is seldom enjoyed; claiming their closest attention by the magic of that subtle thought, that happy expression, and that simple, but unique manner, that have so long charmed and delighted the world—" The historical significance of the moment must, however, have been more impressive than the address. "The striking contrast manifested between the Dean of the School on this occasion, and the spirit of a former one toward Mr. Emerson, was," the scribe observed, "an element which forced itself upon the minds of many present, and in no small degree added to the enjoyment of the occasion—"

By this time even an appearance at the Concord Lyceum could put Emerson into the news. When he read a lecture there on oratory and orators in February of 1875, three hundred people came on a special train from New Hampshire to hear him, and it was said that he spoke "with his old ease and confidence." If he cared to go far from home with a lecture he could count on a much larger fee than he could have expected in his prime. In March of 1875 he received $300 for a lecture in Philadelphia. But he had other and less pleasant reasons to remember that occasion. He was overpowered by the size of the auditorium at the Academy of Music. Ellen saw from the box where she sat with the Furnesses that he was making no effort. She gauged his appeal to the audience by the response to the passages which had been favorites with other listeners and concluded that only a few persons could hear all he said. He had the feeling that it was impossible to give anything its right meaning when he had to struggle to make himself heard. So he did not struggle.

A few weeks later he was making his 19th of April centennial address in Concord at the unveiling of Daniel Chester French's "Minute Man," the first serious work of the young sculptor. It was almost as much his statue as French's. Some two years before, a committee of the town meeting had voted to erect on the American side of the river a statue of a minute man "with the lines of Emerson, that are 'household words,'" engraved on its base. As those lines had perhaps been heard almost as far as the shot his embattled farmers had fired in 1775, it was appropriate that their author should be added to the committee on the monument. He took great interest in the progress of the statue. Granite was discarded for bronze, Congress furnishing some cannon as materials for the completion of the work. On the raw 19th of April, Emerson delivered the short and simple address which, according to his son, was the last he ever composed. Hundreds of visitors, it is true, sought shelter in the hospitable homes of the village and would not stir out even to the tents to hear Lowell's ode and Curtis's oration. But in spite of the rough weather it was a memorable day for Concord. President Grant, cabinet members, governors, regiments of soldiers, and noted authors were among her guests.

In these years Emerson might still go as far as New Hampshire to address the graduating class of an obscure academy, as he did at New Hampton in the summer of 1875, or obediently appear in Boston at some club or at some historic celebration. He had read the poem "Boston" at the centennial Boston Tea Party in 1873, and had soon repeated it at the Radical Club. The much later New Hampton address meant a serious adventure of some days' length. Emerson went shopping for a map of New Hampshire and a new felt hat. The hat was so good a disguise that Ellen could hardly recognize him. At the last moment she got the manuscript of the address in hand and sewed the leaves, thus discouraging any inspirational rearrangement on the spur of the moment. At New Hampton, social and literary fraternities appeared with a band to convoy the Emersons to the academy. A marshal with a portentous baton was personal escort for Emerson; another carrying a cane ornamented with pink ribbons took charge of Ellen. Emerson pleased his audience with a few homely stories.

After the commencement he and Ellen traveled into the mountains, stopping along the road to hunt strawberries. At the Flume House sudden oblivion fell over his memory of a former visit there, and he wanted to know whether the Flume was a mountain, a river, a tree, or a rock. At length he said he remembered having admired something long ago and this was it. Ellen prolonged the vacation, and he was delighted. He suggested, as he often did on such occasions, that they should never go home. She looked for signs of benefit to his health, but when she saw how pale and thin he was, she feared a week would do little for him.

He was unmoved, to all appearances, by his fame. It had been so in earlier years when long experience of it could not have accounted for his unperturbed attitude. He was pursued by autograph-hunters. Literary societies were named for him. He had got used, no doubt, to such outbursts as Benjamin Presbury's in 1867. Presbury, after hearing him lecture, had described him as the greatest teacher of the age in the most bountiful hour of his life. Emerson must have known that Alcott, lecturing on New England authors, had hardly been able to get beyond Emerson. Privately, he was very probably bored. When, at a town meeting in 1874, it was proposed to call a Concord street by his name, he declined being so honored. He suggested that the street be named for Thoreau, and it was. Alcott commented that "We would not name one street Emerson, but all in the village, were this possible, to signify our respect for our fellow-townsman."

Charles Sumner, with almost his last words, sent his love and reverence to his Concord friend. Emerson was a pallbearer, with Whittier for his mate. "Where does one put this crape?" he asked. Whittier, doubtless seeing how helpless Emerson was, replied, "I have put mine in my hat." Ellen was not surprised when her father failed to return to Concord at the expected time. She knew that some of his bodyguard, as she called the numerous friends nowadays on the lookout for his safety, would see that he got back.

He was pleased when Max Müller honored him by dedicating the *Introduction to the Science of Religion* to him in memory of the visit the Emersons had made to Oxford, and again when one of the student parties at Glasgow nominated him for the rectorship of their university. At Glasgow he was under the disadvantage of being a foreigner as well as of being pitted against such a powerful political figure as Disraeli, then prime minister and first lord of the treasury and at the height of his popularity. The Independents, Emerson's sponsors, printed propaganda in *The University Independent,* sang their imprecations against "drivelling 'Dizzy' " to the tune of the "Soldier's Chorus" in Gounod's *Faust,* demanded to know whether the students would permit their souls to be sold for government gold, and urged everybody to vote for the philosopher of the Oversoul instead. The result was that Emerson got more than five hundred votes, and Disraeli's margin of some two hundred was considered small in the circumstances. Emerson, spurred on by his family, had been willing to face the necessity of another voyage to Britain in case of his election but was more than content to stay at home. There, in spite of old age, he continued to be host to visiting celebrities from abroad. In October of 1875 his friend Monckton Milnes, now Lord Houghton, arrived. With Judge Hoar as chief partner in the conversation, Houghton kept the dinner table at Bush in a state of pleased excitement.

Emerson felt his faculties rapidly weakening. Ellen was both his memory and his judgment. Now a notable figure in the village, she rode about on her donkey Graciosa, a native of the island of that name in her beloved Azores, and was busy with public-spirited projects as well as with her father's affairs. But her most important business was to be her father's companion. In conversation Emerson could still seem charming to some, but he confessed that "an old man fears most his best friends." "I have grown silent to my own household under this vexation," he said, "& cannot afflict dear friends with my tied tongue. Happily this embargo does not reach to the eyes, and I read with unbroken pleasure."

W. H. Channing, arriving for a stay of two weeks or more at Bush in the summer of 1877, found that his host could not remember even Alcott's name and noticed that he asked where Henry Thoreau was when he wanted the name of a plant he had known from youth but had now forgotten. But it seemed to Channing that though Emerson's words halted sadly his thoughts were as clear and swift as ever. Ellen continued to find his struggles for words enchanting. He arrived at hen only after zigzagging from cat to fish, fish to bird, and bird to cock. In trying to speak of the Capitol at Washington he could only describe it as "United States—survey of the beauty of eternal Government." More than a year later he had the courage to read the Concord Lyceum a lecture entitled "Memory." He was serene in the face of defeat.

He did not easily lose his interest in the social life he had become used to. As late as 1878, in spite of his difficulty in spelling and in writing, he was sending out invitations in his own hand for the big family festival of Thanksgiving, though he may well have used models prepared by Ellen. Mrs. Gilchrist, a visitor in Concord that autumn, told William Rossetti that, as she had heard, Emerson usually gathered some twenty-two children, grandchildren, and relations about him on Thanksgivings. His daughter Edith Forbes then had five children and his son, Edward, had two, and Mrs. Gilchrist's total was not far from correct. Some of his grandchildren still remember these occasions, when the house was alive with fun by day and the garret was turned into a dormitory for the boys at night. Every August or September Emerson continued to enter his name in the "Island Book" at Naushon.

He did not quite forget his old friends, living or dead. At the grave of Thoreau's sister Sophia in 1876 he wished for "some public service, less hurried, with opportunity for friends of Henry and his sister to have spoken of their worth." He concerned himself with the disposal of Thoreau's manuscripts, he kept up his defense of Thoreau against critics, and helped keep the memory of Thoreau green by reading an account of him to a club in the village. He lived over again his friendship with Carlyle, a pessimist plunged into deepening gloom since the death of Jane Carlyle. As early as 1870 it had been arranged that copies should be made of all Carlyle's letters for greater convenience in rereading them. Some five years later Carlyle had promised Edith that after his death all of her father's letters should be sent back to America.

As late as 1876 Emerson was still jotting down in his memorandum book the street address of Walt Whitman. In the following year the Englishman Edward Carpenter, having made a pilgrimage to Whitman, visited Concord and questioned Emerson closely about his changed relations with Walt. Emerson laughed, a little nervously, Carpenter thought, and admitted that he had once believed Walt had some merit. But now, according to Carpenter's story, he called Walt a wayward, fanciful man and complained of his lack of respect for meter. He took down a volume of Tennyson from the shelf and dwelt upon the beauty of Tennysonian diction and meter as if to point his moral. As the two men sat in the book-lined study or walked in the old-fashioned garden, Carpenter observed Emerson's painful failure of memory and saw the fixed look of age in his eyes yet found him active in body, full of fun, and enjoying intellectual life. Carpenter was struck by what he called "a wonderful bird-like look about the face." This was all the more impressive because Emerson had a way of jerking his head forward as he spoke. Ellen was distressed because her father quite forgot that his British guest had been invited to spend the night. Emerson ostentatiously exhibited his fatigue in the hope that this "most agreeable man" would start for his train. Carpenter, as Ellen sympathetically observed, "had a funny visit, and behaved beautifully through its extraordinary scenes."

When Mrs. Alcott died, Emerson attended the funeral, sitting beside Bronson Alcott. He had been the friend of the Alcotts for forty years. That summer he and Ellen went down Boston Harbor on the *Parthia* to bid farewell to Lowell, now the new American minister to Spain. On returning to shore, Emerson found one of what Ellen called his bodyguard on the alert and was soon put into a barouche and carried uptown to the Athenæum in state. A long chapter in the history of his friendships ended the following year with the loss of Elizabeth Hoar. Having missed what had seemed her destined relation of sister-in-law to him, she had been like a sister to him ever since. A few days before her death, remembering her

Chaucer, she sent Emerson word that she was waiting till the grain should be taken off her tongue. Sam Bradford and William Henry Furness, Emerson's schoolboy friends, still lived. Bradford was the treasurer of a railroad. Furness lived the intellectual life but had, as he himself said, only two ideas. He missed slavery because one lifelong interest of his had been emancipation, and now it was out of date. His other idea, the life of Jesus, remained a hobby; and, he said, one paid for a hobby by becoming a bore. At seventy-six Emerson attended the Holmes birthday breakfast given by *The Atlantic Monthly's* publishers. John Burroughs, seeing him there, thought him the most divine-looking man he had ever seen, not like a saint but like a god.

Though Emerson was no longer very helpful in his role of literary adviser to promising young authors, he had for years occasionally tried to guide the hand of Emma Lazarus, a New York poet. She was still eager for his advice, and it was hard to make her understand that he had no more advice to give. He had needed to use tact in order to preserve his friendly relations with her. Not long since, her admiration for him had been severely shaken by his failure to include any of her verses in *Parnassus*, for, after the warm commendation he had given a few of her poems, she had fully expected to appear in his volume of favorites.

She forgot all her bitterness when, in response to an invitation from the Emersons, she arrived at Concord in the autumn of 1876. Though surprisingly mature in appearance and, to Ellen's eyes, unexpectedly large, she was only twenty-seven years old and was pleasant with her plain, natural manners. She seemed an easy guest to entertain, being "at the very summit of delight & joyful anticipation." Yet she faced some difficult problems of adjustment.

When eight o'clock came on her first night she was astounded to hear that it was, in general, the family bedtime. Learning that Emerson himself would sit up longer, she begged and got the extraordinary privilege of sitting up and talking with him. He was alarmed but got happily through an hour and a half of conversation. She vanished at nine-thirty that night and thereafter tried to accommodate herself to all the customs of Bush as soon as she became aware of them. But she could learn them only with some effort. The old poet, she discovered, still kept hours of seclusion in his study, as he had done in his days of busy literary work. In the morning, after waiting patiently on the doorstep till half past ten or so for him to appear, she was told, to her consternation, "Oh he is always shut up in the study till dinner-time." After an excursion with Ellen to the Cliffs she inquired what Emerson would do that afternoon. "Oh he always spends his afternoons shut up in his study till he takes his walk," was the reply she got.

Having come under the misapprehension that she was Emerson's guest and not Ellen's, she was, it seems, only gradually disillusioned.

But once these disappointments were over, she was constantly delighted and was a delight to the people of Bush. "After that," Ellen said, "everything seemed only to fill her young enthusiastic mind with utter happiness, and her youth & happiness were elixir to us all." The guest had a way of revealing the character of her hosts, as Ellen saw. Lidian was a discovery for Emma. Ellen thought "it was one of the highest entertainments I ever had to hear them together, her ardent persistent questions sometimes and Mother's utterly unexpected answers, which surprised now by their unfathomable innocence, now by their erudition. She got at many a corner of Mother's mind never before visited. Then again Mother's sudden walking right into & onto all Emma's supposed feelings & opinions with such loftly unconsciousness, and the pretty frankness with which Emma would take it." The visitor stirred everybody into new life. "Father & she," Ellen said, "were also a novel spectacle, the peaceful directness of her questions astonished him she didn't see how much, and she got answers out of him that I should have declared he wouldn't give. Not that I think she succeeded in getting at what she wanted to, but he wouldn't have treated anyone else so well. Then think of what nuts it was to me, old S. S. teacher that I am, to get at a real unconverted Jew (who had no objection to calling herself one, and talked freely about 'our Church' and 'we Jews,') and hear how Old Testament sounds to her, & find she has been brought up to keep the Law, and the Feast of the Passover, and the Day of Atonement. The interior view was more interesting than I could have imagined. She says her family are outlawed now, they no longer keep the Law, but Christian institutions don't interest her either."

In a journal of her Concord days which is now lost except for a few excerpts, Emma Lazarus noted every incident and detail. Her sister said of it a dozen years after it was written that it was "touching to read now, in its almost childlike simplicity." It must have given an intimate view of more than one Concord worthy along with personalized portraits of Emerson himself and "the stately, white-haired Mrs. Emerson, and the beautiful, faithful Ellen, whose figure seems always to stand by the side of her august father." Back in her Newport summer home, Emma dispatched fruit to Bush and worried over Ellery Channing's attempt to take Emerson's place as critic of what she called her crude rhymes. From New York she was soon inquiring hopefully for Emerson's opinion of a play of hers she had left in his hands, and was carrying on a correspondence with the amazing Ellery Channing and pondering his morbid and melancholy moods. Concord was henceforth a great capital on her literary map, and she kept Emerson's picture before her on her mantelpiece. In the third summer after her visit, Ellen invited her again, but Emma apparently did not go.

Writing grew more and more difficult for Emerson, and his long-lived journals came finally to an end. One he called "Old Man," apparently meant to record the mind of age, turned out to be a mere fragment. He still read, even going back to his own books. They now seemed new to him. Ellen, finding him poring over them, heard him say, "Why, these things are really very good." His enthusiasm for Oriental lore was still strong, and he was shocked when he learned that even a spurious Oriental work, *The Desatir*, had been allowed to go out of his study without his knowledge. He had something to do with the preparation of his *Selected Poems*, published late in 1876, though he leaned heavily on the advice of others. About the quality of some of his pieces he had very definite opinions still. He disliked the early poem "Good-bye" so much that neither family nor friends could persuade him to include it.

Ellen now carried on much of his correspondence, doubtless most of it. She and Cabot did their best to leave Emerson's own words untouched in what they thought still had to be published, but changes seemed essential. Sometimes the manuscripts, after years of hasty rearrangements for lyceum audiences, were almost hopelessly confused, and it was too late to make sure what order Emerson would really prefer for publication. When *Fortune of the Republic* appeared in proof in a form unfamiliar to Edith, Ellen explained: "The 'original order' was not Father's but Mr Cabot's and mine. We have never changed his order I think where it could be ascertained. This is a collection of every general remark on the country from many lectures of many dates, each full of the moment when it was written and so adapted to that occasion and no other that scarcely a page entire could be saved. When you first heard it at Thanksgiving it was most of it from the lecture named F. of R. which Mr C. had already sifted but there was then no order at all. As read at the Old South it had copious additions from Moral Forces and some from other lectures, one on N. England particularly. As read at Dr Bartol's it had been helped by all we could collect from American Nationality. So don't think this last is any more my version than all the rest for from the beginning I have done as much in arrangement as Mr Cabot."

But Cabot was becoming more important in such matters, especially since he had been asked, in 1877, to write a life of Emerson and had promptly announced his half-way acceptance of the task. He said he felt incompetent to write a life but would be willing to collect materials for the right man whenever he should appear and would meanwhile, if occasion arose, make a sketch that might do for a time.

One of the last attempts of Emerson, Ellen, and Cabot at their now habitual collaboration on printer's copy was in response to the British Sampson Low & Company's request in 1878 for an introduction to *The Hundred Greatest Men*. The ambitious project demanded Emerson's aid, so the publishers assured Ellen, their correspondent. They thought only two men at all fit to write the general introduction, "the two Fathers of the Century," Emerson and Carlyle, and they rejected Carlyle because he was not catholic enough, belonged to only part of the world, not to all of it as Emerson did. A page or two would be enough. By March of 1879 Emerson, in receipt of a new and urgent request for action, was writing to Ellen, then away for a visit, that if he was to do the work for Sampson Low & Company it was "absolutely necessary that you should come home & tell me what hints & what resources Mr Cabot & you have found in my workshop possible to this end." Before the year was over Emerson's general introduction of two or three pages duly appeared in print, with Matthew Arnold's introduction to Volume I immediately following it.

Lecturing, from old manuscripts, sometimes refurbished by the collaborators, continued intermittently. It was hard for the master of the art to quit, and he could be successful still. Rounds of applause greeted his thirty-five-minute lecture to the teachers' convention at Concord in April of 1876. Some weeks later he and Ellen were at the University of Virginia after visiting the centennial exhibition then attracting the world to Fairmount Park in Philadelphia. He was "dazzled & astounded" at the exposition, "had no idea of the glories" he saw with his friends Furness and Bradford at his side. At Charlottesville, almost to the last possible moment he was still working desperately, with Ellen's help, to get his unsatisfactory oration in order. But in their brief intervals of freedom the representatives of the North, so lately the hated enemy country, were received with great friendliness, and all might have gone well had Emerson's voice been stronger and the hall less large and difficult to speak in.

Large as it was, the hall was packed, principally with students from seventeen to nineteen years old and an average of some two belles to each beau. There was also a large sprinkling of children from four years old upwards and due proportions of parents and of professors' families. Ellen felt a mixture of regret and satisfaction. "The uproar of people coming in late and hunting seats," she wrote home, "continued some ten minutes into the address and I saw with dismay that Father's voice seldom rose clear above it, and all the young & gay perceived the same thing, and like the audience at Mr Adams's oration at the Dedication of the Memorial Hall, concluded they couldn't hear very well and had better enjoy themselves, so the noise rather grew than decreased. Eight front rows; two knots of stu-

letermined to hear, who left their seats and came up the two aisles,
od; a like knot above on each side hanging over the gallery rail-
d as many of the faculty, & 'joint-committee-of-the-literary-societies'
latform as were on a line with Father or before him, heard. Here
people strained their ears in vain; and the larger part of the audi-
ispered together, while some talked & laughed aloud all the time.
o bad."

on seemed hurt, but Ellen was in a better position to judge.
thinks if they would only have been quiet he could easily have
m all hear. I don't," she decisively commented. "I think he could
·eached more than two thirds; his voice didn't sound strong enough.
1ow the oration was appreciated by some of the hearers; and in
l... ng Father and in a speech made afterwards things were said just
such as I desired,—that it was a sign of re-union, his coming down,—that
'it was fit that Virginia should hear the sage of the North' &c We have
been treated with every attention, and have seen people from every southern
State, and I have enjoyed all very much. . . . If the oration had been my
first thought in this visit, I should be disappointed, but as I regard the
expedition principally as a right hand of fellowship, I am contented."

In later years, as she looked back on the event and remembered how
unhappy her father had been over the failure of his address, Ellen imagined
that part of the trouble had been a determined hostility on the part of the
hearers; but this view was not in agreement with the full accounts she wrote
immediately after the oration. Her letters at that time were well filled with
evidences of the friendliness shown on every hand. She saw then that the
Southern audience at the University of Virginia behaved just as the New
England audience had done at Harvard's Memorial Hall.

The Charlottesville students and their friends, naturally not realizing
how much crippled by old age the orator was, hardly had patience to sit
and listen to what they could not quite hear. The reports of the occasion
in *The Richmond Enquirer* doubtless expressed well the contradictory moods
he aroused—disappointment "that even those who sat within a few feet of
him were able only to catch at intervals some terse sentence full of strength
and meaning," the feeling that the little that was heard "only served to
increase the desire of every one to hear more," anger because the gaunt
"Abolitionist philosopher of Boston" had visited the university at its expense
but with profit only to himself, suspicion that he was now going back to
Boston with the address in his carpetbag in order to put it into a book and
so receive a more substantial return than expenses and hospitality and
applause. But almost certainly the reporters failed to reflect the full measure
of the Virginians' friendliness, and certainly the university was "vexed and

humiliated" by the exhibition of journalistic bad taste. The whole episode was, however, a memorable landmark in the revival of good feeling after the bitterness Emerson himself had shared during the war of the 1860s.

On the way back through Virginia, Ellen was once more struck most by the kindness and courtesy of the people. "Then the fun," she wrote home from Washington, "which no one but I ever has, as I am the travelling companion, of seeing all the world burn incense to Father was never so great as now, just because it is the South. To hear him constantly called by name . . . To see people come & stand before him in the aisle of the cars & gaze at him, and bring their children & ask him to shake hands with them. People from Tennessee, Alabama, Texas . . ." At Washington more kindness was shown to the Concord travelers. As they entered a horse car to ride to the Capitol, Bret Harte seized upon Emerson. Another willing guide turned up in the person of the librarian of Congress, and Ellen thought her father seemed ten years younger all day. When they returned to the hotel he was delighted to find that they had missed their train and so had the prospect of "an afternoon & night, an oasis of quiet." But whatever peace they enjoyed in Washington that afternoon and night, the next stage of their journey homeward, which brought them to Philadelphia for another look at the exposition, was enlivened by new adventures.

A few somewhat confused notes were got together as the basis for the speech Emerson made at the celebration by the Latin School Association that autumn. He appeared at the Old South Church more than once in these years, with worn wares of his, in obedience to the call of the committee for the preservation of the church. In February of 1878 he practiced faithfully his reading of his lecture on education for a Concord audience, but could not even remember the subject and continually asked what it was. He was keenly aware of the humor of the situation. "A funny occasion it will be—a lecturer who has no idea what he's lecturing about," he commented, "and an audience who don't know what he *can* mean!" But when the day came, though he was hoarse and had to be taken to the hall in his heaviest clothes especially lined with wadding, he had one of his great successes.

He kept on reading "Education" in private and in public, taking it as far away from home as Phillips Exeter Academy in New Hampshire. As late as 1879 he boldly delivered "The Superlative" at Amherst. About the same time the Divinity School Debating Club begged for a lecture or talk, and soon Cabot was at work arranging a manuscript on preaching. But on May 5, when Emerson tried to read it to the club, though he got on well enough for a time, "there was some boggling at words," as Ellen noted, "and a wicked choking cough set in towards the end, so that it was almost impossible to finish." Still undaunted, he was at the Concord celebration of July 4 to read the Declaration of Independence. The occasion was, in spite of his weakness, a triumph for him. The crowd stood and applauded and there was a call for "Three cheers for the man whose voice is heard round the world." He had studied the declaration for three days past and supposed he knew every point of it, but, as he began to read, it seemed suddenly unfamiliar, and he almost feared he was reading in the wrong book. Yet he somehow got through it to the satisfaction of his friendly audience.

As he grew very old, hawk-eyed critics were on the lookout for the expected return to religious orthodoxy of the individualist who had in his younger days stirred up controversy by his quietly issued declaration of independence. He unwittingly encouraged them. Weary of sitting silent in his study, he took to attending church, as he now attended almost any kind of meeting or lecture, in order to break the monotony of his days. By 1876 he liked going to church almost as much as Ellen herself, so she thought. He continued to show his customary toleration toward Protestants and Catholics alike. When Lidian offered Bush for the Catholic wedding of her niece Eugenia Jackson, he "said it was a very proper thing, and he had no objection." He did his part as a witness while the priest in white surplice and black robes officiated. Presumably he contributed nothing to the support of the Roman Catholic Church, though he was solicited even for a subscription to a monastery. Alcott, in 1877, saw his friend's persistent individualism mellowing with age and infirmity but found his temperament still too dominant and determined. Next year he judged Emerson true to his old convictions, resting modestly in his individualism, silent concerning immortality, and deserving to be classed somewhat uncertainly "as an ideal theist, with that film of pantheistic haze that hovers always about that school of thinkers."

The fact that Emerson now signed his name in the list of members of the parish betrayed nothing concerning his religious belief. And his boyish junketing with Ellen to attend a Unitarian convention at Saratoga in 1878 had no greater significance. The convention was only one objective in a journey that was partly a vain search for George Tufts, a disappointing literary protégé of years past, and partly a visit to Niagara Falls. A great stir was caused when the false rumor got round that Emerson was a delegate to the Unitarian convention. It was true that he showed some enthusiasm for the proceedings during the brief time he witnessed them and was much lionized before he could escape. Ellen had her first actual experience of radical Unitarians tirelessly quoting her father in defense of their own thought. But for him the most exciting adventure had been his traveling

alone for several days in search of Tufts. Quite unable to remember such names as Niagara, Saratoga, Buffalo, and Olean, he had managed to get along with the aid of some written directions from Ellen. He had arrived at Saratoga, after a final night of sitting up on the train, fuller of zest than usual, his faculties stimulated by his days of independence.

By 1879 the Rev. Joseph Cook had started the countrywide rumor that Emerson had publicly renounced his liberal religious views, had become a Christian, had accepted the Bible as divine, and had joined an orthodox church. The rumor was good for a year or two of vigorous life. When Emerson returned to Concord, New Hampshire, to read a hymn as his part in the semicentennial of the church to which he had preached some of his earliest sermons, he seemed to many, no doubt, to be making a new gesture toward orthodoxy. But a more significant event of the same year had been his re-election as a vice-president of the Free Religious Association. The secretary reminded him that he had honored the vice-presidency with his name for the past seven years.

Honors, fame, and notoriety came faster now that he did little or nothing to earn them. In 1876 Lowell's second series of *Among my Books* was dedicated to him by way of public acknowledgment of a debt. The younger Oliver Wendell Holmes, future jurist, confessed that his own first interest in philosophical ideas was due to Emerson more than to anyone else. From Germany, Emerson learned that his photograph was wanted for publication in an illustrated magazine at Leipzig. He was punished by being used as an exhibit at public meetings, or at celebrations such as the Whittier birthday dinner of *The Atlantic Monthly* in 1877, where he read "Ichabod" in the face of old Webster partisans and thus seemed to reaffirm his prewar devotion to abolition, Union or no Union.

The Whittier birthday banqueters were, however, more amazed at the temerity of Mark Twain, who read a skit he had written for the occasion. Three ill-favored tramps masquerading under the names of Longfellow, Emerson, and Holmes visited a California miner's cabin, made what Mark Twain regarded as very amusing use of certain verses by their namesakes, and, in general, behaved in ungentlemanlike manner. Or at least this must have been approximately what the banqueters made of it all, and their applause was weak enough to crush the temperamental humorist.

He quickly suffered an acute attack of remorse. The abject plea for forgiveness that he wrote to Concord was answered on Emerson's part by Ellen's confession of her own hurt feelings, now healed by the letter of apology, and her assurance that her father never quite heard the skit in the first place, never quite understood it, and forgot it easily and completely. Doubtless if Emerson had understood it and its humorous intention

he would have been no more offended than Lidian was when she read it. As for Mark Twain, he had, in his apology, unwittingly made up for any lack of humor in his performance at the solemn dinner.

In 1878 Emerson became a member of the moral and political science academy of the Institut de France. Dean Stanley, his guest at Concord that year, had already honored him by posting in Westminster Abbey the verses on England's abbeys from "The Problem." At a meeting of the newly founded Concord School of Philosophy in 1879, Emerson sat with Lidian and listened while Elizabeth Peabody, Frank Sanborn, Wentworth Higginson, and Bronson Alcott gave their reminiscences of him and of Hawthorne and Thoreau. Doubtless Hawthorne and Thoreau were hardly farther back in Concord's past than he himself was as he struggled to catch the meaning of the speakers. The youthful Frank Dempster Sherman, having called upon the poet in Concord, paid him as genuine an honor as any when he sent him a picture of Homer as a token of sincere affection and as a sign of the appreciation of a boy for what Emerson had done "to help him to become a man."

Daniel Chester French, sculptor of the "Minute Man" at the North Bridge, added a memorable bust to the already extensive but very unsatisfying iconography of Emerson. Ellen, though she later lost some of her enthusiasm, at first agreed with Edith that this was a piece of great good fortune. French himself was not pleased. It was only after the work was done that he accidentally discovered on Emerson's face the expression he had vainly set out to capture. He had found the face a remarkable combination of strength and delicacy, and difficult because of its extreme mobility and consequent great variety of expression. Emerson was, he judged, one of the most difficult subjects imaginable to portray adequately, and he believed that he had failed in his attempt. Cabot, much with Emerson at the time, thought French's bust "the best likeness of him . . . by any artist (except the sun), though unhappily so late in his life."

For lack of translations, Emerson had hitherto had no great vogue in Continental Europe, though in England his name was a household word. German versions of a number of his volumes, French of a few, and Danish and Swedish that amounted to the merest samplings had not clearly forecast his future importance in many countries. But now, with the advance of his fame, even such skimmed Emerson as *Letters and Social Aims* could find translators in Germany and France at least. By 1876 an authorized rendering called *Neue Essays* had been published at Stuttgart. The general preoccupation with politics in France made success more doubtful there, and Jeanne Montagnon, finishing her French version of the same book some three years after the German text had appeared, knew that the number of readers could only be very limited. The times proved to be even more unfavorable than she had believed, and she failed to find a publisher.

But the clatter or the silence of the printing presses was not infallible evidence of the growth or decay of ideas. Mental ferment could be going on quietly and obscurely. The half dozen or so volumes of the American essayist to be had in German translation seem to have been potent intellectual yeast for at least one Continental genius—Friedrich Nietzsche, by this time a professor of classical philology in the Swiss university of Basel. As early as 1862, when he was still in his teens, this German pastor's son who rebelled against the creed of his father discovered the rebel of Concord. At times his enthusiasm for Emerson weakened, but his doubts were overbalanced by his delight. The very incomplete record of his opinions pieced out from meager published references to Emerson, and from fresh passages brought up from the as yet inadequately explored depths of the Weimar archives, warrants the belief that the resemblances between some of the best-known doctrines of Nietzsche and the aphorisms on self-reliance which he gleaned from Emerson are significant.

If Nietzsche discovered serious imperfections in Emerson—too much repetition, too much love of life, tasteless extravagance of style learned from Carlyle, regrettable haziness borrowed from German philosophy, and a badly disciplined mind—he discovered far greater virtues. Emerson, named first among his most read authors in 1863, was later, according to Nietzsche's varying moods, an admirable writer, a glorious friend, one of the four masters of prose in the nineteenth century, more enlightened and skillful and more a man of taste than Carlyle, the most richly endowed of Americans, the author in whose book Nietzsche himself felt most at home though he hardly felt at liberty to praise it as it was too near to his own thought, a man richer in ideas than any other of his century, a brother soul. But as Nietzsche once wished that he might have the privilege of re-educating Emerson and of disciplining strictly, according to his own notions, that splendid spiritual and intellectual specimen, so Emerson, had he known Nietzsche's work, would doubtless have been glad of an opportunity to make his German admirer over into a more restrained protagonist of self-reliance and some of its related doctrines. Nietzsche had a systemless style of thinking and writing strikingly resembling Emerson's but transformed Emersonian thought into something far from Emersonian. He separated the most iconoclastic ideas from their large admixture of less unconventional moral doctrine and almost transmuted them in the intense heat of his own fiery brain.

During the last years of Emerson's life there were few letters, few lectures, and no more books. For the Concord School of Philosophy, meeting in what had recently been Alcott's Orchard House, irreverently dubbed Apple Slump by Louisa, Emerson had read "Memory" in 1879. In 1880, when the school began to use its new Hillside Chapel in the Apple Slump orchard, he read "Aristocracy." In the latter year, according to one observer, he still came "often" to the school, passing along the aisle on tiptoe and seating himself "in a huge ear-lap chair at the left of the platform." On at least one Sunday evening the parlor, study, and hall at Bush were filled with friends from both the town and the school. Emerson rapped on a doorjamb and announced that some present would speak and asked them to begin. In 1880, the year of his last lecture at the School of Philosophy, he read his "100th lecture before the Lyceum" in Concord. At the lyceum, as its secretary recorded, a "very large audience . . . rose en masse to receive him," and he "read . . . with a clearness and vigor remarkable, considering his advanced age." His last public reading of any kind may have been that of his paper on Carlyle at the Massachusetts Historical Society in February, 1881. Ellen, doubtless there to see him through the risky adventure, thought that "It was a very pleasant occasion."

He lived only a twilight existence. To a visitor in the summer of 1880 he would hardly give an answer in conversation, but smiled and turned away his head as if another person had been addressed. Next year the octogenarian Alcott conquered his desire to report on his winter campaign of lecturing in the West because he knew Emerson would forget as fast as he was told. But to him Emerson's failure of memory did not seem tragic. "His," he commented, "is a happy euthanasia, and a painless." Sometimes there seemed to be marked but only momentary upsurges of memory. When the sixteen-year-old Edward Bok, with Louisa May Alcott's aid, penetrated Bush as far as the study, the old man rose with great dignity to greet him but had no light in his eyes. As the boy insisted on an autograph, Emerson had him write out exactly what he wanted copied, then proceeded to copy his own name painfully letter by letter; then, the place, Concord; and finally, the date, November 22, 1881. Suddenly transformed at this point, Emerson rewrote both name and place without effort, thanked Bok for coming, shook hands vigorously enough, and let his face and eyes light up as if he had thrown off the weight of years.

The rumor started by Joseph Cook that Emerson had returned to Christianity in old age continued to reverberate. Emerson had habitually avoided public controversy and was now all but oblivious of such matters. But he authorized his son to speak for him, and on February 17, 1880, Edward wrote to Alfred Ferguson, an inquirer in Indianapolis, that the rumor of a change to orthodoxy was "in every respect incorrect." Ralph Waldo Emerson, he stated as explicitly as he could, "has not joined any church, nor has he retracted any views expressed in his writings after his withdrawal from the ministry." George Cooke came to the defense of Emerson in an article aimed at Joseph Cook, and *The Commonwealth* published Edward's letter to the Indianapolis man, as *The Index,* a Boston journal, did a few days later. Ellen was troubled, hating to see the family "appear to rush into print about the matter, but," she explained, "Father said he was glad, he liked to have the truth told." It was good, he declared, to have a son who could defend him.

Perhaps the final attempt to convert Emerson from the supposed error of his ways was made by the founder of Christian Science and author of *Science and Health.* According to her own statement, Mrs. Eddy appeared on the scene some months before Emerson's death. Taking her husband along with her but letting no one else know, she went with the avowed purpose of healing the slowly dying Transcendentalist. But a brief introduction into his mind was sufficient to disabuse her completely of any notion of carrying out her mission. He knew he was breaking up, he made it clear to her, and he considered it simply profane to believe that man was not mortal. If Mrs. Eddy's account was correct, he contradicted her flatly, assuring her that he did not believe that God either could or would prevent the deterioration of old age. She withdrew convinced that he was a long way from being or becoming a Christian Scientist. Alcott, she decided, was far nearer salvation than he.

While the battle over his religious opinions continued, Emerson, quite too old and worn to give serious thought to religion or any other subject, unconcernedly continued to fill his vacant hours as comfortably as he could. He had long ago announced his desire, contrary to Cabot's better judgment in that matter and therefore never complied with, that his own sermons should be destroyed. But he was now quite willing to hear sermons by other men. He would also appear at special Unitarian celebrations. Anniversary week in Boston, a time-honored church festival, seems to have proved alluring to him in 1880 because his friends Furness, Hedge, and W. H. Channing were to speak on his early benefactor Doctor William Ellery Channing. On his seventy-seventh birthday he joined Ellen at a Unitarian anniversary meeting, but, once he had listened through W. H. Channing's address, he made for the door and did not want to return for another meeting. Later the same year he was placed on the platform at the celebration of the 250th anniversary of the First Church in Boston, once his father's. On a Sunday within some two months of his death he was eager for church time to come and asked hopefully, "It is the day of Heaven today, isn't it?"

He arranged in good time for a final settlement of his affairs. In 1876 he had signed his new will, dividing his possessions among his wife and their three children. Lidian, and afterwards Ellen, was to be in control of the homestead; and Edward was to have possession of copyrights and plates and the ownership of all published writings and contracts for publication. Elliot Cabot was to be literary executor with authority, in cooperation with the Emerson children, to permit or to forbid future publications. Emerson's son, Edward, and son-in-law, William Forbes, were to be the executors. In a codicil of March, 1881, a little more than a year before his death, Emerson requested some changes. He asked his family to see that one thousand dollars should be given to each of the children of Elliot Cabot, "in recognition of his goodness in rendering to me a service which no other could render" and that $500 be paid to the hired man, John Clahan, with thanks for his "many years of faithful interest in my affairs." And he wanted new dispositions made of a copy of Montaigne, "the cup that was bought by Charles Sumner because it had belonged to Goethe," "the diamond shaped piece of porphyry from the floor of the Pantheon given to me by Margaret Fuller," his watch, his sole-leather trunk, his teak cane, and his six-volume Molière, once the property of Joseph Bonaparte. But he doubtless made these adjustments mainly at the suggestion of the members of his family in the interest of justice or of good sense.

On his last birthday he had a visit from Bronson Alcott and his daughter Louisa. Alcott came to present his grandchild, Louisa's niece; Louisa brought flowers with verses in honor of the day concealed in their leaves. Emerson could do little but listen approvingly to the tireless Alcott's adventures on lecture tour and, being moved by his habitual anxiety to discover genius, inquire repeatedly whether the traveler had "found any new men in those parts."

In September of the same year Walt Whitman turned up in Concord to gaze, much in the attitude of a worshiper, upon his silent friend. At Sanborn's house, where the literati were gathered, Whitman cared little whether he was thought stupid in the conversation of the roomful of company, for he was spending what he called "a long and blessed evening with Emerson," though this meant almost nothing but staring at his cornered man. "My seat and the relative arrangement were such that, without being rude, or anything of the kind," he explained, "I could just look squarely at E., which I did a good part of the two hours." Next day he was invited to Bush for dinner and had several hours with the family and some friends. Again he was almost completely absorbed in observing, hardly listening to, Emerson. "Of course," he put it, "the best of the occasion (Sunday, September 18, '81) was the sight of E. himself. . . . a healthy color in the cheeks, and good light in the eyes, cheery expression, and just the amount of talking that best suited, namely, a word or short phrase only where needed, and almost always with a smile."

It was in the same autumn that Robert Collyer, visiting Bush, found Emerson "mousing about his study—not for books, as you may think, but for some fine pears he had hidden away till they should grow ripe" or sitting "in his old chair like one in a dream," as he and his guest "looked at each other like persons in a dream."

Emerson did not entirely give up the Saturday Club; and in August of 1881 he was as far from home as Naushon Island, signing his name in the "Island Book" for the last time. Even as late as the following February he got through snowdrifts to a village club to hear Sanborn read from his life of Thoreau then about to be published. Only a month before his death he attended once more a meeting of the Social Circle, the Concord club always highest in his esteem. But he was barely conscious of persons, places, and time.

Alcott, though he found twelve hours without philosophical discussion an unhappy experience, could now only remember better days with Emerson. He recalled in a sonnet the times

> When all the long forenoon we two did toss
> From lip to lip, in lively colloquy,
> Plato, Plotinus, or some schoolman's gloss,
> Disporting in rapt thought and ecstasy.
> Then, by the tilting rail, Millbrook we cross,
> And sally through the field to Walden wave,
> Plunging within the cove, or swimming o'er.
> Through woodpaths wending, he, with gesture quick,
> Rhymes deftly in mid-air with circling stick,
> Skims the smooth pebble from the leafy shore,
> Or deeper ripples raises as we lave—
> Nor will his pillow press, though late at night,
> Till converse with the stars his eyes invite.

At Longfellow's funeral, after he had twice gone to the coffin, Emerson asked Ellen, "Where are we? What house? And who is the sleeper?" When he was told, he understood and was shocked afresh and went a third time to see the face of the poet. Perhaps Conway had heard only a confused report of this incident when he wrote that, after walking twice to the coffin to see the face, Emerson explained, "That gentleman was a sweet, beautiful soul, but I have entirely forgotten his name." "In the evening," Ellen recorded a few days after the event, "Father learned of Mr Longfellow's death once more, and was very sad about it. The next day he remembered everything."

As late as the beginning of the following April, Emerson, still in love with the country roads, would take the first opportunity for a long walk. On April 2, "a delicious spring day after a week of cold," he and Ellen went as far as Walden. Two weeks later he became hoarse, but a growing restlessness drove him to take longer walks than usual. On the 17th he came in only at half past nine at night, just as a search was being started for him. Next day, though his cold affected his voice quite as much as before, he took many walks. On the 19th he walked round the Two-Mile-Square and was caught in the rain. On the 20th he was sick but not seriously as yet, it seemed to Edward, his doctor. He struggled to find his words as he talked to his son about objects in the room. He passed on from a little figure of Psyche to a picture of Carlyle. Hardly more than a year since, Carlyle, in dying, had seemed to Mary Carlyle to verify his belief that death would be "like cataracts of sleep." Emerson remembered Carlyle's picture but not his name. "That is that man—my man," he said, and added regretfully to Edward, "You never saw him." When Edward recalled his meeting with Carlyle in Devonshire, Emerson was greatly delighted and surprised.

In the following days Emerson frequently asked whose house he was in, but, perhaps discovering some familiar portraits by Mrs. Hildreth, would be satisfied for a time that he was at home. Dizziness made him complain "that he didn't wish it to come in this way, he would rather have fallen down cellar." But comfortably settled in his bed, he was happy in the conviction that he was at home in his own house and that he had lived a happy life.

Pneumonia now affected one of his lungs and sealed his doom. But he was much less troubled by the disease than a younger man might have been, and insisted on dressing and coming downstairs as long as he could. At bedtime on the 22d he locked the windows and shutters, raked down the fire, and collected all the letters of the day. He ran lightly upstairs with a lamp in his hand but stumbled badly, to his disgust, before he reached the top.

In his five remaining days he did not come down. He had lucid intervals and recognized many of the friends and relatives who came to tell him good-bye. His cousin Mary Simmons, his attendant, jotted down bulletins of happenings in his sick room. She recorded his visitors one by one and the remarks that were made. Noticing the pictures on the wall, he ventured that there were "a great many seemings here." His neighbor Sam Staples, once the keeper of the town jail, brought him a bottle of choice brandy and said he was ready at any time to help take care of him. Alcott and others came. With great difficulty Emerson tried to communicate something to Lidian, apparently a farewell. He seemed to remember his first son. "Oh that beautiful boy," he exclaimed. On the morning of the 27th he still remembered Ellery Channing as the man who used to come and dine, and he invited him to come again. Once on this last day he sat by the fire for a while. He seemed to recognize Judge Hoar, Cabot, and Sanborn when they came. At ten minutes of nine that evening, after being some time under the influence of ether, he died.

The church bells of the village tolled seventy-nine times to announce his death. It was the 27th of April, 1882, and he would have been seventy-nine years old had he lived four weeks longer. On the 30th, a cool day with a threat of rain in the air, some thousand persons came into Concord, by regular and special trains and other conveyances, to attend the funeral. The first ceremony was in private, with William Furness, Emerson's boyhood friend, in charge. Then the funeral party moved from the home to the Unitarian Church, where most of the townspeople and visitors were waiting. There, since Frederic Hedge could not come, James Clarke made the principal address. Alcott read a sonnet. On the way to Sleepy Hollow, village friends from the Social Circle went before the hearse. The grave was on a high ridge, not far from where Thoreau and Hawthorne lay. Emerson's cousin Samuel Moody Haskins, rector of Saint Mark's Church in Brooklyn, read a part of the Episcopal order for the burial of the dead and threw upon the lowered coffin some ashes he had taken from the fireplace in the study at Bush and had mixed with sand and dust from the walk in front of the house.

Funeral eulogies and memorial addresses and essays recognized the greatness of Emerson but limited the rich complexity of his thought and character almost beyond recognition. Whitman's "just man, poised on himself . . . sane and clear as the sun," who had been one of the few flawless excuses for the existence of the whole literary class, and Lowell's "least vulgar of men, the most austerely genial, and the most independent of opinion," were fragments of the real man. The rough-hewn quartz of the gravestone that was erected within a few years and its inscribed lines on the passive master from "The Problem" were fitting symbols of only two of the many discordant elements which, as this book has tried to show, were harmonized in Emerson.

NOTES

Abbreviations that are not self-explanatory are explained in the index. Letters written by Emerson's daughter Ellen belong to his heirs. With a few rather obvious exceptions—such as official records of towns, churches, and colleges—other manuscripts whose ownership is not given in the notes or index belong to the Ralph Waldo Emerson Memorial Association. In this restricted space it has generally been impossible to discuss the dating of manuscripts. Bold-faced numerals refer to pages in the text.

1: MS *J&Cbk,* 25 May 1803. MS in *FaBi.* MS *J&Cbk,* 1 Jan 1795–25 May 1803. MS in *Fleets* for 1790, Boston, n.d. **2:** MS WmE (f) to PBER (grm), 11 June 1790. MS approbation by Assoc. of Ministers at East Sudbury, Mass., 16 Aug 1791. WmE (f) to HarCh, 17 Mar 1792, copied in MS *HarToRec,* III, 160. MS *HarChRec,* pp. 258–259 (23 May 1792). WmE (f) to HarCh, 27 June 1799, copied *ibid.,* pp. 273–276. MS WmE (f) to EzR, 6 Jan 1796. MS *J&Cbk,* 16 Oct 1795. *Ibid.,* 11 Feb 1796. MS *HarToRec,* III, 209, 212, 216, 236. MS *J&Cbk,* 1 June 1796. MS WmE (f) to EzR, 8 Mar 1796. *Memoir of . . . Eliza S. M. Quincy,* 1861, pp. 93–94, and *CabM,* I, 13–17, *passim.* MS WmE (f) to EzR, 6 Jan 1796. MS *HarChRec,* p. 262. The new hymnal (*cf.* note on p. 140 below) was Dr. Belknap's *Sacred Poetry,* in the making of which WmE (f) had had some slight part, as shown in MS WmE (f) to Belknap, 4 Aug 1794 (owned by MHS); *cf.* WmE (f) to Belknap, 17 Aug 1795 (owned by MHS). MS *HarChRec,* p. 265; MS *J&Cbk,* 11 Feb 1795. **3:** Nourse, p. 384. MS *J&Cbk,* 10 Oct 1795. *Ibid.,* 10 Jan, 14 Apr 1795. *Ibid.,* 9 and 10 Jan, 8 and 27 and 28 Apr, 6 and 19 and 20 and 22 and 28 and 29 May, 1 July 1795. **4:** *Ibid.,* 1 Sept, 13 and 31 Oct, 21 and 26 Nov 1795. *Ibid.,* 4 and 7 and 8 and 25 Jan, 4 May 1796. Nourse,

pp. 213–214. *Cf.* MS WmE (f) to Belknap, 4 Aug 1794 (owned by MHS), and WmE (f) to Belknap, 17 Aug 1795 (owned by MHS). MS MME to WmE (f), 17 M (Mar or May?) 1795. **5:** DGH, pp. 4–5, 145. *Ibid.,* pp. 14–15. MS MME to WmE (f), 17 M (Mar or May?) 1795. MS *J&Cbk,* 8 and 11 June, 25 Oct 1796. DGH, opposite p. 8. **6:** MS *J&Cbk,* 27 Oct, 2 and 26 and 30 Nov 1796. MS WmE (f) to John Haskins, 20 Feb 1797. MS RHE to ElizHas, 24 Apr 1797. t copy (by John L. Cooley) of RH, MS prayer dated Boston, 2 Dec 1792 (in my possession). RHE, MS leaf containing three precepts. MS *J&Cbk,* 9 Feb 1798. **7:** MS WmE (f) to ElizHas, 28 Mar 1799. MS WmE (f) to SamR, 22 Jan 1806. BoFCh to HarCh, June 1799, copied in MS *BoFChRec1786–1815,* following minutes of 11 June 1799. WmE (f), request for dismission, 27 June 1799, copied in MS *HarChRec,* pp. 273–276. Correspondence between HarCh and BoFCh, 13 July 1800 (*i.e.,* 1799) –11 Sept 1799, copied in MS *BoFChRec1786–1815;* and MS *HarToRec,* III, 271–272, 274–275. MS *J&Cbk,* 22 Sept 1799. MS *BoFChRec-1786–1815,* 20 and 24 Sept 1799. WmE (f) to BoFCh, 25 Sept 1799, copied in MS *BoFChRec1786–1815.* BoDir, 1803, gives the number as 27. *Cf.* Ellis, p. 242, and WmE (f), *HistSk,* pp. 241–242, describing conditions nine years later. *CabM,*

I, 3. Drake, p. 381. *CabM*, I, 2. MS *What*, p. 5; MS JLG to OWH, 26 Feb 1883. *CabM*, I, 2–3. **8:** Drake, pp. 360, 381. MS RHE to ElizHas, 13 Aug 1799. MS *What*, p. 5. MS *J&Cbk*, 22 Nov 1799, 28 Sept 1800. RHE, MS untitled and unsigned. MS *J&Cbk*, 31 July 1801. *Ibid.*, 19 Dec 1800, and 30 Jan, 14 Apr, 5 May, 9 June 1801; *cf.* Winsor, IV, 662. MS *J&Cbk*, 10 June 1801. **9:** *Ibid.*, 7 and 9 and 10 July, 19 and 20 Aug, 15 and 30 Oct 1801, and 9 Apr, 11 May, 5 July, 20 Aug, 10 Dec 1802. *Ibid.*, 14 Jan and 1 June 1803. *Ibid.*, 25 Jan and 11 Feb 1803. WmE (f), MS *Pra*, pp. 6–7. WmE (f), *HistSk*, p. 230. **10:** WmE (f), *SerBeede*, pp. 14–17 *passim*. *Poly*, May 1812, p. 221. *SerTh*, p. 13. MS *J&Cbk*, 6 Sept 1803. *BoGaz*, 3 Oct 1803. MS WmE (f) to RHE, 15 and 16 Oct 1799. MS *J&Cbk*, 14 Apr 1795. WmE (f), MS "Catalogue of Books" (ownership of books uncertain). MS WmE (f) to EzR, 20 Nov and 31 Dec 1790. **11:** WmE (f), *SerBow*, p. 6. *ColCen*, 21 Sept 1805. WmE (f), *DisBoFe*, pp. 5 and 15–16. WmE (f), *OrAmIn*, pp. 6–7, 8, 9, 12, 17–19. *Poly*, May 1812, opposite p. 217. J. T. Buckingham, *Personal Memoirs*, 1852, p. 60. **12:** RWE's comment on the picture reproduced in Ellis, opposite p. 230. *J*, I, 363. Pierce, in Sprague, p. 243. Chas. Lowell, in Sprague, p. 244. MS *What*, pp. 4–5. F. Hedge, in MS *CabCon*, p. 19. MS *J&Cbk*, 25 and 26–27 May 1803. *Cf.* Winsor, IV, 672. WmE (f), *SerBow*. Winsor, II, 540. **13:** DGH, pp. 54, 54–55. MS *BoFChBa*, p. 347. DGH, pp. 83–84. MS *J&Cbk*, 30 Mar 1803. **14:** Winthrop Sargent, 1st ed., 1803, p. 5. Puffer, 1803, pp. 7, 9, 12. *BoGaz*, 12 May (Federalist victory) and 7 Nov 1803 ("Extended empire"). **15:** *Ibid.*, 26 May 1803. **16:** *Ibid.*, 26 May 1803. Winthrop Sargent, 1st ed., 1803, pp. 5–17 and 11–16. MS *J&Cbk*, 6 Sept 1803. WmE (f), MS *Pra*, p. 12. **17:** MS *J&Cbk*, 1 June 1803. Ellis, p. 234. Harlow, 1923, pp. 355–356. MS

WmE (f) to Paine, 3 Feb 1806 (owned by MHS), and MS WmE (f) to Paine, 4 Feb 1806 (owned by MHS). *BoGaz*, 6 Oct 1803. *Ibid.*, 2 June 1803. **18:** *ColCen*, 19 and 22 Jan 1803; *BoGaz*, 30 May 1803. *Gazetteer*, Boston, 21 and 28 Dec 1803. *ColCen*, 2 Feb 1803. Ph of MS subscription list, 4 Dec 1801 (owned by MHS). *AnSoJou*, 1910, p. 4. Winsor, III, 638. *Let*, IV, 179. **19:** St. Augustine, Oxford, 1838, p. 5. MS WmE (f) to RHE, 14 Sept 1804. MS WmE (f) to RHE, 25 May 1805. MS RHE to WmE- (f), 3 and 5 Oct 1805. MS WmE (f) to EzR and PBER (grm), 22 Oct 1805. MS WmE (f) to John Clarke Emerson, 13 Dec 1805. MS RHE to PER (a), 9 and 12 Mar 1806. MS RHE to PER (a), 20 Apr 1806. MS WmE (f) to John Clarke Emerson, 17 May 1806. DGH, pp. 55, 56. *ColCen*, 11 Nov 1809. DGH, pp. 53, 55. MS RHE to MME, 5 Jan 1806. MS WmE (f) to RHE, 14 Apr 1810. **20:** MS WmE (f) to RHE, 19 and 20 Sept 1806; MS RHE to PER (a), 10 and 11 Oct 1806. MS WmE (f) to RHE, 16 and 17 June 1806; *cf. BoGaz*, 12 June 1806. *AnSoJou*, pp. 43, 45, 46, *et passim*. *BoGaz*, 27 Feb and 3 and 6 Mar 1806. *BoGaz*, 7 July 1806. MS *What*, pp. 1, 8 (*cf.* back of p. 7, where EWE wrote a slightly different version). MS WmE (f) to MME, 20 Apr 1807. **21:** MS WmE (f) to Lincoln Ripley, 25 Apr 1807. MS WmE (f) to PER (a), 28 and 29 Apr 1807. RHE, MS dated 5 July 1807. MS *What*, p. 5. MS WmE (f) to MME, 11 Nov 1807. MS *J&CbkNo.2-* ("*Dialling*"), 20 Jan 1808. *BuckSer*, p. 8; Sprague, p. 242. **22:** MS WmE (f) to EzR, 18 June 1808. *ColCen*, 9 July 1808. WmE (f), sermon 17 July 1808, *HistSk*, pp. 230, 241–242; *cf. ColCen*, 20 and 23 July 1808. Ellis, pp. 235–238, 242. *SelPs*, p. vi. See below, pp. 37 and 55, for learning hymns. MS *J&CbkNo.2* ("*Dialling*"), 27 Oct and 3 Nov 1808. MS *BoFChPr*, p. 6. MS *J&CbkNo.2* ("*Dialling*"), 8 Nov 1808. MS *PierceExt*, p. 1. **23:** MS in

FaBi. MS *J&CbkNo.2* ("Dialling"), 20 Dec 1808. MS MME to RHE, 15 Aug 1809? MS *What*, p. 3. *Let*, IV, 179. A Susanna Whitwell, 31 Summer St., is in *BoDir*, 1813. *RecLiLong*, pp. 3, 159, 164; MS Furness to "My dear Sir" (doubtless Cabot), 23 Sept 1882. *BradInc*, p. 36. **24:** *ColCen*, 11 Jan 1812 (Lyon's adv.). MS Furness to "Dear children," 22? Mar 1888. MS *EEFchmem; cf. CEd*, VII, 106. MS *EEFchmem*. MS EEF to "Cousin Lizzie" (Elizabeth Cabot?), 29 Apr 1885. *J*, VI, 305. *CabM*, I, 5. **25:** MS WmE-(f) to MME, 23 Oct 1809. *CEd*, X, 400, 411. *MoAn*, I and II, *passim*, as listed in *AnSoJou*, pp. 317–319. *CEd*, X, 404–429, *passim*. **26:** MS WmE (f) to RHE, 14 Apr 1810. *BradInc*, p. 30. MS Furness to Cabot? 23 Sept 1882. MS WmE (grf) to WmE (f), 1776? MS WmE (f) to John Clarke Emerson, 17 May 1806. P. Holmes, p. 430. MS WmE (f) to PBER (grm), 11 Jan 1810. DGH, p. 60. t EllenE to Edith Davidson, 11 Dec 1865. DGH, p. 62. **27:** DGH, pp. 56–64, *passim. Poly*, for May 1812, p. 219. *HistSk*, p. 228. *Poly*, for May 1812, p. 220. *MoAn*, I, ii; *Mott-1741–1850*, pp. 253 ff. *AnSoJou, passim.* **28:** *MoAn*, II, 541–647, *passim*. *AnSoJou*, p. 215 (5 Dec 1809). *ColCen*, 4 Jan 1812. MS WmE (f) to Paine, 3 Feb 1806 (owned by MHS). MS WmE (f) to MME, 26 Feb 1811. MS "Record of Marriages in the First Church." MS *BoFChBa*, p. 359. Sprague, p. 242. MS WmE (f) to RHE, 16 Apr 1811; Ellis, p. 227. MS WmE (f) to EzR and PBER (grm), 18 Apr 1811. **29:** *BuckSer*, p. 8. MS WmE (f) to EzR and PBER (grm), 18 Apr 1811. MS WmE (f) to Mr. and Mrs. Joy, 19 Apr 1811. MME, MS journal, 12 May 1827. MS *BoFChPr*, p. 8 (13 May 1811). *ColCen*, 15 May 1811. MS *What*, pp. 6–7. DGH, p. 51. MS *What*, p. 7. **30:** *The Prelude*, London, 1850, p. 17. MS *BoFChPr*, pp. 7–9. MS RHE to PER (a), 18 June 1811. MS RHE to EzR, 24 June 1811. MS RHE to MME, 13 and 15 Aug 1811. RHE, MS dated 28 July and headed

"May 12. 1811. Died William Emerson." *ColCen*, 24 Aug 1811. *WmE* (f) *BroadCat* (now also printed in *EtheE*, II, 135–137). MS RWE to Mrs. Sturgis, 11 Oct 1854 (owned by HCL). *HistSk*, p. 7 and back of title page. **31:** MS RHE to PER-(a), 27 Jan 1812. *J*, IV, 231–232. *ColCen*, 23 Sept 1809. Emerson, in MS *BPLS8-Nov1876*, says he entered when N. L. Frothingham was usher (1811–1812, according to P. Holmes, appendix XXXI). Rufus Dawes, quoted in P. Holmes, p. 82. P. Holmes, pp. 242–248; Winsor, IV, 241. MS *BPLS8Nov1876*. Jenks, 1886, p. 93. **32:** Rufus Dawes, quoted in P. Holmes, pp. 82–83. MS *BPLS8Nov1876; BradInc*, p. 41. See p. 37 below; P. Holmes, pp. 411, 413. MS Furness to Cabot, 8 Feb 1878; Winsor, II, xxiv. *EinC*, p. 13. MS Furness to Cabot, 8 Feb 1878. *J*, X, 381. **33:** MS copy of "The Sabbath" owned by Mr. A. Le Baron Russell. The copy was made (t signed A. Le B. Russell to me, 5 Aug 1948) by Laura Dewey Russell, daughter of Emerson's friend Andrew Leach Russell of Plymouth, Mass. The copyist, who did not sign her name, described the poem, in a note at its end, as "Written by Ralph Waldo Emerson at the age of nine years." *EinC*, pp. 14–15. MS j "BL," p. 150. t EllenE to EdithE, 29 Mar 1859. *CEd*, VIII, 128. *EinC*, p. 14. **34:** MS j "KL," p. 158. MS j "BL," p. 150. *ColCen*, 27 Apr and 4 May 1814. *Ibid.*, 19 Sept and 10 Oct 1812. MS EEF to "Cousin Lizzie" (Elizabeth Cabot?), 29 Apr 1885; MS *What*, p. 11. MS Sam Bradford to Cabot, 24 May 1882. MS MME to RWE, 21 June 1813. *ColCen*, 2 and 5 June 1813. MS copy of "Perry's Victory," not in Emerson's hand but bearing his name and the date 1814. **35:** *ColCen*, 1 Jan 1814. MS "Perry's Victory," cited above. MS RHE to MME, 28 Mar 1813; *ColCen*, 24 and 27 Mar 1813. "Poetical Essay" (dated 1815), in *Let*, VI, 330–332. MS RHE to PER (a), 3 June 1813. MS RHE to MME, 11 June 1813. RHE, MS *Memo-*

BkWms, 2 Mar, 13 Apr, and 25 May 1813. *ColCen,* 14 July 1813. **36:** MS RHE to MME, 20 July 1813. MS RHE to PER (a), 4 Sept 1813. MS RHE to MME, 28 Dec 1813. MS RHE to PER (a), 27 Jan 1814. MS MME to RHE, 10 July 1810. **37:** MS RWE to MME, 16 Apr 1813. *Let,* I, 4–6. **38:** *RecLiLong,* pp. 178–185. MS records "City of Boston School Committee 1792 to 1814," pp. 193 (9 Apr 1813) and 195 (12 Nov 1813). MS report of subcommittee for Latin School, 18 Mar 1814, MS *BoSchComPa.* MS *BPLS8Nov1876.* Death of Mary Caroline on 30 Apr 1814 (*ColCen,* 4 May 1814; MS in *FaBi*). *BradInc,* p. 40. MS *What,* p. 2. *ColCen, e. g.,* 22 Dec 1813. **39:** MS LydiaJ to Chas. Jackson, 3 Nov 1813. *ColCen,* 4 June, 2 July, 27 Aug, 7 and 14 Sept, 1 Oct, 2 Nov, and 14 Dec 1814. *Ibid.,* 17 Sept 1814. **40:** *ColCen,* 7 Sept–29 Oct 1814, *passim. J,* IX, 42. MS "BL," p. 150. *J,* IX, 42. See above, p. 30; MS *BoFChTr,* pp. 51–54. Ellis, pp. 244–246. MS *BoFChPr,* p. 19. MS RHE to WmE (b), 13 Dec 1814. DGH, p. 85. MS MME to PER (a), 20 Sept 1814. **41:** *Ibid. Let,* I, 48–49. MS RHE to WmE (b), 13 Oct 1814. **42:** *Ibid. ColCen,* 29 Oct 1814. DGH, p. 27. **43:** *CEd,* IX, 145. *ColCen,* 29 Oct 1814; DGH, p. 26. MS RHE to FanHas, 11 Nov 1814. *ColCen,* 30 Nov 1814. EBE to WmE (b), 30 Nov 1814. *OrAmIn,* p. 20. MS WmE (f) to PBER (grm), 22 July 1803. **44:** *CEd,* X, 383, 384, 386. Sprague, p. 117. *CEd,* X, 391. MS notebook "Art," p. 106. *CEd,* X, 390, 394. *IpsEm, passim. CEd,* X, 385–386. *IpsEm,* p. 126. MS *ConFChRec* for 1738/9–1857, p. 72. EWE, *Es,* pp. 249–253; MS WmE (grf) to Phebe Bliss, 27 May 1766; *IpsEm,* p. 126. **45:** *Ibid.* MS *ConToRecfc,* XI, 277 (owned by CFPL). MS "An Inventory . . . William Emerson." MS *ConFChRec,* pp. 71–102; MS of council convened 11 Apr 1769; MS "Covenant sign'd . . . July 11th 1776." MS EllenE to EWE, 9, 11, and 12 Sept 1871. EWE, *Es,* pp. 254–255. MS

WmE (grf) to PBE, *c.* June? 1774? EWE, *Es,* pp. 257–263. *Cf.* Allen French, 1925, *passim.* **46:** Shattuck, pp. 105–106. EWE, *Es,* p. 264. *Cf.* Allen French, 1925, *passim.* MS WmE (grf) to PBE, 17 July 1775. WmE (grf), MS draft of oration for 19 Apr 1776. MS *ConFChRec,* p. 10 (4 Aug 1776). MS MME to LE, 26 July 1850. MS WmE (grf) to PBE, 26 and 28–31 Aug 1776. MS WmE (grf) to PBE, Friday evening, endorsed 12 Sept 1776. For discharge from army by Gen. Gates, 18 Sept 1776, see endorsement on MS WmE (grf) to Lt. Col. Benj. Brown, 18 Sept 1776. MS Lt. Col. Brown to John Flint, 18 Apr 1778. MS WmE (grf) to PBE, 23 Sept 1776. MS Benajah Roots to "Church and People of God at Concord," 21 Oct 1776. Daniel Bliss's ordination, 7 Mar 1738/9, in MS *ConFChRec,* p. 1. Bliss's death, 11 May 1764, *ibid.,* p. 70. MS *ConFChRecfc* (owned by CFPL), pp. 10–45, *passim. Ibid.,* pp. 55–72, *passim.* **47:** *HistSk,* pp. 189–190. *Whitefield's Journals,* ed. Wale, London, Drane, n.d., p. 475. *IpsEm,* p. 34. *CEd,* XI, 61, 63. *IpsEm,* p. 34. C. Mather, 1702, Bk. III, p. 97. *Ibid.,* p. 96; *cf.* MS WmE (f) to Paine, 4 Feb 1806 (owned by MHS). *CEd,* XI, 32, 34, 37–38. C. Mather, 1702, Bk. VII, p. 16; *Winthrop's Journal,* ed. Hosmer, New York, 1908, I, 232. P. Bulkeley, *The Gospel-covenant,* London, 1646, "To the Church and Congregation at Concord" and pp. 335–336. **48:** *Ibid.,* pp. 294–382. *Cf. CEd,* XI, 40. Emerson's extant copy of *The Gospel-covenant* was given him by G. F. Hoar, apparently not earlier than 1869. *CEd,* IX, 35; XI, 30, 41, 557. MS j "GH," p. 123; *IpsEm,* pp. 74–76; Corey, p. 477 *et passim; IpsEm,* p. 74. *J,* III, 432. MS *VBk"P,"* p. 63; *J,* IV, 231. *CabM,* I, 10. *HistSk,* p. 190. MS *J&Cbk,* 3 Mar 1803; *cf. IpsEm,* p. 75. JEofMa, MS diary for 1737–1738, 29 Jan 1738. **49:** MS JEofMa and MaryE to WmE (grf), 26 Oct 1763. MS *VBk"P,"* p. 61. *CabM,* p. 9. *J,* VII, 338–341. *IpsEm,* pp. 50–51. *Let,* I, 247. *EinC,* pp.

2–3. *Antiquarian Papers* (with running head "Ipswich Antiquarian Papers"), Mar 1880. Morris C. Jones, n.d. (1863?), p. 1; Joseph D. Hall, Jr., pp. 8 and 121; *IpsEm*, pp. 50 ff. J. G. Metcalf, 1880, p. 19 *et passim; IpsEm*, pp. 32–36. *CabM*, I, 8. *IpsEm*, pp. 32, 34; *EinC*, p. 2; A. Hammatt, No. 1, 1854, 85 ff.; Thomas was "first" American Emerson of RWE's ancestors, and Eliz. Bulkeley was Jos.'s second wife. A. Hammatt, p. 86; *cf.* T. F. Waters, p. 491. P. H. Emerson, *The English Emersons*, London, 1898, pp. 153–159; *cf. IpsEm*, pp. 18 ff. MS *EWE-SocCirMemLi*, p. 1. *EinC*, p. 2. *Antiquarian Papers*, Ipswich, for Mar 1880, p. 5. MS W. M. Eggleston to EllenE, 25 Feb 1881; P. H. Emerson, *The English Emersons*, pp. 9–10, supported the theory of a connection with Durham Emersons, but, later in the same book, turned against it; *cf. IpsEm*, pp. 9–25, and P. H. Emerson's rejoinder in *A Criticism*, n.d. (1901?). For the bookplate, see DGH, opposite p. 142; *cf.* frontispiece of *IpsEm*. **50:** *J*, II, 41–42. MS *JarvTr* (owned by CFPL), pp. 24–35, 198. *Ibid.*, pp. 62–63, 82–83. *Ibid.*, pp. 36–37, 367. MS EBE to WmE (b), 14 Dec 1814. **51:** *CEd*, IX, 385. *Ibid.*, IX, 146. *Let*, I, frontispiece and p. 7. Shattuck, p. 222. **52:** *EinC*, pp. 16, 17. *Let*, VI, 329. *Let*, I, 9. Facsimile of MS "Valedictory," dated 1815, is in *The Month at Goodspeed's*, VII, 262–263 (Apr 1936). **53:** MS RHE to PER (a), 31 Mar 1815. *Let*, I, 10–11. **54:** MS WmE (f) to PBER (grm), 11 Jan 1810. MS RHE to PER (a), 31 Mar 1815. MS FanHas to RHE, 16 Dec 1815. RHE, MS *MemoBkWms*, pp. 46, 48. *Let*, I, 13. MS *CabCon*, p. 2; MS RHE to PER (a), 5 Oct 1815; Sanborn in *NEMag*, n.s., XV, 465. MS RHE to PER (a), 5 Oct 1815. MS EzR to RHE, 18 Apr 1816. *CabM*, I, 47. **55:** Drake, 1873, pp. 337–344; Winsor, IV, opposite 64, and 65. RHE, MS *MemoBkWms*, p. 61. MS *BoF-ChBa*, 418. MS *BoFChRecfc*, pp. 415–416. MS *AuLoLe*, Feb 1839. MS EEF to

Eliz.? Cabot? July? 1886? MS *What*, pp. 10–11. *J*, IV, 286. **56:** MS FanHas to RHE, 16 Dec 1815. MS EBE to RHE, 19 Oct 1816. MS EBE to RHE, 1 Nov 1816. MS FanHas to EBE, 10 Nov 1816. Thwing, 1920, pp. 234–235. *Let*, I, 12–13. *Let*, I, 18. **57:** MS Gould to BoSch-Com, 1 Sept 1815, in MS *BoSchComPa* for 1815. MS report of 19 Sept 1817, in MS *BoSchComPa* for 1817. MS Furness to Cabot, 8 Feb 1878. MS *BPLS8Nov1876*. *Let*, I, 23. MS *BPLS8Nov1876*. *The Library of the Late Marsden J. Perry*, sale at American Art Association Anderson Galleries, 11 and 12 Mar 1936, pp. 98–100. MS *BPLS8Nov1876*. Broadside *Order of Performances at the Latin School, August 25, 1815*. **58:** MS sheet numbered 1675, verso. *ColCen*, 24 Aug 1816; MS copy titled "Poem on Eloquence by R. W. Emerson" (owned by Lewis S. Gannett). *Let*, I, 32. MS *AutoSkAmCy*, p. 2. *Let*, I, 14. **59:** *Let*, I, 15–16. MS J "AZ," p. 260. *Cf. Let*, I, 15; later comments on mathematics are more positive. *J*, V, 270. MS JLG to OWH, 2 Aug 1883 (owned by HCL). *Let*, I, 35. *Let*, I, 38–40. *EinC*, p. 51. MS *What*, p. 9. *Let*, I, 29. **60:** *CEd*, II, 133. *EtheE*, II, 138, 149, and 152–154. *J*, I, 11 *et passim; Let*, I, 225 and 271. The recently discovered MS RWE to MME, 28 Feb 1816 (owned by the Trustees of Public Reservations, of Mass.), shows Emerson as a juvenile collector of literary anecdote, with the French pulpit orator Massillon as the immediate object of his curiosity. *ColCen*, 4 and 8 Oct 1817. *Let*, I, 20, 33. *BoDir*, 1816. RHE, MS "Notes," p. 12. **61:** *Let*, I, 19, where my note makes the Emersons live in Beacon St. a few weeks longer than they actually did. *Ibid.*, I, 28. MS MME to John Emerson, 26 Feb 1817. MS *BoFChBa*, p. 418. MS RHE to PER-(a), 18 Mar 1817; for Bulkeley, *cf.* other correspondence of RHE. MS RHE to PER (a), 11 May 1817. MS *BoFChBa*, p. 418. RHE, MS "Notes," p. 63. **62:** MS RHE to MME, 28 Aug and 1 and 2 Sept

1817. **63:** Cowley, in "Miscellanies," p. 26 (*The Works*, 5th ed., London, 1678). Montaigne, *Essays*, tr. Cotton, III (London, 1693), 66. MS EBE to RWE, 1 Oct 1817; MS EBE to RWE, 5 Oct 1819; *BoDir*, 1818, and *Bowen's*, 1833, pp. 51–52. MS RHE to MME, 28 Aug and 1 and 2 Sept 1817. *Let*, I, 47. *TickLi*, I, 355, 358–359. **64:** *Cf.* *HCLa*, 1816, p. 36. See above, p. 62. *HCLa*, 1816, pp. 1, 2, 15, 16. *Ibid.*, pp. 6, 22, 27, 28. **65:** MS *HCStewQBk*, bills for quarters ending 2 Oct and 11 Dec 1817 and 2 Apr and 25 June 1818. Broadside *HCCat*, Oct 1817. MS *CabCon*, p. 22. *LoSoRem*, pp. 39–50. Broadside *HCCat*, Oct 1817. *J*, VI, 94, and IX, 303. *Three*, pp. 195–196. *Let*, I, 68. P. Holmes, pp. 2–3. *J*, I, opposite p. 264. *Three*, p. 216. *LoSoRem*, p. 43. **66:** Augustus Peirce, 1863, p. 27. MS *HCFaRecfc*, IX, 121–122. *LoSoRem*, p. 51. *J*, III, 376–377. MS *CabCon*, p. 1. MS j "Z," pp. 43–44. **67:** MS JLG to OWH, 2 Aug 1883 (owned by HCL), quoted less literally than here, but at greater length, in *HolmesRWE*, pp. 39–41. *LoSoRem*, p. 43. *QuiFig*, pp. 16–18. MS *HillSk*, pp. 2–3. *HillLitW*, p. 180. *J*, V, 166. MS *HillSk*, p. 6. T. McDowell, in *PMLA*, XLV, 326–329; *Let*, I, 69–70. **68:** *CEd*, II, 133. MS *BPLS8Nov1876*. MS *HillSk*, p. 5. *Let*, I, 67. *Let*, I, 68. *Let*, I, 48–49; *HCLa*, 1816, p. 37. T. McDowell, in *PMLA*, XLV, 327. MS *HillSk*, p. 5. Broadside *HCCat*, Oct 1817. Everson, 1944, p. 50. *Let*, I, 262; MS j "BL," p. 244. *CEd*, VII, 330. *Let*, I, 66. *HCLa*, 1816, p. 37. MS *HistSk*, p. 5. **69:** *J*, VIII, 123. *LoSoRem*, pp. 50–51, 61, 62. MS *CabCon*, p. 22. *LoSoRem*, p. 62. MS RHE to EBE, 21 Oct 1817. MS EBE to MME, 12 Dec 1817. MS WmE(b) to RHE, 15, 16, 19 Dec 1817. MS WmE(b) to RHE, 24 Jan 1818 (owned by DrHE). *Let*, I, 54–55. **70:** *Let*, I, 57. *Let*, I, 54–57. MS EBE to RHE, 24 Mar 1818. MS EBE to MME, 31 May 1818. *Let*, I, 60, 70–74. MS EBE to WmE(b), 22 and 26 Sept 1818. *Let*, I, 63. *LoSoRem*, p. 62.

Let, I, 63. P. 67 above. MS *What*, pp. 42–43. **71:** *CEd*, IX, 372. MS *What*, p. 14. Broadside *HCCat*, Oct 1818. *HillLitW*, p. 180. MS *HCHolAnRec*, Oct 1818. *HCLa*, 1816, pp. 21–22; *Let*, I, 73. *HillLitW*, p. 180. MS *HCFaRec* for 1816–1820, 23 Nov 1818. *Ibid.*, 2 Nov 1818. **72:** *Ibid.*, 6 and 8 Nov 1818; also, MS *HCFaRecfc*, IX, 172–173 (it is possible that a few of the sophomores who chose to remain were sent home for other reasons than failure to attend chapel). *Let*, I, 74. MS RHE to WmE(b), 30 Nov 1818. *HillLitW*, p. 180. MS *HCFaRec* for 1816–1820, 16 Nov and 7 Dec 1818. *J*, VI, 37. Porcellian Club, *Catalogue*, Aug 1825, pp. 18–19; *cf. Three*, p. 181. Hasty Pudding Club, MS "Catalogue," for 1795 ff., p. 31; *cf. Three*, p. 182 *et passim*. Order of Knights of the Square Table, *Catalogue*, 1827, p. 12; MS *HCFaRecfc*, IX, 207. MS "Pierian Sodality. Book No. IV," *passim*, and *Catalogue*, 1832. MS *HCFaRec* for 1816–1820, 3 Mar 1819 and 5 May 1821; MS *HCFaRecfc*, IX, 232. Harvard Washington Corps, MS "Laws and Records," II, *passim* (records for 1817–June 1819 are wanting). All records of clubs and of the Harvard chapter of Phi Beta Kappa that I have cited are in HCL. **73:** Phi Beta Kappa, Harvard chapter, MS "Records of the Immediate Members," III, 30 June and 5 July 1820. MS records of the Saturday Evening Religious Society (becoming records of the Society of the Christian Brethren on p. 101), *passim*, especially pp. 109–110. MHS, *Proceedings*, L, 123–132. Adelphoi Theologica, MS "Journal," V, meetings of 1820–1821, *passim*, and MS "The Constitution," list of members from the Class of 1821. *HillLitW*, p. 180; *J*, I, 7–9; *Let*, I, 107. *Let*, I, 85, 93. Society without a name, MS journal, pp. 7, 18, 23, 27. MS *HCFaRecfc*, IX, 121–122. *EtheE*, I, 437 ff. Society without a name, MS journal, p. 57. For this society see also *J*, I, 34–51; *Let*, I, 85–86; *EtheE*, I, 437–458. **74:** MS j *NoXVII*,

p. 57; the drinking song is, as Edward W. Forbes showed me, a parody on Moore's "A Canadian Boat-song." MS j *NoXVIII*, pp. 1–3 and 16–17, upside down at the end. *E.g.,* MS RHE to WmE (b), 29 and 30 Dec 1818 and 1 Jan 1819. *Let*, I, 71. MS RHE to WmE (b), 30 Nov 1818. MS deacons of BoFCh to RHE, 9 Jan 1819; *Let*, I, 77. MS RHE to WmE (b), 24 Mar 1819. *Let*, I, 87; MS RHE to WmE (b), 6 Aug 1819. DGH, p. 32. Emerson kept the Penn legacy through his four years at college (MS *BoFChBa*, p. 418. *Let*, I, 80. **75:** *Let*, I, 78. *HCLa*, 1816, p. 24. *Let*, I, 74, 77. MS EBE to RHE, 13 Nov 1818. *Let*, I, 75. MS *CabCon*, p. 2. *J*, VII, 227. Hedge's *Elements* drew heavily on Locke, Reid, Stewart, and Beattie *(Elements,* stereotype ed., 1829, p. v). *NARev*, VI, 423 (Mar 1818); *HCCat*, Oct 1820, "Course of Instruction." *Let*, I, 80, 84–85. *ColCen*, 3 Feb 1819; RHE, MS *MemoBkWms*, p. 39. **76:** Broadside *HCCat*, Oct 1818. *Let*, I, 80–84, *passim.* MS *HCFaRec* for 1816–1820, 13 Aug 1819. *NARev*, VI, 423; *HCCat*, Oct 1820. *ColCen*, 9 Oct 1819; prospectus of the school printed on card and dated 20 Oct 1819; *Let*, I, 90. *HCCat*, Oct 1819, p. 12; *J*, I, 3–4, and picture opposite p. 4; *EtheE*, I, 437 and 439. *Let*, I, 89, 91. MS RHE to EBE, 18 and 24 Feb 1820. RHE, MS "Notes," p. 12. MS RHE to EBE, 18 and 24 Feb 1820. *Bowen's*, 1833, pp. 149–150; Drake, p. 256. *Bowen's*, 1833, pp. 42–43; *EtheE*, II, 138 ff. **77:** *FroEEv*, p. 62. *Let*, I, 89, 90. *Let*, I, 90. Allibone, 1874, I, 569. MS j *Wide*, No. 1, p. 20; *cf. J*, I, 20–22. *CEd*, X, 331–333. MS j "CO," pp. 101–102. *HCCat*, Oct 1819. E. T. Channing, *Lectures*, 1856, pp. viii, x; *Mott50–65*, pp. 225–226. **78:** MS *HCFaRecfc*, IX, 210. *ColCen*, 11 Dec 1819. E. T. Channing, *Inaugural Discourse*, 1819, pp. 12, 21–23, 25, 30–31. MS *CatBksRead*, p. 9. E. T. Channing, *Lectures*, 1856, *passim*, especially pp. 59, 71 245, 257. *CanbyThor*, p. 52. MS j *NoXVII*, pp. 1–5. *TwoUnEs*,

pp. 23–38, *passim; cf. J*, III, 260; *Let*, I, 63; MS "A Dissertation" (owned by HCL); MS CCE to MME, 3 Sept 1820. *ColCen*, 2 Sept 1820. **79:** MS *What*, p. 12. MS *HCHolAnRec*, Oct 1820. MS j "AC," p. 246. MS j "LN," p. 204. Sameness of junior and senior years, in spite of *HCCat*, Oct 1820, pp. 1–2 at the end. EEv, *Synopsis of a Course of Lectures on the History of Greek Literature*, n.d., with MS annotations. *TickLi*, I, 319. *J*, I, 65. MS "Prof. Ticknors Synopsis" (dated Oct 1820), pp. 15, 30, 32–35, 37, 40. **80:** tj *Wide*, No. 2, pp. 11, 16, 23, 33–34. MS j *Wide*, No. 2, p. 28. MS j *NoXVIII*, pp. 86–88, upside down, at end. *HCCat*, Oct 1820. MS *LecEngLit* (course of 1835–1836), X, 11–12. MS MME to RWE, 24 Feb 1821. **81:** *Ibid.* Block, pp. 101–102 *et passim; EtheE*, I, 253–255. MS MME to RWE, 24 Feb 1821. *RemTeach*, p. 29. *FrisCol*, p. xx. *FrisIn*, pp. 10, 12, 21, 24. Frisbie, review of Adam Smith's *The Theory of Moral Sentiments*, repr. from *NARev* in *FrisCol*, pp. 43–88. *FrisCol*, pp. 88, 150–151, 193, 199. **82:** *HCCat*, Oct 1820, p. 14; *cf. FroRip*, p. 13. Winsor, IV, 296–301. *Cf.* Bonar, *passim.* Winsor, IV, 296. *J*, I, 161–162. MS j *NoXV*, pp. 34–35. MS j Cabot's "R," p. 9; MS j *BlotBk*, No. II, p. 5. *HCCat*, Oct 1820; *J*, I, 71–72. *J*, X, 393. MS j *Wide*, No. 2, p. 12. MS j *NoXVII*, p. 49. MS EBE to WmE (b), 22 and 26 Sept 1818. **83:** MS WmE (f) to MME, 28 Sept 1803; *WmE (f) BroadCat.* MS *CatBksRead*, p. 10. J. Everett, *An Oration . . . July 14, 1818*, 1818, p. 6. *Let*, I, 66. MS j *NoXVIII*, pp. 14, 129. MS "Indian Superstition" (owned by John L. Cooley), p. 3. *Let*, I, 99–100. *J*, I, 68. MS "Dissertation . . . Philosophy" (owned by HCL); *cf. Let*, I, 63. *NEPal*, 17 July 1821. *QuiFig*, p. 50. *TwoUnEs*, pp. 43 ff., especially 76. **84:** *QuiFig*, p. 50. MS "Valedictory Poem" of July 1821, pp. 1 *et passim.* Barnwell, MS "Valedictory Oration . . . 17 July 1821" (owned by HCL), pp. 2, 3, 9. *QuiFig*, p. 17;

EinC, p. 27; *J*, I, 95. *QuiFig*, p. 51. MS *HCFaRecfc*, IX, 263. MS *HCFaRec* for 1816–1820, 18 July 1821. MS *HCFaRecfc*, IX, 261. *J*, I, 95. Cushing, *To the Members of the Senior Class* (dated, partly in longhand, at end, 13 July 1821; copy owned by HCL), p. 1. **85:** MS *CatBksRead*, pp. 9–13. MS MME to RWE, 24 Feb 1821. *J*, I, 69, 80, and *cf.* 138, 197–198. MS *MemBk1820&Misc*, unnumbered page. **86:** MS RHE to PER (a), 16 May 1821; RHE, MS "Notes," p. 13. MS EBE to RHE, 15 May 1822, and other MS family letters. *Bowen's*, 1833, p. 141. *RemTeach*, pp. 33, 51, 59. RHE, MS *MemoBkWms*, p. 50. MS RHE to PER- (a), 16 May 1821. *Let*, I, 100–101. MS Sam Bradford to Cabot, 24 May 1882; MS Sam Bradford to Cabot, 14 Feb 1883. Adams, MS "The Influence of Natural Scenery on Poetry" (owned by HCL). John B. Hill, MS "An Essay" (owned by HCL), pp. 3, 6. **87:** Hatch, MS "Colloquial Discussion" (owned by HCL), p. 6. Quincy, MS commencement part on the "elegant literature of France and Great Britain" (owned by HCL), pp. 1, 5. *Let*, I, 101. *NEGal*, 31 Aug 1821. *Let*, III, 74; oration repr. in *EtheE*, II, 9–11. *Let*, I, 101. *J*, I, 116. *Let*, I, 107. **88:** *J*, III, 299. **89:** *The College Chaucer*, ed. MacCracken, 1913, pp. 9–10. *Let*, I, *passim*. MS letters of RHE earlier than 1821, *passim*. MS *CabCon*, p. 8. P. 86 above. MS EEF to "Cousin Lizzie" (Elizabeth Cabot?), 29 Apr 1885 (is in error as to years of Cousin Ralph's residence). *Let*, V, 242. *Let*, I, 101–104. For prospectus of William's school, in newspaper and on card, see notes on p. 76 above. MS *SchReun*, pp. 1–2. **90:** *RemTeach*, pp. 30, 33, 51–54. MS *SchReun*, pp. 3–4. *CookeRWE*, p. 23. MS *StevRec*, pp. IV–VI. t *TilRem* (given me by Lewis S. Gannett), p. 2. MS *SchReun*, p. 5. t *TilRem*, p. 2. MS "Story for September 10th 1823 Ginevra" is in RWE's hand. MS "Stories to be Written by Learners" is in a doubtful hand. Other MS stories

are also among extant RWE papers. t *TilRem*, p. 3. MS *SchReun*, p. 3. **91:** MS *StevRec*, p. V. t *TilRem*, p. 2. MS *StevRec*, p. 5. MS *SchReun*, pp. 8–9. *Ibid.*, pp. 6–7. MS *CabCon*, pp. 24, 25. MS *VBk"P,"* p. 99. *Let*, I, 106. *J*, I, 138. **92:** *Let*, I, 114–115. *Let*, I, 115, 131. *J*, II, 55. MS *CatBksRead*, pp. 13–15; *cf.* index to *Let*, and *EtheE*, II, 158–161. **93:** MS *CatBksRead*, pp. 13–14. *Let*, I, 121–122, 131. MS j *NoXVIII*, p. 64. *J*, I, 145. *Let*, I, 306. MS j *NoXVIII*, p. 46. *Let*, I, 116–117; "A Hymn to Narayena" had been reprinted in *The Asiatic Miscellany*, 1818, pp. 9–13; *cf.* p. 83 above. For Roy, see also Christy, pp. 338–339, and *cf.* MS MME to RWE, 24 May 1822, which shows that MME had recently met Roy and that he had inspired in her a keen interest in Hindu lore. **94:** *Let*, I, 118. *J*, I, 96. *Let*, I, 127. *J*, I, 81. MS j *NoXVIII*, pp. 25–26, 26–28, 48–50, 72–73. *J*, I, 108–109. MS j *Wide*, No. 8, p. 33. *J*, I, 170–173, 177–180. *J*, I, 129. **95:** MS j *NoXVIII*, pp. 62, 74. MS j *Wide*, No. 13, pp. 83–84. There is no longer any doubt about the authorship. Ralph Thompson's conjecture (*AL*, VI, 155–157, and *AmLitAn*, 1936, p. 97) was correct. MS j *NoXVI*, pp. 16–17. MS j *Wide*, No. 6, pp. 39–43, 47–50; MS j *Wide*, No. 7, pp. 7 ff.; *J* references in *Let*, I, 102. *Let*, I, 103. *J*, I, 254–256. tj *NoXVIII*, 31–33. *J*, I, 185. *J*, I, 112–115, 135, 246. **96:** *J*, I, 265. *J*, I, 198. *J*, I, 162–164, 210–211. MS j *Wide*, No. 10, pp. 16–32. MS j *Wide*, No. 7, pp. 3–6, 10–11 and later; MS j *Wide*, No. 8, *passim* to p. 46. P. 92 above; MS j *NoXVIII*, pp. 75–87; *Let*, I, 118. *The Christian Disciple*, n.s., IV, 401, 403–405, 407 (Nov and Dec 1822). MS MME to RWE, 25 and 26 July 1822. MS CCE to MME, Thursday (c. Feb? 1823?); MS MME to CCE, 10 Feb 1823. **97:** *The Century*, XXVI, 458. MS Withington to RWE, 1 Aug 1823, is the latest of the Emerson-Withington letters I have seen. *Cf. Mott1741–1850*, p. 284. *BoSChCom*, p. x. *J*, I, 141–142. *J*,

I, 137, 142. *J,* I, 140–142. RHE, MS *MemoBkWms,* p. 96. **98:** MS CCE to EBE, 12 Mar 1831. *Let,* I, 133–134. MS MME to WmE (b) , 27 May 1823. A bronze tablet in Franklin Park records that "NEAR THIS ROCK A-D-1823–1825 WAS THE HOME OF SCHOOLMASTER RALPH WALDO EMERSON." *Cf.* DGH, p. 149. *Let,* I, 132, 135. MS Sam Bradford to Cabot, 2 Mar 1883; *CabM,* I, 83–84. MS EBE to WmE- (b) , 21 May 1824 (owned by DrHE). MS CCE to MME, 7 Dec 1823; MS RHE to WmE (b) , 24 June and 23 July and 1 Aug 1824 (owned by DrHE). DGH, pp. 86–87. *Bowen's,* 1833, pp. 98–100. *Let,* I, 133. MS j *Wide,* No. 13, pp. 14– 15. **99:** *Ibid. J,* I, 268–284. *The Century,* XXVI, 457. *J,* II, 28–29. *Let,* I, 128. **100:** *Let,* I, 132. *The Christian Disciple,* V, 313–314 (July-Aug 1823). MS MME to RWE, 13 June? 1822. MS Furness to Cabot, 8 Feb 1878. MS *BoF-ChRec1786–present* (with omissions) , pp. 3–12. **101:** MS CCE to MME, 7 Dec 1823. MS *What,* pp. 14–15. *FroRip,* pp. 20–21. MS CCE to MME, 16 Oct 1823; *Let,* I, 135. *Let,* I, 136, 141. MS CCE to MME, 7 Dec 1823; MS EBE to WmE (b) , 21 May 1824 (owned by DrHE). EBE, MS "The Encouragement of a Sound Literature the Duty of the Patriot" (owned by HCL) , pp. 3–11; *cf. University in Cambridge. Order of Performances* for 16 Aug 1823, p. 4. MS *HCCorpRec,* VI, 156. **102:** *Ibid.,* VI, 159. *QuiFig,* p. 56. *Order of Exercises for Commencement, XXV August, MDCCCXXIV. QuiFig,* p. 56; *Let,* I, 149. MS F. Hedge to Cabot, 30 Sept 1882. MS *What,* pp. 23–24. The MS "Oration in English by Edward B. Emerson," still preserved by the family, is a juvenile piece of eloquence in the style of its period. The opening passage, commemorating the benefactors of Harvard, was, as is shown by *Let,* I, 147, written at the direction of the college authorities. The oration asserts the idea of progress and ends with a burst of praise for the New World. The

manuscript has been wrongly identified as that of EBE's Master's oration of 1827. *Let,* I, 146; MS CCE to WmE (b) , 11 Sept 1824 (owned by DrHE). *Let,* I, 148. *Let,* I, 143, 144, 146. **103:** MS RHE to WmE (b) , 24 June and 22 July and 1 Aug 1824 (owned by DrHE). *Let,* I, 146. *J,* I, 290–291. MS *CabCon,* p. 21. MS endorsed by RWE "Dr. Channing's list . . . books for a theological student, given by Dr. C. to me, probably in 1824." *Cf.* T. P. Doggett's MS "Dr Channing's Course of Study for Students in Divinity" (owned by AnHarTheoLib). The date of this formidable list was presumably soon after 1830. *J,* I, 360–367. **104:** *J,* I, 361–363. **105:** *J,* I, 364–365. *J,* I, 379–380. It was several months later than the passage last cited that Emerson was urged (27 Aug 1824) by his brother William to "Read all of Herder you can get" (*Let,* I, 153). The same idea of "the full and regular series of animals" could, no doubt, have come from Buffon, or others, quite as well as from Herder. MS MME to RWE, 10 Aug 1824. *J,* I, 382– 386. *Let,* I, 141. MS WmE (b) to RWE, 1 Apr 1824 (owned by DrHE). **106:** MS WmE (b) to RWE, 29 May 1824 (owned by DrHE). MS WmE (b) to EBE, 27 June 1824 (owned by DrHE). MS WmE (b) to RWE, 27 Aug 1824 (owned by DrHE). *Let,* I, 149–150. *Let,* I, 152. **107:** *Let,* I, 154–155, 160–162. MS WmE (b) to RWE, 10 Oct and 6 Nov 1824 (owned by DrHE). *Let,* I, 161. **108:** MS WmE (b) to RWE, 17 and 22 Jan 1825 (owned by DrHE). MS WmE- (b) to RWE, 2 Mar 1825 (owned by DrHE). *Let,* I, 158–159. *J,* II, 36, 55. *J,* I, 367. **109:** *Let,* I, 159. *J,* II, 54. *CEd,* IX, 384–385; these verses, also printed in *J,* II, 39, were written, I conjecture, late in Dec 1824 or early in the following month. **110:** Herbert, *The Temple,* 2d ed., 1633, p. 154. MS *HCDivSFaRecfc* (owned by AnHarTheoLib) , 16 Feb 1825. MS *HCDivSStuRec* (owned by AnHarTheoLib) , pp. 3–5; MS "Records of the Trustees of the Society for Promoting Theological Education in Harvard University" (owned by HCL); *HCDivSGenCat*, pp. vii–viii, 2; *cf.* R. S. Morison in *Addresses . . . Harvard Divinity School,* 1917. *ChrEx,* IV, 193–195 (Mar-Apr 1827). MS *HCDivSStuRec* (owned by AnHarTheoLib), *passim.* RHE, MS *MemoBkWms,* p. 96; *Let,* I, 159; MS *CabCon,* pp. 10, 21; *J,* II, 68, 70. **111:** MS *HCStewQBk,* Mar, June, Dec 1825; MS *HCStewLedg,* p. 45. MS *Autobbovo,* under Mar 1825. MS *CabCon,* p. 21. *NTWake,* opposite pp. 17, 23, 38, 131, 181, and on leaf following the half title "Notes." MS MME to RWE, 23 Aug 1825. **112:** MS MME to RHE, 27? Sept 1825. MS MME to RWE, 23 Aug 1825. *J,* II, 68. The inscriptions are described as I saw them in 1945. DGH, p. 88. MS Webster to EBE, 5 Dec 1824. **113:** MS CCE to MME, 12 Sept 1825 (the word I have transcribed as "sad" may possibly be read as "safe"). *Let,* I, 164. MS CCE to MME, 12 Sept 1825. RHE, MS "Notes," p. 17, where the date of William's arrival is given as 18 Oct 1825. MS *What,* pp. 15–16. MS WmE (b) to MME, 27 Oct 1825 (owned by DrHE). MS *What,* p. 16. MS MME to RWE, 24?–25 Sept and late Oct? or Nov? or early Dec? and 13 Dec 1825. MS Cabot to EllenE, 15 July 1882. **114:** *J,* IX, 235–236. *HolmesRWE,* pp. 49–50. MS RHE to MME, 6 and 22 Jan and 12 Feb 1826; Reynolds was presumably Dr. Edward Reynolds (*BoDir,* 1826). *Let,* I, 163–165; MS RHE to MME, 6 and 22 Jan and 12 Feb 1826. *Ibid.;* DGH, p. 110, opposite p. 110, p. 151. MS RHE to MME, 6 and 22 Jan and 12 Feb 1826. **115:** DGH, pp. 109–111. *J,* II, 70, 72. *J,* II, 77; *Let,* I, 166. *J,* II, 81, 83–85. *ThayRip,* p. 39. MS RHE to MME, 6 and 22 Jan and 12 Feb 1826. tj Cabot's "Q," p. 19. *J,* II, 86. **116:** *J,* II, 86. MS CCE to MME, 30 Jan 1826. *Ibid.;* MS *EBEjEur,* 21 Nov 1825. MS *EBEjEur,* 15 Mar ff. and 5 Apr ff., 1826. MS *Cab-*

Con, pp. 18, 21; MS *CabLedgJEC,* p. 117 (has map). DGH, p. 110. MS *Autobbovo,* 1 Apr 1826. *AdDana,* I, 2–3, 5. *Holmes-RWE,* p. 50. *Let,* I, 168. *J,* II, 96. MS MME to RWE, 27 Apr 1826. **117:** MS MME to RWE, 21? May 1826. MS MME to RWE, 13 June 1826. *J,* II, 97, 98. MS j Cabot's "Q," p. 58. On last page of MS sermon No. I, Emerson wrote: "Association of Camb & vic." MS *AutoSk-AmCy,* p. 3, records the approbation. *EinC,* p. 33. MS *PrRec,* 15 Oct 1826. *J,* I, 14–16. **118:** MS copy of MME to WmE (b), 5 Nov 1826. *Let,* I, 170–175. MS *VBkRhymer,* leaf now inserted at p. 97. MS *BoFChBa,* p. 418. *Let,* I, 172. **119:** MS EBE to RWE, 14 July 1826. MS *EBEjEur,* 21 July and 4 and 24 Aug 1826. *Let,* I, 177; RHE, MS *MemoBkWms,* p. 62. *Let,* I, 312. MS EBE to ———, 18 Nov 1826 (possibly a diary entry and not a letter). MS EBE to RWE, 27 Dec 1826. *Let,* I, 178; meantime, *HCCat,* Sept 1826, p. 11, lists RWE, not as a theological student, but only as a resident graduate rooming at "Mrs. Emerson's." MS *PrRec,* 12 Nov 1826; MS WmE (b) to RWE, 23 Dec 1826. MS *HCDivSStuRec* (owned by AnHarTheoLib), 29 Aug 1826. *Let,* I, 179–180. MS j *NoXVIII,* verso of title leaf. *J,* II, 134. *Let,* I, 179. *J,* II, 141–142. **120:** *Let,* I, 180. MS Gilman to RWE, 21 Dec 1826. *DuyCyc,* II, 180. MS *PrRec,* Dec 1826. *Let,* I, 180–185. *J,* II, 149–151, 163–164, 166. *J,* II, 167 ff.; *Let,* I, *e.g.,* 187 ff. *Let,* I, 189. MS *PrRec,* Mar 1827. **121:** *J,* II, 177, 180. *Let,* I, 192. For a general account of Murat, see Hanna, 1946, *passim. Let,* I, 193–194. MS *What,* p. 30. *Let,* I, 193. **122:** *J,* II, 183. MS Murat to Hopkinson, 17 Apr 1827 (owned by HistSocPa; I am indebted to Hanna for a photostat). *J,* II, 195–196. *J,* II, 188, 190. Achille Murat, *The United States,* 2d ed., London, 1833, pp. 124–125. **123:** *J,* II, 195. *Let,* I, 194. *Let,* I, 196; MS *PrRec,* Apr 1827. *Let,* I, 194, 196–199. *Let,* I, 200; MS *PrRec,* May 1827. *Let,*

I, 172, 185, 199, 201; MS *PrRec,* June 1827. MS sermon No. III. MS sermon No. IV, pp. 1 ff. and p. 19. MS sermon No. V, especially p. 1. **124:** MS sermons; 171 sermons, and a few unnumbered fragments, are preserved. *Let,* I, 201–202. MS EBE to RWE, 18 Feb 1827; MS EBE to RWE, 5 Apr 1827. *Let,* I, 201–202, 210; MS Webster to EBE, 2 Dec 1827; MS Webster to EBE, 15 and 16 Jan 1828; MS Webster to EBE, 17 Jan 1828; MS Webster to EBE, 17 and 18 Jan 1828; MS Webster to EBE, 23 Jan 1828. MS J. T. Kirkland to EBE, 7 July 1827. *Let,* I, 206, 209; *Illustrissimo Levi Lincoln* (p. 2 has title "Order of Exercises for . . . XXIX August, MDCCCXXVII") , p. 3. MS *HCCorpRec,* VII, 22. *Let,* I, 208, 211. MS *What,* pp. 43–44. *Let,* I, 211–218; MS *PrRec,* 9 Sept–28 Oct 1827, where Lenox is omitted. MS incomplete copy of RWE to EzR, 10 Nov 1827, in MS *CabBlBkCal-RWE,* under 1827. MS *PrRec,* 6 Nov–16 Dec 1827. **125:** *Let,* I, 222; MS j Cabot's "R," p. 115. MS *VBk"P",* p. 39, where the date is given as "Cambridge 1827." Printed in *CEd,* IX, 381, and in *J,* II, 217–218, where it is dated from 14 Divinity Hall, 7 Dec 1827. *Let,* I, 221–225; MS *PrRec,* 23 Dec 1827–6 Jan 1828. *Let,* I, 222; L. V. Briggs, 1898, p. 80; *EtheE,* I, 437. *Let,* I, 223, 225–226. *Cf.* tj Cabot's "R," p. 97; *J,* II, 236; *Let,* I, 226, 228. *HCCat* for 1827–1828, pp. 7–9, does not list Emerson as a candidate. *ThayRip,* pp. 39–40. **126:** *Let,* I, 234. *HCCat* for 1827–1828, p. 8; *LoHedge,* p. 2. t room lists of Divinity Hall (owned by AnHarTheoLib) . *Let,* I, 227. *Let,* I, 223, 229. *NortonLet,* I, 11. *Cf. Bowen's,* 1833, p. 164. MS CCE to RHE, Feb 1828. *Let,* I, 229. *Cf.* Block, pp. 144–149. *NJ-Mag,* Boston, I (copy at Bush in 1945) , *passim. Let,* I, 223, 224. **127:** EBE, MS *Jou1827-8,* pp. 13–14, 18–19, and entry of 8 May 1828. *Let,* I, 235. MS *What,* p. 27. *Let,* I, 235–236; MS *PrRec,* 25 May and 15 and 22 June 1828. MS *What,* p.

27. *CabM,* I, 140–141. **128:** *J,* II, 245. MS MME to RWE and CCE, 15? July 1828. *Let,* I, 215–224, *passim.* MS CCE to RHE, Feb 1828. *Let,* I, 237, 238–240, 245. MS *HCPhiBetaKRec,* II, 12. *Let,* I, 237. MS *HedgeRem,* p. 5. *HCCat* for 1828–1829, p. 8. **129:** MS *AcctBk1828-ff.,* 8 Aug 1828, 17 Jan and 22 Apr 1829. MS *CabCon,* p. 23. *HCDivSGenCat,* pp. 34, 35. t room lists of Divinity Hall (owned by AnHarTheo Lib) . *LoSoRem,* p. 63. MS *HedgeRem,* pp. 1–3. *Let,* I, 250. *Let,* I, 216; see also p. 123 above. MS fragment CCE to MME, 1828, postmarked 2 Nov. *Let,* I, 249, 251–252. **130:** *Let,* I, 222, 252–254. MS *AcctBk-1828ff.,* 6 Dec 1828. The *Forget me not* may have been either the Philadelphia or the London gift book of that name. **131:** Leconte de Lisle, *Poésies complètes . . . Poèmes barbares,* Paris, 1927, p. 102. *Let,* I, 256. Miniature of Ellen Tucker (owned by RWEMA; now lent to the Concord Antiquarian Society) , presumably the same painted by Sarah Goodridge and all but finished on 10 Apr 1829 (*Let,* I, 269) and the same "Miniature of E. L. T." that Emerson paid $30 for on the 16th of that month (MS *AcctBk1828ff.*) ; the black-and-white reproduction in *J,* II, opposite p. 256, is less attractive than the original. *Let,* I, 256. See above, p. 125. *Let,* I, 234, 235, 236; MS *PrRec,* 25 May and 15 and 22 June 1828. Ellen's MS *Album,* with printed title page dated New Haven, 1826, and with the name "Ellen L. Tucker," apparently in Emerson's hand, on the second flyleaf and, on an early page, *a* poem "To Ellen," signed "Dad" and dated Dec 1826. *Ibid.,* recto of 4th leaf following title page. **132:** *Ibid.,* leaves 38 and 39. **133:** MS ELT to RWE, n.d., postmarked 29 Dec and endorsed by RWE Dec 1828. *Let,* I, 256. *J,* II, 252. *J,* II, 252–253. *Let,* I, 254. *J,* VI, 379. *J,* II, 257. MS sermon No. XXVI, finished, it seems, on 13 Nov 1828 (p. 19) , and preached at Concord, N. H., on 21 Dec

(MS *PrRec*) . MS sermon No. XXVI, p. 8. **134:** *Ibid.*, pp. 9, 10–15. *Let*, I, 256. *DrakeRox*, pp. 351–352. MS *BoFChPr*, p. 4. *DrakeRox*, pp. 111, 352. *Let*, I, 256. MS *VerBkJouGWT–ELT*, 15 Aug 1825. Clipping "Poetry" inserted in MS *VerBkElTuck*. *Let*, VI, 169. *Let*, I, 330 et *passim*. MS *PrRec*. MS *AcctBk1828ff.*, 26 Dec 1828. As early as 1878, F. Hedge stated that Emerson wrote "2 poems & a prose piece" that were published in *The Offering* (MS *CabCon*, p. 20) ; for the identity of the three pieces see Ralph Thompson in *AL*, VI, 151–157, and his *AmLitAn*, pp. 96 ff.; see also p. 95 above. **135:** MS ELT to RWE, n.d., postmarked 29 Dec and endorsed Dec 1828 by Emerson. MS ELT to RWE, 5 and 6 May 1829. MS ELT to RWE, 2 and 3 June 1829. MS ELT to RWE, July 1829. MS ELT to RWE, 30? July 1829. MS ELT to RWE, *c.* 3? or *c.* 8? Aug 1829; MS MME to CCE, 9 Feb 1828; *Let*, I, 274. MS RHE to CCE, 20 Jan 1829. MS EBE to MME dated 24 Jan 1829 by EBE but 17 Jan by, apparently, the postmaster. *Let*, I, 257. **136:** *J*, VI, 456. *Let*, I, 259–260. *ThayRip*, p. 40. MS MME to ELT and RWE, 24 Jan 1829. *Let*, I, 259–261, 265–266. **137:** *Let*, I, 264–265; MS CCE to WmE (b) , 12 Mar 1829. Ezra Gannett, MS "Address . . . March 11, 1829" (owned by Lewis S. Gannett) , pp. 4, 5–6. John Milton, *A Selection*, Boston, 1826, I, 207, in a paragraph marked by Emerson in his copy. *Let*, I, 265. "Holy & happy" from my MS copy made from the panel. *Bowen's*, 1833, pp. 126–127, and opposite p. 128. **138:** Drake, p. 155. The pulpit and pews of Emerson's church were later sold, and I have described them as I saw them, 14 Sept 1947, in the church of the First Parish in Billerica, Unitarian. *YoungEm*, especially pp. 28, 29, 31–33. **139:** *Let*, I, 267, 269, 270. *AlcJou*, p. 19. W. C. Gannett, "Ralph Waldo Emerson," *The Union and Advertiser*, Rochester, N. Y., 27 May 1893. *CabM*, I, 154. *CookeRWE*, p. 27. *Let*, I,

273. Chandler Robbins, in MS *CabCon*, p. 11. MS notes of RWE in a book of psalms and hymns now without title page but with RHE's name and the date 1796. MS F. Hedge to Cabot, 30 Sept 1882. **140:** No. 539 in *A Collection of Psalms and Hymns*, ed. F. W. P. Greenwood, Boston, 1830. MS *What*, pp. 47–48. E. Stebbins, Boston, 1878, pp. 14, 19. *YoungEm*, pp. 146–149, 247; *Sacred Poetry*, ed. Jeremy Belknap, Boston, 1795 (or a later edition of that book) , was the hymnal and psalter that Emerson wanted to discard; for his father's aid to Belknap as its editor, see above, notes on p. 2. MS *BoSChPropRec1804–1845*, p. 129 (16 Oct 1831) . MS F. Hedge to Cabot, 30 Sept 1882. Capt. Francis Green (sometimes spelled Greene) of 157 Hanover St. died 5 Sept 1831 at the age of 81 (Heitman, 1914, p. 259; *BoDaAdv*, 6 Sept 1831; *BoDir*, 1828, 1829, 1830; *StimBoDir*, 1831) . MS *CabCon*, p. 11. MS j "K," pp. 88–89. **141:** *J*, III, 475. MS *AcctBk1828ff.*, 30 Mar 1829; *cf. Let*, I, 266. MS *What*, p. 46. *Let*, I, 270; MS ELT to RWE, postmarked and endorsed May 1829; MSS ELT to RWE of later dates. *Let*, I, 271. MS ELT to RWE, postmarked 17? May and endorsed by Emerson May 1829. *Let*, I, 271–276. MS *RhymJouNH*, *passim; Let*, I, 276–279. **142:** *Let*, I, 282–284; MS *PrRec*, 13 Sept 1829. *Let*, I, 283–286. MS *AcctBk1828ff.*, 7 Nov 1829, 27 and 30 Nov 1829, 1 Dec 1829, 1 Jan 1830, also *passim. Let*, I, 285, 287–289. **143:** MS *AcctBk1828ff.*, 20 Jan, 29 Apr, 7 and 18 Nov, and 29 Dec 1829. *RWE's-Re*, p. 47; for Herder, *cf. Let*, I, 153. MS *AcctBk1828ff.*, 19? and 20 Jan and 23 July 1829. *EtheE*, II, 162–163. *RWE's-Re*, pp. 17 ff. tj *NoXVII*, p. 28; tj *NoXVIII*, p. 53; *Let*, I, 286; F. T. Thompson in *Studies in Philology*, XXIII, 55–76. *J*, II, 277; *Let*, I, 286. *J*, II, 278–279. *Let*, I, 291. MS CCE to MME, 9 Jan 1830. MS copy of a letter of MME's on same sheet with a copy of MME to CCE, 24 Dec 1829. **144:** MS MME to SABR

and SamR, 31 Dec 1829. MS *AcctBk1828-ff.*, 9 and 20 and 22 Feb, 19 and 29 Apr, 28 May, and 24 June 1830, and Jan 1831. *Ibid.*, 15 Jan and 22 Feb 1830 (but the whole record of payments of rent is confusing). *Let,* I, 193; MS *PrRec,* 14 Mar 1830. MS *RhymJouPhila.* MS MME to EBE, 15 Mar 1830. MS copy of MME to WmE (b), 10 Apr 1834. MS MME to EBE, 15 Mar 1830. *Let,* I, 295. **145:** MS *RhymJouPhila. Let,* I, 296–297. MS *RhymJouPhila.* MS Furness to Cabot, 29 Sept 1882. *Let,* I, 296–299, 302; MS *PrRec,* 21 and 28 Mar 1830; MS *RhymJouPhila;* MS *MemBk1820&Misc,* 10–27 Mar 1830. *Let,* I, 302 ff.; *J,* II, 298–309, *passim.* MS CCE to WmE (b), 28 May 1830 (owned by DrHE). MS CCE to WmE (b), 27 June 1830 (owned by DrHE). *Let,* I, 302. MS *EllVer,* folio 64. *Let,* I, 303. MS CCE to MME, 12 Sept 1830. MS CCE to WmE (b), 30 Oct 1830 (owned by DrHE). **146:** *Let,* I, 302, 303. *Let,* I, 270. MS *BoSchComRec1815-1836,* p. 268; ColCen, 16 Dec 1829. *Regulations of the School Committee of the City of Boston,* 1830, pp. 3–5. MS *BoSchComRec1815–1836,* pp. 268 ff., 281–282. MS *BoSchComPa,* May and Nov 1830. MS *BoSchComRec1815–1836,* pp. 294–295. *J,* II, 309. **147:** *J,* II, 310–311, 315, 327. *Let,* I, 310–313; MS RHE to EBE, 21 and 22 Dec 1830; Hanna, pp. 165–166, 266; *New-York Spectator,* 18 Jan 1831 (shows Murat sailed for London that month, apparently on the 13th). *Let,* I, 310–313; MS RHE to EBE, 21 and 22 Dec 1830. MS partial copy of RWE to EzR, 8 Oct 1830, in MS *CabBlBkCalRWE* under 1830. *J,* VII, 357. **148:** MS *VerBkJouGWT-ELT,* 25? Oct 1829 and p. 36 (or what might be so numbered). MS *EllVer,* folio 7 (or 77, upside down). MS version of "Lines" on sheet now inserted in MS *VerBkJouGWT-ELT.* MS *EllVer,* p. 5, following p. 10 (the pagination is erratic). *The Dial,* I, 72, 314. MS RHE to EBE, 21 and 22 Dec 1830. MS *EllVer,* folio 27

(upside down); remembered by Charles in MS *CCEJouFrags,* entry of perhaps 1835. MS RHE to EBE, 21 and 22 Dec 1830; MS RHE to EBE, 1 and 3 Mar 1831. **149:** *Let,* I, 316. MS CCE to MME, 6 Feb 1831. MS RHE to EBE, 11 Feb 1831. MS fragmentary copy of RWE to H. Ware, Jr., 15 Feb 1831, in MS *CabLedgJEC,* p. 202. *Boston Commercial Gazette,* 10 Feb 1831. MS RHE to EBE, 1 and 3 Mar 1831. RWE's partial MS copy of CCE to ElizH, 7 Dec 1833, in MS *ETEVer,* p. 11. DGH, pp. 111–112. **150:** MS *EllVer,* verso of folio 25, upside down. MS j *BlotBk,* No. III (also marked "Ω" by Emerson), p. 36 (19 Sept 1831). *J,* II, 469. *J,* IV, 401. *J,* III, 453–454. **151:** MS j "Q," p. 76. MS RHE to EBE, 7 Mar 1831. MS *PrRec,* 20 Feb 1831; MS dated 19 Feb 1831, written for this occasion. *YoungEm,* pp. 138–144. MS *PrRec,* 1 Mar 1831; MS RHE to EBE, 7 Mar 1831; MSS *LecScr,* I (8 Mar 1831), III (presumably of 22 Mar 1831), IV (29 Mar 1831), V (5 Apr 1831), VIII (26 Apr 1831), IX (3 May 1831). MS sermon CVIII, completed 26 Feb 1831 (p. 20) and preached next day (MS *PrRec*). **152:** MS sermon CVIII, p. 15. MS copy by Cabot of part of RWE to WmE (b), 5 Apr 1830, in MS *BlBkI.Ex,* p. 16. *ColCen,* 15 and 18 Dec 1830 (Emerson re-elected from the fourth ward in a pretty general National Republican victory on 13 Dec). MS *BoSchComRec1815–1836,* pp. 300, 301. MS report (in Emerson's hand) of subcommittee for the Mayhew School, 9 Aug 1831, in MS *BoSchComPa.* MS *BoSchComRec1815–1836,* pp. 313–314; and pamphlet *City of Boston . . . Committee . . . Uniform Mode of Classification . . . Report,* dated 29 Nov 1831, *passim,* but especially p. 15. *Let,* I, 337. MS undated petition of Thomas Appleton, H. G. Ware, Levi Cushing, Charles Warren, and others, in 1831 file of MS *BoSchComPa.* MS undated petition of Moses Jaquith in 1831 file of MS *BoSchCom-*

Pa. **153:** MS *BoSchComRec1815–1836,* pp. 320, 322. *J,* II, 431. MS *BoSchCom-Rec1815–1836,* p. 326. MS report of 4 May on BPLS (in Emerson's hand), in MS *BoSchComPa* for 1831. *Let,* I, 337, 339. *J,* II, 408. *Let,* I, 330. *J,* II, 528. MS CCE to EBE, 4 Jan 1831; *Let,* I, 317. Slavery, in, *e.g.,* MS sermons XCVI, XCVII, XCIX, and C–all preached Nov–Dec 1830 (MS *PrRec*). *AlcJou,* p. 418. *ChrReg,* 28 May and 4 June 1831. MS CCE to EBE, 12 Mar 1831. **154:** *CEd,* IX, 391–392; *cf. J,* II, 367. MS CCE to EzR, 17 June 1831. *Cf.* MS CCE to MME, 12 June 1831; MS CCE to EBE, 16 June 1831; and *Let,* I, 323, 324, 325. *J,* II, 384. MS *VBk"P,"* p. 5 (dated 1 June 1831); slightly different texts are in *CEd,* IX, 391, and *J,* II, 383. **155:** MS EBE to RWE, 4 Aug 1830. *Cf.* Freneau's poem. MS *NoStC&PR* for Jan 1831. *Ibid., e.g.,* Jan and Feb 1831; MS DrWEC to Andrews Norton, 24 Jan 1831 (owned by HCL); MS DrWEC to EBE, 13 Feb 1831. MS *NoStC&PR,* 24 Feb, 1 and 18 Mar, and 5 and 6 Apr 1831. *Ibid.,* Apr, May, June, July, and Sept 1831, *passim,* and 17 Nov 1831; *Let,* I, 313–337, *passim.* MS MME to CCE, 2 Nov 1830. **156:** MS MME to CCE, 9 Feb? 1831. MS CCE to MME, 7 May 1831. *Let,* I, 322–324, 326. MS CCE to MME, 15 Aug 1831. *Let,* I, 330. *J,* II, 401, 415–416; Emerson marked the passage in his Montaigne, *Essays,* tr. Cotton, 2d ed., 1693, I, 261. *J,* II, 440. **157:** *J,* II, 440–441. *Let,* I, 327, 349. *Let,* I, 338, 344. Review of Burton's *Cheering Views of Man and Providence,* 1832 (title and date from the review), *ChrEx,* XIII, 394–399. *Let,* I, 215, 338, 346, 348; MS CCE to EBE, 31 Aug and 2 Sept 1831. **158:** MS CCE to WmE(b), 17 May 1832 (owned by Dr-HE). MS sermon XVI, p. 8 (written 1828, preached at BoSch 6 Sept 1829, according to MS *PrRec*). MS sermons XXX, pp. 2–3; XXXVII, pp. 11–15; XLV, pp. 2–3; XLVI, p. 12; XLIX, p. 3; XCVI, pp. 16–18; CXIX, pp. 4, 7; CXXIII, pp.

10, 13; CXXIX, pp. 11–14; CXL, pp. 11, 12, 20–21, 22. **159:** MS sermon CLV, p. 22. For Emerson's reading of Carlyle on German literature as early as Oct 1827, see *Let,* I, 218–219. *J,* II, 424, 444. Emerson wrote his record of the 36 lectures in the margins of the four Gospels in his copy, still among his books, of *The New Testament in the Common Version Conformed to Griesbach's Standard Greek Text,* Boston, 1828. *ChrReg,* 31 Oct 1829, 20 Nov 1830, 30 Apr 1831, 24 Dec 1831. **160:** *J,* II, 448–449, 463. MS CCE to WmE(b), 29 May 1832 (owned by Dr-HE). *J,* II, 481, 491–492 (2 June 1832). *Let,* I, 351. *ChrEx,* V, 203–208. MS WmE(f) to SamR, 22 Jan 1806. MS WmE(b) to EzR, 4 Apr 1830. **161:** *Let,* I, 352, and MS report of the committee, 16 June 1832 (owned by BoSCh); endorsement on that MS report, and MS J. Mackintosh, Jr., to RWE, 21 June 1832 (owned by BoFCh); the endorsement and the letter seem to differ as to the date of the meeting of the church. MS WmE(b) to RWE, 17 and 22 Jan 1825 (owned by DrHE, quoted above, pp. 107–108). MS *PrRec,* 24 June–29 July 1832. *Let,* I, 353. "Lovewell's Fight," *Collections, Historical and Miscellaneous; and Monthly Literary Journal,* III, 64–66 (Feb 1824). MS CCE to WmE(b), 6 July 1832 (owned by DrHE). *Let,* I, 353. *J,* II, 492. MS CCE to WmE(b), 6 July 1832 (owned by DrHE); MS *PrRec.* **162:** *J,* II, 492. MS *JouEur4,* p. 48. MS MME to RWE, 14 or 15 July 1832. *J,* II, 495–497. MS *JouEur4,* p. 40 (16 July 1832); *cf.* Baedeker, *Les Etats-Unis,* 12th ed., 1905, p. 157. *Let,* I, 353. MS CCE to MME, 16 Aug 1832. MS *PrRec,* 5 Aug–2 Sept 1832; *Let,* I, 351–352. **163:** *Let,* I, 352–354. MS EBE to WmE(b), 7 Sept 1832. *Let,* I, 355. *CEd,* XI, 4–5, 9–10, 13–15, 17, 19, 20, 22. **164:** *Ibid.,* XI, 24. *Let,* I, 355–357. MS CCE to WmE(b), 26 Sept 1832 (owned by DrHE); *Let,* II, 330. MS CCE to WmE(b), 9 Oct 1832 (owned by DrHE). MS CCE to RWE,

11 Jan 1833. *The Dial,* I, 47; printed more fully in *CEd,* IX, 258–260. *YoungEm,* pp. 180–190, especially 183–184, 188. *J,* II, 459, 497–500. *YoungEm,* p. 186. Luther copied in MS j "Q," p. 76, from *FraM,* II, 743 (Jan 1831). **165:** *J,* II, 515. MS *PrRec,* 21 Oct 1832. MS CCE to MME, 24 Oct 1832; Mrs. W. L. Watts, of the American Unitarian Association Historical Library, informs me that Rev. William Steile Brown, a native of England, was a Unitarian minister at Buffalo from 1832 to 1834, died at Columbia, Texas, 4 Aug 1835, and was highly praised in an obituary printed in *Chr-Reg,* 24 Oct 1835. *Let,* I, 356–358. **166:** *Let,* I, 358. MS CCE to EzR, 1 Oct 1832, and later letters. *Let,* I, 358, 359. MS *PrRec,* 28 Oct–30 Dec 1832. MS CCE to EzR, 10 Dec 1832. *Let,* I, 361. *Let,* I, 360. **167:** MS *HedgeRem,* p. 6. MS CCE to MME, 20 Sept 1832; MS CCE to MME, 11 Apr 1833. MS MME to CCE, 10 Feb 1833. MS MME to CCE, 6 Dec 1832. *J,* II, 525. MS MME to CCE, 8 Jan 1833. **168:** *CEd,* II, 81–82. *Let,* I, 359–360. *NortonLet,* I, 510. *Let,* I, 359. *Let,* I, 337. For complicated but pretty convincing evidence that, in spite of a change of captains, the "mule bearing Jasper" of 1831 was Emerson's brig *Jasper* of 1832, see in addition to passages in *Let* referred to, *ColCen,* 14 and 17 Dec 1831 and 3 Nov 1832. *BoDaAdv, IndepChron, DaEvTrans,* and presumably other Boston papers for approximately the same dates, give all or parts of the same evidence. *J,* III, 3. *Let,* I, 360. *J,* III, 3, and X, 251. **169:** *DAB* and *ApCAB. J,* III, 33. *Specimens,* ed. Kettell, Boston, 1829, I, v. *J,* III, 7, 8. *Let,* I, 359, 361, 418, 421. *J,* III, 10, 11. **170:** MS *Man-Globe,* p. 22. *J,* III, 23. EPP's reminiscences in MS Cabot to EllenE, 15 July 1882, and in Cabot's MS notes "Miss E. P. Peabody, July 14' 1882." MS "Prudence," 17 Jan 1838, p. 48. *The Malta Government Gazette,* 6 Feb 1833. MS *JouEur4,* p. 9, 15 Feb 1833. *J,* III, 26–

27, 30, 31. **171:** *J,* III, 32, 33, 35. Inscription at entrance to palace, as I saw it in 1939, says Coleridge lived and worked "IN THIS BUILDING . . . BETWEEN MAY 1804 AND SEPTEMBER 1805." *J,* III, 35, 36. MS *JouEur4,* pp. 8–10; but for the spelling "Vicary's" and for location, see Bigelow, p. 113. *J,* III, 37–38. The name of the Via Amalfitania is misspelled by Emerson in *J,* III, 41, and in *Let,* I, 366. Inscription "VENNE . . ." as I copied it in 1939 from tablet placed on the building in 1896. *Let,* I, 362, 363. **172:** *Let,* I, 363. **173:** *Let,* I, 363. *J,* III, 39–41, 43–47, 49. *CEd,* IX, 353; Strauch in *Modern Language Notes,* LVIII, 64–67; *J,* III, 467. *J,* III, 50–51, 53. **174:** *J,* III, 54. *Let,* I, 366. *J,* III, 55. *Let,* I, 364. *J,* III, 55, 56. *Let,* I, 367. *Let,* I, 363. *J,* III, 55. *Let,* I, 364. MS *JouEur4,* p. 11. *Let,* I, 364; *J,* III, 56–60. **175:** *J,* III, 59. *La Cerere,* Palermo, 21, 25, 26, 28 Feb 1833. *J,* III, 480–481. *J,* III, 58, 60–61. *Let,* I, 369; MS *ItalyI,* p. 11. *J,* III, 66. MS *JouEur4,* p. 12. *J,* III, 66–67. *Let,* I, 367. *J,* III, 67. *Let,* I, 367. *J,* III, 62. MS *ArtBeauty,* p. 17. **176:** *Let,* I, 369. *J,* III, 73. tj "Journal in Europe 1833," No. 4, p. 8. MS *ItalyI,* pp. 45–46, 49–51. MS j "E," p. 256. MS j "D," p. 333. *Let,* I, 371. MS *JouEur4,* p. 11. MS *ItalyI,* p. 53. *J,* III, 74, 76, 97. *Let,* I, 368. **177:** Copy of *Officium,* Rome, 1799, still among the books of Emerson, bears his signature dated Rome, 1833. *J,* III, 81–82, 85–86. Newman, *Letters and Correspondence,* ed. Anne Mozley, London, 1891, I, 380, 390. *J,* III, 87–89. **178:** *J,* III, 99. *Let,* I, 374. *Let,* I, 372–374; the misspelling "Thorwalsden's" is probably chargeable to CCE, whose copy of RWE's letter is here quoted (see *Let,* I, 372, 374). *J,* III, 78–79. **179:** *J,* III, 77, 91, 92. *J,* III, 84, *J,* III, 76. *Let,* I, 380, 381. *J,* III, 79–80. *Let,* I, 374, 380. *Let,* I, 373. *J,* III, 83, 95. *J,* III, 92. **180:** *Let,* I, 373–374. *J,* III, 103, 106. *Let,* I, 374. *J,* III, 103–108. *Let,* I, 384. *J,* III, 110, 119, 121. *Let,* I,

382; *J*, III, 120. *J*, III, 105, 111, 119, 124. **181:** *Let*, I, 377. *J*, III, 122. *Let*, I, 384–385. *J*, III, 120–121. *J*, III, 109. *J*, III, 105, 108. *Let*, I, 382; VI, index. **182:** *J.* III, 112–113. *J*, III, 111–112. *Let*, I, 381–382. MS j Cabot's "1833" (Italian and French journey), p. 24. *Let*, I, 382–383. *Let*, I, 378, 384, 385. *J*, III, 125–129 (Caldani's name is misspelled). **183:** *J*, III, 130, 131. Weather reports in *Gazzetta privilegiata di Venezia*, 4, 5 June 1833. *J*, III, 132–133. H. Cary, *Memoir of the Rev. Henry Francis Cary*, London, 1847, II, 215, 240–243. T. W. Reid, *The Life . . . Milnes*, I, 137–143. *Gazzetta privilegiata*, 7 June 1833, gives day of Cary and Milnes's departure as 3 June. Emerson's arrival in Venice and departure, *ibid.*, 7, 8 June 1833. *J*, III, 139, 140. **184:** *J*, III, 142–145. Emerson, in MS *ItalyII*, p. 57, remembered his frustrated desire to meet Manzoni. *J*, III, 146–152, 154–155. *Let*, I, 388. *J*, III, 165. *Le Temps*, 11 July 1833. *JouDéb*, 14 July 1833. **185:** *J*, III, 155–156; *Let*, I, e.g., 386–388. *J*, III, 155, 159. *Let*, I, 388. *Let*, I, 387; *J*, III, 156. *Let*, I, 388, 390. *Let*, I, 387–388, 389. *J*, III, 167. *JouDéb*, 25 June, 6 and 14 July 1833. *Let*, I, 390–391; *Le Temps*, 22 June 1833. *J*, III, 156–157. **186:** *J*, III, 167. *Le Temps*, 20, 23 June and 7 July 1833. *Ibid.*, 28 June 1833. *Ibid.*, 1 July 1833. *Ibid.*, 28 June and 1 July 1833. *JouDéb*, 1 July 1833; *Le Temps*, 8 and 12 July 1833. *Let*, I, 390. *J*, III, 168. *Le Temps*, 22 June 1833. *Ibid.*, 21 June 1833. *Let*, I, 389. *J*, III, 168–169. **187:** *J*, III, 160. *Let*, I, 391; *J*, III, 170. *JouDéb*, 10 July 1833. *J*, III, 156. Emerson tells in *The Dial*, III, 512–513, the story of his first acquaintance with the Sorbonne and its vicinity. Among his papers are still preserved his copies of the *Programme des cours* of the Sorbonne for the second semester, 1833, and *Programme du Collège Royal de France* for the same semester. I owe to Louis Cazamian (letter of 21 Nov 1948) some illuminating notes

on the neighborhood where, as a student, he knew the Café Procope. The café, rechristened in 1928 and now abandoned, once had an important part in the intellectual activity of Paris, much such a part as that played by some of the coffee houses of London in the literary life of that city. The shop of Papinot, the bookseller, quite obscure in comparison with the Café Procope, was, in the 1830s, at No. 14 in the rue de Sorbonne, as the present rue de la Sorbonne was then called. *J*, III, 156; *Let*, I, 387. *J*, III, 164. *Let*, I, 387. *J*, III, 161. **188:** MS *UsNaH*, pp. 9, 10. *Ibid.*, p. 22; a somewhat altered version is in *The Gift*, Phila., 1844, p. 146. Mrs. R. Lee, *Memoirs of Baron Cuvier*, New York, 1833, pp. 45–46, 56–57. *J*, I, 379; see above, p. 105 and a note on that page. As for Herder's *Ideen*, on 1 Feb 1829 Emerson had borrowed T. Churchill's English translation, *Outlines of a Philosophy of the History of Man*, London, 1800 (see above, p. 143, and a note on that page). **189:** MS *HuSci*, p. 8. *J*, III, 170–171; *Let*, I, 392. *J*, III, 171; MS j "Visits," p. 34; MS j Cabot's "1833" (Italian and French journey), verso of back flyleaf; the address in Russell Square, No. 63, had been given to Emerson by a Mr. Webb of Albany. MS RHE to EBE, 31 Oct 1833; *J*, III, 80. MS *MemBk1833*, 23 July. *Let*, I, 374. *The Letters of John Stuart Mill*, ed. H. S. R. Elliot, London, 1910, I, 57. **190:** *Ibid.*, I, 60. *J*, II, 455. *J*, III, 173. *The Times*, London, 23 July 1833. *Ibid.*, 22, 24, 29 July 1833. *Ibid.*, 26 July 1833. *Ibid.*, 24 and 27 July 1833. *CEd*, II, 143. *The Times*, 22 July 1833. *The News*, London, 4 Aug 1833. *Ibid.*, 21 July 1833. *The Observer*, London, 4 Aug 1833. **191:** *Let*, I, 392–393; *cf.* above, p. 183. *Let*, I, 393; undated entry in MS *MemBk1833*; *ConwayAut*, I, 434–435. *Let*, I, 393. Hazlett, 2d ed., London, 1825, pp. 90–91. *J*, III, 173; MS *MemBk1833*, 25 and 28 July 1833; *CEd*, V, 4; *cf.* p. 190, above. *J*, III, 172. *CEd*, V, 12.

MS j "Visits," pp. 23–31, for account of Coleridge here and on p. 192. **192:** *CEd*, V, 14. *Ibid.*, V, 4. *J*, III, 175–176; Scott, *Marmion*, Canto I, stanza xi. *J*, XII, 174. *Let*, I, 394; MS *MemBk1833*, 15 Aug 1833. *Let*, I, 394. **193:** *IreRWE*, pp. 140–141, 142. *Marmion*, Canto IV, stanza xxiv. *IreRWE*, pp. 143–144, 146–147. *The Edinburgh Observer*, 16 and 20 Aug 1833, shows that the Scottish Athens was at that time having its sense of propriety offended by one Carlyle—quite other than Thomas—who was preaching on High Street, in front of St. Giles's Church. *J*, III, 177; *Let*, I, 394. **194:** *J*, III, 177–179. *J*, III, 179–180; MS *JouEur4*, p. 9. MS *MemBk1833*, back flyleaf. *CEd*, V, 14–15. *Let*, I, 394. **195:** *CEd*, V, 15. *Let*, I, 394. *J*, III, 182. *Let*, I, 378, 394, 395. *C-ECor*, I, 192. *EatH&A*, p. 77. TC to Mill in *CartoFrR*, p. 335. *C-ECor*, passim. *CabM*, I, 197. *J*, III, 186. **196:** *J*, III, 182; *Let*, I, 394. *CEd*, V, 19–23; *Let*, I, 395. *J*, III, 184, 187, 190–191. *J*, III, 187. MS copy of James Martineau to A. Ireland, 31 Dec 1882. MS *MemBk-1833*. **197:** *J*, III, 187, 188, 190, 193; *Let*, I, 396. *J*, III, 194, 196–197, 199–201; cf. *Let*, I, 386. *J*, III, 185. MS *VBkX*, pp. 98–99, 104–105; another version of the poem in *J*, III, 206–207. *Let*, I, 396. MS RHE to EBE, 31 Oct 1833, for Emerson's arrival at the Tremont House in Boston on 9 Oct. **198:** *Areopagitica*, ed. T. Holt White, London, 1819, p. 180. *CEd*, XI, 217. *Let*, I, 397. *J*, III, 232. *StimBoDir*, 1833 and 1834. MS CCE to EBE, 24 Dec 1833. *Let*, I, 410; *StimBoDir*, 1833, lists Jerusha Palmer, keeper of a boarding house at 18 Franklin Place. MS RHE to EBE, 1 May 1834. MS RHE to EBE, 30 May 1834; *Let*, I, 415; MS CCE to EBE, 30 Apr and 1 and 3 May 1834; *J*, III, 291. *NEMag*, IV, 241 (Mar 1833). **199:** E. S. Gannett, *ibid.*, IV, 409–410 (May 1833); MS CCE to RWE, 9 and 11 May 1833; cf. W. C. Gannett, *Ezra Stiles Gannett*, 1875, pp. 187–188. MS *PrRec*, 27 Oct 1833. *YoungEm*, pp.

191–192, 195–202, *passim*. MS *PrRec*, 9 Nov 1833–30 Mar 1834, *passim; Let*, I, 397–408, *passim. Let*, I, 420. I am indebted to William M. Emery of Fairhaven, Mass. (letter of 8 Jan 1942), for pertinent extracts from the MS records of the First Congregational Society (Unitarian) in New Bedford. MS *CabCon*, p. 18. *Let*, I, 400; Emery, *One Hundred Years*, New Bedford, Mass., 1938, p. 9. *Let*, I, 415–417, 421–423. MS *PrRec*, 6–27 July and 19 Oct–10 Nov 1834. *Let*, I, 399. MS *PrRec*, 15 Dec 1833. MS CCE to RWE, 18 and 22 Jan 1833. **200:** MS CCE to RWE, 4 and 5 Apr 1833. MS CCE to RWE, 27 June 1833. MS CCE to WmE (b), 25 Jan 1834 (owned by DrHE). MS record of decree "Supreme Judicial Court Suffolk ss. March Term, 1834—Ralph W. Emerson Adm^r in Equity v Pliny Cutler & als." *Let*, I, 413. MS record of decree entitled "March Term S. J. C *1837*"; *Let*, I, 413–414. *Let*, I, 414–V, 154, *passim*. MS *UsNaH*, p. 70. **201:** Bliss Perry, *Emerson Today*, Princeton, N. J., 1931, p. 46. *Let*, I, 397. MS *ManGlobe*, p. 22. *Ibid.*, pp. 7, 9, 40–41, 52. MS CCE to EBE, 11 and 15 Jan (and perhaps 21 Jan and 5 Feb) 1834. *Let*, I, 402. MS "Water," p. 79. *Let*, I, 414. MS *AdNatHis*, pp. 2, 7, 9, 15, 27. **202:** *Ibid.*, pp. 31–32. Cf. *Let*, III, 224. Hodgin, p. 27; cf. p. 179 *et passim* above. MS *ItalyI*, pp. 5, 28, 81. MS *ItalyII*, *passim. Let*, I, 435. MSS *TGM, Miang, MarLu, GFo*, and *EdBu*. For Emerson's use of the lectures on Michelangelo and Milton as articles in *NARev*, see *Let*, III, 359, and index. *J*, III, 394, 400–401, 439. **203:** MS *ConLyRecBk28–59*, 11 Feb 1835, records the debate (I am indebted to Sarah R. Bartlett for checking this entry). *CEd*, IX, 37–38. Early versions of "The Rhodora" differ from the text in *CEd*—cf. *Let*, II, 189; *LitMWF*, I, 183; and tj Cabot's "U," p. 8, dated "Newton 1834"; but many other poems mentioned in the present book are preserved in variant forms that I cannot record.

Let, I, 418. *J,* III, 333. *Let,* I, 417–418, 419. *Let,* I, 402. *J,* III, 226–227, 272, 452, *e.g.* **204:** *Let,* I, 412–413, 433. *J,* III, 266. *Let,* I, 430; *J,* III, 430–432. *Let,* I, 430. *J,* III, 369. *J,* III, 350. *J,* III, 325. *J,* III, 308. **205:** *Let,* III, 357. *J,* III, 446. *Let,* I, 417. MS *PrRec,* 3 Aug 1834–end. MS sermon CLXVIII, p. 7. *Ibid.,* p. 6. *Ibid.,* p. 3. *Let,* I, 417. MS EBE to RWE, 20 Jan 1833. **206:** *CEd,* IX, 262. *Let,* I, 422. *EdRev,* XLVI, 304–351 (Oct 1827), especially 341–343, 343 ff., 348. *Cf.* above, p. 203. TC to RWE, 12 Aug 1834 (*C-ECor,* I, 18–26); RWE to TC, 14 May 1834 (*ibid.,* I, 11–17). MS CCE to MME, 7 July 1834. *Let,* I, 424. **207:** *HolmesRWE,* p. 79. *C-ECor,* I, 20–21. *Sartor Resartus,* London, 1869 (Vol. I of *CarlyleCoWks*), pp. 28, 50, 53, 65, 188. *Ibid.,* pp. 171, 184. *Ibid.,* pp. 163, 185, 244. *Let,* I, 432. *J,* III, 300–301. *ChrEx,* XV, 193–218 (Nov 1833). *Ibid.,* XIV, 108–129 (Mar 1833). *Let,* I, 402. *ChrEx,* XV, 194, 196, 209 ff., 216–217. **208:** *Ibid.,* XV, 218. *Ibid.,* XIV, 122–126. *JFC-Auto,* p. 85. *Let,* I, 425; II, 32. MS SMF to F. Hedge, 1 Feb 1835, in Fuller MSS, X, 99 (owned by HCL). *AlcJou,* p. 56. *Let,* I, 409. MS CCE to RWE, 15 Nov 1833. **209:** *Let,* I, 420–421. RHE, MS "Notes," p. 40. MS *PrRec,* 19 and 26 Oct and 3 and 10 Nov 1834. MS *VBk-"E.L.,"* p. 47. *J,* III, 361, 422 (apparently corrects *CEd,* I, 400). *J,* III, 425–426. **210:** *Let,* I, 436, 439. Emerson preached at the Twelfth Congregational Church once each year of his regular pastorate and always in the afternoon (MS *PrRec,* 30 Aug 1829, 26 Sept 1830, 30 Jan 1831, and 27 May 1832). "Chambers" is the usual spelling, though *Bowen's,* 1833, p. 173, has "Chamber"; *cf.* Thwing, p. 205. MS *Lidian,* p. 76. *Ibid.,* pp. 82–83; MS CCE to WmE(b), 13 Feb 1834 (owned by DrHE). MS CCE to EBE, 25 Jan 1834. *Cf.* MS *PrRec,* 26 Jan; 2, 9, 16 Feb; and 9, 16, 23, 30 Mar 1834. MS CCE to WmE(b), 13 Feb 1834 (owned by DrHE). MS *Lidian,* pp. 82–

83. MS *PrRec,* 13? Mar 1834. MS *Lidian,* p. 83. **211:** *Ibid.,* p. 84. MS LydiaJ to LJB, 3 Oct 1834. t copy, by Viola C. White, of MS material sent by Le Baron Russell to OWH and now in AbLib. *Let,* I, 441. *Let,* I, 439. MS *PrRec,* 21 Jan 1835. *J,* III, 445. MS *Lidian,* pp. 84–85, 266. *J,* III, 446. **212:** *Let,* I, 435 ff. MS *Lidian,* p. 86. *Let,* I, 434–435. **213:** *Let,* I, 435. MS RWE to LydiaJ, 3 Feb 1835. Dykema, in *American Speech,* XVII, 285–286, suggests that Emerson had perhaps "had as much of Ralph Waldo-r-Emerson as he could stand." t EllenE to EEF, 24 Aug 1885. **214:** MS RWE to LydiaJ, 12 Feb 1835. *Let,* I, 436–437. MS LydiaJ to CTJ, 29 July 1830. *Let,* I, 439–441. MS LydiaJ to LJB, 5 Mar 1835; MS *Lidian,* p. 87. MS LydiaJ to LJB, 23 May 1835. *Let,* I, 436. **215:** *Let,* I, 439. t excerpts from S. F. Clarke to JFC, 28 Feb 1835, inserted in MS *Lidian.* MS L. M. Child to LE, 22 May, n.y. MS SMF to F. Hedge, 6 Mar 1835, in Fuller MSS, X, 100 (owned by HCL). *Let,* I, 439–441; MS *Lidian,* p. 87; MS LydiaJ to LJB, 5 Mar 1835. L. C. Cooley, 1945, p. 37; broadside *Pedigree of Cotton.* t *Lidian,* p. 15. **216:** *Plymouth Church Records,* II (New York, 1923), 506; broadside *Pedigree of Cotton.* t *Lidian,* p. 16. MS *Lidian,* pp. 23, 30. *Ibid.,* pp. 24–25; t *Lidian,* pp. 19, 26. MS *Lidian,* p. 10. P. L. Ford, ed., p. 65 (text of 1727). MS *Lidian,* p. 21. *ColCen,* 19 Aug 1812. MS bill, Dorchester, 15 Dec 1813, for instruction, books, etc., of Lucy and Lydia for three months. A copy of N. G. Dufief's *Nature Displayed . . . A New and Infallible Method,* 3d ed., Phila., 1810, Vol. I, still among the Emerson books, is inscribed "L. C. and L. Jackson's." MS receipt signed by J. F. Saunders & C. Beach, 8 Sept 1813, on behalf of J. Falcone, acknowledging payment of $30 for one quarter's instruction of Lucy and Lydia in dancing. MS *Lidian,* pp. 14–15. MS LydiaJ to Mrs. Lucy Jackson, 18 June 1813. **217:** MS

LydiaJ to Mrs. Lucy Jackson, 16 July 1813. MS LydiaJ to Mrs. Lucy Jackson, 29 July 1813. MS LydiaJ to Charles Jackson, Sr., 3 Nov 1813. MS LydiaJ to Mrs. Lucy Jackson, 19 Nov 1813. MS *Lidian*, p. 27. LydiaJ's MS composition and commonplace book for 1815–1816, and a similar one mainly for 1817; also MS copybook of Lydia's verse for 1819. "Trust in Providence Recommended," signed by Lydia and dated 23 Nov 1815, is on the same loose sheet with a poem called "Resignation," dated 22 Nov 1815 and also signed by Lydia. MS *Lidian*, pp. 16, 39, 41. *Ibid.*, pp. 43–44; *Plymouth Church Records*, II (New York, 1923), 611, 638, 666. **218:** t *Lidian*, p. 18. MS *Lidian*, p. 43. *Ibid.*, pp. 42, 47, 58. *Ibid.*, p. 49. *Ibid.*, pp. 48–52; *ColCen*, 27 Apr 1816. MS *Lidian*, p. 52, according to which "Next year," spent with aunts and uncles, was 1819. t *Lidian*, p. 19. MS *Lidian*, pp. 52–54. MS LydiaJ to LJB, 5 Oct 1821. **219:** MS *Lidian*, pp. 56–58. LydiaJ to LJB, 14 Oct 1823. MS *Lidian*, pp. 58, 70–72. *Ibid.*, p. 59. MS LydiaJ to LJB, 10 July 1825. MS LydiaJ to CTJ, 28 Feb 1832. MS *Lidian*, p. 74. **220:** MS CTJ to LydiaJ, May 1835. MS LydiaJ to EPP, 28 July 1835. t *Lidian*, p. 23; *BoDir*, 1826, 1827, 1828, 1829. t *Lidian*, p. 24; MS ChasB to LJB, Constantinople, 11 Jan 1837, says he has been absent for three and one-fourth years. **221:** MSS ChasB to LJB, 11 Jan 1837, 19 Aug 1853, 20 Jan 1854; MSS ChasB to LE, 25 Sept and 2 Oct 1838, 11 Dec 1838, 16 Aug 1851, 6 Aug 1852, Oct 1853, 11 July 1854; t *Lidian*, p. 27; various entries in MS *AcctBk40–44*, MS *AcctBk45–49*, MS *Acct-Bk65–72*. MS *Lidian*, p. 91; MS *AcctBk-36–40*, p. 15. MS *Lidian*, pp. 90–91. *Ibid.*, pp. 88–89. MS LydiaJ to LJB, 23 May 1835. MS *ConToRec*, VIII, 37–38, 43. *J*, III, 497. *Let*, I, 452. *J*, III, 499 *et passim;* but especially *Let*, I, 455. *J*, III, 507–508, 516. **222:** *Let*, I, 455. *Let*, I, 452. *ConFre*, 5 Sept 1835. *Let*, I, 453. MS Joseph Willard to RWE, 26 Sept 1835.

MS *Lidian*, pp. 92–93; *I Chronicles*, 17: 10. **223:** MS CCE to WmE (b), 7 July 1835 (owned by DrHE) ; *J*, III, 540; MS *Lidian*, p. 93. MS CCE to WmE (b), 14 and 18 Sept 1835 (owned by DrHE). t EllenE to EEF, 24 Aug 1885. MS *Lidian*, pp. 98–101; *cf. Let*, I, 454. MS "A Plan of the House Lot with the Buildings thereon, Belonging to Mr Charles Coolidge . . . Surveyed March the 29th 1832 by Cyrus Hubbard." *Ibid.*; *J*, III, 540–541; MS *Lidian*, p. 103. *Let*, I, 448. *Let*, I, 447. *Let*, I, 454, 456; and II, 19, 21. **224:** MS LE to LJB, 16 Sept 1835. MS LE to LJB, 22 Sept 1835. MS *Con-AsBk* for 1835. MS CCE to RWE, 22 Sept 1835; *Let*, II, 66 *et passim.* MS LE to LJB, 28 Sept 1835. MS LE to LJB, 30 Sept 1835. **225:** *Ibid.* MS without signature, date, beginning, or close, but presumably copied from a letter of 13 Sept 1835. **226:** MS *Lidian*, pp. 123–124. For Asia, see also *Let*, II, 112, 410, 427; *J*, IV, 182 and 206, and V, 93–94 and 97; *C-ECor*, I, 161. For Palestine, see *Let*, II, 112, 113. MS *Lidian*, pp. 147–148. MS LE to LJB, 10 (*i.e.*, 9?) Oct 1835, reported that "to-day . . . a 'transcendental' also dined with us." **227:** Plato, *The Dialogues*, tr. Jowett, 3d ed., Oxford, 1892, I, 489 (where, however, the names of the speakers are abbreviated). *EinC*, pp. 96–97. *Cf.* Shattuck, p. 211, and *YeoGaz*, 1 July 1837. *ConFree*, 11 ff. and 20 Dec 1834 and 14 Nov 1835. *Ibid.*, 3, 10, and 31 Jan and 7 Feb 1835. **228:** MS CCE to WmE (b), 29 Apr 1835 (owned by DrHE). MS LE to LJB, 10 (*i.e.*, 9?) Oct 1835; MS CCE to WmE-(b), 10 Oct 1835 (owned by DrHE); *J*, III, 546. *William Lloyd Garrison . . . Told by his Children*, New York, 1885, II, 11–28, 49–50. *J*, IV, 73. *Cf. EinC*, pp. 99–100. *Ibid.*, pp. 71–73. MS *ConTo-Rec*, VIII, 58; *EinC*, p. 67. MS *ConTo-Rec*, VIII, 46, 64. *YeoGaz*, 9 Apr 1836. *ECitCon*, pp. 370–371. Broadside *Report of the Selectmen . . . Concord . . . up to March 24, 1837;* MS *AcctBk36–40*, p.

31. MS *ConToRec*, VIII, 71–72. *Let*, II,
19, 21. MS *AcctBk36–40*, p. 29; *EinC*,
p. 67. **229:** *Social Library,* printed and
MS certificate of Emerson's share, No. 44,
dated 4 Jan 1836 (owned by CFPL).
MS *ConSoLibRec* (owned by CFPL), pp.
20, 118, 120. *Ibid., passim,* showing Emerson was committeeman or officer 4 Jan
1836–3 Jan 1842, and 7 Jan 1850–20
Jan 1851, and presumably till 29 Nov
1851, when the library was taken over
by the town. After his marriage Emerson
preached at Dr. Ripley's church once in
1835, eleven times in 1836, twice in 1837,
twice in 1838, and twice in 1839 (MS
PrRec). In 1836, *e.g.*, Emerson lectured
not fewer than three times for the Concord Lyceum, according to MS *ConLy-
Rec28–59* (owned by CFPL), 27 Jan and
2 and 28 Dec. MS MME to RWE, 15
May 1841; *Let,* II, 397. MS MME to
RWE, 31? Mar 1836 (owned by AbLib).
230: MS MME to CCE, 10 Feb 1833.
For MME's incipient consciousness of
what she called "transcendentalism," see
MS MME to CCE, 29 Apr 1833. *Let,* I,
429. MS RHE to CCE, 3 Mar 1836. *Let,*
I, 429. MS CCE to RWE, 3 May 1836.
Let, II, 9–20. **231:** *Let,* II, 20. Holmes,
The Poetical Works, Boston and New
York, n.d., cop. 1892, I (XII of *HolStan-
Lib*), 58. *Let,* II, 24, 31, 34. *J,* IV, 40.
Let, II, 59. *The Dial,* I, 13–16; III, 522–
526; IV, 88–92 (these ascriptions to CCE
were made by Emerson in his own copy
of the magazine, now in HCL). *Let,* II,
24–25. MS *AcctBk36–40,* p. 9, mentions
Lucy's boarding with the Emersons for
twenty-two weeks, up to Mar 1836. **232:**
J, IV, 134–135. *Let,* II, 30. *J,* III, 501.
AlcJou, pp. 57–58; *Pedlar'sP,* pp. 24, 34,
et passim. Let, I, 447–448. *J,* III, 501;
AlcJou, p. 68. *AlcJou,* pp. 68–69; *J,* III,
559–560. *AlcJou,* p. 70; *J,* III, 573. **233:**
AlcJou, pp. 70, 75. *Let,* II, 4–6; *EtheE,*
II, 101–125. *J,* II, 109, alludes to Wordsworth's famous "Ode," which is, significantly, quoted in MS j "F No 1" (dated
1836–1837), p. 57. *AlcJou,* pp. 75–76.

Let, II, 32; *AlcJou,* pp. 77–78. *Let,* II,
138–141; *AlcJou,* p. 102. *J,* IV, 69. *Let,*
II, 60–62. *Let,* II, 27–28, and VI, index;
MS *AcctBk36–40, passim.* W. E. Channing the Younger, MS "Poetry," III, 92
(owned by HCL); Frederick T. McGill,
the best knower of the younger Channing's life and writings, first made me
acquainted with these verses. **234:** *Cf.*
p. 232 above. *Let,* II, 32. *IreRWE,* p.
83. *Let,* II, 32; *J,* IV, 79–80. *Let,* II, 32.
MS SMF to Ellen Fuller, 25 Aug 1836,
in Fuller MSS, IX, 43 (owned by HCL).
235: MS LE to EPP, n.d. (July or Aug
1836); I have supplied in square brackets
portions of words torn away with the
seal. *LoHedge,* pp. 3–15. *Let,* I, 446.
236: *Let,* II, 29. MS sermon CLXXI,
the last of the extant sermons of Emerson, was first preached 17 July 1836, according to MS *PrRec.* MS *AcctBk36–40,*
p. 9. *J,* IV, 131–132. *J,* III, 505–506, 512
ff.; *EtheE,* II, 83–87, 88–99, *passim.* MS
RWE to EPP, 12 June 1835 (owned by
HCL), may relate to an at least partial
English translation of *The True Messiah*
in EPP's possession and possibly by her.
J, III, 432, 524–525. *IreRWE,* p. 21. *J,*
IV, 10–11; MS j "B," pp. 132 ff. Among
Emerson's books there is still a copy of
the first volume of *Cabinets-Bibliothek
der deutschen Classiker. Anthologie aus
den Werken Jean Paul's,* Hildburghausen
and New York, 1829, inscribed with the
name "Lidian Jackson," in Emerson's
hand. *J,* IV, 17, 27; MS j "B," pp. 141–
148. MS j "B," especially pp. 142, 143;
J, IV, 28. *Let,* II, 32–33. **237:** MS MME
to LE, Wednesday, Aug n.y. (1837?). *J,*
IV, 94. Long afterwards Emerson remembered the impress of Goethe on the Transcendental movement as of first importance—"Goethe,—the one efficient source
of influence, twenty years ago" (MS
RWE to Charles Leland, 23 Dec 1861,
owned by HistSoPa). MS GPB to RWE,
10 Oct 1835. *C-ECor,* I, 48–49. Incomplete MS copy ᵇʸ Cabot of Le Baron
Russell to RWE, 16 Dec 1835. *C-ECor,*

I, 86–87. *J,* III, 477; IV, 89. *Cf.* p. 156 above. **238:** MS *CCEJouFrags,* 2 Aug 1835. *J,* III, 536. MS F. Hedge to Cabot, 20 Nov 1883. *Let,* I, 449. *Let,* I, 447; *BoDaAdv,* 3 Nov 1835–14 Jan 1836, *passim.* MS CCE to WmE (b), 7 Nov 1835 (owned by DrHE). **239:** MS *LecEng-Lit,* IV, pp. 3–45, *passim. Ibid.,* VIII, pp. 33, 38; IX, p. 48; X, pp. 22, 27, 31. MS *AcctBk36–40,* p. 2. MS *PrRec.* MS *AcctBk36–40,* p. 4; *Let,* II 9. **240:** *Let,* II, 26, 37. *CEd,* I, 3, 9, 10. *Select Works of Plotinus,* tr. Thomas Taylor, London, 1817, p. 365; *cf.* J. S. Harrison, p. 105. A notation on a back flyleaf of the copy of the *Select Works* that belonged to Emerson (now in HCL) refers to the passage in question but is not very clearly in his hand. *CEd,* I, 11, 12–14, 24. **241:** *CEd,* I, 70, 71, 72, 76. *Let,* II, 29. *Let,* II, 26–27, 29, 30, 32. For discussion of the Orphic poet, see *EtheE,* I, 361 ff., and my review in *AL,* XVII, 273. **242:** *AlcJou,* p. 78. *C-ECor,* I, 112. *Let,* II, 42. *ChrReg,* 24 Sept 1836. *WMess,* II, 385–393, but especially 392; Osgood's identity in *PerTran,* p. 22. *ChrEx,* XXI, 372, 376, 377, 380–381, 385. **243:** *DemRev,* I, 319–329, but especially 320. *The Intellectual Repository and New Jerusalem Magazine,* I (n.s.), 188–191 (Apr 1840). *NJMag,* XV, 48–52, *passim. J,* IV, 85–87; *Let,* II, 37; *StimBoDir,* 1835 and 1837; *AlcJou,* p. 78. *J,* IV, 87. **244:** *AlcJou,* pp. 78–79; *HCDivSGenCat, passim; CooDw,* p. 11; *WHCMemWEC,* III, 313; *ChadChan,* pp. 29, 380–381. *J,* IV, 87. *J,* IV, 113–114; *AlcJou,* p. 79; MS *FraJouEx,* p. 1. **245:** *Let,* II, 48. MS W. C. Martin to RWE, 5 Nov 1836. *Bowen's,* 1833, pp. 87–89 and 166, and pictures opposite pp. 144, 180; for Alcott's school, *Pedlar'sP,* pp. 164–165 *et passim,* and picture opposite p. 168. *Let,* II, 43. **246:** *J,* IV, 189; Shakespeare, *MSND,* II, i, 175–176. MS *PhHis,* I, 23, 25; II, 8, 21, 27. *Ibid.,* XII, 24. *Ibid.,* V, *passim,* but especially 10–12, 36–38; VI, 11, 18–22. **247:** *Ibid.,* VII, 35; IX, 33–38, *passim;* X, 9–

10, 33–34. *AlcJou,* pp. 81–82. MS *FraJouEx,* pp. 4–5. *PeaRemChan,* pp. 365–366. **248:** *MannMann,* pp. 51–52. **249:** Whitman, *Leaves of Grass,* New York, 1867, p. 10. *Let,* II, 81, 83. MS j "U," pp. 56–57; Emerson read and indexed the passage on Harvey in his copy of *Letters Written by Eminent Persons . . . to which are Added . . . Lives of Eminent Men, by John Aubrey,* London, 1813, II, 380. MS RHE to CCE, 3 Mar 1836; *J,* IV, 57–58. MS *TreesMajor,* p. 3. MS *AcctBk36–40,* p. 17. MS *TreesMajor, passim;* MS *TreesMinor, passim.* **250:** *J,* IV, 236, 251, 260. *C-ECor,* I, 161. *J,* V, 6. MS account books, *passim.* MS *Ledger49–72,* p. 60; a note in *Let,* III, 371, confuses the "heater piece" with a neighboring parcel of land later purchased by Emerson. *Let,* II, 66. MS W. D. Sohier to RWE, 27 July 1837; *Let,* II, 87, 92. MS W. D. Sohier to RWE, 30 June 1837. **251:** *Let,* II, 86 *et passim,* and later volumes, *passim.* MS *ConAsBk* for 1839. *Let,* II, 69, 95; VI, 81, 166. *J,* V, 43. MS LE to EPP, 4 Dec 1837. *J,* IV, 398; V, 49–50. *Let,* II, 203. *J,* IV, 232. MS LE to LJB, 6 and 8 Oct 1837. *J,* V, 114–115. **252:** *Let,* II, 185; *J,* V, 167. *J,* IV, 290, 469; V, 23. *EinC,* p. 146. *Let,* II, 168. *Let,* II, *passim; Pedlar'sP,* pp. 203–210. *J,* IV, 225. **253:** *Let,* II, 68–82, *passim. J, e.g.,* V, 14. *Let,* II, 181–184. MS SMF to Eugene Fuller, 31 Mar 1839, in Fuller MSS, IX, 59 (owned by HCL). MS ElizH to MME, 23 Apr 1839. MS SMF to CKN, 18 Apr 1839, in Fuller MSS, X, 128 (owned by HCL). MS SMF to Eugene Fuller, 31 Mar 1839, in Fuller MSS, IX, 59 (owned by HCL). *Let,* II, 197, 203, 234; II–IV, *passim.* MS ElizH to MME, 23 Apr 1839. *J,* IV, 474; *Let,* II, 135 and 137, and, in general, II ff.; MS RWE to CS, 3 Mar 1838 (owned by HCL), and MS RWE to CS, 23 Mar 1838 (owned by HCL), and much other correspondence between RWE and CS that has become available and has been placed in HCL since the publication of

Let in 1939. *Let,* II, 205. *Cf. HigFul,* pp.
36, 37. *J,* V, 279. *Let,* II, 338 *et passim.*
254: *Cf. LetFriend,* p. 9. *EarlySClub,*
pp. 109 ff.; *TickLi,* II, 85, 99–100. *Let,*
II–V, *passim;* VI, index. *Let,* II, 226–
228; MS RWE to SGW, 27 Oct 1839 (MS
owned by HCL; much other correspondence between RWE and SGW has become available since 1939 and is now in
HCL). *Let,* II–VI, *passim. Let,* II, 446;
III, 80–81 *et passim.* MS *Lidian,* pp.
120–121; in MS LE to LJB, "Wednesday
Eveg." ("1836" added in pencil), Lidian
was sorry to be packing Lucy's things,
realized that Lucy would not be back in
Concord that winter, and was especially
sorry because Lucy would now be unable
to see baby Waldo (born 30 Oct 1836),
and she also said that Mrs. and Miss
Ward reported Mrs. Thoreau's kind feelings toward Lucy. On the other hand,
Sanborn (*SanLiThor,* pp. 128–129) quoted Emerson as saying in conversation:
"My first intimacy with Henry began
after his graduation in 1837. Mrs. Brown,
Mrs. Emerson's sister from Plymouth,
then boarded with Mrs. Thoreau . . ."
SanHDT, pp. 52–54. *ThorWr,* VII, 3;
cf. CanbyThor, pp. 65, 461. *J,* IV, 395,
397, 406. *J,* V, 128–130; *cf. CEd,* I, 230
ff. and 306 ff. *Let,* II, 182. **255:** MS
G. B. Loring to JRL, 24? Feb 1839
(owned by HCL). *J,* V, 241. *Let,* II, 225.
MS JRL to G. B. Loring, 22 Dec 1837
(owned by HCL). MS LE to LJB, 19
and 21 July 1838. *Let,* II, 147, 159. *J,*
IV, 191, 236, 239. MS LE to LJB, 19 and
21 July 1838. That Emerson was too selfish and too earthy for Very emerges from
the whole record of the friendship of the
two men. MS LE to LJB, Fast Day, 5?
Apr 1838; *VeryPo,* pp. 18–19. **256:** MS
G. B. Loring to JRL, 19 Sept 1838
(owned by HCL). *Let,* II, 170–171. *J,*
V, 105; Very had by this time begun the
short series of letters to Emerson now in
the Wellesley College Library, and some
weeks after the visit of late October he
wrote him an admonition to bind "the

strong man within you (that is your
will)" and so receive a spiritual weapon
with which to "plunder the goods of the
evil one" (MS Very to RWE, 30 Nov
1838, owned by Wellesley College Library) ; Very's letters to Emerson are often
Biblical in style, and, though not im-
passioned, have a tone of authority suggesting the speech of a Hebrew prophet.
Let, II, 171; *BartlettJoVe,* pp. 59, 80.
Let, II, 179, 204, 209. *J,* IV, 235; V, 103.
J, IV, 361. *J,* IV, 356. *Let,* II, 134. MS
LE to LJB, 19 and 21 July 1838. *J,* IV,
491. **257:** *J,* V, 195, ed. note. *Let,* II,
98–99 *et passim. J,* IV, 363. *Let,* II, 108;
MS Brownson to RWE, 10 Nov 1837.
J, IV, 405. *Let,* II, 122. *Let,* II, 109.
C-ECor, I, 141. *St-ECor,* pp. 23–25 *et pas-
sim. C-ECorSup,* p. 6. *J,* IV, 137–138.
258: *J,* IV, 207, 235–236. *CEd,* IX, 38–
40. *J,* IV, 243. MS j "C," p. 84. **259:**
J, IV, 304. *J,* III, 369. MS *HuLi,* I, 15;
Let, II, 177. MS LE to LJB, "Tuesday
Evening," early 1838? *J,* V, 86–87, 233.
Herald, Vol. I, No. 4, is for 25 Apr 1838.
Let, II, 170–171; *J,* V, 234. *J,* V, 76. MS
PresAge, I, 5, 54, 65, 76. **260:** MS copy,
by F. B. Sanborn, of TheoP to C. Francis, 6 Dec 1839. *AlcJou,* p. 137. MS LE
to Sophia Brown, 9 Sept 1837; *The Liberator,* 25 Aug 1837, shows the Grimkés
were visiting neighboring towns; and
they presumably arrived in Concord on
1 Sept 1837 (*cf. Letters of Theodore
Dwight Weld . . . 1822–1844,* ed. Barnes
and Dumond, n.d. [cop. 1934], I, 440,
442) ; the sisters no longer lived in the
South. *CabM,* II, 425–426. *J,* IV, 371–
372, 374; V, 26–27, 301. *J,* IV, 316–319,
400, 411–412. *J,* V, 261. *Let,* II, 235 *et
passim.* Kant, *Critick of Pure Reason,*
London, William Pickering, 1838, pp.
431–432; a notation in Emerson's copy
indicates that the price was $6, the same
amount charged Emerson for the book
in MS *MunAcct37–39,* 19 Nov 1838; the
pertinent marginal marking on p. 432
of Emerson's autographed copy is in a
cramped, and therefore dubious, hand.

J, IV, 185. **261:** *J*, IV, 247, 248. MS
j "C," p. 91 (17 July 1837). MS LE to
EPP, 20 Jan 1839. *Let*, II, 104. **262:**
Let, II, 177, 244. *AlcJou*, p. 107. *Thay-
Rip*, pp. 46–47. See below, pp. 269 ff.,
for the "recent attacks." *ThayRip*, p. 46;
Let, II, 177. MS LE to LJB, 2 Jan 1839;
Let, II, 177. MS *AcctBk36-40*, pp. 140–
141. *Let*, II, 60. MS *AcctBk36-40*, pp.
34, 36, 38; MS *MunAcct37-39*, under
"Tickets to Lectures, 1838-9." *J*, V, 373.
Let, II, 94. *J*, III, 537. **263:** MS j "Concord L.," p. 144. *J*, IV, 56. *Let*, II, 94.
MS "Memoirs by John Pierce" (owned
by MHS), VII, 155–156; MS *HCPhiBeta-
KRec*, II, 59. *CookeRWE*, p. 60. MS LE
to LJB, 2 Sept 1837. *LowLitEs*, pp. 366–
367; Lowell may well have heard the
oration, but I have no definite proof.
HolmesRWE, p. 115; as Holmes was at
the dinner (see p. 265 below), he presumably had heard the oration. MS *Cab-
Con*, p. 12. **264:** *CEd*, I, 81, 84, 100,
113, 114–115. *Ibid.*, I, 91. *Ibid.*, I, 89, 94.
265: *Ibid.*, I, 94–95. Copy of Emerson's
Miscellanies, Boston, 1868, bears the signature of William James and his mark
on this passage, p. 90 (owned by HCL);
John Dewey, as a young man, read Emerson, but does not remember that he was
directly influenced by the passage I have
quoted (letter to me, 16 Sept 1948). *CEd*,
I, 102, 106, 108, 109–115. MS *HCPhiBeta-
KRec*, II, 59. **266:** *J*, IV, 294. *FroEEv*,
p. 367. MS LE to LJB, 2 Sept 1837. *J*,
IV, 289. MS LE to LJB, 2 Sept 1837. *J*,
IV, 341; *Let*, II, 99–100. MS LE to LJB,
6 and 8 Oct 1837. *Let*, II, 104. MS LE to
LJB, 23 Apr 1838. **267:** *J*, IV, 427.
MS RWE to John Pierpont, 7 June 1838
(owned by NYPL). *J*, IV, 430; *Let*, II,
126–127. *J*, III, 502, 518. MS *PrRec*. *J*,
IV, 413. *Let*, II, 147. According to *ChrEx*,
XXV, 266, there were seven graduates;
and seven are named in *HCDivSGenCat*,
pp. 52–53. **268:** MS *HCDivSStuRec*, p.
96 (owned by AnHarTheoLib); printed
in *RWE'sRe*, p. 130. MS *HCDivSStuRec*,
pp. 27, Jan 1831, and 98, 15 July 1838

(owned by AnHarTheoLib); description
of the chapel as I found it 3 July 1945;
a tablet, set in the wall, now commem-
orates the address of 15 July 1838. *CEd*,
I, 119, 120, 122–131, 145, 149–151. **269:**
PeaRemChan, p. 373. *Let*, II, 147. MS N.
Hale, Jr., to JRL, 24 July 1838 (owned
by HCL). MS JRL to G. B. Loring, 2
Aug 1838 (owned by HCL). *ScudLowell*,
I, 57–58. MS G. B. Loring to JRL, 19
Sept 1838 (owned by HCL). MS JRL to
G. B. Loring, 22 Sept 1838 (owned by
HCL). MS G. B. Loring to JRL, 5 Oct
1838 (owned by HCL). *Let*, II, 147.
270: *Let*, II, 149–150. *Let*, II, 148–149.
ThayRip, p. 45. *Let*, II, 149. MS LE to
LJB, Aug? 1838. *J*, V, 30. *Let*, II, 149;
cf. Commager in *NEQ*, VIII, 29–41, and
The Evening Post, New York, 27 June
1838, where the petition is given without
the names of the signers, as it is in *The
Liberator*, 6 July 1838. *J*, V, 34, 91–92.
271: *Let*, II, 166; *The Personality* was
published on 4 Oct 1838, according to
MS *HCDivSStuRec* (owned by AnHar-
TheoLib), p. 100. *Let*, II, 166–167.
WMess, VI, 37–42; this review begins
with a summary of the controversy to
date (Nov 1838). *BoQR*, I, 501, 514.
ChrEx, XXV, 266–268. *PrincetonRev*, XI,
43–90, 91, 95, 97. "Unitarian Pope" was
Carlyle's epithet, according to *SanHarris-
Alc*, II, 360. A. Norton, *Inaugural Discourse*, 1819, p. 12. **272:** A. Norton, *A
Discourse . . . Infidelity*, 1839, especially
pp. 9 ff. and 39 ff. Cf. *CookeRWE*, pp.
74–75. GR, *"The Latest Form of Infidel-
ity" Examined*, 1839, especially pp. 19,
22, 43, 119, 122, 125, 150. *Let*, II, 225.
MS MME to WmE (b), 13 June 1840. *J*,
V, 123. *ThayRip*, p. 45. MS *FraJouEx*,
p. 13. *J*, V, 83, 123. Incomplete rough
draft of "Uriel," almost illegible, MS j
"V," p. 147 (1845?). *MannMann*, p. 52;
the comparison suggested by ed. note in
J, IV, 362. *CEd*, IX, 13–15. **273:** *Ibid.*,
IX, 14–15. MS F. Hedge to OWH, 22
Dec 1884 (owned by HCL). MS *PrRec*.
Let, II, 144–145, 153. *CEd*, I, 153–187.

Let, II, 176, 189–190; *LitMWF,* I, 182–183. *Let,* II, 85. **274:** MS *ConToRec,* VIII, 165–166; *ChrReg,* 17 Dec 1836; *Yeo-Gaz,* 8 July 1837; *BoCou,* 8 July 1837; *Let,* II, 85. *YeoGaz,* 8 July 1837. Verses quoted are from broadside text of "Original Hymn" as reproduced in facsimile in *The Critic,* XLII, 431 (May 1903); *CookeBib,* p. 63, gives an entirely erroneous date. *J,* V, 226, 227, 343. **275:** *Goethe's Werke,* Stuttgart and Tübingen, 1827, II, 85, 86, 87. *C-ECor,* I, 48. *Let,* II, 225. MS *ParkerJou* (owned by American Unitarian Association Historical Library), volume for 1838–1840, under Sept 1839. *Let,* II, 231, 243. **276:** MS F. Hedge to SMF, 16 Jan 1840, in Fuller MSS, XVI, 23 (owned by HCL). Cabot's notes on F. Hedge to SMF, 24 Mar 1840, in MS *CabBlBkCal. Let,* II, 270–271. *Let,* II, 249, 276. *Let,* II, 253. *Let,* II, 285–286; *The Dial,* I, 1, in Emerson's annotated copy (owned by HCL); names of contributors mentioned in the present chapter are from Emerson's notes in the four volumes of this set of *The Dial. Let,* II, 310. *The Dial,* I, 84 ("To Eva" is there entitled "To * * * *"), 122–123. *Ibid.,* I, 5–11, 14, 47, 71–72. **277:** *Ibid.,* I, 117–121. *Ibid.,* I, 72. *Ibid.,* I, 83, 84; other contributions by Ward are *ibid.,* I, 121, 123. *Ibid.,* I, 86, 87, 89, 94. *Let,* II, 294, 313, 322. *C-ECor,* I, 304. *The Dial,* I, 137–158. MS *PresAge,* II. *The Dial,* I, 242–245. *Ibid.,* I, 220–232. *C-ECor,* I, 313–314. *The Dial,* I, 348–350. "An After-dinner Poem" (OWH, *Poems,* new rev. ed., Boston, 1878, p. 68). *The Dial,* I, 497–519, 523–538. *Ibid.,* I, 536. **278:** *Ibid.,* II, 207–214. *Let,* II, 456–458; *The Dial,* II, No. 3 (Jan 1842), back cover. *J,* V, 506, 513–514. *Let,* II, 387. *CEd,* II, 318. *Let,* II, 387. Hegel, *The Philosophy of History,* tr. Sibree, rev. ed., New York, 1899, especially p. 457. Cousin, *Introduction,* tr. Linberg, Boston, 1832, *e.g.,* p. 312. *Let,* I, 322, 346. **279:** Emerson's new words and obsolete words seemed particularly striking to a contributor to

A New English Dictionary (MS G. M. Philips to RWE, 8 Jan 1880). *CEd,* II, 45–47, 49, 50, 53, 57, 61, 81, 83–85, 89–90. **280:** Hindu law (*The Dial,* III, 336; but earlier quoted in MS *PhHis,* VI, 22). Montaigne, *Essays,* tr. Cotton, 2d ed., London, 1693, I, 199. *J,* V, 484. *CEd,* II, 68, 70, 94. **281:** *CEd,* II, 96, 98. *Job,* 42:3. *CEd,* II, 126, 131. **282:** *Ibid.,* II, 188. Aristotle, *The Nicomachean Ethics,* especially Bks. VIII and IX. Emerson must also have been familiar enough with Cicero on friendship. Montaigne, *Essays,* tr. Cotton, 2d ed., London, 1693, I, 296 (passage marked in Emerson's copy of the book). *CEd,* II, 208, 217. *Ibid.,* II, 214. For Stoics, *cf.* Diogenes Laertius, *Lives of Eminent Philosophers,* tr. Hicks, London and New York, 1925, II, 229. **283:** *CEd,* II, 222, 240, 268, 279, 304–306, 308. *J,* V, 485. *CEd,* II, 328, 336, 342, 351–353, 367. **284:** MS MME to ElizH, 8 Apr 1841. MS Wm. Foster to RWE, 12 Apr 1841. *J,* VI, 297. *LowLitEs,* I, 67. *ChrEx,* XXX, 253, 262. *Ibid.,* XXX, 255. MS EdEv to Sarah Everett Hale, 2 Jan 1843 (owned by MHS). *C-ECor,* I, 263. *WestmRev,* XXXIII, 345, 346. **285:** *Ibid.,* XXXIII, 361, 363, 364. *Essays,* London, 1841, p. v. *C-ECor,* I, 351. *Ibid.,* I, 326. MS H. Martineau to RWE, 8 Aug 1841. *C-ECor,* II, 61–62; *CookeBib,* p. 77. MS Chas. Sumner to RWE, 23 Aug 1841. *St-ECor,* pp. 45, 46. C. Fox, *Memories,* ed. Pym, Phila., 1882, p. 140. *Let,* II, 444. *Let,* II, 260, 262. MS RWE to LE, 18 and 19 Mar 1840. *Let,* II, 266. **286:** CKN, *The Journals,* ed. J. K. Johnson, 1946, p. 24. *Let,* II, 266, 272, 419, 421, 434, 439–440, 454, 468. *The Dial,* III, 301. *Ibid.,* III, 297–300, 302, 306–307, 311–313. **287:** *Let,* III, 65. *Let,* III, 11, 13–14, 21. *J,* VI, 163. *PartGree,* pp. 1–91, *passim,* and 158, 166–167. *ThorWr,* VI, 81. **288:** *Let,* III, 15–23, *passim; PartGree,* p. 169. *Let,* III, 18, 19–21, 23. *Let,* III, 23; *WarJa,* pp. 28–41, *passim; PerWJ,* I, 20–21. *Let,* III, 26, 33. Henry James, *A Small Boy,* New York, 1913, p. 8. *Cf.*

Baumgarten, n.d. (1938), *passim;* and see F. I. Carpenter in *NEQ*, II, 458–474. **289:** *Let,* III, 20. *Let,* II, 323–324. *J,* V, 473. *Let,* II, 360–361, 364–365, 368–372, 382, 387, 389, 394. **290:** *Let,* II, especially 394, 402, 403. *J,* VI, 152. *Thor-Wr,* VI, 328–329; for marriage of the Watsons, in 1846, see *Let,* II, 85; for Thoreau's sending a message to Mary in 1842 and his comment that "You must not blame me if I do *talk to the clouds* . . ." see *ThorWr,* VI, 43. *J,* V, 558; VI, 74. *HawAmNbkSt,* p. 166. MS LE to LJB, n.d. (Jan 1842). *HawAmNbkSt,* p. 176. *ThorWr,* VI, 53. *E.g.,* MS LE to LJB, "Tuesday evening" (11 and 12 Jan 1842). *ThorWr,* VI, 76–78, 87–89, 112–113. On the Staten Island letters and on "A Sister," a brief composition left by Thoreau in a manuscript of uncertain date, H. S. Canby (*CanbyThor,* pp. 155–163 *et passim*), has based the theory—to me, entirely unconvincing—of a one-sided love affair on Thoreau's part, lasting, one judges, half a dozen years or more. "A Sister," if taken literally, is a surprisingly erotic outpouring to come from such a born bachelor and almost maidenly moral purist as Thoreau and so deserves comment. But it offers no substantial ground for conjecture as to the identity of the woman addressed, if any real woman was. If a person of flesh and blood has to be found to explain the dreamlike figure that Thoreau created, the Mary Russell who was under the Emerson roof and in the Emerson family circle at the same time with him in 1841 would seem, in the present state of our knowledge, to be the most likely choice (*cf. Let,* II, 402, 403, 420; and VI, index). She was younger than Thoreau (she was born in 1820, according to M. Stockwell, pp. 122 and 264), and he described his sister as older than he. But such a discrepancy was presumably immaterial to him. In a fragment apparently related to "A Sister," he made the significant confession that he always thought of a woman as older than

himself, no matter what her age (*cf. CanbyThor,* p. 163). **291:** MS "Prolegomena of Sketch of Thoreau" (dated 29 June 1862), p. 45. *Let,* III, 41. *HawAmNbkSt,* p. 78. *CEd,* X, 364. *CaryCurt,* p. 19. MS GWC to Cabot, 10 June 1885. *Cf. Let,* III, 99; *J,* VI, 416–417. MS *CKNNbk,* pp. 134–135. MS GR to RWE, 25 Feb 1842; MS GR to RWE, 25 May 1842. *J,* VI, 396, 441–442. **292:** *Let,* III, 203. *Let,* III, 4. *J,* VI, 303. MS *AcctBk40–44,* p. 29. *J,* VI, 303. *J,* VI, 181, 201. *AtlMo,* LXIX, 592–593. *J,* VI, 419. *J,* V, 422–423, 538. *Repub,* 28 May and 4 June 1841. MS *AcctBk40–44,* pp. 45, 71. **293:** MS "Address to the Temperance Society at Harvard, (Mass.) 4 July 1843," pp. 1, 5–6, 32–33. MS j "H," p. 86. MS RWE to CS, 1? Dec? 1840 (owned by HCL); *cf. Let,* II, 360. *CEd,* X, 373–377; *Let,* III, 41. *HawAmNbkSt,* p. 156. *J,* VI, 234–235, 363. MS account books, *passim.* MS *AcctBk40–44,* p. 137. *J,* VI, 497–498; *CabM,* II, 411–412. *Let,* II, 257. **294:** MS *ConFChRecfc* (owned by CFPL), p. 300; *Let,* II, 450–451. *Let,* II, 465; III, 6 ff. *EatH&A,* p. 141. *EinC,* p. 167. Especially *Let,* III, *passim.* *J,* VI, 166. *Thay-Rip,* p. 51. *Let,* III, 68. *Mosses* (*Haw-StanLib,* II), p. 42. *Let,* II, 332, 335. MS RWE to CS, 26 Feb 1841 (owned by HCL); MS *AcctBk40–44,* pp. 35, 37; *Let,* II, 384. *Let,* II, 459, 460; for an early version of the well-known anecdote, see H. Barnes, p. 256. **295:** *J,* VI, 89–91; some months later Emerson told John Sterling the theater was "now so dead" that he wondered why "so many English poets of this time" should choose to write tragedy (MS RWE to Sterling, 15 Aug 1842, owned by NYPL). *Let,* III, 33–38, 98. *Let,* III, 43–44, 54–55 *et passim. Let,* III, *passim. Let,* III, 85. *Let,* III, 29–82, *passim.* MS Very to RWE, 23 Nov 1842 (owned by Wellesley College Library). **296:** *Let,* III, 33–288, *passim;* Emerson's MS notes in his own copy of *The Dial* (owned by HCL), III, IV. *Let,* III, 154, 159–160, 165. MS RWE to SGW, 23 Oct

1843 (owned by HCL). *EarlyCurt*, p. 167. *Let*, III, 40, 88, 107–108, 110 ff., 116. *Let*, III, 112, 114, 125, 128, 131. **297:** *Let*, III, 120–124. *Let*, III, 119 *et passim*, 144, 149, 154–157. *Let*, II, 281; *C-ECor*, I, 285–286. MS LE to LJB, 15 and 22 Mar 1842; *AlcJou*, p. 142. *J*, VI, 173. MS *AcctBk40–44*, pp. 24, 97. *J*, VI, 253. *Alc-Jou*, p. 160. *Ibid.*, pp. 161 ff.; *C-ECor*, II, 7–8, 17–18; *EatH&A*, pp. 317–318; *Pedlar'sP*, pp. 323 ff. *J*, VII, 179. *The Dial*, III, 545–548. **298:** *Let*, III, 88 *et passim*. *AlcJou*, p. 152. *Cf. Let*, III, 221. *J*, VI, 451–453. *J*, VI, 421. *Cf. St-ECor*, p. 78. *Let*, III, 235. *Cf. Pedlar'sP*, pp. 381 ff. *Let*, III, 231–IV, 290, *passim*, and a few later pages; Emerson's MS account books; MS receipts relating to Lane's affairs. *Let*, III, 246–252. *J*, VI, 258 ff.; *HawAmNbkSt*, pp. 170–171. *MemHaw*, p. 53. MS *AcctBk40–44*, pp. 93, 128. *Atl-Mo*, LXIX, 589. *HawStanLib*, II, 224. *Let*, III, 174. *Let*, III, 160 ff., 197, 181. MS *AcctBk40–44*, pp. 138, 146. **299:** *Let*, III, 268 ff. *Let*, III, 254. MS CS to RWE, 23 Aug 1842 (owned by HCL). MS *AuLoLe*, leaf for 1843–1844. MS *Lidian*, p. 175; *cf. Let*, II, 252; MS *AcctBk40–44*, pp. 95 *et ante*. *Let*, II, 413; III, 263 *et passim*. *Let*, III, 257. MS *ConAthRec* (owned by CFPL), pp. 1, 5. *J*, VI, 506. MS *AcctBk40–44*, p. 119 *et passim*. *Let*, III, 256. *J*, VI, 322. MS *AcctBk40–44*, p. 151; MS *Ledger49–72*, p. 60. *Let*, III, 74–75. MS j "R," p. 53. *J*, VI, 360, 403; *Let*, III, 179. *E.g.*, *J*, VI, 293–294. MS C. S. Wheeler to RWE, 11 June 1842. **300:** *Let*, III, 212. *Let*, III, 102, 183. MS "The New Life of Dante Alighieri"; this MS, which I did not discover till after the publication of *Let*, seems too neat to be a first draft, though it shows numerous alterations and its verse (the Englished canzoni) is very rough; I have no proof that Emerson actually copied translations of the canzoni by Ellery Channing. *Let*, III, 183. MS "The New Life," sheet 36. *Let*, III, 397–398. MS RWE to CS, 20 July (presumably 1844; owned by HCL).

Let, III, 214, 264–265. *C-ECor*, II, 69. *CookeBib*, pp. 82–83. *Let*, III, 273. Especially *CEd*, III, 179–182. See above, p. 278. *The Dial*, IV, 93–95. **301:** In Melville's annotated copy of *Essays: Second Series*, Boston, 1844 (owned by HCL), the most significant comments are on pp. 10, 20, 23, 24–25, 31, 32, and 33–34; a general study of Melville's annotations on Emerson's works has been made by Braswell, *AL*, IX, 317 ff. *CEd*, III, 23–24, 37, 125, 247. MS CS to RWE, 29 Aug 1844 (owned by HCL). *CEd*, II, 267. *Let*, III, 9. *CEd*, III, 48. **302:** *J*, VI, 158. *CEd*, III, 50, 55, 65, 72, 75, 82–83. *CEd*, III, 83–84; *PlatoJow*, I, 454. See above, pp. 146, 153; also a note on p. 152. *E.g.*, *Let*, II, 357. MS separate leaf headed "New England Capitalist"; the poem mentions both the telegraph and the phototype. **303:** *Ibid. J*, VI, 338. *EarlyCurt*, p. 193. *J*, VI, 541. *CEd*, III, 200, 205. *Ibid.*, III, 204, 207. **304:** *Ibid.*, III, 209–210, 214, 215–216. *ChildLet*, pp. 44, 56–57. *Let*, III, 269. See above, p. 242. *ChrEx*, XXXVIII, 87–106. *DemRev*, n.s., XVI, 595, 598, 599. *C-ECor*, II, 80–82. **305:** *CEd*, III, 23–24. MS Griswold to RWE, 18 Sept 1841; Bayless, 1943, pp. 37–45, *passim*. Poe, *Complete Works*, ed. Harrison, New York, n.d. (cop. 1902), XV, 260; XVI, index. *C-ECor*, II, 119. *Laz-Let*, p. 48. *Kalendarium*, London, 1706, still among Emerson's books, bears Alcott's inscription to Emerson; for Emerson's reading in the book, see MS RWE to SGW, 17 June 1844 (owned by HCL). **306:** Middlesex South District Registry of Deeds, MS book 454, p. 447 (official t copy in my possession). MS *AcctBk45–49*, p. 5. *Let*, IV, 234; MS *AcctBk45–49*, p. 5. *CabM*, II, 575. *J*, VII, 5. *J*, VII, 4, 26. MS RWE to CS, 1 Feb 1845 (owned by HCL). MS RWE to CS, endorsed Feb 1845 (owned by HCL). *Let*, III, 279, from Cabot's incomplete copy; original MS, endorsed 1845, now owned by HCL. *J*, VII, 7. *Let*, III, 283; *J*, VII, 52, 69. *Let*, III, 288, 290, 303–304. **307:** *Let*, III,

281. MS RWE to Anna B. Ward, 30 Apr 1845 (owned by HCL). *ThorWr*, VII, 361. *Let*, III, 285–286. MS CS to RWE, 10 July 1845 (owned by HCL). MS RWE to Anna B. Ward, 30 Apr 1845 (owned by HCL). MS RWE to CS, 2 Aug 1845 (owned by HCL). *Let*, III, 305. *J*, VII, 50. MS will dated 13 Sept 1845. *Ibid.*, pp. 1–2; *cf. Let*, III, 334. MS will of 13 Sept 1845, paragraph 5 and marginal note dated 5 Nov 1848. *Let*, III, 294–295; *Ire-RWE*, pp. 299–300. **308:** MS RWE to CS, 17 Aug 1845 (owned by HCL); *Let*, III, 294–296; MS *AcctBk45–49*, p. 41. MS *AcctBk45–49*, pp. 17, 45, 46, 47. *Let*, III, 293–294, 298–299, 303–304, 343, 345, 346. *J*, VII, 54, 99. *J*, VII, 87. *CabM*, II, 575–577; *Let*, III, 306. *Let*, III, 306–307. *J*, VII, 115. MS *AcctBk45–49*, p. 55. *J*, VII, 133–135. *Let*, III, 312, 322–323. MS *AcctBk45–49*, p. 61. **309:** *Ibid.*, p. 57. *Let*, III, 287, 288, 296 ff., *passim*, but especially 307–308. *Let*, III, 315–332, *passim; C-ECor*, II, 106–107. *J*, VII, 106. *Let*, III, 306. MS *AcctBk45–49*, p. 49; signatures of Lane are in all volumes of the Sydenham and Taylor edition, and signatures of Emerson are in four. *RWE'sRe*, p. 26. **310:** MS CS to SMF, Thanksgiving Day and 10 Dec 1845, in Fuller MSS, X, 27 (owned by HCL). MS *AcctBk45–49*, pp. 14, 18; *Let*, III, 304, 380; *cf.* p. 262 above. *Let*, III, 326–327, 340. *C-ECor*, II, 115. *J*, V, 562. *Let*, III, 212. MS *AcctBk45–49*, p. 81 (9 Apr 1846); Emerson's autographed copy of *Der Diwan*, 2 vols., Stuttgart and Tübingen, 1812 and 1813 (now owned by HCL), has notes in his hand and contains some loose sheets of his own translations. *J*, VII, 170–171. *Cf.* Yohannan, in *AL*, XIV, 407–420, and XV, 25–41. *Let*, III, 341. *J*, VII, 193, 206. **311:** *ThorWr*, II, 190; *Let*, III, 340. *J*, VII, 223. *AlcJou*, p. 183. *Let*, III, 338. MS *Lidian*, p. 192; *Let*, III, 331 and 415; and IV, 117; MS bill paid to Mrs. Goodwin by Emerson, 27 Aug 1846. *Cf.* MS *EllenEJou*, 25 July 1846. MS *Lidian*, p. 197. *Let*, III, 362, 371 (but *cf.* above, p.

250 and note), 389–390; MS *AcctBk45–49*, p. 107. **312:** *Let*, III, 353 ff. MS "Memorandum of an Agreement," 21 Oct 1846; MS j "E," p. 374. MS "Memorandum of an Agreement," 21 Oct 1846. *Let*, III, 356, 358–359. MS j "E," p. 374; *Let*, III, 366. **313:** HDT, untitled MS about "The Sphinx," p. 13. *ThorWr*, VII, 237 (the printed version of Thoreau's commentary on "The Sphinx," *ibid.*, pp. 229–237, contains both more and less than is to be found in the MS version just cited). MS *VBk"P."* *CEd*, IX, 24. MS *VBk"P."* *CEd*, IX, 412. *Ibid.*, IX, 20–25. **314:** *Ibid.*, IX. **315:** *Ibid.*, IX. **316:** *Ibid.*, IX. *J*, VII, 127–129; *Let*, III, 293. *CEd*, IX. **317:** *Ibid.*, IX. Evidence (unconvincing to me) against the identification of the forest seer as Thoreau is in *CookeRWE*, p. 245, and *SanPer*, p. 70; *cf. CEd*, IX, 420. Wordsworth, *The Prelude*, London, 1850, pp. 122–123; the lines on the boy of Winander had been published as early as 1800. *CEd*, IX. **318:** *Ibid.*, IX. Coleridge, *Biographia Literaria*, Chapter XVII. *CEd*, IX. **319:** *Ibid.*, IX. *ThorWr*, VI, 115. *CEd*, IX. **320:** *CEd*, IX. Dante, "Paradise," ii, 20–21, *The Vision*, tr. Cary, Oxford, 1916. *CEd*, IX. **321:** *Ibid.*, IX. *LongLong*, II, 69. *Let*, III, 364. *J*, VII, 234. MS OWH to RWE, 18 Jan "1846," *i.e.*, 1847 (owned by HCL). MS Greeley to RWE, 26 Jan 1847. **322:** MS MME to RWE, 17 July 1847. MS CS to RWE, 15 no month 1847? or 1846? (endorsed "Lenox 1846"; owned by HCL). *C-ECor*, II, 121–122. *Fuller-Lit&Art*, p. 132. *Let*, III, 366. **323:** *Brownson'sQR*, n.s., I, 276; *cf.* Maynard, pp. 215–216. *LitWorldNY*, I, 197–199; *cf.* MS Mathews to RWE, 8 Apr 1847. *LitWorldNY*, I, 197. *NARev*, LXIV, 402–434. *LowPo*, III, 38. MS *EllenEJou*, 26 Dec 1846, 2 Jan 1847. MS *AcctBk45–49*, pp. 99, 100. **324:** *Let*, III, 381 *et passim. Let*, III, 366–367, 378. *Let*, III, 366–367, 379. *Let*, III, 367, 379–380. *C-ECor*, II, 126–127. *Let*, III, 369–370, 392, 397. *Let*, III, 405–406, 409; *J*, VII, 314–315;

PerTran, pp. 160–163; *CEd*, XI, 381, 393.
325: MS *TreesMinor, passim;* MS *Acct-Bk45–49*, p. 107; *J*, VII, 248; MS *Trees-Major*, pp. 9, 19. MS *TreesMajor*, pp. 32–33. *AlcJou*, pp. 196–197. *Let*, III, 411. *Let*, III, 407, 417–418. **326:** *Let*, III, 409; MS *AcctBk45–49*, p. 121. *Let*, III, 415. *EinC*, p. 156; *SanPer*, p. 8; pictures and numerous accounts by observers. *J*, V, frontispiece; VII, frontispiece. *SanPer*, frontispiece and pp. 8–9; *AlcJou*, p. 485. *Lonely*, frontispiece. MS *NbkEngParis*, p. 61. *AlcJou*, p. 225. MS *T.* Ballantyne to RWE, 3 Dec 1842. MS Samuel Brown to RWE, Portobello, Scotland, 12 July 1843. *AlcJou*, p. 175. **327:** MS Heraud to RWE, 28 Nov 1846; *cf. Let*, III, 363. *Em-CloughLet*, p. v and No. 1. Arnold, *The Strayed Reveller, and Other Poems*, London, 1849, p. 53. *MemMFO*, II, 207. Chazin, in *PMLA*, XLVIII, 147, 160. *Ibid.*, p. 148. Hans Keller, 1932, p. 77. Quinet, *Le Christianisme*, Paris, n.d., pp. 195–196. Chazin, pp. 159–160. **328:** For convenient summaries of facts and authorities relating to Emerson's early vogue in France, see Hans Keller, *passim*, and Chazin, pp. 147–163. Chasles, in *Revue des deux mondes*, n.s., VII, 497–545. *Ibid.*, 498–499. Chazin, p. 162. Hans Keller, pp. 84, 100. SMF, "De la Littérature américaine," in *La Revue indépendante*, 2d ser., 6th year, VI, 341 ff. Daniel Stern (*i.e.*, Comtesse d'Agoult), *ibid.*, 2d ser., 6th year, IV, 195–209, but especially 195–196, 198, 209. **329:** Montégut, in *Revue des deux mondes*, n.s., XIX, 462–493, but especially 466, 468, 470, 480–482, 486, 493. MS *MemBk1820&Misc*, Oct 1847; *IreIn*, p. 79; *Let*, III, 419. **330:** *CEd*, V, 41. MS *Lidian*, p. 199; RHE, MS "Notes," folded sheet sewed into front. *ThorWr*, VI, 133. *CEd*, V, 26, 28. *Let*, III, 420–421; MS *SeaNo1847*, p. 9. *J*, VII, 338–341. **331:** MS *SeaNo1847*, p. 9 *et passim; Let*, III, 421; *CEd*, V, 26, 28, and VI, 68. *J*, VII, 342–343; *CEd*, V, 40, 41. Carlyle, *Latter-day Pamphlets*, London, 1870 (Vol. XIX of *CarlyleCoWks*) . *Let*,

III, 422–423, 452. **332:** *Let*, III, 423, 424. Mrs. William Elder to me, 7 Sept 1948; Laughlin, 2d ed., revised, Boston, 1948, p. 388. *Let*, III, 425–426, 437. MS *NbkEngParis*, pp. 5, 8. **333:** *Let*, III, 437, 439; *PhilEm*, p. 41. MS copy of J. Martineau to A. Ireland, 31 Dec 1882. *AtlMo*, LXIX, 742. *Let*, III, 430–431; *ChronList*, pp. 244–245. *Let*, III, 444. *EatH&A*, p. 321. Smithson to RWE, 2 Nov 1847. Hotson, in *NewChMag*, LII, 52–55. *Let*, III, 444. **334:** *EatH&A*, pp. 321–322. *PhilEm*, p. 39. *EatH&A*, p. 322. *Let, III,* 439. For Cobden's triumphal tour, ending 11 Oct 1847, see John Morley, *The Life of Richard Cobden*, abridged ed., London, etc., n.d., pp. 236–238. *Cf. EspLitRec*, p. 158, mainly about a later banquet. *CEd*, V, 309–311; *Let*, III, 436–437; *Lonely*, pp. 74–86. MS *NbkEng-Paris*, p. 1. *Let*, III, 452–453. **335:** *Let*, III, 442 *et passim; ChronList*, pp. 245–246. *Let*, III, 454, 455. *J*, VII, 361. *Let*, IV, 3. MS J. H. Shaw to RWE, 12 Jan 1848. *Let*, IV, 3–5; *J*, VII, 376. For all the English and Scottish lectures, see *ChronList* and *Let*, III and IV. *Let*, III, 454. *Let*, III, 437, 440, 444, 458; IV, 8, 12. *Let*, IV, 9; MS *NbkEngParis*, p. 16. *AtlMo*, LXIX, 745–746; *cf. Let*, IV, 12. *Let*, III, 451, 455. *Let*, III, 447; V, 219; VI, 312–313. **336:** *J*, VII, 358; *IreRWE*, pp. 165–169. *Let*, III, 451. *PhilEm*, p. 44. A copy of *The Evangel*, London, 1847, is among Emerson's books. *Let*, III, 451. *Let*, IV, 11, 15; *PhilEm*, p. 44. *Lonely*, pp. 92–93. *IreRWE*, p. 164; *Let*, IV, 15. *Let*, III, 447, and IV, 15; *PhilEm*, p. 45. *EspLitRec*, p. 163; *Lonely*, pp. 48–49. *Let*, III, 447. *PhilEm*, p. 42; *Lonely*, p. 90. *IreRWE*, p. 163. *PhilEm*, pp. 41–47. *Ibid.*, p. 41. *EspLitRec*, p. 159. *PhilEm*, pp. 42, 43–45. **337:** *PhilEm*, p. 46; *IreRWE*, p. 164. *PhilEm*, pp. 46, 47. *IreRWE*, pp. 162–163. *Let*, IV, 15. *Let*, IV, 13 ff.; *ChronList*, p. 247. *Let*, IV, 15–16. *Let*, III, 460; IV, 16, 18, 23, 24. **338:** *Let*, IV, 18 ff.; *ChronList*, pp. 247–248. *Let*, IV, 18. MS Wm. Johnston to RWE,

23 Feb 1848. MS Samuel Brown to RWE, 6 Dec 1847; *Let*, III, 449. *J*, VII, 392. *Let*, IV, 18–19. **339:** *Let*, IV, 19–22. **340:** *Let*, IV, 20. *Let*, IV, 19. MS De Quincey to Derwent Coleridge, 21 Feb 1848. *Let*, IV, 25, 26. *CEd*, V, 294. *Let*, IV, 27. *CEd*, V, 298. **341:** *Let*, IV, 27, 29, 32, 33. Jane Carlyle, *New Letters*, ed. Thomas and Alexander Carlyle, London and New York, 1903, I, 244–245. *Post Office London Directory*, 1849, p. 675. For Chapman, his house, and his life, see Haight, *passim*. *J*, VII, 406–407. MS Hugh Whelan to RWE, n.d. (1847 or 1848). *J*, III, 173. **342:** *J*, VII, 403. *Let*, IV, 34, 54. *J*, VII, 402–403, 414. *Let*, IV, 34–35. *J*, VII, 428, 429. *Let*, IV, *passim*. *Let*, IV, 38. MS Milnes to RWE, 15 Jan 1848. MS Milnes to RWE, 20 Jan 1848. *Let*, IV, 42. *Let*, IV, 41–42. **343:** *Let*, IV, 43, 46. *Let*, IV, 42. *Athenæum. Rules and Regulations*, 1847, pp. 7, 12. MS D. Simpson to E. W. Field, 7 Apr 1848. **344:** *Let*, IV, 55. MS Eliza Gillies to RWE, 6 May 1848; *Let*, VI, index. *Letters of Matthew Arnold 1848–1888*, ed. Russell, New York and London, 1895, I, 8. *Let*, IV, 47–49. *Let*, IV, 47–48. **345:** The grace is quoted from MS j "DO," p. 104; *cf. CEd*, V, 200. *Let*, IV, 48; VI, 192. *J*, VII, 428. *Let*, IV, 47, 55. *J*, VII, 434. *LetFriend*, p. 66. *Let*, IV, 55–56; MS *NbkEngParis*, pp. 20 ff.; *J*, VII, 443. *J*, VII, 420, 421, 480; *Let*, IV, 41. For Owen's attending a lecture of Emerson's, and for his wife's preference of Emerson the conversationalist to Emerson the lecturer, whose manner she thought "studiously flat and cold," see R. Owen, *The Life of Richard Owen*, London, 1894, I, 326; for Emerson's visit to the museum, see *ibid.*, I, 327. *J*, VII, 420, 421, 480; *Let*, IV, 41. *Let*, IV, 41–42, 51. *Let*, IV, 42, 87. *Let*, IV, 51. **346:** *Let*, IV, 49–50; *J*, VII, 438–439. MS Henry Crabb Robinson to RWE, 2 May 1848; *Let*, IV, 66. *Let*, IV, 66, 74; *J*, VII, 440–441, 444–449. *Let*, IV, 28. MS *NbkEngParis*, p. 20. *Let*, IV, 72. *EatH&A*, p. 335; *Let*, IV, 16–17; *Ped-*

lar'sP, pp. 321–322. *Let*, IV, 72; *J*, VII, 450, 459; Petit, *Nomenclature des voies*, 5th ed., Paris, 1911, p. 893. *Let*, III, 436, 443, and IV, 3, 72, 519; *Lonely*, p. 109. MS *NbkEngParis*, p. 24. *J*, VII, 470. *CloughP&PR*, I, 131, 133. *Let*, IV, 74. *CloughP&PR*, I, 126. **347:** *Ibid.*, frontispiece and pp. 3–8. *Let*, IV, 72, 74, 519. *Let*, IV, 72. *J*, VII, 560. *J*, VII, 459–460. *J*, VII, 440–441. *JouDéb*, 22 May 1848; Jean-Jacques Ampère had been elected to the academy 22 Apr 1847, according to Franqueville, I (Paris, 1895), 270. MS *NbkEngParis*, pp. 23–25. *Let*, IV, 73, 75, 77. MS "France or Urbanity," 17 Jan 1854, p. 16. *J*, VII, 468. **348:** MS *NbkEngParis*, p. 26. *J*, VII, 455–456. *J*, VII, 452, 454–455. *Let*, IV, 72, 73. MS Lardner to RWE, 12? May? 1848; *Let*, IV, 73. *JouDéb*, 14 May 1848. *Let*, IV, 72, 73; *CloughP&PR*, I, 122; *J*, VII, 464. *J*, VII, 487. *J*, VII, 456. *CloughP&PR*, I, 131. **349:** *Let*, IV, 72, 73. MS LE to RWE, 4 June 1848. *CloughP&PR*, I, 125. *Let*, IV, 76, 77. *Let*, IV, 67, 73. *Let*, IV, 77; *J*, VII, 469–470. *Let*, IV, 73. **350:** *Let*, IV, 75. *Let*, IV, 78; *J*, VII, 451. *J*, VII, 485. *Let*, IV, 78. *CloughP&PR*, I, 127. *Let*, III, 395. *J*, VII, 464. *J*, VII, 415. *Let*, IV, 80. *MemMFO*, II, 233; *Wade*, p. 227. *Let*, IV, 78, 80. *J*, VII, 495–496; *Let*, IV, 80. **351:** *IreRWE*, p. 55; *EatH&A*, p. 329. *Let*, IV, 79, 80. *Let*, IV, 75–76, 79. *Let*, IV, 50–51. *IreIn*, p. 82. *Let*, IV, 55, 65. *EspLitRec*, p. 162. MS Forster No. 193, Victoria and Albert Museum (partly printed by Scudder in *AL*, VIII, 26). *Let*, IV, 80. MS *NbkEngParis*, p. 23. *Let*, IV, 80. MS "Natural History of Intellect," I (1848 version), p. 35. **352:** *Ibid.*, pp. 39, 59, 66, 68. *IreRWE*, pp. 169–170. *IreRWE*, pp. 171–175; *Let*, IV, 86. *IreRWE*, pp. 175–176. *Ibid.*, p. 171. *CookeRWE*, pp. 115–116. *IreRWE*, p. 55. **353:** *Let*, IV, 85. *Let*, IV, 84. A. Ireland in *The Manchester Guardian*, 3 Dec 1889. *J*, VII, 478. *EspLitRec*, pp. 163–164. *Let*, IV, 84. *EspLitRec*, p. 163. MS j "LN," p. 185; *Let*, IV, 86, 94. *Let*, IV, 85, 86, 89. *Esp-*

LitRec, p. 162. *Let*, IV, 84. **354:** MS F. B. Barton to RWE, 2 June 1848; *Let*, IV, 84, 103. *Let*, IV, 84, 86–87, 103. *Let*, IV, 87. *Let*, IV, 84, 87. MS W. M. Rossetti to Conway, 9 June 1882 (owned by CUL) ; *cf. EatH&A*, pp. 334–335. *Let*, IV, 84, 94. *EatH&A*, p. 325; *J*, VII, 485–486. *Let*, IV, 103. **355:** *Let*, IV, 92–94. *Let*, IV, 97; *J*, VII, 490–492. *CEd*, V, 273–276. MS *NbkEngParis*, p. 48 (upside down). *CEd*, V, 277. *Let*, III, 460. *PhilEm*, p. 47. *J*, VII, 441, 442. Mary Ann Evans to Sara Hennell, Dec 1848, in *CrossEliot*, I, 193. *CEd*, V, 279. **356:** *Ibid.*, V, 280–283, 284. *Ibid.*, V, 285–287; *Let*, IV, 93, 94, 97. *CEd*, V, 288. *Let*, IV, 97–99. Bray, *Phases*, n.d., p. 72; *Let*, IV, 98–99; *EatH&A*, pp. 337–338; *The Cornhill*, n.s., XX, 225–236. *CrossEliot*, I, 191; *EatH&A*, p. 339. *EatH&A*, pp. 337–340; Bray, *Phases*, p. 72; *Let*, IV, 98, 139. *CrossEliot*, II, 270. *AmberleyPa*, II, 68. **357:** *IreIn*, p. 18. *Let*, IV, 99, 101. *HaleLowFr*, pp. 136–137; *Let*, IV, 99. *CloughP&PR*, I, 133. *Let*, V, 361; *cf.* p. 344 above. Kingsley, *Alton Locke*, New York, 1850, pp. 196–197 (in Chapter XXII, "An Emersonian Sermon"). *Alton Locke*, p. 342. **358:** MS MME to LE, 23? Jan ? 1848. *Let*, IV, 101. *J*, VII, 494. *Let*, IV, 101–102. See pp. 218–219 above. MS *Lidian*, p. 199. *AtlMo*, LXIX, 746–747. *Let*, IV, 28, 32, 33, 54. *Cf.* LE to RWE, 6 Mar 1848 (t in possession of EWF). **359:** *EspLitRec*, p. 159. *Let*, IV, 101. *EatH&A*, p. 337. **360:** *The Bhagavad-gita*, Chicago, n.d. (cop. 1929), p. 28. MS CKN to SMF, 23 Jan 1849, in Fuller MSS, X, 148 (owned by HCL). MS *Chan2Nbk-57–64* (owned by HCL), final leaf. **361:** MS *Ledger49–72*, pp. 60–61. MS *AcctBk-49–53*, pp. 156, 193. *J*, VIII, 31–32, 47–48. MS EEF to Elizabeth Cabot? July? 1886? MS *AcctBk49–53*, p. 161. MS *AcctBk53-59*, Oct 1855. Sarah Hosmer Lunt, as reported in *Somerville Journal*, 11 Aug 1911; Swayne, pp. 217–218; broadside describing the Concord grape, dated Mar 1859 (copy owned by CFPL). MS ac-

count books, *passim*, especially entries of 1847–1850. MS *AcctBk45–49*, p. 138. *E.g.*, MS *AcctBk49–53*, p. 43. MS account books *passim;* MS *Lidian*. p. 205. MS *Lidian*, p. 200; *cf. Let*, III, 432. **362:** MS *Acct-Bk49–53*, p. 220. MS "Entries of Neat Stock and Swine at the Cattle Show in Concord" for 1842 ff. (owned by CFPL), entry of 1854. MS account books, *passim; Let*, IV, *passim. Let*, IV, 215. MS *AcctBk49–53*, pp. 155, 186, 197. MS account books, *passim; Let*, IV, 350 *et passim;* V, 250, 264; *J*, VIII, 580–581. *Let*, IV, 109–110; MS *AcctBk45–49*, p. 42. MS account books, *passim*. MS *AcctBk49–53*, p. 240. See p. 360 above. **363:** MS *EEF-ChMem*. MS EWE to EllenE, 27 June 1853. *Let*, IV, 362–468, *passim*. DGH, p. 106. MS *AcctBk49–53*, p. 223. MS LE to RWE, "No 2," spring of 1848. MS LE to EllenE, 28 June 1853. *Let*, IV, 289. DGH, pp. 104–105. *Let*, IV, 252–253. *Clough-P&PR*, I, 183. *Let*, IV, 403. **364:** *Let*, IV, 401. *Let*, IV, 384, 388; *J*, VIII, 398 ff. *E.g.*, MS MME to LE, 6 Apr 1849. *Let*, IV, 452. MS MME to ElizH, 29 Sept 1849. *Cf. Let*, III, 456–457. *E.g.*, *Let*, IV, 57; V, 317, 367–368. *Let*, IV, 140, 141–142, 146, 234, 291–292, 366. *J*, VII, 498. *Let*, IV, 145, 151. *J*, VIII, 303. *J*, VIII, 228. **365:** *Let*, IV, 512. *J*, VII, 552. *J*, VIII, 362–363. *J*, VIII, 303. *AlcJou*, pp. 211–212, 269, 274. *Ibid.*, p. 258. *J*, VIII, 93–94, 96. *AlcJou*, p. 270. *Let*, IV, 511 *et passim*, and V, 159–160; MS F. Beck to RWE, 30 June 1855. *J*, VII, 506. For long walks, see especially *J*, VIII, *passim. Let*, IV, 389. *J*, VIII, 10. *EarlySClub*, pp. 7 ff. *Cf.* MS RWE and others to "Sir," 12 Mar 1850 (owned by Trustees of the Longfellow House in Cambridge, Mass.) . *Let*, IV, 146. *EarlySClub*, pp. 6–7. *AlcJou*, p. 223. MS *AcctBk49–53*, p. 108. MS *Chan-2Nbk57–64* (owned by HCL), last leaf. **366:** H. James, Sr., *The Literary Remains*, ed. Wm. James, Boston and New York, n.d. (cop. 1884), pp. 293–294. *J*, VII, 547–548; VIII, 99–100, 111. MS *Lidian*, p. 205. MS RWE to Edmund Quin-

cy, 16 Sept 1850 (owned by CUL). *Let,*
IV, 229. *The Liberty Bell,* 1851, pp. 78–
81, 156–157; cf. *AmLitAn,* pp. 83, 89.
WhittStanLib, IV, 62–63. *J,* VIII, 182,
198. **367:** *J,* VIII, 202. *CEd,* XI, 210–
214. *Ibid.,* XI, 206. *Ibid.,* XI, 179, 184,
204, 208, 209. *Let,* IV, 250; MS *AcctBk-
49–53,* p. 60. *The Liberator,* 23 May 1851;
MS J. B. Thayer to Cabot, 5 Dec 1886.
J, VIII, 236. MS *AcctBk49–53,* p. 157.
Let, IV, 265. **368:** MS *ConToRec,* IX,
election of 10 Nov 1851 and 2d trial;
ECitCon, p. 378. MS Philadelphia Anti-
Slavery Society's committee to RWE, 31
Dec 1851; MS Lucretia Mott and others
to RWE, 25 Nov 1852. MS Phillips to
RWE, 24 Mar 1852. MS *AcctBk49–53,* p.
203. MS *Lidian,* p. 207E; *CEd,* XI, 395–
401. MS *Lidian,* p. 207F. *J,* VIII, 316,
335. MS J. T. Fisher to RWE, 19 Nov
1852. MS Lucretia Mott and others to
RWE, 25 Nov 1852. **369:** *Let,* IV, 302,
343. *CloughP&PR,* I, 190. *J,* VIII, 442–
443. *CEd,* XI, especially 217, 235, 244. MS
AcctBk53–59, 21 June 1854. MS *Lidian,*
pp. 216–217. Haynes, *Charles Sumner,*
Phila., n.d. (cop. 1909), pp. 180–181. MS
FraJouEx, 27 Jan 1855. *RecLiLong,* p.
106. **370:** *Let,* IV, 230, 260–261, 345–
346. *Let,* IV, 230. *CEd,* XI, especially 423–
426. MS Watson G. Haynes to RWE, 19
Mar 1850. *J,* VIII, 351. For articles signed
by Marx, see, *e.g., New-York Weekly
Tribune,* 4 and 11 Sept 1852, and *New-
York Daily Tribune,* 25 Nov and 22 Dec
1852. **371:** *CEd,* IX, 357. DGH, pp.
103–104, 106. *J,* VIII, 69, 530. *Let,* IV,
248 *et passim,* especially 350–351. *J,* VIII,
113–114, 416. *Let,* IV, 194. *J,* VIII, 163,
455; some five years later, when the first
series of *Idylls of the King* was published,
Emerson commented, "What benefits still
come to us from the old island! . . ."
(MS RWE to Eliza T. Clapp, 10 Aug
1859, owned by LC). *LongLong,* II, 151.
372: *Ibid.,* II, 294–295. *Whitman1855-
Fac,* editor's introd., pp. v, viii, xii. MS
RWE to Ward, 10 July 1855 (owned by
HCL). *Whitman1855Fac,* pp. 13, 15, 26,

45. *Ibid.,* pp. 29, 39, 54. **373:** RWE to
Whitman, 21 July 1855, an incomplete
facsimile reproduction of the original,
The Bookman, New York, VI, 435 (Jan
1898). *NortonLet,* I, 135. *Let,* IV, 531.
RecLiLong, p. 107. For Emerson's later
relations with Whitman, see below, *passim,* and, *e.g., Let,* IV, 520–521, and *The
Shock,* ed. Edmund Wilson, Garden City,
1943, pp. 244–295. *Let,* IV, 520–521. MS
RWE to S. Longfellow, 24 Oct 1855
(owned by Trustees of the Longfellow
House, Cambridge, Mass.). *Whitman1855-
Fac,* opposite p. xvi of editor's introduction. *PerryWhit,* opposite p. 114. *Let,* IV,
521. **374:** *ConwayAut,* I, 215–216. *Eat-
H&A,* p. 360. MS *MemBk1855,* 11 Dec
1855; MS WmE (b) to RWE, 5 Dec 1855
(owned by DrHE); MS WmE (b) to
RWE, 11? Dec? 1855 (owned by DrHE).
CarpDays, pp. 166–167. Trowbridge, p.
367. *J,* VIII, 48; *Let,* IV, 158. *CookeBib,*
p. 81. *Let,* IV, 149, 153. MS *AcctBk49–
53,* p. 55. *Let,* IV, 174. *CEd,* IV, 8, 27–30.
375: *Ibid.,* IV, pp. 23, 49, 51, 52, 54, 58.
Ibid., IV, pp. 40, 61, 62. *Ibid.,* IV, 58, 76,
78. For a key to the not very important
use Emerson made of the new Bohn version of Plato, see *CEd,* IV, 80–89. The
history of his use of various translations
—the Dacier, Sydenham and Taylor,
Cousin, Bohn, and Jowett versions—can
be traced through the index to *Let* (Vol.
VI). In 1861 Emerson confirmed and
added to his early impressions. The Dacier version he knew in his youth was "a
translation of a translation." Sydenham
and Taylor, "which I knew best, is not
yet English, but very Greekish & pedan-
tic," he said. Cousin's French version was,
as he put it, "elegant, &, I believe, faithful." He "found or fancied Bohn's translators great benefactors," and their work
was in "good English" and had a "tone
of sense & culture." But the truth was
that he made no pretense to exact scholarship in such matters. Of the Bohn version he confessed characteristically: "I
have not, to be sure, looked into the book

to criticize, or even to compare, but only for Plato." (MS RWE to WmE[n], 29 Mar 1861, owned by Scripps College Library.) *CEd,* IV, 97–98, 106, 121. *J,* IX, 579. **376:** *CEd,* IV, 162, 164. *Cf.* C. L. Young, New York, 1941, pp. 16–51. *CEd,* IV, 170 ff., 183, 191 ff. Carlyle, *On Heroes (CarlyleCoWks,* XII), p. 131. *CEd,* IV, pp. 217, 219, 224–225, 257, 258. **377:** *Ibid.,* IV, 270, 280, 284, 285, 287, 289. *J,* VIII, 88. *Let,* IV, 175. *The Eclectic Review,* n.s., III, 568–582. *C-ECor,* II, 187–189. Montégut, in *Revue des deux mondes,* new period, VII, especially 722 (15 Aug 1850), 725–726, 728–729. **378:** *MemMFo,* I, 217. *Let,* IV, 198–199. *Let,* IV, 219–221; MS *AcctBk49–53,* p. 40. MS "Ossoli," p. 1. MS *Lidian,* p. 215b. *J,* VIII, 250. *Let,* IV, 222, 225, 228 *et passim;* MS RWE to CS, 9 Oct 1850 (owned by HCL). *Let,* IV, 222. MS "Ossoli," p. 273. *Let,* IV, 257, 310; *C-ECor,* II, 209. **379:** *Cf. Let,* IV, 257–258, 281, 384. *Let,* IV, 281, 384. MS *MemBk1848,* 22 Nov–27 Dec 1848. *Let,* IV, 125–126, 178. **380:** *Let,* IV, 183, 193. MS *AcctBk49–53,* p. 72. *Let,* IV, 224. *Let,* IV, 201, 207. *Let,* IV, 203, 204–205, 207. **381:** *Let,* IV, 211–214. *Let,* IV, 209–210. **382:** *Let,* IV, 210–211, 214, 216–217. MS *AcctBk49–53,* pp. 34, 91, 293. *Let,* IV, 242–244, 245–246, 270. **383:** *Let,* IV, 267–268, 272–273, 290–291. *J,* VIII, 283–286. *Let,* IV, 291. *Let,* IV, 314 ff.; *cf.* MS *AcctBk49–53,* p. 294. *Let,* IV, 330, 336–337, 338. *Let,* IV, 336, 342. **384:** *Let,* IV, 342, 343. MS *AcctBk49–53,* p. 198. MS now labeled "Anglo-American" and dated Jan 1853 (pagination irregular). *Let,* IV, *passim. Let,* IV, 397. MS *MemBk1854,* Jan–Feb, *passim; Let,* IV, 423 ff. **385:** *C-ECor,* II, 233–234. MS HDT and others to RWE, 30 Mar 1854. MS *ConLyRecBk28–59* (owned by CFPL), 5 and 12 Apr 1854. *Let,* IV, 455, 456, 460. MS, dictated, Edw. Atkinson to J. B. Thayer, 3 May 1882; Theo. C. Smith, New Haven, 1925, I, 76; R. G. Caldwell, New York, 1931, p. 33. *Let,* IV, 484–485, 524. *CEd,* XI, 427–436;

Let, IV, 530. *Let,* IV, 473 ff., especially 491–492, 540. **386:** *J,* VIII, 585. *EatH&A,* pp. 178–179. Parker, *The American Scholar,* ed. G. W. Cooke, Boston, n.d. (cop. 1907), p. 121. *Ibid.,* pp. 62, 63, 69, 70, 80–83, 84, 93. *Ibid.,* pp. 87, 94, 96, 97, 124. *Ibid.,* p. 121. **387:** *Let,* IV, 176, 177. *J,* VIII, 318 *et passim; Let,* IV, 271, 272, 306, 312. *Let,* IV, 295 *et passim. EatH&A,* pp. 6–7 *et passim; ConwayAut,* I, 134–138 *et passim; Let,* IV, 438, and V and VI, *passim; SanRec,* I–II, *passim. CloughP&PR,* I, 199, 207. *HawStanLib,* III, 495. **388:** *CEd,* IX, 76, 78. **389:** *Let,* IV, 249–250, 347, 536. MS OWH to RWE, 26 Mar 1856 (owned by HCL). *CEd,* XI, 251. *Ibid.,* XI, 247. *Let,* V, 23. **390:** *Let,* V, 23. MS EllenE to RWE, 17 Jan 1857. MS *AcctBk53–59,* 6 Sept 1856. *J,* IX, 51. *CEd,* XI, 255, 256, 258 ff. *Let,* V, 46; MS EllenE to "Dear Addy," 8 Sept 1856. MS Garrison to RWE, 20 Nov 1856; Sanborn in *NEMag,* n.s., XV, 453, 466. *Let,* V, 4, 6. *J,* IX, 7. **391:** *Let,* V, 7. *Let,* V, 4, 9. *Let,* V, 15, 23; MS *AcctBk53–59,* 5 May 1856. MS j "T Transcript," p. 93; MS OWH to RWE, 4 Apr 1856 (owned by HCL). *EarlySClub,* pp. 124–127. *Let,* VI, 126. MS *AcctBk53–59,* 9 May 1856; MS *Ledger49–72,* p. 150. *Let,* V, 3–4. MS *MemBk1856,* 26 Sept 1856 (but concerns Feb). *Poems,* Boston, 5th ed., 1856 (Lidian's copy is among Emerson's books). MS EdithE to EWE, 13 Aug 1856. **392:** MS *AcctBk53–59,* 17 Oct 1856; *Let,* IV, 528. MS *AcctBk53–59,* 19, 22, 23 Oct 1856, and 1856, *passim. EarlySClub,* pp. 21–127. *Cf. Let,* V, 23; later, Edith attended Agassiz's school (*Let,* V, 121 *et passim). EarlySClub,* pp. 19 *et passim. J,* IX, 33. *Em-CloughLet,* No. 29. **393:** *Let,* V, 87 (RWE to CST, 13 Oct 1857); a longer MS version, also unsigned, and endorsed by Emerson "Unsent," has now come to light (owned by HCL) but, except for length, does not differ significantly from the version in *Let. Grimm-RWECor,* pp. 16, 17, 74, 75, 76, 77; for the early vogue of Emerson in Germany, see also Julius

Simon, pp. 108–112. *Let,* V, 157–158. In some of the gift copies from Grimm still among Emerson's books there are numerous uncut leaves. *Essays von Herman Grimm,* Hannover, 1859. MS *AcctBk53-59,* 18 July 1859; also later MS account books. *C-ECor,* II, 219. *Let,* IV, 533; V, 29, 30. *C-ECor,* II, 261–262. **394:** *Let,* V, 30. *Em-CloughLet,* No. 29. *Let,* V, 33. *CEd,* V, 146. *Ibid.,* V, 60, 84, 125. *Ibid.,* V, 124. *Ibid.,* V, 105. *Ibid.,* V, 102, 112, 155–166. **395:** *Ibid.,* V, 82–83, *e.g.,* 248–249. *Ibid.,* V, 98, 230. *Ibid.,* V, 220–221, 227. *C-ECor,* II, 262. *CEd,* V, 172, 299, 304. *Let,* V, 34, 52, 56, 59, 63. MS EdithE to "Dear Lizzy," 30 May 1857. *Cf.* MS *AcctBk59-65,* p. 115. *Cf. Let,* V, 31–34, 132–133. MS *Lidian,* p. 236. *Ibid.,* p. 220; for repairing the house, *cf. Let,* V, 74 *et passim.* **396:** MS EWF to me, 4 Dec 1947, in my possession. *Cf. Let,* V, 23–24; *J,* IX, 54–55. MS *IslandBk,* II, 18 Aug 1857 (at Naushon). The best-known account of Naushon Island was written by Holmes about the time when Emerson's visits began (*HolStanLib,* I, 39–41, in *The Autocrat*). *J,* IX, 15, 34. MS RWE to CST, 13 Oct 1857 (owned by HCL); *J,* IX, 110, 274. *AlcJou,* pp. 300–301; *Let,* V, 76. *Let,* V, 79. *AlcJou,* p. 301. t EllenE to WmE(n), 17 Nov 1857; *AlcJou,* p. 307. *Cf.* Christy, pp. 164 ff. **397:** MS EllenE to HavenE, 3 Dec 1858. MS *Acct-Bk53-59,* 27 Dec 1858; also later MS accounts. *J,* IX, 117. *J,* IX, 81. *J,* IX, 81–83; *ThorWr,* VI, 358; *SanRec,* I, 104–110. *Let,* V, 69; MS cited there is now in AbLib. MS Burritt to RWE, 21 May 1857; *cf.* Curti, New York, 1937, pp. 120, 133. Broadside *Fourth of July Breakfast; CEd,* IX, 199–200. *Let,* V, 95–97; MS *MemBk1857,* MS *MemBk1858. Let,* V, 101. MS *FraJouEx,* 10 Apr 1858. MS *Acct-Bk53-59,* 22 Apr 1858. MS EllenE to HavenE, 7 and 11 May 1858; *Let,* V, *passim; J,* IX, 154. Both Rowse's sketch and his finished crayon portrait are reproduced in *NEMag,* n.s., XV, 456–457. The finished portrait appears as frontispiece

in *C-ECor,* II, and in *CabM,* II; in both books it is dated 1857, not 1858. MS Louisa F. Dewey to MME, 15 Mar 1858. **398:** *Let,* V, 111–112; *J,* VIII, 580; MS j "Δ," p. 65. *Let,* V, 114. MS *IslandBk,* II, 2 Sept 1858; *Let,* V, 118–119. MS *Acct-Bk53-59,* 18 Aug 1858. *EarlySClub,* pp. 169 ff. *CEd,* IX, 182–183, 186. **399:** *Ibid.,* IX, 463–464. *Let,* V, 117–118. *CEd,* VII, *e.g.,* 153–154. MS *FraJouEx,* 2 Oct 1858. MS *AcctBk53-59,* program pasted inside front cover. *AlcJou,* p. 310; MS EllenE to Annie Fields, 12 Feb 1884 (owned by Huntington Library). *Let,* V, 122, 124. *Let,* V, 125–126, 325; *J,* IX, 508. MS Lucretia Mott to Martha Wright, 26 and 27 Dec 1858 (owned by Friends Historical Library of Swarthmore College); Frederick Tolles has used this letter in *AL,* X, 157. *Let,* V, 128. **400:** MS *Ledger-49-72,* p. 145. *Let,* V, 130–133. *CEd,* XI, 437–443. *Let,* V, 142. *Let,* V, 139; MS RWE to H. Woodman, 24 May 1859 (owned by MHS). *J,* IX, 181, 183. t EllenE to EdithE, 22 Apr 1859. *Let,* V, 148–152. *E.g., Let,* V, 137, 138, 231. *Early-SClub,* pp. 200–202. *Ibid.,* pp. 203–205; *J,* IX, 226–229. *Let,* V, 139. *CEd,* VII, 243, 245, 246. **401:** *Ibid.,* VII, 250. *Let,* V, 152–153. *Let,* V, 166; Emerson paid assessments to the Adirondack Club as late as 1862 (MS *AcctBk59-65,* 31 May 1862); MS SGW to RWE, 28 Mar 1876, inclosed Emerson's share of the funds of the club, which had then practically ceased to exist. *Let,* V, 168. *Let,* V, 161. MS RWE to CST, 7? July? 1859? (owned by HCL). MS RWE to SGW, 9 July 1859 (owned by HCL). *J,* IX, 223; *Let,* V, 171. *Let,* V, 174. *Let,* I, 287, 288. *AlcJou,* pp. 315–316; *SanRec,* I, 163 *et passim. Let,* V, 178, 179–180. **402:** *Let,* V, 179, 193–194, 210. *NYDaTrib,* 14 Nov 1859. *Canby-Thor,* p. 390. *Let,* V, 182 *et passim. CEd,* XI, 269. *NYDaTrib,* 12 Nov 1859. *Alc-Jou,* pp. 322–323. *HawStanLib,* XII, 327. *Let,* V, 190–203. **403:** *Let,* V, 196, 199. *Let,* V, 197, 206–207. *Let,* V, 195. *Specimen,* p. 191; *cf. PerryWhit,* p. 127. *Leaves* of *Grass*, 1860–61, pp. 287–314. *Let*, V, 214–216. **404:** *Ibid.*, V, 215. MS *Mem-Bk1860*, 18 Mar 1860; *CabM*, II, 769. *Let*, V, 72 *et passim*. *Let*, V, 220–221; *CEd*, XI, 283–293. MS "Domestic Life" (owned by CUL). *Let*, V, 221. *J*, IX, 273. *LMAedCheney*, p. 122. *AlcJou*, p. 328; *cf. Let*, V, 222. *LowLet*, I, 305; *HowLitFrAc*, p. 67. *Ibid.*, p. 60. **405:** *Ibid.*, pp. 60–64. t EllenE to "Dear Alice," 24 Oct 1860. Broadside *Wide-awake!!* (copy owned by CFPL). *AlcJou*, p. 330. *J*, IX, 286. *Let*, V, 233; MS *Ledger49–72*, p. 32. *Let*, V, 233; *NortonLet*, I, 215. **406:** *C-ECor*, II, 275–276. *AlcJou*, pp. 330–331. *C-ECor*, II, 275. MS *AcctBk59–65*, p. 82; *Let*, V, 177–178. *CEd*, VI, 3, 201. *Ibid.*, VI, 7, 8. *Ibid.*, VI, 5, 53 ff., 101, 105, 126. **407:** *Ibid.*, VI, 213, 290. *Ibid.*, VI, 4, 165–166, 258. *Ibid.*, VI, *e.g.*, 134. *Ibid.*, VI, 28, 49. **408:** *Henry V*, III, i, 5–6, text of *The Dramatic Works of William Shakespeare*, ed. Samuel Johnson, G. Steevens, and others, rev. by Isaac Reed, New York, 1821, VI, 41. *J*, IX, 366. *J*, IX, 362. *Let*, V, 236–238; MS *MemBk1861*. **409:** *The Liberator*, 1 Feb 1861, p. 18; I have capitalized the first word of each quoted phrase. *J*, IX, 305. t EdithE to EllenE, 14 Jan 1861. *Let*, V, *e.g.*, 240, 256. *Let*, V, 243; MS EllenE to EdithE, 6, 8, and 9 Apr 1861. Leaflet *Exhibition of the Schools of Concord . . . March 16th, 1861*. *J*, IX, 315. Lincoln, *Complete Works*, ed. Nicolay and Hay, New York, n.d. (cop. 1905), VI, 103–168 *passim*, 169–185 *passim*. **410:** *CEd*, XI, 166–169. *Em-CloughLet*, No. 32. Copies of the two handbills dated 17 Apr 1861 and of the one dated 22 Apr 1861 are owned by CFPL. *Let*, V, 246, 247. **411:** MS *Life&Lit*, I, 9; III, 1. *Let*, V, 247. MS *Life&Lit*, III, 59, 78, 97, 124, 135, 160. MS EllenE to EdithE, 9 May 1861. MS EllenE to EdithE, 10 May 1861. *CabM*, II, 601. *ThorWr*, VI, 383–384; MS EllenE to EdithE, 10 May 1861. MS *Ledger49–72*, p. 140. *Let*, V, 250, 256–257. **412:** MS *AcctBk59–65*, p. 98. *J*, IX, 330. *Grimm-RWECor*, pp.

61–62. *Let*, V, 249. *Em-CloughLet*, No. 33. MS Emily M. Drury to RWE, 19 Aug 1861. t EllenE to WmE (n), 29 and 31 July 1861. *Let*, V, 253. MS j "War & Politics & Washington City," p. 4. MS EllenE to EWE, 2 Aug 1861; MS EdithE to EWE, 2 Aug 1861; MS EdithE to EWE, 4 and 5 Aug 1861. MS EdithE to EWE, 20 and 23? Sept 1861. **413:** MS *AcctBk59–65*, p. 116. *E.g., J*, IX, 320. MS EdEv to RWE, 23 Sept 1861; MS EllenE to EWE, 27 Sept 1861. Concord Soldiers Aid Society, MS list of members (owned by CFPL). MS EllenE to EWE, 19 Oct 1861. *Let*, V, 257, 263–264. MS *MemBk1861*, 12 Nov 1861. MS "American Nationality," 12 Nov 1861, pp. 39, 69, 108, 111–112. *MatherHaw*, p. 317. *Let*, V, 259. *AlcJou*, pp. 342–343. *J*, IX, 361. *Let*, V, 260. *Let*, V, 257. MS WmE (b) to RWE, 24 Nov 1861 (owned by DrHE). **414:** *Let*, V, 249. *Let*, V, 258, 263. *Let*, V, 265; *J*, IX, 372–374; evidence as to whether Lincoln heard this lecture is either unconvincing or negative. *J*, IX, 375–394. *J*, IX, 393. *J*, IX, 375. *HawStanLib*, XII, 309. *J*, IX, 375–376. **415:** *J*, IX, 375, 385–386, 387–388. Bush was pretty obviously a familiar name for the Emerson home by early 1863 (*cf.* MS EdithE to RWE, 7 and 13 Jan 1863). *Let*, V, 279, 289–290. MS *Lidian*, p. 246c; MS *AcctBk59–65*, p. 166. MS j "VA," p. 156. MS *AcctBk59–65*, p. 130. MS EllenE to EWE, 11 and 17 June 1862. MS EWE to EdithE, 9 and 11 Feb 1862. t excerpts by EWF from EdithE to EWE, 26 Mar 1863. MS EllenE to EWE, 11 and 17 June 1862. *J*, IX, 401, 413. *Let*, V, 272. **416:** *AlcJou*, pp. 347–348. *ChanThor*, pp. 350–351. *J*, IX, 430. MS "Prolegomena of Sketch of Thoreau" dated 29 June 1862; *CabM*, II, 787–788. *Let*, V, 413, 423–424. MS EdithE to EWE, 12? and 13? June 1862. MS j "War & Politics & Washington City," p. 194. *J*, IX, 434, 442. **417:** *CEd*, XI, 317. *Cf. Let*, V, 290. *CEd*, XI, 320–321. *J*, IX, 457. Lincoln, *Complete Works*, ed. Nicolay and Hay, New York, n.d. (cop. 1905),

VIII, 16. *Let,* V, 271–290, *passim.* MS *EWESocCirMemLi,* p. 2. *Let,* V, 271–290, *passim. Let,* V, 290, 290–291. MS *Lidian,* pp. 243–244. **418:** t EllenE to EdithE, 24 Jan 1859. *Let,* V, 301. *CEd,* IX, 204. MS Higginson to RWE, 7 Jan 1864, quoting an entry of 9 Feb 1863 in the diary of his surgeon. *Let,* V, 320. *Let,* V, 300–312; MS Edward W. Russell to RWE, 30 Dec 1862. **419:** *Let,* V, 304; MS "Concord Atheneum" (a record book, owned by CFPL), p. 1; *MemMemSocCir,* 3d ser., p. 146. *Let,* V, 308–311. *Let,* V, 310, 311, 313. *J,* IX, 492–494. MS *AcctBk59–65,* p. 198. *J,* IX, 499, 556, 557. **420:** *Let,* V, 322. *Let,* V, 319–325. *J,* IX, 501. *Let,* V, 325–326, 329–331. *Cf. J,* IX, 511–518. MS *Waterville1863,* pp. 86–87. MS j "DL," p. 99. MS *Waterville1863,* pp. 87–88. MS "West Point" (a single leaf). **421:** *BarrusLiBur,* I, 63. MS Burroughs to Cabot, 29 Mar 1883; *BarrusLiBur,* I, 63, 72–73. *Let,* V, 329. *J,* IX, 525–526 and 528; *Let,* V, 334–335. MS *Waterville1863,* pp. 191–192. *J,* IX, 552. *J,* IX, 532, 555. **422:** *Let,* V, 336. *CEd,* IX, 205, 207. MS Hallowell to RWE, 29 Oct 1863; Hallowell was colonel of the Fifty-fourth Regiment Infantry, Massachusetts Volunteers, as successor to Robert Gould Shaw, who had been killed while leading his Negro troops (*Record of the Massachusetts Volunteers. 1861–1865,* II [1870], 846); *cf. Let,* V, 318, 320, 336. *J,* IX, 541. *J,* IX, 522; *Let,* V, 336, 339, 344. **423:** MS "Fortune of the Republic" (Dec 1863), pp. 31–171, *passim.* MS memorandum books, Dec 1863, and 1864, *passim. Let,* V, *passim.* MS Sumner to RWE, 11 Nov 1863; *EarlySClub,* p. 288, however, gives the year of Sumner's election as 1862. *Let,* V, 302–303. RWE to Chase, 10 Jan 1863, printed by Carlos Baker in *The Princeton University Library Chronicle,* VII, 108. *Let,* V, 302; *PerryWhit,* p. 153. *Let,* V, 354. MS *ConToRec,* IX, 288. MS RWE to Bancroft, 28 Sept 1863 (owned by MHS). MS *TreesMajor,* p. 96. *J,* X, 43. **424:** *Let,* V, 355–375, *passim.* MS, con-

sisting of two separate parts–a single folded sheet, "Shakspeare," and an untitled group of about a dozen unsewed leaves. *CabM,* II, 621–622. MS j "ML," p. 196. *J,* X, 39, 40. *J,* IX, 503. *AlcJou,* p. 306 *et passim.* MS EdithE to RWE, 29 Jan and 5 Feb 1865. **425:** *J,* X, 56. MS "Alcott Fund," giving a "Statement of monies received by Samuel G. Ward from sundry persons, and held by him for the benefit of A. Bronson Alcott Esq." *Let,* V, 378; MS *AcctBk59–65,* p. 249. *Let,* V, 392–393, 395–397; MS RWE to G. W. Curtis, 15 Dec 1864 (owned by HCL). *Let,* V, 406. MS EllenE to RWE, 24 Jan 1865. *Let,* V, 361–362, 376. RWE, MS undated draft of petition asking the faculty of Harvard College to allow Edward to do guard duty at a fort; presumably used as the basis of the petition Edward actually presented; *cf. Let,* V, 376. MS EdithE to EWE, 13 July 1864. EWE, *Es,* p. xi. **426:** *J,* X, 56–57. *C-ECor,* II, 285. *Let,* V, 382. *Let,* V, 384; *J,* X, 72. *Let,* V, 385–386. *AlcJou,* p. 365. *Let,* V, 387, 389. *J,* X, 82–83. MS EllenE to SHE, 5 Jan 1865. *Let,* V, 389 *et passim.* MS *MemBk1864–1865,* Dec 1864. **427:** *Let,* V, 397–407, 412. *J,* X, 93–94. Whitman, *When Lilacs Last in the Door-yard Bloom'd,* 1865–6, p. 4. Broadside *Surrender of Lee!!* (copy owned by CFPL). Handbill dated 18 Apr 1865, issued by authority of the selectmen of Concord (copy owned by CFPL). Leaflet *Order of Services . . . Concord, at the Hour of the Funeral . . . April 19, 1865* (copy owned by CFPL). *CEd,* XI, 332–335. *Ibid.,* XI, 333, 334, 336. **428:** *J,* IX, 366. MS j "KL," p. 203. **429:** *CEd,* IX, 251. *J,* X, 361; MS EllenE to EEF, 22 Aug 1872. *CEd,* XI, 342, 345. *C-ECor,* II, 296. **430:** *Let,* V, 468. *J,* X, 132, 155–156. *Let,* V, 420. *J,* X, 107. *Let,* V, 429. *Let,* V, 433–434; Woodbury, *passim. Let,* V, 425–426. Three broadsides (copies owned by CFPL) relating to the Cattle Show of 21 Sept 1865. *Let,* V, 426–427; MS in *FaBi,* recto of 2d leaf pasted in.

431: t EllenE to Miss Waterman, 3 and 25 Jan 1866. MS EllenE to EEF, 3 and 4 Nov 1865. MS EllenE to EEF, 10 Oct 1865. *J*, X, 160; *cf. Let*, II, 95, and III–VI, *passim*, but especially VI, 81, 166. *Let*, V, 440–441, 443. *Let*, V, 435, 447–458; MS *MemBk1866*. *ECitCon*, pp. 371–372; *Let*, V, 430, 437; MS WmE (b) to Sam Bradford, 28 June 1865; leaflet, *Concord Free Public Library*, showing tenure of officers; *Concord Free Public Library Seventy-fifth Anniversary*, n.d. (1948), *passim*. **432:** MS EllenE to EEF, 6 Apr 1866. MS EllenE to HavenE, 12 May 1866; MS EllenE to Miss Waterman, 17 May 1866; MS EEF to EWE, 19 May 1866. *Let*, V, 461. MS EllenE to Sally Gibbons Emerson, 5 May 1866. *Let*, V, 464. MS EllenE to EEF, 29 June 1876 (*i.e.*, 1866) ; *Let*, V, 467. MS *Lidian*, p. 255; *cf. Let*, V, 471–473, 478, 482. MS EllenE to EWE, 21, 23, and 25 July 1866. *BoDaAdv*, 19 July 1866. Carbon or similar record of the original hand, Hill to RWE, 18 July 1866 (owned by HCL) ; incomplete MS copy of same letter (owned by HCL). *Let*, V, 487–509. **433:** *Let*, V, 493–494. *Let*, V, 513–514; *cf. AlcJou*, p. 420. *Let*, V, 521. *Let*, V, 508–509. *Let*, V, 504. *CEd*, XI, 353 ff., 355, 357–374. Handbill with dates 19 Apr 1861 and 19 Apr 1867 (copy owned by CFPL) ; broadside *Order of Procession . . . April 19th, 1867* (copy owned by CFPL). MS *ConToRec*, IX, 331; *CEd*, XI, 347–379. *J*, X, 231. MS EllenE to HavenE, 29 Apr 1867. MS EllenE to EWE, 4, 8, and 10 Oct 1866. *E.g., Let*, V, 506–507; *Fields-An*, p. 83. **434:** *J*, X, 231. *Let*, VI, 63. Apparently as late as 1867, Whitman placed Emerson, but no other major author, decisively in the front rank of American poets: "With the names of our so-far noblest poets, Bryant, Emerson, Whittier, Longfellow, I should put on the scroll at any rate immediately below the others, Edgar Poe and Bret Harte though the scope of their song is limited and its direction special" (MS, undated

and without title, owned by LC). *CEd*, XI, 475–481, 486, 488. *Let*, V, 521. *AmberleyPa*, II, 65. *Let*, V, 449. **435:** *Comm*, 27 Feb 1869. *E.g.*, MS J. Donaldson to RWE, 14 Mar 1870. *AmberleyPa*, II, 67. *E.g.*, MS EdithE to RWE, 29 Jan and 5 Feb 1865. MS EllenE to EWE, 27, 29, and 30 Jan 1872. MS *HCDivSStuRec*, p. 359. P. 432 above. MS *HCOvRec*, X, 241; *cf. Let*, VI, 26. MS *HCPhiBetaKRec*, III, 18 July 1867. *CEd*, VIII, 208–210, *e.g.* 211–213, *e.g.* 225 ff., 229–230. *CookeRWE*, p. 184. MS EllenE to EEF, 2 Apr 1867; MS EllenE to EEF, 30 Mar 1868; *Let*, V, 511, 532; MS *AcctBk1865–1872*, p. 149. MS EllenE to Annie Fields, 12 Feb 1884. MS *MemBk1867*, Sept and Nov 1867. *Let*, V, 539–546. *Let*, V, 545; *cf.* VI, 18–19. *J*, X, 248. *Let*, VI, 10. MS EllenE to EEF, 20 Apr 1868. **436:** *Ibid.* **437:** *Ibid.* **438:** *Ibid. Let*, VI, 24–26, 28–29. *Let*, VI, 30; t EllenE to EEF, 17 Aug 1868. *Let*, VI, 30, 32. *Let*, VI, 30–31. *CEd*, XI, 469–474. Clapp's MS narrative and the MS Emerson wrote from memory for the press (both in Clapp's scrapbook, largely about the Chinese banquet, owned by HCL). *Let*, V, 523–524, 529. **439:** t *Lidian*, p. 26. *Let*, VI, 4, 33–34. *J*, IX, 319. MS EllenE to EEF, *c.* 17? Sept 1868. *Let*, VI, 35. *LowLitEs*, I, 360. *Let*, VI, 35, 54–55. **440:** *Let*, VI, 43–44, 46, 52–53. *Let*, VI, 48, 52. *Let*, VI, 52–53; extant manuscripts of this course are fragmentary and in disorder. MS EEF to EWE, 11 Feb 1869. *Let*, VI, 39, 55, 56, 58, 64. *J*, X, 280, 288; *Let*, VI, 65. *Let*, VI, 86; *CEd*, XI, 455–459. *Let*, VI, 78. *AlcJou*, p. 389. **441:** *BoDaAdv*, 27 May 1869; *cf. Let*, VI, 78. MS EllenE to EWE, 17, 18, 19, 20, 21 Nov 1871. *J*, X, 258–259; *Let*, VI, 56–57. MS *HCOvRec*, X, 327, 333–335. MS EWE to EllenE, 19 Sept 1869. MS *HCOvRec*, *e.g.*, X, 358–366, *passim*. MS *HCFaRec*, volume for 1869–1872, p. 118, mentions the overseers' action of 15 Feb 1870. MS *HCOvRec*, X, 338–340 (3 June 1869). MS *HCCorpRec*, XI, 195. *RWEMA* owns a proof sheet, corrected by Emerson's hand, of recommendations of the committee, appointed by the corporation, on the Master's degree; *cf. Three*, p. 334. *Let*, VI, *passim. C-ECor*, II, 306–328, *passim; Let*, VI, 97–98, 104–108, 111–112. *J*, X, 301. **442**: *Let*, VI, 94, 96, 110. *CEd*, VII, 1–16. *J*, X, 312. *C-ECor*, II, 324–325. *Let*, VI, 73, 114–115; MS *HCOvRec*, X, 343; MS *PeaNbkPhil* (owned by HCL), *passim. J*, X, 321. There were only seven registrants, it seems, at the beginning of the course, some months before Emerson's first lecture (*Let*, VI, 104). **443**: MS *PeaNbkPhil* (owned by HCL), *passim.* MS EllenE to EEF, 27 May 1870. MS *PeaNbkPhil* (owned by HCL), *passim.* MS EllenE to HavenE, 6 May 1870. MS *HCCorpRec*, XI, 209. MS *AcctBk65–72*, p. 214. *C-ECor*, II, 326–327. **444**: MS *WHChanRem*, leaves 1–10, dated 20 June 1870. *Let*, VI, 119. MS EllenE to HavenE, 21 July 1870. *Let*, VI, 126; *Grimm-RWE-Cor*, pp. 85–86. *Let*, VI, 124–125, 134, 136, 180–181; MS A. Ireland to Conway, 24 Apr 1870 (owned by CUL); the letter from Ireland shows that he was at once suspicious of Hotten. *J*, X, 309; *Let*, VI, 128. *CEd*, X, 295, 306. **445**: MS EllenE to EEF, 19 Aug 1870. MS *AcctBk65–72*, p. 216. *J*, X, 225, 227–228. MS EWE to EEF, 2 and 3 Sept 1870. MS EWE to LE, 4 Sept 1870. MS *MemBk1870–1871*, Dec 1870. *Let*, VI, 138. MS *MemBk1871; Let*, VI, 144. *J*, X, 347; MS *MemBk1871*, 3 Feb 1871. MS EllenE to EEF, 17 Feb 1871. *J*, X, 347–348; *Let*, VI, 145; according to MS *AcctBk65–72*, p. 234, Emerson received $340 from the college for this year's lectures. **446**: *Let*, VI, 145, 147–149; *ForbesLetRec*, II, 175–176; *ThayerWest*, p. 9. *ThayerWest*, p. 10. *J*, X, 351. *ThayerWest* (based, at least partly, on Thayer's letters written during the journey), pp. 5, 36, 40–41, 43, 50. *Let*, VI, 149, 152. **447**: *Let*, VI, 152; the much-debated passage about the mouse trap may well be authentic and may have been used in one of Emerson's California lectures; its lineage might, perhaps, be traced from a journal entry as early as 1840 (*J*, V, 392) to one of some fifteen years later (*J*, VIII, 528–529); but the problem receives adequate attention in *The Home Book of Quotations*, New York, 1937; for a suggestion that the mouse trap owed something to a remark of Daniel Webster's about Emerson's brother Charles, see R. Adams, in *Modern Language Notes* for Nov 1947 (pp. 483–486). *Let*, VI, 152, 157–158. *Let*, VI, 154–155. **448**: *Let*, VI, 155; *cf.* Linnie Wolfe, New York, 1945, pp. 146 ff. *Let*, VI, 158. *Let*, VI, 155–156. *J*, X, 357. *Let*, VI, 183. *J*, X, 362–363; *CEd*, VII, 21. **449**: MS EllenE to EWE, 3 and 6 Nov 1871. *MerwHarte*, p. 227. *ThayerWest*, p. 61. MS EllenE to EWE, 16 and 17 Oct 1871; MS EllenE to EWE, 3 and 6 Nov 1871. *CEd*, XI, 461–467. *Let*, VI, 188. MS EllenE to EWE, 27 and 28 Nov 1871. *Let*, VI, 187–197. **450**: *Let*, VI, 193; *BarrusWhit&Bur*, pp. 64–66, where the date is slightly erroneous. *Let*, VI, 193, 195. MS *AcctBk53–59*, 14 Jan 1858; MS *AcctBk59–65*, pp. 84, 159; *cf. Let*, V, 58. Agassiz, *Contributions*, Boston, 1860, III, 89. *Let*, VI, 195; MS EllenE to EEF, 5, 8, and 9 Feb 1872; *J*, X, 377–378. **451**: *Concord Lyceum. Course of 1871 and '72* (copy in CFPL). MS *MemBk1872*, 7 Feb 1872. *AlcJou*, p. 425. MS EllenE to EEF, 7, 8, and 9 Mar 1872. MS EllenE to EEF, 14? Mar 1872. MS EllenE to EEF, 7, 8, and 9 Mar 1872. *Let*, VI, 172–173, 176, 179. MS James R. Osgood & Co. to RWE, 15 Feb 1872. MS EllenE to EEF, 7, 8, and 9 Mar 1872. *Let*, VI, 207. t EllenE to EWE, 26 Mar 1872. *Let*, VI, 209. t EllenE to EEF, 25 and 26 Apr 1872. **452**: MS EllenE to EWE, 7 May 1872. t EllenE to EEF, 10 May 1872. t EllenE to EWE, 15 and 16 Apr 1872. MS EllenE to EEF, 10 May 1872. *Let*, VI, 209; *Fields-An*, p. 91. MS EllenE to EWE, 14 May 1872. MS EllenE to EEF, 17 May 1872. MS EllenE to HavenE, 27 and 29 July 1872. **453**: *Ibid.;* MS EllenE to EWE, 30 July and 2 Aug 1872. *Let*, VI, 214. t extracts, by EWF, of Annie Keyes to EllenE, 2 Mar 1873. MS EllenE to HavenE, 27 and 29 July 1872; MS EllenE to EWE, 30 July and 2 Aug 1872. **454:** MS EllenE to HavenE, 16 Aug 1872; *Let,* VI, 218; *CabM,* II, 703–705. MS EllenE to EWE, 30 July and 2 Aug 1872. MS Arinori Mori (of the Japanese Legation in Washington) to RWE, 3 Feb 1872; *Comm,* 10 Aug 1872. *Let,* VI, 217. MS EllenE to EEF, 20 Aug 1872; *Let,* VI, 109, 173 *et passim.* MS EllenE to EEF, 22 Aug 1872. **455:** *Ibid. Let,* VI, 219–221. t EllenE to EWE, 9 and 10 Apr 1872. *E.g., J,* X, 391–392. t EllenE to Edward H. Clarke, 1 Sept 1872, where the doctor's name is given as Clark. **456:** *Ibid.* The 8th folded sheet of MS EEF to Elizabeth Cabot? July? 1886? *HoweBan,* II, 261–262. The $17,000 or $18,000 would include the $11,020 accounted for in *CabM,* II, 705–707, together with the $5000 brought by Francis Lowell and Bancroft's $1000. *Let,* VI, 218–219. *ConwayAut,* II, facsimile between pp. 358 and 359; MS *CabLedgJEC,* p. 128. t EllenE to EWE? 22 and 23 Sept 1872. Fragmentary MS EllenE to EWE, presumably 30 Sept 1872. MS EllenE to EWE, 7 Oct 1872. MS EWE to RWE and LE, 11 Aug 1872; MS EllenE to EWE, 7 Oct 1872; MS copy of EWE, presumably to Annie Keyes, 7 and 10 Oct 1872; *J,* X, 387, 395. *Let,* VI, 219–220; *ConwayAut,* II, between pp. 358 and 359. MS EWE to EEF, 20 Oct 1872. **457:** *Let,* VI, 150, 173–174, 222. *Cf., e.g., J,* X, 222. *J,* X, 216. *Cf. Let,* VI, 93. MS Arnold to Conway, 8 Nov 1865 (in CUL), partly printed in *ConwayAut,* II, 340. *J,* X, 364. *AlcJou,* p. 428. *EatH&A,* p. 150; *CookeRWE,* p. 186; *cf. Let,* VI, 122–123. **458:** MS "NQ," p. 284; *J,* X, 405; for the possibility that Emerson here remembered part of a passage in Diodorus Siculus, see, below, a note on pp. 468–469. **459:** *CEd,* VI, 94. *Let,* VI, 224; MS EllenE to LE, 23 Oct 1872; EllenE's MS *LongLet. Let,* VI, 225. **460:** *Let,* VI, 225. MS *LongLet. Let,* VI, 226. MS El-

lenE to LE, 4 Nov 1872; *Let,* VI, 226. MS EllenE to LE, 5, 6, and 8 Nov 1872. MS EWE to EEF, 20 Oct 1872; MS EllenE to LE, 5, 6, and 8 Nov 1872. *Let,* VI, 226. Incomplete MS EWE to LE, 10 Nov 1872. **461:** MS EllenE to EEF, "finished" 9 Nov 1872; MS EllenE to EEF, 14 Nov 1872; *Let,* VI, 227. MS EWE to EllenE, 13 Nov 1872; MS EllenE to EEF, 14 Nov 1872. MS Una Hawthorne to LE, 17 Nov 1872. MS EllenE to LE, 16 and 22 Nov 1872. *Le Figaro,* 14, 15, and 16 Nov 1872. MS EllenE to EEF, 26 and 28 Nov 1872; *Let,* VI, 228. **462:** MS EllenE to EEF, 26 and 28 Nov 1872. MS EllenE to LE, 16 and 22 Nov 1872; MS EllenE to EEF, 26 and 28 Nov 1872. **463:** *Let,* VI, 228–229. *Let,* VI, 228; MS EllenE to EEF, 26 and 28 Nov 1872. *La Nazione,* Florence, 27 and 28 Nov 1872. *Ibid.,* 27 and 30 Nov and 2 Dec 1872. MS *MemBk1872,* 27–28 Nov 1872. MS EllenE to LE, 4 Dec 1872. MS EllenE to EEF, 3 Dec 1872; MS EllenE to LE, 4 Dec 1872; *Let,* VI, 229. MS EllenE to EEF, 6 Dec 1872; *Let,* VI, 229. **464:** *La Nazione,* Florence, 27 Nov 1872. MS George P. Marsh to RWE, 4 Dec 1872; *L'Opinione,* Rome, 5 Dec 1872, *e.g.* MS EllenE to EWE, 14 Dec 1872. MS EllenE to LE, 25 Dec 1872. *Ibid.; J,* X, 406. *L'Omnibus,* Naples, 17 (and later) Dec 1872. MS EllenE to LE, 25 Dec 1872. **465:** *Ibid. Le Nil,* Alexandria, 29 Dec 1872. MS EllenE to EWE, 1, 2, and 4 Jan 1873. *Le Nil,* Alexandria, 29 Dec 1872. MS EllenE to EWE, 1, 2, and 4 Jan 1873; MS EllenE to EEF, 3 and 4 Jan 1873; *Let,* VI, 230–232. **466:** MS Bancroft to OWH, 19 Jan 1855 (owned by HCL). *Let,* VI, 230–231; MS EllenE to EWE, 1, 2, and 4 Jan 1873. *Let,* VI, 231–232; MS EllenE to EWE, 1, 2, and 4 Jan 1873. E. S. Bradley, *George Henry Boker,* 1927, pp. 289–290. MS EllenE to EWE, 1, 2, and 4 Jan 1873. *Le Nil,* Alexandria, 2 and 5 Jan 1873. *J,* X, 406; MS EllenE to EWE, 1, 2, and 4 Jan 1873. MS EllenE to LE, 29 and 30 Jan and 1

Feb 1873. MS EllenE to LE, 13 Jan 1873. **467:** *Ibid.* MS EllenE to EEF, 21 Jan 1873. *J*, X, 407–408. MS EllenE to EEF, 21 Jan 1873. MS EllenE to EWE, 23? Jan 1873. **468:** *Ibid.;* in *Die Geschichte meines Lebens*, 1893, Ebers was concerned with the years prior to 1864, and Emerson seems not to be mentioned. MS EllenE to LE, 29 and 30 Jan and 1 Feb 1873. *J*, X, 409. MS EllenE to "My dear daughter" (Edith Davidson?) , 27 and 29 Jan 1873. MS EllenE to LE, 29 and 30 Jan and 1 Feb 1873. **469:** MS "Egypt" and another manuscript numbered "2," on the same subject. Emerson, lover of Plutarch and author of an introduction to *Plutarch's Morals*, doubtless was, or had been, familiar with the chapter on Isis and Osiris, where Philae is, however, only one of many towns claiming the honor of being the god's final resting place. I owe to La Rue Van Hook the suggestion of Diodorus Siculus as the inspirer of Emerson's lively preference for the legend that Osiris was buried at Philae. *Cf. The Historical Library of Diodorus the Sicilian*, tr. G. Booth, London, 1700, pp. 9–10. MS EllenE to LE, 29 and 30 Jan and 1 Feb 1873. MS EllenE to EWE, 31 Jan and 6, 10, and 18 Feb 1873. Laporte, Boston, 1872, p. 135. MS EllenE to LE, 29 and 30 Jan and 1 Feb 1873. MS EllenE to EWE, 31 Jan and 6, 10, and 18 Feb 1873. MS EllenE to LE, 29 and 30 Jan and 1 Feb 1873. MS EllenE to LE, 19, 24, and 25 Feb 1873. **470:** MS EllenE to LE, 29 and 30 Jan and 1 Feb 1873; MS EllenE to EEF, 3 Feb 1873; MS EllenE to LE, 19, 24, and 25 Feb 1873. Theodore Roosevelt, New York, 1920, p. 19; a sister of young Theodore was struck by Emerson's "lovely smile, somewhat vacant . . . but very gentle, with which he received the little children of his fellow countryman" (Corinne R. Robinson, New York, 1921, p. 62) . MS EllenE to LE, 19, 24, and 25 Feb 1873. MS EllenE to EWE, 31 Jan and 6, 10, and 18 Feb 1873. Brugsch, Berlin, 1894,

tells of experiences in Egypt but does not mention Emerson. MS EllenE to LE, 19, 24, and 25 Feb 1873. *Let*, VI, 234, 235. **471:** *Let*, VI, 236. *Let*, VI, 234. MS EllenE to LE, 19, 24, and 25 Feb 1873. In *Let*, VI, 234–235, I was misled by an error in R. Owen, *The Life of Richard Owen*, 1894, II, 222, into the belief that it was "almost certain that Emerson revisited Malta on the way to Italy"; but the "Emerson" there mentioned, certainly not Ralph Waldo, was presumably a J. T. Emmerson, as I learned when, a few weeks after the publication of *Let*, I visited Malta and studied the movements of J. T. Emmerson as recorded in the Malta newspapers *Public Opinion* (26 Feb 1873) and *Il Portafoglio maltese* (25 Feb 1873) . As the Royal Malta Library, at Valetta, proved to be rich in files covering the months of Feb and Mar 1873, I also examined *The Malta News* and other local papers for that period and found numerous notices of the activities of both Owen and Emmerson but nothing about Emerson. *Let*, I, 362. MS EllenE to LE, 19, 24, and 25 Feb 1873. MS EllenE to EEF, 1 and 8? Mar 1873. **472:** MS EllenE to LE, 11 and 17 Mar 1873; *Let*, VI, 236–237; "Music," under a somewhat different title, is in Strode, ed. Dobell, London, 1907, pp. 2–3, where the text is from a manuscript version. MS EllenE to EEF, 14? Mar 1873. MS EllenE to LE, 11 and 17 Mar 1873; MS EllenE to EEF, 18, 19, and 21 Mar 1873. MS EllenE to EWE, 28 and 29 Mar 1873. MS EllenE to LE, 21 Mar and 8 Apr 1873. **473:** *Let*, VI, 228; MS EllenE to EEF, 1, 3, and 7 Apr 1873, mentions an earlier visit of Mar 1873 to the Laugels. MS EllenE to EWE, 28 and 29 Mar 1873; *J*, X, 413. *Let*, VI, 228; *J*, X, 413. MS EllenE to LE, 16 and 18 Apr 1873. MS EllenE to LE, 21 Mar and 8 Apr 1873; *J*, X, 413. MS EllenE to EEF, 1, 3, and 7 Apr 1873. MS EllenE to LE, 21 Mar and 8 Apr 1873. MS EllenE to LE, 16 and 18 Apr 1873. **474:** *Ibid.* MS EllenE to LE, 6?–16? Apr 1873 (a diary letter covering 6–16 Apr 1873; at top of p. 1, in different ink but apparently in Ellen's hand, is "London April 1873"). **475:** *Ibid.;* in the original manuscript ditto marks are used instead of my "Mr Browning" in the second of the two consecutive sentences in which that name occurs. MS EllenE to "Dear Family," dated "R. R. May 1 1873." **476:** *Ibid.* MS EllenE to EEF, 26 Apr 1873. *EatH&A,* p. 343. **477:** *Let,* VI, 238–241. *J,* X, 417–418. MS EllenE to "My dear childy" (Edith Davidson?), 3 May 1873. MS EllenE to EEF, 5 May 1873. **478:** *Let,* VI, 242; *IreRWE,* pp. 177–178. *Let,* VI, 242. *IreRWE,* p. 179; *Let,* VI, 242. *Let,* VI, 242–243. *NortonLet,* I, 502, 503, 506, and, *e.g.,* 508. *Ibid.,* I, 488, 508, 510, 511. **479:** *Ibid.,* I, 511–512. MS EllenE to "Dear Miss Clara" (Dabney?), 27 May and 7 June 1873. MS bills submitted to the "Committee on Reception of R. W. Emerson" by A. B. Warren dated 27 May 1873, by A. W. Hosmer dated 28 May 1873, and by Samuel W. Brown dated 3 June 1873 (owned by CFPL). Broadside *A Public Reception,* dated 24 May 1873 (copy owned by CFPL). *AlcJou,* p. 432. MS EllenE to "Dear Miss Clara" (Dabney?), 27 May and 7 June 1873. **480:** *Ibid.* MS *ConToRec,* IX, 437. MS EllenE to "Dear Miss Clara" (Dabney?), 27 May and 7 June 1873; *AlcJou,* p. 433. *AlcJou,* pp. 432–433. *EinC,* p. 187. *AlcJou,* p. 433. Conway, *Life of Nathaniel Hawthorne,* London, n.d. (1890?), p. 98. **481:** *Marcus Aurelius . . . Meditations,* 1635, p. 209. From Aug 1872 to July 1873, John S. Keyes spent $6519.43 in rebuilding the Emerson house; and of this amount, $2500 had been received as insurance (MS *AcctBk72–82,* p. 19). MS *Lidian,* pp. 277, 279. MS LE to EllenE, 29 July 1873. t EllenE to Sarah G. Emerson, 16 Jan 1874. MS EllenE to Miss Dabney, 17 Sept 1875. Two Gutekunst photographs are reproduced in *RecLiLong,* opposite pp. 165 and 166; the date given *ibid.,* pp.

xi–xii, is some weeks too late (*ibid.,* pp. 165–167; and t EllenE to HavenE, 29 Mar 1873). **482:** Clipping from an unidentified newspaper of 1882 (p. 9 of Drury clippings owned by CUL). J. H. W. Stuckenberg, London, 1882, pp. 430–431. *AlcJou,* pp. 454, 457. MS *AcctBk72–82,* pp. 17, 24. *Let,* VI, 272. MS *ConAsBk,* 1 May 1875. **483:** MS bankbook for 1874–1878. *Let,* VI, *passim.* MS *TreesMajor,* p. 47 *et passim.* The descriptions are from Emerson's fellow townsmen Simon Brown and Albert Stacy's leaflet *Pear Trees for Sale,* a copy of which is inserted loosely in MS *TreesMajor.* MS *MemBk1873,* 7 July 1873. MS EllenE to EWE, 27, 29, and 30 Jan 1872. *AmberleyPa,* II, 67; MS *Lidian,* p. 226. MS *Lidian,* pp. 225–226, 261. *Ibid.,* pp. 261–262, 301. Edward was married 19 Sept 1874 (MS in *FaBi,* verso of 2d leaf). MS *Lidian,* pp. 287–288. **484:** MS *IslandBkWHF* (at Naushon), entries in 1873, 1874, 1876, 1877, 1878, 1879, 1880, 1881. MS EllenE to Edith (Davidson?), 24 Apr 1874. *Let,* VI, 259, 261. MS EllenE to EEF, 8 Jan 1875; MS EllenE to EEF, 3 Feb 1875. MS *HCOvRec,* XI, 116. *Let,* V, 469–471, 476–482, *passim. J,* X, 266, 332–333. *Let,* VI, 68–72, *passim. Let,* VI, *passim;* MS *HCOvRec,* X and XI, *passim;* MS reports to overseers. MS records of corporation, overseers, and faculty in the 1870s, *passim. Comm,* 14 Mar 1874 (the date 7 Mar also appears on the same issue). **485:** *CabM,* II, 630. MS copy or rough draft, by EllenE, of EllenE to Gisela Grimm, with date 2 Mar 1868 added by another hand, together with what seems to be "to 1871." *Let,* VI, *passim; J,* X, 437–438. MS EllenE to EEF, 17 Nov 1874. MS EEF to EllenE, 18 Dec 1874; *Let,* VI, 267. **486:** MS EllenE to HavenE, 15 and 23 Feb 1875. MS Hillard to RWE, 1 Jan 1875. MS JFC to RWE, 10 Jan 1875. MS Stirling to RWE, 26 Feb 1875. MS Rolfe to RWE, 30 Aug 1875. MS J. W. Morris to RWE, 16 Sept 1875. *AlcJou,* p. 460. MS EllenE to EEF,

16 and 17 Aug 1875. *Let,* VI, 180–181. *EmStanLib,* VIII, iii, iv. **487:** MS EllenE to EEF, 8 Sept and "Wednesday," 1875; *cf.* MS EllenE to EEF, 15 Nov 1875. *J,* X, 442. MS EllenE to EEF, 25 Sept 1875. *Let,* VI, 286. *Letters and Social Aims,* Boston, 1876. *EmStanLib,* VIII, i–v; reprinted in *CEd,* VIII, ix–xiii. *Cf.* Hegel, *The Philosophy of History,* tr. J. Sibree, revised ed., New York, n.d. (cop. 1899), pp. xi–xiii. *CEd,* XI, 493–508; *Let,* VI, 249. *CEd,* XI, 500–501. MS EllenE to EEF, 2 Oct 1873. *Let,* VI, *e.g.,* 253. *Comm,* 28 Feb 1874. **488:** MS *HCDivSStuRec* (owned by AnHarTheoLib), p. 359. MS *HCDivSFaRecfc* (owned by AnHarTheoLib), 28 Oct 1873; MS *HCDivSStuRec* (owned by AnHarTheoLib), p. 365. *Let,* VI, 261. *NortonLet,* II, 43. MS *HCDivSStuRec* (owned by AnHarTheoLib), pp. 367–368. MS *ConLyRecBk59–81* (owned by CFPL), 10 Feb 1875 (gives no subject). MS EllenE to HavenE, 15 and 23 Feb 1875. MS *AcctBk72–82,* p. 26. **489:** MS EllenE to LE, 20 and 21 Mar 1875. MS *ConToRec,* IX, 441–442, 449, 451. *Ibid.,* IX, 442; MS EllenE to EEF, 18 Jan 1875; MS RWE to G. W. Curtis, 15 Mar 1875 (owned by HCL); *Let,* VI, 264–265, 271; *CookeRWE,* p. 183. MS EllenE to HavenE, 24 Apr and 20 June 1875. *Let,* VI, 271; *CookeRWE,* pp. 182–183. MS EllenE to HavenE, 24 Apr and 20 June 1875; *J,* X, 443–444. *Let,* VI, 277, 279. *Let,* VI, 253–255; *CookeRWE,* pp. 178–179. MS EllenE to EEF, 2 and 4 July 1875. **490:** *Ibid. Let,* VI, *passim,* and various MS letters to Emerson. MS Presbury to RWE, 15 May 1867. *AlcJou,* pp. 403–404, 447–448. MS E. R. Hoar to RWE, 11 Mar 1874. MS EllenE to EEF, 18? and 19 Mar 1874. *Let,* VI, 245–247. Monypenny and Buckle, London, 1920, V, 266–288, *passim. The University Independent,* 2d ser., No. 2, is dated 31 Mar 1874. Leaflet *Glasgow University Rectorial Election,* 1874, pp. 2–3. *Let,* VI, 258–270, *passim; J,* X, 436–437; MS EEF to EllenE, 15 Mar 1874; MS EEF to

EllenE, 17 Nov 1874; MS W. H. Fish to RWE, 15 Nov 1875. **491:** MS EllenE to EEF, 12 Oct 1875; *Let,* VI, 283–284. MS *Lidian,* p. 304; MS *AcctBk72–82,* p. 81. *AlcJou,* p. 466. *Let,* VI, 296, and *cf.* 304, 306, 307. MS *WHChanRem,* leaves 11–13 (20? July 1877). MS EllenE to ElizH, 30 Oct and 3 Nov 1877. MS *ConLyRecBk59–81,* 5 Mar 1879. *Let,* VI, 315. MS in *FaBi.* MS *IslandBkWHF,* 1876–1881, *passim.* **492:** *AlcJou,* p. 471. *Let,* VI, 298–300, 303. MS EllenE to ElizH, 30 Oct and 3 Nov 1877. *Cf. C-ECor,* II, 298. *Let,* VI, 120–121. MS *MemBk1876,* 7 Apr and 12 June 1876. *CarpDays,* pp. 3, 166–167. MS EllenE to EEF, 9 June 1877. *AlcJou,* p. 480. MS EllenE to EEF, 16 July 1877; *cf. ScudLowell,* II, 220. **493:** Incomplete MS EllenE to EEF, 2 and 9 Apr 1878; MS *Lidian,* p. 312. *BradInc,* p. 69. MS Furness to RWE, 5 Sept 1878. *BarrusLiBur,* I, 213. *Let,* VI, *passim;* also in *LazLet,* pp. 3–16. *Let,* VI, 296, 297. MS EllenE to EEF, 26 Aug 1876. MS EllenE to "Edith" (presumably EEF but possibly Edith Davidson), 6 Sept 1876. **494:** *Ibid. The Poems of Emma Lazarus,* 1889, I, 12–15. MS Emma Lazarus to EllenE, 7 Sept 1876; *LazLet,* p. 21. MS Emma Lazarus to EllenE, 2 Nov 1876. **495:** MS EllenE to EEF, 18 July 1879; Ellen later thought she recalled Emma's visiting Bush another time, in the summer of 1881, but Ellen's remembrance of this was too hazy to offer any satisfactory evidence (MS *Lidian,* p. 324). Only a few pages of MS j "Old Man" have any interest. *J,* X, 476. MS EllenE to EEF, 16 Mar 1876. *AlcJou,* p. 470; *Let,* VI, 268; MS Sanborn to EllenE, 4 Mar 1876. MS EllenE to "My dear Sally" (Sarah Gibbons Emerson, presumably), 27 Feb 1877. MS EllenE to EEF, n.d. ("May 18? 78" supplied in pencil). *Ibid.; Let,* VI, 309–311. MS EWE to Cabot, 10 Nov 1877; MS Cabot to EWE, 13 Nov 1877. **496:** *Let,* VI, 318. MS EllenE to EEF, 14 Apr 1876. MS EllenE to EEF, 22 and 23 June 1876; MS EllenE to Cabot, 12–26 Sept 1882. MS EllenE to EEF, 1 July 1876. MS Ellen E to LE, 29 June 1876. **497:** *Ibid.* MS EllenE to Cabot, 12–26 Sept 1882. MS EllenE to LE, 29 June 1876; MS EllenE to EEF, 1 July 1876. *Let,* VI, 295. **498:** MS EllenE to EEF, 1 July 1876. MS EllenE to EWE, 30 June and 1 July 1876. t signed EWF to me, 16 Dec 1947, pp. 3–4. MS *BPLSNo8Nov1876;* MS Joseph Healy to RWE, 20 Oct 1876; *CabM,* II, 676–677; *J,* X, 450. *Let,* VI, 304, 309, 311; *AlcJou,* p. 484. MS EllenE to EEF, 6 Feb 1878. MS EllenE to EEF, 8, 9, and 11 Feb 1878. MS EllenE to EEF, 9 Mar 1878; MS EllenE to HavenE, 17 June 1878. *Let,* VI, 317. MS Henry W. Robinson to RWE, 11 Feb 1879. MS EllenE to EEF, 9 and 10 Apr 1879. MS EllenE to EEF, 7 May 1879. **499:** MS EllenE to EEF, 5 July 1879. MS EllenE to EEF, 17 June 1876; MS *Lidian,* p. 326. MS EllenE to EEF, 29 Aug 1877. MS EllenE to "Dearest girl" (EEF, presumably), 26 and 27 Sept 1877. MS Mary Pauline Alden to RWE, 20 Feb 1879. *AlcJou,* pp. 475, 485. *ECitCon,* p. 369. MS EllenE to LE, 16 Sept 1878. MS EllenE to EEF, 25 Sept 1878. MS EllenE to EEF, 23 Sept 1878; MS EllenE to LE, 17 Sept 1878; MS EllenE to EEF, 23 Sept 1878; MS EllenE to EEF, 25 Sept 1878. **500:** MS EllenE to HavenE and SusyE, 17 Oct 1878. MS EllenE to EEF, 23 Sept 1878. MS EllenE to EEF, 25 Sept 1878. MS B. B. Marshall to RWE, 3 June 1879. MS EllenE to EEF, 26 Sept 1879; MS EllenE to "Cousin Sarah," 4 Oct 1879. MS W. J. Potter to RWE, 23 June 1879. *Let,* VI, 290. MS OWHjr to RWE, 16? Apr 1876. MS Otto Zacharias? to RWE, 25 July 1876. *AlcJou,* p. 481. *Mark Twain's Speeches,* with introduction by W. D. Howells, New York and London, 1910, pp. 1–16. A. B. Paine, New York, 1912, II, 603–610; DeVoto, Boston, 1935, pp. 196–205. MS Clemens to RWE (also addressed, in same manuscript, to Longfellow and Holmes), 27 Dec 1877. A. B. Paine, New York, 1912, II, 608–609.

501: *Let,* VI, 311; Franqueville, Paris, II (1896), 102; Emerson had been elected to the Institut de France 29 Dec 1877, was notified in a French Presidential decree of 9 Jan 1878, and accepted in his letter of 6 Mar 1878 (so dated in extant rough draft). MS Stanley to RWE, 1877, quoted in MS EllenE to EEF, 12 July 1883; MS EllenE to Sarah Gibbons Emerson, 30 Oct 1878; MS J. W. Sharp to RWE, 14 July 1879. *AlcJou,* p. 498; *Genius&Char,* p. xi. Sherman to RWE, 5 Aug 1879. t EllenE to HavenE and Susan Tompkins Emerson, 11 and 12 June 1879; MS EllenE to EEF, 18 July 1879. MS French to Cabot, 17 Feb 1887. *CabM,* II, 678–679. *Cf. CookeBib, passim. Let,* VI, 274–287, *passim,* and 320–321. **502:** *Let,* VI, 320–321. Julius Simon, pp. 137–139; Hummel, pp. 64–66, 68, and 71–73; see also Baumgarten, pp. 81 ff.; the problem of Nietzsche's relation to Emerson needs much further study, to which Hummel offers the most convenient introduction. **503:** MS *Lidian,* pp. 314 ff. *Genius&Char,* pp. x–xiii, xxi. *Ire-RWE,* pp. 288–290. MS *ConLyRecBk-59–81,* 4 Feb 1880. *CEd,* X, 487–498, 617 ff.; *J,* X, 476; MS EllenE to EEF, 12 Feb 1881. MS EllenE to EEF, 25 Aug 1880. *AlcJou,* pp. 523–524. Bok, pp. 53–58. **504:** MS EllenE to EEF, 4 Mar 1880; *cf.* MS EllenE to EEF, 25 Aug 1880; *Comm,* 28 Feb 1880; *The Index,* 4 Mar 1880, pp. 114–115. Mary Baker Eddy to "Miss" Lane, printed without date in *The Autograph,* Vol. I, No. 7 (Sept–Oct 1912), pp. 148–149, and reprinted in E. S. Bates and J. V. Dittemore, New York, 1932, p. 171; other pertinent facts, and comment on the untenable theory that Mrs. Eddy derived much of her doctrine from Emerson, are in Bates and Dittemore, pp. 156 and 168; see also especially Lyman P. Powell, New York, 1930, pp. 131, 133, 284–285; I. C. Tomlinson, Boston, n.d. (cop. 1945), p. 43, cites no documentary authority for his statement that the Eddys had Emerson's own invitation to visit him; *AlcJou,* p. 463 *et passim,* shows Alcott's attitudes toward Christian Science. MS EllenE to EEF, 30 May–2 June 1880. Ellis, p. 318. MS EllenE to EEF, 27 Feb 1882. **505:** MS will signed by Emerson 14 Apr 1876 (in files of Register of Probate Court of Middlesex County at East Cambridge, Mass.). MS codicil, or formal request, dated 26 Mar 1881 (apparently never probated; on the same sheet there follows a request, signed by Lidian, Ellen, Edith, and Edith's son Ralph, that Emerson's executors comply with the new provision). *AlcJou,* p. 524. Whitman, *Specimen,* pp. 189–190. **506:** *Ibid.,* p. 190. Unidentified newspaper clipping of 1882 (p. 9 of Drury clippings, owned by CUL). MS EllenE to EEF, 28 June 1880; MS EllenE to EEF, 26? Feb? 1881? MS *IslandBkWHF,* 18 Aug 1881. EWF's t extracts from Annie Keyes Emerson to EEF, 5 Feb 1882. *EinC,* p. 146. *AlcJou,* p. 532. MS EllenE to EEF, 28

and 29 Mar 1882. *EatH&A,* p. 382. **507:** MS EllenE to EEF, 28 and 29 Mar 1882. MS EllenE to Clara Dabney, 2 Apr 1882. MS EllenE to Cabot, 16 Aug 1882. MS EllenE to EEF, 20 Apr 1882. MS EWE to Cabot, 17 Oct 1886. t EllenE to EWE, 6 May 1881. MS EWE to Cabot, 17 Oct 1886. MS EllenE to EEF, 22 Apr 1882. MS EllenE to "Dear Cousin Sarah" (Sarah Gibbons Emerson?), 22 Apr 1882. MS EllenE to HavenE, 24 Apr 1882. MS Mary E. Simmons to EEF, 25 Apr 1882. **508:** MS Mary E. Simmons to EEF, 26 Apr 1882. MSS Mary E. Simmons to EEF (two separate letters), 27 Apr 1882. *New-York Tribune,* 28 Apr 1882. *Ibid.,* 1 May 1882. MS F. Hedge to OWH, 22 Dec 1884 (owned by HCL). *New-York Tribune,* 1 May 1882. DGH, pp. 134–136. Whitman, *Specimen,* p. 197. *LowLit&-PolAd,* p. 32. *Cf.* t EllenE to Miss Dabney, 2 Apr 1885, and t EllenE to EEF, 3 Sept 1885.

INDEX AND BIBLIOGRAPHY

This list includes the names of the persons and of the towns and other geographical divisions mentioned in the text, together with the titles of books, essays, poems, etc. Though not an index of the notes and without any page reference to them, it is related to them. It includes the titles of Emerson's holograph writings, other than letters, that are cited there. Other titles not followed by page numbers appear in this list only because they have been abbreviated in the notes to avoid repetition and save space. Dates and places of publication are not generally given here unless they have been omitted from the notes. Published works that are fully cited there are not mentioned here unless they also appear in the text.

No adequate description of printed books, printed articles, and manuscripts by or about Emerson has yet been compiled; but there are some bibliographical aids, and a few of them are important. Manuscripts of Emerson's correspondence that were available before 1938 are, in general, described in the six volumes of *The Letters of Ralph Waldo Emerson,* New York, 1939. And those volumes refer to, or quote, many sources which the present book uses but, for lack of space, cites only indirectly, through *The Letters.* Much useful information is to be found in G. W. Cooke, *A Bibliography of Ralph Waldo Emerson,* Boston and New York, 1908; in the bibliography by H. R. Steeves, published in *The Cambridge History of American Literature,* ed. W. P. Trent and others, New York and Cambridge, England, 1917 and later, I, 551–566; in the quarterly dissertation lists printed in *American Literature* from 1929 to the present (but especially in the numbers for January, 1933, and May, 1948) and in the same journal's bibliographies from 1946 to the present time; in *Ralph Waldo Emerson Representative Selections,* ed. F. I. Carpenter, New York, Cincinnati, and elsewhere, cop. 1934, pp. xlix–lvi; in the bibliography by H. Hartwick, published as part of W. F. Taylor, *A History of American Letters,* Boston, Atlanta, and elsewhere, cop. 1936, pp. 509–513; in K. W. Cameron's *Ralph Waldo Emerson's Reading,* Raleigh, N. C., 1941, and in his *Emerson the Essayist,* Raleigh, N. C., 1945; in Lewis Leary, *Articles on American Literature Appearing in Current Periodicals. 1920–1945,* Durham, N. C., 1947, pp. 48–57; and in *Literary History of the United States,* ed. R. E. Spiller and others, New York, 1948, III (*Bibliography,* ed. T. H. Johnson), 492–501.

Though they contain no formal bibliographical lists, the *Centenary Edition The Complete Works of Ralph Waldo Emerson,* ed. E. W. Emerson, Boston and New York, n. d. (1903–1904), and the *Journals of Ralph Waldo Emerson,* ed. E. W. Emerson and W. E. Forbes, Boston and New York, 1909–1914, are invaluable to readers concerned with Emerson or with the American cultural and literary scene of his day. There is, however, no edition of either works or journals that approaches completeness (*cf.* "journals," "lectures," and "sermons" below). Typescript copies of most of the extant journals, including a great deal that has never been printed, are in the Harvard College Library and in the Columbia University Libraries.